Praise for *Introduction to Android™ Application Development, Fifth Edition*

"*Introduction to Android Application Development* is a great resource for developers who want to understand Android app development but who have little or no experience with mobile software. This fifth edition has a bunch of great changes, from using Android Studio to understanding and implementing navigation patterns, and each chapter has quiz questions to help make sure you're picking up the vital info that fills this book."
—*Ian G. Clifton, author of* Android User Interface Design

"Revamped, revitalized, and refreshed! *Introduction to Android Application Development, Fifth Edition,* is a wonderful upgrade to an already impressive compendium. Common pitfalls are explained, new features are covered in depth, and the knowledge that the book is geared to cover everything from introduction of a concept to learning how to implement it into your app makes this a great choice for new developers who are ready to make the jump into Android development. Being already accustomed to the professional work and experience that Annuzzi et al., bring to the table, you will be grateful to have expert insight along with the care and instruction that developers of all skill levels can benefit from."
—*Phil Dutson, solution architect, ICON Health & Fitness*

"Best technical summary of Material Design implementation I've seen outside the Android sample docs."
—*Ray Rischpater, software development manager, Uber*

"*Introduction to Android Application Development* is well written and fulfills the requirements of developers, project managers, educators, and entrepreneurs in developing fully featured Android applications. In addition, it emphasizes quality assurance for mobile applications, teaches you how to design and plan your Android application, and teaches the software development process through a step-by-step, easy-to-understand approach. I recommend this book to anyone who wants to not just focus on developing apps, but also to apply tips and tricks and other tools for project management in their development of successful applications."
—*Bintu Harwani, founder of MCE (Microchip Computer Education)*

Introduction to Android™ Application Development

Fifth Edition

Developer's Library Series

Visit **developers-library.com** for a complete list of available products

The **Developer's Library Series** from Addison-Wesley provides practicing programmers with unique, high-quality references and tutorials on the latest programming languages and technologies they use in their daily work. All books in the Developer's Library are written by expert technology practitioners who are exceptionally skilled at organizing and presenting information in a way that's useful for other programmers.

Developer's Library books cover a wide range of topics, from open-source programming languages and databases, Linux programming, Microsoft, and Java, to Web development, social networking platforms, Mac/iPhone programming, and Android programming.

Introduction to Android™ Application Development

Android Essentials

Fifth Edition

Joseph Annuzzi, Jr.
Lauren Darcey
Shane Conder

✦ Addison-Wesley

Boston • Columbus • Indianapolis • New York • San Francisco • Amsterdam • Cape Town
Dubai • London • Madrid • Milan • Munich • Paris • Montreal • Toronto • Delhi • Mexico City
Sao Paulo • Sidney • Hong Kong • Seoul • Singapore • Taipei • Tokyo

For information about buying this title in bulk quantities, or for special sales opportunities (which may include electronic versions; custom cover designs; and content particular to your business, training goals, marketing focus, or branding interests), please contact our corporate sales department at corpsales@pearsoned.com or (800) 382-3419.

For government sales inquiries, please contact governmentsales@pearsoned.com.

For questions about sales outside the U.S., please contact international@pearsoned.com.

Visit us on the Web: informit.com/aw

Library of Congress Cataloging-in-Publication Data
Names: Annuzzi, Joseph, Jr., author. | Darcey, Lauren, 1977- author. |
    Conder, Shane, 1975- author.
Title: Introduction to Android application development : Android essentials /
    Joseph Annuzzi, Jr., Lauren Darcey, Shane Conder.
Description: Fifth edition | New York : Addison-Wesley, [2016] | Includes
    bibliographical references and index.
Identifiers: LCCN 2015037913 | ISBN 9780134389455 (pbk. : alk. paper)
Subjects: LCSH: Application software—Development. | Android (Electronic
    resource) | Mobile computing. | Wireless communication systems.
Classification: LCC QA76.76.A65 A56 2016 | DDC 005.3—dc23
LC record available at http://lccn.loc.gov/2015037913

ISBN-13: 978-0-13-438945-5
ISBN-10: 0-13-438945-X

Text printed in the United States on recycled paper at RR Donnelley in Crawfordsville, Indiana.
First printing December 2015

Editor-in-Chief
Mark L. Taub

Executive Editor
Laura Lewin

Development Editor
Songlin Qiu

Managing Editor
John Fuller

Senior Project Editor
Kesel Wilson

Copy Editor
Deborah Thompson

Indexer
Jack Lewis

Proofreader
Sue Boshers

Technical Reviewers
Douglas Jones
Ray Rischpater
Valerie Shipbaugh

Editorial Assistant
Olivia Basegio

Cover Designer
Chuti Prasertsith

Compositor
codeMantra

❖

This book is dedicated to Cleopatra (Cleo).
—Joseph Annuzzi, Jr.

This book is dedicated to ESC.
—Lauren Darcey and Shane Conder

❖

Contents at a Glance

Contents

Acknowledgments

This book is the result of collaboration among the finest group of professionals: from the efforts of the team at Pearson Education (Addison-Wesley); from the suggestions made by the technical reviewers; and from the support of family, friends, coworkers, and acquaintances alike. We'd like to thank the Android developer community, Google, and the Android Open Source Project for their vision and expertise. Special thanks go to Mark Taub for believing in the vision for extending this book to another edition; Laura Lewin, who was the driving force behind the book—without her this book would not have become a reality; Olivia Basegio, who was instrumental in orchestrating all of the efforts among everyone involved; and Songlin Qiu for performing countless iterations combing through the manuscript to make this book ready for production. And to the technical reviewers: Ray Rischpater, who surprised us yet again with quality recommendations; Doug Jones, whose expertise uncovered needed improvements to the fine details; and Valerie Shipbaugh, who was able to provide tips on desperately needed clarification (as well as Mike Wallace, Mark Gjoel, Dan Galpin, Tony Hillerson, Ronan Schwarz, and Charles Stearns, who reviewed previous editions). For previous editions, Dan Galpin graciously provided the clever Android graphics used for Tips, Notes, and Warnings. Amy Badger must be commended for her wonderful waterfall illustration, and we also thank Hans Bodlaender for letting us use the nifty chess font he developed as a hobby project.

About the Authors

Joseph Annuzzi, Jr. is a code warrior, graphic artist, entrepreneur, and author. He usually can be found mastering the Android platform; implementing cutting-edge HTML5 capabilities; leveraging various cloud technologies; speaking in different programming languages; working with diverse frameworks; integrating with various APIs; tinkering with peer-to-peer, cryptography, and biometric algorithms; or creating stunningly realistic 3D renders. He is always on the lookout for disruptive Internet and mobile technologies. He graduated from the University of California, Davis, with a BS in managerial economics and a minor in computer science, and lives where much of the action is, Silicon Valley.

When he is not working with technology, he has been known to lounge in the sun on the beaches of the Black Sea with international movie stars; he has trekked through the Bavarian forest in winter, has immersed himself in the culture of the Italian Mediterranean, and has narrowly escaped the wrath of an organized crime ring in Eastern Europe after his taxi dropped him off in front of the bank ATM they were liquidating. He also lives an active and healthy lifestyle, designs and performs custom fitness training routines to stay in shape, and adores his loyal beagle, Cleopatra.

Lauren Darcey is responsible for the technical leadership and direction of a small software company specializing in mobile technologies, including Android and iOS consulting services. With more than two decades of experience in professional software production, Lauren is a recognized authority in application architecture and the development of commercial-grade mobile applications. Lauren received a BS in computer science from the University of California, Santa Cruz.

She spends her copious free time traveling the world with her geeky mobile-minded husband and pint-sized geekling daughter. She is an avid nature photographer. Her work has been published in books and newspapers around the world. In South Africa, she dove with 4-meter-long great white sharks and got stuck between a herd of rampaging hippopotami and an irritated bull elephant. She's been attacked by monkeys in Japan, has gotten stuck in a ravine with two hungry lions in Kenya, has gotten thirsty in Egypt, narrowly avoided a coup d'état in Thailand, geocached her way through the Swiss Alps, drank her way through the beer halls of Germany, slept in the crumbling castles of Europe, and has gotten her tongue stuck to an iceberg in Iceland (while being watched by a herd of suspicious wild reindeer). Most recently, she can be found hiking along the Appalachian Trail with her daughter and documenting the journey with Google Glass.

Shane Conder has extensive application development experience and has focused his attention on mobile and embedded development for well over a decade. He has designed and developed many commercial applications for Android, iOS, BREW, BlackBerry, J2ME, Palm, and Windows Mobile—some of which have been installed on millions of phones worldwide. Shane has written extensively about the tech industry and is known for his keen insights regarding mobile development platform trends. Shane received a BS in computer science from the University of California, Santa Cruz.

A self-admitted gadget freak, Shane always has the latest smartphone, tablet, or wearable. He enjoys traveling the world with his geeky wife, even if she did make him dive with 4-meter-long great white sharks and almost get eaten by a lion in Kenya. He admits that he has to take at least three devices with him when backpacking ("just in case")—even where there is no coverage. Lately, his smartwatch collection has exceeded his number of wrists. Luckily, his young daughter is happy to offer her own. Such are the burdens of a daughter of engineers.

Introduction

Android is a popular, free, open-source mobile platform that has taken the world by storm. This book provides guidance for software development teams on designing, developing, testing, debugging, and distributing professional Android applications. If you're a veteran mobile developer, you can find tips and tricks to streamline the development process and take advantage of Android's unique features. If you're new to mobile development, this book provides everything you need to make a smooth transition from traditional software development to mobile development—specifically, the most promising platform: Android.

Who Should Read This Book

This book includes tips for successful mobile development based upon our years in the mobile industry and covers everything you need to know in order to run a successful Android project from concept to completion. We cover how the mobile software process differs from traditional software development, including tricks to save valuable time and pitfalls to avoid. Regardless of the size of your project, this book is for you.

This book was written for several audiences:

- **Software developers who want to learn to develop professional Android applications.** The bulk of this book is targeted at software developers with Java experience who do not necessarily have mobile development experience. More-seasoned developers of mobile applications can learn how to take advantage of Android and how it differs from the other technologies on the mobile development market today.

- **Quality assurance personnel tasked with testing Android applications.** Whether they are black-box or white-box testing, quality assurance engineers can find this book invaluable. We devote several chapters to mobile QA concerns, including topics such as developing solid test plans and defect-tracking systems for mobile applications, how to manage handsets, and how to test applications thoroughly using all the Android tools available.

- **Project managers planning and managing Android development teams.** Managers can use this book to help plan, hire for, and execute Android projects from start to finish. We cover project risk management and how to keep Android projects running smoothly.

- **Other audiences.** This book is useful not only to the software developer, but also to the corporation looking at potential vertical market applications, the entrepreneur thinking about a cool phone application, and the hobbyist looking for some fun with his or her new phone. Businesses seeking to evaluate Android for their specific needs (including feasibility analysis) can also find the information provided valuable. Anyone with an Android handset and a good idea for a mobile application can put the information in this book to use for fun and profit.

Key Questions Answered in This Book

This book answers the following questions:

1. What is Android? How do the SDK versions differ?
2. How is Android different from other mobile technologies? How should developers take advantage of these differences?
3. How do developers use Android Studio and the Android SDK tools to develop and debug Android applications on the emulator and handsets?
4. How are Android applications structured?
5. How do developers design robust user interfaces for mobile—specifically, for Android?
6. What capabilities does the Android SDK have and how can developers use them?
7. What is material design and why does it matter?
8. How does the mobile development process differ from traditional desktop development?
9. What strategies work best for Android development?
10. What do managers, developers, and testers need to look for when planning, developing, and testing a mobile application?
11. How do mobile teams deliver quality Android applications for publishing?
12. How do mobile teams package Android applications for distribution?
13. How do mobile teams make money from Android applications?
14. And, finally, what is new in this edition of the book?

How This Book Is Structured

Introduction to Android Application Development, Fifth Edition, focuses on Android essentials, including setting up the development environment, understanding the application lifecycle, user interface design, developing for different types of devices, and the mobile software process from design and development to testing and publication of commercial-grade applications.

The book is divided into six parts. Here is an overview of the various parts:

- **Part I: Platform Overview**

  Part I provides an introduction to Android, explaining how it differs from other mobile platforms. You become familiar with the Android SDK tools, install the development tools, and write and run your first Android application—on the emulator and on a handset. This section is of primary interest to developers and testers, especially white-box testers.

- **Part II: Application Basics**

  Part II introduces the principles necessary to write Android applications. You learn how Android applications are structured and how to include resources, such as strings, graphics, and user interface components, in your projects. You learn about the core user interface element in Android: the View. You also learn about the most common user interface controls and layouts provided in the Android SDK. This section is of primary interest to developers.

- **Part III: Application Design Essentials**

  Part III dives deeper into how applications are designed in Android. You learn about material design, styling, and common design patterns found among applications. You also learn how to design and plan your applications. This section is of primary interest to developers.

- **Part IV: Application Development Essentials**

  Part IV covers the features used by most Android applications, including storing persistent application data using preferences, working with files and directories, SQLite, and content providers. This section is of primary interest to developers.

- **Part V: Application Delivery Essentials**

  Part V covers the software development process for mobile, from start to finish, with tips and tricks for project management, software developers, user-experience designers, and quality assurance personnel.

- **Part VI: Appendixes**

  Part VI includes several helpful appendixes to help you get up and running with the most important Android tools. This section consists of tips and tricks for Android Studio, an overview of the Android SDK tools, three helpful quick-start guides for the Android development tools—the emulator, Device Monitor, and Gradle—as well as answers to the end-of-chapter quiz questions.

An Overview of Changes in This Edition

When we began writing the first edition of this book, there were no Android devices on the market. Today, there are hundreds of millions of Android devices (with thousands of different device models) shipping all over the world every quarter—phones, tablets, e-book readers, smartwatches, and specialty devices such as gaming consoles, TVs, and Google Glass. Other devices such as Google Chromecast provide screen sharing between Android devices and TVs.

The Android platform has gone through extensive changes since the first edition of this book was published. The Android SDK has many new features, and the development tools have received many much-needed upgrades. Android, as a technology, is now the leader within the mobile marketplace.

In this new edition, we took the opportunity to add a wealth of information. But don't worry, it's still the book readers loved the first, second, third, and fourth time around; it's just much bigger, better, and more comprehensive, following many best practices. In addition to adding new content, we've retested and upgraded all existing content (text and sample code) for use with the latest Android SDKs available, while still remaining backward compatible. We included quiz questions to help readers ensure they understand each chapter's content, and end-of-chapter exercises for readers to perform to dig deeper into all that Android has to offer. The Android development community is diverse and we aim to support all developers, regardless of which devices they are developing for. This includes developers who need to target nearly all platforms, so coverage in some key areas of older SDKs continues to be included because it's often the most reasonable option for compatibility.

Here are some of the highlights of the additions and enhancements we've made to this edition:

- The entire book has been overhauled to include coverage of the Android Studio IDE. Previous editions of this book included coverage of the Eclipse IDE. Where applicable, all content, images, and code samples have been updated for Android Studio. In addition, coverage of the latest and greatest Android tools and utilities is included.

- The chapter on defining the manifest includes coverage of the new Android 6.0 Marshmallow (API Level 23) permission model, and it provides a code sample demonstrating the new permission model.

- A brand new chapter on material design has been added and demonstrates how developers can integrate common material design features into their application, and it includes a code sample.

- A brand new chapter on working with styles has been included with tips on how to best organize styles and reuse common UI components for optimized display rendering, and it provides a code sample.

- A brand new chapter on common design patterns has been added with details on various ways to architect your application, and it offers a code sample.

- A brand new chapter on incorporating SQLite for working with persistent database-backed application data has been added, and it includes a code sample.

- An appendix providing tips and tricks for using Android Studio has been included.

- An appendix on the Gradle build system has been included to help you understand what Gradle is and why it's important.

- The `AdvancedLayouts` code sample has been updated so that the `GridView` and `ListView` components make use of `Fragment` and `ListFragment` classes respectively.

- Some code samples include an `ActionBar` by making use of the new `Toolbar`, and have done so using the support library for maintaining compatibility on devices running older APIs. When necessary, application manifests have been updated to support parent-child `Activity` relationships that support up-navigation.
- Many code samples make use of the `AppCompatActivity` class and the `appcompat-v7` support library.
- All chapters and appendixes include quiz questions and exercises for readers to test their knowledge of the subject matter presented.
- All existing chapters have been updated, often with some entirely new sections.
- All sample code and accompanying applications have been updated to work with the latest SDK.

As you can see, we cover many of the hottest and most exciting features that Android has to offer. We didn't take this review lightly; we touched every existing chapter, updated content, and added new chapters as well. Finally, we included many additions, clarifications, and, yes, even a few fixes based on the feedback from our fantastic (and meticulous) readers. Thank you!

Development Environments Used in This Book

The Android code in this book was written using the following development environments:

- Windows 7, 8, and Mac OS X 10.9
- Android Studio 1.3.2
- Android SDK API Level 23 (referred to in this book as Android Marshmallow)
- Android SDK Tools 24.3.4
- Android SDK Platform Tools 23.0.0
- Android SDK Build Tools 23.0.0
- Android Support Repository 17 (where applicable)
- Java SE Development Kit (JDK) 7 Update 55
- Android devices: Nexus 4, 5, and 6 (phones), Nexus 7 (first- and second-generation 7-inch tablet), Nexus 9 and 10 (large tablet), including various other popular devices and form factors.

The Android platform continues to grow aggressively in market share against competing mobile platforms, such as Apple iOS, Windows Phone, and BlackBerry OS. New and exciting types of Android devices reach consumers' hands at a furious pace. Developers have embraced Android as a target platform to reach the device users of today and tomorrow.

Android's latest major platform update, Android Marshmallow, brings many new features. This book covers the latest SDK and tools available, but it does not focus on them to the detriment of popular legacy versions of the platform. The book is meant to be an overall reference to help developers support as many popular devices as possible on the market today. As of the writing of this book, approximately 9.7% of users' devices are running a version of Android Lollipop, 5.0 or 5.1, and Android Marshmallow has yet to be released on real devices. Of course, some devices will receive upgrades, and users will purchase new Lollipop and Marshmallow devices as they become available, but for now, developers need to straddle this gap and support numerous versions of Android to reach the majority of users in the field. In addition, the next version of the Android operating system is likely to be released in the near future.

So what does this mean for this book? It means we provide legacy API support and discuss some of the newer APIs available in later versions of the Android SDK. We discuss strategies for supporting all (or at least most) users in terms of compatibility. And we provide screenshots that highlight different versions of the Android SDK, because each major revision has brought with it a change in the look and feel of the overall platform. That said, we are assuming that you are downloading the latest Android tools, so we provide screenshots and steps that support the latest tools available at the time of writing, not legacy tools. Those are the boundaries we set when trying to determine what to include and leave out of this book.

Supplementary Materials for This Book

The source code that accompanies this book is available for download from our book's website: *http://introductiontoandroid.blogspot.com/2015/08/5th-edition-book-code-samples.html*. The code samples are organized by chapter and downloadable in zip format or accessible from the command line with Git. You'll also find other Android topics discussed on our book's website (*http://introductiontoandroid.blogspot.com*).

Conventions Used in This Book

This book uses the following conventions:

- Code and programming terms are set in monospace text.
- Java import statements, exception handling, and error checking are often removed from printed code examples for clarity and to keep the book to a reasonable length.

This book also presents information in the following sidebars:

Tip

Tips provide useful information or hints related to the current text.

Note

Notes provide additional information that might be interesting or relevant.

Warning

Warnings provide hints or tips about pitfalls that may be encountered and how to avoid them.

Where to Find More Information

There is a vibrant, helpful Android developer community on the Web. Here are a number of useful websites for Android developers and followers of the mobile industry:

- Android Developer website: the Android SDK and developer reference site: *http://d.android.com/index.html* and *http://d.android.com*
- Google Plus: Android Developers Group: *https://plus.google.com/+AndroidDevelopers/posts*
- YouTube: Android Developers and Google Design: *https://www.youtube.com/user/androiddevelopers* *https://www.youtube.com/channel/UClKO7be7O9cUGL94PHnAeOA*
- Google Material Design: *https://www.google.com/design/spec/material-design/introduction.html*
- Stack Overflow: the Android website with great technical information (complete with tags) and an official support forum for developers: *http://stackoverflow.com/questions/tagged/android*
- Android Open Source Project: *https://source.android.com/index.html*
- Open Handset Alliance: Android manufacturers, operators, and developers: *http://openhandsetalliance.com*
- Google Play: buy and sell Android applications: *https://play.google.com/store*
- tuts+: Android development tutorials: *http://code.tutsplus.com/categories/android*
- Google Sample Apps: open-source Android applications hosted on GitHub: *https://github.com/googlesamples*
- Android Tools Project Site: the tools team discusses updates and changes: *https://sites.google.com/a/android.com/tools/recent*
- FierceDeveloper: a weekly newsletter for wireless developers: *http://fiercedeveloper.com*
- XDA-Developers Android Forum: *http://forum.xda-developers.com/android*
- Developer.com: a developer-oriented site with mobile articles: *http://developer.com*

Contacting the Authors

We welcome your comments, questions, and feedback. We invite you to visit our blog at:

- *http://introductiontoandroid.blogspot.com*

Or email us at:

- *introtoandroid5e@gmail.com*

Find Joseph Annuzzi on LinkedIn:

- Joseph Annuzzi, Jr.: *https://www.linkedin.com/in/josephannuzzi*

Circle Joseph Annuzzi on Google+:

- Joseph Annuzzi, Jr.: *http://goo.gl/FBQeL*

Platform Overview

1

Presenting Android

The mobile development community has helped transform the Android operating system (OS) into the global leader. Mobile device users have shown their passion for Android. Developing for Android is now a primary focus for companies that would like to target and retain a mobile user base for their businesses. Handset manufacturers and mobile operators have invested heavily in Android to create unique experiences for their customers. Entrepreneurs and startups are delivering Android-application user experiences that you cannot find on other mobile platforms or other platforms such as desktops. Further, new device categories continue to emerge, and the creators of those devices are showing favor for powering these devices with Android.

Android has dominated the market as a game-changing platform for the mobile development community. An innovative and open platform, Android is addressing the increasing demands of the marketplace as it continues to expand to new types of devices beyond phones and tablets, and further penetrates the far regions of the globe. This chapter introduces the Android OS and where the platform fits into the marketplace, and discusses how the platform operates.

The Android Open Source Project (AOSP)

The Android Open Source Project (AOSP) is an initiative led by Google that makes the source code of the Android OS available for all to read, review, and modify to your liking. You may make contributions of your own custom code for everyone else to use if you so desire. The main goal of the AOSP is to provide a set of compatibility guidelines—for OEMs and device manufacturers—for porting Android to custom devices and for building accessories that comply with Android's open accessory standard, allowing those OEMs and manufacturers to deliver a standard experience.

Although anyone is free to fork the Android OS source code, maintaining a consistent OS experience is important for the Android ecosystem because making radical changes to that experience introduces fragmentation in the marketplace and competing Android distributions. To learn more about the AOSP and to review the OS source code, see *https://source.android.com/index.html.*

The Open Handset Alliance

Google has been busy spreading its vision, its brand, its search and ad-revenue-based platform, and its suite of tools to the mobile marketplace. The company's business model has been amazingly successful on the Internet and, technically speaking, mobile isn't that different.

Google Goes Mobile First

The company's initial forays into mobile were beset with many problems. The freedoms Internet users enjoyed were not shared by mobile phone subscribers of older platforms because the mobile operating systems of those times were closed ecosystems—not open source like Android—so developing applications for those closed-ecosystem mobile operating systems was limited to a few players.

Internet users can choose from a wide variety of computer brands, operating systems, Internet service providers, and Web browser applications. Nearly all Google services are free and ad driven. Many applications created by Google directly competed with the applications available on the mobile operating systems of those closed ecosystems. The applications ranged from simple calendars and calculators to navigation with Google Maps—not to mention other services such as Gmail and YouTube.

When Google's approach to application creation within those closed ecosystems didn't yield the intended results, Google decided on a different approach—to revamp the entire ecosystem upon which mobile application development was based, hoping to provide a more open environment for users and developers: the Internet model. The Internet model allows users to choose among freeware, shareware, and paid software. This enables free-market competition among services.

Fast forward to today: Google's Android efforts have come to the forefront. Google's search engine algorithm has been modified to penalize websites that are not mobile compatible. Mobile search traffic has exceeded that of desktop search traffic and it is only going to continue to grow. Google's mobile first philosophy surely makes sense.

Introducing the Open Handset Alliance

With its user-centric, democratic design philosophies, Google has led a movement to turn the closely guarded mobile market of the past into one where phone users can move between carriers easily and have unfettered access to applications and services. With its vast resources, Google has taken a broad approach, examining the mobile infrastructure—from the FCC's wireless spectrum policies to the handset manufacturers' requirements, application developer needs, and mobile operator desires.

Years ago, Google joined with other like-minded members in the mobile community and posed the following question: What would it take to build a better mobile phone? The Open Handset Alliance (OHA) was formed in November 2007 to answer that very question. The OHA is a business alliance composed of many of the largest and most successful mobile companies on the planet. Its members include chip makers, handset manufacturers, software developers, and service providers. The entire mobile supply chain is well represented.

Andy Rubin has been credited as the father of the Android platform. His company, Android, Inc., was acquired by Google in 2005. Working together, OHA members, including Google, began developing an open-standard platform based on technology developed at Android, Inc., that would aim to alleviate the aforementioned problems hindering the mobile community. The result was the AOSP described previously.

Google's involvement in the AOSP has been so extensive that who should take responsibility for the Android platform (the OHA or Google) is unclear. Google provides the initial code for the AOSP and provides online Android documentation, tools, forums, the Software Development Kit (SDK), tools, and platforms for developers. Most major Android news originates from Google. The company has also hosted a number of events at conferences (Google I/O, Mobile World Congress, and CTIA Wireless) for millions of dollars in prizes to spur development on the platform. That's not to say Google is the only organization involved, but it is the driving force behind the platform.

Joining the Open Handset Alliance

The AOSP provides the entire source code for the Android OS as well as instructions for meeting device compatibility requirements, but does not include the source code for many of Google's proprietary suite of applications. The benefits of joining the Open Handset Alliance include the ability to license Google Mobile Services (GMS), which include proprietary Google applications such as Google Play, YouTube, Google Maps, Gmail, and many other Google branded applications and services. GMS is not included in the AOSP and must be licensed directly from Google. Becoming part of the OHA allows you to bundle GMS on Android-compatible devices.

Manufacturers: Designing Android Devices

More than half the members of the OHA are device manufacturers, such as Samsung, Motorola, Dell, Sony Ericsson, HTC, and LG, as well as semiconductor companies, such as Intel, Texas Instruments, ARM, NVIDIA, and Qualcomm.

The first Android handset to ship—the T-Mobile G1—was developed by handset manufacturer HTC with service provided by T-Mobile. It was released in October 2008. Many other Android handsets were slated for 2009 and early 2010. The platform gained momentum relatively quickly. By the fourth quarter of 2010, Android had come to dominate the smartphone market, gaining ground steadily against competitive platforms such as RIM BlackBerry, Apple iOS, and Windows Mobile.

Google normally announces Android platform statistics at its annual Google I/O conference each year and at important events, such as financial earnings calls. As of May 2015, Android devices were being shipped to more than 130 countries, and Google Play had more than 1 billion active users, with 50 billion app installs in the previous 12 months. The advantages of widespread manufacturer and carrier support appear to be really paying off at this point.

Manufacturers continue to create new generations of Android devices—from phones and tablets with HD displays, to watches for enhancing your mobile experience or managing your fitness level, to dedicated e-book readers, to full-featured televisions, netbooks, integration with automobiles, and almost any other "smart" device you can imagine.

Mobile Operators: Delivering the Android Experience

After you have developed the devices, you have to get them out to the users. Mobile operators from North, South, and Central America as well as Europe, Asia, India, Australia, Africa, and the Middle East have joined the OHA, ensuring a worldwide market for the Android movement. With nearly 1 billion subscribers alone, telephony giant China Mobile is a founding member of the alliance.

Much of Android's success is also due to the fact that many Android handsets don't come with the traditional smartphone price tag—quite a few are offered free with activation by carriers. Competitors such as the Apple iPhone have struggled to provide competitive offerings at the low end of the market. For the first time, the average Jane or Joe can afford a feature-full smart device. We've heard so many people, from waitstaff to grocery store clerks, say how much their lives have changed for the better after receiving their first Android phone. This phenomenon has only added to Android's status.

Manufacturers have contributed significantly to the growth of Android. In July 2015, according to International Data Corporation (IDC), Samsung shipped 73.2 million smartphones worldwide in the second quarter of 2015 (*http://www.idc.com/getdoc. jsp?containerId=prUS25804315*), with the majority of those devices most likely powered by Android.

Google has also created its own Android brand known as Nexus. There are currently multiple devices that have been introduced through the Nexus line—the 4, 5, 6, 7, 9, 10, and Player—each created in partnership with the manufacturers LG (4, 5), Motorola (6), ASUS (7, Player), HTC (9), and Samsung (10). The Nexus devices provide the full, authentic Android experience as Google intends. Many developers use these devices for building and testing their applications because they are the only devices in the world that receive the latest Android operating system upgrades as they are released. If you, too, would like your applications to work on the latest Android operating system version, you should consider investing in one or more of these devices when they become available.

Apps Drive Device Sales: Developing Android Applications

When users acquire Android devices, they need those killer apps, right?

Initially, Google led the pack in developing Android applications. It also developed the first successful distribution platform for third-party Android applications, originally called the Android Market, now known as Google Play. Google Play remains the primary method by which users download apps, but it is no longer the only distribution mechanism for Android apps.

As of May 2015, there have been more than 50 billion application installations from Google Play within the previous 12 months. This takes into account only applications published through this one app store—not the many other applications sold individually or on other app markets across the globe. These numbers also do not take into account all the Web applications that target mobile devices running the Android platform. This opens up even more application choices for Android users and more opportunities for Android developers.

Google Play has been working to increase the exposure and sales of game applications and has provided the Play Game Services SDK. This SDK allows developers to add real-time social features to games, and application programming interfaces (APIs) for implementing leaderboards and achievements to help drive new users to applications, while continuing to engage existing users. An effort to help drive sales of content has also been undertaken. Users are always looking for new music, movies, TV shows, books, magazines, and more, and Google Play's focus on content has placed it in a position to keep up with user demand for such services.

Taking Advantage of All Android Has to Offer

Android's open platform has been embraced by much of the mobile development community—extending far beyond the members of the OHA.

As Android devices and applications have become more readily available, many other mobile operators and device manufacturers have jumped at the chance to sell Android devices to their subscribers, especially given the cost benefits compared to the older proprietary platforms. The Android platform's open standard has resulted in reduced operator costs in licensing and royalties, and we are now seeing a migration to more open devices. The market has cracked wide open; new types of users are able to consider smartphones for the first time. Android is well suited to fill this demand.

Android: Where We Are Now

Android continues to grow at an aggressive rate on all fronts (devices, developers, and users). Lately, the focus has been on several specific topics:

- **Upgrades to competitive hardware and software features:** The Android SDK developers have focused on providing APIs for features that are not available on competing platforms to move Android ahead in the market. For example, recent releases of the Android SDK have featured significant improvements to Notifications to bring you the information that matters most to you when you need it.

- **Expansion beyond phones and tablets:** Smartwatch usage is on the rise with Android users. There are many new Android Wear devices on the market that come in many different sizes and form factors. Hardware manufacturers are even using Android for gaming consoles, TVs, and dashboards for automobiles, in addition to many other types of devices that require an operating system. Google has even announced Project Brillo, a version of Android designed for the Internet of Things (IoT), along with Weave, an IoT protocol for connecting these devices.

- **Improved user-facing features:** The Android development team has shifted its focus from feature implementation to providing user-facing usability upgrades and "chrome." It has invested heavily in creating a smoother, faster, more responsive user interface, in addition to updating its design documentation with excellent training in best practices for developers to follow. Following these principles should help any application increase usability.

> **Note**
>
> Some may wonder about various legal battles surrounding Android that appear to involve almost every industry player in the mobile market. Although most of these issues do not affect developers directly, some have—in particular, those dealing with in-app purchases. This is typical of any popular platform. We can't provide any legal advice here. What we can recommend is keeping informed on the various legal battles and hope they turn out well, not just for Android, but for all platforms they impact.

Android Platform Uniqueness

The Android platform itself is hailed as "the first complete, open, and free mobile platform."

- **Complete:** The designers took a comprehensive approach when they developed the Android platform. They began with a secure operating system and built a robust software framework on top that allows for rich application-development opportunities.
- **Open:** The Android platform is provided through open-source licensing. Developers have unprecedented access to the device features when developing applications.
- **Free:** Android applications are free to develop. There are no licensing fees for developing on the platform, no required membership fees, no required testing fees, and no required signing or certification fees. Android applications can be distributed and commercialized in a variety of ways. There is no cost for distributing your applications on your own, and there are app stores that do not require fees for publishing your application for download. But to publish your applications on Google Play requires registration and paying a small, one-time $25 fee. (The term "free" implies there might actually be costs for development, but they are not mandated by the Android platform. Costs for designing, developing, testing, marketing, and maintaining are not included. If you provide all of these, you may not be laying out cash, but there is a cost associated with them. The $25 developer registration fee is designed to encourage developers to create quality applications for Google Play.)

Android: The Code Names

The Android mascot is a little green robot, shown in Figure 1.1. This little robot is often used to depict Android-related materials.

Figure 1.1   The official Android mascot.

Since the Android 1.0 SDK was released, Android platform development has continued at a fast and furious pace. For quite some time, a new Android SDK came out every couple of months! In typical tech-sector jargon, each Android SDK has had a project name. In Android's case, the SDKs are named alphabetically after sweets.

Free and Open Source

Android is an open-source platform. Neither developers nor device manufacturers pay royalties or license fees to develop for the platform.

The underlying operating system of Android is licensed under GNU General Public License Version 2 (GPLv2), a strong "copyleft" license where any third-party improvements must continue to fall under the open-source licensing agreement terms. The Android framework is distributed under the Apache Software License (ASL/Apache2), which allows for the distribution of both open- and closed-source derivations of the source code. Platform developers (device manufacturers especially) can choose to enhance Android without having to provide their improvements to the open-source community. Instead, platform developers can profit from enhancements such as device-specific improvements and redistribute their work under whatever licensing they want.

Android application developers have the ability to distribute their applications under whatever licensing scheme they prefer, too. They can write open-source freeware or traditional licensed applications for profit and everything in between.

Familiar and Inexpensive Development Tools

Unlike some proprietary platforms that require developer registration fees, vetting, and expensive compilers, there are no up-front costs to developing Android applications.

Freely Available Software Development Kit

The Android SDK, tools, and platforms are freely available. Developers can download the Android SDK from the Android website after agreeing to the terms and conditions of the Android Software Development Kit License Agreement.

Familiar Language, Familiar Development Environments

Developers now have access to an official integrated development environment (IDE) for Android application development, Android Studio, which comes bundled with the Android SDK tools, the most recent Android Platform, and the most recent Android emulator system image with Google APIs. Android Studio is based on the free Community Edition of IntelliJ IDEA, developed by the company JetBrains s.r.o.

Before Android Studio became the official IDE for Android development, many developers chose to use the popular and freely available Eclipse IDE to design and develop Android applications. Eclipse has been one of the most popular IDEs for Android development, and the Android Developer Tools (ADT) plugin has been available for facilitating Android development with Eclipse.

You may also choose to use the Android SDK tools from the command-line as a stand-alone application, without being tied to a particular IDE, or if you prefer running command-line build scripts.

Android Studio is the recommended IDE for Android application development and is supported on the following operating systems:

- Windows 2003, Vista, 7, and 8 (32-bit or 64-bit)
- Mac OS X 10.8.5 up to 10.9
- Linux GNOME or KDE desktops (Tested on Ubuntu Linux 14.04 64-bit)

Reasonable Learning Curve for Developers

Android applications are written in a well-respected programming language: Java. The Android application framework includes traditional programming constructs, such as threads and processes and specially designed data structures to encapsulate objects commonly used in mobile applications. Developers can rely on familiar class libraries such as `java.net` and `java.text`. Specialty libraries for tasks such as graphics and database management are implemented using well-defined open standards such as OpenGL Embedded Systems (OpenGL ES) and SQLite.

Enabling Development of Powerful Applications

In the past, device manufacturers often established special relationships with trusted third-party software developers (OEM/ODM relationships). This elite group of software developers wrote native applications, such as messaging and Web browsers that shipped on the device as part of its core feature set. To design these applications, the manufacturer would grant the developer privileged inside access to and knowledge of the internal software framework and firmware.

On the Android platform, there is no distinction between native and third-party applications, thus helping to maintain healthy competition among application developers. All Android applications use the same APIs. Android applications have unprecedented access to the underlying hardware, allowing developers to write much more powerful applications. Applications can be extended or replaced altogether.

Rich, Secure Application Integration

One of the Android platform's most compelling and innovative features is well-designed application integration. Android provides all the tools necessary to build a better "mousetrap," if you will, by allowing developers to write applications that seamlessly leverage core functionality such as Web browsing, contact management, and messaging. Applications can also become content providers and share their data with each other in a secure fashion.

No Costly Obstacles for Development

Android applications require none of the costly and time-intensive testing and certification programs that other platforms such as iOS do. To create Android applications, there is no cost whatsoever other than your time. All you need is a computer, an Android device, a good idea, and an understanding of Java.

If you want to publish applications within Google Play, a one-time, low-cost ($25) developer fee is required, but you may choose to publish your application in an app store that does not require a developer fee for publishing or you may host the application for download on your own.

A "Free Market" for Applications

Android developers are free to choose any kind of revenue model they want. They can develop freeware, shareware, trial-ware or ad-driven applications, and paid applications. Android was designed to fundamentally change the rules about what kind of mobile applications could be developed. On mobile platforms preceding Android, developers faced many restrictions that had little to do with the application's functionality or features such as:

- Store limitations on the number of competing applications of a given type
- Store limitations on pricing, revenue models, and royalties
- Operator unwillingness to provide applications for smaller demographics

With Android, developers can write and successfully publish any kind of application they want. Developers can tailor applications to small demographics, instead of just large-scale moneymaking markets often insisted on by mobile operators. Vertical market applications can be deployed to specific, targeted users.

Because developers have a variety of application distribution mechanisms to choose from, they can pick the methods that work for them instead of being forced to play by others' rules. Android developers can distribute their applications to users in a variety of ways:

- Google developed Google Play (formerly the Android Market), a generic Android application store with a revenue-sharing model. Google Play also has a Web store for browsing and buying apps online. Google Play also sells movies, music, and books, so your application will be in good company.
- Amazon Appstore for Android launched in 2011 with a lineup of exciting Android applications using its own billing and revenue-sharing models.
- Numerous other third-party application stores are available. Some are for niche markets; others cater to many different mobile platforms.
- Developers can come up with their own delivery and payment mechanisms, such as distributing from a website or within an enterprise.

Mobile operators and carriers are still free to develop their own application stores and enforce their own rules, but these will no longer be the only opportunities developers have to distribute their applications. Be sure to read any application store's agreements carefully before distributing your applications on them.

A Growing Platform

Early Android developers have had to deal with the typical roadblocks associated with a new platform: frequently revised SDKs, lack of good documentation, market uncertainties, and mobile operators and device manufacturers that have been extremely slow in rolling out new upgrades of Android, if ever. This means that Android developers often need to target several different SDK versions to reach all users. Luckily, the continuously evolving Android SDK tools have made this easier than ever, and now that Android is a well-established platform, many of these issues have been ironed out. The Android forum community is lively, friendly, and very supportive when it comes to helping one another over these bumps in the road.

Each new version of the Android SDK has provided a number of substantial improvements to the platform. In recent revisions, the Android platform has received some much-needed enhancements in terms of visual appeal, performance, and user experience. Popular types of devices such as smartwatches and TVs are now fully supported by the platform, in addition to new categories such as automobiles.

Although most of these upgrades and improvements were welcome and necessary, new SDK versions often cause some upheaval within the Android developer community. A number of published applications have required retesting and resubmission to Google Play to conform to new SDK requirements, which are rolled out to select Android devices in the field as a firmware upgrade, rendering older applications obsolete and sometimes unusable.

Although these pains are expected, and most developers have endured them, it's important to remember that Android was a latecomer to the mobile marketplace compared to the iOS platform. The Apple App Store boasts many applications, but users demand these same applications on their Android devices. Few developers can afford to deploy exclusively to one platform or the other—they must support both.

The Android Platform

Android is an operating system and a software platform upon which applications are developed. A core set of applications for everyday tasks, such as Web browsing and email, are included on Android devices.

As a product of the OHA's vision for a robust and open-source development environment for mobile, Android is a leading development platform. The platform was designed for the sole purpose of encouraging a free and open market that users might want to have and software developers might want to develop for. So far the platform has lived up to that potential.

Android's Underlying Architecture

The Android platform is designed to be more fault tolerant than many of its predecessors. The device runs a Linux operating system upon which Android applications are executed in a secure fashion. Each Android application runs in its own Application Sandbox (see Figure 1.2). Android applications are managed code; therefore, they are much less likely to cause the device to crash, leading to fewer instances of device corruption (also called "bricking" the device, or rendering it useless).

The Linux Operating System

The Linux kernel handles core system services and acts as a hardware abstraction layer (HAL) between the physical hardware of the device and the Android software stack.

Some of the core functions the kernel handles include

- Enforcement of application permissions and security
- Low-level memory management
- Process management and threading
- The network stack
- Display, keypad input, camera, Wi-Fi, Flash memory, audio, binder interprocess communication (IPC), and power-management driver access

Android Runtime (ART)

Each Android application runs in a separate process, within its own Application Sandbox. The Android Runtime (ART) is the runtime successor of Dalvik. One of the main feature improvements introduced by ART is ahead-of-time compilation (AOT) rather than the just-in-time compilation (JIT) of Dalvik. With ART, applications are compiled during installation. The compiled files are stored on the device as an executable without requiring compilation prior to launching the application. On the other hand, Dalvik would compile application files prior to launching the application. ART was officially introduced in Android 5.0, and brings significant performance enhancements not previously available with Dalvik.

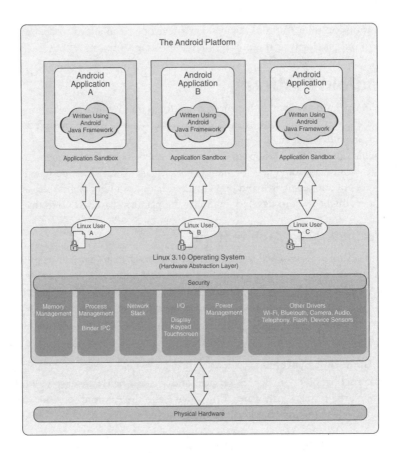

Figure 1.2   Diagram of the Android platform architecture.

Security and Permissions

The integrity of the Android platform is maintained through a variety of security measures. These measures help ensure that the user's data is secure and that the device is not subjected to malware or misuse.

Applications as Operating-System Users

When an application is installed, the operating system creates a new user profile associated with the application. Each application runs as a different user, with its own private files on the file system, a user ID, and a secure operating environment.

The application executes in its own process within its own Application Sandbox and under its own user ID on the operating system.

SELinux Kernel Security Module

Android 4.3 introduced a modified version of the Security-Enhanced Linux (SELinux) kernel module. This edition provides enhanced security for the Android OS and further confines applications to their own sandbox while enforcing mandatory access control (MAC) over all processes.

Explicitly Defined Application Permissions

To access shared resources on the system, Android applications request registration for the specific privileges they require. Some of these privileges enable the application to use device functionality to make calls, access the network, and control the camera and other hardware sensors. Applications also require permission to access shared data containing private and personal information, such as user preferences, the user's location, and contact information.

Applications might also enforce their own permissions by declaring them for other applications to use. An application can declare any number of different permission types, such as read-only or read-write permissions, for finer control over the application.

Android 6.0 (API Level 23) introduced a streamlined permission process. Rather than requiring users to grant all permissions upon application installation, you are now able to request permissions at runtime when your application actually needs access to a particular permission. Permissions with a protection level of normal are granted at installation and any permission that has a protection level other than normal must be requested at runtime.

Application Signing for Trust Relationships

All Android application packages are signed with a certificate, so users know that the application is authentic. The private key for the certificate is held by the developer. This helps establish a trust relationship between the developer and the user. It also enables the developer to control which applications can grant access to one another on the system. No certificate authority is necessary; self-signed certificates are acceptable.

Multiple Users and Restricted Profiles

Android 4.2 (API Level 17) brought support for multiple user accounts on shareable Android devices such as tablets. With the new release of Android 4.3 (API Level 18), primary device users are now able to create restricted profiles for limiting a user profile's access to particular applications. Developers may also leverage restricted profile capabilities in their applications to provide primary users the ability to further prohibit particular device users from accessing specific in-app content.

Google Play Developer Registration

To publish applications on Google Play, developers must create a developer account. Google Play is managed closely and no malware is tolerated.

Exploring Android Applications

The Android SDK provides an extensive set of APIs that are both modern and robust. Android device core system services are exposed and accessible to all applications. When granted the appropriate permissions, Android applications can share data with one another and access shared resources on the system securely.

Android Programming Language Choices

Android applications are written in Java. For now, the Java language is the developer's only choice for accessing the entire Android SDK.

> **Tip**
>
> There has been some speculation that other programming languages, such as C++, might be added in future versions of Android. If your application must rely on native code in another language such as C or C++, you might want to consider integrating it using the Android Native Development Kit (NDK).

You can also develop mobile Web applications that will run on Android devices. These applications can be accessed through an Android browser application, or an embedded WebView control within a native Android application (still written in Java). This book focuses on Java application development. You can find out more about developing Web applications for Android devices at the Android developer website: *http://d.android.com/guide/webapps/index.html*.

Got a Flash app you want to deploy to the Android platform? Check out Adobe's AIR support for the Android platform. Users install the Adobe AIR application from the Google Play store and then load their compatible applications using it. For more information, see the Adobe website: *http://adobe.com/devnet/air/air_for_android.html*.

Developers even have the option to build applications using certain scripting languages. There is an open-source project that is working to use scripting languages such as Python and others as options for building Android applications, but the project has not been updated in quite some time. For more information, see the android scripting project: *https://github.com/damonkohler/sl4a*. As with Web apps and Adobe AIR apps, developing SL4A applications is outside the scope of this book.

No Distinctions Made between Native and Third-Party Applications

Unlike other mobile development platforms, the Android platform makes no distinction between native applications and developer-created applications. Provided they are granted the appropriate permissions, all applications have the same access to core libraries and the underlying hardware interfaces.

Android devices ship with a set of native applications such as a Web browser and contact manager. Third-party applications might integrate with these core applications, extend them to provide a rich user experience, or replace them entirely with alternative applications. The idea is that any of these applications is built using the exact same APIs available to third-party developers, thus ensuring a level playing field, or as close to one as we can get.

Note that although this has been Google's line since the beginning, there are some cases where Google has used undocumented APIs. Because Android is open, there are no private APIs. Google has never blocked access to such APIs but has warned developers that using them may result in incompatibilities in future SDK versions. See the blog post at *http://android-developers.blogspot.com//2011/10/ics-and-non-public-apis.html* for some examples of previously undocumented APIs that have become publicly documented.

Commonly Used Packages

With Android, mobile developers no longer have to reinvent the wheel. Instead, developers use familiar class libraries exposed through Android's Java packages to perform common tasks involving graphics, database access, network access, secure communications, and utilities. The Android packages include support for the following:

- A wide variety of user interface controls (buttons, spinners, text input)
- A wide variety of user interface layouts (tables, tabs, lists)
- Integration capabilities (notifications, widgets)
- Secure networking and Web browsing features (SSL, WebKit)
- XML support (DOM, SAX, XML Pull Parser)
- Structured storage and relational databases (App Preferences, SQLite)
- Powerful 2D and 3D graphics (including SGL, OpenGL ES, and RenderScript)
- Multimedia frameworks for playing and recording stand-alone or network streaming (`MediaPlayer`, `JetPlayer`, `SoundPool`, `AudioManager`)
- Extensive support for many audio and visual media formats (MPEG4, H.264, MP3, AAC, AMR, JPG, and PNG)
- Access to optional hardware such as location-based services (LBS), USB, Wi-Fi, Bluetooth, NFC, and hardware sensors

Android Application Framework

The Android application framework provides everything necessary to implement an average application. The Android application lifecycle involves the following key components:

- Activities are functions that the application performs.
- Fragments are reusable and modular sections of activities.
- Loaders are for loading data asynchronously into fragments or activities.
- Groups of views define the application's layout.
- Intents inform the system about an application's plans.
- Services allow for background processing without user interaction.
- Notifications alert the user when something interesting happens.
- Content providers facilitate data transmission among different applications.

Android Platform Services

Android applications can interact with the operating system and underlying hardware using a collection of managers. Each manager is responsible for keeping the state of some underlying system service. For example:

- The `LocationManager` facilitates interaction with the location-based services available on the device.
- The `ViewManager` and `WindowManager` manage display and user interface fundamentals related to the device.

- The `AccessibilityManager` manages accessibility events, facilitating device support for users with physical impairments.
- The `ClipboardManager` provides access to the global clipboard for the device, for cutting and pasting content.
- The `DownloadManager` manages HTTP downloads in the background as a system service.
- The `FragmentManager` manages the fragments of an activity.
- The `AudioManager` provides access to audio and ringer controls.

Google Services

Google provides APIs for integrating with many different Google services. Prior to the addition of many of these services, developers would need to wait for mobile operators and device manufacturers to upgrade Android on their devices in order to take advantage of many common features such as maps or location-based services. Now developers are able to integrate the latest and greatest updates of these services by including the required SDKs in their application projects. Some of these Google services include:

- Maps
- Places
- Play Game services
- Google Sign-In
- In-app Billing and Subscriptions
- Google Cloud Messaging
- Mobile App Analytics SDK
- AdMob Ads

Android beyond the OHA and GMS

One of the primary benefits for device manufacturers becoming members of the OHA is the ability to license the GMS suite of Google branded applications such as Google Play. GMS provides features and capabilities not found on devices without GMS. With that said, there are other popular versions of Android not associated with the OHA and therefore they do not have access to GMS without resorting to aftermarket installations. Just because a device based on a custom fork of Android is not part of the OHA, and does not include GMS or Google Play, does not mean you should overlook supporting your applications on those devices. Here are some areas of interest that involve custom forks of Android.

Amazon Fire OS

Amazon has created its own version of Android named Fire OS. Fire OS is a fork of the AOSP that is installed on all Amazon Fire branded devices, such as the Fire Phone, Fire

Tablet, and Fire TV. Recently, Amazon released the Fire OS 5 developer preview that is based on Android Lollipop.

According to a report by Strategy Analytics, Inc., there are close to 4.5 million Amazon Fire TVs that have shipped since launch (*http://www.prnewswire.com/news-releases/amazon-fires-to-the-top-of-the-us-digital-media-streamer-market-says-strategy-analytics-300094475.html*). With millions of devices available, supporting your Android applications on Amazon Fire OS is definitely worth consideration.

You can learn more about the Amazon Fire OS version of Android here: *https://developer.amazon.com/public/solutions/platforms/android-fireos*.

Cyanogen OS and CyanogenMod

Another version of Android to keep an eye on is Cyanogen OS. Cyanogen OS is based on the CyanogenMod project that is a community-driven fork of the Android OS, without GMS, although there are aftermarket instructions and tools provided by the user community for installing apps such as Google Play. The Cyanogen, Inc., blog (*https://cyngn.com/blog/an-open-future*) boasts having over 50 million users in over 190 countries running different versions of CyanogenMod. CyanogenMod is classified as replacement firmware that requires manual installation by a user, for replacing the stock firmware that comes bundled when purchasing a device. Cyanogen OS, on the other hand, is stock firmware that will come preinstalled on Android devices.

Cyanogen, Inc., the company behind Cyanogen OS, is working to create a competing Android ecosystem to that of Google. Currently, Cyanogen, Inc., has received $80 million in venture-capital financing from investors such as Qualcomm Incorporated, Twitter Ventures, Rupert Murdoch, Andreesen Horowitz, and Tencent, just to name a few.

You can learn more about CyanogenMod at *http://www.cyanogenmod.org* and Cyanogen OS at *https://cyngn.com*.

Maker Movement and Open-Source Hardware

Another area to keep an eye on is the "Maker Movement," which is a community of do-it-yourself technology hobbyists, often referred to as "Makers." A subculture of this community involves projects that are based on open-source hardware. Similar to the beginnings of the open-source software movement, the hardware industry has been experiencing similar open-source trends amongst enthusiasts—mainly in the area of electronics and printed circuit board (PCB) design. The barriers to entry for designing sophisticated electronic devices such as computers, laptops, tablets, or devices for IoT seem to be limited only to one's imagination and the desire to innovate.

Major hardware-component companies that have traditionally guarded electronic PCB designs are now realizing the potential for innovation by open-sourcing some designs. Processor manufacturers such as Intel, as well as other companies that license and manufacture components based on the ARM processor, have been releasing open-source PCB designs and providing full PCB schematics with the list of required components for completing the circuit. There is an incentive for component manufacturers to provide working PCB designs to help drive sales of those components.

Quite a few companies that manufacture ARM processors have developed open-source PCBs—for devices like tablets—with Android as the OS. This makes designing a sophisticated device—a tablet running Android—accessible to anyone capable of working with a PCB design. PCB software design tools—such as Altium Designer—are used for working with PCB designs.

Powerful tools, combined with open-source PCB designs and the AOSP, may bring about new generations of devices that we are not yet capable of envisioning. The future for Android application development sure looks bright and the possibility for developing innovative applications for Android seems nearly limitless.

Maintaining Awareness

Although this book is about developing Android applications, we wanted to provide background of the overall Android ecosystem—as we see it. We think it is always a good idea to maintain awareness about what is occurring in the ever-expanding Android ecosystem, as these happenings affect everyone involved. There are many exciting occurrences for Android worth following today, and hopefully there will be many more to come.

Summary

Android software development has evolved rapidly over the last few years. Android has become a leading mobile development platform, building on past successes and avoiding the past failures of other platforms. Android was designed to empower the developer to write innovative applications. The platform is open source, with no up-front fees, and developers enjoy many benefits over other competing platforms. There are also a few promising areas of the Android ecosystem to watch. Now it's time to dive deeper into application development so you can evaluate what Android can do for you.

Quiz Questions

1. What does the acronym AOSP stand for?

2. True or false: Joining the Open Handset Alliance allows device makers to bundle Google Mobile Services.

3. What was the name of the company that Google purchased that is credited for developing much of the technology used in the Android operating system?

4. What was the first Android device called? Which manufacturer created it? Which mobile operator sold it?

5. What is the name of the Amazon OS based on Android?

Exercises

1. Describe the benefits of Android being open source.

2. In your own words, describe Android's underlying architecture.

3. Familiarize yourself with the Android documentation, which can be found at *http://d.android.com/index.html*.

References and More Information

Android Developers:
> *http://d.android.com/index.html*

Android Open Source Project:
> *https://source.android.com/index.html*

Open Handset Alliance:
> *http://openhandsetalliance.com*

Official Android Developers Blog:
> *http://android-developers.blogspot.com*

This book's blog:
> *http://introductiontoandroid.blogspot.com*

Intel Open Source: Android on Intel Platforms:
> *https://01.org/android-IA*

ARM Connected Community: Android Community:
> *http://community.arm.com/groups/android-community*

Altium Designer:
> *http://www.altium.com/altium-designer/overview*

Wikipedia: Maker Culture:
> *https://en.wikipedia.org/wiki/Maker_culture*

2

Setting Up for Development

Android developers write and test applications on their computers and then deploy those applications onto the actual device hardware for further testing.

In this chapter, you'll become familiar with all the tools you need to master in order to develop Android applications. You'll learn information about configuring your development environment both on a virtual device and on real hardware. You'll also explore the Android SDK and all it has to offer.

> **Note**
>
> The Android SDK and Android Studio are updated frequently. We have made every attempt to provide the latest steps for the latest tools. However, these steps and the user interfaces described in this chapter may change at any time. Please refer to the Android development website (*http://d.android.com/sdk/index.html*) and our book's website (*http://introductiontoandroid.blogspot.com*) for the latest information.

Configuring Your Development Environment

To write Android applications, you must configure your programming environment for Java development. The software is available online for download at no cost. Android applications can be developed on Windows, Macintosh, or Linux systems.

To develop Android applications, you need to have the following software installed on your computer:

- The Java Development Kit (JDK), Version 7, available for download at *http://oracle. com/technetwork/java/javase/downloads/index.html* (or *http://java.sun.com/javase/ downloads/index.jsp*, if you're nostalgic). If you are developing on Mac OS X, you should use the Java Runtime Environment (JRE), Version 6, to run Android Studio, and then configure your projects to run JDK 7.

- The latest Android SDK. In this book, we will cover using the Android SDK included with Android Studio, which is available for Windows, Mac, or Linux and can be downloaded at *http://d.android.com/sdk/index.html*. Android Studio includes everything you will need for working on the examples in this book and for developing Android applications. Other items included with Android Studio are the SDK Tools, Platform Tools, the latest Android platform, and the latest Android System image for the emulator.

- A compatible Java IDE is required. Luckily, Android Studio is provided, and is based on the free Community Edition of IntelliJ IDEA, and IDE for Java Development. Android Studio comes with the most recent Android SDK already installed. This book focuses on using Android Studio. An alternative to using Android Studio would be to use IntelliJ IDEA Community or Ultimate Edition, or your own copy of Eclipse, but unfortunately, the Eclipse Android Developer Tools plugin is no longer supported so we can only recommend that you use Android Studio for this reason.

An up-to-date and complete list of Android development system requirements is available at *http://d.android.com/sdk/index.html*.

Tip

Developers should use Android Studio for Android development, as this is the official IDE for Android application development. The JetBrains development team has integrated the Android development tools directly into Android Studio. Although previous editions of this book covered how to develop Android applications with Eclipse, this edition will only cover using Android Studio. For information on using Android Studio, read the overview at *http://d.android.com/tools/studio/index.html*.

For information on managing your projects from the command-line, begin by reading *http://d.android.com/tools/projects/projects-cmdline.html*; that link discusses using the command-line tools, which may be useful for developing with other environments. You may download the stand-alone SDK tools here: *http://d.android.com/sdk/index.html#Other*. In addition, read *http://d.android.com/tools/debugging/debugging-projects-cmdline.html* for information on debugging from other IDEs, and *http://d.android.com/tools/testing/testing_otheride.html* for testing from other IDEs.

The basic installation process follows these steps:

1. Download and install the appropriate JRE/JDK for your operating system.

2. Download and install or unzip the appropriate Android Studio package for your operating system. When installing Android Studio, make sure to select all the available components for your system setup, as seen on the `Choose Components` dialog of the `Android Studio Setup` wizard seen in Figure 2.1. The last component, `Performance (Intel® HAXM)` may not be available on your device for installation, but don't worry if that particular component is not available. Make sure the `Android SDK` and the `Android Virtual Device` are selected for installation.

3. Launch Android Studio and use the Android SDK Manager to download and install specific Android platform versions and other components you might use, including the documentation, USB drivers, and additional tools. The Android SDK Manager has been integrated directly into Android Studio and is also available

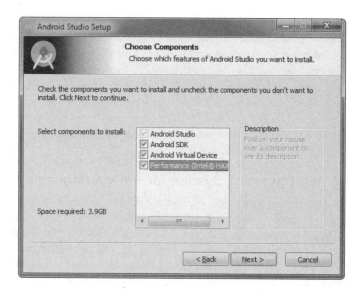

Figure 2.1   The `Choose Components` dialog of the `Android Studio Setup` installation wizard.

as a stand-alone tool accessible from within Android Studio. In terms of which components you'll want to choose for installing, we recommend a full installation (choose everything).

4. Configure your computer for device debugging by installing the appropriate USB drivers, if necessary.

5. Configure your Android device(s) for device debugging.

6. Start developing Android applications.

In this book, we do not give you detailed, step-by-step instructions for installing each and every component listed in the preceding steps for these main reasons:

- This is an intermediate/advanced book, and we expect you to have some familiarity with installing Java development tools and SDKs.

- The Android Developer website provides fairly extensive information about installing development tools and configuring them on a variety of different operating systems. Instructions for installing Android Studio are available at *http://d.android.com/sdk/installing/index.html?pkg=studio* and instructions for installing the stand-alone SDK are available at *http://d.android.com/sdk/installing/index.html?pkg=tools*.

- The exact steps required to install the Android SDK tend to change subtly with each release, so you're always better off checking the Android Developer website for the latest information.

Keep in mind that the Android SDK, Android Studio, and tools are updated frequently and may not exactly match the development environment used in this book, as defined in the Introduction, and may look different on your machine than what has been presented in this book. That said, we will help you work through some of the later steps in the process described in this section, starting after you've installed and configured the JDK and Android Studio in step 2 of the basic installation process listed above. We'll poke around in the Android SDK and look at some of the core tools you'll need to use to develop applications. Then, in the next chapter, you'll test your development environment and write your first Android application.

Configuring Your Operating System for Device Debugging

To install and debug Android applications on Android devices, you need to configure your operating system to access the device via the USB cable (see Figure 2.2). On some operating systems, such as Mac OS X, this may just work automatically. However, for Windows installations, you need to install the appropriate USB driver. You can learn how to download and install the Windows USB driver for any Google Nexus device from the following link: *http://d.android.com/sdk/win-usb.html*. If you are using the Galaxy Nexus device, you may download the drivers here: *http://www.samsung.com/us/support/owners/product/ GT-I9250TSGGEN*. For other manufacturer's devices, you can learn more about the appropriate USB drivers here: *http://d.android.com/tools/extras/oem-usb.html*. Under Linux, there are some additional steps to perform; see *http://d.android.com/tools/device.html* for more information.

Configuring Your Android Hardware for Debugging

Android devices have debugging disabled by default. Your Android device must be enabled for debugging via a USB connection to allow the tools to install and launch the applications you deploy.

Figure 2.2   Android application debugging using an IDE
and the device emulator on a development machine and an
Android handset connected to a development machine.

Devices that have Android 4.2+ require enabling Developer Options for testing your applications on real hardware. We will be discussing how to configure your hardware for working with Android 4.2+, but if you are working with a different version of Android, check out the following link to learn how to get set up with your version: *http://d.android.com/tools/device.html#setting-up*. Different versions of Android use different setup methods, so just perform the method for the version you have.

> **Note**
>
> You can enable the `Developer Options` by navigating to `Settings`, then choosing `About Phone` (or `About Tablet`); then scroll down to `Build Number`, and press `Build Number` seven times. After a few presses, you will notice a message displaying "You are now X steps away from being a developer," where X is the quantity of presses you have remaining. Continue to press `Build Number` until you are told that `Developer Options` have been enabled. If you do not enable the `Developer Options`, you will not be able to install your applications on your device.

You'll need to enable your device to install Android applications other than those from the Google Play store. This setting is reached by navigating to `Settings`, then choosing `Security`. Here, you should check (enable) the option called `Unknown sources`, as shown in Figure 2.3. If you do not enable this option, you cannot install developer-created applications, the sample applications, or applications published on alternative markets without the developer tools. Loading applications from servers or even email is a great way to test deployments.

Several other important development settings are available on the Android device by selecting `Settings`, and then `Developer options` (see Figure 2.4).

Here, you should enable the `USB debugging` option. This setting enables you to debug your applications via the USB connection.

Upgrading Android Studio

Android Studio is updated fairly frequently. By default, Android Studio is configured to check for updates to the IDE automatically. When there is an update, you will be notified of the new update, and prompted to install the update upon opening the IDE. You may also configure from which channel to install the update. The options are: `Stable Channel`, `Beta Channel`, `Dev Channel`, and `Canary Channel`. Unless you already know what the other channels are for, you should only consider installing from the default update channel named `Stable Channel`, which has features that are known to be stable.

The `Beta Channel` is reserved for installing features that are near the stable, beta features of Android Studio. The `Dev Channel` is for installing features that were once bleeding edge features that have survived the cut. The `Canary Channel` is for installing the most recent bleeding edge features. With that said, expect to run into many bugs and issues if you decide to use the `Canary Channel`.

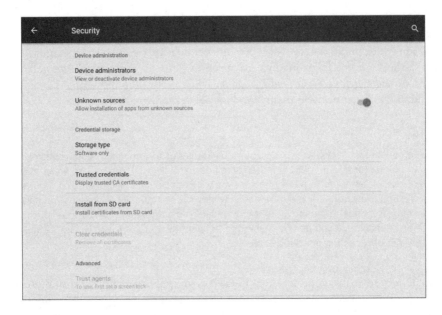

Figure 2.3   Enabling Unknown sources on the device.

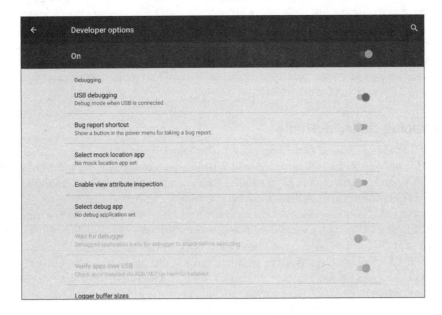

Figure 2.4   Enabling Android developer settings on the device.

Upgrading the Android SDK

The Android SDK is upgraded from time to time. You can easily upgrade the Android SDK platform and tools from within Android Studio using the built-in SDK Manager or by launching the stand-alone SDK Manager, which is installed as part of the Android SDK.

Changes to the Android SDK might include addition, update, and removal of features; package name changes; and updated tools. With each new version of the SDK, Google provides the following useful documents:

- An Overview of Changes: A brief description of the major changes to the SDK
- An API Diff Report: A complete list of specific changes to the SDK
- Release Notes: A list of known issues with the SDK

These documents are available with every new release of the Android SDK. For instance, Android 5.1 information is available at *http://d.android.com/about/versions/android-5.1.html*, and Android 5.0 information is available at *http://d.android.com/about/versions/android-5.0.html*.

You can find out more about adding and updating SDK packages at *http://d.android.com/sdk/installing/adding-packages.html*.

Problems with Android Studio

When developing with the `Stable Channel` of Android Studio, you may not experience any bugs during development, but even with stable software, an occasional bug may creep in. On the other hand, when you use any of the other channels of Android Studio, the odds of encountering a bug increase. Luckily, Android Studio has a reporting mechanism built into the IDE. When such an error occurs, you will receive a notification informing you that you have encountered an error. If you follow the notification instructions, you will be led to a dialog for submitting the bug report to JetBrains. Submitting bug reports not only helps JetBrains and the Android developer community, but it will also benefit you when JetBrains is made aware of any issues encountered, so that it may follow up with a fix. You may submit these reports anonymously or through your JetBrains account if you have one.

Problems with the Android SDK

Because the Android SDK is constantly under active development, you might come across problems with it. If you think you've found a problem, you can find a list of open issues and their status at the Android project's Issue Tracker website. You can also submit new issues for review.

The Issue Tracker website for the Android open-source project is *https://code.google.com/p/android/issues/list*. For more information about logging your own bugs or defects for consideration by the Android platform development team, check out the following website: *http://source.android.com/source/report-bugs.html*.

Tip

Frustrated with how long it takes for your Android SDK bug to get fixed? It can be helpful to understand how the Android bug-resolution process works. For more information on this process, see *http://source.android.com/source/life-of-a-bug.html*.

IntelliJ IDEA as an Android Studio Alternative

Because Android Studio is based on the Community Edition of IntelliJ IDEA, you may also use the Community or Ultimate Edition of IntelliJ IDEA for developing Android applications. Both of these IDEs support Android application development. There is not much of an advantage to using IntelliJ IDEA Community Edition over Android Studio if you only program with the Android SDK. If that is the case, you are better off using Android Studio.

However, IntelliJ IDEA Ultimate Edition may be worth considering if the project you are working on involves other aspects such as Web development or backend server development using languages like Python, Ruby, PHP, HTML, CSS, or JavaScript, or if you use Web frameworks such as Spring, GWT, Node.js, Django, Rails, or others. Having a single IDE may be beneficial, rather than having to manage a single project across many different IDEs. If you find your project and job duties extend beyond just Android development, take a look at IntelliJ IDEA Ultimate.

IntelliJ IDEA Community Edition is free to download and use, but the Ultimate Edition requires purchasing a commercial or personal license. JetBrains does offer special pricing to qualifying startups, and offers Ultimate for free to qualifying students and teachers, open-source projects, and for education and training purposes. To learn more about IntelliJ IDEA or pricing information, please see *https://www.jetbrains.com/idea*. For a full list of the differences between the Community and Ultimate Edition of IntelliJ, see *https://www.jetbrains.com/idea/features/editions_comparison_matrix.html*.

Exploring the Android SDK

The Android SDK comes with several major components: the Android SDK Platform by version, SDK Platform Tools, SDK Build Tools, System Images, Google APIs, Sources for Android SDK, extras, and sample applications.

Understanding the Android SDK License Agreement

Before you can download Android Studio, you must review and agree to the Android SDK License Agreement. This agreement is a contract between you (the developer) and Google (copyright holder of the Android SDK).

Even if someone at your company has agreed to the licensing agreement on your behalf, it is important for you, the developer, to be aware of a few important points:

- Rights granted: Google (as the copyright holder of Android) grants you a limited, worldwide, royalty-free, nonassignable, and nonexclusive license to use the SDK solely to develop applications for the Android platform. Google (and third-party contributors) are granting you the license, but they still hold all copyrights and intellectual property rights to the material. Using the Android SDK does not grant you permission to use any Google brands, logos, or trade names. You may not remove any of the copyright notices therein. Third-party applications that your applications interact with (other Android apps) are subject to separate terms and fall outside this agreement.

- SDK usage: You may only develop Android applications. You may not make derivative works from the SDK or distribute the SDK on any device, or distribute part of the SDK with other software.

- SDK changes and backward compatibility: Google may change the Android SDK at any time, without notice and without regard to backward compatibility. Although Android API changes were a major issue with prerelease versions of the SDK, recent releases have been reasonably stable. That said, each SDK update does tend to affect a small number of existing applications in the field, thus necessitating updates.

- Android application developer rights: You retain all rights to any Android software you develop with the SDK, including intellectual property rights. You also retain all responsibility for your own work.

- Android application privacy requirements: You agree that your application will protect the privacy and legal rights of its users. If your application uses or accesses personal and private information about the user (usernames, passwords, and so on), your application must provide an adequate privacy notice and keep that data stored securely. Note that privacy laws and regulations may vary by user location; you as a developer are solely responsible for managing this data appropriately.

- Android application malware requirements: You are responsible for all applications you develop. You agree not to write disruptive applications or malware. You are solely responsible for all data transmitted through your application.

- Additional terms for specific Google APIs: Use of the Google Maps Android API is subject to further Terms of Service. You must agree to these additional terms before using those specific APIs and always include the Google Maps copyright notice provided. Use of Google APIs (Google apps such as Gmail, Blogger, Google Calendar, YouTube, and so on) is limited to accessing what the user has explicitly granted permission for during installation time.

- Develop at your own risk: Any harm, financial or otherwise, that comes about from developing with the Android SDK is your own fault and not Google's.

Reading the Android SDK Documentation

The Android documentation is provided in HTML format online at *http://d.android.com/ index.html*. If you would like to have a local copy of the docs, you need to download them using the SDK Manager. Once you have downloaded them, a local copy of the Android documentation is provided in the `docs` subfolder of the Android installation directory (see Figure 2.5).

Exploring the Core Android Application Framework

The Android SDK platform is provided in the `android.jar` file. This file is made up of several important packages, which are listed in Table 2.1.

Several optional third-party APIs are available outside the core Android SDK. These packages must be installed separately from their respective websites or from within the Android SDK Manager when available. Some packages are from Google, whereas others are from device manufacturers and other providers. Some of the most popular third-party APIs are described in Table 2.2.

For a complete list of Google Play services APIs, see *https://developers.google.com/ android/guides/setup*. For a complete list of all Google products that may have Android APIs, see *https://developers.google.com/products/*.

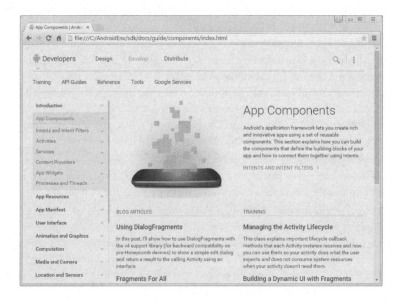

Figure 2.5   The Android SDK documentation viewed offline.

Table 2.1 **Important Packages in the Android SDK**

Top-Level Package Name	Description
android.*	Android application fundamentals
dalvik.*	Dalvik virtual machine support classes
java.*	Core classes and familiar generic utilities for networking, security, math, and so on
javax.*	Encryption support
junit.*	Unit-testing support
org.apache.http.*	HTTP protocol support
org.json	JavaScript Object Notation (JSON) support
org.w3c.dom	W3C Java bindings for the Document Object Model Core (XML and HTML)
org.xml.*	Simple API for XML (SAX) support for XML
org.xmlpull.*	High-performance XML pull parsing

Table 2.2 **Just a Few Popular Third-Party Android APIs**

Optional Android SDKs	Description
Android Support Library Packages: various	Adds several components available in recent SDKs to legacy versions of the SDKs. For example, the Various Loader APIs and Fragment APIs introduced in API Level 11 can be used, in compatibility form, as far back as API Level 4 using this add-on.
Google Mobile Ads SDK Package: com.google.android. gms.ads.*	Allows developers to insert Google Mobile Ads to monetize their applications. This SDK requires agreement to additional Terms of Service and registration for an account. For more information, see *https://developers.google.com/mobile-ads-sdk/*.
Google Analytics SDK for Android Package: com.google.android. gms.analytics.*	Allows developers to collect and analyze information about how their Android applications are used with the popular Google Analytics service. This SDK requires agreement to additional Terms of Service and registration for an account. For more information, see *https://developers.google.com/analytics/devguides/collection/android/v4/app*.
Google Cloud Messaging for Android (GCM) Package: com.google.android. gms.gcm	Provides access to a service for developers to push data from the network to their applications installed on devices. This SDK requires agreement to additional Terms of Service and registration for an account. For more information, see *https://developers.google.com/cloud-messaging/*.

(Continues)

Table 2.2 **Continued**

Optional Android SDKs	Description
Google App Indexing Package: `com.google.android. gms.appindexing`	This SDK helps you prepare your application for indexing in Google Search so that your application may be found by users. For more information, see *https://developers.google.com/ app-indexing/*.
Google App Invites Package: `com.google.android. gms.appinvite`	This SDK allows you to integrate app invite functionality so that your users may invite their Google contacts using SMS and email. For more information, see *https://developers.google. com/app-invites/*.
Google Play Games Services Package: `com.google.android. gms.games`	Provides achievement, leaderboard, and multiplayer functionality to your games. This SDK requires agreement to additional Terms of Service and registration for an account. For more information, see *https://developers.google.com/games/ services/*.
Google Fit Package: `com.google.android. gms.fitness`	Allows users to integrate fitness tracking functionality in their applications. This SDK requires agreement to additional Terms of Service and registration for an account. For more information, see *https://developers.google.com/fit/*.
Numerous device and manufacturer-specific add-ons and SDKs	You'll find a number of third-party add-ons and manufacturer-specific SDKs available within the Android SDK and Android Virtual Device (AVD) add-ons and SDK Manager's Available Packages. Still others can be found at third-party websites. If you are targeting features available from a specific device or manufacturer, or services from a known service provider, check to see if they have add-ons available for the Android platform.

Exploring the Core Android Tools

The Android SDK provides many tools to design, develop, debug, and deploy your Android applications. For now, we want you to focus on familiarizing yourself with the core tools you need to know about to get up and running with Android applications. We discuss many Android tools in greater detail in Appendix D, "Mastery: Android SDK Tools."

Android Studio

You'll spend most of your development time in your IDE. This book assumes you are using Android Studio because this is the official development environment configuration.

Android Studio incorporates many of the most important Android SDK tools seamlessly and provides various wizards for creating, debugging, and deploying Android applications. The Android SDK tools add useful functions to Android Studio. Buttons are available on the toolbar, including those that perform the following Android actions (see Figure 2.6):

- Launch the Android Virtual Device Manager
- Launch the Android SDK Manager
- Launch the Android Device Monitor

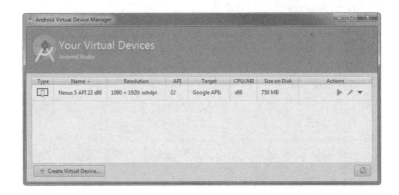

Figure 2.6 Android features on the Android Studio toolbar.

Figure 2.7 The Android Virtual Device Manager.

Android SDK and AVD Managers

In Figure 2.6, note the left-most icon within the red border that looks like a tiny phone with an Android head in the lower-right corner; this will launch the Android Virtual Device Manager (see Figure 2.7). The second Android toolbar icon within the red border, with the little green Android head at the top and the down arrow, will launch the built-in Android SDK Manager (see Figure 2.8) that also includes a link to launch the stand-alone SDK Manager (see Figure 2.9).

These tools perform two major functions: management of the developer's AVD configurations and management of Android SDK components installed on the development machine.

Much like desktop computers, different Android devices run different versions of the Android operating system. Developers need to be able to target different Android SDK versions with their applications. Some applications target a specific Android SDK, whereas others try to provide simultaneous support for as many versions as possible.

The Android Virtual Device Manager organizes and provides tools to create and edit AVDs. To manage applications in the Android emulator, you must configure different AVD profiles. Each AVD profile describes what type of device you want the emulator to simulate, including which Android platform to support as well as what the device specifications should be. You can specify different screen sizes and orientations, and you can specify whether the emulator has an SD card and, if so, what its capacity is, among many other device configuration settings.

The Android SDK Manager facilitates Android development across multiple platform versions simultaneously. When a new Android SDK is released, you can use this tool to

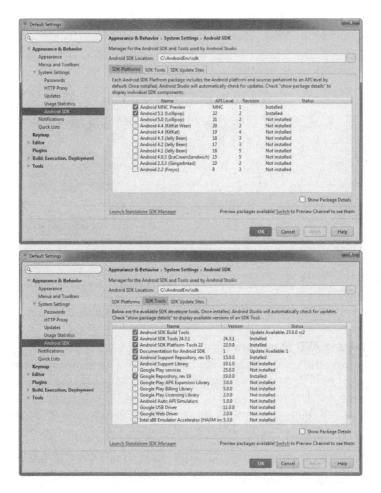

Figure 2.8   The built-in Android SDK Manager shows the currently installed
Android SDK Platforms (top) and SDK Tools (bottom).

download and update your tools while still maintaining backward compatibility and use
older versions of the Android SDK.

Android Emulator

The Android emulator is one of the most important tools provided with the Android
SDK. You will use this tool frequently when designing and developing Android
applications. The emulator runs on your computer and behaves much as a mobile device
would. You can load Android applications into the emulator, test, and debug them.

The emulator is a generic device and is not tied to any one specific phone
configuration. You describe the hardware and software configuration details that the

Figure 2.9   The stand-alone Android SDK Manager.

emulator is to simulate by providing an AVD configuration. Figure 2.10 shows what the emulator might look like with a typical Android 5.1 smartphone-style AVD configuration.

Figure 2.11 shows what the emulator might look like with a typical Android 5.1 tablet-style AVD configuration. Both Figures 2.10 and 2.11 show how the Settings application behaves differently on different devices.

Tip

You should be aware that the Android emulator is a substitute for a real Android device, but it's an imperfect one. The emulator is a valuable tool for testing, but cannot fully replace testing on actual target devices.

Exploring the Android Sample Applications

The Android SDK provides many samples and demo applications to help you learn the ropes of Android development. These demo applications are not provided as part of the

Figure 2.10   The Android emulator (Nexus 5 smartphone-style, Android
API 22 AVD configuration).

Figure 2.11   The Android emulator (Nexus 9 tablet-style, Android API 22
AVD configuration).

Android SDK by default. Android Studio provides a dialog for importing the sample applications—from GitHub—as a project.

Tip

To learn how to import an Android SDK sample application using Android Studio, in Chapter 3, "Creating Your First Application," read the section titled "Importing the `BorderlessButtons` Sample into Android Studio."

Many sample applications are available to demonstrate different aspects of the Android SDK. Some focus on generic application development tasks while others focus on demonstrating specific APIs.

As of API 23, some of the sample code that you should look into further is categorized as follows:

- **Getting started:** includes samples demonstrating common Android components such as the action bar, floating action button, and more

- **Background:** includes samples demonstrating common tasks that should be run in the background

- **Input:** includes samples demonstrating common input methods such as gestures, multitouch, and swipes

- **Media:** includes samples demonstrating media-related features such as the camera, recording, effects, and others

- **Connectivity:** includes samples demonstrating various networking methods such as Bluetooth and HTTP

- **Notification:** includes samples demonstrating various Notification APIs

- **Wearable:** includes many samples demonstrating the various features available to developers for wearable devices

The examples above are just a few of the many categories of applications that are available as samples that demonstrate various features of the Android APIs.

Tip

We discuss how to import a sample application in Chapter 3, "Creating Your First Application." Once Android Studio is installed, to add a sample project from the "Welcome to Android Studio" screen, select `Import an Android Code Sample`, select the sample application to import, click `Next`, then click `Finish` and you should now be in the editor with your sample project ready for editing. Proceed as you normally would, compiling and running the application in the emulator or on a device. You will see these steps performed in detail in the next chapter when you test your development environment and write your first application.

Summary

In this chapter, you installed, configured, and began to explore the tools you will need to start developing Android applications, including the appropriate JDK, the Android SDK, and Android Studio. You also learned that there are alternative development environments you can choose from, such as IntelliJ IDEA Community or Ultimate Edition. You learned how to configure your Android hardware for debugging. In addition, you explored many of the tools provided with the Android SDK and now understand their basic purposes. Finally, you perused the sample applications provided with the Android SDK. You should now have a reasonable development environment configured to write Android applications. In the next chapter, you'll be able to take advantage of all this setup and write an Android application.

Quiz Questions

1. What version of the Java JDK is required for Android development?
2. What security option must be selected on an Android hardware device for installing your own applications without using an Android marketplace?
3. What option must be enabled on your hardware device to debug your applications?
4. What is the name of the `.jar` file that comprises the Android application framework?
5. What is the top-level package name for unit-testing support?
6. Which optional Android SDK is provided by Google for integrating advertising in your applications?

Exercises

1. Open a local copy of the Android documentation provided with the Android SDK.
2. Launch the Android Studio SDK Manager of Android Studio and install at least one other version of Android.
3. Name five sample applications provided with the Android SDK.

References and More Information

Google's Android Developers Guide:
   http://d.android.com/guide/components/index.html
Android SDK download site:
   http://d.android.com/sdk/index.html
Android SDK License Agreement:
   http://d.android.com/sdk/terms.html

The Java Platform, Standard Edition:
   http://oracle.com/technetwork/java/javase/overview/index.html
JetBrains:
   https://www.jetbrains.com/
Android Developer Tools:
   https://developer.android.com/tools/help/adt.html
The Eclipse Project:
   http://eclipse.org

3

Creating Your First Application

You should now have a workable Android development environment set up on your computer. Ideally, you have an Android device as well. Now it's time for you to start writing some Android code. In this chapter, you learn how to verify that your Android development environment is set up correctly. You also learn how to add and create Android projects from within Android Studio. You then write and debug your first Android application in the software emulator and on an Android device.

> **Note**
>
> The Android SDK tools are updated frequently. We have made every attempt to provide the latest steps for the latest tools. However, these steps and the user interfaces described in this chapter may change at any time. Please refer to the Android development website (*http://d.android.com/sdk/index.html*) for the latest information.

Testing Your Development Environment

The best way to make sure you setup your development environment correctly is to run an existing Android application. You can do this easily by importing one of the sample applications available when you choose the `Import Sample` option of Android Studio. The sample applications are hosted on Google's GitHub account, a popular source-control service, and because Android Studio has built-in integration with GitHub, the sample is automatically grabbed from GitHub and imported into Android Studio for you without any extra configuration setup for you to perform.

Within the sample applications available for import, you will find an application named `BorderlessButtons`. To build and run the `BorderlessButtons` application, you must import the sample into Android Studio, launch an appropriate Android Virtual Device (AVD) profile, and run a launch configuration for that project. Luckily, all of these things should be setup for you already, so you can quickly build the application and run it on the Android emulator and on an Android device. By testing your development environment with a sample application, you can rule out system configuration and coding issues, and focus on determining whether the tools are set up properly for Android development. After this fact has been established, you can move on to writing and compiling your own applications. If you are not able to get the sample working, you may have missed a configuration step when preparing your system for development.

Importing the `BorderlessButtons` Sample into Android Studio

To import the `BorderlessButtons` sample into Android Studio, follow these steps:

1. Launch Android Studio and wait for the `Welcome to Android Studio` screen to appear (see Figure 3.1).

2. Click `Import an Android code sample` on the `Welcome to Android Studio` screen (see Figure 3.1).

3. On the `Browse Samples` screen, enter the keyword `Borderless Buttons` in the search bar to locate the sample. You should see two results appear in the Browse Samples listing. Select either of the `Borderless Buttons` keyword results (see Figure 3.2) as they both link to the same sample application. We selected the `Borderless Buttons` listing of the `Design` section. Once you have selected the sample, click `Next`.

4. On the `Sample Setup` screen (see Figure 3.3), you should see the `Application` name of `BorderlessButtons` already filled out, and a `Project location` already selected. Feel free to change the `Project location` to a directory of your choosing and then click `Finish`.

Figure 3.1   The `Welcome to Android Studio` **screen.**

Figure 3.2   Selecting the `Borderless Buttons` sample application to import into Android Studio.

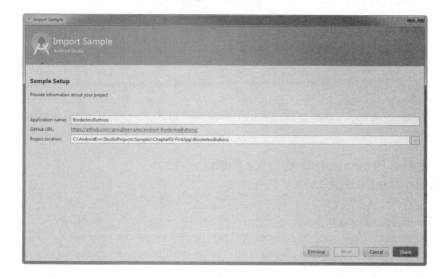

Figure 3.3   Reviewing the `Application name` and `Project location` before importing into Android Studio.

You should now see Android Studio import the `BorderlessButtons` sample application, and if everything worked correctly, there should not be any errors appearing in the `Gradle Build` messages (see Figure 3.4). If there are any errors listed, you must fix them before you'll be able to proceed.

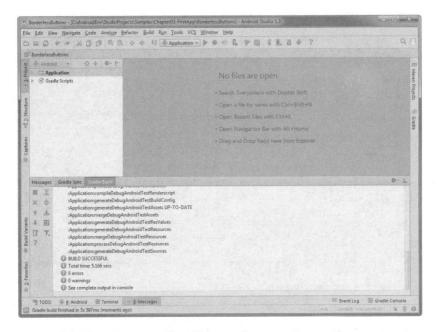

Figure 3.4   The `BorderlessButtons` sample application imported into Android Studio with no errors reported.

Now you know how to import a sample application into Android Studio. The sample applications are useful for learning how to write code using particular Android APIs. Feel free to import other samples to review how they have been developed. This is one of the fastest ways to learn how to write Android applications.

Using the Preinstalled AVD for Running Your `BorderlessButtons` Project

In Chapter 2, "Setting Up for Development," in the second step of the basic installation process of the "Configuring Your Development Environment" section, we recommended selecting all components for installation when installing Android Studio. One of the optional components for installation was a preconfigured Android Virtual Device. You will want to emulate this AVD profile when running the `BorderlessButtons` application. This AVD profile describes a default emulator configuration, and at the time of this writing, the preinstalled AVD configuration was a Nexus 5 running API 22 compatible with an x86 CPU. For the purposes of this example and other examples in this book, the provided AVD bundled with the default installation of Android Studio suffices. Just note that the AVD configuration bundled with your installation may be different from the one used in these examples. You may also opt to create your own AVDs, too.

You do not need to create new AVDs for each application, only for each device you want to emulate. You can specify different screen sizes and orientations, and you can specify whether the emulator has an SD card, and if it does, what capacity the card has. For the exact steps to configure an AVD for your BorderlessButtons project and to learn about the different configuration options, check out the section titled "Creating an AVD" in Appendix B, "Quick-Start: Android Emulator."

In the next section, you will learn how to launch an emulator for running your applications.

Running the BorderlessButtons Application in the Android Emulator

Since you already have an AVD for your BorderlessButtons project, you can run the BorderlessButtons application using the following steps:

1. With your application now open in Android Studio, press the Run icon on the toolbar (▶).

2. A dialog will appear that prompts you to choose a device. Make sure the Launch emulator option is chosen, and that the Android virtual device selected is the Nexus 5 API 22 x86, and then click OK.

3. The Android emulator starts up; this might take a few moments to initialize (see Figure 3.5). Once started, the application will be installed onto the emulator.

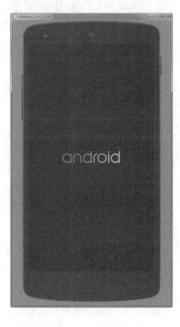

Figure 3.5   The Android emulator starting up.

Tip

It can take a long time for the emulator to start up, even on very fast computers. You might want to leave it running while you work and reattach to it as needed. The tools in Android Studio handle reinstalling the application and relaunching it, so you can more easily keep the emulator loaded all the time. This is good reason to enable the Snapshot feature for each AVD. You can also use the Start button on the Android Virtual Device Manager to load an emulator before you need it. You can learn more about the Snapshot feature and configuring and launching AVD's in Appendix B, "Quick-Start: Android Emulator."

4. If necessary, swipe the screen from bottom to top to unlock the emulator where it reads Swipe up to unlock, as shown in Figure 3.6.

5. The BorderlessButtons application starts and you can begin using the application, as shown in Figure 3.7.

You can interact with the BorderlessButtons application through the emulator and use the application. You can also launch the BorderlessButtons application from the All Apps screen at any time by clicking its application icon. There is no need to shut down and restart the emulator every time you rebuild and reinstall your application for testing.

Figure 3.6 The Android emulator launching (locked).

Figure 3.7   The `BorderlessButtons` sample application running on the
Android emulator.

Simply leave the emulator running on your computer in the background while you work
in Android Studio and then redeploy it using the `Run` button again.

Building Your First Android Application

Now it's time to write your first Android application from scratch. To get your feet wet,
you will start with a simple "Hello world" application and build on it to explore some of
the features of the Android platform in more detail.

> **Tip**
>
> The code examples provided in this chapter are taken from the `MyFirstAndroidApp`
> application. The source code for the `MyFirstAndroidApp` application is provided for
> download on the book's website (*http://introductiontoandroid.blogspot.com*).

Creating and Configuring a New Android Project

You can create a new Android application in much the same way that you added the
`BorderlessButtons` application to Android Studio.

The first thing you need to do is create a new project in Android Studio. The New Project creation wizard creates all the required files for an Android application. Follow these steps within Android Studio to create a new project:

1. From the Welcome to Android Studio dialog that appears after launching Android Studio, choose Start a new Android Studio project listed within the Quick Start options shown in Figure 3.8. If you launch Android Studio and are brought into an already-open project, rather than the Welcome to Android Studio dialog, be sure to close out of the project before launching Android Studio by selecting File, Close Project.

2. Choose an application name as shown in Figure 3.9. The application name is the "friendly" name of the application and the name shown with the icon on the application launcher. Name the application My First Android App. This will automatically create a Project location folder named MyFirstAndroidApp, but you are free to change this name and location to one of your choosing.

3. You should also change the package name, using reverse domain name notation (*http://en.wikipedia.org/wiki/Reverse_domain_name_notation*), to com.introtoandroid.myfirstandroidapp. To do this, edit the Company Domain field to something like introtoandroid.com. You will see the Package name change automatically when you modify the Company Domain field. You may also edit the Package name field directly by clicking the Edit link located to the far right of the Package name listing. Once you are finished, click Next.

Figure 3.8   **Selecting the** Start a new Android Studio project **from the** Welcome to Android Studio **dialog.**

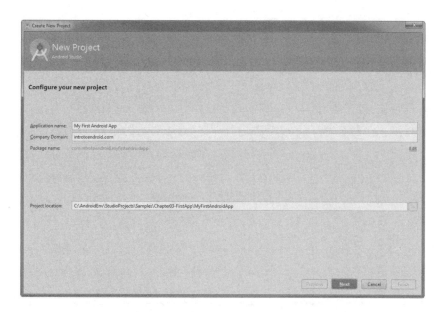

Figure 3.9   Configuring a new Android project.

4. On the `Target Android Devices` screen (see Figure 3.10), you should have the `Phone and Tablet` option selected, in addition to choosing the `Minimum SDK` you want your application to support. At the time of this writing, Android 4.0.3 API Level 15 is the default `Minimum SDK` option preselected for us. This will allow us to support 94.0% of all devices compatible with Google Play Store applications. You are free to choose a different `Minimum SDK`, but for this application, keep it set to the `API 15: Android 4.0.3 (IceCreamSandwich)` if it is not already selected. You are also able to choose other form factors for your application to support, such as Wear, TV, Android Auto, and Glass, in addition to selecting a `Minimum SDK` for most of those options, but we are only interested in `Phone and Tablets`. Click `Next`.

5. On the `Add an activity to Mobile` screen (see Figure 3.11), you are able to select what type of Activity you want to add to your application from a few common options, or you are free to choose `Add No Activity`, but for this example, keep the `Blank Activity` option selected. Choose `Next`.

6. The `Customize the Activity` screen (see Figure 3.12) allows you to provide an `Activity Name`. Name the `Activity` `MyFirstAndroidAppActivity`. You will notice the `Layout Name`, `Title`, and `Menu Resource Name` fields change as you edit the `Activity Name` field. You are now ready to create your application. Finally, click the `Finish` button to create the application.

7. Android Studio may take a short while to build your project, but once it is complete, your first application will display with your layout file open and ready for editing (see Figure 3.13).

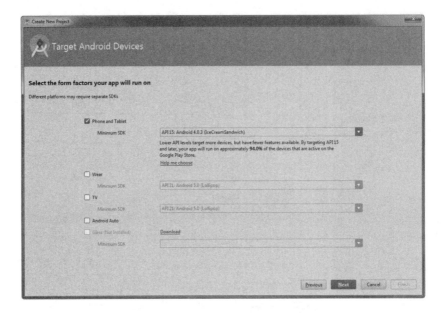

Figure 3.10   Choosing the form factors and `Minimum SDK` options on the
`Target Android Devices` screen.

Figure 3.11   Choosing the `Blank Activity` from the `Add an activity`
`to Mobile` screen.

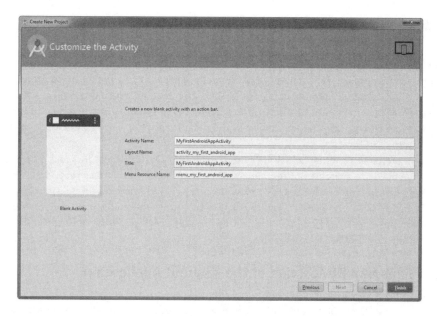

Figure 3.12   Customizing the `Activity`.

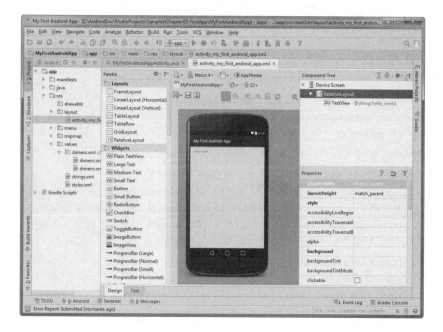

Figure 3.13   Your first application created and open in Android Studio.

Understanding the `Android` Symbolic View and the Traditional `Project` View

When you created your first application in Android Studio, your project was opened in the `Android` project view. The project hierarchy represented in the `Android` project view is only a symbolic representation of file and directory names, and not their actual file system location. Figure 3.14 (left) shows the `Android` symbolic project view of the `MyFirstAndroidApp`. This `Android` view is the default view for managing your projects with Android Studio.

If you prefer to view the actual file system location of your project files and directories, you may choose to switch from the `Android` view to the traditional `Project` view. You can do so by clicking on the `Android` view drop-down and selecting the `Project` view seen in Figure 3.14 (top center). Figure 3.14 (right) shows the traditional `Project` view displaying the `MyFirstAndroidApp` project listing the actual file system location of the files and directories for easy navigation.

Core Files and Directories of the Android Application

Every Android application has a set of core files that are created and used to define the functionality of the application. The files you want to understand are located inside the app module directory of the `MyFirstAndroidApp` project. The following are some of the files created by default when you created the application and are located inside the app module:

- **`build/`**—Required folder for all autogenerated files.
- **`libs/`**—Folder for including any `.jar` library projects.
- **`src/`**—Required folder for all source code.
- **`src/main/AndroidManifest.xml`**—The central configuration file for the application. It defines your application's capabilities and permissions as well as how it runs.
- **`src/main/java/`**—Folder for the main `Activity` file and other `.java` and `.aidl` files.
- **`src/androidTest/`**—Folder for all instrumentation test source code.
- **`src/main/res/`**—Required folder where all application resources are managed. Application resources include animations, color definitions, drawable graphics, mipmap launcher icons, layout files, menu definitions, data such as strings and numbers, xml, and raw files.
- **`src/main/res/drawable`**—Application graphic resources that define `Drawable` objects and shapes.
- **`src/main/res/layout`**—Required folder that comprises one or more layout resource files, each file managing a different UI or App Widget layout for your application.

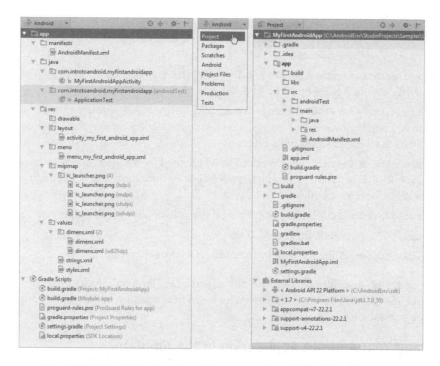

Figure 3.14   The `Android` symbolic view (left); the traditional `Project` view (right); switching from the `Android` symbolic view to the traditional `Project` view (top center).

- **src/main/res/layout/activity_my_first_android_app.xml**—Layout resource file used by MyFirstAndroidAppActivity to organize controls on the main application screen.

- **src/main/res/menu**—Folder for including XML files for defining Android application menus.

- **src/main/res/menu/menu_my_first_android_app.xml**—Menu resource file used by MyFirstAndroidAppActivity to define a menu item for Settings.

- **src/main/res/mipmap-***—Folders for including different resolution, density-specific app launcher icons.

- **src/main/res/values***—Folders for including XML files for defining Android application dimensions, strings, and styles.

- **src/main/res/values/dimens.xml**—Dimension resource file used by MyFirstAndroidAppActivity defining default screen margins.

- **src/main/res/values/strings.xml**—String resource file used by MyFirstAndroidAppActivity defining string variables that may be reused throughout the application.

- **src/main/res/values/styles.xml**—Style resource file used by MyFirstAndroidAppActivity to define the application theme.

- **src/main/res/values-w820dp/dimens.xml**—Dimension resource file for overriding the res/values/dimens.xml for defining dimensions for 7-inch and 10-inch tablets in landscape mode.

- **proguard-rules.pro**—A generated build file used by Android Studio and ProGuard. Edit this file to configure your code optimization and obfuscation settings for release builds.

- **build.gradle**—A file for customizing the gradle build system's properties.

- **app.iml**—A module for IntelliJ IDEA.

- **.gitignore**—A file for defining what files Git should ignore.

A number of other files are saved on disk as part of the Android Studio project. However, the files and resource directories included in this list are the important project files you will use on a regular basis.

Running Your Android Application in the Emulator

Now you can run the MyFirstAndroidApp project using the following steps:

1. With the Run/Debug Configuration named app (see Figure 3.15) already selected, click the Run icon (▶) on the toolbar.

2. You are now prompted to Choose a running device (see Figure 3.16). The default emulator you launched for the previous example should be listed as a running device. If it is not already running, select Launch emulator and choose the appropriate AVD if it is not already selected. Then click OK.

3. If not already started, the Android emulator starts up, which might take a moment.

4. Unlock the emulator if it is locked.

5. The application starts, as shown in Figure 3.17.

6. Click the Back button in the emulator to end the application, or click Home to suspend it.

7. Click the All Apps button (see Figure 3.18) found in the Favorites tray to browse all installed applications from the All Apps screen.

8. Your screen should now look something like Figure 3.19. Click the My First Android App icon to launch the application again.

Figure 3.15 The Run/Debug Configuration named app selected.

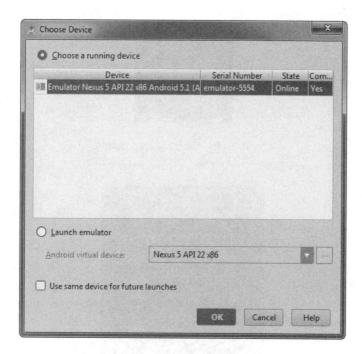

Figure 3.16   Choosing the running emulator previously launched.

Figure 3.17   `My First Android App` running in the emulator.

Figure 3.18   The `All` `Apps` button.

Figure 3.19   The `My First Android App` icon is shown on the `All Apps` screen.

Debugging Your Android Application in the Emulator

Before going any further, you need to become familiar with debugging in the emulator. To illustrate some useful debugging tools, let's manufacture an error in the `My First Android App`.

In your project, edit the source file called `MyFirstAndroidAppActivity.java`. Create a new method called `forceError()` in your class and make a call to this method in your `Activity` class's `onCreate()` method. The `forceError()` method forces a new unhandled error in your application.

The forceError() method should look something like this:

```
public void forceError() {

    if(true) {

        throw new Error("Whoops");

    }

}
```

It's probably helpful at this point to Run (▶) the application and watch what happens. In the emulator, you see that the application has stopped unexpectedly. You are prompted by a dialog that notifies you that the application has stopped, as shown in Figure 3.20.

Shut down the application but keep the emulator running. Now it's time to debug. You can Debug the MyFirstAndroidApp application using the following steps:

1. With the Run/Debug Configuration named app selected (see Figure 3.15), click the Debug icon (✳) on the toolbar.

2. Continue as you did when launching the Run configuration and choose the appropriate emulator, unlocking it if needed.

It takes a moment for the debugger to attach. If this is the first time you've debugged an Android application, you may need to progress through some dialogs, such as the one shown in Figure 3.21, the first time your application attaches to the debugger.

In Android Studio, use the Debugger tab (see Figure 3.22) to view breakpoints, step through code, and watch the Logcat logging information about your application. This time, when the application fails, you can determine the cause using the debugger. If you allow the application to continue after throwing the exception, you can examine the results in the Debugger of Android Studio. If you examine the Debugger tab, you'll see that your application was forced to exit due to an unhandled exception.

Specifically, there's an uncaughtException() error of java.lang.Error: Whoops. Back in the emulator, click the Force Close button. Now set a breakpoint on the line that starts with throw of the forceError() method by clicking inside the column to the left side of the line of code so that a red circle appears (see Figure 3.22).

Tip

In Android Studio, you can set a breakpoint by clicking in the column to the left side of the line of code, so that a red circle appears, or you can use the keyboard shortcut to toggle a breakpoint—Ctrl+F8 on Windows and Command+F8 on Mac. You can also step through code using Step Into (F7), Step Over (F8), or Step Out (Shift+F8).

In the emulator, restart your application and step through your code. You see that your application has thrown the exception, and then the exception shows up in the Debugger. Expanding the exception variable's contents shows that it is the "Whoops" error. This is a great time to crash your application repeatedly and get used to the controls.

Figure 3.20 My First Android App crashes gracefully.

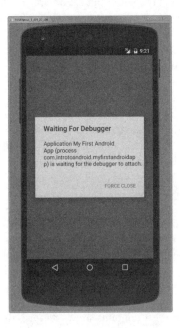

Figure 3.21 Waiting for the debugger to attach to the emulator.

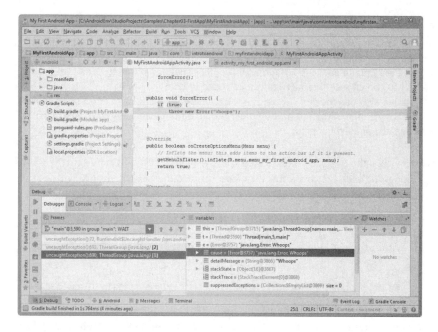

Figure 3.22   Debugging `MyFirstAndroidApp` in Android Studio.

Adding Logging Support to Your Android Application

Before you start diving into the various features of the Android SDK, you should familiarize yourself with logging, a valuable resource for debugging and learning Android. Android logging features are in the `Log` class of the `android.util` package. See Table 3.1 for some helpful methods in the `android.util.Log` class.

To add logging support to `MyFirstAndroidApp`, edit the file `MyFirstAndroidApp.java`. First, you must add the appropriate import statement for the `Log` class:

```
import android.util.Log;
```

Table 3.1 **Commonly Used Logging Methods**

Method	Purpose
`Log.e()`	Log errors
`Log.w()`	Log warnings
`Log.i()`	Log informational messages
`Log.d()`	Log debug messages
`Log.v()`	Log verbose messages

Tip

To save time in Android Studio, you can use the classes in your code and add the imports needed by hovering over the class name and pressing `Alt+Enter`. This will automatically import the required packages. If a naming conflict arises, as it often does with the `Log` class, you can choose the package you intended to use.

You can also use the `Optimize imports` command (`Ctrl+Alt+O` on Windows or `^+Option+O` on the Mac) to have Android Studio automatically organize your imports. This removes any unused imports.

Next, within the `MyFirstAndroidApp` class, declare a constant string that you'll use to tag all logging messages from this class. You can use the `Logcat` utility within Android Studio to filter your logging messages to this `DEBUG_TAG` tag string:

```
private static final String DEBUG_TAG= "MyFirstAppLogging";
```

Now, within the `onCreate()` method, you can log something informational:

```
Log.i(DEBUG_TAG,
    "In the onCreate() method of the MyFirstAndroidAppActivity Class");
```

While you're here, you must comment out or remove your previous `forceError()` call so that your application doesn't fail. Now you're ready to run `MyFirstAndroidApp`. Save your work and `Debug` (🐞) it in the emulator. Notice that your logging messages appear in the `Logcat` listing, with the `DEBUG_TAG` field of `MyFirstAppLogging` (see Figure 3.23).

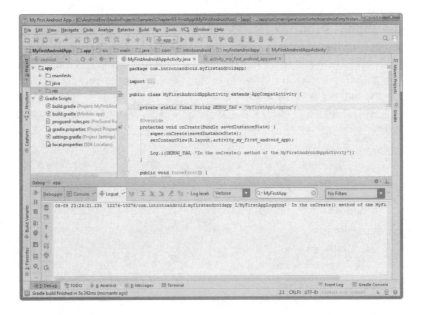

Figure 3.23   A `Logcat` log for `MyFirstAndroidApp`.

Debugging Your Application on Hardware

You have mastered running applications in the emulator. Now let's put the application on real hardware. This section discusses how to install the application on a Nexus 4 device with Android 5.1.1. To learn how to install on a different device or different Android version, read *http://d.android.com/tools/device.html*.

Connect an Android device to your computer via USB and relaunch the application using the `Debug` option. You should now see a real Android device listed as an option in the `Choose Device` dialog (see Figure 3.24).

Choose the Android device and you'll see that the `My First Android App` application gets loaded onto the Android device and launched, just as before. Provided you have enabled the development debugging options on the device, you can debug the application here as well. To allow USB debugging, go to the `Settings` application, then choose `Developer Options`, and under `Debugging`, turn on `USB debugging`. A dialog prompt will appear (see Figure 3.25) requesting that USB debugging be allowed. Click `OK` to allow debugging.

Once the USB-connected Android device is recognized, you may be prompted with another dialog asking you to confirm the development computer's RSA key fingerprint. If so, select the option `Always allow from this computer` and click `OK` (see Figure 3.26).

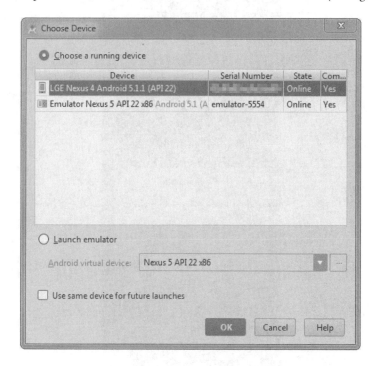

Figure 3.24   `Choose Device` dialog with a USB-connected Android device listed.

Figure 3.25   Allowing USB debugging.

Figure 3.26   Remembering the computer's RSA key fingerprint.

Figure 3.27   `My First Android App` running on Android device hardware.

Once enabled, you can tell that the device is actively using a USB debugging connection because a little Android bug-like icon appears in the `status bar` (![icon]). Depending on your version of Android, the bug-like icon might appear slightly different to resemble the code name of the version of Android, in this case, a lollipop with bug eyes and antennae. Figure 3.27 shows a screenshot of the application running on a real device (in this case, a phone running Android 5.1.1).

Debugging on the device is much the same as debugging on the emulator, but with a couple of exceptions. You cannot use the emulator controls to do things such as send an SMS or configure the location to the device, but you can perform real actions (true SMS, actual location data) instead.

Summary

This chapter showed you how to add, build, run, and debug Android projects using Android Studio. You started by installing the sample applications from within Android Studio. You then began testing your development environment using a sample application, importing the project from GitHub, and then you created a new Android application from scratch using Android Studio. You also learned how to make some quick modifications to the application, demonstrating some exciting Android features you will learn about in future chapters.

In the next few chapters, you will learn about the tools available for use in developing Android applications and then focus on the finer points of defining your Android application using the application manifest file. You will also learn how to organize your application resources, such as images and strings, for use within your application.

Quiz Questions

1. What do the e, w, i, v, and d letters stand for in relation to the android.util.Log class, for example, Log.e()?

2. What are the Debug breakpoint keyboard shortcuts for Step into, Step over, and Step out?

3. What is the keyboard shortcut for optimizing imports?

4. What is the keyboard shortcut for toggling a breakpoint in Android Studio?

5. What are the steps to allow USB debugging on an Android device?

Exercises

1. Describe the purpose of the Minimum SDK options listed in the Create New Project creation wizard.

2. Found in the Create New Project creation wizard, is an Activity option listed on the Add an activity to Mobile screen named Fullscreen Activity. Create a new application with that Activity, and then describe the difference between a Blank Activity and a Fullscreen Activity.

3. Describe the difference between the symbolic Android project view and the traditional Project view of Android Studio.

References and More Information

Android Training: "Getting Started":
  http://d.android.com/training/index.html
Android SDK Reference regarding the application Activity class:
  http://d.android.com/reference/android/app/Activity.html
Android SDK Reference regarding the application Log class:
  http://d.android.com/reference/android/util/Log.html
Android Tools: "Using Hardware Devices":
  http://d.android.com/tools/device.html
Android Tools: "Managing Projects Overview":
  http://d.android.com/tools/projects/index.html
Android Samples: "Samples":
  http://d.android.com/samples/index.html

II

Application Basics

4

Understanding Application Components

Classical computer science classes often define a program in terms of functionality and data, and Android applications are no different. They perform tasks, display information on the screen, and act upon data from a variety of sources.

Developing Android applications for mobile devices with limited resources requires a thorough understanding of the application lifecycle. Android uses its own terminology for these application building blocks—terms such as *context*, *activity*, *fragment*, and *intent*. This chapter familiarizes you with the most important terms and their related Java class components, used by Android applications.

Mastering Important Android Terminology

This chapter introduces you to the terminology used in Android application development and provides you with a more thorough understanding of how Android applications function and interact with one another. Here are some of the important terms covered in this chapter:

- **Context:** The context is the central command center for an Android application. Most application-specific functionality can be accessed or referenced through the context. The Context class (android.content.Context) is a fundamental building block of any Android application and provides access to application-wide features such as the application's private files and device resources, as well as system-wide services. The application-wide Context object is instantiated as an Application object (android.app.Application).

- **Activity:** An Android application is a collection of tasks, each of which is called an activity. Each activity within an application has a unique task or purpose. The Activity class (android.app.Activity) is a fundamental building block of any Android application, and most applications are made up of several activities. Typically, the purpose is to handle the display of a single screen, but thinking only in terms of "an activity is a screen" is too simplistic. An Activity class extends the Context class, so it also has all of the functionality of the Context class.

- **Fragment:** An activity has a unique task or purpose, but it can be further componentized; each component is called a fragment. Each fragment within an application has a unique task or purpose within its parent activity. The `Fragment` class (`android.app.Fragment`) is often used to organize activity functionality in such a way as to allow a more flexible user experience across various screen sizes, orientations, and aspect ratios. A fragment is commonly used to hold the code and screen logic for placing the same user interface component in multiple screens, which are represented by multiple `Activity` classes.

- **Intent:** The Android operating system uses an asynchronous messaging mechanism to match task requests with the appropriate activity. Each request is packaged as an intent. You can think of each such request as a message stating an intent to do something. Using the `Intent` class (`android.content.Intent`) is the primary method by which application components such as activities and services communicate with one another.

- **Service:** Tasks that do not require user interaction can be encapsulated in a service. A service is most useful when the operations are lengthy (offloading time-consuming processing) or need to be done regularly (such as checking a server for new mail). Whereas activities run in the foreground and generally have a user interface, the `Service` class (`android.app.Service`) is used to handle background operations related to an Android application. The `Service` class extends the `Context` class.

The Application `Context`

The application `Context` is the central location for all top-level application functionality. The `Context` class can be used to manage application-specific configuration details as well as application-wide operations and data. Use the application `Context` to access settings and resources shared across multiple `Activity` instances.

Retrieving the Application `Context`

You can retrieve the `Context` for the current process using the `getApplicationContext()` method, found in common classes such as `Activity` and `Service`, like this:

```
Context context = getApplicationContext();
```

Using the Application `Context`

After you have retrieved a valid application `Context` object, it can be used to access application-wide features and services, including the following:

- Retrieving application resources such as strings, graphics, and XML files
- Accessing application preferences
- Managing private application files and directories

- Retrieving uncompiled application assets
- Accessing system services
- Managing a private application database (SQLite)
- Working with application permissions

Warning

Because the `Activity` class is derived from the `Context` class, you can sometimes use this instead of retrieving the application `Context` explicitly. However, don't be tempted to use just your `Activity` `Context` in all cases, because doing so can lead to memory leaks. You can find a great article on this topic at *http://android-developers.blogspot. com/2009/01/avoiding-memory-leaks.html*.

Retrieving Application Resources

You can retrieve application resources using the `getResources()` method of the application `Context`. The most straightforward way to retrieve a resource is to use its resource identifier, a unique number automatically generated within the `R.java` class. The following example retrieves a `String` instance from the application resources by its resource ID:

```
String greeting = getResources().getString(R.string.hello);
```

We talk more about different types of application resources in Chapter 6, "Managing Application Resources."

Accessing Application Preferences

You can retrieve shared application preferences using the `getSharedPreferences()` method of the application `Context`. The `SharedPreferences` class can be used to save simple application data, such as configuration settings or persistent application-state information. We talk more about application preferences in Chapter 14, "Using Android Preferences."

Accessing Application Files and Directories

You can use the application `Context` to access, create, and manage application files and directories private to the application as well as those on external storage. We talk more about application file management in Chapter 15, "Accessing Files and Directories."

Retrieving Application Assets

You can retrieve application resources using the `getAssets()` method of the application `Context`. This returns an `AssetManager` (`android.content.res.AssetManager`) instance that can then be used to open a specific asset by its name.

Performing Application Tasks with Activities

The Android `Activity` class (`android.app.Activity`) is the core of any Android application. Much of the time, you define and implement an `Activity` class for each screen in your application. For example, a simple game application might have the following five activities, as shown in Figure 4.1.

- **A startup or splash screen:** This activity serves as the primary entry point to the application. It displays the application name and version information, and transitions to the main menu after a short interval.
- **A main menu screen:** This activity acts as a switch to drive users to the core activities of the application. Here, users must choose what they want to do within the application.
- **A game play screen:** This activity is where the core game play occurs.
- **A high scores screen:** This activity might display game scores or settings.
- **A help/about screen:** This activity might display the information users might need to play the game.

The Lifecycle of an Android `Activity`

Android applications can be multiprocess, and the Android operating system allows multiple applications to run concurrently, provided memory and processing power are available. Applications can have background behavior, and applications can be interrupted and paused when events such as phone calls occur. Only one active application can be visible to the user at a time—specifically, a single application `Activity` is in the foreground at any given time.

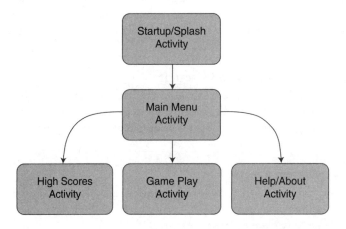

Figure 4.1　A simple game with five activities.

I am the top Activity.
User can see and interact with me!

I am the second Activity in the stack.
If the user hits Back or the top Activity is destroyed,
the user can see and interact with me again!

I am an Activity in the middle of the stack.
Users cannot see and interact with me until everyone
above me is destroyed.

I am an Activity at the bottom of the stack.
If those Activities above me use too many resources,
I will be destroyed!

Figure 4.2   The Activity stack.

The Android operating system keeps track of all Activity objects running by placing them on an Activity stack (see Figure 4.2). This Activity stack is referred to as the "back stack." When a new Activity starts, the Activity on the top of the stack (the current foreground Activity) pauses and the new Activity pushes onto the top of the stack. When that Activity finishes, it is removed from the Activity stack and the previous Activity in the stack resumes.

Android applications are responsible for managing their state as well as their memory, resources, and data. They must pause and resume seamlessly. Understanding the different states within the Activity lifecycle is the first step in designing and developing robust Android applications.

Using Activity Callbacks to Manage Application State and Resources

Different important state changes within the Activity lifecycle are punctuated by a series of important method callbacks. These callbacks are shown in Figure 4.3.

Here are the method stubs for the most important callbacks of the Activity class:

```
public class MyActivity extends Activity {

    protected void onCreate(Bundle savedInstanceState);

    protected void onStart();

    protected void onRestart();

    protected void onResume();

    protected void onPause();

    protected void onStop();

    protected void onDestroy();

}
```

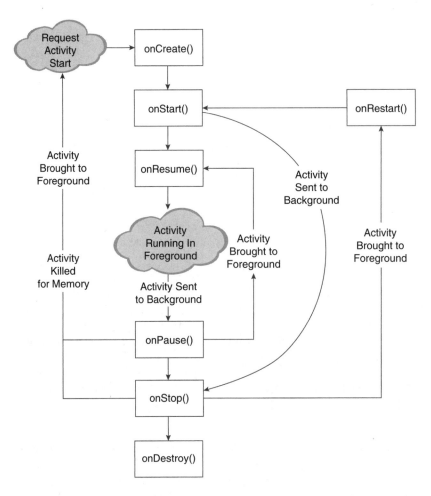

Figure 4.3   The lifecycle of an Android `Activity`.

Now let's look at each of these callback methods, when they are called, and what they are used for.

Initializing Static **Activity** Data in **onCreate()**

When an `Activity` first starts, the `onCreate()` method is called. The `onCreate()` method has a single parameter, a `Bundle`, which is null if this is a newly started `Activity`. If this `Activity` was killed for memory reasons and is now restarted, the `Bundle` contains the previous state information for this `Activity` so that it can reinitiate. It is appropriate to perform any setup, such as layout and data binding, in the `onCreate()` method. This includes calls to the `setContentView()` method.

Confirming Features in `onStart()`

When confirming features for the first time, after the call to `onCreate()`, or reconfirming after a call to `onStop()`, then `onRestart()`, the `onStart()` method is where you should confirm that the appropriate features are enabled on a user's device. For example, if Bluetooth is required for your application to function properly, the `onStart()` method is where you would check to verify that Bluetooth has been enabled, and if not, you would request that the user enable Bluetooth before proceeding with your application.

Initializing and Retrieving **Activity** Data in `onResume()`

When the `Activity` reaches the top of the `Activity` stack and becomes the foreground process, the `onResume()` method is called. Although the `Activity` might not be visible yet to the user, this is the most appropriate place to retrieve any instances of resources (exclusive or otherwise) that the `Activity` needs to run. Often, these resources are the most process intensive, so we keep them around only while the `Activity` is in the foreground.

Tip

The `onResume()` method is often the appropriate place to start audio, video, and animations.

Stopping, Saving, and Releasing **Activity** Data in `onPause()`

When another `Activity` moves to the top of the `Activity` stack, the current `Activity` is informed that it is being pushed down the `Activity` stack by way of the `onPause()` method.

Here, the `Activity` should stop any audio, video, and animations it started in the `onResume()` method. This is also where you must deactivate resources such as database `Cursor` objects or other objects that should be cleaned up should your `Activity` be terminated. The `onPause()` method may be the last chance for the `Activity` to clean up and release any resources it does not need while in the background. You need to save any uncommitted data here, in case your application does not resume. The system reserves the right to kill an `Activity` without further notice after the call on `onPause()`.

The `Activity` can also save state information to `Activity`-specific preferences or application-wide preferences. We talk more about preferences in Chapter 14, "Using Android Preferences."

The `Activity` needs to perform anything in the `onPause()` method in a timely fashion because the new foreground `Activity` is not started until the `onPause()` method returns.

Warning

Generally speaking, any resources and data retrieved in the `onResume()` method should be released in the `onPause()` method. If they aren't, there is a chance that these resources can't be cleanly released if the process is terminated.

Avoiding Activities Being Killed

Under low-memory conditions, the Android operating system can kill the process for any Activity that has been paused, stopped, or destroyed. This essentially means that any Activity not in the foreground is subject to a possible shutdown.

If the Activity is killed after onPause(), the onStop() and onDestroy() methods will not be called. The more resources released by an Activity in the onPause() method, the less likely the Activity is to be killed while in the background without further state methods being called.

The act of killing an Activity does not remove it from the Activity stack. Instead, the Activity state is saved to a Bundle object, assuming the Activity implements and uses onSaveInstanceState() for custom data, although some View data is automatically saved. When the user returns to the Activity later, the onCreate() method is called again, this time with a valid Bundle object as the parameter.

Tip

So why does it matter if your application is killed when it is straightforward to resume? Well, it's primarily about responsiveness. The application designer must maintain the data and resources the application needs to resume quickly without degrading the CPU and system resources while paused in the background.

Saving **Activity** State into a **Bundle** with **onSaveInstanceState()**

If an Activity is vulnerable to being killed by the Android operating system due to low memory, or in response to state changes like a keyboard opening, the Activity can save state information to a Bundle object using the onSaveInstanceState() callback method. This call is not guaranteed under all circumstances, so use the onPause() method for essential data commits. What we recommend doing is saving important data to persistent storage in onPause(), but using onSaveInstanceState() to start any data that can be used to rapidly restore the current screen to the state it was in (as the name of the method might imply).

Tip

You might want to use the onSaveInstanceState() method to store nonessential information such as uncommitted form-field data or any other state information that might make the user's experience with your application less cumbersome.

When this Activity is returned to later, this Bundle is passed in to the onCreate() method, allowing the Activity to return to the exact state it was in when the Activity paused. You can also read Bundle information after the onStart() callback method using the onRestoreInstanceState() callback. Thus, when the Bundle information is there, restoring the previous state will be faster and more efficient than starting from scratch.

Destroying Static **Activity** Data in **onDestroy()**

When an Activity is being destroyed in the normal course of operation, the onDestroy() method is called. The onDestroy() method is called for one of two reasons: the Activity has completed its lifecycle voluntarily, or the `Activity` is being killed by the Android operating system because it needs the resources but still has the time to gracefully destroy the `Activity` (as opposed to terminating it without calling the `onDestroy()` method).

Tip

The `isFinishing()` method returns `false` if the `Activity` has been killed by the Android operating system. This method can also be helpful in the `onPause()` method to know if the `Activity` is not going to resume right away. However, the `Activity` might still be killed in the `onStop()` method at a later time, regardless. You may be able to use this as a hint as to how much instance-state information to save or permanently persist.

Backward-Compatibile `Activity` with `AppCompatActivity`

When a new version of Android is released, there are many new APIs added that are specifically designed for that version—and newer versions—provided those features are not deprecated or removed in future versions. The `Activity` class has received frequent updates with new features, but the downside of that means those features will not work on older versions of Android. That is where the `AppCompatActivity` class comes in. `AppCompatActivity` provides the same functionality as the `Activity` class and makes those same features available through the support library, bringing those new features to old versions of Android.

The code samples provided with this book make use of the `Activity` class frequently, and in many cases, the `AppCompatActivity` is used to bring new `Activity` feature support to older versions of Android. Even though the APIs are nearly the same, there are minor differences in their implementations, which you will learn about in this book and in the code samples provided with the book, which are available for download on the book's website (*http://introductiontoandroid.blogspot.com*). When APIs are identical, we sometimes use `Activity` and `AppCompatActivity` interchangeably, but where APIs are specific to a certain implementation, we make sure to note this fact.

To use `AppCompatActivity`, simply extend your custom `Activity` from `AppCompatActivity` instead of `Activity` and import the class from `android.support. v7.app.AppCompatActivity`. You also need to add the appcompat-v7 support library as a dependency to your Gradle build file. To learn how to add app support libraries to your Gradle build file, in Appendix E, "Quick-Start: Gradle Build System," see the section titled "Configuring Application Dependencies."

Organizing `Activity` Components with Fragments

Until Version 3.0 (API Level 11) of the Android SDK, usually a one-to-one relationship existed between an `Activity` class and an application screen. In other words, for each screen in your app, you defined an `Activity` to manage its user interface. This worked well enough for small-screen devices such as smartphones, but when the Android SDK started adding support for other types of devices such as tablets and televisions, this relationship did not prove flexible enough. There were times when screen functionality needed to be componentized at a lower level than the `Activity` class.

Therefore, Android 3.0 introduced a new concept called fragments. A fragment is a chunk of screen functionality or user interface with its own lifecycle that can exist within an activity and is represented by the `Fragment` class (`android.app.Fragment`) and several supporting classes. A `Fragment`-class instance must exist within an `Activity` instance (and its lifecycle), but fragments need not be paired with the same `Activity` class each time they are instantiated.

Tip

Even though fragments were not introduced until API Level 11, the Android SDK includes a Compatibility Package (also called the Support Package) that enables `Fragment` library usage on all currently used Android platform versions (as far back as API Level 4). Fragment-based application design is considered a best practice when designing applications for maximum device compatibility. Fragments do make application design more involved, but your user interfaces will be much more flexible when designing for different-size screens.

Fragments, and how they make applications more flexible, are best illustrated by example. Consider a simple MP3 music-player application that allows the user to view a list of artists, drill down to a list of their albums, and drill down further to see each track in an album. When the user chooses to play a song at any point, that track's album art is displayed along with the track information and progress (with "Next," "Previous," "Pause," and so on).

Now, if you were using the simple one-screen-to-one-activity rule of thumb, you'd count four screens here, which could be called List Artists, List Artist Albums, List Album Tracks, and Show Track. You could implement four activities, one for each screen. This would likely work just fine for a small-screen device such as a smartphone. But on a tablet or a television, you're wasting a whole lot of space. Or, thought of another way, you have the opportunity to provide a much richer user experience on a device with more screen real estate. Indeed, on a large-enough screen, you might want to implement a standard music library interface:

- Column 1 displays a list of artists. Selecting an artist filters the second column.
- Column 2 displays a list of that artist's albums. Selecting an album filters the third column.
- Column 3 displays a list of that album's tracks.
- The bottom half of the screen, below the columns, always displays the artist, album, or track art and details, depending on what is selected in the columns above. If the user ever chooses the "Play" function, the application can display the track information and progress in this area of the screen as well.

This type of application design requires only a single screen, and thus a single `Activity` class, as shown in Figure 4.4.

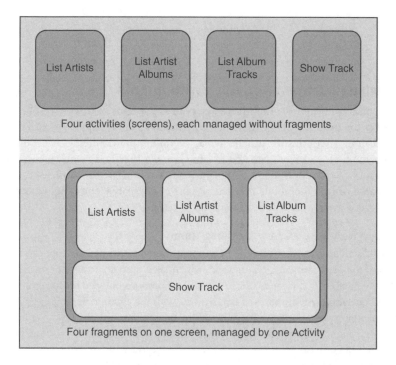

Figure 4.4   How fragments can improve application workflow flexibility.

But then you're stuck with having to develop basically two separate applications: one to work on smaller screens, and another to work on larger ones. This is where fragments come in. If you componentize your features and make four fragments (List Artists, List Artist Albums, List Album Tracks, Show Track), you can mix and match them on the fly, while still having only one code base to maintain.

We discuss fragments in detail in Chapter 9, "Partitioning with Fragments."

Managing `Activity` Transitions with Intents

Throughout the lifetime of an Android application, the user might transition between a number of different `Activity` instances. At times, there might be multiple `Activity` instances on the `Activity` stack. Developers need to pay attention to the lifecycle of each `Activity` during these transitions.

Some `Activity` instances—such as the application splash/startup screen—are shown and then permanently discarded when the main menu screen `Activity` takes over. The user cannot return to the splash screen `Activity` without relaunching the application. In this case, use the `startActivity()` and appropriate `finish()` methods.

Other `Activity` transitions are temporary, such as a child `Activity` displaying a dialog and then returning to the original `Activity` (which was paused on the

Activity stack and now resumes). In this case, the parent Activity launches the child Activity and expects a result. For this, use the startActivityForResult() and onActivityResult() methods.

Transitioning between Activities with Intents

Android applications can have multiple entry points. A specific Activity can be designated as the main Activity to launch by default within the AndroidManifest.xml file; we talk more about this file in Chapter 5, "Defining the Manifest."

Other activities might be designated to launch under specific circumstances. For example, a music application might designate a generic Activity to launch by default from the Application menu but also define specific, alternative entry-point activities for accessing specific music playlists by playlist ID or artists by name.

Launching a New Activity by Class Name

You can start activities in several ways. The simplest method is to use the application Context object to call the startActivity() method, which takes a single parameter, an Intent.

An Intent (android.content.Intent) is an asynchronous message mechanism used by the Android operating system to match task requests with the appropriate Activity or Service (launching it, if necessary) and to dispatch broadcast Intent events to the system at large.

For now, though, we focus on the Intent object and how it is used with activities. The following line of code calls the startActivity() method with an explicit Intent. This Intent requests the launch of the target Activity named MyDrawActivity by its class. This class is implemented elsewhere within the package.

```
startActivity(new Intent(getApplicationContext(),

    MyDrawActivity.class));
```

This line of code might be sufficient for some applications, which simply transition from one Activity to the next. However, you can use the Intent mechanism in a much more robust manner. For example, you can use the Intent structure to pass data between activities.

Creating Intents with Action and Data

You've seen the simplest case of using an Intent to launch a class by name. Intents need not specify the component or class they want to launch explicitly. Instead, you can create an intent filter and register it within the Android manifest file. An intent filter is used by activities, services, and broadcast receivers to specify which intents each is interested in receiving (and filter out the rest). The Android operating system attempts to resolve the Intent requirements and launch the appropriate Activity based on the filter criteria.

The guts of the Intent object are composed of two main parts: the action to be performed and, optionally, the data to be acted upon. You can also specify action/data pairs using Intent action types and Uri objects. As you saw in Chapter 3, "Creating Your First Application," a Uri object represents a string that gives the location and name of an object. Therefore, an Intent is basically saying "do this" (the action) to "that" (the URI describing to what resource the action will be performed).

The most common action types are defined in the `Intent` class, including `ACTION_MAIN` (describes the main entry point of an `Activity`) and `ACTION_EDIT` (used in conjunction with a URI to the data edited). You will also find action types that generate integration points with activities in other applications, such as the browser or Phone Dialer.

Launching an `Activity` Belonging to Another Application

Initially, your application might launch only those activities defined within its own package. However, with the appropriate permissions, applications might also launch external activities within other applications. For example, a customer relationship management (CRM) application might launch the Contacts application to browse the Contacts database, choose a specific contact, and return that contact's unique identifier to the CRM application for use.

Here is an example of how to create a simple `Intent` with a predefined action (`ACTION_DIAL`) to launch the Phone Dialer with a specific phone number to dial in the form of a simple `Uri` object:

```
Uri number = Uri.parse("tel:5555551212");

Intent dial = new Intent(Intent.ACTION_DIAL, number);

startActivity(dial);
```

You can find a list of commonly used Google application intents at *http://d.android. com/guide/components/intents-common.html*. Also available is the developer-managed Registry of Intents protocols at OpenIntents, found at *http://www.openintents.org/*. A growing list of intents is available from third-party applications and those within the Android SDK.

Passing Additional Information Using Intents

You can also include additional data in an `Intent`. The extras property of an `Intent` is stored in a `Bundle` object. The `Intent` class also has a number of helper methods for getting and setting name/value pairs for many common data types.

For example, the following `Intent` includes two extra pieces of information— a `String` value and a `Boolean`:

```
Intent intent = new Intent(this, MyActivity.class);

intent.putExtra("SomeStringData","Foo");

intent.putExtra("SomeBooleanData",false);

startActivity(intent);
```

Then, in the `onCreate()` method of the `MyActivity` class, you can retrieve the extra data sent as follows:

```
Bundle extras = getIntent().getExtras();

if (extras != null) {

    String myStr = extras.getString("SomeStringData");

    Boolean myBool = extras.getBoolean("SomeBooleanData");

}
```

Tip

The strings you use to identify your `Intent` object extras can be whatever you want. However, the Android convention for the key name for "extra" data is to include a package prefix—for example, `com.introtoandroid.Multimedia.SomeStringData`. We also recommend defining the extra string names in the `Activity` for which they are used. (We've skipped doing this in the preceding example to keep it short.)

Organizing Application Navigation with Activities, Fragments, and Intents

As previously mentioned, your application likely has a number of screens, each with its own `Activity`. There is a close relationship between activities and intents, and application navigation. You often see a kind of menu paradigm used in several different ways for application navigation:

- **Main menu or list-style screen:** Acts as a switch in which each menu item launches a different `Activity` in an application, for instance, menu items for launching the Play Game `Activity`, the High Scores `Activity`, and the Help `Activity`.

- **Navigation-drawer-style screen:** A drawer acts as a list of items that are either hidden or shown, and when shown, it presents a list of items that, when pressed, controls what is viewable in the main area of an `Activity` by switching between fragments.

- **Master-detail-style screen:** Acts as a directory in which each menu item launches the same `Activity` or `Fragment`, but each item passes in different data as part of the `Intent` (for example, a menu of all database records). Choosing a specific item might launch the Edit Record `Activity` or `Fragment` passing in that particular item's unique identifier.

- **Click or Swipe actions:** Sometimes you want to navigate between screens in the form of a wizard. You might set a click handler for a user interface control, such as a "Next" button, to trigger a new `Activity` or `Fragment` to start and the current one to finish.

- **Action-bar-style navigation:** Action bars are functional title bars with navigational button options, each of which spawns an `Intent` and launches a specific `Activity`. To support action bars on devices running Android versions all the way back to 2.1 (API Level 7), you should use the `android-support-v7-appcompat` Support Library that comes packaged with the SDK.

We'll talk more about application navigation in Chapter 10, "Architecting with Patterns," which discusses many different but common navigation-design patterns for Android applications.

Working with Services

Trying to wrap your head around activities and intents when you start with Android development can be daunting. We have tried to distill everything you need to know to start writing Android applications with multiple `Activity` or `Fragment` classes, but we'd be remiss if we didn't mention that there's a lot more here, much of which is discussed throughout this book using practical examples. However, we need to give you a "heads up" about some of these topics now because we begin to touch on them in the next chapter when we cover configuring the Android manifest file for your application.

One application component we have briefly discussed is the service. An Android `Service` (`android.app.Service`) can be thought of as a developer-created component that has no user interface of its own. An Android `Service` can be one of two things, or both. It can be used to perform lengthy operations that may go beyond the scope of a single `Activity`. Additionally, a `Service` can be the server of a client/server for providing functionality through remote invocation via interprocess communication (IPC). Although often used to control long-running server operations, the processing could be whatever the developer wants. Any `Service` classes exposed by an Android application must be registered in the Android manifest file.

You can use services for different purposes. Generally, you use a `Service` when no input is required from the user. Here are some circumstances in which you might want to implement or use an Android `Service`:

- A weather, email, or social network app might implement a service to routinely check for updates on the network. (Note: There are other implementations for polling, but this is a common use of services.)

- A game might create a service to download and process the content for the next level before the user actually needs it.

- A photo or media app that keeps its data in sync online might implement a service to package and upload new content in the background when the device is idle.

- A video-editing app might offload heavy processing to a queue on its service in order to avoid affecting overall system performance for nonessential tasks.

- A news application might implement a service to "preload" content by downloading news stories before the user launches the application, to improve performance and responsiveness.

A good rule of thumb is that if the task requires the use of a worker thread, if it might affect application responsiveness and performance, and it is not time sensitive to the application, consider implementing a `Service` to handle the task outside the main application and any individual activity lifecycles.

Tip

In addition to deferring certain tasks with services, Android 5.0 Lollipop introduced the new `JobScheduler` API which allows you to schedule a `Service` to execute when certain conditions are met.

Receiving and Broadcasting Intents

Intents serve yet another purpose. You can broadcast an `Intent` (via a call to the `sendBroadcast()` method of the `Context` class) to the Android system at large, allowing any interested application (called a `BroadcastReceiver`) to receive that broadcast and act upon it. Your application might send off as well as listen for `Intent` broadcasts. Broadcasts are generally used to inform the system that something interesting has happened. For example, a commonly listened-for broadcast `Intent` is `ACTION_BATTERY_LOW`, which is broadcast as a warning when the battery is low. If your application has a battery-hogging service of some kind, or might lose data in the event of an abrupt shutdown, it might want to listen for this kind of broadcast and act accordingly. There are also broadcast events for other interesting system events, such as SD-card state changes, applications being installed or removed, and the wallpaper being changed.

Your application can also share information using this same broadcast mechanism. For example, an email application might broadcast an `Intent` whenever a new email arrives so that other applications (such as spam filters or antivirus apps) that might be interested in this type of event can react to it.

Summary

We have tried to strike a balance between providing a thorough reference and over-whelming you with details you won't need to know when developing a typical Android application. We have focused on the details you need to know to move forward with developing Android applications and to understand every example provided within this book.

The `Activity` class is the core building block of any Android application. Each `Activity` performs a specific task within the application. Each `Activity` is responsible for managing its own resources and data through a series of lifecycle callbacks. Meanwhile, you can break your `Activity` class into functional components using the `Fragment` class. This allows more than one `Activity` to display similar components of a screen without duplicating code across multiple `Activity` classes. The transition from one `Activity` to the next is achieved through the `Intent` mechanism. An `Intent` object acts as an asynchronous message that the Android operating system processes and responds to by launching the appropriate `Activity` or `Service`. You can also use `Intent` objects to broadcast system-wide events to any interested applications listening.

Quiz Questions

1. Which class does the `Activity` class extend?
2. What is the method for retrieving the application `Context` discussed in this chapter?
3. What is the method for retrieving application resources discussed in this chapter?
4. What is the method for accessing application preferences discussed in this chapter?
5. What is the method for retrieving application assets discussed in this chapter?
6. What is another name for the `Activity` stack?
7. What is the method for saving the `Activity` state discussed in this chapter?
8. What is the method for broadcasting an `Intent` discussed in this chapter?

Exercises

1. For each of the `Activity` callback methods, describe the method's overall purpose during the `Activity` lifecycle.

2. Using the online documentation, determine the method names responsible for the lifecycle of a `Fragment`.

3. Create a list of ten `Activity` action intents using the online documentation, where an `Activity` is the target component of the `Intent` action.

4. Using the online documentation, determine the method names responsible for the lifecycle of a `Service`.

References and More Information

Android SDK Reference regarding the application `Context` class:
   http://d.android.com/reference/android/content/Context.html
Android SDK Reference regarding the `Activity` class:
   http://d.android.com/reference/android/app/Activity.html
Android SDK Reference regarding the `Fragment` class:
   http://d.android.com/reference/android/app/Fragment.html
Android API Guides: "Fragments":
   http://d.android.com/guide/components/fragments.html
Android Tools: Support Library:
   http://d.android.com/tools/support-library/index.html
Android API Guides: "Intents and Intent Filters":
   http://d.android.com/guide/components/intents-filters.html
Android SDK Reference regarding the `JobScheduler` class:
   http://d.android.com/reference/android/app/job/JobScheduler.html

5

Defining the Manifest

Android projects use a special configuration file called the Android manifest file to determine application settings, such as the application name and version, as well as what permissions the application requires to run and what application components it is composed of. In this chapter, you explore the Android manifest file in detail and learn how applications use it to define and describe application behavior.

Configuring Android Applications Using the Android Manifest File

The Android application manifest file is a specially constructed XML file that must accompany each Android application. This file contains important information about the application's identity. Here, you define the application's name and version information as well as what application components the application relies on, what permissions the application requires to run, and other application configuration information.

The Android manifest file is named `AndroidManifest.xml`. The easiest way to find this file is by making the `1: Project` tab the `Active Tool Window` of Android Studio and then selecting the `Android` tab from the drop down list (see Figure 5.1 left), so that the app folder is shown as the root for navigating your project structure. You should see a `manifests` folder inside the `app` folder that includes the `AndroidManifest.xml` file (see Figure 5.1, right).

The information in this file is used by the Android system to

- Install and upgrade the application package
- Display the application details to users, such as the application name, description, and icon
- Specify application system requirements, including which Android SDKs are supported, what device configurations are required (for example, D-pad navigation), and which platform features the application relies on (for example, multitouch capabilities)
- Specify what features are required by the application for app store-filtering purposes
- Register application activities and when they should be launched

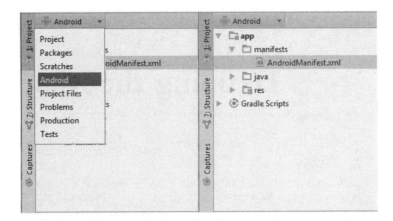

Figure 5.1   Selecting the `Android` tab from the `Active Tool Window`
drop-down list (left) and showing the `AndroidManifest.xml` file inside the
`app/manifests` directory (right).

- Manage application permissions
- Configure other advanced application component configuration details, including defining services, broadcast receivers, and content providers
- Specify intent filters for your activities, services, and broadcast receivers
- Enable application settings such as debugging and configuring instrumentation for application testing

Tip

When you create a project using Android Studio, the initial `AndroidManifest.xml` file is created for you. If you are using the `android` command-line tool, the Android manifest file is also created for you.

Editing the Android Manifest File

You can edit the Android manifest file, `AndroidManifest.xml`, by manually editing the XML. The Android manifest file is a specially constructed XML file.

Android manifest files include a single `<manifest>` tag with a single `<application>` tag. The following is a sample `AndroidManifest.xml` file for an application called Simple Hardware:

```
<?xml version="1.0" encoding="utf-8"?>

<manifest xmlns:android="http://schemas.android.com/apk/res/android"

    package="com.introtoandroid.simplehardware" >
```

```
<uses-permission android:name="android.permission.BATTERY_STATS" />

<uses-feature android:name="android.hardware.sensor.accelerometer" />
<uses-feature android:name="android.hardware.sensor.barometer" />
<uses-feature android:name="android.hardware.sensor.compass" />
<uses-feature android:name="android.hardware.sensor.gyroscope" />
<uses-feature android:name="android.hardware.sensor.light" />
<uses-feature android:name="android.hardware.sensor.proximity" />
<uses-feature android:name="android.hardware.sensor.stepcounter" />
<uses-feature android:name="android.hardware.sensor.stepdetector" />

<application
    android:allowBackup="true"
    android:icon="@mipmap/ic_launcher"
    android:label="@string/app_name"
    android:theme="@style/AppTheme" >
    <activity
        android:name=".SimpleHardwareActivity"
        android:label="@string/app_name" >
        <intent-filter>
            <action android:name="android.intent.action.MAIN" />
            <category android:name="android.intent.category.LAUNCHER" />
        </intent-filter>
    </activity>
    <activity
        android:name=".SensorsActivity"
        android:label="@string/title_activity_sensors"
        android:parentActivityName=".SimpleHardwareActivity" >
        <meta-data
            android:name="android.support.PARENT_ACTIVITY"
            android:value="com.introtoandroid.simplehardware.
SimpleHardwareActivity" />
    </activity>
    <activity
```

(Continues)

(Continued)

```
              android:name=".BatteryActivity"

              android:label="@string/title_activity_battery"

              android:parentActivityName=".SimpleHardwareActivity" >

              <meta-data

                  android:name="android.support.PARENT_ACTIVITY"

              android:value="com.introtoandroid.simplehardware.
SimpleHardwareActivity" />

          </activity>

      </application>

  </manifest>
```

Note

Within the previous manifest code listing, you may be wondering why there is a dot (.) in front of the `<activity>` tag `name` attributes. The dot is used as shorthand to specify that the `SimpleHardware`, `SensorsActivity`, and `BatteryActivity` classes belong to the package name specified in the manifest. We could have specified the entire package name path, but we have used the shorthand to save on typing the extra characters.

Here is a summary of what this file tells us about the `SimpleHardware` application:

- The application uses the package name `com.introtoandroid.simplehardware`.
- The application name and label are stored in the resource string called `@string/app_name` within the `res/values/strings.xml` resource file.
- The application theme is stored in the resource string called `@style/AppTheme` within the `res/values/styles.xml/styles.xml` files (there are two default files created for supporting devices' themes).
- The application supports backup and restore with `allowBackup` set to `true`.
- The application icon is the PNG file called `ic_launcher.png` stored within the `res/mipmap/ic_launcher.png` directory (there are actually multiple versions for different pixel densities).
- The application has four activities (`MenuActivity`, `SimpleHardwareActivity`, `SensorsActivity`, and `BatteryActivity`).
- `SimpleHardwareActivity` is the primary entry point for the application because it handles the action `android.intent.action.MAIN`. This `Activity` shows in the application launcher because its category is `android.intent.category.LAUNCHER`. Each `<activity>` tag also defines a `name` and a `label` attribute.
- `SensorsActivity` and `BatteryActivity` both have a `parentActivityName` of `SimpleHardwareActivity`, defined once with the `android:parentActivityName` attribute of the `<activity>` tag to support the Up navigation feature on API 17+, and once in the `<meta-data>` tag to support this same feature on API versions 4 to 16.

- The application requires the BATTERY_STATS permissions to run with the `<uses-permission>` tag.

- Finally, the application requests to use various different hardware sensors with the `<uses-feature>` tag.

Tip

When using the `<uses-feature>` tag, you can specify an optional attribute of android:required and set the value to `true` or `false`. This is used for configuring Google Play store filtering. If this attribute were set to `true`, Google Play would show your application listing only to users with devices that have that particular hardware or software feature, in this case, various sensors. To learn more about Google Play store filtering, visit *http://d.android.com/google/play/filters.html*.

Now let's talk about some of these important configurations in detail.

Managing Your Application's Identity

Your application's Android manifest file defines the application properties. The package name must be defined in the Android manifest file within the `<manifest>` tag using the `package` attribute:

```
<manifest

    xmlns:android="http://schemas.android.com/apk/res/android"

    package="com.introtoandroid.simplehardware">
```

Setting the Application Name and Icon

Overall application settings are configured with the `<application>` tag of the Android manifest file. Here, you set information such as the application icon (android:icon) and friendly name (android:label). These settings are attributes of the `<application>` tag.

For example, here we set the application icon to an image resource provided with the application package, and the application label to a string resource:

```
<application android:icon="@mipmap/ic_launcher"

    android:label="@string/app_name">
```

You can also set optional application settings as attributes in the `<application>` tag, such as the application description (android:description).

Tip

Android Marshmallow introduced an auto backup feature. To leverage this feature in your application, use the `<application>` attribute android:fullBackupContent and specify an XML file as the value that defines a data backup scheme your application should follow. This will help protect information your user cares about by backing up and restoring the information automatically, in case the user loses a device. To learn more about this feature and how to implement this functionality, see *http://d.android.com/preview/backup/index.html*.

Enforcing Application System Requirements

In addition to configuring your application's identity, the Android manifest file is used to specify any system requirements necessary for the application to run properly. For example, an augmented reality application might require that the device have GPS, a compass, and a camera.

These types of system requirements can be defined and enforced in the Android manifest file. When an application is installed on a device, the Android platform checks these requirements and will error out if necessary. Similarly, the Google Play store uses information in the Android manifest file to filter which applications to offer to which devices so that users install applications that should work on their devices.

Some of the application system requirements that developers can configure through the Android manifest file include:

- The Android platform features used by the application
- The Android hardware configurations required by the application
- The screen sizes and pixel densities supported by the application
- Any external libraries included in the application

Enforcing Application Platform Requirements

Android devices have different hardware and software configurations. Some devices have built-in hardware controls and others rely on the software only controls. Similarly, certain Android devices support the latest 3D graphics libraries and others provide little or no graphics support. The Android manifest file has several informational tags for flagging the system features and hardware configurations supported or required by an Android application.

Specifying Supported Input Methods

The `<uses-configuration>` tag can be used to specify which hardware and software input methods the application supports. There are different configuration attributes for five-way navigation: the hardware keyboard and keyboard types, navigation devices such as the directional pad, and touchscreen settings.

There is no "OR" support within a given attribute. If an application supports multiple input configurations, there must be multiple `<uses-configuration>` tags defined in your Android manifest file—one for each configuration supported.

For example, if your application requires a physical keyboard and touchscreen input using a finger or a stylus, you need to define two separate `<uses-configuration>` tags in your manifest file, as follows:

```
<uses-configuration android:reqHardKeyboard="true"

    android:reqTouchScreen="finger" />

<uses-configuration android:reqHardKeyboard="true"

    android:reqTouchScreen="stylus" />
```

For more information about the `<uses-configuration>` tag of the Android manifest file, see the Android SDK Reference at *http://d.android.com/guide/topics/manifest/ uses-configuration-element.html.*

Warning

Make sure to test your application with all of the available types of input methods, as not all devices support all types. For example, TVs do not have touchscreens, and if you design your application for touchscreen inputs, your app will not work properly on TV devices.

Specifying Required Device Features

Not all Android devices support every Android feature. Put another way, there are a number of APIs (and related hardware) that Android device manufacturers and carriers may optionally include. For example, not all Android devices have multitouch capability or a camera flash.

The `<uses-feature>` tag is used to specify which Android features your application uses to run properly. These settings are for informational purposes only—the Android operating system does not enforce these settings, but publication channels such as the Google Play store use this information to filter the applications available to a given user. Other applications might check this information as well.

If your application requires multiple features, you must create a `<uses-feature>` tag for each feature. For example, an application that requires both a light and a proximity sensor requires two tags:

```
<uses-feature android:name="android.hardware.sensor.light" />

<uses-feature android:name="android.hardware.sensor.proximity" />
```

One common reason to use the `<uses-feature>` tag is for specifying the OpenGL ES versions supported by your application. By default, all applications function with OpenGL ES 1.0 (which is a required feature of all Android devices). However, if your application requires features available only in later versions of OpenGL ES, such as 2.0 or 3.0, you must specify this feature in the Android manifest file. This is done using the `android:glEsVersion` attribute of the `<uses-feature>` tag. Specify the lowest version of OpenGL ES that the application requires. If the application works with 1.0, 2.0, and 3.0, specify the lowest version (so that the Google Play store allows more users to install your application).

For more information about the `<uses-feature>` tag of the Android manifest file, see the Android SDK Reference at *http://d.android.com/guide/topics/manifest/uses-feature-element.html.*

Tip

If a certain feature is not required for your application to function properly, rather than providing filters for the Google Play store to limit access to specific devices, you could check for certain device features at runtime and allow specific application functionality only if those particular features are present on the user's device. That way, you maximize the number of users who can install and use your application. To check for specific features at runtime, use the `hasSystemFeature()` method. For example, to see if the device your application is running on has touchscreen capabilities and returns a Boolean value: `getPackage Manager().hasSystemFeature("android.hardware.touchscreen");`

Specifying Supported Screen Sizes

Android devices come in many shapes and sizes. Screen sizes and pixel densities vary tremendously across the wide range of Android devices available on the market today. The `<supports-screens>` tag can be used to specify which Android screen types the application supports. The Android platform categorizes screen types in terms of sizes (small, normal, large, and xlarge) and pixel density (LDPI, MDPI, HDPI, XHDPI, XXHDPI, and XXXHDPI, representing low-, medium-, high-, extra-high-, extra-extra-high-, and extra-extra-extra-high-density displays). These characteristics effectively cover the variety of screen types available within the Android platform.

For example, if the application supports small screens and normal screens regardless of pixel density, the application's `<supports-screens>` tag is configured as follows:

```
<supports-screens android:resizable="false"
                   android:smallScreens="true"
                   android:normalScreens="true"
                   android:largeScreens="false"
                   android:xlargeScreens="false"
                   android:compatibleWidthLimitDp="320"
                   android:anyDensity="true"/>
```

For more information about the `<supports-screens>` tag of the Android manifest file, see the Android SDK Reference at *http://d.android.com/guide/topics/manifest/supports-screens-element.html* as well as the Android Developers Guide on screen support at *http://d.android.com/guide/practices/screens_support.html#DensityConsiderations*.

Other Application-Configuration Settings and Filters

You'll want to be aware of several other lesser-used manifest file settings because they are also used by the Google Play store for application filtering:

- The `<supports-gl-texture>` tag is used to specify the GL texture compression format supported by the application. This tag is used by applications that use the graphics libraries and are intended to be compatible only with devices that support a specific compression format. For more information about this manifest file tag, see the Android SDK documentation at *http://d.android.com/guide/topics/manifest/supports-gl-texture-element.html*.

- The `<compatible-screens>` tag is used solely by the Google Play store to restrict installation of your application to devices with specific screen sizes. This tag is not checked by the Android operating system, and usage is discouraged unless you absolutely need to restrict the installation of your application on certain devices. For more information about this manifest file tag, see the Android SDK documentation at *http://d.android.com/guide/topics/manifest/compatible-screens-element.html*.

Registering Activities in the Android Manifest

Each `Activity` within the application must be defined within the Android manifest file with an `<activity>` tag. For example, the following XML excerpt registers an `Activity` class called `SensorActivity`:

```
<activity android:name="SensorsActivity" />
```

This `Activity` must be defined as a class within the `com.introtoandroid.simplehardware` package—that is, the package specified in the `<manifest>` element of the Android manifest file. You can also enforce the scope of the `Activity` class by using the dot as a prefix in the `Activity` class name:

```
<activity android:name=".SensorsActivity" />
```

Or, you can specify the complete class name:

```
<activity android:name="com.introtoandroid.simplehardware.SensorsActivity" />
```

> **Warning**
>
> You must define the `<activity>` tag for each `Activity` or it will not run as part of your application. It is quite common for developers to implement an `Activity` and then forget to do this. They then spend a lot of time troubleshooting why it isn't running properly, only to realize they forgot to register it in the Android manifest file.

Designating a Primary Entry-Point `Activity` for Your Application Using an Intent Filter

You designate an `Activity` class as the primary entry point by configuring an intent filter using the Android manifest tag `<intent-filter>` in the Android manifest file with the `MAIN` action type and the `LAUNCHER` category.

For example, the following XML configures an `Activity` called `SimpleHardwareActivity` as the primary launching point of the application:

```
<activity android:name=".SimpleHardwareActivity"
    android:label="@string/app_name">
    <intent-filter>
        <action android:name="android.intent.action.MAIN" />
        <category android:name="android.intent.category.LAUNCHER" />
    </intent-filter>
</activity>
```

Configuring Other Intent Filters

The Android operating system uses intent filters to resolve implicit intents—that is, intents that do not specify a specific activity or other component type to launch. Intent filters can be applied to activities, services, and broadcast receivers. An intent filter declares that this application component is capable of handling or processing a specific type of intent when it matches the filter's criteria.

Different applications have the same sorts of intent filters and are able to process the same sorts of requests. In fact, this is how the "share" features and the flexible application launch system of the Android operating system work. For example, you can have several different Web browsers installed on a device, all of which can handle "browse the Web" intents by setting up the appropriate filters.

Intent filters are defined using the `<intent-filter>` tag and must contain at least one `<action>` tag, but can also contain other information such as `<category>` and `<data>` blocks. Here, we have a sample intent filter block that might be found within an `<activity>` block:

```
<intent-filter>

    <action android:name="android.intent.action.VIEW" />

    <category android:name="android.intent.category.BROWSABLE" />

    <category android:name="android.intent.category.DEFAULT" />

    <data android:scheme="geoname"/>

</intent-filter>
```

This intent filter definition uses a predefined action called VIEW, the action for viewing particular content. It also handles Intent objects in the BROWSABLE or DEFAULT category, and uses a scheme of geoname so that when a URI starts with geoname://, the Activity with this intent filter can be launched to view the content.

Tip

You can define custom actions unique to your application. If you do so, be sure to document these actions if you want them to be used by third parties. You can document these how-ever you want: your SDK documentation could be provided on your website, or confidential documents could be given directly to a client.

Registering Other Application Components

All application components must be defined within the Android manifest file. In addition to activities, all services and broadcast receivers must be registered within the Android manifest file.

- Services are registered using the `<service>` tag.
- Broadcast receivers are registered using the `<receiver>` tag.
- Content providers are registered using the `<provider>` tag.

Both services and broadcast receivers use intent filters. If your application acts as a content provider, effectively exposing a shared data service for use by other applications, it must declare this capability within the Android manifest file using the `<provider>` tag.

Configuring a content provider involves determining what subsets of data are shared and what permissions are required to access them, if any. We begin our discussion of content providers in Chapter 17, "Leveraging Content Providers."

> **Tip**
>
> Many of the code examples provided in this chapter are taken from the SimplePermissions application. The source code for this application is provided for download on the book's website (*http://introductiontoandroid.blogspot.com*).

Working with Permissions

The Android operating system has been locked down so that applications have limited capability to adversely affect operations outside their process space. Instead, Android applications run within the bubble of their own virtual machine, with their own Linux user account (and related permissions).

Registering Permissions Your Application Requires

Android applications have no permissions by default. Instead, any permissions for shared resources or privileged access—whether it's shared data, such as the Contacts database, or access to underlying hardware, such as the built-in camera—must be explicitly registered within the Android manifest file. For devices running versions of Android prior to Marshmallow 6.0 API Level 23, these permissions are granted when the application is installed. For devices running Android Marshmallow 6.0 API Level 23 and newer, permissions with a level of PROTECTION_NORMAL, and some with PROTECTION_SIGNATURE, are granted at installation, while those with a PROTECTION_DANGEROUS must be requested and verified at runtime.

The following XML excerpt for inclusion in the Android manifest file defines a permission using the <uses-permission> tag to read from and write to the contact database, both having a permission level of PROTECTION_DANGEROUS:

```
<uses-permission android:name="android.permission.READ_CONTACTS" />

<uses-permission android:name="android.permission.WRITE_CONTACTS" />
```

A complete list of the permissions can be found in the android.Manifest.permission class. Your application manifest should include only the permissions required to run.

> **Tip**
>
> You might find that, in certain cases, permissions are not enforced (you can operate without the permission) by one device or another. In these cases, it is prudent to request the permission anyway for two reasons. First, the user is informed that the application is performing those sensitive actions, and second, that permission could be enforced in a later device update. Also be aware that in early SDK versions, not all permissions were necessarily enforced at the platform level.

Warning

If the application description or type of application you are providing does not clearly justify the permissions requested, you may get low ratings simply for requesting unnecessary permissions. We see many applications asking for permissions they do not need or have no reason to request. Many people who realize this will not follow through and install the application. Privacy is a big concern for many users, so be sure to respect it.

Requesting Permissions at Runtime

Android Marshmallow introduced a new permissions model allowing users to install your application and to accept your applications permissions once they interact with the features that require them. This new permissions model is important because it reduces the amount of friction permissions may have caused in the past, such as users abandoning the installation of your application because they are not comfortable accepting a particular permission.

With the Android Marshmallow permissions model, a user does not need to grant permissions prior to installing, allowing him or her to install and start interacting with your application. Once the user comes across a feature that requires a particular permission, he or she is presented with a dialog requesting that the permission be granted. If the permission is granted, the system notifies the application and permission is then granted to the user. If the permission is not granted, the user will not be able to access that particular functional area of your application that requires the denied permission. Permissions are declared as normal with the `<uses-permission>` tag in the Android manifest file. Your applications code is where you check to see if the permission has been granted. This permissions model allows users to revoke access to particular permissions in the application settings, without having to uninstall your application. Even if a user grants a particular permission, he or she is able to revoke permissions at any time, so your application must always check that a particular permission is granted, and if not, make a request for the permission.

To request permissions at runtime, you must first add the following dependencies to your `build.gradle` app module file (we talk more about Gradle and dependencies in Appendix E, "Quick-Start: Gradle Build System"):

```
compile 'com.android.support:support-v4:23.0.0'
compile 'com.android.support:appcompat-v7:23.0.0'
```

Then your `Activity` must extend from `AppCompatActivity` and implement the `ActivityCompat.OnRequestPermissionsResultCallback` interface as shown here:

```
public class PermissionsActivity extends AppCompatActivity

      implements ActivityCompat.OnRequestPermissionsResultCallback {

   // Activity code here

}
```

Then you must check if the permission has been granted yet, and if not, request the permission. This is performed as shown below:

```
if (ActivityCompat.checkSelfPermission(this, Manifest.permission.READ_CONTACTS)

      != PackageManager.PERMISSION_GRANTED)
```

```
        || ActivityCompat.checkSelfPermission(this, Manifest.permission.WRITE_
CONTACTS)

        != PackageManager.PERMISSION_GRANTED) {
    Log.i(DEBUG_TAG, "Contact permissions not granted. Requesting permissions.");
    ActivityCompat.requestPermissions(GridListMenuActivity.this, {
                Manifest.permission.READ_CONTACTS,
                Manifest.permission.WRITE_CONTACTS}, 0);
} else {
    Log.i(DEBUG_TAG,
            "Contact permissions granted. Displaying contacts.");
    // Do work here
}
```

This if statement checks if the READ_CONTACTS and WRITE_CONTACTS permissions have been granted, and if not, calls the requestPermissions() method of ActivityCompat. You then must implement the OnRequestPermissionsResultCallback by overriding the onRequestPermissionsResult() method in your Activity as shown below:

```
@Override
public void onRequestPermissionsResult(int requestCode,
        @NonNull String[] permissions, @NonNull int[] grantResults) {
    if (requestCode == REQUEST_CONTACTS) {
        Log.d(DEBUG_TAG, "Received response for contact permissions request.");

        // All Contact permissions must be checked
        if (verifyPermissions(grantResults)) {
            // All required permissions granted, proceed as usual
            Log.d(DEBUG_TAG, "Contacts permissions were granted.");
            Toast.makeText(this, "Contacts Permission Granted",
                    Toast.LENGTH_SHORT).show();
        } else {
            Log.d(DEBUG_TAG, "Contacts permissions were denied.");
            Toast.makeText(this, "Contacts Permission Denied",
                    Toast.LENGTH_SHORT).show();

        }

    } else {
        super.onRequestPermissionsResult(requestCode, permissions, grantResults);
    }

}
```

This method handles the result input by the user, and if the user accepted, the permission is now available to your application; if the user denied the request, the permission will not be available. Whatever features you develop that require those denied permissions will not be made available until the user chooses to grant the appropriate permission.

Note

Android Marshmallow introduced a permission for fingerprint authentication. To add this permission to your applications manifest, use the `android.permission.USE_FINGERPRINT` value. This will allow your application to support fingerprint authentication on devices that have the appropriate hardware support.

Registering Permissions Your Application Enforces

Applications can also define and enforce their own permissions via the `<permission>` tag to be used by other applications. Permissions must be described and then applied to specific application components, such as activities, using the `android:permission` attribute.

Tip

Use Java-style scoping for unique naming of application permissions (for example, `com.introtoandroid.media.ViewMatureMaterial`).

Permissions can be enforced at several points:

- When starting an `Activity` or `Service`
- When accessing data provided by a content provider
- At the method call level
- When sending or receiving broadcasts by an `Intent`

Permissions can have three primary protection levels: normal, dangerous, and signature. The normal protection level is a good default for fine-grained permission enforcement within the application. The dangerous protection level is used for higher-risk activities, which might adversely affect the device. Finally, the signature protection level permits any application signed with the same certificate to use that component for controlled application interoperability. You will learn more about application signing in Chapter 22, "Distributing Your Applications."

Permissions can be broken down into categories, called permission groups, which describe or warn why specific activities require permission. For example, permissions might be applied for activities that expose sensitive user data such as location and personal information (`android.permission-group.LOCATION` and `android.permission-group.PERSONAL_INFO`), access underlying hardware (`android.permission-group.HARDWARE_CONTROLS`), or perform operations that might incur fees to the user (`android.permission-group.COST_MONEY`). A complete list of permission groups is available within the `Manifest.permission_group` class.

For more information about applications and how they can enforce their own permissions, check out the `<permission>` manifest tag SDK documentation at *http://d.android .com/guide/topics/manifest/permission-element.html.*

Exploring Other Manifest File Settings

We have now covered the basics of the Android manifest file, but many other settings are configurable within the Android manifest file using different tag blocks, not to mention attributes within each tag that we have already discussed.

Some other features you can configure within the Android manifest file include

- Setting application-wide themes within the `<application>` tag attributes
- Configuring unit-testing features using the `<instrumentation>` tag
- Aliasing activities using the `<activity-alias>` tag
- Creating broadcast receivers using the `<receiver>` tag
- Creating content providers using the `<provider>` tag, along with managing content-provider permissions using the `<grant-uri-permission>` and `<path-permission>` tags
- Including other data within your activity, service, or receiver-component registrations with the `<meta-data>` tag

For more detailed descriptions of each tag and attribute available in the Android SDK (and there are many), please review the Android SDK Reference on the Android manifest file at *http://d.android.com/guide/topics/manifest/manifest-intro.html.*

Summary

Each Android application has a specially formatted XML configuration file called `AndroidManifest.xml`. This file describes the application's identity in great detail. Some information that you must define within the Android manifest file includes the application's package and name information, what application components it contains, which device configurations it requires, and what permissions it needs to run. The Android manifest file is used by the Android operating system to install, upgrade, and run the application package. Some details of the Android manifest file are also used by third parties, including the Google Play publication channel. In addition, the new Android Marshmallow permission model allows users to grant access to permissions at runtime and revoke access to particular permissions.

Quiz Questions

1. What is the manifest XML tag for specifying the input methods your application supports?
2. What is the manifest XML tag for specifying the required device features for your application?

3. What is the manifest XML tag for specifying screen sizes supported by your application?

4. What is the manifest XML tag for registering permissions that your application enforces?

5. What is the manifest XML `<uses-permission>` attribute for supporting fingerprint authentication?

Exercises

1. Define a fictitious `<application>` manifest XML tag; include the `icon`, `label`, `allowBackup`, `enabled`, and `testOnly` attributes; and then include values for each.

2. Using the Android documentation, list all the potential string values available for defining the `reqNavigation` attribute of the `<uses-configuration>` tag.

3. Using the Android documentation, create a list of five hardware features of the `name` attribute of the `<uses-feature>` tag.

4. Using the Android documentation, name all of the possible attributes and their value types of the `<supports-screens>` manifest XML tag.

5. Using the Android documentation, create a list of ten different values that could be used for defining the `name` attribute of the `<uses-permission>` manifest XML tag.

References and More Information

Android Developers Guide: "The `AndroidManifest.xml` File":
   http://d.android.com/guide/topics/manifest/manifest-intro.html
Android Developers Guide: "Supporting Multiple Screens":
   http://d.android.com/guide/practices/screens_support.html
Android Developers Guide: "Security Tips: Using Permissions":
   http://developer.android.com/training/articles/security-tips.html#Permissions
Android Google Services: "Filters on Google Play":
   http://d.android.com/google/play/filters.html
Android Preview: "Permissions":
   http://d.android.com/preview/features/runtime-permissions.html

6

Managing Application Resources

The well-written application accesses its resources programmatically instead of the developer hard-coding them into the source code. This is done for a variety of reasons. Storing application resources in a single place is a more organized approach to development and makes the code more readable and maintainable. Externalizing resources such as strings makes it easier to localize applications for different languages and geographic regions. Finally, different resources may be necessary for different devices.

In this chapter, you learn how Android applications store and access important resources such as strings, graphics, and other data. You also learn how to organize Android resources within the project files for localization and different device configurations.

What Are Resources?

All Android applications are composed of two things: functionality (code instructions) and data (resources). The functionality is the code that determines how your application behaves. This includes any algorithms that make the application run. Resources include text strings, styles and themes, dimensions, images and icons, audio files, videos, and other data used by the application.

> **Tip**
>
> Many of the code examples provided in this chapter are taken from the `SimpleResourceView`, `ResourceRoundup`, and `ParisView` applications. The source code for these applications is provided for download on the book's website (*http://introductiontoandroid .blogspot.com*).

Storing Application Resources

Android resource files are stored separately from the `.java` class files in the Android project. Most common resource types are stored in XML format. You can also store raw data files and

Table 6.1 **Default Android Resource Directories**

Resource Subdirectory	Purpose
res/drawable/	Graphics resources
res/layout/	User interface resources
res/menu/	Menu resources for showing options or actions in activities
res/mipmap/	App launcher icon resources
res/values/	Simple data such as strings, styles and themes, and dimensions

graphics as resources. Resources are organized in a strict directory hierarchy. All resources must be stored under the res project directory in specially named subdirectories whose names must be lowercase.

Different resource types are stored in different directories. The resource subdirectories generated when you create an Android project are shown in Table 6.1.

Each resource type corresponds to a specific resource subdirectory name. For example, all graphics are stored under the res/drawable directory structure. Resources can be further organized in a variety of ways using even more specially named directory qualifiers. For example, a res/drawable-hdpi directory would be used to store graphics for high-density screens; a res/drawable-ldpi directory is used to store graphics for low-density screens; a res/drawable-mdpi directory stores graphics for medium-density screens; a res/drawable-xhdpi directory stores graphics for extra-high-density screens; and a res/drawable-xxhdpi directory stores graphics for extra-extra-high-density screens. If you had a graphics resource that was shared by all screens, you would simply store that resource in the res/drawable directory. We talk more about resource directory qualifiers later in this chapter.

If you use the Android Studio, you will find that adding resources to your project is simple. Android Studio automatically detects new resources when you add them to the appropriate project resource subdirectory under res. These resources are compiled, resulting in the generation of the R.java source file, which enables you to access your resources programmatically.

Resource Value Types

Android applications rely on many different types of resources—such as text strings, graphics, and color schemes—for user interface design.

These resources are stored in the res directory of your Android project in a strict (but reasonably flexible) set of directories and files. All resource filenames must be lowercase and simple (letters, numbers, and underscores only).

The resource types supported by the Android SDK and how they are stored within the project are shown in Table 6.2.

Table 6.2 **How Common Resource Types Are Stored in the Project File Hierarchy**

Resource Type	Required Directory	Suggested Filenames	XML Tag
Strings	`res/values/`	`strings.xml`	`<string>`
Quantity strings (pluralization)	`res/values/`	`strings.xml`	`<plurals>`, `<item>`
String array	`res/values/`	`strings.xml` or `arrays.xml`	`<string-array>`, `<item>`
Booleans	`res/values/`	`bools.xml`	`<bool>`
Colors	`res/values/`	`colors.xml`	`<color>`
Color state lists	`res/color/`	Examples include `buttonstates.xml`, `indicators.xml`	`<selector>`, `<item>`
Dimensions	`res/values/`	`dimens.xml`	`<dimen>`
IDs	`res/values/`	`ids.xml`	`<item>`
Integers	`res/values/`	`integers.xml`	`<integer>`
Integer array	`res/values/`	`integers.xml`	`<integer-array>`, `<item>`
Typed arrays	`res/values/`	`arrays.xml`	`<array>`, `<item>`
Simple drawables (paintables)	`res/values/`	`drawables.xml`	`<drawable>`
Graphics definition XML files such as shapes	`res/drawable/`	Examples include `icon.png`, `logo.jpg`	Supported graphics files or drawables
Tween animations	`res/anim/`	Examples include `fadesequence.xml`, `Spinsequence.xml`	`<set>`, `<alpha>`, `<scale>`, `<translate>`, `<rotate>`
Property animations	`res/animator/`	`mypropanims.xml`	`<set>`, `<objectAnimator>`, `<valueAnimator>`
Frame animations	`res/drawable/`	Examples include `sequence1.xml`, `sequence2.xml`	`<animation-list>`, `<item>`
Menus	`res/menu/`	Examples include `mainmenu.xml`, `helpmenu.xml`	`<menu>`, `<item>`, `<group>`
XML files	`res/xml/`	Examples include `data.xml`, `data2.xml`	Defined by the developer
Raw files	`res/raw/`	Examples include `jingle.mp3`, `somevideo.mp4`, `helptext.txt`	Defined by the developer
Layouts	`res/layout/`	Examples include `main.xml`, `help.xml`	Varies; must be a layout control
Styles	`res/values/`	`styles.xml`, `themes.xml`	`<style>`, `<item>`

Tip

Some resource files, such as animation files and graphics, are referenced by variables named from their filenames (regardless of file suffix), so name your files appropriately. Check the Android Developer website at *http://d.android.com/guide/topics/resources/ available-resources.html* for more details.

Storing Primitive Resource Types

Simple resource value types, such as strings, colors, dimensions, and other primitives, are stored under the `res/values` project directory in XML files. Each resource file under the `res/values` directory should begin with the following XML header:

```
<?xml version="1.0" encoding="utf-8"?>
```

Next comes the root node `<resources>` followed by the specific resource element types such as `<string>` or `<color>`. Each resource is defined using a different element name. Primitive resource types simply have a unique name and a value, like this color resource:

```
<color name="myFavoriteShadeOfRed">#800000</color>
```

Tip

Although the XML filenames are arbitrary, the best practice is to store your resources in separate files to reflect their types, such as `strings.xml`, `colors.xml`, and so on. However, there is nothing stopping developers from creating multiple resource files for a given type, such as two separate XML files called `bright_colors.xml` and `muted_colors.xml`, if they so choose. You will learn later in Chapter 13, "Designing Compatible Applications," about alternative resources that also influence how the files may be named and subdivided.

Storing Graphics and Files

In addition to simple resource types stored in the `res/values` directory, you can also store numerous other types of resources, such as graphics, arbitrary XML files, and raw files. These types of resources are not stored in the `res/values` directory but instead are stored in specially named directories according to their type. For example, graphics are stored as files in the `res/drawable` directory structure. XML files can be stored in the `res/xml` directory, and raw files can be stored in the `res/raw` directory.

Make sure you name resource files appropriately because the resource name for graphics and files is derived from the filename of the specific resource. For example, a file called `flag.png` in the `res/drawable` directory is given the name `R.drawable.flag`.

Storing Other Resource Types

All other resource types—whether they are tween animation sequences, color state lists, or menus—are stored in special XML formats in various directories, as shown in Table 6.2. Again, each resource must be uniquely named.

Understanding How Resources Are Resolved

The Android platform has a very robust mechanism for loading the appropriate resources at runtime. You can organize Android project resources based on more than a dozen different criteria. It can be useful to think of the resources stored in the directory hierarchy discussed in this chapter as the application's *default resources*. Under certain conditions, you can also supply special versions of your resources to load instead of the defaults. These specialized resources are called *alternative resources*.

Two common reasons that developers use alternative resources are for internationalization and localization purposes, and to design an application that runs smoothly on different device screens and orientations. We focus on default resources in this chapter and discuss alternative resources in Chapter 13, "Designing Compatible Applications."

Default and alternative resources are best illustrated by example. Let's presume that we have a simple application with its requisite string, graphics, and layout resources. In this application, the resources are stored in the top-level resource directories (for example, `res/values/strings.xml`, `res/drawable/mylogo.png`, and `res/layout/main.xml`). No matter what Android device (huge hi-def screen, postage-stamp-size screen, portrait or landscape orientation, and so on) you run this application on, the same resource data is loaded and used. This application uses only default resources.

But what if we want our application to use different graphics sizes based on the screen density? We could use alternative graphics resources to do this. For example, we could provide different logos for different device screen densities by providing many versions of `mylogo.png`:

- `res/drawable-ldpi/mylogo.png` (low-density screens)
- `res/drawable-mdpi/mylogo.png` (medium-density screens)
- `res/drawable-hdpi/mylogo.png` (high-density screens)
- `res/drawable-xhdpi/mylogo.png` (extra-high-density screens)
- `res/drawable-xxhdpi/mylogo.png` (extra-extra-high-density screens)
- `res/drawable-xxxhdpi/mylogo.png` (extra-extra-extra-high-density screens)
- `res/drawable-nodpi/mylogo.png` (do not scale for any screens)
- `res/drawable-tvdpi/mylogo.png` (between medium-and high-density screens)

Let's look at another example. Let's say we find that the application would look much better if the layout were fully customized for portrait versus landscape orientation. We could change the layout, moving controls around, in order to achieve a more pleasant user experience and provide two layouts:

- `res/layout-port/main.xml` (layout loaded in portrait mode)
- `res/layout-land/main.xml` (layout loaded in landscape mode)

We are introducing the concept of alternative resources now because they are hard to avoid completely, but we will work primarily with default resources for most of this book, simply in order to focus on specific programming tasks without the clutter that results from trying to customize an application to run beautifully on every device configuration one might use.

Accessing Resources Programmatically

Developers access specific application resources using the R.java class file and its subclasses, which are automatically generated when you add resources to your project (if you use Android Studio). You can refer to any resource identifier in your project by its name (which is why it must be unique). For example, a String named strHello defined within the resource file called res/values/strings.xml is accessed in the code as follows:

```
R.string.strHello
```

This variable is not the actual data associated with the String named strHello. Instead, you use this resource identifier to retrieve the resource of that type (which happens to be String) from the project resources associated with the application.

First, you retrieve the Resources instance for your application Context (android.content.Context), which is, in this case, this because the Activity class extends Context. Then you use the Resources instance to get the appropriate kind of resource you want. You find that the Resources class (android.content.res.Resources) has helper methods for handling every kind of resource.

For example, a simple way to retrieve the String text is to call the getString() method of the Resources class, like this:

```
String myString = getResources().getString(R.string.strHello);
```

Before we go any further, we find it can be helpful to dig in and create some resources, so let's create a simple example.

Adding Simple Resource Values in Android Studio

To illustrate how to add resources in Android Studio, let's look at an example. Create a new Android project and navigate to the res/values/strings.xml file in the Android Studio and double-click the file to edit it. Alternatively, you can use the Android project included with the book called ResourceRoundup to follow along. Your strings.xml resource file opens in the editor and should look something like Figure 6.1, but with fewer strings.

Now add some resources to the XML. Specifically, create the following resources:

- A color resource named prettyTextColor with a value of #ff0000
- A dimension resource named textPointSize with a value of 14pt
- A drawable resource named redDrawable with a value of #F00

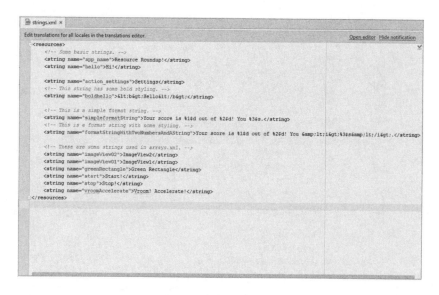

Figure 6.1   A sample string resource file in the Android Studio editor (XML).

Now you have several resources of various types in your `strings.xml` resource file, which now should look something like this:

```xml
<?xml version="1.0" encoding="utf-8"?>

<resources>

    <string name="app_name">ResourceRoundup</string>

    <string
        name="hello">Hello World, ResourceRoundupActivity</string>

    <color name="prettyTextColor">#ff0000</color>

    <dimen name="textPointSize">14pt</dimen>

    <drawable name="redDrawable">#F00</drawable>

</resources>
```

Save the `strings.xml` resource file. Android Studio automatically generates the `R.java` file in your project, with the appropriate resource IDs, which enables you to access your resources programmatically after they are compiled into the project. You may navigate to your `R.java` file by switching the `Active Tool Window` of the `Project` tab of Android Studio to the `Project Files` selection. Then expand the `app` folder so that the `build` folder is visible. Then expand further into `r/debug`, and finally expand into `com/introtoandroid/samples/resourceroundup`, and you should see the `R.java` file listing (see Figure 6.2).

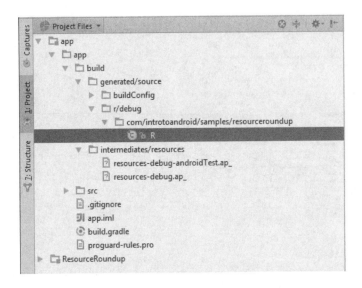

Figure 6.2   Showing the R.java file within Android Studio.

Double-click to open the R.java file, which should look something like this:

```
package com.introtoandroid.resourceroundup;
public final class R {
    public static final class attr {
    }
    public static final class color {
        public static final int prettyTextColor=0x7f050000;
    }
    public static final class dimen {
        public static final int textPointSize=0x7f060000;
    }
    public static final class drawable {
        public static final int icon=0x7f020000;
        public static final int redDrawable=0x7f020001;
    }
    public static final class layout {
        public static final int main=0x7f030000;
    }
    public static final class string {
```

```
    public static final int app_name=0x7f040000;
    public static final int hello=0x7f040001;

    }

}
```

Now you are free to use these resources in your code. If you navigate to your ResourceRoundupActivity.java source file, you can add some lines to retrieve your resources and work with them, like this:

```
String myString = getResources().getString(R.string.hello);
int myColor =
    ContextCompat.getColor(context, R.color.prettyTextColor);
float myDimen =
    getResources().getDimension(R.dimen.textPointSize);
ColorDrawable myDraw = (ColorDrawable) ContextCompat.
    getDrawable(R.drawable.redDrawable);
```

If we go back to the strings.xml file, we can add a string array to our resource listing by adding the following XML element:

```
<?xml version="1.0" encoding="utf-8"?>
<resources>
    <string name="app_name">Use Some Resources</string>
    <string
        name="hello">Hello World, UseSomeResources</string>
    <color name="prettyTextColor">#ff0000</color>
    <dimen name="textPointSize">14pt</dimen>
    <drawable name="redDrawable">#F00</drawable>
    <string-array name="flavors">
        <item>Vanilla</item>
        <item>Chocolate</item>
        <item>Strawberry</item>
    </string-array>
</resources>
```

Save the strings.xml file and now the string array named flavors is available in your source file R.java, so you can use it programmatically in ResourceRoundupActivity.java, like this:

```
String[] aFlavors =
    getResources().getStringArray(R.array.flavors);
```

You now have a general idea of how to add simple resources using the Android Studio editor, but there are quite a few different types of data available to add as resources. It is a common practice to store different types of resources in different files. For example, you might store the strings in `res/values/strings.xml`, but store the `prettyTextColor` color resource in `res/values/colors.xml` and the `textPointSize` dimension resource in `res/values/dimens.xml`. Reorganizing where you keep your resources in the resource directory hierarchy does not change the names of the resources or the code used earlier to access the resources programmatically.

Now let's take a closer look at how to add some of the most common types of resources to your Android applications.

Working with Different Types of Resources

In this section, we look at the specific types of resources available for Android applications, how they are defined in the project files, and how you can access this resource data programmatically. For each type of resource, you learn what types of values can be stored and in what format.

Working with String Resources

String resources are among the simplest resource types available to the developer. String resources might be used to show text labels on form views and for help text. The application name is also stored as a string resource, by default.

String resources are defined in XML under the `res/values` project directory and compiled into the application package at build time. All strings with apostrophes or single straight quotes need to be escaped or wrapped in double straight quotes. Some examples of well-formatted string values are shown in Table 6.3.

You can edit the XML by double-clicking the file and opening it in the Android Studio editor. After you save the file, the resource identifiers are automatically added to your `R.java` class file.

String values are appropriately tagged with the `<string>` tag and represent a name/value pair. The `name` attribute is how you refer to the specific string programmatically, so name these resources wisely.

Table 6.3 **String Resource Formatting Examples**

String Resource Value	Displays As
`Hello, World`	Hello, World
`"User's Full Name:"`	User's Full Name:
`User\'s Full Name:`	User's Full Name:
`She said, \"Hi.\"`	She said, "Hi."
`She\'s busy but she did say, \"Hi.\"`	She's busy but she did say, "Hi."

Here is an example of the string resource file `res/values/strings.xml`:

```xml
<?xml version="1.0" encoding="utf-8"?>
<resources>
    <string name="app_name">Resource Viewer</string>
    <string name="test_string">Testing 1,2,3</string>
    <string name="test_string2">Testing 4,5,6</string>
</resources>
```

Bold, Italic, and Underlined Strings

You can also add three HTML-style attributes to string resources: bold, italic, and underlining. You specify the styling using the `<b>`, `<i>`, and `<u>` tags, respectively; for example:

```xml
<string
    name="txt"><b>Bold</b>,<i>Italic</i>,<u>Line</u></string>
```

Using String Resources as Format Strings

You can create format strings, but you need to escape all bold, italic, and underlining tags if you do so. For example, this text shows a score and the "win" or "lose" string:

```xml
<string
    name="winLose">Score: %1$d of %2$d! You %3$s.</string>
```

If you want to include bold, italic, or underlining in this format string, you need to escape the format tags. For example, if you want to italicize the "win" or "lose" string at the end, your resource would look like this:

```xml
<string name="winLoseStyled">
    Score: %1$d of %2$d! You &lt;i&gt;%3$s&lt;/i&gt;.</string>
```

> **Note**
>
> Those of you who are familiar with XML will recognize this as standard XML escaping. Indeed, that's all it is. After the standard set of XML escape characters is parsed, the string is then interpreted with the formatting tags. As with any XML document, you'd also need to escape single quotes (`'` is `&apos;`), double quotes (`"` is `&quot;`), and ampersands (`&` is `&amp;`).

Using String Resources Programmatically

As shown earlier in this chapter, accessing string resources in code is straightforward. There are two primary ways in which you can access a string resource.

The following code accesses your application's string resource named `hello`, returning only the `String`. All HTML-style attributes (bold, italic, and underlining) are stripped from the `String`.

```
String myStrHello =
    getResources().getString(R.string.hello);
```

You can also access the `String` and preserve the formatting by using this alternative method:

```
CharSequence myBoldStr =
    getResources().getText(R.string.boldhello);
```

To load a format `String`, you need to make sure any format variables are properly escaped. One way you can do this is by using the `htmlEncode()` method of the `TextUtils` (`android.text.TextUtils`) class:

```
String mySimpleWinString;

mySimpleWinString =
    getResources().getString(R.string.winLose);

String escapedWin = TextUtils.htmlEncode(mySimpleWinString);

String resultText = String.format(mySimpleWinString, 5, 5, escapedWin);
```

The resulting text in the `resultText` variable is

```
Score: 5 of 5! You Won.
```

Now, if you have styling in this format `String` like the preceding string resource `winLoseStyled`, you need to take a few more steps to handle the escaped italic tags. For this, you might want to use the `fromHtml()` method of the `Html` class (`android.text.Html`), as shown here:

```
String myStyledWinString;

myStyledWinString =
    getResources().getString(R.string.winLoseStyled);

String escapedWin = TextUtils.htmlEncode(myStyledWinString);

String resultText =
    String.format(myStyledWinString, 5, 5, escapedWin);

CharSequence styledResults = Html.fromHtml(resultText);
```

The resulting text in the `styledResults` variable is

```
Score: 5 of 5! You <i>Won</i>.
```

This variable, `styledResults`, can then be used in user interface controls such as `TextView` objects, where styled text is displayed correctly.

Working with Quantity Strings

A special resource type called <plurals> can be used to define strings that are useful for changing a word's grammatical quantity form. Here is an example string resource file with the resource path of res/values/strings.xml that defines two different quantity forms of a particular animal name that changes based on the context of the quantity:

```
<resources>

    <plurals name="quantityOfGeese">

        <item quantity="one">You caught a goose!</item>

        <item quantity="other">You caught %d geese!</item>

    </plurals>

</resources>
```

The singular form for this particular animal is goose, and the plural form is geese. The %d value is used so we can display the exact quantity of geese to the user. To work with pluralized resources in your code, the method getQuantityString() can be used to retrieve a plural string resource as shown here:

```
int quantity = getQuantityOfGeese();

Resources plurals = getResources();

String geeseFound = plurals.getQuantityString(

        R.plurals.quantityOfGeese, quantity, quantity);
```

getQuantityString() takes three variables. The first is the plural resource; the second is the quantity value, which is used to tell the application which grammatical form of the word to display; and the third value is defined only when the actual quantity is to be displayed to the user, substituting %d with the actual integer value.

When internationalizing your application, managing the translation of words properly and accounting for quantity in a particular language is very important. Not all languages follow the same rules for quantity, so in order to make this process manageable, using plural string resource files will definitely help.

For a particular word, you are able to define many different grammatical forms. To define more than one quantity form of a given word in your string resource file, you simply specify more than one <item> element and provide a value for the quantity attribute for that particular <item> denoting the word's quantity. The values that you can use to specify the <item>'s quantity are shown in Table 6.4.

Working with String Arrays

You can specify lists of strings in resource files. This can be a good way to store menu options and drop-down list values. String arrays are defined in XML under the res/values project directory and compiled into the application package at build time.

Table 6.4 **String `quantity` Values**

Value	Description
zero	Used for languages that have words with a zero `quantity` form
one	Used for languages that have words with a singular `quantity` form
two	Used for languages that have words for specifying two
few	Used for languages that have words for specifying a small `quantity` batch
many	Used for languages that have words for specifying a large `quantity` batch
other	Used for languages that have words that do not have a `quantity` form

String arrays are appropriately tagged with the `<string-array>` tag and a number of `<item>` child tags, one for each `String` in the array. Here is an example of a simple array resource file, `res/values/arrays.xml`:

```xml
<?xml version="1.0" encoding="utf-8"?>

<resources>

    <string-array name="flavors">

        <item>Vanilla</item>

        <item>Chocolate</item>

        <item>Strawberry</item>

        <item>Coffee</item>

        <item>Sherbet</item>

    </string-array>

    <string-array name="soups">

        <item>Vegetable minestrone</item>

        <item>New England clam chowder</item>

        <item>Organic chicken noodle</item>

    </string-array>

</resources>
```

As shown earlier in this chapter, accessing string-array resources is easy. The method `getStringArray()` retrieves a string array from a resource file, in this case, one named `flavors`:

```
String[] aFlavors =
    getResources().getStringArray(R.array.flavors);
```

Working with Boolean Resources

Other primitive types are supported by the Android resource hierarchy as well. Boolean resources can be used to store information about application game preferences and default values. Boolean resources are defined in XML under the `res/values` project directory and compiled into the application package at build time.

Defining Boolean Resources in XML

Boolean values are appropriately tagged with the `<bool>` tag and represent a name/value pair. The `name` attribute is how you refer to the specific Boolean value programmatically, so name these resources wisely.

Here is an example of the Boolean resource file `res/values/bools.xml`:

```xml
<?xml version="1.0" encoding="utf-8"?>

<resources>

    <bool name="onePlusOneEqualsTwo">true</bool>

    <bool name="isAdvancedFeaturesEnabled">false</bool>

</resources>
```

Using Boolean Resources Programmatically

To use a Boolean resource in code, you can load it using the `getBoolean()` method of the `Resources` class. The following code accesses your application's Boolean resource named `bAdvancedFeaturesEnabled`:

```java
boolean isAdvancedMode =

    getResources().getBoolean(R.bool.isAdvancedFeaturesEnabled);
```

Working with Integer Resources

In addition to strings and Boolean values, you can also store integers as resources. Integer resources are defined in XML under the `res/values` project directory and compiled into the application package at build time.

Defining Integer Resources in XML

Integer values are appropriately tagged with the `<integer>` tag and represent a name-value pair. The `name` attribute is how you refer to the specific integer programmatically, so name these resources wisely.

Here is an example of the integer resource file `res/values/nums.xml`:

```xml
<?xml version="1.0" encoding="utf-8"?>

<resources>

    <integer name="numTimesToRepeat">25</integer>

    <integer name="startingAgeOfCharacter">3</integer>

</resources>
```

Using Integer Resources Programmatically

To use the integer resource, you must load it using the `Resources` class. The following code accesses your application's integer resource named numTimesToRepeat:

```java
int repTimes = getResources().getInteger(R.integer.numTimesToRepeat);
```

> **Tip**
>
> Similar to string arrays, you can create integer arrays as resources using the
> `<integer-array>` tag with child `<item>` tags, defining one for each item in the array. You
> can then load the integer array using the `getIntArray()` method of the `Resources` class.

Working with Colors

Android applications can store RGB color values, which can then be applied to other
screen elements. You can use these values to set the color of text or other elements, such as
the screen background. Color resources are defined in XML under the `res/values` project directory and compiled into the application package at build time.

Defining Color Resources in XML

RGB color values always start with the hash symbol (#). The alpha value can be given for
transparency control. The following color formats are supported:

- #RGB (for example, `#F00` is 12-bit color, red)
- #ARGB (for example, `#8F00` is 12-bit color, red with alpha 50%)
- #RRGGBB (for example, `#FF00FF` is 24-bit color, magenta)
- #AARRGGBB (for example, `#80FF00FF` is 24-bit color, magenta, with alpha 50%)

Color values are appropriately tagged with the `<color>` tag and represent a name/value
pair. Here is an example of a simple color resource file, `res/values/colors.xml`:

```
<?xml version="1.0" encoding="utf-8"?>

<resources>

    <color name="background_color">#006400</color>

    <color name="text_color">#FFE4C4</color>

</resources>
```

Using Color Resources Programmatically

The example at the beginning of the chapter accessed a color resource. Color resources
are simply integers. You should use the `ContextCompat` class to access colors as of Android
Marshmallow 6.0 API Level 23, and pass in the application context. The following example shows the method `getColor()` retrieving a color resource called `prettyTextColor`:

```
int myResourceColor =

    ContextCompat.getColor(context, R.color.prettyTextColor);
```

Working with Dimensions

Many user interface layout controls, such as text controls and buttons, are drawn to specific dimensions. These dimensions can be stored as resources. Dimension values always
end with a unit of measurement tag.

Defining Dimension Resources in XML

Dimension values are tagged with the `<dimen>` tag and represent a name/value pair.
Dimension resources are defined in XML under the `res/values` project directory and
compiled into the application package at build time.

The dimension units supported are shown in Table 6.5.

Here is an example of a simple dimension resource file called `res/values/dimens.xml`:

```
<?xml version="1.0" encoding="utf-8"?>

<resources>

    <dimen name="FourteenPt">14pt</dimen>

    <dimen name="OneInch">1in</dimen>

    <dimen name="TenMillimeters">10mm</dimen>

    <dimen name="TenPixels">10px</dimen>

</resources>
```

> **Note**
>
> Generally, dp is used for layouts and graphics, whereas sp is used for text. A device's
> default settings will usually result in dp and sp being the same. However, because the user
> can control the size of text when it's in sp units, you would not use sp for text where the
> font layout size was important, such as with a title. Instead, it's good for content text where
> the user's settings might be important (such as a really large font for the vision impaired).

Using Dimension Resources Programmatically

Dimension resources are simply floating-point values. The `getDimension()` method
retrieves a dimension resource called `textPointSize`:

```
float myDimension =

    getResources().getDimension(R.dimen.textPointSize);
```

Table 6.5 **Dimension Unit Measurements Supported**

Unit of Measurement	Description	Resource Tag Required	Example
Pixels	Actual screen pixels	px	20px
Inches	Physical measurement	in	1in
Millimeters	Physical measurement	mm	1mm
Points	Common font measurement unit	pt	14pt
Screen density-independent pixels	Pixels relative to 160dpi screen (preferable for dimension screen compatibility)	dp	1dp
Scale-independent pixels	Best for scalable font display	sp	14sp

Warning

Be cautious when choosing dimension units for your applications. If you are planning to target multiple devices, with different screen sizes and resolutions, you need to rely heavily on the more scalable dimension units, such as dp and sp, as opposed to pixels, points, inches, and millimeters.

Drawable Resources

The Android SDK supports many different types of drawable resources for managing the different types of graphics files that your project requires. These resource types are also useful for managing the presentation of your project's drawable files. Table 6.6 presents some of the different types of drawable resources that you can define.

Working with Simple Drawables

You can specify simple colored rectangles by using the drawable resource type, which can then be applied to other screen elements. These drawable resource types are defined in specific paint colors, much as the color resources are defined.

Defining Simple Drawable Resources in XML

Simple paintable drawable resources are defined in XML under the res/values project directory and compiled into the application package at build time. Paintable drawable resources use the <drawable> tag and represent a name/value pair. Here is an example of a simple drawable resource file called res/values/drawables.xml:

```
<?xml version="1.0" encoding="utf-8"?>

<resources>

    <drawable name="red_rect">#F00</drawable>

</resources>
```

Table 6.6 **Different Drawable Resources**

Drawable Class	Description
ShapeDrawable	A geometric shape such as a circle or rectangle
ScaleDrawable	Defines the scaling of a Drawable
TransitionDrawable	Used to cross-fade between drawables
ClipDrawable	Drawable used to clip a region of a Drawable
StateListDrawable	Used to define different states of a Drawable such as pressed or selected
LayerDrawable	An array of drawables
BitmapDrawable	Bitmap graphics file
NinePatchDrawable	Stretchable PNG file

Although it might seem a tad confusing, you can also create XML files that describe other `Drawable` subclasses, such as `ShapeDrawable`. `Drawable` XML definition files are stored in the `res/drawable` directory within your project, along with image files. This is not the same as storing `<drawable>` resources, which are paintable drawables. `ShapeDrawable` resources are stored in the `res/values` directory, as explained previously.

Here is a simple `ShapeDrawable` described in the file `res/drawable/red_oval.xml`:

```xml
<?xml version="1.0" encoding="utf-8"?>
<shape xmlns:android="http://schemas.android.com/apk/res/android"
    android:shape="oval">
    <solid android:color="#f00"/>
</shape>
```

Of course, we don't need to specify the size because it will scale automatically to the layout it's placed in, much like any vector graphics format.

Using Simple Drawable Resources Programmatically

Drawable resources defined with `<drawable>` are simply rectangles of a given color, which is represented by the `Drawable` subclass `ColorDrawable`. As of Android Marshmallow 6.0 API Level 23, you should use the `ContextCompat` class to access drawable resources and pass in the application context as the first parameter. The following code retrieves a `ColorDrawable` resource called `redDrawable`:

```java
ColorDrawable myDraw = (ColorDrawable) ContextCompat.
    getDrawable(context, R.drawable.redDrawable);
```

Note

To learn how to define XML resources for a particular type of drawable and to learn how to access the different types of drawable resources in your code, see the Android documentation at *http://d.android.com/guide/topics/resources/drawable-resource.html*.

Tip

Use the `res/mipmap/` directory for placing your application launcher icons. In the past, app launcher icons were stored in the drawables directory, but the `mipmap` folder is now the best-practice location for these assets.

Working with Images

Applications often include visual elements such as icons and graphics. Android supports several image formats that can be directly included as resources for your application. These image formats are shown in Table 6.7.

Table 6.7 **Image Formats Supported in Android**

Supported Image Format	Description	Required Extension
Portable Network Graphics (PNG)	Preferred format (lossless)	`.png`
Nine-Patch Stretchable Graphics	Preferred format (lossless)	`.9.png`
Joint Photographic Experts Group (JPEG)	Acceptable format (lossy)	`.jpg, .jpeg`
Graphics Interchange Format (GIF)	Discouraged format	`.gif`
WebP (WEBP)	Android 4.0+	`.webp`

These image formats are all well supported by popular graphics editors such as Adobe Photoshop, GIMP, and Microsoft Paint. Adding image resources to your project is easy. Simply drag the image asset into the `res/drawable` resource directory hierarchy and it will automatically be included in the application package.

Warning

All resource filenames must be lowercase and simple (letters, numbers, and underscores only). This rule applies to all files, including graphics.

Working with Nine-Patch Stretchable Graphics

Android device screens, be they smartphones, tablets, wearables, TVs, or auto displays, come in various dimensions. It can be handy to use stretchable graphics to allow a single graphic that can scale appropriately for different screen sizes and orientations or different lengths of text. This can save you or your designer a lot of time in creating graphics for many different screen sizes.

Android supports Nine-Patch Stretchable Graphics for this purpose. Nine-Patch graphics are simply PNG graphics that have patches, or areas of the image, defined to scale appropriately, instead of the entire image scaling as one unit. Often the center segment is transparent or has a solid color for a background because it's the stretched part. As such, a common use for Nine-Patch graphics is to create frames and borders. Little more than the corners are needed, so a very small graphics file can be used to frame any size image or `View` control.

Nine-Patch Stretchable Graphics can be created from PNG files using the `draw9patch` tool included with the `tools` directory of the Android SDK. We talk more about compatibility and using Nine-Patch graphics in Chapter 13, "Designing Compatible Applications."

Using Image Resources Programmatically

Image resources are simply another kind of `Drawable` called a `BitmapDrawable`. Most of the time, you need only the resource ID of the image to set as an attribute on a user interface control.

For example, if we drop the graphics file `flag.png` into the `res/drawable` directory and add an `ImageView` control to the main layout, we can interact with that control programmatically in the layout by first using the `findViewById()` method to retrieve a control by its identifier and then casting it to the proper type of control—in this case, an ImageView (`android.widget.ImageView`) object:

```
ImageView flagImageView =

    (ImageView)findViewById(R.id.ImageView01);

flagImageView.setImageResource(R.drawable.flag);
```

Similarly, if you want to access the BitmapDrawable (`android.graphics.drawable.BitmapDrawable`) object directly, you can request that resource directly using the `getDrawable()` method, as follows:

```
BitmapDrawable bitmapFlag = (BitmapDrawable)

    ContextCompat.getDrawable(context, R.drawable.flag);

int iBitmapHeightInPixels =

    bitmapFlag.getIntrinsicHeight();

int iBitmapWidthInPixels = bitmapFlag.getIntrinsicWidth();
```

Finally, if you work with Nine-Patch graphics, the call to `getDrawable()` will return a NinePatchDrawable (`android.graphics.drawable.NinePatchDrawable`) object instead of a BitmapDrawable object:

```
NinePatchDrawable stretchy = (NinePatchDrawable)

    ContextCompat.getDrawable(context, R.drawable.pyramid);

int iStretchyHeightInPixels =

    stretchy.getIntrinsicHeight();

int iStretchyWidthInPixels = stretchy.getIntrinsicWidth();
```

Working with Color State Lists

A special resource type called `<selector>` can be used to define different colors or drawables to be used, depending on a control's state. For example, you could define a color state list for a Button control: gray when the button is disabled, green when it is enabled, and yellow when it is being pressed. Similarly, you could provide different drawables based on the state of an ImageButton control.

The `<selector>` element can have one or more child `<item>` elements that define different colors for different states. There are quite a few attributes that you are able to define for the `<item>` element, and you can define one or more for supporting many different states for your View objects. Table 6.8 shows many of the attributes that you are able to define for the `<item>` element.

Defining a Color State List Resource

You first must create a resource file defining the various states that you want to apply to your View object. To do so, you define a color resource that contains the `<selector>`

Table 6.8 **Color State List `<item>` Attributes**

Attribute	Values
color	Required attribute for specifying a hexadecimal color in one of the following formats: #RGB, #ARGB, #RRGGBB, or #AARRGGBB, where A is alpha, R is red, G is green, and B is blue
state_enabled	Boolean value denoting whether this object is capable of receiving touch or click events, true or false
state_checked	Boolean value denoting whether this object is checked or unchecked, true or false
state_checkable	Boolean value denoting whether this object is checkable or not checkable, true or false
state_selected	Boolean value denoting whether this object is selected or not selected, true or false
state_focused	Boolean value denoting whether this object is focused or not focused, true or false
state_pressed	Boolean value denoting whether this object is pressed or not pressed, true or false

element and the various `<item>`s and their attributes that you want to apply. Following is an example file named `text_color.xml` that resides under the color resource directory, `res/color/text_color.xml`:

```
<selector xmlns:android="http://schemas.android.com/apk/res/android">
    <item android:state_disabled="true"
        android:color="#C0C0C0"/>
    <item android:state_enabled="true"
        android:color="#00FF00"/>
    <item android:state_pressed="true"
        android:color="#FFFF00"/>
    <item android:color="#000000"/>
</selector>
```

We have defined four different state values in this file: disabled, enabled, pressed, and a default value, provided by just defining an `<item>` element with only a `color` attribute.

Defining a `Button` for Applying the State List Resource

Now that we have a color state list resource, we can apply this value to one of our `View` objects. Here, we define a `Button` and set the `textColor` attribute to the state list resource file `text_color.xml` that we defined previously:

```
<Button

    android:layout_width="match_parent"

    android:layout_height="wrap_content"

    android:text="@string/text"

    android:textColor="@color/text_color" />
```

When a user interacts with our `Button` view, the disabled state is gray, the enabled state is green, the pressed state is yellow, and the default state is black.

Working with Animation

Android provides two categories of animations. The first category, property animation, allows you to animate an object's properties. The second category of animation is view animation. There are two different types of view animations: frame-by-frame animation and tween animations.

Frame-by-frame animation involves the display of a sequence of images in rapid succession. Tweened animation involves applying standard graphical transformations such as rotations and fades to a single image.

The Android SDK provides some helper utilities for loading and using animation resources. These utilities are found in the `android.view.animation.AnimationUtils` class. Let's look at how you define the different view animations in terms of resources.

Defining and Using Frame-by-Frame Animation Resources

Frame-by-frame animation is often used when the content changes from frame to frame. This type of animation can be used for complex frame transitions—much like a kid's flip book.

To define frame-by-frame resources, take the following steps:

1. Save each frame graphic as an individual drawable resource. It may help to name your graphics sequentially, in the order in which they are displayed—for example, `frame1.png`, `frame2.png`, and so on.

2. Define the animation set resource in an XML file within the `res/drawable/` resource directory hierarchy.

3. Load, start, and stop the animation programmatically.

Here is an example of a simple frame-by-frame animation resource file called `res/drawable/juggle.xml` that defines a simple three-frame animation that takes 1.5 seconds to complete a single loop:

```
<?xml version="1.0" encoding="utf-8" ?>

<animation-list

    xmlns:android="http://schemas.android.com/apk/res/android"
```

(Continues)

(Continued)

```
    android:oneshot="false">

    <item

        android:drawable="@drawable/splash1"

        android:duration="500" />

    <item

        android:drawable="@drawable/splash2"

        android:duration="500"/>

    <item

        android:drawable="@drawable/splash3"

        android:duration="500"/>

</animation-list>
```

Frame-by-frame animation set resources defined with `<animation-list>` are represented by the `Drawable` subclass `AnimationDrawable`. The following code retrieves an `AnimationDrawable` resource called `juggle`:

```
AnimationDrawable jugglerAnimation = (AnimationDrawable) ContextCompat.

    getDrawable(context, R.drawable.juggle);
```

After you have a valid `AnimationDrawable` (`android.graphics.drawable.Animation Drawable`), you can assign it to a `View` control on the screen and start and stop animation.

Defining and Using Tweened Animation Resources

Tweened animation features include scaling, fading, rotation, and translation. These actions can be applied simultaneously or sequentially and might use different interpolators.

Tweened animation sequences are not tied to a specific graphics file, so you can write one sequence and then use it for a variety of different graphics. For example, you can make moon, star, and diamond graphics all pulse using a single scaling sequence, or you can make them spin using a rotate sequence.

Defining Tweened Animation Sequence Resources in XML

Graphics animation sequences can be stored as specially formatted XML files in the `res/anim` directory and are compiled into the application binary at build time.

Here is an example of a simple animation resource file called `res/anim/spin.xml` that defines a simple rotate operation—rotating the target graphic counterclockwise four times in place, taking 10 seconds to complete:

```
<?xml version="1.0" encoding="utf-8" ?>

<set xmlns:android="http://schemas.android.com/apk/res/android"

    android:shareInterpolator="false">

    <rotate

        android:fromDegrees="0"
```

```
    android:toDegrees="-1440"

    android:pivotX="50%"

    android:pivotY="50%"

    android:duration="10000" />

</set>
```

Using Tweened Animation Sequence Resources Programmatically

If we go back to the earlier example of a `BitmapDrawable`, we can now include some animation simply by adding the following code to load the animation resource file `spin.xml` and set the animation in motion:

```
ImageView flagImageView =

    (ImageView)findViewById(R.id.ImageView01);

flagImageView.setImageResource(R.drawable.flag);

...

Animation an =

    AnimationUtils.loadAnimation(this, R.anim.spin);

flagImageView.startAnimation(an);
```

Now you have your graphic spinning. Notice that we loaded the animation using the base class object `Animation`. You can also extract specific animation types using the subclasses that match: `RotateAnimation`, `ScaleAnimation`, `TranslateAnimation`, and `AlphaAnimation` (found in the `android.view.animation` package). There are a number of different interpolators you can use with your tweened animation sequences.

Working with Menus

You can also include menu resources in your project files. Similar to animation resources, menu resources are not tied to a specific control but can be reused in any menu control.

Defining Menu Resources in XML

Each menu resource (which is a set of individual menu items) is stored as a specially formatted XML file in the `res/menu` directory and is compiled into the application package at build time.

Here is an example of a simple menu resource file called `res/menu/speed.xml` that defines a short menu with four items in a specific order:

```
<menu xmlns:android="http://schemas.android.com/apk/res/android">

    <item

        android:id="@+id/start"

        android:title="Start!"

        android:orderInCategory="1"></item>
```

(Continues)

(*Continued*)

```
    <item
        android:id="@+id/stop"
        android:title="Stop!"
        android:orderInCategory="4"></item>
    <item
        android:id="@+id/accel"
        android:title="Vroom! Accelerate!"
        android:orderInCategory="2"></item>
    <item
        android:id="@+id/decel"
        android:title="Decelerate!"
        android:orderInCategory="3"></item>
</menu>
```

You can create menus using Android Studio, which can access the various configuration attributes for each menu item. In the previous case, we set the title (label) of each menu item and the order in which the items display. Now, you can use string resources for those titles instead of typing in the strings. For example:

```
<menu xmlns:android=
    "http://schemas.android.com/apk/res/android">
    <item
        android:id="@+id/start"
        android:title="@string/start"
        android:orderInCategory="1"></item>
    <item
        android:id="@+id/stop"
        android:title="@string/stop"
        android:orderInCategory="2"></item>
</menu>
```

Using Menu Resources Programmatically

To access the preceding menu resource called res/menu/speed.xml, simply override the method onCreateOptionsMenu() in your Activity class, returning true to cause the menu to be displayed:

```
public boolean onCreateOptionsMenu(Menu menu) {
    getMenuInflater().inflate(R.menu.speed, menu);
    return true;
}
```

That's it. Now, if you run your application and press the Menu button, you see the menu. A number of other XML attributes can be assigned to menu items. For a complete list of these attributes, see the Android SDK Reference for menu resources at the website *http://d.android.com/guide/topics/resources/menu-resource.html*. You will learn a lot more about menus and menu event handling in Chapter 7, "Exploring Building Blocks."

Working with XML Files

You can include arbitrary XML resource files to your project. You should store these XML files in the res/xml directory, and they are compiled into the application package at build time.

The Android SDK has a variety of packages and classes available for XML manipulation. You will learn more about XML handling in Chapter 15, "Accessing Files and Directories." For now, we create an XML resource file and access it through code.

Defining Raw XML Resources

First, put a simple XML file in the res/xml directory. In this case, the file my_pets.xml with the following contents can be created:

```
<?xml version="1.0" encoding="utf-8"?>

<pets>

    <pet name="Bit" type="Bunny" />

    <pet name="Nibble" type="Bunny" />

    <pet name="Stack" type="Bunny" />

    <pet name="Queue" type="Bunny" />

    <pet name="Heap" type="Bunny" />

    <pet name="Null" type="Bunny" />

    <pet name="Nigiri" type="Fish" />

    <pet name="Sashimi II" type="Fish" />

    <pet name="Kiwi" type="Lovebird" />

</pets>
```

Using XML Resources Programmatically

Now you can access this XML file as a resource programmatically in the following manner:

```
XmlResourceParser myPets =
    getResources().getXml(R.xml.my_pets);
```

You can then use the parser of your choice to parse the XML. We discuss working with files, including XML files, in Chapter 15, "Accessing Files and Directories."

Working with Raw Files

Your application can also include raw files as part of its resources. For example, your application might use raw files such as audio files, video files, and other file formats not supported by the Android SDK.

Tip

For a full list of supported media formats, have a look at the following Android documentation: *http://d.android.com/guide/appendix/media-formats.html*.

Defining Raw File Resources

All raw resource files are included in the `res/raw` directory and are added to your package without further processing.

Warning

All resource filenames must be lowercase and simple (letters, numbers, and underscores only). This also applies to raw file filenames even though the tools do not process these files other than to include them in your application package.

The resource filename must be unique to the directory and should be descriptive because the filename (without the extension) becomes the name by which the resource is accessed.

Using Raw File Resources Programmatically

You can access raw file resources from the `res/raw` resource directory and any resource from the `res/drawable` directory (bitmap graphics files or anything not using the `<resource>` XML definition method). Here is one way to open a file called `the_help.txt`:

```
InputStream iFile =
    getResources().openRawResource(R.raw.the_help);
```

References to Resources

You can reference resources instead of duplicating them. For example, your application might need to reference a single string resource in multiple string arrays.

The most common use of resource references is in layout XML files, where layouts can reference any number of resources to specify attributes for layout colors, dimensions, strings, and graphics. Another common use is within style and theme resources.

Resources are referenced using the following format:

```
@resource_type/variable_name
```

Recall that earlier we had a string array of soup names. If we want to localize the soup listing, a better way to create the array is to create individual string resources for each soup name and then store the references to those string resources in the string array (instead of the text).

To do this, we define the string resources in the `res/strings.xml` file like this:

```
<?xml version="1.0" encoding="utf-8"?>

<resources>

    <string name="app_name">Application Name</string>

    <string name="chicken_soup">Organic chicken noodle</string>

    <string name="minestrone_soup">Veggie minestrone</string>

    <string name="chowder_soup">New England clam chowder</string>

</resources>
```

Then we can define a localizable string array that references the string resources by name in the `res/arrays.xml` file like this:

```
<?xml version="1.0" encoding="utf-8"?>

<resources>

    <string-array name="soups">

        <item>@string/minestrone_soup</item>

        <item>@string/chowder_soup</item>

        <item>@string/chicken_soup</item>

    </string-array>

</resources>
```

Tip

Save the `strings.xml` file first so that the string resources (that are included in the R.java class) are defined prior to trying to save the `arrays.xml` file, which references those particular string resources. Otherwise, you might get the following error:

```
Error: No resource found that matches the given name.
```

You can also use references to make aliases to other resources. For example, you can alias the system resource for the OK String to an application resource name by including the following in your `strings.xml` resource file:

```
<?xml version="1.0" encoding="utf-8"?>

<resources>

    <string id="app_ok">@android:string/ok</string>

</resources>
```

You learn more about all the different system resources available later in this chapter.

> **Tip**
>
> Much as with string and integer arrays, you can create arrays of any type of resource by using the `<array>` tag with child `<item>` tags, defining one item for each resource in the array. You can then load the array of miscellaneous resources using the `obtainTypedArray()` method of the `Resources` class. The typed array resource is commonly used for grouping and loading a bunch of drawable resources with a single call. For more information, see the Android SDK documentation on typed array resources.

Working with Layouts

Much as Web designers use HTML, user interface designers can use XML to define Android application screen elements and layout. A layout XML resource is where many different resources come together to form the definition of an Android application screen. Layout resource files are included in the `res/layout/` directory and are compiled into the application package at build time. Layout files might include many user interface controls and define the layout for an entire screen or describe custom controls used in other layouts.

Following is a simple example of a layout file (`res/layout/activity_simple_resource_view.xml`) that sets the screen's background color and displays some text in the middle of the screen (see Figure 6.3).

The `activity_simple_resource_view.xml` layout file that displays this screen references a number of other resources, including colors, strings, and dimension values, all of which were defined in the `strings.xml`, `styles.xml`, `colors.xml`, and `dimens.xml` resource files. The color resource for the screen background color and resources for a `TextView` control's color, string, and text size follow:

```xml
<?xml version="1.0" encoding="utf-8"?>

<LinearLayout xmlns:android=
    "http://schemas.android.com/apk/res/android"
    android:orientation="vertical"
    android:layout_width="match_parent"
    android:layout_height="match_parent"
    android:background="@color/background_color">
    <TextView
        android:id="@+id/TextView01"
        android:layout_width="match_parent"
        android:layout_height="match_parent"
        android:text="@string/test_string"
        android:textColor="@color/text_color"
        android:gravity="center"
        android:textSize="@dimen/text_size" />
</LinearLayout>
```

Figure 6.3   How the `activity_simple_resource_view.xml` layout file
displays in the emulator.

The preceding layout describes all the visual elements on a screen. In this example,
a `LinearLayout` control is used as a container for other user interface controls—here, a
single `TextView` that displays a line of text.

Tip

You can encapsulate common layout definitions in their own XML files and then include those
layouts within other layout files using the `<include>` tag. For example, you can use the
following `<include>` tag to include another layout file called `res/layout/mygreenrect.xml`
within the `activity_resource_roundup.xml` layout definition:

```
<include layout="@layout/mygreenrect"/>
```

Designing Layouts in Android Studio

Layouts can be designed and previewed in Android Studio by using the resource editor
functionality (see Figure 6.4). If you click the project file
`res/layout/activity_simple_resource_view.xml`, you see the `Design` tab, which

Figure 6.4   Designing a layout file using Android Studio.

shows a preview of how the `activity_simple_resource_view.xml` will appear on a device, and the `Text` tab, which shows the raw XML of the layout file.

As with most user interface editors, Android Studio works well for your basic layout needs, enables you to create user interface controls such as `TextView` and `Button` controls easily, and enables you to set the controls' properties in the `Properties` pane.

Now is a great time to get to know the layout editor. Try creating a new Android project called `ParisView` (available as a sample project). Navigate to the `res/layout/activity_paris_view.xml` layout file and double-click it to open it in the editor. It's quite simple by default.

To the right of the `Design` preview, you notice the `Component Tree` section. This outline is the XML hierarchy of this layout file. By default, you see a `LinearLayout`. If you expand it, you see it contains one `TextView` control. Click the `TextView` control. You see that the `Properties` section of Android Studio now has all the properties available for that object. If you scroll down to the property called `text`, you see that it's set to the string resource variable `@string/hello_world`.

Tip

You can also select specific controls by clicking them in the layout editor preview area. The currently selected control is highlighted. We prefer to use the `Component Tree`, so we can be sure we are clicking what we expect.

You can use the layout editor to set and preview layout control properties. For example, you can modify the TextView property called textSize by typing 18pt (a dimension). You see the results of your change to the property immediately in the preview area.

Take a moment to switch to the Text view. Notice that the properties you set are now in the XML. If you save and run your project in the emulator now, you will see similar results to what you see in the layout editor preview.

Now within the Palette, found under the Widgets section, drag and drop the ImageView object within the preview editor. Now you have a new control in your layout.

Drag two PNG (or JPG) graphics files into your res/drawable project directory, naming them flag.png and background.png. Now go to the Component Tree to make sure the ImageView is selected, then browse the properties of your ImageView control, and then set the src property manually by typing @drawable/flag.

While we're at it, select the LinearLayout object and set its background property to the background drawable you added.

If you save the layout file and run the application in the emulator (as shown in Figure 6.5) or on the phone, you will see results much like those in the layout editor Design view.

Figure 6.5   A layout with a LinearLayout, TextView, and ImageView shown in the Android emulator.

Using Layout Resources Programmatically

Objects within layouts, whether they are `Button` or `ImageView` controls, are all derived from the `View` class. Here is how you would retrieve a `TextView` object named `TextView01`, called in an `Activity` class after the call to `setContentView()`:

```
TextView txt = (TextView)findViewById(R.id.TextView01);
```

You can also access the underlying XML of a layout resource much as you would any XML file. The following code retrieves the `main.xml` layout file for XML parsing:

```
XmlResourceParser myMainXml =

    getResources().getLayout(R.layout.activity_paris_view);
```

Developers can also define custom layouts with unique attributes. We talk much more about layout files and designing Android user interfaces in Chapter 8, "Positioning with Layouts."

Warning

The Java code associated with your project is pretty much unaware of which version of a resource is loaded—whether it's the default or some alternative version. Take special care when providing alternative layout resources. Layout resources tend to be more complicated; the child controls within them are often referred to in code by name. Therefore, if you begin to create alternative layout resources, make sure each named child control that is referenced in code exists in each alternative layout. For example, if you have a user interface with a `Button` control, make sure the `Button` control's identifier (`android:id`) is the same in the landscape, portrait, and other alternative layout resources. You may include different controls and properties in each layout and rearrange them as you like, but those controls that are referred to and interacted with programmatically should exist in all layouts so that your code runs smoothly, regardless of the layout loaded. If they don't, you'll need to code conditionally, or you may even want to consider whether the screen is so different it should be represented by a different `Activity` class.

Referencing System Resources

In addition to the resources included in your project, you can also take advantage of the generic resources provided as part of the Android SDK. You can access system resources much as you would your own resources. The `android` package contains all kinds of resources, which you can browse by looking in the `android.R` subclasses. Here, you find system resources for

- Animation sequences for fading in and out
- Arrays of email/phone types (home, work, and such)
- Standard system colors
- Dimensions for application thumbnails and icons

- Many commonly used drawable and layout types
- Error strings and standard button text
- System styles and themes

You can reference system resources in other resources such as layout files by specifying the @android package name before the resource. For example, to set the background to the system color for darker gray, you set the appropriate background color attribute to @android:color/darker_gray.

You can access system resources programmatically through the android.R class. If we go back to our animation example, we could have used a system animation instead of defining our own. Here is the same animation example again, except it uses a system animation to fade in:

```
ImageView flagImageView =

    (ImageView)findViewById(R.id.ImageView01);

flagImageView.setImageResource(R.drawable.flag);

Animation an = AnimationUtils.

    loadAnimation(this, android.R.anim.fade_in);

flagImageView.startAnimation(an);
```

Warning

Although referencing system resources can be useful to give your application a look that is more consistent with the rest of a particular device's user interface (something users will appreciate), you still need to be cautious when doing so. If a particular device has system resources that are dramatically different or it fails to include specific resources your application relies on, your application may not look right or behave as expected. An installable application, called rs:ResEnum (*https://play.google.com/store/apps/details?id=com .risesoftware.rsresourceenumerator*), can be used to enumerate and display the various system resources available on a given device. Thus, you can quickly verify system resource availability across your target devices.

Summary

Android applications rely on various types of resources, including strings, string arrays, colors, dimensions, drawable objects, graphics, animation sequences, layouts, and more. Resources can also be raw files. Many of these resources are defined with XML and organized into specially named project directories. Both default and alternative resources can be defined using this resource hierarchy.

Resources are compiled and accessed using the R.java class file, which is automatically generated by the Android Studio when the application resources are saved, allowing developers to access the resources programmatically.

Quiz Questions

1. True or false: All graphics are stored under the `res/graphics` directory structure.
2. What are the various resource types supported by the Android SDK?
3. What `Resources` method would you use to retrieve a string resource?
4. What `Resources` method would you use to retrieve a string array resource?
5. What image formats does the Android SDK support?
6. What is the format for referencing resources?

Exercises

1. Using the Android documentation, create a list of the different types of drawable resources.
2. Using the Android documentation, create a list of the available keyword values for the `quantity` attribute of the `<item>` element for quantity strings (`<plurals>`).
3. Provide an example of `TypedArray` defined in XML.

References and More Information

Android API Guides: "App Resources":
   http://d.android.com/guide/topics/resources/index.html
Android API Guides: "Resource Types":
   http://d.android.com/guide/topics/resources/available-resources.html

7

Exploring Building Blocks

Most Android applications inevitably need some form of user interface. In this chapter, we discuss the user interface elements available within the Android SDK. Some of these elements display information to the user, whereas others are input controls that can be used to gather information from the user. In this chapter, you learn how to use a variety of common user interface controls to build different types of screens.

Introducing Android Views and Layouts

Before we go any further, we need to define a few terms to give you a better understanding of certain capabilities provided by the Android SDK before they are fully introduced. First, let's talk about the `View` and what it is to the Android SDK.

The Android `View`

The Android SDK has a Java package named `android.view`. This package contains a number of interfaces and classes related to drawing on the screen. However, when we refer to the `View` object, we're actually referring to only one of the classes within this package: the `android.view.View` class.

The `View` class is the basic user interface building block within Android. It represents a rectangular portion of the screen. The `View` class serves as the base class for nearly all the user interface controls and layouts within the Android SDK.

The Android Controls

The Android SDK contains a Java package named `android.widget`. When we refer to controls, we are typically referring to a class within this package. The Android SDK includes classes to draw most common objects, including `ImageView`, `FrameLayout`, `EditText`, and `Button` classes. As mentioned previously, all these controls are derived from the `View` class.

This chapter is primarily about controls that display and collect data from the user. We cover many of these basic controls in detail.

Your layout resource files are composed of different user interface controls. Some are static and you don't need to work with them programmatically. Others you'll want to be able to access and modify in your Java code. Each control you want to be able to access programmatically must have a unique identifier specified using the `android:id` attribute. You use this identifier to access the control with the `findViewById()` method in your `Activity` class. Most of the time, you'll want to cast the `View` returned to the appropriate control type. For example, the following code illustrates how to access a `TextView` control using its unique identifier:

```
TextView tv = (TextView) findViewById(R.id.textview01);
```

> **Note**
>
> Do not confuse the user interface controls in the `android.widget` package with App Widgets. An `AppWidget` (`android.appwidget`) is an application extension, often displayed on the Android `Home` screen.

The Android Layout

One special type of control found within the `android.widget` package is called a layout. A layout control is still a `View` object, but it doesn't actually draw anything specific on the screen. Instead, it is a parent container for organizing other controls (children). Layout controls determine how and where on the screen child controls are drawn. Each type of layout control draws its children using particular rules. For instance, the `LinearLayout` control draws its child controls in a single horizontal row or a single vertical column. Similarly, a `TableLayout` control displays each child control in tabular format (in cells within specific rows and columns).

In Chapter 8, "Positioning with Layouts," we organize various controls within layouts and other containers. These special `View` controls, which are derived from the `android.view.ViewGroup` class, are useful only after you understand the various display controls these containers can hold. By necessity, we use some of the layout `View` objects within this chapter to illustrate how to use the controls previously mentioned. However, we don't go into the details of the various layout types available as part of the Android SDK until Chapter 8.

> **Note**
>
> Many of the code examples provided in this chapter are taken from the `ViewSamples` application. The source code for the `ViewSamples` application is provided for download on the book's website (*http://introductiontoandroid.blogspot.com*).

Displaying Text to Users with `TextView`

One of the most basic user interface elements, or controls, in the Android SDK is the `TextView` control. You use it to draw text on the screen. You primarily use it to display fixed text strings or labels.

Frequently, the `TextView` control is a child control within other screen elements and controls. As with most of the user interface elements, it is derived from `View` and is within the `android.widget` package. Because it is a `View`, the standard attributes such as width, height, padding, and visibility can be applied to the object. However, because this is a text-displaying control, you can apply many other `TextView` attributes to control behavior and how the text is viewed in a variety of situations.

First, though, let's see how to put some quick text up on the screen. `<TextView>` is the XML layout file tag used to display text on the screen. You can set the `android:text` property of the `TextView` to be either a raw text string in the layout file or a reference to a string resource.

Here are examples of both methods you can use to set the `android:text` attribute of a `TextView`. The first method sets the text attribute to a raw string; the second method uses a string resource called `sample_text`, which must be defined in the `strings.xml` resource file.

```
<TextView
    android:id="@+id/TextView01"
    android:layout_width="wrap_content"
    android:layout_height="wrap_content"
    android:text="Some sample text here"/>
<TextView
    android:id="@+id/TextView02"
    android:layout_width="wrap_content"
    android:layout_height="wrap_content"
    android:text="@string/sample_text"/>
```

To display this `TextView` on the screen, all your `Activity` needs to do is call the `setContentView()` method with the layout resource identifier where you defined the preceding XML shown. You can change the text displayed programmatically by calling the `setText()` method on the `TextView` object. Retrieving the text is done with the `getText()` method.

Now let's talk about some of the more common attributes of `TextView` objects.

Configuring Layout and Sizing

The `TextView` control has some special attributes that dictate how the text is drawn and flows. You can, for instance, set the `TextView` to be a single line high and a fixed width. If, however, a string of text is too long to fit, the text truncates abruptly. Luckily, there are some attributes that can handle this problem.

Tip

When looking through the attributes available to `TextView` objects, you should be aware that the `TextView` class contains all the functionality needed by editable controls. This means that many of the attributes apply only to input fields, which are used primarily by the subclass `EditText` object. For example, the `autoText` attribute, which helps the user by fixing common spelling mistakes, is most appropriately set on editable text fields (`EditText`). There is no need to use this attribute normally when you are simply displaying text.

The width of a `TextView` can be controlled in terms of the `ems` measurement rather than in pixels. An *em* is a term used in typography that is defined in terms of the point size of a particular font. (For example, the measure of an em in a 12-point font is 12 points.) This measurement provides better control over how much text is viewed, regardless of the font size. Through the `ems` attribute, you can set the width of the `TextView`. Additionally, you can use the `maxEms` and `minEms` attributes to set the maximum width and minimum width, respectively, of the `TextView` in terms of `ems`.

The height of a `TextView` can be set in terms of lines of text rather than pixels. Again, this is useful for controlling how much text can be viewed regardless of the font size. The `lines` attribute sets the number of lines that the `TextView` can display. You can also use `maxLines` and `minLines` to control the maximum height and minimum height, respectively that the `TextView` displays.

Here is an example that combines these two types of sizing attributes. This `TextView` is two lines of text high and 12 ems of text wide. The layout width and height are specified to the size of the `TextView` and are required attributes in the XML schema:

```
<TextView

    android:id="@+id/TextView04"

    android:layout_width="wrap_content"

    android:layout_height="wrap_content"

    android:lines="2"

    android:ems="12"

    android:text="@string/autolink_test"/>
```

Instead of having the text only truncate at the end, as happens in the preceding example, we can enable the `ellipsize` attribute to replace the last couple of characters with an ellipsis (. . .) so the user knows that not all text is displayed.

Creating Contextual Links in Text

If your text contains references to email addresses, Web pages, phone numbers, or even street addresses, you might want to consider using the attribute `autoLink` (see Figure 7.1). The `autoLink` attribute has six values that you can use. When enabled, these `autoLink` attribute values create standard Web-style links to the application that can act on that data type. For instance, setting the attribute to `web` automatically finds and links any URLs to Web pages.

Your text can contain the following values for the `autoLink` attribute:

- **none**: disables all linking
- **web**: enables linking of URLs to Web pages
- **email**: enables linking of email addresses to the mail client with the recipient filled in
- **phone**: enables linking of phone numbers to the dialer application with the phone number filled in, ready to be dialed

Figure 7.1   Three TextView types: Simple, autoLink none (not
clickable), and autoLink all (clickable).

- **map**: enables linking of street addresses to the map application to show the location
- **all**: enables all types of linking

Turning on the autoLink feature relies on the detection of the various types within the Android SDK. In some cases, the linking might not be correct or might be misleading.

Here is an example that links email and Web pages, which, in our opinion, are the most reliable and predictable:

```
<TextView
    android:id="@+id/TextView02"
    android:layout_width="wrap_content"
    android:layout_height="wrap_content"
    android:text="@string/autolink_test"
    android:autoLink="web|email"/>
```

Two helper values are available for this attribute as well. You can set it to none to make sure no type of data is linked. You can also set it to all to have all known types linked. Figure 7.2 illustrates what happens when you click these links. The default for a TextView is not to link any types. If you want the user to see the various data types highlighted, but you don't want the user to click them, you can set the linksClickable attribute to false.

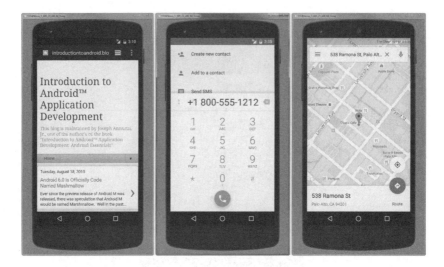

Figure 7.2   Clickable `autoLinks`: a URL launches the browser, a phone number launches the dialer, and a street address launches Google Maps.

Retrieving Data from Users with Text Fields

The Android SDK provides a number of controls for retrieving data from users. One of the most common types of data that applications often need to collect from users is text. One frequently used text field control to handle this type of job is the `EditText` control.

Retrieving Text Input Using `EditText` Controls

The Android SDK provides a convenient control called `EditText` to handle text input from a user. The `EditText` class is derived from `TextView`. In fact, most of its functionality is contained within `TextView`, but is enabled when created as an `EditText`. The `EditText` object has a number of useful features enabled by default, many of which are shown in Figure 7.3.

First, though, let's see how to define an `EditText` control in an XML layout file:

```
<EditText
    android:id="@+id/EditText01"
    android:layout_height="wrap_content"
    android:hint="type here"
    android:lines="4"
    android:layout_width="match_parent"/>
```

Figure 7.3   Various styles of `EditText`, `Spinner`, and `Button` controls.

This layout code shows a basic `EditText` element. There are a couple of interesting things to note. First, the `hint` attribute puts some text in the edit box that goes away when the user starts entering text (run the sample code to see an example of a `hint` in action). Essentially, this gives a hint to the user as to what should go there. Next is the `lines` attribute, which defines how many lines tall the input box is. If this is not set, the entry field grows as the user enters text. However, setting a size allows the user to scroll within a fixed size to edit the text. This also applies to the width of the entry.

By default, the user can perform a long press to bring up a context menu. This provides some basic copy, cut, and paste operations to the user as well as the ability to change the input method and add a word to the user's dictionary of frequently used words (shown in Figure 7.4). You do not need to provide any additional code for this useful behavior to benefit your users. You can also highlight a portion of the text from code. A call to `setSelection()` does this, and a call to `selectAll()` highlights the entire text entry field.

The `EditText` object is essentially an editable `TextView`. This means that you can read text from it in the same way as you did with `TextView` by using the `getText()` method. You can also set initial text to draw in the text entry area using the `setText()` method.

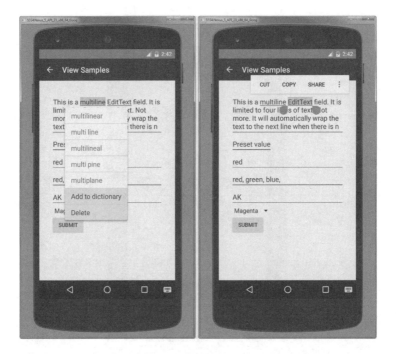

Figure 7.4   A long press on an `EditText` control typically launches
a context menu for selections, cutting, and copying. (The `Paste` option
appears when you have copied text.)

Constraining User Input with Input Filters

There are times when you don't want the user to type just anything. Validating input after
the user has entered something is one way to do this. However, a better way to avoid
wasting the user's time is to filter the input. The `EditText` control provides a way to set an
`InputFilter` that does only this.

The Android SDK provides some `InputFilter` objects for use. `InputFilter` objects
enforce such rules as allowing only uppercase text and limiting the length of the text
entered. You can create custom filters by implementing the `InputFilter` interface, which
contains the single method called `filter()`. Here is an example of an `EditText` control
with two built-in filters that might be appropriate for a two-letter state abbreviation:

```
final EditText text_filtered = (EditText) findViewById(R.id.input_filtered);

text_filtered.setFilters(new InputFilter[] {

    new InputFilter.AllCaps(),

    new InputFilter.LengthFilter(2)

});
```

The `setFilters()` method call takes an array of `InputFilter` objects. This is useful for combining multiple filters, as shown. In this case, we convert all input to uppercase. Additionally, we set the maximum length to two characters long. The `EditText` control looks the same as any other, but if you try to type in lowercase, the text is converted to uppercase, and the string is limited to two characters. This does not mean that all possible inputs are valid, but it does help users to avoid making the input too long or bothering with the case of the input. This also helps your application by guaranteeing that any text from this input is a length of two characters. It does not constrain the input to only letters, though.

Helping the User with Autocompletion

In addition to providing a basic text editor with the `EditText` control, the Android SDK provides a way to help the user with entering commonly used data into forms. This functionality is provided through the autocomplete feature.

There are two forms of autocomplete. One is the more standard style of filling in the entire text entry based on what the user types. If the user begins typing a string that matches a word in a developer-provided list, the user can choose to complete the word with just a tap. This is done through the `AutoCompleteTextView` control (see Figure 7.5, left). The second method allows the user to enter a list of items, each of which has

Figure 7.5   Using `AutoCompleteTextView` (left)
and `MultiAutoCompleteTextView` (right).

autocomplete functionality (see Figure 7.5, right). These items must be separated in some way by providing a `Tokenizer` to the `MultiAutoCompleteTextView` object that handles this method. A common `Tokenizer` implementation is provided for comma-separated lists and is used by specifying the `MultiAutoCompleteTextView.CommaTokenizer` object. This can be helpful for lists of specifying common tags and the like.

Both of the autocomplete text editors use an `Adapter` to get the list of text they use to provide completions to the user. This example shows how to provide an `AutoComplete TextView` that can help users type some of the basic colors from an array in the code:

```
final String[] COLORS = { "red", "green", "orange", "blue", "purple",
    "black", "yellow", "cyan", "magenta" };
ArrayAdapter<String> adapter = new ArrayAdapter<String>(this,
    android.R.layout.simple_dropdown_item_1line, COLORS);
AutoCompleteTextView text = (AutoCompleteTextView)
    findViewById(R.id.AutoCompleteTextView01);
text.setAdapter(adapter);
```

In this example, when the user starts typing in the field, if he or she starts with one of the letters in the COLORS array, a drop-down list shows all the available completions. Note that this does not limit what the user can enter. The user is still free to enter any text (such as "puce"). The `Adapter` controls the look of the drop-down list. In this case, we use a built-in layout made for such things. Here is the layout resource definition for this `AutoCompleteTextView` control:

```
<AutoCompleteTextView
    android:id="@+id/AutoCompleteTextView01"
    android:layout_width="match_parent"
    android:layout_height="wrap_content"
    android:completionHint="Pick a color or type your own"
    android:completionThreshold="1"/>
```

There are a few more things to notice here. First, you can choose when the completion drop-down list shows by filling in a value for the `completionThreshold` attribute. In this case, we set it to a single character, so it displays immediately if there is a match. The default value is two characters of typing before it displays autocompletion options. Second, you can set some text in the `completionHint` attribute. This displays at the bottom of the drop-down list to help users. Finally, the drop-down list for completions is sized to the `TextView`. This means that it should be wide enough to show the completions and the text for the `completionHint` attribute.

The `MultiAutoCompleteTextView` is essentially the same as the regular autocomplete, except that you must assign a `Tokenizer` to it so that the control knows where each autocompletion should begin. The following is an example that uses the same `Adapter` as the previous example but includes a `Tokenizer` for a list of user color responses, each separated by a comma:

```
MultiAutoCompleteTextView mtext =
    (MultiAutoCompleteTextView) findViewById(R.id.MultiAutoCompleteTextView01);
mtext.setAdapter(adapter);
mtext.setTokenizer(new MultiAutoCompleteTextView.CommaTokenizer());
```

As you can see, the only change is setting the `Tokenizer`. Here, we use the built-in comma `Tokenizer` provided by the Android SDK. In this case, whenever a user chooses a color from the list, the name of the color is completed, and a comma is automatically added so that the user can immediately start typing in the next color. As before, this does not limit what the user can enter. If the user enters "maroon" and places a comma after it, the autocompletion starts again as the user types another color, regardless of the fact that it didn't help the user type in the color maroon. You can create your own `Tokenizer` by implementing the `MultiAutoCompleteTextView.Tokenizer` interface. You can do this if you prefer entries separated by a semicolon or some other more complex separator.

Giving Users Choices Using Spinner Controls

Sometimes you want to limit the choices available for users to type. For instance, if users are going to enter the name of a state, you might as well limit them to only the valid states, because this is a known set. Although you could do this by letting them type something and then blocking invalid entries, you can also provide similar functionality with a `Spinner` control. As with the autocomplete method, the possible choices for a spinner can come from an `Adapter`. You can also set the available choices in the layout definition by using the `entries` attribute with an array resource (specifically a string array that is referenced as something such as `@array/state-list`). The `Spinner` control isn't actually an `EditText`, although it is frequently used in a similar fashion. Here is an example of the XML layout definition for a `Spinner` control for choosing a color:

```
<Spinner
    android:id="@+id/Spinner01"
    android:layout_width="wrap_content"
    android:layout_height="wrap_content"
    android:entries="@array/colors"
    android:prompt="@string/spin_prompt"/>
```

This places a `Spinner` control on the screen. A closed `Spinner` control is shown in Figure 7.5, with just the first choice, red, displayed. An open `Spinner` control is shown in Figure 7.6, which shows all the color selections available. When the user selects this control, a pop-up shows the prompt text followed by a list of the possible choices. This list

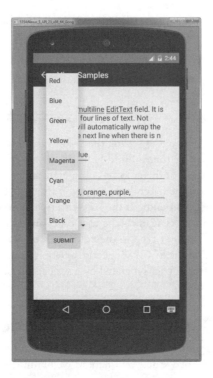

Figure 7.6   Filtering choices with a `Spinner` control.

allows only a single item to be selected at a time, and when one is selected, the pop-up goes away.

There are a couple of things to notice here. First, the `entries` attribute is set to the value of a string array resource, referred to here as `@array/colors`. Second, the `prompt` attribute is defined as a string resource. Unlike some other string attributes, this one is required to be a string resource. The `prompt` displays when the `Spinner` control is opened and all selections are displayed. The `prompt` can be used to tell the user what kinds of values can be selected.

Because the `Spinner` control is not a `TextView`, but a list of `TextView` objects, you can't directly request the selected text from it. Instead, you have to retrieve the specific selected option (each of which is a `TextView` control) and extract the text directly from it:

```
final Spinner spin = (Spinner) findViewById(R.id.Spinner01);

TextView textSel = (TextView) spin.getSelectedView();

String selectedText = textSel.getText().toString();
```

Alternatively, we could have called the `getSelectedItem()`, `getSelectedItemIndex()`, or `getSelectedItemId()` method to deal with other forms of selection.

Allowing Simple User Selections with Buttons and Switches

Other common user interface elements are buttons and switches. In this section, you learn about different kinds of buttons and switches provided by the Android SDK. These include the basic `Button`, `CheckBox`, `ToggleButton`, and `RadioButton`.

- A basic `Button` is often used to perform some sort of action, such as submitting a form or confirming a selection. A basic `Button` control can contain a text or image label.

- A `CheckBox` is a button with two states—checked and unchecked. You often use `CheckBox` controls to turn a feature on or off, or to pick multiple items from a list.

- A `ToggleButton` is similar to a `CheckBox`, but you use it to show the state visually. The default behavior of a toggle is like that of a power on/off button.

- A `Switch` is similar to a `CheckBox` in that it is a two-state control. The default behavior of a control is like a slider switch that can be moved between the "on" and "off" positions.

- A `RadioButton` provides selection of an item. Grouping `RadioButton` controls together in a container called a `RadioGroup` enables the developer to enforce that only one `RadioButton` is selected at a time.

You can find examples of each type of control in Figure 7.7.

Using Basic Buttons

The `android.widget.Button` class provides a basic `Button` implementation in the Android SDK. Within the XML layout resources, buttons are specified using the `Button` element. The primary attribute for a basic `Button` is the text field. This is the label that appears on the middle of the button's face. You often use basic `Button` controls for buttons with text such as "OK," "Cancel," or "Submit."

Tip

You can find many common application string values in the Android system resource strings, exposed in `android.R.string`. There are strings for common button text such as "Yes," "No," "OK," "Cancel," and "Copy." For more information on system resources, see Chapter 6, "Managing Application Resources."

The following XML layout resource file shows a typical `Button` control definition:

```
<Button
    android:id="@+id/basic_button"
    android:layout_width="wrap_content"
    android:layout_height="wrap_content"
    android:text="Basic Button"/>
```

Figure 7.7   Various types of `Button` controls.

Tip

One popular styling method for buttons is the borderless button. To create a button without borders, all you need to do is set the `style` attribute of your Button in your layout file to `style: "?android:attr/borderlessButtonStyle"`. To learn more about styling your buttons, see *http://d.android.com/guide/topics/ui/controls/button.html#Style*.

A `Button` control won't do anything, other than animate, without some code to handle the click event. Here is an example of some code that handles a click for a basic `Button` and displays a `Toast` message on the screen:

```
setContentView(R.layout.buttons);

final Button basicButton = (Button) findViewById(R.id.basic_button);

basicButton.setOnClickListener(new View.OnClickListener() {

    public void onClick(View v) {

        Toast.makeText(ButtonsActivity.this,

            "Button clicked", Toast.LENGTH_SHORT).show();

    }

});
```

Tip

A `Toast` (`android.widget.Toast`) is a simple dialog-like message that displays for a second or so and then disappears. `Toast` messages are useful for providing the user with nonessential confirmation messages; they are also quite handy for debugging. Figure 7.7 shows an example of a `Toast` message that displays the text "Image button clicked."

To handle the click event for when a `Button` control is pressed, we first get a reference to the `Button` by its resource identifier. Next, the `setOnClickListener()` method is called. It requires a valid instance of the class `View.OnClickListener`. A simple way to provide this is to define the instance right in the method call. This requires implementing the `onClick()` method. Within the `onClick()` method, you are free to carry out whatever actions you need. Here, we simply display a message to the users telling them that the button was, in fact, clicked.

A `Button`-like control whose primary label is an image is an `ImageButton`. An `ImageButton` is, for most purposes, almost exactly like a basic `Button`. Click actions are handled in the same way. The primary difference is that you can set its `src` attribute to be an image. Here is an example of an `ImageButton` definition in an XML layout resource file:

```
<ImageButton
    android:layout_width="wrap_content"
    android:layout_height="wrap_content"
    android:id="@+id/image_button"
    android:src="@drawable/droid"
    android:contentDescription="@string/droidSkater"/>
```

In this case, a small drawable resource is referenced. Refer to Figure 7.7 to see what this "Android" button looks like. (It's to the right of the basic `Button`.)

Tip

You can also use the `onClick` XML attribute to set the name of your click method within your `Activity` class and implement it that way. Simply specify the name of your `Activity` class's click method using this attribute—`android:onClick="myMethod"`—and define a public void method that takes a single `View` parameter and implement your click handling.

Using `CheckBox` and `ToggleButton` Controls

The `CheckBox` button is often used in lists of items where the user can select multiple items. The Android `CheckBox` contains a `text` attribute that appears to the side of the check box. Because the `CheckBox` class is derived from the `TextView` and `Button` classes, most of the attributes and methods behave in a similar fashion.

Here is an XML layout resource definition for a simple `CheckBox` control with some default text displayed:

```
<CheckBox
    android:id="@+id/checkbox"
    android:layout_width="wrap_content"
    android:layout_height="wrap_content"
    android:text="Check me?"/>
```

The following example shows how to check for the state of the button programmatically and how to change the text label to reflect the change:

```
final CheckBox checkButton = (CheckBox) findViewById(R.id.checkbox);
checkButton.setOnClickListener(new View.OnClickListener() {
    public void onClick (View v) {
        CheckBox cb = (CheckBox) findViewById(R.id.checkbox);
        cb.setText(checkButton.isChecked() ?
            "This option is checked" :
            "This option is not checked");
    }
});
```

This is similar to the basic `Button` control. A `CheckBox` control automatically shows the state as checked or unchecked. This enables us to deal with behavior in our application rather than worrying about how the button should behave. The layout shows that the text starts out one way, but after the user clicks the button, the text changes to one of two different things, depending on the checked state. You can see how this `CheckBox` is displayed once it has been clicked (and the text has been updated) in Figure 7.7 (center).

A `ToggleButton` is similar to a `CheckBox` in behavior but is usually used to show or alter the "on" or "off" state of something. Like the `CheckBox`, it has a state (checked or not). Also like the `CheckBox`, the act of changing what displays on the `ToggleButton` is handled for you. Unlike the `CheckBox`, it does not show text next to it. Instead, it has two text fields. The first attribute is `textOn`, which is the text that displays on the `ToggleButton` when its checked state is on. The second attribute is `textOff`, which is the text that displays on the `ToggleButton` when its checked state is off. The default text for these is "ON" and "OFF," respectively.

The following layout code shows a definition for a `ToggleButton` control that shows "Enabled" or "Disabled" based on the state of the button:

```
<ToggleButton
    android:id="@+id/toggle_button"
```

```
android:layout_width="wrap_content"

android:layout_height="wrap_content"

android:text="Toggle"

android:textOff="Disabled"

android:textOn="Enabled"/>
```

This type of button does not actually display the value for the text attribute, even though it's a valid attribute to set. Here, the only purpose it serves is to demonstrate that it doesn't display. You can see what this `ToggleButton` looks like in Figure 7.7 ("Disabled").

The `Switch` control (`android.widget.Switch`), which was introduced in API Level 14, provides two-state behavior similar to that of the `ToggleButton` control, only instead of the control being clicked to toggle between the states, it looks more like a slider. The following layout code shows a definition for a `Switch` control with a prompt ("Switch Me?") and two states: "Wax On" and "Wax Off":

```
<Switch android:id="@+id/switch1"

    android:layout_width="wrap_content"

    android:layout_height="wrap_content"

    android:text="Switch me?"

    android:textOn="Wax On"

    android:textOff="Wax Off"/>
```

Using `RadioGroup` and `RadioButton`

You often use radio buttons when a user should be allowed to select only one item from a small group of items. For instance, a question asking for gender can give three options: male, female, and unspecified. Only one of these options should be checked at a time. The `RadioButton` objects are similar to `CheckBox` objects. They have a text label next to them, set via the `text` attribute, and they have a state (checked or unchecked). However, you can group `RadioButton` objects inside a `RadioGroup` that handles enforcing their combined states so that only one `RadioButton` can be checked at a time. If the user selects a `RadioButton` that is already checked, it does not become unchecked. However, you can provide the user with an action to clear the state of the entire `RadioGroup` so that none of the buttons are checked.

Here, we have an XML layout resource with a `RadioGroup` containing four `RadioButton` objects (shown in Figure 7.7, toward the bottom of the screen). The `RadioButton` objects have text labels: "Option 1," "Option 2," and so on. The XML layout resource definition is shown below:

```
<RadioGroup

    android:id="@+id/RadioGroup01"

    android:layout_width="wrap_content"
```

(Continues)

(*Continued*)

```
        android:layout_height="wrap_content">
    <RadioButton
        android:id="@+id/RadioButton01"
        android:layout_width="wrap_content"
        android:layout_height="wrap_content"
        android:text="Option 1"/>
    <RadioButton
        android:id="@+id/RadioButton02"
        android:layout_width="wrap_content"
        android:layout_height="wrap_content"
        android:text="Option 2"/>
    <RadioButton
        android:id="@+id/RadioButton03"
        android:layout_width="wrap_content"
        android:layout_height="wrap_content"
        android:text="Option 3"/>
    <RadioButton
        android:id="@+id/RadioButton04"
        android:layout_width="wrap_content"
        android:layout_height="wrap_content"
        android:text="Option 4"/>
</RadioGroup>
```

You can handle actions on these RadioButton objects through the RadioGroup object. The following example shows registering for clicks on the RadioButton objects within the RadioGroup, and setting the text of a TextView called TextView01, which is defined elsewhere in the layout file:

```
final RadioGroup group = (RadioGroup) findViewById(R.id.RadioGroup01);
final TextView tv = (TextView) findViewById(R.id.TextView01);
group.setOnCheckedChangeListener(new RadioGroup.OnCheckedChangeListener() {
    public void onCheckedChanged(RadioGroup group, int checkedId) {
        if (checkedId !=-1) {
            RadioButton rb = (RadioButton) findViewById(checkedId);
            if (rb != null) {
                tv.setText("You chose: " + rb.getText());
            }
```

```
        } else {
            tv.setText("Choose 1");
        }
    }
});
```

As this layout example demonstrates, there is nothing special you need to do to make the `RadioGroup` and internal `RadioButton` objects work properly. The preceding code illustrates how to register to receive a notification whenever the `RadioButton` selection changes.

The code demonstrates that the notification contains the resource identifier for the specific `RadioButton` chosen by the user, as defined in the layout resource file. To do something interesting with this, you need to provide a mapping between this resource identifier (or the text label) and the corresponding functionality in your code. In the example, we query for the button that was selected, get its text, and assign its text to another `TextView` control that we have on the screen.

As mentioned, the entire `RadioGroup` can be cleared so that none of the `RadioButton` objects are selected. The following example demonstrates how to do this in response to a button click outside the `RadioGroup`:

```
final Button clearChoice = (Button) findViewById(R.id.Button01);
clear_choice.setOnClickListener(new View.OnClickListener() {
    public void onClick(View v) {
        RadioGroup group = (RadioGroup) findViewById(R.id.RadioGroup01);
        if (group != null) {
            group.clearCheck();
        }
    }
}
```

The action of calling the `clearCheck()` method triggers a call to the `onCheckedChangedListener()` callback method. This is why we have to make sure that the resource identifier we received is valid. Right after a call to the `clearCheck()` method, it is not a valid identifier but instead is set to the value -1 to indicate that no `RadioButton` is currently checked.

Tip

You can also handle `RadioButton` clicks using specific click handlers on individual `RadioButtons` within a `RadioGroup`. The implementation mirrors that of a regular `Button` control.

Retrieving Dates, Times, and Numbers from Users with Pickers

The Android SDK provides a couple of controls for getting date, time, and number input from the user. The first is the `DatePicker` control (see Figure 7.8, top). It can be used to get a month, day, and year from the user.

The basic XML layout resource definition for a `DatePicker` follows:

```
<DatePicker
    android:id="@+id/DatePicker01"
    android:layout_width="wrap_content"
    android:layout_height="wrap_content"
    android:calendarViewShown="false"
    android:datePickerMode="spinner"
    android:spinnersShown="true"/>
```

Tip

If you want to control the minimum or maximum date that a user can choose from a `DatePicker`, you can set the `android:minDate` or `android:maxDate` values in your layout file, or you can set these values programmatically using `setMinDate()` or `setMaxDate()`.

Figure 7.8   Date and time controls.

As you can see from this example, a couple of attributes help control the look of the picker. Setting the `calenderViewShown` attribute to `true`, when using API Level 11 and up, will show a full calendar, including week numbers, but may take up more space than you can allow. Try it in the sample code, though, to see what it looks like.

The attribute `datePickerMode` was added in API Level 21. This attribute was added because when using the Material theme, the `calendar` layout is configured by default, so setting the value of `spinner` forces a spinner to be used. As with many of the other controls, your code can register to receive a method call when the date changes. You do this by implementing the `onDateChanged()` method:

```
final DatePicker date = (DatePicker) findViewById(R.id.DatePicker01);

Calendar cal = Calendar.getInstance();

date.init(2015, 7, 17,

    new DatePicker.OnDateChangedListener() {

        public void onDateChanged(DatePicker view, int year,

                int monthOfYear, int dayOfMonth) {

            Calendar calendar = Calendar.getInstance();

            calendar.set(year, monthOfYear, dayOfMonth,

                    time.getCurrentHour(), time.getCurrentMinute());

            text.setText(calendar.getTime().toString());

        }

});
```

The preceding code sets the `DatePicker.OnDateChangedListener` via a call to the `DatePicker.init()` method. The `DatePicker` control is initialized to a specific date (note that the month field is zero based, so May is month number 4, not 5). In our example, a `TextView` control is set with the date value that the user entered into the `DatePicker` control.

A `TimePicker` control (also shown in Figure 7.8, bottom) is similar to the `DatePicker` control. It also doesn't have any unique attributes. However, to register for a method call when the values change, you call the more traditional method of `TimePicker.setOnTimeChangedListener()`, as shown here:

```
time.setOnTimeChangedListener(new TimePicker.OnTimeChangedListener() {

    public void onTimeChanged(TimePicker view, int hourOfDay, int minute) {

        Calendar calendar = Calendar.getInstance();

        calendar.set(calendar.get(Calendar.YEAR),

                calendar.get(Calendar.MONTH),

                calendar.get(Calendar.DAY_OF_MONTH),

                hourOfDay, minute);
```

(Continues)

(Continued)

```
        text.setText(calendar.getTime().toString());
    }
});
```

As in the previous example, this code also sets a `TextView` to a string displaying the time value that the user entered. When you use the `DatePicker` control and the `TimePicker` control together, the user can set both a date and a time.

Android also provides a `NumberPicker` widget, which is very similar to the `TimePicker` widget. You can use a `NumberPicker` to present users with a selection mechanism for choosing a number from a predefined range. There are two different types of `NumberPickers` you can present, both of which are entirely based on the theme your application is using. To learn more about the `NumberPicker`, see *http://d.android.com/reference/android/widget/NumberPicker.html*.

Using Indicators to Display Progress and Activity to Users

The Android SDK provides a number of controls that can be used to show some form of information to the user. These indicator controls include the `ProgressBar`, activity bars, activity circles, clocks, and other similar controls.

Indicating Progress with `ProgressBar`

Applications commonly perform actions that can take a while. A good practice during this time is to show the user some sort of progress indicator to indicate that the application is off "doing something." Applications can also show how far a user has progressed through some operation, such as playing a song or watching a video. The Android SDK provides several types of progress indicators.

The standard `ProgressBar` is a circular indicator that only animates. It does not show how complete an action is. It can, however, show that something is taking place. This is useful when an action is indeterminate in length. There are three sizes of this type of progress indicator (see Figure 7.9).

The second type is a horizontal `ProgressBar` that shows how far an action has progressed toward completion. (For example, you can see how much of a file has downloaded.) This horizontal `ProgressBar` can also have a secondary progress indicator on it. This can be used, for instance, to show the completion of a downloading media file while that file plays.

Here is an XML layout resource definition for a basic indeterminate `ProgressBar`:

```
<ProgressBar
    android:id="@+id/progress_bar"
    android:layout_width="wrap_content"
    android:layout_height="wrap_content"/>
```

Figure 7.9   Various types of progress and rating indicators.

The default style is for a medium-size circular progress indicator—not a "bar" at all. The other two styles for an indeterminate `ProgressBar` are `progressBarStyleLarge` and `progressBarStyleSmall`. These styles animate automatically. The next example shows the layout definition for a horizontal progress indicator:

```
<ProgressBar
    android:id="@+id/progress_bar"
    style="?android:attr/progressBarStyleHorizontal"
    android:layout_width="match_parent"
    android:layout_height="wrap_content"
    android:max="100"/>
```

We have also set the attribute for `max` in this example to `100`. This can help mimic a percentage `ProgressBar`—that is, setting the progress to `75` shows the indicator at 75% complete.

We can set the indicator progress status programmatically as follows:

```
mProgress = (ProgressBar) findViewById(R.id.progress_bar);
mProgress.setProgress(75);
```

Adding Progress Indicators to the `ActionBar`

You can also put a `ProgressBar` in your application's `ActionBar` or `Toolbar` (as shown in Figure 7.9). This can save screen real estate and can also make it easy to turn an indeterminate progress indicator on and off without changing the look of the screen. Indeterminate progress indicators are commonly used to display progress on pages where items need to be loaded before the page can finish drawing. This is often employed on Web browser screens. The following XML allows you to set two different progress bars on a `Toolbar`—found in the `appcompat-v7` Support Library—which is set up as the `ActionBar` of your `Activity`:

```
<android.support.v7.widget.Toolbar xmlns:app="http://schemas.android.com/apk/
res-auto"
    android:id="@+id/toolbar_progress"
    android:background="@color/bg_color"
    android:layout_width="match_parent"
    android:layout_height="wrap_content"
    android:minHeight="?attr/actionBarSize"
    app:popupTheme="@style/ThemeOverlay.AppCompat.Light"
    app:theme="@style/ToolbarTheme">

    <ProgressBar
        android:id="@+id/toolbar_spinner"
        android:layout_width="wrap_content"
        android:layout_height="wrap_content"
        android:layout_gravity="end"
        android:indeterminate="true"
        android:visibility="gone" />
</android.support.v7.widget.Toolbar>
```

The following code demonstrates how to place this type of indeterminate progress indicator on the `ActionBar` of your `Activity` screen:

```
supportRequestWindowFeature(Window.FEATURE_INDETERMINATE_PROGRESS);
supportRequestWindowFeature(Window.FEATURE_PROGRESS);
setContentView(R.layout.indicators);
Toolbar toolbar = (Toolbar) findViewById(R.id.toolbar_progress);
toolbar.setTitleTextColor(Color.WHITE);
setSupportActionBar(toolbar);
```

```
if (getSupportActionBar() != null) {

    getSupportActionBar().setDisplayHomeAsUpEnabled(true);
}
ProgressBar toolbarProgress = (ProgressBar) findViewById(R.id.toolbar_spinner);
toolbarProgress.setVisibility(View.VISIBLE);
toolbarProgress.setProgress(5000);
```

To use the indeterminate indicator on your `Activity` object's `ActionBar`, you need to request the feature `Window.FEATURE_INDETERMINATE_PROGRESS`, as previously shown. This shows a small circular indicator in the right side of the `ActionBar`. For a horizontal `ProgressBar` style that shows in the `ActionBar`, you need to enable `Window.FEATURE_PROGRESS`. These features must be enabled before your application calls the `setContentView()` method, as shown in the preceding example.

You also need to know about a couple of important default behaviors. First, the indicators are visible by default. Calling the visibility methods shown in the preceding example can set visibility to on or off, or to indeterminate using the `setProgress()`. The horizontal `ProgressBar` defaults to a maximum progress value of `10000`. In the preceding example, we set it to `5000`, which is equivalent to 50%. When the value reaches the maximum value, the indicators fade from view. This happens for both indicators.

Indicating Activity with Activity Bars and Activity Circles

When there is no telling how long an operation will take to complete, but you need a way to indicate to the user that an operation is taking place, you should use an activity bar or an activity circle. You define an activity bar or circle exactly like you define a `ProgressBar`, with one small change: you need to tell Android that the operation running will continue for an indeterminate amount of time by either setting the attribute within your layout file using `android:indeterminate`, or from within your code by setting the `ProgressBar`'s visibility to indeterminate using the `setIndeterminate()` method.

Tip

When using an activity circle, there is no need to display any text to users to let them know that an operation is taking place. The activity circle alone is enough for users to understand that an operation is taking place.

Adjusting Progress with Seek Bars

You have seen how to display progress to the user. However, what if you want to give the user some ability to move the indicator—for example, to set the current cursor position in a media file that's playing or to tweak a volume setting? You accomplish this by using the SeekBar control provided by the Android SDK. It's like the regular horizontal ProgressBar, but includes a thumb, or selector, that can be dragged by the user. A default thumb selector is provided, but you can use any Drawable item as a thumb. In Figure 7.9 (center), we replaced the default thumb with a little Android graphic.

Here, we have an example of an XML layout resource definition for a simple SeekBar:

```
<SeekBar
    android:id="@+id/seekbar1"
    android:layout_height="wrap_content"
    android:layout_width="240dp"
    android:max="500"
    android:thumb="@drawable/droidsk1"/>
```

With this sample SeekBar, the user can drag the thumb named droidsk1 to any value between 0 and 500. Although this is represented visually, it might be useful to show the user the exact value selected. To do this, you can provide an implementation of the onProgressChanged() method, as shown here:

```
SeekBar seek = (SeekBar) findViewById(R.id.seekbar1);
seek.setOnSeekBarChangeListener(
    new SeekBar.OnSeekBarChangeListener() {
        public void onProgressChanged(
            SeekBar seekBar, int progress, boolean fromTouch) {
            ((TextView) findViewById(R.id.seek_text))
                .setText("Value: "+progress);
            seekBar.setSecondaryProgress(
                (progress+seekBar.getMax())/2);
        }
    });
```

There are two interesting things to notice in this example. The first is that the fromTouch parameter tells the code if the change came from the user input or, instead, if it came from a programmatic change as demonstrated with the regular ProgressBar controls. The second interesting thing is that the SeekBar still enables you to set a secondary progress value. In this example, we set the secondary indicator to be halfway between the user's selected value and the maximum value of the ProgressBar. You might use this feature to show the progress of a video and the buffer stream.

Note

If you want to create your own activity indicator, you can define a custom indicator. For most situations, the default indicators that Android provides should be enough.

Other Valuable User Interface Controls

Android has a number of other ready-to-use user interface controls to incorporate into your applications. This section is dedicated to introducing the `RatingBar` and various time controls, such as the `Chronometer`, `DigitalClock`, `TextClock`, and `AnalogClock`.

Displaying Rating Data with `RatingBar`

Although the `SeekBar` is useful for allowing a user to set a value, such as the volume, the `RatingBar` has a more specific purpose: showing ratings or getting a rating from a user. By default, this `ProgressBar` uses the star paradigm, with five stars by default. A user can drag across this horizontally to set a rating. A program can set the value as well. However, the secondary indicator cannot be used because it is already used internally by this particular control.

Here is an example of an XML layout resource definition for a `RatingBar` with four stars:

```
<RatingBar
    android:id="@+id/ratebar1"
    android:layout_width="wrap_content"
    android:layout_height="wrap_content"
    android:numStars="4"
    android:stepSize="0.25"/>
```

This layout definition for a `RatingBar` demonstrates setting both the number of stars and the increment between each rating value. Figure 7.9 (center) illustrates how the `RatingBar` behaves. In this layout definition, a user can choose any rating value between 0 and 4.0, in increments of 0.25, the `stepSize` value. For instance, users could set a value of 2.25. This is visualized for users, by default, with the stars partially filled.

Although the value is indicated to the user visually, you might still want to show its numeric representation. You can do this by implementing the `onRatingChanged()` method of the `RatingBar.OnRatingBarChangeListener` class, as shown here:

```
RatingBar rate = (RatingBar) findViewById(R.id.ratebar1);
rate.setOnRatingBarChangeListener(new RatingBar.OnRatingBarChangeListener() {
    public void onRatingChanged(RatingBar ratingBar,
            float rating, boolean fromTouch) {
        ((TextView)findViewById(R.id.rating_text))
            .setText("Rating: "+ rating);
    }
});
```

The preceding example shows how to register the listener. When the user selects a rating using the control, a `TextView` is set to the numeric rating the user entered. One interesting thing to note is that, unlike the `SeekBar`, the implementation of the onRatingChange() method is called after the change is complete, usually when the user lifts a finger—that is, while the user is dragging across the stars to make a rating, this method isn't called. It is called only when the user stops pressing the control.

Showing Time Passage with the `Chronometer`

Sometimes you want to show time passing instead of incremental progress. In this case, you can use the `Chronometer` control as a timer (see Figure 7.9, near the bottom). This might be useful if it's the user who is taking time doing some task or playing a game where some action needs to be timed. The `Chronometer` control can be formatted with text, as shown in this XML layout resource definition:

```
<Chronometer
    android:id="@+id/Chronometer01"
    android:layout_width="wrap_content"
    android:layout_height="wrap_content"
    android:format="Timer: %s"/>
```

You can use the `Chronometer` object's `format` attribute to put text around the time that displays. A `Chronometer` won't show the passage of time until its `start()` method is called. To stop it, simply call its `stop()` method. Finally, you can change the time from which the timer is counting—that is, you can set it to count from a particular time in the past instead of from the time it was started. You call the `setBase()` method to do this.

Tip

The `Chronometer` uses the `elapsedRealtime()` method's time base. Passing `android.os.SystemClock.elapsedRealtime()` in to the `setBase()` method starts the `Chronometer` control at 0.

In this next code example, the timer is retrieved from the `View` by its resource identifier. We then check its base value and reset it to 0. Finally, we start the timer counting up from there.

```
final Chronometer timer = (Chronometer)findViewById(R.id.Chronometer01);
long base =  timer.getBase();
Log.d(ViewsMenu.debugTag, "base = "+ base);
timer.setBase(0);
timer.start();
```

Tip

You can listen for changes to the `Chronometer` by implementing the `Chronometer.OnChronometerTickListener` interface.

Displaying the Time

Displaying the time in an application is often not necessary because Android devices have a status bar to display the current time. However, two clock controls are available to display this information: the `TextClock` and `AnalogClock` controls.

Using the `TextClock`

The `TextClock` control was added in API Level 17 and is meant to be a replacement for the `DigitalClock`, which was deprecated in API Level 17. The `TextClock` has many more features than the `DigitalClock` and allows you to format the display of the date and/or time. In addition, the `TextClock` allows you to display the time in 12-hour mode or 24-hour mode and even allows you to set the time zone.

By default, the `TextClock` control does not show the seconds. Here is an example of an XML layout resource definition for a `TextClock` control:

```
<TextClock
    android:id="@+id/TextClock01"
    android:layout_width="wrap_content"
    android:layout_height="wrap_content"/>
```

Using the `AnalogClock`

The `AnalogClock` control (Figure 7.9, bottom) is a dial-based clock with a basic clock face with two hands. It updates automatically as each minute passes. The image of the clock scales appropriately with the size of its `View`.

Here is an example of an XML layout resource definition for an `AnalogClock` control:

```
<AnalogClock
    android:id="@+id/AnalogClock01"
    android:layout_width="wrap_content"
    android:layout_height="wrap_content"/>
```

The `AnalogClock` control's clock face is simple. However, you can set its minute and hour hands. You can also set the clock face to specific drawable resources, if you want to jazz it up. Neither of these clock controls accepts a different time or a static time to display. They can show only the current time in the current time zone of the device, so they are not particularly useful.

Playing Video with `VideoView`

The `VideoView` control is a video player `View` used for playing video in your application. This `View` has controls to play, pause, skip forward, skip backward, and seek. Figure 7.10 shows a `VideoView` playing a video inside an `Activity`.

Figure 7.10 A `VideoView` playing a recording of a user interacting with an Application.

Here is an example XML layout resource definition for a `VideoView` control:

```
<VideoView
    android:id="@+id/video_view"
    android:layout_width="match_parent"
    android:layout_height="match_parent" />
```

And here is the `onCreate()` method of the `Activity`:

```
@Override
protected void onCreate(Bundle savedInstanceState) {
    super.onCreate(savedInstanceState);
    setContentView(R.layout.activity_simple_video_view);
    VideoView vv = (VideoView) findViewById(R.id.videoView);
    MediaController mc = new MediaController(this);
    Uri video = Uri.parse("http://andys-veggie-garden.appspot.com/vid/reveal.
mp4");
    vv.setMediaController(mc);
    vv.setVideoURI(video);
}
```

You first want to get the `VideoView` from the layout, then you need to create a `MediaController` object. In our case, we are grabbing the video from the Internet so we first need to parse the URL of the video using the `Uri.parse` method so that our code uses a valid `Uri` object. We then use the `setMediaController()` method for adding the `MediaController` object to your `VideoView`, and then we use the `setVideoURI()` method to pass the `Uri` to our `VideoView`.

Since this example pulls the video from a location on the Internet, be sure to add the `INTERNET` permission of your Android manifest file as shown here:

```
<uses-permission android:name="android.permission.INTERNET" />
```

Summary

The Android SDK provides many useful user interface components that developers can use to create compelling and easy-to-use applications. This chapter introduced you to many of the most useful controls and discussed how each behaves, how to style them, and how to handle input events from the user.

You learned how controls can be combined to create user entry forms. Important controls for forms include `EditText`, `Spinner`, and various `Button` controls. You also learned about controls that can indicate progress or the passage of time to users. We talked about many common user interface controls in this chapter; however, there are many others. In the next chapter, you will learn how to use various layout and container controls to organize a variety of on-screen controls easily and accurately.

Quiz Questions

1. What `Activity` method would you use to retrieve a `TextView` object?
2. What `TextView` method would you use to retrieve the text of that particular object?
3. What user interface control is used for retrieving text input from users?
4. What are the two different types of autocompletion controls?
5. True or false: A `Switch` control has three or more possible states.
6. True or false: The `DateView` control is used for retrieving dates from users.

Exercises

1. Create a simple application that accepts text input from a user with an `EditText` object and, when the user clicks an update `Button`, displays the text within a `TextView` control.
2. Create a simple application that has an integer defined in an integer resource file and, when the application is launched, displays the integer within a `TextView` control.

3. Create a simple application with a red color value defined in a color resource file. Define a `Button` control in the layout with a default blue `textColor` attribute. When the application is launched, have the default blue `textColor` value change to the red color value you defined in the color resource file.

References and More Information

Android API Guides: "User Interface":
   http://d.android.com/guide/topics/ui/index.html
Android SDK Reference regarding the application `View` class:
   http://d.android.com/reference/android/view/View.html
Android SDK Reference regarding the application `TextView` class:
   http://d.android.com/reference/android/widget/TextView.html
Android SDK Reference regarding the application `EditText` class:
   http://d.android.com/reference/android/widget/EditText.html
Android SDK Reference regarding the application `Button` class:
   http://d.android.com/reference/android/widget/Button.html
Android SDK Reference regarding the application `CheckBox` class:
   http://d.android.com/reference/android/widget/CheckBox.html
Android SDK Reference regarding the application `Switch` class:
   http://d.android.com/reference/android/widget/Switch.html
Android SDK Reference regarding the application `RadioGroup` class:
   http://d.android.com/reference/android/widget/RadioGroup.html
Android SDK Reference regarding the support v7 `Toolbar` class:
   http://d.android.com/reference/android/support/v7/widget/Toolbar.html
Android SDK Reference regarding the application `VideoView` class:
   http://d.android.com/reference/android/widget/VideoView.html

8

Positioning with Layouts

In this chapter, we discuss how to design user interfaces for Android applications. Here, we focus on the various layout controls you can use to organize screen elements in different ways. We also cover some of the more complex View controls that we call container views. These are View controls that can contain other View controls.

Creating User Interfaces in Android

Application user interfaces can be simple or complex, involving many different screens or only a few. Layouts and user interface controls can be defined as application resources or created programmatically at runtime.

Although it's a bit confusing, the term *layout* is used for two different but related purposes in Android user interface design:

- In terms of resources, the res/layout/ directory contains XML resource definitions often called layout resource files. These XML files provide a template for how to arrange and draw controls on the screen; layout resource files may contain any number of controls.

- The term is also used to refer to a set of ViewGroup classes, such as LinearLayout, FrameLayout, TableLayout, RelativeLayout, and GridLayout. These controls are used to organize other View controls. We talk more about these classes later in this chapter.

Creating Layouts Using XML Resources

As discussed in previous chapters, Android provides a simple way to create layout resource files in XML. These resources are stored in res/layout/. This is the most common and convenient way to build Android user interfaces and is especially useful for defining screen elements and default control properties that you know about at compile time. These layout resources are then used much like templates. They are loaded with default attributes that you can modify programmatically at runtime.

You can configure almost any View or ViewGroup subclass attribute using the XML layout resource files. This method greatly simplifies the user interface design process, moving much of the static creation and layout of user interface controls, and basic definition of control attributes, to the XML instead of littering the code. Developers reserve the ability to alter these layouts programmatically as necessary, but they should set all the defaults in the XML template whenever possible.

You'll recognize the following as a simple layout file with a `RelativeLayout` and a single `TextView` control. Here is the default layout file provided with any new Android project in Android Studio, referred to as `res/layout/activity_main.xml`, assuming your `Activity` is named `MainActivity`:

```
<RelativeLayout xmlns:android="http://schemas.android.com/apk/res/android"

    xmlns:tools="http://schemas.android.com/tools"

    android:layout_width="match_parent"

    android:layout_height="match_parent"

    android:paddingBottom="@dimen/activity_vertical_margin"

    android:paddingLeft="@dimen/activity_horizontal_margin"

    android:paddingRight="@dimen/activity_horizontal_margin"

    android:paddingTop="@dimen/activity_vertical_margin"

    tools:context=".MainActivity">


    <TextView

        android:layout_width="wrap_content"

        android:layout_height="wrap_content"

        android:text="@string/hello_world" />


</RelativeLayout>
```

This block of XML shows a basic layout with a single `TextView` control. The first line, which you might recognize from most XML files, is required with the `android` layout namespace, as shown. Because it's common across all the files, we do not show it in any other examples.

Next, we have the `RelativeLayout` element. `RelativeLayout` is a `ViewGroup` that shows each child `View` relative to other views. When applied to a full screen, it merely means that each child `View` is drawn relative to the specified `View`.

Finally, there is a single child `View`—in this case, a `TextView`. A `TextView` is a control that is also a `View`. A `TextView` draws text on the screen. In this case, it draws the text defined in the `"@string/hello"` string resource.

If you create your own XML file, though, that file won't actually draw anything on the screen. A particular layout is usually associated with a particular `Activity`. In your default Android project, there is only one `Activity`, which sets the `activity_main.xml` layout by default. To associate the `activity_main.xml` layout with the `Activity`, use the method call `setContentView()` with the identifier of the `activity_main.xml` layout.

The ID of the layout matches the XML filename without the extension. In this case, the preceding example came from `activity_main.xml`, so the identifier of this layout is simply `activity_main.xml`, and this layout will actually display on the screen as it has been created for us during project creation:

```
setContentView(R.layout.activity_main);
```

> **Warning**
>
> The Android tools team has made every effort to make the Android Studio `Design` view layout editor feature complete, and this tool can be helpful for designing and previewing how layout resources will look on a variety of different devices. However, the preview can't replicate exactly how the layout appears to end users. For this, you must test your application on a properly configured emulator and, more important, on your target devices.

Creating Layouts Programmatically

You can create user interface components such as layouts at runtime programmatically, but for organization and maintainability, it's best to leave this for the odd case rather than the norm. The main reason is that the creation of layouts programmatically is onerous and difficult to maintain, whereas the XML resources are visual and more organized, and could be used by a separate designer with no Java skills.

> **Tip**
>
> The code examples provided in this section are taken from the `SameLayout` application. The source code for the `SameLayout` application is provided for download on the book's website (*http://introductiontoandroid.blogspot.com*).

The following example shows how to have an `Activity` instantiate a `LinearLayout` programmatically and place two `TextView` controls within it as child controls. The same two string resources are used for the contents of the controls; these actions are done at runtime instead.

```
public void onCreate(Bundle savedInstanceState) {
    super.onCreate(savedInstanceState);

    assert getSupportActionBar() != null;
    getSupportActionBar().setDisplayHomeAsUpEnabled(true);

    TextView text1 = new TextView(this);
    text1.setText(R.string.string1);

    TextView text2 = new TextView(this);
```

(Continues)

(Continued)

```
    text2.setText(R.string.string2);

    text2.setTextSize(TypedValue.COMPLEX_UNIT_SP, 60);


    int pixelDimen = (int) TypedValue.applyDimension(

        TypedValue.COMPLEX_UNIT_DIP, 16,

        getResources().getDisplayMetrics());


    LinearLayout ll = new LinearLayout(this);

    ll.setOrientation(LinearLayout.VERTICAL);

    ll.setPadding(pixelDimen, pixelDimen,

        pixelDimen, pixelDimen);

    ll.addView(text1);

    ll.addView(text2);


    setContentView(ll);

}
```

The onCreate() method is called when the Activity is created. The first thing
this method does is some normal housekeeping by calling the super class onCreate()
method.

Next, the ActionBar is configured and two TextView controls are instantiated. The
Text property of each TextView is set using the setText() method. All TextView
attributes, such as TextSize, are set by making method calls on the TextView control.
These actions perform the same function of setting the properties Text and TextSize as
in the Android Studio layout editor, except these properties are set at runtime instead of
defined in the layout files compiled into your application package.

Tip

The XML property name is usually similar to the method calls for getting and setting
that same control property programmatically. For instance, android:visibility
maps to the methods setVisibility() and getVisibility(). In the preceding
sample TextView, the methods for getting and setting the TextSize property are
getTextSize() and setTextSize().

To display the TextView controls appropriately, we need to encapsulate them within a
container of some sort (a layout). In this case, we use a LinearLayout with the orientation
set to VERTICAL so that the second TextView begins beneath the first, each aligned to the

left of the screen. The two TextView controls are added to the LinearLayout in the order we want them to display.

Finally, we call the setContentView() method, part of the Activity class, to draw the LinearLayout and its contents on the screen.

As you can see, the code can rapidly grow in size as you add more View controls and you need more attributes for each View. Here is that same layout, now in an XML layout file:

```xml
<?xml version="1.0" encoding="utf-8"?>

<LinearLayout

    xmlns:android="http://schemas.android.com/apk/res/android"

    android:orientation="vertical"

    android:layout_width="match_parent"

    android:layout_height="match_parent">

    <TextView

        android:id="@+id/TextView1"

        android:layout_width="match_parent"

        android:layout_height="wrap_content"

        android:text="@string/string1" />

    <TextView

        android:id="@+id/TextView2"

        android:layout_width="match_parent"

        android:layout_height="wrap_content"

        android:textSize="60sp"

        android:text="@string/string2" />

</LinearLayout>
```

You might notice that this isn't a literal translation of the code example from the previous section, although the output is identical, as shown in Figure 8.1.

First, in the XML layout files, layout_width and layout_height are required attributes. Next, you see that each TextView control has a unique id property assigned so that it can be accessed programmatically at runtime. Finally, the textSize property needs to have its units defined. The XML attribute takes a dimension type.

The end result differs only slightly from the programmatic method. However, it's far easier to read and maintain. Now you need only one line of code to display this layout view. Again, the layout resource is stored in the res/layout/resource_based_layout.xml file:

```java
setContentView(R.layout.resource_based_layout);
```

Figure 8.1   Two different methods of creating a screen have the same exact display result seen here.

Organizing Your User Interface

In Chapter 7, "Exploring Building Blocks," we talked about how the class View is the building block for user interfaces in Android. All user interface controls, such as Button, Spinner, and EditText, derive from the View class.

Now we consider a special kind of View called a ViewGroup. The classes derived from ViewGroup enable developers to display View controls such as TextView and Button controls on the screen in an organized fashion.

It's important to understand the difference between View and ViewGroup. Like other View controls, including the controls from the previous chapter, ViewGroup controls represent a rectangle of screen space. What makes a ViewGroup different from a typical control is that ViewGroup objects contain other View controls. A View that contains other View controls is called a *parent view*. The parent View contains View controls called *child* views, or *children*.

You add child View controls to a ViewGroup programmatically using the method addView(). In XML, you add child objects to a ViewGroup by defining the child View control as a child node in the XML (within the parent XML element, as we've seen various times using the LinearLayout ViewGroup).

`ViewGroup` subclasses are broken down into two categories:

- Layout classes
- `View` container controls

Using `ViewGroup` Subclasses for Layout Design

Many of the most important subclasses of `ViewGroup` used for screen design end with "Layout." For example, the most common layout classes are `LinearLayout`, `RelativeLayout`, `TableLayout`, `FrameLayout`, and `GridLayout`. You can use each of these classes to position other `View` controls on the screen in different ways. For example, we've been using the `LinearLayout` to arrange various `TextView` and `EditText` controls on the screen in a single vertical column. Users do not generally interact with the layouts directly. Instead, they interact with the `View` controls they contain.

Using `ViewGroup` Subclasses as `View` Containers

The second category of `ViewGroup` subclasses is the indirect "subclasses"—some formal and some informal. These special `View` controls act as `View` containers like `Layout` objects do, but they also provide some kind of active functionality that enables users to interact with them like other controls. Unfortunately, these classes are not known by any handy names; instead, they are named for the kind of functionality they provide.

Some of the classes that fall into this category include `RecyclerView`, `GridView`, `ImageSwitcher`, `ScrollView`, and `ListView`. It can be helpful to consider these objects as different kinds of `View` browsers, or container classes. The `ListView` and `RecyclerView` display each `View` control as a list item, and the user can browse the individual controls using vertical scrolling capability.

Using Built-in Layout Classes

We have talked a lot about the `LinearLayout` layout, but there are several other types of layouts. Each layout has a different purpose and order in which it displays its child `View` controls on the screen. Layouts are derived from `android.view.ViewGroup`.

The types of layouts built into the Android SDK framework include the following:

- `LinearLayout`
- `RelativeLayout`
- `FrameLayout`
- `TableLayout`
- `GridLayout`

Tip

Many of the code examples provided in this section are taken from the `SimpleLayout` application. The source code for the `SimpleLayout` application is provided for download on the book's website.

All layouts, regardless of their type, have basic layout attributes. Layout attributes apply to any child `View` control within that layout. You can set layout attributes at runtime programmatically, but ideally you set them in the XML layout files using the following syntax:

```
android:layout_attribute_name="value"
```

There are several layout attributes that all `ViewGroup` objects share. These include size attributes and margin attributes. You can find basic layout attributes in the `ViewGroup.LayoutParams` class. The margin attributes enable each child `View` within a layout to have margin padding on each side. Find these attributes in the `ViewGroup.MarginLayoutParams` class. There are also a number of `ViewGroup` attributes for handling child `View` drawing bounds and animation settings.

Some of the important attributes shared by all `ViewGroup` subtypes are shown in Table 8.1.

Here is an XML layout resource example of a `LinearLayout` set to the size of the screen with an orientation of `vertical` so that all child elements will be displayed vertically in a linear fashion, containing one `TextView` that is set to the full height and width of the `LinearLayout` (and therefore the screen):

```
<LinearLayout xmlns:android=
    "http://schemas.android.com/apk/res/android"
    android:layout_width="match_parent"
    android:layout_height="match_parent"
    android:orientation="vertical">
    <TextView
        android:id="@+id/TextView01"
        android:layout_height="match_parent"
        android:layout_width="match_parent" />
</LinearLayout>
```

Here is an example of a `Button` object with some margins set via XML used in a layout resource file:

```
<Button
    android:id="@+id/Button01"
    android:layout_width="wrap_content"
    android:layout_height="wrap_content"
    style="?android:button"
    android:text="Press Me"
    android:layout_marginRight="20dp"
    android:layout_marginTop="60dp" />
```

Table 8.1 **Important `ViewGroup` Attributes**

Attribute Name (all begin with `android:`)	Applies to	Description	Value
`layout_height`	Parent View Child View	Height of the `View`. Used on attribute for child `View` controls within layouts. Required in some layouts, optional in others.	Dimension value or `match_parent` or `wrap_content`.
`layout_width`	Parent View Child View	Width of the `View`. Used on attribute for child `View` controls within layouts. Required in some layouts, optional in others.	Dimension value or `match_parent` or `wrap_content`.
`layout_margin`	Parent View Child View	Extra space around all sides of the `View`.	Dimension value. Use more specific margin attributes to control individual margin sides, if necessary.

Remember that a layout element can cover any rectangular space on the screen; it doesn't need to fill the entire screen. Layouts can be nested within one another. This provides great flexibility when developers need to organize screen elements. It is common to start with a `RelativeLayout`, `FrameLayout`, or `LinearLayout` as the parent layout for the entire screen and then organize individual screen elements inside the parent layout using whichever layout type is most appropriate.

Now let's talk about each of the common layout types individually and how they differ from one another.

Using `LinearLayout`

A `LinearLayout` view organizes its child `View` controls in a single row, as shown in Figure 8.2, or a single column, depending on whether its `orientation` attribute is set to `horizontal` or `vertical`. This is a very handy layout method for creating forms.

You can find the layout attributes available for `LinearLayout` child `View` controls in `android.widget.LinearLayout.LayoutParams`. Table 8.2 describes some of the important attributes specific to `LinearLayout` views.

Note

To learn more about `LinearLayout`, see the Android API Guides discussion at *http://d.android.com/guide/topics/ui/layout/linear.html*.

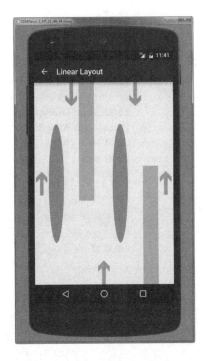

Figure 8.2   An example of LinearLayout (horizontal orientation).

Table 8.2 **Important LinearLayout View Attributes**

Attribute Name (all begin with android:)	Applies to	Description	Value
orientation	Parent View	The layout is a single row (horizontal) or single column (vertical) of controls.	Either horizontal or vertical.
gravity	Parent View	The gravity of child views within a layout.	One or more constants separated by " | ". The constants available are top, bottom, left, right, center_vertical, fill_vertical, center_horizontal, fill_horizontal, center, fill, clip_vertical, clip_horizontal, start, and end.

(Continues)

Table 8.2 **Continued**

Attribute Name (all begin with android:)	Applies to	Description	Value
weightSum	Parent View	The sum of all child control weights.	A number that defines the sum of all child control weights. Default is 1.
layout_gravity	Child View	The gravity for a specific child View. Used for positioning of views.	One or more constants separated by " | ". The constants available are top, bottom, left, right, center_vertical, fill_vertical, center_ horizontal, fill_ horizontal, center, fill, clip_vertical, clip_horizontal, start, and end.
layout_weight	Child View	The weight for a specific child View. Used to provide the ratio of screen space used within the parent control.	The sum of values across all child views in a parent View must equal the weightSum attribute of the parent LinearLayout control. For example, one child control might have a value of .3 and another a value of .7.

Note

The v7 appcompat library provides a LinearLayoutCompat class that provides backward-compatible LinearLayout capabilities found in more recent API versions, making the features available all the way back to API Level 7. You can learn more about the class here: *http://d.android.com/reference/android/support/v7/widget/ LinearLayoutCompat.html*.

Using **RelativeLayout**

The RelativeLayout view enables you to specify where the child View controls are in relation to each other. For instance, you can set a child View to be positioned "above" or "below" or "to the left of" or "to the right of" another View, referred to by its unique identifier. You can also align child View controls relative to one another or to the parent layout edges. Combining RelativeLayout attributes can simplify the creation of interesting user interfaces without resorting to multiple layout groups to achieve a desired effect. Figure 8.3 shows where the Button controls are relative to each other.

Figure 8.3   An example of RelativeLayout usage.

You can find the layout attributes available for RelativeLayout child View controls in android.widget.RelativeLayout.LayoutParams. Table 8.3 describes some of the important attributes specific to RelativeLayout views.

Here is an example of an XML layout resource with a RelativeLayout and two child View controls—a Button object aligned relative to its parent, and an ImageView aligned and positioned relative to the Button (and the parent):

```
<?xml version="1.0" encoding="utf-8"?>

<RelativeLayout xmlns:android=

    "http://schemas.android.com/apk/res/android"

    android:id="@+id/RelativeLayout01"

    android:layout_height="match_parent"

    android:layout_width="match_parent">

    <Button

        android:id="@+id/ButtonCenter"

        android:text="Center"
```

```
        android:layout_width="wrap_content"

        android:layout_height="wrap_content"

        android:layout_centerInParent="true" />

    <ImageView

        android:id="@+id/ImageView01"

        android:layout_width="wrap_content"

        android:layout_height="wrap_content"

        android:layout_above="@id/ButtonCenter"

        android:layout_centerHorizontal="true"

        android:src="@drawable/arrow" />

</RelativeLayout>
```

Note

To learn more about `RelativeLayout`, see the Android API Guides discussion at *http://d.android.com/guide/topics/ui/layout/relative.html.*

Table 8.3 **Important RelativeLayout View Attributes**

Attribute Name (all begin with `android:`)	Applies to	Description	Value
`gravity`	Parent `View`	The gravity of child views within a layout.	One or more constants separated by " | ". The constants available are `top`, `bottom`, `left`, `right`, `center_vertical`, `fill_vertical`, `center_horizontal`, `fill_horizontal`, `center`, `fill`, `clip_vertical`, `clip_horizontal`, `start`, and `end`.
`layout_centerInParent`	Child `View`	Centers the child `View` horizontally and vertically within the parent `View`.	True or false.
`layout_centerHorizontal`	Child `View`	Centers the child `View` horizontally within the parent `View`.	True or false.

(Continues)

Table 8.3 **Continued**

Attribute Name (all begin with android:)	Applies to	Description	Value
layout_ centerVertical	Child View	Centers the child View vertically within the parent View.	True or false.
layout_ alignParentTop	Child View	Aligns the child View with the top edge of the parent View.	True or false.
layout_ alignParentBottom	Child View	Aligns the child View with the bottom edge of the parent View.	True or false.
layout_ alignParentLeft	Child View	Aligns the child View with the left edge of the parent View.	True or false.
layout_ alignParentRight	Child View	Aligns the child View with the right edge of the parent View.	True or false.
layout_ alignParentStart	Child View	Aligns the child View with the start edge of the parent View.	True or false.
layout_ alignParentEnd	Child View	Aligns the child View with the end edge of the parent View.	True or false.
layout_alignRight	Child View	Aligns the right edge of the child View with the right edge of another child View, specified by ID.	A View ID; for example, @id/Button1.
layout_alignLeft	Child View	Aligns the left edge of the child View with the left edge of another child View, specified by ID.	A View ID; for example, @id/Button1.
layout_alignStart	Child View	Aligns the start edge of the child View with the start edge of another child View, specified by ID.	A View ID; for example, @id/Button1.
layout_alignEnd	Child View	Aligns the end edge of the child View with the end edge of another child View, specified by ID.	A View ID; for example, @id/Button1.

Table 8.3 **Continued**

Attribute Name (all begin with `android:`)	Applies to	Description	Value
`layout_alignTop`	Child `View`	Aligns the top edge of the child `View` with the top edge of another child `View`, specified by ID.	A `View` ID; for example, `@id/Button1`.
`layout_alignBottom`	Child `View`	Aligns the bottom edge of the child `View` with the bottom edge of another child `View`, specified by ID.	A `View` ID; for example, `@id/Button1`.
`layout_above`	Child `View`	Positions the bottom edge of the child `View` above another child `View`, specified by ID.	A `View` ID; for example, `@id/Button1`.
`layout_below`	Child `View`	Positions the top edge of the child `View` below another child `View`, specified by ID.	A `View` ID; for example, `@id/Button1`.
`layout_toLeftOf`	Child `View`	Positions the right edge of the child `View` to the left of another child `View`, specified by ID.	A `View` ID; for example, `@id/Button1`.
`layout_toRightOf`	Child `View`	Positions the left edge of the child `View` to the right of another child `View`, specified by ID.	A `View` ID; for example, `@id/Button1`.

Using `FrameLayout`

A `FrameLayout` view is designed to display a stack of child `View` items. You can add multiple views to this layout, but each `View` is drawn from the top-left corner of the layout. You can use this to show multiple images within the same region, as shown in Figure 8.4, and the layout is sized to the largest child `View` in the stack.

You can find the layout attributes available for `FrameLayout` child `View` controls in `android.widget.FrameLayout.LayoutParams`. Table 8.4 describes some of the important attributes specific to `FrameLayout` views.

Here is an example of an XML layout resource with a `FrameLayout` and two child `View` controls, both `ImageView` controls. The green rectangle is drawn first and the red

Figure 8.4   An example of `FrameLayout` usage.

oval is drawn on top of it. The green rectangle is larger, so it defines the bounds of the
FrameLayout:

```
<FrameLayout xmlns:android=
    "http://schemas.android.com/apk/res/android"
    android:id="@+id/FrameLayout01"
    android:layout_width="wrap_content"
    android:layout_height="wrap_content"
    android:layout_gravity="center">
    <ImageView
        android:id="@+id/ImageView01"
        android:layout_width="wrap_content"
        android:layout_height="wrap_content"
        android:src="@drawable/green_rect"
        android:contentDescription="@string/green_rect"
        android:minHeight="300dp"
        android:minWidth="300dp" />
    <ImageView
```

```
            android:id="@+id/ImageView02"

            android:layout_width="wrap_content"

            android:layout_height="wrap_content"

            android:src="@drawable/red_oval"

            android:contentDescription="@string/red_oval"

            android:minHeight="150dp"

            android:minWidth="150dp"

            android:layout_gravity="center" />

</FrameLayout>
```

Table 8.4 **Important `FrameLayout` View Attributes**

Attribute Name (all begin with `android:`)	Applies to	Description	Value
foreground	Parent View	Drawable to draw over the content.	Drawable resource.
foregroundGravity	Parent View	The gravity of the foreground drawable.	One or more constants separated by "`|`". The constants available are `top`, `bottom`, `left`, `right`, `center_vertical`, `fill_vertical`, `center_horizontal`, `fill_horizontal`, `center`, `fill`, `clip_vertical`, and `clip_horizontal`.
measureAllChildren	Parent View	Restricts the size of the layout to all child views or just the child views set to `VISIBLE` (and not those set to `INVISIBLE`).	True or false.
layout_gravity	Child `View`	A gravity constant that describes the child `View` within the parent.	One or more constants separated by "`|`". The constants available are `top`, `bottom`, `left`, `right`, `center_vertical`, `fill_vertical`, `center_horizontal`, `fill_horizontal`, `center`, `fill`, `clip_vertical`, `clip_horizontal`, `start`, and `end`.

Using `TableLayout`

A `TableLayout` view organizes children into rows, as shown in Figure 8.5. You add individual `View` controls within each row of the table using a `TableRow` layout `View` (which is basically a horizontally oriented `LinearLayout`) for each row of the table. Each column of the `TableRow` can contain one `View` (or layout with child `View` controls). You place `View` items added to a `TableRow` in columns in the order they are added. You can specify the column number (zero based) to skip columns as necessary (the bottom row shown in Figure 8.5 demonstrates this); otherwise, the `View` control is put in the next column to the right. Columns scale to the size of the largest `View` of that column. You can also include normal `View` controls instead of `TableRow` elements, if you want the `View` to take up an entire row.

You can find the layout attributes available for `TableLayout` child `View` controls in `android.widget.TableLayout.LayoutParams`. You can find the layout attributes available for `TableRow` child `View` controls in `android.widget.TableRow.LayoutParams`. Table 8.5 describes some of the important attributes specific to `TableLayout` controls.

Here is an example of an XML layout resource with a `TableLayout` with two rows (two `TableRow` child objects). The `TableLayout` is set to stretch the columns to the size of

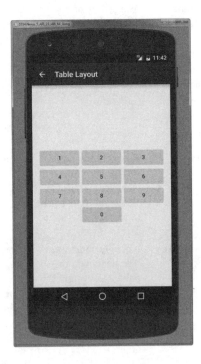

Figure 8.5   An example of `TableLayout` usage.

Table 8.5 **Important `TableLayout` and `TableRow` View Attributes**

Attribute Name (all begin with `android:`)	Applies to	Description	Value
collapseColumns	TableLayout	A comma-delimited list of column indices to collapse (zero based).	String or string resource; for example, `"0,1,3,5"`.
shrinkColumns	TableLayout	A comma-delimited list of column indices to shrink (zero based).	String or string resource. Use `"*"` for all columns; for example, `"0,1,3,5"`.
stretchColumns	TableLayout	A comma-delimited list of column indices to stretch (zero based).	String or string resource. Use `"*"` for all columns; for example, `"0,1,3,5"`.
layout_column	TableRow child View	Index of the column this child `View` should be displayed in (zero based).	Integer or integer resource; for example, `1`.
layout_span	TableRow child View	Number of columns this child `View` should span.	Integer or integer resource greater than or equal to `1`; for example, `3`.

the screen width. The first `TableRow` has three columns; each cell has a `Button` object. The second `TableRow` puts only one `Button` control into the second column explicitly:

```
<TableLayout xmlns:android=
    "http://schemas.android.com/apk/res/android"
    android:id="@+id/TableLayout01"
    android:layout_width="match_parent"
    android:layout_height="match_parent"
    android:gravity="center_vertical"
    android:stretchColumns="*">
<TableRow
    android:id="@+id/TableRow01"
    android:layout_width="match_parent"
    android:layout_height="match_parent">
    <Button
        android:id="@+id/ButtonLeft"
```

(Continues)

(Continued)

```
                    style="?android:button"

                    android:text="Left Door" />

            <Button

                    android:id="@+id/ButtonMiddle"

                    style="?android:button"

                    android:text="Middle Door" />

            <Button

                    android:id="@+id/ButtonRight"

                    style="?android:button"

                    android:text="Right Door" />

        </TableRow>

        <TableRow

            android:id="@+id/TableRow02"

            android:layout_width="match_parent"

            android:layout_height="match_parent">

            <Button

                    android:id="@+id/ButtonBack"

                    style="?android:button"

                    android:text="Go Back"

                    android:layout_column="1" />

        </TableRow>

    </TableLayout>
```

Using `GridLayout`

Introduced in Android 4.0 (API Level 14), the `GridLayout` organizes its children inside a grid. But don't confuse it with `GridView`; this layout grid is dynamically created. Unlike a `TableLayout`, child `View` controls in a `GridLayout` can span rows and columns, and are flatter and more efficient in terms of layout rendering. In fact, it is the child `View` controls of a `GridLayout` that tell the layout where the child views are to be placed. Figure 8.6 shows an example of a `GridLayout` with five child controls.

You can find the layout attributes available for `GridLayout` child `View` controls in `android.widget.GridLayout.LayoutParams`. Table 8.6 describes some of the important attributes specific to `GridLayout` controls.

The following is an example of an XML layout resource with a `GridLayout` view resulting in four rows and four columns. Each child control occupies a certain number of rows and columns. Because the default span attribute value is 1, we only specify when the element will take up more than one row or column. For instance, the first `TextView`

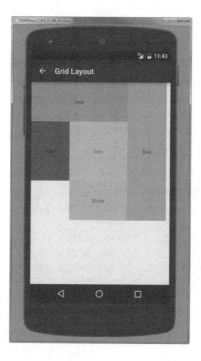

Figure 8.6   An example of GridLayout usage.

Table 8.6 **Important GridLayout View Attributes**

Attribute Name (all begin with android:)	Applies to	Description	Value
columnCount	GridLayout	Defines a fixed number of columns for the grid.	A whole number; for example, 4.
rowCount	GridLayout	Defines a fixed number of rows for the grid.	A whole number; for example, 3.
orientation	GridLayout	When a row or column value is not specified on a child, this is used to determine whether the next child is down a row or over a column.	Can be vertical (down a row) or horizontal (over a column).
layout_column	Child View of GridLayout	Index of the column this child View should be displayed in (zero based).	Integer or integer resource; for example, 1.

(Continues)

Table 8.6 **Continued**

Attribute Name (all begin with `android:`)	Applies to	Description	Value
`layout_columnSpan`	Child `View` of `GridLayout`	Number of columns this child `View` should span.	Integer or integer resource greater than or equal to 1; for example, 3.
`layout_row`	Child `View` of `GridLayout`	Index of the row this child `View` should be displayed in (zero based).	Integer or integer resource; for example, 1.
`layout_rowSpan`	Child `View` of `GridLayout`	Number of rows this child `View` should span down.	Integer or integer resource greater than or equal to 1; for example, 3.
`layout_gravity`	Child `View` of `GridLayout`	Specifies the "direction" in which the `View` should be placed within the grid cells it will occupy.	One or more constants separated by "`|`". The constants available are `baseline`, `top`, `bottom`, `left`, `right`, `center_vertical`, `fill_vertical`, `center_horizontal`, `fill_horizontal`, `center`, `fill`, `clip_vertical`, `clip_horizontal`, `start`, and `end`. Defaults to `LEFT|BASELINE`.

is one row high and three columns wide. The height and width of each of the `View` controls are specified to control the look of the result; otherwise, the `GridLayout` control will automatically assign sizing.

```xml
<?xml version="1.0" encoding="utf-8"?>
<GridLayout xmlns:android="http://schemas.android.com/apk/res/android"
    android:id="@+id/gridLayout1"
    android:layout_width="match_parent"
    android:layout_height="match_parent"
    android:columnCount="4"
    android:rowCount="4" >
    <TextView
        android:layout_width="250dp"
```

```
        android:layout_height="100dp"
        android:layout_column="0"
        android:layout_columnSpan="3"
        android:layout_row="0"
        android:background="#f44336"
        android:gravity="center"
        android:text="one" />
    <TextView
        android:layout_width="150dp"
        android:layout_height="150dp"
        android:layout_column="1"
        android:layout_columnSpan="2"
        android:layout_row="1"
        android:layout_rowSpan="2"
        android:background="#ff9800"
        android:gravity="center"
        android:text="two" />
    <TextView
        android:layout_width="150dp"
        android:layout_height="100dp"
        android:layout_column="2"
        android:layout_row="3"
        android:background="#8bc34a"
        android:gravity="center"
        android:text="three" />
    <TextView
        android:layout_width="100dp"
        android:layout_height="150dp"
        android:layout_column="0"
        android:layout_row="1"
        android:background="#673ab7"
        android:gravity="center"
        android:text="four" />
    <TextView
```

(Continues)

(Continued)

```
        android:layout_width="100dp"
        android:layout_height="350dp"
        android:layout_column="3"
        android:layout_row="0"
        android:layout_rowSpan="4"
        android:background="#03a9f4"
        android:gravity="center"
        android:text="five" />
</GridLayout>
```

Tip

You may add a `GridLayout` to legacy applications all the way back to Android 2.1 (API Level 7) using the `v7 gridlayout` library. To learn more about the support version of this layout, see the following: *http://d.android.com/reference/android/support/v7/widget/GridLayout.html*.

Using Multiple Layouts on a Screen

Combining different layout methods on a single screen can create complex layouts. Remember that because a layout contains `View` controls and is, itself, a `View` control, it can contain other layouts.

Tip

Want to create a certain amount of space between `View` controls without using a nested layout? Check out the `Space` view (`android.widget.Space`).

Figure 8.7 demonstrates a combination of layout views used in conjunction to create a more complex and interesting screen.

Warning

Keep in mind that individual screens of mobile applications should remain sleek and relatively simple. This is not just because this design results in a more positive user experience; cluttering your screens with complex (and deep) `View` hierarchies can lead to performance problems. Use the Hierarchy Viewer tool to inspect your application layouts; you can also use the `lint` tool to help optimize your layouts and identify unnecessary components. In addition, you can use `<merge>` and `<include>` tags in your layouts for creating a common set of reusable components instead of duplicating them. `ViewStub` can be used to add more complex views to your layouts during runtime as they are needed, rather than building them directly into your layouts.

Figure 8.7   An example of multiple layouts used together.

Using Container Control Classes

Layouts are not the only controls that can contain other View controls. Although layouts are useful for positioning other View controls on the screen, they aren't interactive. Now let's talk about the other kind of ViewGroup: the containers. These View controls encapsulate other, simpler View types and give the user the ability to interactively browse the child View controls in a standard fashion. Much like layouts, each of these controls has a special, well-defined purpose.

Some ViewGroup containers built into the Android SDK framework include

- Lists and grids
- ScrollView and HorizontalScrollView for scrolling
- ViewFlipper, ViewSwitcher, ImageSwitcher, and TextSwitcher for switching

Tip

Many of the code examples provided in this chapter are taken from the AdvancedLayouts application. The source code for the AdvancedLayouts application is provided for download on the book's website.

Using Data-Driven Containers

Some of the `View` container controls are designed for displaying repetitive `View` controls in a particular way. Examples of this type of `View` container control include `ListView` and `GridView`:

- **ListView:** Contains a vertically scrolling, horizontally filled list of `View` controls, each of which typically contains a row of data. The user can choose an item to perform some action.
- **GridView:** Contains a grid of `View` controls, with a specific number of columns. This container is often used with image icons; the user can choose an item on which to perform some action.

These containers are all types of `AdapterView` controls. An `AdapterView` control contains a set of child `View` controls to display data from some data source. An `Adapter` generates these child `View` controls from a data source. Because this is an important part of all these container controls, we talk about the `Adapter` objects first.

In this section, you learn how to bind data to `View` controls using `Adapter` objects. In the Android SDK, an `Adapter` reads data from some data source and generates the data for a `View` control based on certain rules, depending on the type of `Adapter` used. This `View` is used to populate the child `View` controls of a particular `AdapterView`.

The most common `Adapter` classes are the `CursorAdapter` and the `ArrayAdapter`. The `CursorAdapter` gathers data from a `Cursor`, whereas the `ArrayAdapter` gathers data from an array. A `CursorAdapter` is a good choice when using data from a database. The `ArrayAdapter` is a good choice when there is only a single column of data or when the data comes from a resource array.

You should know some common elements of `Adapter` objects. When creating an `Adapter`, you provide a layout identifier. This layout is the template for filling in each row of data. The template you create contains identifiers for particular controls to which the `Adapter` assigns data. A simple layout can contain as little as a single `TextView` control. When making an `Adapter`, refer to both the layout resource and the identifier of the `TextView` control. The Android SDK provides some common layout resources for use in your application.

Using ArrayAdapter

An `ArrayAdapter` binds each element of the array to a single `View` control within the layout resource. Here is an example of creating an `ArrayAdapter`:

```
private String[] items = {"Item 1", "Item 2", "Item 3" };

ArrayAdapter adapt = new ArrayAdapter<>(this, R.layout.textview, items);
```

In this example, we have a string array called `items`. This is the array used by the `ArrayAdapter` as the source data. We also use a layout resource, which is the `View` that is repeated for each item in the array. This is defined as follows:

```
<TextView xmlns:android="http://schemas.android.com/apk/res/android"

    android:layout_width="match_parent"
```

```
android:layout_height="wrap_content"

android:textSize="20sp" />
```

This layout resource contains only a single TextView. However, you can use a more complex layout with constructors that also take the resource identifier of a TextView within the layout. Each child View within the AdapterView that uses this Adapter gets one TextView instance with one of the strings from the string array.

If you have an array resource defined, you can also directly set the entries attribute for an AdapterView to the resource identifier of the array to provide the ArrayAdapter automatically.

Using **CursorAdapter**

A CursorAdapter binds one or more columns of data to one or more View controls within the layout resource provided. This is best shown with an example. We also discuss Cursor objects in Chapter 17, "Leveraging Content Providers," where we provide a more in-depth discussion of content providers.

The following example demonstrates creating a CursorAdapter by querying the Contacts content provider. The CursorAdapter requires the use of a Cursor.

```
CursorLoader loader = new CursorLoader(
    this, ContactsContract.CommonDataKinds.Phone.CONTENT_URI,
    null, null, null, null);
Cursor contacts = loader.loadInBackground();
ListAdapter adapter = new SimpleCursorAdapter(this,
    R.layout.scratch_layout,
    contacts,
    new String[] {
        ContactsContract.CommonDataKinds.Phone.DISPLAY_NAME,
        ContactsContract.CommonDataKinds.Phone.NUMBER
    }, new int[] {
        R.id.scratch_text1,
        R.id.scratch_text2
    }, 0);
```

In this example, we present a couple of new concepts. First, you need to know that the Cursor must contain a field named _id. In this case, we know that the ContactsContract content provider does have this field. This field is used later when we handle the user selecting a particular item.

> **Note**
>
> The `CursorLoader` class was introduced in Android 3.0 (API Level 11). If you need to sup-
> port applications prior to Android 3.0, you can use the Android Support Library to add the
> `CursorLoader` class (`android.support.v4.content.CursorLoader`) to your appli-
> cation. We talk more about the Android Support Library in Chapter 13, "Designing Compat-
> ible Applications."

We instantiate a new `CursorLoader` to get the `Cursor`. Then, we instantiate a
`SimpleCursorAdapter` as a `ListAdapter`. Our layout, `R.layout.scratch_layout`, has
two `TextView` controls in it, which are used in the last parameter.
`SimpleCursorAdapter` enables us to match up columns in the database with particular
controls in our layout. For each row returned from the query, we get one instance of the
layout within our `AdapterView`.

Binding Data to the `AdapterView`

Now that you have an `Adapter` object, you can apply this to one of the `AdapterView`
controls. Either of them will work. Here is an example of this with a `ListView`, continuing from the previous sample code:

```
ListView adapterView = (ListView) findViewById(R.id.scratch_adapter_view)

adapterView.setAdapter(adapter);
```

The call to the `setAdapter()` method of the `AdapterView`, a `ListView` in this case,
should come after your call to `setContentView()`. This is all that is required to bind data
to your `AdapterView`. Figure 8.8 shows the same data in a `GridView` and `ListView`.

Handling Selection Events

You often use `AdapterView` controls to present data from which the user should select.
Both of the discussed controls—`ListView` and `GridView`—enable your application to
monitor for click events in the same way. You need to call `setOnItemClickListener()`
on your `AdapterView` and pass in an implementation of the
`AdapterView.OnItemClickListener` class. Here is a sample implementation of this class:

```
    adapterView.setOnItemClickListener(

        new AdapterView.OnItemClickListener() {

        @Override

        public void onItemClick(AdapterView<?> parent,

                View view, int position, long id) {

            Toast.makeText(ListAdapterSampleActivity.this,

                "Clicked _id=" + id, Toast.LENGTH_SHORT).show();

        }

});
```

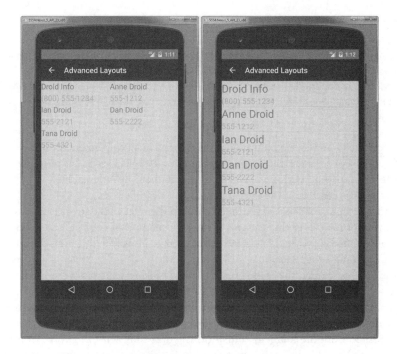

Figure 8.8   `GridView` and `ListView`: same data, same list item,
different layout views.

In the preceding example, `adapterView` is our `AdapterView`. The implementation
of the `onItemClick()` method is where all the interesting work happens. The `parent`
parameter is the `AdapterView` where the item was clicked. This is useful if your screen has
more than one `AdapterView` on it. The `View` parameter is the specific `View` within the
item that was clicked. The position is the zero-based position within the list of items that
the user selects. Finally, the `id` parameter is the value of the `_id` column for the particular
item that the user selects. This is useful for querying for further information about the
particular row of data that the item represents.

Your application can also listen for long-click events on particular items. Additionally,
your application can listen for selected items. Although the parameters are the same, your
application receives a call as the highlighted item changes. This can be in response to the
user scrolling with the arrow keys and not selecting an item for action.

Using `ListView` with `ListFragment`

The `ListView` control is commonly used for full-screen menus or lists of items from
which a user selects. Thus, you might consider using `ListFragment` as the base class for
such screens and adding the `ListFragment` to your `View`. Using the `ListFragment` can
simplify these types of screens. We discuss Fragments in Chapter 9, "Partitioning with
Fragments."

Warning

Before the `ListFragment` class was added to the Android SDK, the `ListActivity` class was available for making use of a `ListView`. Using a `ListActivity` is no longer recommended; the use of a `ListFragment`, which provides greater flexibility for your applications, is preferred. The `AdvancedLayouts` sample application provided with this chapter implements both a `ListView` using a `ListFragment`, and a `GridView` using a `Fragment`.

First, to handle item events, you now need to provide an implementation in your `ListFragment`. For instance, the equivalent of `OnItemClickListener` is to implement the `onItemClick()` method within your `ListFragment` that implements the `AdapterView.OnItemClickListener` interface.

Second, to assign an `Adapter`, you need a call to the `setListAdapter()` method. You do this after the call to the `setContentView()` method of your `Activity`, in the `ListFragment` method named `onActivityCreated()`. However, this hints at some of the limitations of using `ListFragment`.

To use `ListFragment`, the layout that is inflated inside your `View` fragment with the `onCreateView()` method of the `ListFragment` must contain a `ListView` with the identifier set to `@android:id/list`; this cannot be changed. Second, you can also have a `View` with an identifier set to `@android:id/empty` to have a `View` display when no data is returned from the `Adapter`. Finally, this works only with `ListView` controls, so it has limited use. However, when it does work for your application, it can save some coding.

Tip

You can create `ListView` headers and footers using the `ListView` methods `addHeaderView()` and `addFooterView()`.

Adding Scrolling Support

One of the easiest ways to provide vertical scrolling for a screen is by using the `ScrollView` (vertical scrolling) and `HorizontalScrollView` (horizontal scrolling) controls. Either control can be used as a wrapper container, causing all child `View` controls to have one continuous scroll bar. The `ScrollView` and `HorizontalScrollView` controls can have only one child, though, so it's customary to have that child be a layout, such as a `Linear Layout`, which then contains all the "real" child controls to be scrolled through.

Tip

The code examples of scrolling in this section are provided in the `SimpleScrolling` application. The source code for the `SimpleScrolling` application is available for download on the book's website.

Figure 8.9 shows a screen with and without a `ScrollView` control.

Figure 8.9   A screen without (left) and with (right) a `ScrollView` control.

Exploring Other `View` Containers

Many other user interface controls are available within the Android Support Library, providing backward-compatible features all the way back to a particular API level noted by its particular Support Library package. Some of the controls you should familiarize yourself with are available in the various support libraries, and a few are listed here:

- **Toolbar:** A `Toolbar` can be used as your application's `ActionBar` or may also be used anywhere else in your application's view hierarchy. If your application has media controls, for example, you may want to embed your media controls inside a `Toolbar`, and place the `Toolbar` at the bottom of your application. To use a `Toolbar`, you need to add the v7 appcompat library to your project.

- **SwipeRefreshLayout:** A `SwipeRefreshLayout` is a useful `View` container for when your application supports vertical swipe gestures for updating the contents of your application. Your `Activity` must implement the `OnRefreshListener` to know how to handle the swipe gesture. To use the `SwipeRefreshLayout`, you need to add the v4 support library to your project.

- **RecyclerView:** A `RecyclerView` is similar to a `ListView` container that provides more efficient scrolling when rendering a list that contains a large amount of data to display. To use a `RecyclerView`, you need to add the `v7 recyclerview library` to your project. We talk more about `RecyclerView` in Chapter 12, "Embracing Material Design."

- **CardView:** A `CardView` is a `FrameLayout` container that allows you to apply rounded corners and shadows. To use a `CardView`, you need to add the `v7 cardview library` to your project. We talk more about `CardView` in Chapter 12, "Embracing Material Design."

- **ViewPager:** A `ViewPager` is a useful `View` container for when your application has many different pages of data and you need to support swiping left and right through that data. To use a `ViewPager`, you must create a `PagerAdapter` that provides the data for the `ViewPager`. Fragments are typically used for paging data with `View Pager`.

- **DrawerLayout:** A layout pattern that has been embraced by the Android team is the `DrawerLayout`. This layout is especially useful for providing a list of navigation items that are hidden off the screen but presented when users swipe from the left or the right, or when they press the `Home` button from the action bar if the `DrawerLayout` resides to the left. `DrawerLayout` should really be used only for navigation and only when there are more than three top-level views within your application. To use the `DrawerLayout`, you must add the `v4 support library` to your project.

Summary

The Android SDK provides a number of powerful methods for designing usable and great-looking screens. This chapter introduced you to many of them. You first learned about some of the Android layout controls that can manage the placement of your controls on the screen. `LinearLayout` and `RelativeLayout` are two of the most common, but others such as `FrameLayout`, `GridLayout`, and `TableLayout` provide great flexibility for your layouts. In many cases, these layout controls enable you to have a single screen design that works on most screen sizes and aspect ratios.

You then learned about other objects that contain views and how to group or place them on the screen in a particular way. These included a variety of different controls for placing data on the screen in a readable and browsable way. In addition, you learned how to use `ListView` and `GridView` as data-driven containers for displaying repetitive content. You now have all the tools you need to develop applications with usable and exciting user interfaces.

Quiz Questions

1. True or false: `LinearLayout`, `FrameLayout`, `TableLayout`, `RelativeLayout`, and `GridLayout` refer to a set of `ViewControl` classes.

2. True or false: A `LinearLayout` is used for showing each child `View` either in a single column or in a single row.

3. What is the method name for associating an XML layout resource file with an `Activity`?

4. True or false: The only way to create an Android user interface is by defining one in a layout resource XML file.

5. What is the syntax for assigning values to attributes within a layout resource XML file?

6. True or false: A `FrameLayout` is used for wrapping images within a picture frame.

7. What is the name of the control for adding horizontal or vertical scrolling?

8. What are a few `View` containers available within the Android Support Library?

Exercises

1. Use the Android documentation to determine the difference between a `CursorAdapter` and a `SimpleCursorAdapter`, and provide an explanation of that difference.

2. Use the Android documentation to determine the difference between a `GridView` and a `GridLayout`, and provide an explanation of that difference.

3. Create a simple Android application demonstrating how to use the `ViewSwitcher` control. In the `ViewSwitcher`, define two layouts. The first is a `GridLayout` defining a login form with a `Login` button; when the `Login` button is clicked, switch to a `LinearLayout` displaying a welcome message. The second layout has a `Logout` button; when the `Logout` button is clicked, switch back to the `GridLayout`.

References and More Information

Android API Guides: "Layouts":
  http://d.android.com/guide/topics/ui/declaring-layout.html
Android SDK Reference regarding the application `ViewGroup` class:
  http://d.android.com/reference/android/view/ViewGroup.html
Android SDK Reference regarding the application `LinearLayout` class:
  http://d.android.com/reference/android/widget/LinearLayout.html
Android SDK Reference regarding the application `RelativeLayout` class:
  http://d.android.com/reference/android/widget/RelativeLayout.html
Android SDK Reference regarding the application `FrameLayout` class:
  http://d.android.com/reference/android/widget/FrameLayout.html
Android SDK Reference regarding the application `TableLayout` class:
  http://d.android.com/reference/android/widget/TableLayout.html
Android SDK Reference regarding the application `GridLayout` class:
  http://d.android.com/reference/android/widget/GridLayout.html

Android SDK Reference regarding the application `ListView` class:
http://d.android.com/reference/android/widget/ListView.html

Android SDK Reference regarding the application `ListActivity` class:
http://d.android.com/reference/android/app/ListActivity.html

Android SDK Reference regarding the application `ListFragment` class:
http://developer.android.com/reference/android/app/ListFragment.html

Android SDK Reference regarding the application `GridView` class:
http://d.android.com/reference/android/widget/GridView.html

Android SDK Reference regarding the application `Toolbar` class:
http://d.android.com/reference/android/support/v7/widget/Toolbar.html

Android SDK Reference regarding the application `SwipeRefreshLayout` class:
http://d.android.com/reference/android/support/v4/widget/SwipeRefreshLayout.html

Android SDK Reference regarding the application `RecyclerView` class:
http://d.android.com/reference/android/support/v7/widget/RecyclerView.html

Android SDK Reference regarding the application `CardView` class:
http://developer.android.com/reference/android/support/v7/widget/CardView.html

Android SDK Reference regarding the application `ViewPager` class:
http://d.android.com/reference/android/support/v4/view/ViewPager.html

Android SDK Reference regarding the application `PagerAdapter` class:
http://d.android.com/reference/android/support/v4/view/PagerAdapter.html

Android SDK Reference regarding the application `DrawerLayout` class:
http://d.android.com/reference/android/support/v4/widget/DrawerLayout.html

Android Tools: "Support Library":
http://d.android.com/tools/support-library/index.html

Partitioning with Fragments

Traditionally, each screen within an Android application was tied to a specific `Activity` class. However, in Android 3.0 (Honeycomb), the concept of a `Fragment` was introduced. Fragments were then included in the Android Support Library for use with Android 1.6 (API Level 4) and up. Fragments decouple user interface components or behaviors (without a user interface) from a specific `Activity` lifecycle. Instead, `Activity` classes can mix and match user interface components or behaviors to create more flexible user interfaces. This chapter explains what fragments are and how you can use them. We also introduce the concept of nested fragments.

Understanding Fragments

Fragments were added to the Android SDK at a crucial time when consumers were experiencing an explosion in the variety of Android devices coming to market. We now see not just smartphones but other larger-screen devices such as tablets and televisions that run the platform. These larger devices come with substantially more screen real estate for developers to take advantage of. Your typical streamlined and elegant smartphone user interface often looks oversimplified on a tablet, for example. By incorporating `Fragment` components into your user interface design, you can write one application that can be tailored to these different screen characteristics and orientations instead of different applications tailored for different types of devices. This greatly improves code reuse, simplifies application testing needs, and makes publication and application package management much less cumbersome.

As we stated in the introduction to this chapter, the basic rule of thumb for developing Android applications used to be to have one `Activity` per screen of an application. This ties the underlying "task" functionality of an `Activity` class very directly to the user interface. However, as bigger device screens came along, this technique faced some issues. When you had more room on a single screen to do more, you had to implement separate `Activity` classes, with very similar functionality, to handle the cases where you wanted to provide more functionality on a given screen. Fragments help manage this problem by encapsulating screen functionality into reusable components that can be mixed and matched within `Activity` classes.

Let's look at a theoretical example. Say you have a traditional smartphone application with two screens. Perhaps it's an online news-journal application. The first screen contains

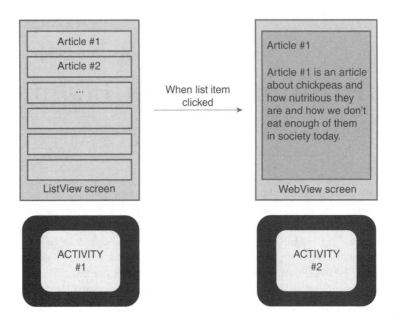

Figure 9.1   Traditional screen workflow without fragments.

a `ListActivity` with a `ListView` control. Each item in the `ListView` represents an article available from the journal that you might want to read. When you click a specific article, since this is an online news-journal application, you are sent to a new screen that displays the article contents in a `WebView` control. This traditional screen workflow is illustrated in Figure 9.1.

This workflow works fine for small-screen smartphones, but it's a waste of all the space on a tablet or a television. Here, you might want to be able to peruse the article list and preview or read the article on the same screen. If we organize the `ListView` and the `WebView` screen functionality into two stand-alone `Fragment` components, we can easily create a layout that includes both on the same screen when screen real estate allows, as shown in Figure 9.2.

Understanding the `Fragment` Lifecycle

We discussed the `Activity` lifecycle back in Chapter 4, "Understanding Application Components." Now let's look at how a `Fragment` fits into the mix. First of all, a `Fragment` must be hosted within an `Activity` class. It has its own lifecycle, but it is not a stand-alone component that can exist outside the context of an `Activity`.

The responsibilities of `Activity` class management are greatly simplified when the entire user interface state is moved off into individual fragments. `Activity` classes with only fragments in their layouts no longer need to spend a lot of time saving and restoring their state because the `Activity` object now keeps track of any `Fragment` that is currently

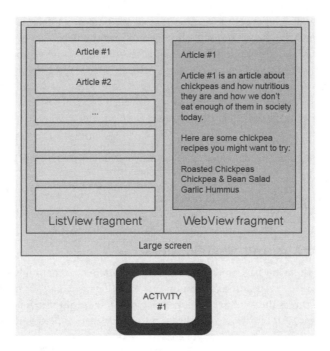

Figure 9.2   Improved screen workflow with fragments.

attached automatically. The `Fragment` components themselves keep track of their own state using their own lifecycle. Naturally, you can mix fragments with `View` controls directly in an `Activity` class. The `Activity` class will be responsible for managing the `View` controls, as normal.

The `Activity` must focus on managing its `Fragment` classes. Coordination between an `Activity` and its `Fragment` components is facilitated by the `FragmentManager` (`android.app.FragmentManager`). The `FragmentManager` is acquired from the `getFragmentManager()` method, which is available within the `Activity` and `Fragment` classes. When using the support library, coordinatiocn is facilitated by the `FragmentManager` (`android.support.v4.app.FragmentManager`) and is acquired from the `getSupportFragmentManager()` method of the `FragmentActivity` support APIs.

Defining Fragments

`Fragment` implementations that have been defined as regular classes within your application can be added to your layout resource files by using the `<fragment>` XML tag and then loaded into your `Activity` using the standard `setContentView()` method, which is normally called in the `onCreate()` method of your `Activity`.

When you reference a `Fragment` class that you have defined in your application package in an XML layout file, use the `<fragment>` tag. This tag has a few important attributes.

Specifically, you will need to set the android:name attribute of the fragment to the fully qualified Fragment class name. You will also need to give the item a unique identifier using the android:id attribute so that you can access that component programmatically, if needed. You still need to set the component's layout_width and layout_height attributes as you would for any other control in your layout. Here is a simple example of a <fragment> layout reference that refers to a class called VeggieGardenListFragment, which is defined as a .java class in the package:

```
<fragment
    android:name="com.introtoandroid.simplefragments.VeggieGardenListFragment"
    android:id="@+id/list"
    android:layout_width="match_parent"
    android:layout_height="match_parent" />
```

Managing Fragment Modifications

As you can see, when you have multiple Fragment components on a single screen, within a single Activity, user interaction on one Fragment (such as our news ListView Fragment) often causes the Activity to update another Fragment (such as our article WebView Fragment). An update or modification to a Fragment is performed using a FragmentTransaction (android.app.FragmentTransaction or android.support.v4.app.FragmentTransaction). A number of different actions can be applied to a Fragment using a FragmentTransaction operation, such as the following:

- A Fragment can be attached or reattached to the parent Activity.
- A Fragment can be hidden and unhidden from view.

Perhaps at this point you are wondering how the Back button fits into the Fragment-based user interface design. Well, now the parent Activity class has its own back stack. As the developer, you can decide which FragmentTransaction operations are worth storing in the back stack and which are not by using the addToBackStack() method of the FragmentTransaction object. For example, in our news application example, we might want each of the articles displayed in the WebView Fragment to be added to the parent Activity class's back stack so that if the user hits the Back button, he or she traverses the articles already read before backing out of the Activity entirely.

Attaching and Detaching Fragments with Activities

After you have a Fragment that you want to include within your Activity class, the lifecycle of the Fragment comes into play. The following callback methods are important to managing the lifecycle of a Fragment, as it is created and then destroyed when it is no longer used. Many of these lifecycle events mirror those in the Activity lifecycle:

- The onAttach() callback method is called when a Fragment is first attached to a specific Activity class.

- The onCreate() callback method is called when a Fragment is first being created.

- The onCreateView() callback method is called when the user interface layout, or View hierarchy, associated with the Fragment should be created.

- The onActivityCreated() callback method will inform the Fragment when its parent Activity class's onCreate() method has completed.

- The onStart() callback method is called when the Fragment's user interface becomes visible but is not yet active.

- The onResume() callback method makes the Fragment's user interface active for interaction after the Activity has resumed or the Fragment was updated using a FragmentTransaction.

- The onPause() callback method is called when the parent Activity is paused, or the Fragment is being updated by a FragmentTransaction. It indicates that the Fragment is no longer active or in the foreground.

- The onStop() callback method is called when the parent Activity is stopped, or the Fragment is being updated by a FragmentTransaction. It indicates the Fragment is no longer visible.

- The onDestroyView() callback method is called to clean up any user interface layout, or View hierarchy resources, associated with the Fragment.

- The onDestroy() callback method is called to clean up any other resources associated with the Fragment.

- The onDetach() callback method is called just before the Fragment is detached from the Activity class.

Working with Special Types of Fragments

Recall from Chapter 8, "Positioning with Layouts," that there are a number of special Activity classes for managing certain common types of user interfaces. For example, the ListActivity class simplifies the creation of an Activity that manages a ListView control. Similarly, the PreferenceActivity class simplifies the creation of an Activity to manage shared preferences. And as we saw in our news reader application example, we often want to use user interface controls such as ListView and WebView within our Fragment components.

Because fragments are meant to decouple this functionality from the Activity class, you'll now find equivalent Fragment subclasses that perform this functionality instead. Some of the specialty Fragment classes you'll want to familiarize yourself with include the following:

- **ListFragment (android.app.ListFragment)**: Much like a ListActivity, this Fragment class hosts a ListView control.

- **PreferenceFragment (android.preference.PreferenceFragment)**: Much like a PreferenceActivity, this Fragment class lets you easily manage user preferences.

- **WebViewFragment (`android.webkit.WebViewFragment`)**: This type of `Fragment` hosts a `WebView` control to easily render Web content. Your application will still need the `android.permission.INTERNET` permission to access the Internet.

- **DialogFragment (`android.app.DialogFragment`)**: Decoupling user interface functionality from your `Activity` classes means you won't want your dialogs managed by the `Activity` either. Instead, you can use this class to host and manage `Dialog` controls as fragments. Dialogs can be traditional pop-ups or embedded. We discuss dialogs in Chapter 10, "Architecting with Patterns."

> **Note**
>
> For a complete list of the different types of special fragments, see the `Fragment` reference documentation and look for the different subclasses available here: *http://d.android.com/ reference/android/app/Fragment.html*.

Designing `Fragment`-Based Applications

At the end of the day, `Fragment`-based applications are best learned by example. Therefore, let's work through a fairly straightforward example to help nail down the many concepts we have discussed thus far in the chapter. To keep things simple, we will target a specific version of the Android platform: Android Marshmallow. However, you will soon find that you can also create `Fragment`-based applications for almost any device by using the Android Support Package.

> **Tip**
>
> Many of the code examples provided in this section are taken from the `SimpleFragments` application. The source code for the `SimpleFragments` application is provided for download on the book's website (*http://introductiontoandroid.blogspot.com*).

Andy (a fictitious robot) is a fan of gardening and has many fruits and vegetables growing in his garden. Let's make a simple application with a `ListView` of fruit and vegetable names. Clicking a `ListView` item will load a `WebView` control and display a specific webpage associated with that fruit or vegetable. To keep things simple, we'll store our fruit and vegetable list, and Web-page URLs in string array resources. (See the sample code provided for download on this book's website for a complete implementation.)

So how will our fragments work? We will use a `ListFragment` for the fruit and vegetable list, and a `WebViewFragment` to display each associated Web page. In portrait mode, we will display one fragment per screen, requiring two `Activity` classes, as shown in Figure 9.3. In this sample, we will be using the `AppCompatActivity` class (`android.support.v7.app.AppCompatActivity`).

In landscape mode, we will display both fragments on the same screen within the same `AppCompatActivity` class, as shown in Figure 9.4.

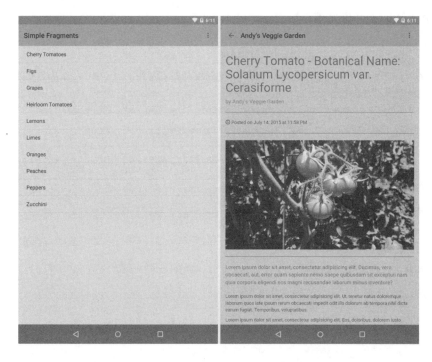

Figure 9.3   One fragment per `Activity`/screen.

Figure 9.4   Both fragments in a single `Activity`/screen.

Implementing a `ListFragment`

Let's begin by defining a custom `ListFragment` class called `VeggieGardenListFragment` to host our fruit and vegetable names. This class will need to determine whether the second `Fragment`, the `VeggieGardenWebViewFragment`, should be loaded or if `ListView` clicks should simply cause the `VeggieGardenViewActivity` to be launched:

```java
public class VeggieGardenListFragment extends ListFragment implements
        FragmentManager.OnBackStackChangedListener {

    private static final String DEBUG_TAG = "VeggieGardenListFragment";
    int mCurPosition = 1;
    boolean mShowTwoFragments;

    @Override
    public void onActivityCreated(Bundle savedInstanceState) {
        super.onActivityCreated(savedInstanceState);

        getListView().setChoiceMode(ListView.CHOICE_MODE_SINGLE);
        String[] veggies = getResources().getStringArray(
                R.array.veggies_array);
        setListAdapter(new ArrayAdapter<>(getActivity(),
                android.R.layout.simple_list_item_activated_1, veggies));

        View detailsFrame = getActivity().findViewById(R.id.veggieentry);
        mShowTwoFragments = detailsFrame != null
                && detailsFrame.getVisibility() == View.VISIBLE;

        if (savedInstanceState != null) {
            mCurPosition = savedInstanceState.getInt("curChoice", 0);
        }

        if (mShowTwoFragments == true || mCurPosition != 1) {
            viewVeggieInfo(mCurPosition);
        }
```

```
        getFragmentManager().addOnBackStackChangedListener(this);
    }


    @Override
    public void onBackStackChanged() {
        VeggieGardenWebViewFragment details =
            (VeggieGardenWebViewFragment) getFragmentManager()
                .findFragmentById(R.id.veggieentry);
        if (details != null) {
            mCurPosition = details.getShownIndex();
            getListView().setItemChecked(mCurPosition, true);


            if (!mShowTwoFragments) {
                viewVeggieInfo(mCurPosition);
            }
        }
    }


    @Override
    public void onSaveInstanceState(Bundle outState) {
        super.onSaveInstanceState(outState);
        outState.putInt("curChoice", mCurPosition);
    }


    @Override
    public void onListItemClick(ListView l, View v, int position, long id) {
        viewVeggieInfo(position);
    }


    void viewVeggieInfo(int index) {
        mCurPosition = index;
        if (mShowTwoFragments == true) {
            // Check what fragment is currently shown, replace if needed.
```

(Continues)

(Continued)

```
            VeggieGardenWebViewFragment details =
                (VeggieGardenWebViewFragment) getFragmentManager()
                    .findFragmentById(R.id.veggieentry);
        if (details == null || details.getShownIndex() != index) {

            VeggieGardenWebViewFragment newDetails = VeggieGardenWebViewFragment
                .newInstance(index);

            FragmentManager fm = getFragmentManager();
            FragmentTransaction ft = fm.beginTransaction();
            ft.replace(R.id.veggieentry, newDetails);
            if (index != 1) {
                String[] veggies = getResources().getStringArray(
                        R.array.veggies_array);
                String strBackStackTagName = veggies[index];
                ft.addToBackStack(strBackStackTagName);
            }

            ft.setTransition(FragmentTransaction.TRANSIT_FRAGMENT_FADE);
            ft.commit();
        }

    } else {
        Intent intent = new Intent();
        intent.setClass(getActivity(), VeggieGardenViewActivity.class);
        intent.putExtra("index", index);
        startActivity(intent);
    }
  }
}
```

Most of the Fragment control's initialization happens in the onActivityCreated()
callback method so that we initialize the ListView only once. We then check to see
which display mode we want to be in by checking to see if our second component is

defined in the layout. Finally, we leave the display details to the helper method called `viewVeggieInfo()`, which is also called whenever an item in the `ListView` control is clicked.

The logic for the `viewVeggieInfo()` method takes into account both display modes. If the device is in portrait mode, the `VeggieGardenViewActivity` is launched via `Intent`. However, if the device is in landscape mode, we have some `Fragment` finagling to do.

Specifically, the `FragmentManager` is used to find the existing `VeggieGardenWebViewFragment` by its unique identifier (`R.id.veggieentry`, as defined in the layout resource file). Then, a new `VeggieGardenWebViewFragment` instance is created for the new fruit or vegetable Web page being requested. Next, a `FragmentTransaction` is started, in which the existing `VeggieGardenWebViewFragment` is replaced with the new one. We put the old one on the back stack so that the `Back` button works nicely, set the transition animation to fade between the blog entries, and commit the transaction, thus causing the screen to update asynchronously.

Finally, we can monitor the back stack with a call to the `addOnBackStackChangedListener()` method. The callback `onBackStackChanged()` updates the list to the current selected item. This provides a robust way to keep the `ListView` item selection synchronized with the currently displayed `Fragment` both when adding a new `Fragment` to the back stack and when removing one, such as when the user presses the `Back` button.

Implementing a `WebViewFragment`

Next, we create a custom `WebViewFragment` class called `VeggieGardenWebViewFragment` to host the webpage related to each fruit or vegetable. This `Fragment` class does little more than determine which Web page URL to load and then load it in the `WebView` control:

```
public class VeggieGardenWebViewFragment extends WebViewFragment {

    private static final String DEBUG_TAG = "VGWebViewFragment";

    public static VeggieGardenWebViewFragment newInstance(int index) {
        Log.v(DEBUG_TAG, "Creating new instance: " + index);
        VeggieGardenWebViewFragment fragment =
                new VeggieGardenWebViewFragment();

        Bundle args = new Bundle();
        args.putInt("index", index);
        fragment.setArguments(args);
        return fragment;
    }
```

(Continues)

(Continued)

```java
    public int getShownIndex() {

        int index = 1;

        Bundle args = getArguments();

        if (args != null) {

            index = args.getInt("index", -1);

        }

        if (index == -1) {

            Log.e(DEBUG_TAG, "Not an array index.");

        }


        return index;

    }


    @Override

    public void onActivityCreated(Bundle savedInstanceState) {

        super.onActivityCreated(savedInstanceState);


        String[] veggieUrls = getResources().getStringArray(

                R.array.veggieurls_array);

        int veggieUrlIndex = getShownIndex();


        WebView webview = getWebView();

        webview.setPadding(0, 0, 0, 0);

        webview.getSettings().setLoadWithOverviewMode(true);

        webview.getSettings().setUseWideViewPort(true);


        if (veggieUrlIndex != 1) {

            String veggieUrl = veggieUrls[veggieUrlIndex];

            webview.loadUrl(veggieUrl);

        } else {

            String veggieUrl = "http://andys-veggie-garden." +

                                "appspot.com/cherrytomatoes";

            webview.loadUrl(veggieUrl);

        }

    }

}
```

Most of the `Fragment` control's initialization happens in the `onActivityCreated()` callback method so that we initialize the `WebView` only once. The default configuration of the `WebView` control doesn't look so pretty, so we make some configuration changes, remove the padding around the control, and make some settings so the browser fits nicely in the screen area provided. If we've received a request for a specific fruit or vegetable to load, we look up the URL and load it; otherwise, we load the "default" Web page of Andy's Veggie Garden about cherry tomatoes.

Defining the Layout Files

Now that you've implemented your `Fragment` classes, you can place them in the appropriate layout resource files. You'll need to create two layout files. In landscape mode, you'll want a single `activity_simple_fragments.xml` layout file to host both `Fragment` components. In portrait mode, you'll want a comparable layout file that hosts only the `ListFragment` you implemented. The user interface of the `WebViewFragment` you implemented will be generated at runtime.

Let's start with the landscape-mode layout resource, called `res/layout-land/activity_simple_fragments.xml`. Note that we store this `activity_simple_fragments.xml` resource file in a special resource directory for landscape mode use only. We discuss how to store alternative resources in this way in depth in Chapter 13, "Designing Compatible Applications." For now, suffice it say that this layout will be automatically loaded whenever the device is in landscape mode.

```xml
<?xml version="1.0" encoding="utf-8"?>

<LinearLayout

    xmlns:android="http://schemas.android.com/apk/res/android"

    android:orientation="vertical"

    android:layout_width="match_parent"

    android:layout_height="match_parent">

    <include

        android:id="@+id/toolbar"

        layout="@layout/tool_bar" />

    <LinearLayout

        android:orientation="horizontal"

        android:layout_width="match_parent"

        android:layout_height="match_parent"

        android:baselineAligned="false">

        <fragment

android:name="com.introtoandroid.simplefragments.VeggieGardenListFragment"

            android:id="@+id/list"

            android:layout_weight="1"
```

(Continues)

(*Continued*)

```
            android:layout_width="200dp"

            android:layout_height="match_parent" />

        <FrameLayout

            android:id="@+id/veggieentry"

            android:layout_weight="4"

            android:layout_width="match_parent"

            android:layout_height="match_parent" />

    </LinearLayout>

</LinearLayout>
```

Here, we have a fairly straightforward LinearLayout control wrapping another LinearLayout that has two child controls. One is a static Fragment component that references the custom ListFragment class you implemented. For the second region, where we want to put the WebViewFragment, we include a FrameLayout region that we will replace with our specific VeggieGardenWebViewFragment instance programmatically at runtime.

The resources stored in the normal layout directory will be used whenever the device is not in landscape mode (in other words, portrait mode). Here, we need to define two layout files. First, let's define our static ListFragment in its own res/layout/activity_simple_fragments.xml file. It looks much like the previous version, without the second FrameLayout control:

```
<?xml version="1.0" encoding="utf-8"?>

<LinearLayout

    xmlns:android="http://schemas.android.com/apk/res/android"

    android:orientation="vertical"

    android:layout_width="match_parent"

    android:layout_height="match_parent"

    tools:context=".SimpleFragmentActivity">

    <include

        android:id="@+id/toolbar"

        layout="@layout/tool_bar" />

    <fragment

android:name="com.introtoandroid.simplefragments.VeggieGardenListFragment"

        android:id="@+id/list"

        android:layout_weight="1"

        android:layout_width="0dp"

        android:layout_height="match_parent"

        tools:layout="@layout/activity_simple_fragments" />

</LinearLayout>
```

Defining the `Activity` Classes

You're almost done. Now you need to define your `Activity` classes to host your `Fragment` components. You'll need two `Activity` classes: a primary class as well as a secondary class that is used only to display the `VeggieGardenWebViewFragment` when in portrait mode. Let's call the primary `Activity` class `SimpleFragmentsActivity` and the secondary `Activity` class `VeggieGardenViewActivity`.

As mentioned earlier, moving all your user interface logic to `Fragment` components greatly simplifies your `Activity` class implementation. For example, here is the complete implementation for the `SimpleFragmentsActivity` class:

```
public class SimpleFragmentsActivity extends AppCompatActivity {

    @Override

    public void onCreate(Bundle savedInstanceState) {

        super.onCreate(savedInstanceState);

        setContentView(R.layout.activity_simple_fragments);

        Toolbar toolbar;

        Toolbar = (Toolbar) findViewById(R.id.toolbar);

        getSupportActionBar(toolbar);

    }

}
```

Yup. That's all that is required. The `VeggieGardenViewActivity` class is only slightly more interesting:

```
public class VeggieGardenViewActivity extends AppCompatActivity {

    @Override

    public void onCreate(Bundle savedInstanceState) {

        super.onCreate(savedInstanceState);


        if (getResources().getConfiguration().orientation ==

            Configuration.ORIENTATION_LANDSCAPE) {

                finish();

                return;

        }


        if (savedInstanceState == null) {

            setContentView(R.layout.activity_simple_fragments);
```

(Continues)

(Continued)

```java
        Toolbar toolbar = (Toolbar) findViewById(R.id.toolbar);

        getSupportActionBar(toolbar);

        getSupportActionBar().setDisplayHomeAsUpEnabled(true);

        VeggieGardenWebViewFragment details = new VeggieGardenWebViewFragment();

        details.setArguments(getIntent().getExtras());


        FragmentManager fm = getFragmentManager();

        FragmentTransaction ft = fm.beginTransaction();

        ft.replace(R.id.list, details);

        ft.commit();

    }

}


@Override

public boolean onOptionsItemSelected(MenuItem item) {

    if (item.getItemId() == android.R.id.home) {

        onBackPressed();

        return true;

    }

    return super.onOptionsItemSelected(item);

}

}
```

Here, we check that we're in the appropriate orientation to be using this `Activity`.
Then we create an instance of the `VeggieGardenWebViewFragment` and programmatically
add it to the `Activity`, generating its user interface at runtime by replacing the
`R.id.list` view, which is the root view of any `Activity` class. That's all that's needed to
implement this simple sample application with `Fragment` components while including
the `Toolbar` component as an `ActionBar`.

Using the Android Support Library Package

Fragments are so important to the future of the Android platform that the Android team
provided a compatibility library so that developers can update their legacy applications as
far back as Android 1.6, if they so choose. This library was originally called the Compatibility Package and is now called the Android Support Library package.

Adding `Fragment` Support to Legacy Applications

The choice of whether or not to update older applications is a personal one for the development team. Non-`Fragment` applications should continue to function for the foreseeable future without error, mostly due to the Android team's continued policy of supporting legacy applications as much as possible when new platform versions are released. Here are some considerations for developers with legacy applications who are considering whether or not to revise their existing code:

- Leave your legacy application as is, and the ramifications are not catastrophic. Your application will not be using the latest and greatest features that the Android platform has to offer (and users will notice this), but it should continue to run as well as it always has without any additional work on your part. If you have no plans to update or upgrade your old applications, this may very well be a reasonable choice. The potentially inefficient use of screen space may be problematic but should not create new errors.

- If your application has a lot of market traction and you've continued to update it as the Android platform has matured, you're more likely to want to consider the Android Support Library package. Your users may demand it. You can certainly continue to support your legacy application and create a separate new-and-improved version that uses the new platform features, but this means organizing and managing different source code branches and different application packages, and it complicates application publication and reporting, not to mention maintenance and marketing complications. Better to revise your existing application to use the Android Support Library package and do your best to keep your single code base manageable. The size and resources of your organization may be contributing factors to the decision described here.

- Just because you start using the Android Support Library package in your applications does not mean you have to implement every new feature (fragments, loaders, toolbars, and so on) immediately. You can simply pick and choose the features that make the most sense for your application and add others over time via application updates when your team has the resources and inclination.

- Choosing not to update your code to new controls could leave your legacy application looking dated compared to other applications. If your application is already completely customized and isn't using stock controls—often the case with games and other highly graphical apps—it may not need updating. If, however, you conform to stock system controls, look, and feel, it may be more important for your application to get a fresh look.

Using Fragments in New Applications Targeting Older Platforms

If you're just starting to develop a new application and plan to target some of the older platform versions, incorporating fragments into your design is a much easier decision. If you're just starting a project, there's little reason not to use them and quite a few reasons why you should:

- Regardless of what devices and platforms you are targeting now, there will be new ones in the future that you cannot foresee. Fragments give you the flexibility to easily adjust your user interface screen workflows without rewriting or retesting all your application code.

- Incorporating the Android Support Library package into your applications early means that if other important platform features are added later, you'll be able to update the libraries and start using them easily.

- By using the Android Support Library package, your application will not show its age nearly as quickly since you will be incorporating the newer features of the platform and providing them to users on older platforms.

Linking the Android Support Package to Your Project

The Android Support Library package is simply a set of static support libraries (available as a `.jar` file) that you can link to your Android application and use. You can download the Android Support Library package using the Android SDK Manager and then add it to the projects of your choice. It is an optional package and not linked by default. Android Support Library packages are versioned like everything else, and they are updated occasionally with new features—and more important, bug fixes.

Tip
You can find out more about the latest version package at the Android Developer website: *http://d.android.com/tools/support-library/index.html.*

There are actually seven Android Support Packages: v4, v7, v8, v13, v17, Annotation, and Design. The v4 package aims to provide new classes introduced in Honeycomb and beyond to platform versions as far back as API Level 4 (Android 1.6). This is the package you want to use when supporting your legacy applications. The v7 package provides additional APIs that are not found within the v4 package and is for supporting newer features all the way back to API Level 7 (Android 2.1); it is organized into the following groups: `appcompat`, `cardview`, `gridlayout`, `mediarouter`, `palette`, and `recyclerview`. The v8 package provides the `renderscript` package to support `RenderScript` computation all the way back to API Level 8 (Android 2.2). The v13 package provides more efficient implementations of some items, such as the `FragmentCompat`, when running on API Level 13 and later. If you're targeting API Level 13 or later, use this package instead. The v17 package provides widgets for building TV user interfaces, such as the `BrowseFragment`, `DetailsFragment`, `PlaybackOverlayFragment`, and `SearchFragment`. The `Annotation` package allows you to add metadata annotations to your code, and the `Design` package allows you to add material design patterns and user interface elements.

To use the Android Support Library package with your application, take the following steps:

1. Use the Android SDK Manager to download the Android Support Repository if you are developing with Android Studio. The Android Support Library item is for use with Eclipse.

2. Find your `build.gradle` module file (not the `build.gradle` project file) of your project listed in the `Project` view of Android Studio and open the file.

3. In the dependencies section, add any support library features that your project needs to include by using their appropriate identifier and version number. For the `SimpleFragments` application, we have added the `support-v4`, `appcompat-v7`, and the `design` support library packages, each with a specified version of `23.0.0`, as shown here:

```
dependencies {
    compile fileTree(dir: 'libs', include: ['*.jar'])
    compile "com.android.support:support-v4:23.0.0"
    compile "com.android.support:appcompat-v7:23.0.0"
    compile 'com.android.support:design:23.0.0'
}
```

4. Begin using the additional support APIs available to your project. For example, to create a class extending `FragmentActivity`, you need to import `android.support.v4.app.FragmentActivity`.

Note

A few differences exist between the APIs used by the Android Support Library package and those found in the later versions of the Android SDK. However, there are some classes that are renamed to avoid name collisions, and not all classes and features are currently incorporated into the Android Support Library package.

Additional Ways to Use Fragments

Fragments are great for creating reusable interface components, but there are other ways to use fragments within your application. You can create reusable behavior components without a user interface, in addition to nesting fragments within fragments.

Behavior Fragments without a User Interface

Fragments are not only for decoupling a user interface component from an `Activity`. You may also want to decouple application behaviors, such as background processing, into a reusable `Fragment`. Rather than providing the ID of a resource, you simply provide a unique string tag when adding or replacing a `Fragment`. Because you are not adding a particular `View` to your layout, the call to the `onCreateView()` method is never called. Just make sure to use the `findFragmentByTag()` to retrieve this behavior `Fragment` from your `Activity`.

Exploring Nested Fragments

Android 4.2 (API Level 17) introduced the ability to nest fragments within fragments. Nested fragments have also been added to the Android Support Library, making this API capability available all the way back to Android 1.6 (API Level 4). In order to add a `Fragment` within another `Fragment`, you must invoke the `Fragment` method `getChildFragmentManager()`, which returns a `FragmentManager`. Once you have the `FragmentManager`, you can start a `FragmentTransaction` by calling `beginTransaction()` and then invoking the `add()` method, including the `Fragment` to add and its layout, followed by the `commit()` method. You can even use the `getParentFragment()` method from within a child `Fragment` to get the parent `Fragment` for manipulation.

This opens many possibilities for creating dynamic and reusable nested components. Some examples include tabbed fragments within tabbed fragments, paging from one `Fragment` item/`Fragment` detail screen to the next `Fragment` item/`Fragment` detail screen with `ViewPager`, paging fragments with `ViewPager` within tabbed fragments, or nesting a behavior `Fragment` without a UI inside a `Fragment` with a UI, along with a host of many other nesting possibilities.

Summary

Fragments were introduced into the Android SDK to help address the different types of device screens that application developers need to target now and in the future. A `Fragment` is simply a self-contained user interface or behavior, with its own lifecycle, that can be independent of a specific `Activity` class. Fragments must be hosted within `Activity` classes, but they give the developer a lot more flexibility when it comes to breaking screen workflow into components that can be mixed and matched in different ways, depending on the screen real estate available on the device. Fragments were introduced in Android 3.0, but legacy applications can use them if they take advantage of the Android Support Library package, which allows applications that target API Level 4 (Android 1.6) and higher to use these more recent additions to the Android SDK. In addition, the APIs with nested fragments provide even greater flexibility when creating reusable components for your applications.

Quiz Questions

1. What class facilitates coordination between an `Activity` and its `Fragment` components?

2. What method call is used for acquiring the class that facilitates coordination between an `Activity` and its `Fragment` components?

3. To what value should the android:name attribute of the <fragment> XML tag be set?

4. True or false: The onActivityAttach() callback method is called when a Fragment is first attached to a specific Activity class.

5. What are some subclasses of the Fragment (android.app.Fragment) class?

6. What type of control does a ListFragment (android.app.ListFragment) host?

7. Fragments were introduced in API Level 11 (Android 3.0). How would you add Fragment support to your application to support devices running versions of Android older than API Level 11?

Exercises

1. Using the Android documentation, review how to add a Fragment to the back stack. Create a simple application with a layout consisting of one Fragment for inserting a number (start with 1 in the first Fragment) and a button below it. Upon clicking the button, replace the first Fragment with a second Fragment and insert the number 2 in that Fragment. Continue this capability all the way up to 10, and while doing so, add each Fragment to the back stack to support back navigation.

2. Using Android Studio, create a new Phone and Tablet Android project using the new project creation wizard, and on the Add an activity to Mobile page, select the Master/Detail Flow option, then select Finish. Launch this application on both a handset and a tablet-size screen to see what it does, and then analyze the code to get a feel for how fragments have been used.

3. Create a two-pane Fragment layout where both fragments are generated and inserted programmatically into a layout at runtime. Have each Fragment take up 50% of the screen space, and use different colors for each Fragment.

References and More Information

Android Training: "Building a Dynamic UI with Fragments":
   http://d.android.com/training/basics/fragments/index.html
Android API Guides: "Fragments":
   http://d.android.com/guide/components/fragments.html
Android SDK Reference regarding the application Fragment class:
   http://d.android.com/reference/android/app/Fragment.html
Android SDK Reference regarding the application ListFragment class:
   http://d.android.com/reference/android/app/ListFragment.html
Android SDK Reference regarding the application PreferenceFragment class:
   http://d.android.com/reference/android/preference/PreferenceFragment.html
Android SDK Reference regarding the application WebViewFragment class:
   http://d.android.com/reference/android/webkit/WebViewFragment.html

Android SDK Reference regarding the application `DialogFragment` class:
   http://d.android.com/reference/android/app/DialogFragment.html
Android Tools: "Support Library":
   http://d.android.com/tools/support-library/index.html
Android Developers Blog: "The Android 3.0 Fragments API":
   http://android-developers.blogspot.com/2011/02/android-30-fragments-api.html

Application Design Essentials

10

Architecting with Patterns

In this chapter, you are going to develop common architectural design patterns using different classes, views, and layouts. This is important because the architecture of your application determines how users navigate and act within your application. You're going to learn about many different navigation patterns and how to implement them, and we'll also discuss many different ways to encourage your users to take action within your application. After completing this chapter, you should be comfortable creating a basic architecture for your application.

Architecting Your Application's Navigation

First, let's take some time to figure out how to implement navigation so users can reach the tasks that you will be providing.

Tip

Before we talk about how to design navigation within your own application, you should take a moment to read about how users navigate within the Android System UI, if you have not already done so. You can learn more at the following URL: *http://d.android.com/design/ handhelds/index.html*. This article will help you learn about the different screens within Android—the Home, All Apps, and Recents screens—in addition to different system bars such as the status bar and navigation bar.

Tip

Many of the code examples provided in this section are taken from the SimpleParentChildSibling application. The source code for this application is provided for download on the book's website (*http://introductiontoandroid.blogspot.com*).

Android Application Navigation Scenarios

In order to understand how to program navigation within your application, you first must understand the different types of navigation that Android provides. There is more than one way that Android allows users to navigate to and within an application as well as to and from one application and another. The following sections describe the navigation scenarios that Android allows.

Entry Navigation

Entry navigation is how a user navigates into an application. There are many different ways this can occur, such as from a Home screen widget, from the All Apps screen, from a notification listed within the status bar, or even from another application altogether.

Lateral Navigation

Lateral navigation is mainly for applications that have screens residing on the same hierarchy level within an application. If your application has more than one screen residing on the same level, you may want to provide users the ability to navigate laterally across that particular hierarchy level by launching an Intent, implementing swipe navigation, tabs, or a combination of those. Figure 10.1 is a depiction of lateral navigation.

To implement lateral navigation for activities, all you need to do is make a call to startActivity() using an Intent with the lateral Activity and ensure that each of the activities is on the same hierarchy level. If your activities are on the same hierarchy level but not the top level, you can define the parentActivityName attribute in your manifest and set the parent Activity to be the same for each of the activities that should reside on the same hierarchy level.

Descendant Navigation

Descendant navigation is used when your application has more than one hierarchy level. This means that users can navigate deeper into your application's hierarchy levels. Usually, this is done by creating a new Activity with startActivity(). Figure 10.2 shows a depiction of navigating from a top-level Activity to a lower-level Activity.

To implement descendant navigation, make sure that the descendant Activity declares parentActivityName in your application manifest and set the Activity to be

Figure 10.1 A depiction of navigating an Android application laterally.

Figure 10.2   A depiction of performing descendant navigation within
an Android application.

the ancestor. Then, from the ancestor Activity, create an Intent with the descendant
Activity, and simply call startActivity().

Back Navigation

Back navigation is used when a user clicks the Back button located on the Android
navigation bar or presses a hardware Back button. The default behavior navigates the
user to the last Activity or Fragment that was placed on the back stack. To override
this behavior, call onBackPressed() from within your Activity. Figure 10.3 shows a
depiction of navigating back within an application after having performed the lateral
navigation seen in Figure 10.1.

You do not have to do anything special to implement back navigation in your
application, unless you are working with fragments. With fragments, if you want to
navigate back, you need to make sure that you add your Fragment to the back stack with
a call to addToBackStack().

Ancestral Navigation

Ancestral navigation, or up navigation, is used when your application has more than one
hierarchy level and you must provide a means for navigating to a higher level. Figure 10.4
shows up navigation enabled within an application, and Figure 10.5 shows a depiction

Figure 10.3   A depiction of navigating back after having navigated laterally
as in Figure 10.1.

Figure 10.4   Showing up navigation as enabled.

of performing ancestral navigation after having performed descendant navigation as in Figure 10.2.

To implement ancestral navigation within your application, you must do two things. The first is to make sure that your descendant Activity defines the correct parentActivityName attribute within your application manifest. Then, in the onCreate() method of your Activity, simply call the setDisplayHomeAsUpEnabled() method of your action bar as shown here:

```
myActionBar.setDisplayHomeAsUpEnabled(true);
```

External Navigation

External navigation occurs when the user navigates from one application to another. Sometimes this is done in order to retrieve a result from another application using startActivityForResult(), or it could be done to leave the current application altogether.

Launching Tasks and Navigating the Back Stack

A task is one or more activities that are used for accomplishing a specific goal. The back stack is where Android manages these activities with a last-in-first-out ordering. As the activities of a task are created, they are added to the back stack in order. If the default behavior applies to an Activity, and the user presses the Back button, Android removes

Figure 10.5   A depiction of performing ancestral navigation within an
Android application.

the last `Activity` added to the stack. In addition, if the user were to press the `Home` button instead, the task would then move itself and the activities to the background. The task may be resumed by the user at a later time, as moving it to the background does not destroy the `Activity` or task.

Tip

You may customize the default behavior of activities in the back stack. To learn how this can be done, you should read the following Android documentation: *http://d.android.com/ guide/components/tasks-and-back-stack.html#ManagingTasks*.

Navigating with Fragments

We have covered extensively how the various navigation scenarios work when using activities. With fragments, let's just say that how navigation should be handled depends. If you have implemented a descendant `ViewPager` with fragments, and there are dozens or potentially hundreds of fragments that a user could page through, it is probably not a good idea to add each of the fragments to the back stack just to give the user the ability to navigate back up to its ancestor `Activity`. If so, and the user has a habit of using the `Back` button rather than the `Up` button, he or she may become extremely frustrated at having to navigate through dozens of fragments just to get to the ancestral Activity. It is clear that ancestral navigation should be used to handle this scenario, but not every user knows to use the Up button.

When the Fragment count is small, supporting back navigation should be OK. When designing your application, think about what a user would experience if you do support adding each and every Fragment to the back stack. After all, your application may require supporting that for various reasons, but be sure to be conscious of how users may experience your application.

Relationships between Screens

Figure 10.6 shows an extremely simple screen map of the hierarchical relationship between the screens for the SimpleParentChildSibling sample application accompanying this chapter.

For your application to understand the hierarchical relationship among your activities, all you need to do is add the android:parentActivityName to your

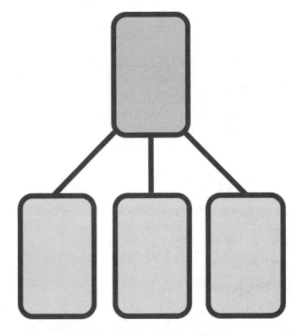

Figure 10.6   An extremely simple screen map shows the hierarchical relationship of the activities of the SimpleParentChildSibling code sample.

<activity> tag of your Android manifest file. To ensure proper support on older versions of Android, you should also define a <meta-data> tag with the name of android.support.PARENT_ACTIVITY. The complete manifest entry should look like this:

```
<activity
    android:name=".FirstChildActivity"
    android:label="@string/title_activity_first_child"
    android:parentActivityName=".SimpleParentChildSiblingActivity" >
    <meta-data
        android:name="android.support.PARENT_ACTIVITY"
        android:value="com.introtoandroid.simpleparentchildsibling.
SimpleParentChildSiblingActivity" />
</activity>
```

Android Navigation Design Patterns

There are many design patterns commonly found within Android applications. Many of these patterns are highlighted within the Android documentation due to their effectiveness. We describe a few of these common navigation design patterns here.

Targets

Use targets such as buttons when your application needs to replace the current screen entirely and none of the other patterns listed in this chapter apply. Figure 10.7 shows the SimpleParentChildSibling application launcher Activity (left) with three target navigational buttons and the FirstChildActivity (right) with two sibling target navigational buttons.

To implement, simply wire up a Button with an OnClickListener() and create an Intent with the application context and the Activity to navigate to, and launch the Intent with the startActivity() method as follows:

```
Button firstChild = (Button) findViewById(R.id.firstChild);
firstChild.setOnClickListener(new View.OnClickListener() {
    @Override
    public void onClick(View v) {
        Intent intent = new Intent(getApplicationContext(), FirstChildActivity.
class);
        startActivity(intent);
    }
});
```

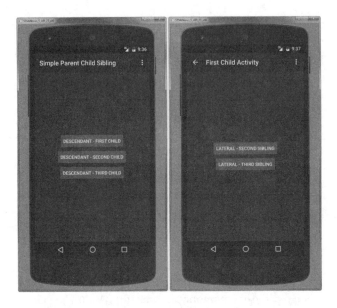

Figure 10.7   A screenshot of the `SimpleParentChildSibling` sample application displays three descendant `Activity` navigation buttons (left), two sibling `Activity` navigation buttons (right), and the up button on the `ActionBar` (right).

Tip

Many of the code examples provided in this section are taken from the `SimpleViewPager`, `SimpleTabs`, `SimpleNavDrawer`, and `SimpleMasterDetailFlow` applications. The source code for these applications is provided for download on the book's website.

Swipe Views

Use swipe views when you need to page through potentially lots of information such as a picture gallery that may have a lot of images. Although this is implemented similar to the tab example by using a `ViewPager`, this pattern is different in that it may have an unlimited number of pages to page through, whereas a `TabLayout` usually has a specified number of tabs to page through. In Figure 10.8, the screenshot on the left is the first image, and the screenshot on the right is the second image, while the screenshot in the middle shows swiping between the two images.

Here is a layout file called `activity_simple_view_pager.xml` where we add a `ViewPager` to the layout:

```
<android.support.v4.view.ViewPager

    xmlns:android="http://schemas.android.com/apk/res/android"
```

Figure 10.8   The `SimpleViewPager` application swiping between two
views, implemented with a `ViewPager`.

```
xmlns:tools="http://schemas.android.com/tools"

android:id="@+id/pager"

android:layout_width="match_parent"

android:layout_height="match_parent" />
```

Then, in your `AppCompatActivity`, you need to implement a `FragmentPagerAdapter`,
which keeps track of the `Fragment` views that are being paged during swipes. This requires
creating an additional layout resource and inflating this layout into a `Fragment` in the
`onCreateView()` method of our `Fragment`. Here is the `fragment_simple_view_pager.xml`
file we inflate into our fragment:

```
<LinearLayout xmlns:android="http://schemas.android.com/apk/res/android"

    xmlns:tools="http://schemas.android.com/tools"

    android:layout_width="match_parent"

    android:layout_height="match_parent"

    android:gravity="center"

    android:orientation="vertical"

    tools:context=".SimpleViewPagerActivity$PlaceholderFragment">


    <ImageView

        android:id="@+id/image_view"
```

(Continues)

(*Continued*)

```
        android:layout_width="match_parent"

        android:layout_height="wrap_content" />


    <TextView

        android:id="@+id/section_label"

        android:layout_width="wrap_content"

        android:layout_height="wrap_content"

        android:gravity="center_horizontal"

        android:paddingBottom="@dimen/activity_vertical_margin"

        android:paddingLeft="@dimen/activity_horizontal_margin"

        android:paddingRight="@dimen/activity_horizontal_margin"

        android:paddingTop="@dimen/activity_vertical_margin"

        android:textSize="16sp"

        android:textStyle="bold" />


</LinearLayout>
```

To see how the `AppCompatActivity`, `Fragment`, and `FragmentPagerAdapter` are implemented, refer to the `SimpleViewPager` code sample provided with the chapter downloads.

Tabs

Use fixed or scrollable tabs when you have three or fewer related content sections within the same hierarchy level. Implementing fixed tabs with swipe functionality using `ViewPager` is recommended (see Figure 10.9).

Implementing tabs is similar to the `ViewPager` example, but we must add a `TabLayout` to our view. Here's how to add a `TabLayout`:

```
<android.support.design.widget.TabLayout

    android:id="@+id/tab_layout"

    android:layout_width="match_parent"

    android:layout_height="wrap_content" />
```

And, in our `AppCompatActivity`, we must add a `ViewPagerOnTabSelectedListener()` to our `TabLayout`. We do this as follows:

```
tabLayout.setOnTabSelectedListener(

    new TabLayout.ViewPagerOnTabSelectedListener(mViewPager));
```

To see how the full functionality is implemented, refer to the `SimpleTabs` code sample provided with the chapter downloads.

Figure 10.9   The `SimpleTabs` application implements a `TabLayout`
and `ViewPager`.

Navigation Drawer

Use the navigation drawer when you have more than three top-level sections within your application and if you need to provide quick access to lower-level sections in addition to the top-level sections. Figure 10.10 shows an application using a navigation drawer. More information on using the navigation drawer can be found at the Android documentation website: *http://d.android.com/training/implementing-navigation/nav-drawer.html*.

To add a navigation drawer, you must first add the appcompat-v7 and design support libraries as dependencies in your `build.gradle` app module file. Here is what the dependencies look like after adding them:

```
dependencies {

    compile fileTree(dir: 'libs', include: ['*.jar'])

    compile 'com.android.support:appcompat-v7:23.0.0'

    compile 'com.android.support:design:23.0.0'

}
```

Figure 10.10   A screenshot of the `SimpleNavDrawer` application shows
the navigation drawer as open.

Then simply add the `DrawerLayout` and the `NavigationView` widgets as shown here:

```
<android.support.v4.widget.DrawerLayout
    xmlns:android="http://schemas.android.com/apk/res/android"
    xmlns:drawer="http://schemas.android.com/apk/res-auto"
    xmlns:tools="http://schemas.android.com/tools"
    android:id="@+id/drawer_layout"
    android:layout_width="match_parent"
    android:layout_height="match_parent"
    android:fitsSystemWindows="true"
    tools:context=".SimpleNavDrawerAndViewActivity">

    <LinearLayout
        android:layout_width="match_parent"
        android:layout_height="match_parent"
        android:orientation="vertical">
```

```
<TextView

        android:id="@+id/text_view"

        android:layout_width="wrap_content"

        android:layout_height="wrap_content"

        android:padding="16dp"

        android:text="@string/instructions"

        android:textSize="24sp"/>

</LinearLayout>


<android.support.design.widget.NavigationView

    android:id="@+id/nav_view"

    android:layout_width="wrap_content"

    android:layout_height="match_parent"

    android:layout_gravity="start"

    drawer:headerLayout="@layout/drawer_headers"

    drawer:menu="@menu/menu_nav_drawer" />

</android.support.v4.widget.DrawerLayout>
```

Finally, you need to implement the
`NavigationView.OnNavigationItemSelectedListener()` in your `AppCompatActivity`
so that your application is able to handle navigation selections. See the `SimpleNavDrawer`
application for the full implementation.

Master Detail Flow

Use the master detail flow with fragments when using views such as lists or grids,
one `Fragment` for the list or grid and the other `Fragment` for the associated detail
view. When selecting an item in the `Fragment` list or grid on a single-pane layout,
launch a new `Activity` to display the `Fragment` detail view. Figure 10.11 shows the
`SimpleMasterDetailFlow` application running in a single-pane layout; the left side shows
the master list `Activity` and the right side shows the detail `Activity`. In a multipane
layout, touching an item within the list or grid should display the accompanying detail
`Fragment` alongside the list or grid. Figure 10.12 shows the same master detail flow
application from Figure 10.11, only this time within a multipane layout with the master
list `Fragment` on the left and the detail `Fragment` on the right. This application was made
using the Android Studio new project creation wizard and choosing the
`Blank Activity with Fragment` option, with minor modifications. This is the fastest
way to implement `Fragment`-based design in your application.

Figure 10.11   Two screenshots of the `SimpleMasterDetailFlow`
application shown in a single-pane layout.

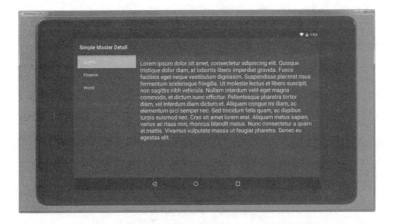

Figure 10.12   A screenshot of the `SimpleMasterDetailFlow`
application shown in a multipane layout.

Encouraging Action

Determining how to navigate your application is only half the battle when designing your product. The other challenge is figuring out how to get your users to perform the actions made available within your application.

Actions differ from navigation as they are usually designed to alter the user's data permanently. With that said, there are a few common design patterns that have evolved on the Android platform for presenting actions to users.

Menus

The concept of presenting menus to users to prompt them to take a particular action has been around since Android API Level 1. With Android API Level 11, menus have been replaced with a newer design pattern known as the `ActionBar` that presents actions to users. API Level 21 added a generalized version of an `ActionBar` called a `Toolbar`. For applications prior to API Level 11, you may want to consider implementing the support version of the `Toolbar`. We talk more about action bars and toolbars in the following section. As for menus, there are three different types of menus available for use:

- **Options menu:** An options menu is where you should present actions available to a particular `Activity`. The maximum number of actions that you can present within an options menu is six. If you need to include more than six menu items, an overflow menu will be created and your actions will be accessible from there. It is a good idea to order your most common actions to be presented in the options menu first.

- **Context menu:** You can use a context menu to present actions when a selection event is initiated by a long press from a user. If your `Activity` supports a context menu upon a selection event, once an item has been selected, a `Dialog` will be displayed presenting the various actions that your application supports.

- **Pop-up menu:** A pop-up menu looks like an overflow-style menu item and is used for displaying actions relevant to the content displayed within an `Activity`.

Action Bars

As mentioned in the preceding section, the `ActionBar` has become the preferred way to present actions to users. The `ActionBar` is where to place actions that you want to make available to a particular `Activity`. You can add actions to or remove them from the `ActionBar` from within an `Activity` or `Fragment`.

Tip

Many of the code examples provided in this section are taken from the `SimpleActionMenu` application. The source code for this application is provided for download on the book's website.

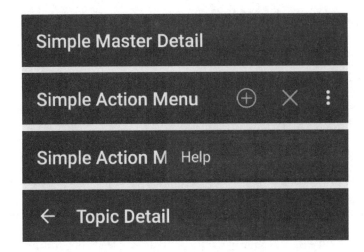

Figure 10.13   Various representations of the action bar.

You can use an `ActionBar` to display various elements, which are detailed in the following sections. Figure 10.13 shows four different states of the `ActionBar` from some of the applications discussed in this chapter. The top `ActionBar` is the default state that just shows the application name. The second from top shows an `ActionBar` with action buttons and an overflow icon. The third from top shows the overflow menu open. The bottom shows an `ActionBar` with the up button enabled.

Application Icon

You may place your application's icon within the `ActionBar`. If your application supports up navigation, the application icon would be placed near where a user would press to navigate up a level.

View Control

A `View` control may be placed on your `ActionBar` for enabling actions such as search or navigation using tabs or a drop-down menu.

Action Buttons

Action buttons are usually icons, text, or both icons and text for displaying the actions you would like to make available to users from within your `Activity`. The second `ActionBar` from the top in Figure 10.13 shows two actions, the `Add` and `Close` buttons, each with an associated icon.

To add action buttons to the `ActionBar`, you must add a menu layout to your `Activity`. Here is the menu layout used in the `SimpleActionMenu` application:

```
<menu xmlns:android="http://schemas.android.com/apk/res/android" >

    <item

        android:id="@+id/menu_add"
```

```
        android:icon="@android:drawable/ic_menu_add"

        android:orderInCategory="2"

        android:showAsAction="ifRoom|withText"

        android:title="@string/action_add"/>

    <item

        android:id="@+id/menu_close"

        android:icon="@android:drawable/ic_menu_close_clear_cancel"

        android:orderInCategory="4"

        android:showAsAction="ifRoom|withText"

        android:title="@string/action_close"/>

    <item

        android:id="@+id/menu_help"

        android:icon="@android:drawable/ic_menu_help"

        android:orderInCategory="5"

        android:showAsAction="never"

        android:title="@string/action_help"/>

</menu>
```

Then, in your `Activity`, you need to inflate the menu using the `onCreateOptionsMenu()` method as follows:

```
@Override

public boolean onCreateOptionsMenu(Menu menu) {

    getMenuInflater().inflate(R.menu.simple_action_bar, menu);

    return true;

}
```

This will add the action items to the `ActionBar`. Notice the item icon attributes in our menu layout. Android provides default icons for many common action types such as add, close, clear, cancel, or help. Using these default icons will save you a great amount of time, in addition to providing a consistent user experience across all applications that use those icons. Using your own icons may seem desirable, but doing so may confuse users who are not used to seeing the icon you provide for a common action.

Action Overflow

Action items that you are not able to fit on the main `ActionBar` will be placed within the overflow section. Make sure to order your action items in the order of their importance and frequency of use. The third `ActionBar` from the top of Figure 10.13 also shows an action overflow menu item named `Help`. This action item is accessible only after the overflow icon in the upper-right corner of the screen is touched.

If your application supports both small screens and large tablets, you may want your `ActionBar` to display differently based on the type of device. Since large tablets have more room on the `ActionBar`, you are able to fit more actions. With smaller screens, rather than having all of the actions displayed in the overflow, you should add a `Toolbar` to the bottom of your `View` and add the additional action items there. Before Android 5.0, support for a split `ActionBar` was available, but if your application makes use of the `Theme.Material` default theme of Android 5.0 and above, this is no longer supported and inserting a `Toolbar` at the bottom of your `View` is the preferred way for achieving the same result.

In certain scenarios, you may want to hide the `ActionBar`. This can be useful if your application requires going into full-screen mode, or if you have designed a game and don't always want the `ActionBar` to be present. In order to hide the `ActionBar`, just add the following to your `Activity`:

```
getActionBar().hide();
```

If you need to show the `ActionBar` again at a later point, you can do so with the following:

```
getActionBar().show();
```

In Figure 10.14, the left and center screenshots display the `ActionBar`; in the right screenshot, the `ActionBar` is hidden.

In order to make your action item respond to touch events, you need to override the `onOptionsItemSelected()` method in your `Activity`. Here is how we defined the method in the `SimpleActionMenu` sample application:

```
@Override
public boolean onOptionsItemSelected(MenuItem item) {
    switch (item.getItemId()) {
        case R.id.menu_add:
            Toast.makeText(this, "Add Clicked", Toast.LENGTH_SHORT).show();
            return true;
        case R.id.menu_close:
            finish();
            return true;
        case R.id.menu_help:
            Toast.makeText(this, "Help Clicked", Toast.LENGTH_SHORT).show();
            return true;
        default:
            return super.onOptionsItemSelected(item);
    }
}
```

Figure 10.14   Three screenshots of the `SimpleActionMenu` sample application show (left and center) a visible `ActionBar` with two action buttons, (center) the overflow item on top of the `ActionBar` and action buttons, and (right) no visible `ActionBar` after the `Hide Action Bar` button is pressed.

The `onOptionsItemSelected()` allows us to detect which item in the menu was interacted with, and we use a simple `switch()` statement to determine which item was selected using the IDs we defined within the menu layout file. Our example is very simple. For the `Add` and `Help` action items, we simply make a `Toast` display to the screen, and the `Close` action item actually ends the `Activity` by calling the `finish()` method.

ActionBar Compatibility

To add an `ActionBar` to legacy applications running on devices with Android versions all the way back to 2.1 (API Level 7), you can use the Android support library in your project. Rather than using the regular `Activity` or `FragmentActivity` classes, you must use the `AppCompatActivity` class, which extends the `FragmentActivity` class of the v4 Support Library. The `ActionBarActivity` class found in older support libraries was used for adding the `ActionBar` to older versions of Android, but this class has since been deprecated for the new `AppCompatActivity`. In addition, you must set the theme of your application or `Activity` to `Theme.AppCompat`.

Toolbar as ActionBar

To add a `Toolbar` to your application, you need to have added the `appcompat-v7` support library as a dependency in your `build.gradle` app module file and then add the toolbar to your layout as shown here:

```
<android.support.v7.widget.Toolbar

    android:id="@+id/toolbar"
```

(Continues)

(*Continued*)

```
    android:layout_width="match_parent"

    android:layout_height="?attr/actionBarSize"

    android:background="?attr/colorPrimary" />
```

A `Toolbar` can be placed anywhere within the `View` hierarchy of your layout using the preceding code. If you want the `Toolbar` to be used as the `ActionBar`, there is an additional step you need to take in the `onCreate()` method of your `AppCompatActivity`. Add the following to set the `Toolbar` as your `ActionBar`:

```
Toolbar toolbar = (Toolbar) findViewById(R.id.toolbar);

setSupportActionBar(toolbar);
```

Finally, in order to access the support version of the `ActionBar` in your code, you must call the `getSupportActionBar()` method.

Contextual Action Mode

Contextual action mode is useful for displaying actions you would like to make available to users when they have selected something from within an `Activity`.

Floating Action Button

The `FloatingActionButton` is a recent addition to the Android design support library. The `FloatingActionButton` is used to perform a primary action of a particular `Activity`. For example, a contacts application would use a `FloatingActionButton` as the primary action for initiating the addition of a new contact by launching an "add contact" `Activity`.

Tip

Many of the code examples provided in this section are taken from the `SimpleFloatingActionButton` application. The source code for this application is provided for download on the book's website.

Once you've added the design support library as a dependency or in your `build.gradle` file, you can add a `FloatingActionButton` to your layout:

```
<android.support.design.widget.FloatingActionButton

    android:id="@+id/fab"

    android:layout_width="wrap_content"

    android:layout_height="wrap_content"

    android:layout_alignParentBottom="true"

    android:layout_alignParentEnd="true"

    android:layout_alignParentRight="true"

    android:layout_marginBottom="25dp"
```

```
android:layout_marginEnd="25dp"

android:layout_marginRight="25dp"

android:clickable="true"

android:contentDescription="@string/fab"

android:elevation="6dp"

android:src="@android:drawable/ic_input_add"

android:tint="@android:color/white" />
```

Figure 10.15 shows a representation of the `FloatingActionButton` and Figure 10.16 shows where the `FloatingActionButton` has been placed.

Actions Originating from Your Application's Content

You may need to make certain actions available from within your application's content areas. If so, there are various UI elements that you can use for enabling actions. These UI elements include:

- Buttons
- Check boxes
- Radio buttons
- Toggle buttons and switches
- Spinners
- Text fields
- Seek bars
- Pickers

For a detailed look at these various user interface controls, see Chapter 7, "Exploring Building Blocks."

Figure 10.15   A `FloatingActionButton`.

Figure 10.16   Viewing the `SimpleFloatingActionButton` application.

Dialogs

Dialogs are yet another way to present actions to your users. One important technique developers can use is to implement dialogs to inform the user or allow the user to perform actions such as edits without redrawing the main screen. Further, the best time to use a `Dialog` is when your application needs to confirm or acknowledge an action a user has taken that will permanently alter the user's data.

If you allow users to edit their application data directly from within a `Dialog`, you should present actions within the `Dialog` for the user to either confirm or deny the changes before actually committing them. Let's take a look at how to incorporate dialogs into your applications.

Tip

Many of the code examples provided in this section are taken from the `SimpleFragDialog` application. The source code for this application is provided for download on the book's website.

Choosing Your `Dialog` Implementation

The Android platform has grown and changed quickly. New revisions to the Android SDK are released on a frequent basis. This means that developers are always struggling to keep up with the latest that Android has to offer. The Android platform has been in a period of transition from a traditional smartphone platform to a "smart device" platform that will support a much wider variety of devices, such as tablets, TVs, wearables, autos, and toasters. To this end, one of the most important additions to the platform is the concept of the `Fragment`. We discussed fragments in detail in the previous chapter, but they have wide ramifications in terms of the user interface design of an Android application. One area of application design that has received an overhaul during this transition is the way in which dialogs now make use of fragments.

Using the `Fragment`-based method, which was introduced in API Level 11 (Android 3.0), dialogs are managed using the `FragmentManager` class (`android.app.FragmentManager`). A `Dialog` becomes a special type of `Fragment` that must still be used within the scope of an `Activity` class, but its lifecycle is managed like that of any other `Fragment`. This type of `Dialog` implementation works with the newest versions of the Android platform and is backward compatible with older devices as long as you incorporate the latest Android Support Package into your application to gain access to these new classes for use with older Android SDKs.

Exploring the Different Types of Dialogs

A number of different `Dialog` types are available within the Android SDK. Each type has a special function with which most users should be somewhat familiar. The `Dialog` types available as part of the Android SDK include the following:

- **`Dialog`**: the basic class for all `Dialog` types. A basic `Dialog` (`android.app.Dialog`) is shown in the top left of Figure 10.17. To learn more about the `Dialog` class, see the Android SDK reference here: *http://d.android.com/reference/android/app/Dialog.html*.

- **`AlertDialog`**: a `Dialog` with one, two, or three `Button` controls. An `AlertDialog` (`android.app.AlertDialog`) is shown in the top center of Figure 10.17. To learn more about the `AlertDialog` class, see the Android SDK reference here: *http://d. android.com/reference/android/app/AlertDialog.html*.

- **`ProgressDialog`**: a `Dialog` with a determinate or indeterminate `ProgressBar` control. An indeterminate `ProgressDialog` (`android.app.ProgressDialog`) is shown in the top right of Figure 10.17. To learn more about the `ProgressDialog` class, see the Android SDK reference here: *http://d.android.com/reference/android/app/ ProgressDialog.html*.

- **`DatePickerDialog`**: a `Dialog` with a `DatePicker` control. A `DatePickerDialog` (`android.app.DatePickerDialog`) is shown in the bottom left of Figure 10.17. To learn more about the `DatePickerDialog` class, see the Android SDK reference here: *http://d.android.com/reference/android/app/DatePickerDialog.html*.

Figure 10.17   Different implementations of dialogs.

- **TimePickerDialog**: a Dialog with a TimePicker control. A TimePickerDialog (android.app.TimePickerDialog) is shown in the bottom center of Figure 10.17. To learn more about the TimePickerDialog class, see the Android SDK reference here: *http://d.android.com/reference/android/app/TimePickerDialog.html*.

- **CharacterPickerDialog**: a Dialog for choosing an accented character associated with a base character. A CharacterPickerDialog (android.text.method.CharacterPickerDialog) is shown in the center right of Figure 10.17. To learn more about the CharacterPickerDialog class, see the Android SDK reference here: *http://d.android.com/reference/android/text/method/ CharacterPickerDialog.html*.

If none of the existing Dialog types is adequate, you can create custom Dialog windows, with your specific layout requirements. Figure 10.17 shows a custom Dialog window in the bottom right requesting the user to set a password.

Working with Dialogs and Dialog Fragments

An Activity can use dialogs to organize information and react to user-driven events. For example, an Activity might display a dialog informing the user of a problem or asking the user to confirm an action such as deleting a data record. Using dialogs for simple tasks helps keep the number of application activities manageable.

Most Activity classes should be "Fragment aware." In most cases, dialogs should be coupled with user-driven events within specific fragments. There is a special subclass of Fragment called a DialogFragment (android.app.DialogFragment) that can be used for this purpose.

A DialogFragment is the best way to define and manage dialogs for use within your user interface.

Tip

Many of the code examples provided in this section are taken from the SimpleFragDialog application. The source code for the SimpleFragDialog application is provided for download on the book's website.

Tracing the Lifecycle of a **Dialog** and **DialogFragment**

Each Dialog must be defined within the DialogFragment in which it is used. A Dialog may be launched once or used repeatedly. Understanding how a DialogFragment manages the Dialog lifecycle is important to implementing a Dialog correctly.

The Android SDK manages a DialogFragment in the same way that fragments are managed. We can be sure that a DialogFragment follows nearly the same lifecycle as a Fragment. Let's look at the key methods that a DialogFragment must use to manage a Dialog:

- The show() method is used to display the Dialog.
- The dismiss() method is used to stop showing the Dialog.

Adding a DialogFragment with a Dialog to an Activity involves several steps:

1. Define a class that extends DialogFragment. You can define this class within your Activity, but if you plan to reuse this DialogFragment in other activities, define this class in a separate file. This class must define a new DialogFragment class method that instantiates and returns a new instance of itself.

2. Define a Dialog within the DialogFragment class. Override the onCreateDialog() method and define your Dialog here. Simply return the Dialog from this method. You are able to define various Dialog attributes for your Dialog using methods such as setTitle(), setMessage(), or setIcon().

3. In your Activity class, instantiate a new DialogFragment instance, and once you have the DialogFragment instance, show the Dialog using the show() method.

Defining a **DialogFragment**

A DialogFragment class can be defined within an Activity or within a Fragment. The type of Dialog you are creating will determine the type of data that you must supply to the Dialog definition inside the DialogFragment class.

Setting **Dialog** Attributes

A Dialog is not too useful without setting the contextual elements. One way of doing this is by defining one or more of the attributes made available by the Dialog class. The base `Dialog` class and all of the `Dialog` subclasses define a `setTitle()` method. Setting the title usually helps a user determine what the `Dialog` is used for. The particular type of `Dialog` you are implementing determines the other methods that are made available to you for setting different `Dialog` attributes. In addition, setting attributes is also important for accessibility purposes, for example, to translate text to speech.

Showing a **Dialog**

You can display any `Dialog` within an `Activity` by calling the `show()` method of the `DialogFragment` class on a valid `DialogFragment` object identifier.

Dismissing a **Dialog**

Most types of dialogs have automatic dismissal circumstances. However, if you want to force a `Dialog` to be dismissed, simply call the `dismiss()` method on the `Dialog` identifier.

Here's an example of a simple class called `SimpleFragDialogActivity` that illustrates how to implement a simple `DialogFragment` with a `Dialog` control that is launched when a `Button` called `Button_AlertDialog` (defined in a layout resource) is clicked:

```
public class SimpleFragDialogActivity extends Activity {

    @Override

    public void onCreate(Bundle savedInstanceState) {

        super.onCreate(savedInstanceState);

        setContentView(R.layout.main);

        // Handle Alert Dialog Button

        Button launchAlertDialog = (Button) findViewById(
            R.id.Button_AlertDialog);

        launchAlertDialog.setOnClickListener(new View.OnClickListener() {

            @Override

            public void onClick(View v) {

                DialogFragment newFragment =
                    AlertDialogFragment.newInstance();

                showDialogFragment(newFragment);

            }

        });

    }


    public static class AlertDialogFragment extends DialogFragment {

        public static AlertDialogFragment newInstance() {

            AlertDialogFragment newInstance = new AlertDialogFragment();

            return newInstance;
```

```
        }

        @Override

        public Dialog onCreateDialog(Bundle savedInstanceState) {


            AlertDialog.Builder alertDialog =
                    new AlertDialog.Builder(getActivity());

            alertDialog.setTitle("Alert Dialog");

            alertDialog.setMessage("You have been alerted.");

            alertDialog.setIcon(android.R.drawable.btn_star);

            alertDialog.setPositiveButton(android.R.string.ok,
                    new DialogInterface.OnClickListener() {

                @Override

                public void onClick(DialogInterface dialog, int which) {

                    Toast.makeText(getActivity(),
                            "Clicked OK!", Toast.LENGTH_SHORT).show();

                    return;

                }

            });

            return alertDialog.create();

        }

    }


    void showDialogFragment(DialogFragment newFragment) {

        newFragment.show(getFragmentManager(), null);

    }

}
```

The full implementation of this AlertDialog, as well as many other types of dialogs, can be found in the sample code provided on the book's website.

Working with Custom Dialogs

When the Dialog types do not suit your purpose exactly, you can create a custom Dialog. One easy way to create a custom Dialog is to begin with an AlertDialog and use an AlertDialog.Builder class to override its default layout. In order to create a custom Dialog this way, the following steps must be performed:

1. Design a custom layout resource to display in the AlertDialog.
2. Define the custom Dialog identifier in the Activity or Fragment.

3. Use a `LayoutInflater` to inflate the custom layout resource for the `Dialog`.

4. Launch the `Dialog` using the `show()` method.

Figure 10.17 (bottom right) shows a custom `Dialog` implementation that accepts values into two `EditText` controls and, when `OK` is clicked, displays whether the two input values are equal.

Working with Support Package Dialog Fragments

The previous example will work only on devices that are running Android 3.0 (API Level 11) or newer. If you want your `DialogFragment` implementation to work on devices running older versions of Android, you must make a few small changes to the code. Doing so will allow your `DialogFragment` to work on devices all the way back to Android 1.6 (API Level 4).

Tip

Many of the code examples provided in this section are taken from the `SupportFragDialog` application. The source code for the `SupportFragDialog` application is provided for download on the book's website.

Let's look at a quick example of how you might implement a simple `AlertDialog`. First, import the support version of the `DialogFragment` class (`android.support.v4.app.DialogFragment`) that is part of the Support Library. Then, just as before, you need to implement your own `DialogFragment` class. This class simply needs to be able to return an instance of the object that is fully configured and it needs to implement the `onCreateDialog` method, which returns the fully configured `AlertDialog`, much as it did using the legacy method. The following code is a full implementation of a simple `DialogFragment` that manages an `AlertDialog`:

```
public class MyAlertDialogFragment extends DialogFragment {


    public static MyAlertDialogFragment

        newInstance(String fragmentNumber) {

        MyAlertDialogFragment newInstance = new MyAlertDialogFragment();

        Bundle args = new Bundle();

        args.putString("fragnum", fragmentNumber);

        newInstance.setArguments(args);

        return newInstance;

    }


    @Override
```

```
public Dialog onCreateDialog(Bundle savedInstanceState) {
    final String fragNum = getArguments().getString("fragnum");


    AlertDialog.Builder alertDialog = new AlertDialog.Builder(
        getActivity());
    alertDialog.setTitle("Alert Dialog");
    alertDialog.setMessage("This alert brought to you by "
        + fragNum );
    alertDialog.setIcon(android.R.drawable.btn_star);
    alertDialog.setPositiveButton(android.R.string.ok,
            new DialogInterface.OnClickListener() {
        @Override
        public void onClick(DialogInterface dialog, int which) {
            ((SimpleFragDialogActivity) getActivity())
                .doPositiveClick(fragNum);
            return;
        }
    });
    return alertDialog.create();
}
}
```

Now that you have defined your DialogFragment, you can use it within your
Activity much as you would any Fragment—but this time, you must use the support
version of the FragmentManager class, by calling the getSupportFragmentManager()
method.

In your Activity, you need to import two support classes for this implementation to
work: android.support.v4.app.DialogFragment and
android.support.v7.app.AppCompatActivity. Be sure to extend your Activity class
from AppCompatActivity, and not Activity as in the previous example, or your code
will not work. The AppCompatActivity class is a special class that makes fragments available with the Support Package.

The following AppCompatActivity class, called SupportFragDialogActivity, has a
layout resource that contains two Button controls, each of which triggers a new instance
of the MyAlertDialogFragment to be generated and shown. The show() method of the
DialogFragment is used to display the Dialog, adding the Fragment to the support version of the FragmentManager, and passing in a little bit of information to configure the
specific instance of the DialogFragment and its internal AlertDialog, as shown here:

```java
public class SupportFragDialogActivity extends FragmentActivity {
    @Override
    public void onCreate(Bundle savedInstanceState) {
        super.onCreate(savedInstanceState);
        setContentView(R.layout.main);

        // Handle Alert Dialog Button
        Button launchAlertDialog = (Button) findViewById(
            R.id.Button_AlertDialog);
        launchAlertDialog.setOnClickListener(new View.OnClickListener() {
            public void onClick(View v) {
                String strFragmentNumber = "Fragment Instance One";
                DialogFragment newFragment = MyAlertDialogFragment
                    .newInstance(strFragmentNumber);
                showDialogFragment(newFragment, strFragmentNumber);
            }
        });

        // Handle Alert Dialog 2 Button
        Button launchAlertDialog2 = (Button) findViewById(
            R.id.Button_AlertDialog2);
        launchAlertDialog2.setOnClickListener(new View.OnClickListener() {
            public void onClick(View v) {
                String strFragmentNumber = "Fragment Instance Two";
                DialogFragment newFragment = MyAlertDialogFragment
                    .newInstance(strFragmentNumber);
                showDialogFragment(newFragment, strFragmentNumber);
            }
        });
    }

    void showDialogFragment(DialogFragment newFragment,
            String strFragmentNumber) {
        newFragment.show(getSupportFragmentManager(), strFragmentNumber);
    }
```

```
public void doPositiveClick(String strFragmentNumber) {

    Toast.makeText(getApplicationContext(),

        "Clicked OK! (" + strFragmentNumber + ")",

        Toast.LENGTH_SHORT).show();

    }

}
```

DialogFragment instances can be traditional pop-ups (as shown in the example provided) or they can be embedded like any other Fragment. Why might you want to embed a Dialog? Consider the following example: You've created a picture-gallery application and implemented a custom Dialog that displays a larger image when you click a thumbnail. On small-screen devices, you might want this to be a pop-up Dialog, but on a tablet or TV, you might have the screen space to show the larger graphic off to the right or below the thumbnails. This would be a good opportunity to take advantage of code reuse and simply embed your Dialog.

Summary

In this chapter, you learned many different ways to develop navigation and encourage action within your application. You learned about different navigation design patterns and how to implement them, in addition to learning about how to encourage your users to take action. You should now be comfortable creating a basic architecture for your application so that your users are able to navigate two different areas of your application and take action when they have reached those particular areas.

Quiz Questions

1. What is required to perform lateral navigation between activities?
2. What must you define in your application manifest for supporting lateral, descendant, or ancestral navigation?
3. What method should you override to change the default behavior of a Back press within your application?
4. What method do you call in your Activity to support up navigation?
5. What method do you use in an Activity to hide the ActionBar?
6. True or false: When using a DialogFragment, you define the Dialog in the Activity onCreateDialog() method.
7. What is the method used to stop showing a Dialog?
8. What Dialog type should you use when creating a custom Dialog?

Exercises

1. Use the Android documentation to determine other common architectural patterns not mentioned in this chapter.

2. Use the Android documentation to determine what interface classes the
    DialogFragment class implements.

3. Create an application that is single-pane on small devices and two-pane on large
    devices. Implement a simple DialogFragment with text that displays as a Dialog on
    small devices, but on large devices, embed the Fragment into the right pane of the
    two-pane layout.

References and More Information

Android Design: Pure Android: "Confirming & Acknowledging":
http://d.android.com/design/patterns/confirming-acknowledging.html
Android Design: Pure Android: "Notifications":
http://d.android.com/design/patterns/notifications.html
Android Training: "Designing Effective Navigation":
http://d.android.com/training/design-navigation/index.html
Android Training: "Implementing Effective Navigation":
http://d.android.com/training/implementing-navigation/index.html
Android Training: "Notifying the User":
http://d.android.com/training/notify-user/index.html
Android Training: "Managing the System UI":
http://d.android.com/training/system-ui/index.html
Android API Guides: "Dialogs":
http://d.android.com/guide/topics/ui/dialogs.html
Android DialogFragment Reference: "Selecting Between Dialog or Embedding":
http://d.android.com/reference/android/app/DialogFragment.html#DialogOrEmbed

11

Appealing with Style

One aspect of Android application development that is frequently overlooked is styles and themes. With a little bit of effort, the most boring-looking application can be transformed by applying styles and themes. Understanding how styles and themes work is important because it is easy to make them overly complex when they are actually fairly simple. In this chapter, you will learn how to make use of colors, styles, and themes. An example will be presented showing the default Android styling applied to a basic layout followed by the application of color styles and themes to that same layout. You will see how performing a few actions could change the entire feel of your application, and by the end of the chapter, you should be able to apply these concepts to your own application with ease.

> **Tip**
>
> Many of the code examples provided in this chapter are taken from the `StylesAndThemes` application. The source code for this application is provided for download on the book's website (*http://introductiontoandroid.blogspot.com*).

Styling with Support

In this chapter, you will make use of two Android support libraries. To learn about adding support libraries to your application, see Appendix E, "Quick-Start: Gradle Build System." We will be adding the `appcompat-v7` support library and the design support library as Gradle module dependencies. To do so, add the following two lines to the dependencies section of the `build.gradle` app module file:

```
compile 'com.android.support:appcompat-v7:23.0.0'
compile 'com.android.support:design:23.0.0'
```

In addition, your application activities should extend the `AppCompatActivity` support class rather than `Activity`.

Themes and Styles

Although many people confuse themes and styles, they are actually two very different things. A theme is applied to an application or `Activity` as a whole, or even to a `Toolbar`, and is usually best suited for the branding of your application. A style is usually applied to one particular `View`, or a collection of similar views, rather than an entire application or `Activity`. For example, if you set the color of a particular attribute of a theme via `android:textColor`, whatever color you choose will be applied to all text in the application. However, if you apply the `textColor` attribute directly to a `TextView` that `textColor` will only be applied to that particular `TextView`. Further, if you define a style that defines the `textColor` and you apply the style to a `TextView`, only the `TextView` will have that color applied.

In this chapter, we will be working with both themes and styles. The themes reside in the `res/values/themes.xml` and `res/values-v21/themes.xml` files and the styles reside in the `res/values/styles.xml` and `res/values-v21/styles.xml` files.

Defining the Default Application Themes

We will be placing all backward-compatible themes in the `res/values/themes.xml` file, and for any styles for API Level 21 or newer, we will be placing them in the `res/values-v21/themes.xml` file. The default application theme will inherit from `Theme.AppCompat` and we will be using a `Toolbar` as the `ActionBar` so the `NoActionBar` theme must be selected. Here's how our default theme named `Brand` looks, and this is placed in the `res/values/themes.xml` file:

```
<style name="Brand" parent="Theme.AppCompat.NoActionBar"/>
```

We also need to choose the theme for the `Toolbar`, and that theme will inherit directly from `Theme.AppCompat` and is also placed in the `res/values/themes.xml` file as before. This theme will have the name of `Toolbar` and is defined as shown here:

```
<style name="Toolbar" parent="Theme.AppCompat"/>
```

Figure 11.1 shows the `StylesAndThemes` application this chapter covers with the default themes described above applied, aside from the basic positioning of the views. With the themes and styles applied, this application will look like a professionally designed application.

In Figure 11.1, you will notice an `ActionBar` at the top that we define using a `Toolbar`. There is also a main content area with multiple `TextView`'s and `EditText` views, and a bottom bar that we also define using a `Toolbar`. The bottom bar includes three icons that can be accessed from one of the icons provided with Android. You will also notice that the `ActionBar` has a menu and there is also a `FloatingActionButton` in the lower-right corner of the application. You will also notice circles to the left of the `TextView`'s and `EditText` views. These act as image placeholders and are defined using a shape drawable. Finally, you will notice an info icon to the right of the `TextView`'s and `EditText` views that we can also access from one of the icons provided with Android.

Defining a Circle-Shape Drawable

In the `StylesAndThemes` application, a circular-shaped drawable is used to act as a placeholder for something like a visually descriptive icon or image. Rather than using a circle,

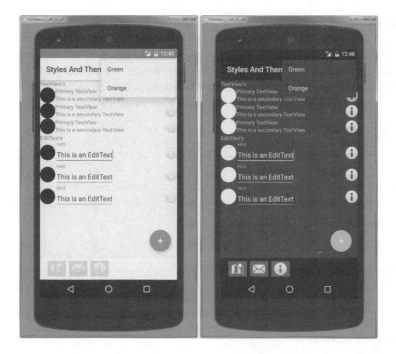

Figure 11.1   The `StylesAndThemes` application with only default themes
applied and basic positioning; the left screenshot shows a light-colored
theme, and the right shows a dark-colored theme.

you would insert your icon or image where this drawable is positioned. Here is the shape
drawable defined in the `res/drawable/circle.xml` file:

```
<?xml version="1.0" encoding="utf-8"?>

<shape xmlns:android="http://schemas.android.com/apk/res/android"

    android:shape="oval">

    <solid

        android:color="@color/circle" />

    <size

        android:width="40dp"

        android:height="40dp"/>

</shape>
```

Theme and Style Inheritance

Just like Java classes can inherit functionality from other classes, the same goes for themes
and styles. This means you can apply attributes to a theme or style, and inherit a new

theme or style from the one you defined; you can also override any existing attributes or define new attributes.

All themes for the StylesAndThemes application will inherit from the Brand or Toolbar theme that we applied earlier. There will be two themes, one Green and one Orange, but the majority of this chapter will focus on the Green theme. To create a Green theme for the application branding that inherits from Brand, add this to your themes.xml file:

```
<style name="Brand.Green" parent="Brand">

    <!-- Define your green brand theme here -->

</style>
```

To create a Green theme for the Toolbar that inherits from default Toolbar theme, add this to your themes.xml file:

```
<style name="Toolbar.Green" parent="Toolbar">

    <!-- Define your green toolbar theme here -->

</style>
```

All application theme attributes will be included in both the Brand.Green and Toolbar.Green themes seen above.

Colors

The colors for the application are defined in the res/values/colors.xml file. We talked about color resources in Chapter 6, "Managing Application Resources." To define a color, you simply add an RGB value to a color tag in the colors.xml file as shown here:

```
<color name="black">#000000</color>
```

This adds the #000000, which sets the RGB value of the color black, to a color resource named black. You may also reference defined color resources that you specify in this way:

```
<color name="circle">@color/black</color>
```

This references the black color you defined with the @color/black value and applies that color to the circle color resource. This is useful for creating a master list of colors and then referencing that specific color rather than using the RGB value all across your application, so that if you have to change the color, all you need to do is change the color in one location.

In addition, Android Studio is helpful because it shows you what color an XML element has. Figure 11.2 shows colors defined in the colors.xml file, and in the far-left column, the actual color is visible for the particular element.

Figure 11.3 shows colors applied to particular style attributes and, again, you see Android Studio displays the color applied to the attribute in the far-left column.

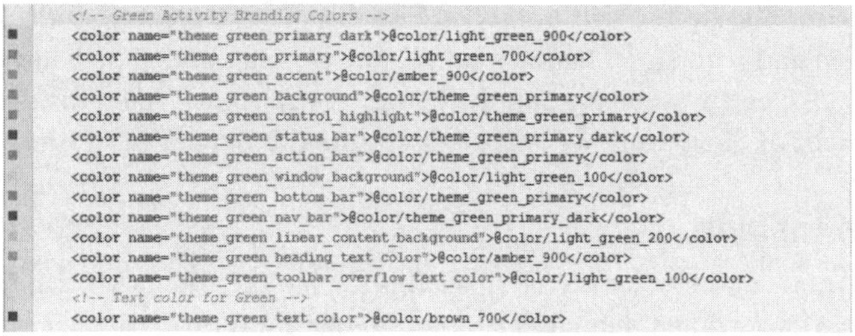

Figure 11.2   Android Studio showing the colors of color resources in the far-left column.

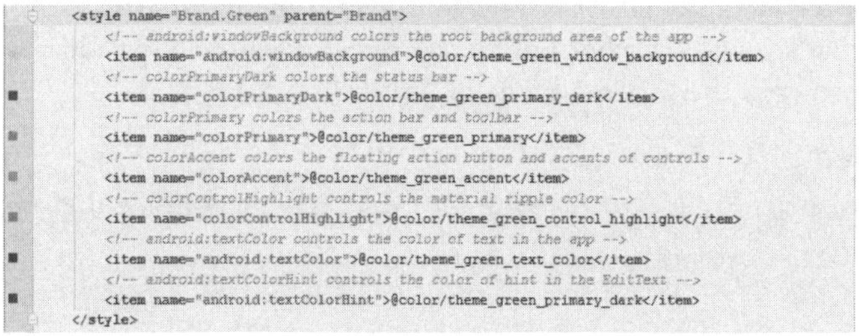

Figure 11.3   Android Studio showing the colors of style attributes in the far-left column.

There are a few theme attributes you should be aware of for color branding your application. These attributes are useful when you have chosen a color palette for styling system attributes beyond the style color attributes:

- **colorPrimary:** Colors the ActionBar.
- **colorAccent:** Colors the accent color of View controls.
- **colorPrimaryDark:** Colors the status bar.
- **colorControlHighlight:** Colors the highlight that occurs when a View is touched.
- **statusBarColor:** Colors the status bar, but this attribute is only available for API Level 21+.
- **navigationBarColor:** Colors the navigation bar; may not be definable on devices with a hardware navigation bar and is only available on devices with API Level 21+.
- **android:windowBackground:** Colors the root background area of the application.

Layout

Rather than discussing every detail of how the layouts seen in Figure 11.1 have been created, we ask that you refer to the StylesAndThemes application layout files. The activity_styles_and_themes.xml and the toolbar.xml file show the default layout

with basic positioning applied without styles. Use this file as a guide to see how this layout
has been created and compare it to, for example, the Green theme. The equivalent layout
is the activity_green_brand.xml and the green_toolbar.xml files. Instead of delving
into all the details of the layouts, we will be discussing the layouts' most notable features.

Merge and Include

You may have noticed the toolbar.xml file. This file has the root XML tag of <merge>
with a child Toolbar widget defined. The <merge> tag allows you to make reusable
components for your application. Rather than defining the same component multiple
times in a layout, you could define it once in its own file with <merge> as the root tag
and then include that layout in another layout with the <include> tag. You can also use
something like a LinearLayout or RelativeLayout as the root of the Toolbar and
then include that layout in another, but the <merge> tag will not add additional resource
consumption, whereas the LinearLayout or RelativeLayout will.

Merge Applied

Here, we show the toolbar.xml file with the Toolbar widget inside the <merge> tag:

```xml
<?xml version="1.0" encoding="utf-8"?>

<merge>

    <android.support.v7.widget.Toolbar

        xmlns:android="http://schemas.android.com/apk/res/android"

        xmlns:tools="http://schemas.android.com/tools"

        android:id="@+id/toolbar"

        android:layout_width="match_parent"

        android:layout_height="wrap_content"

        android:layout_alignParentTop="true"

        android:background="@color/default_toolbar"

        android:elevation="@dimen/highEle"

        android:minHeight="?attr/actionBarSize"

        tools:showIn="@layout/activity_styles_and_themes" />

</merge>
```

Include Applied

Here, we show the toolbar.xml included in the activity_styles_and_themes.xml file
with the include statement that references the toolbar layout:

```xml
<RelativeLayout xmlns:android="http://schemas.android.com/apk/res/android"

    xmlns:tools="http://schemas.android.com/tools"

    android:id="@+id/relative_layout"
```

```
    android:layout_width="match_parent"

    android:layout_height="match_parent"

    tools:context=".DefaultBrandActivity">


    <include layout="@layout/toolbar" />


</RelativeLayout>
```

TextInputLayout

A new widget that was added to the design support library is the TextInputLayout. This widget wraps an EditText and allows the android:hint attribute of the EditText to float above the EditText for constant viewing, rather than the hint disappearing once a user begins entering text into the EditText field. Here's an implementation of the TextInputLayout that can be found in the StylesAndThemes application:

```
<android.support.design.widget.TextInputLayout

    android:id="@+id/input_layout02"

    android:layout_width="match_parent"

    android:layout_height="wrap_content"

    android:layout_centerVertical="true"

    android:layout_toEndOf="@id/circle05">


    <EditText

        android:id="@+id/editText02"

        android:layout_width="wrap_content"

        android:layout_height="wrap_content"

        android:hint="@string/hint"

        android:text="@string/editText" />
</android.support.design.widget.TextInputLayout>
```

FloatingActionButton

The FloatingActionButton was introduced as a pattern in Chapter 10, "Architecting with Patterns." Here, you can see the FloatingActionButton defined and notice the android:elevation attribute with a value of @dimen/highEle, which is a dimension of 6dp defined in the res/values/dimens.xml file:

```
<android.support.design.widget.FloatingActionButton

    android:id="@+id/fab"
```

(Continues)

(Continued)

```
    android:layout_width="wrap_content"

    android:layout_height="wrap_content"

    android:layout_above="@+id/bottom_bar"

    android:layout_alignParentEnd="true"

    android:layout_marginBottom="@dimen/mediumdp"

    android:layout_marginEnd="@dimen/mediumdp"

    android:contentDescription="@string/fab"

    android:elevation="@dimen/highEle"

    android:src="@android:drawable/ic_input_add"

    android:tint="@color/default_fab_tint" />
```

The elevation attribute determines how much of a shadow will be applied to a particular view emphasizing the importance of that view through elevation. A 0dp elevation means there is no shadow at all and would be considered that of a background, whereas the recommended elevation for a FloatingActionButton is 6dp, alerting the user of the button's importance. FloatingActionButton's are used for emphasizing a primary action of an activity such as adding or creating, and that emphasis occurs by applying elevation.

Toolbar as Bottom Bar

On older versions of Android, you were able to split an ActionBar. This was useful if your application needed to include action items on the ActionBar where—on smaller screens—there may not be enough room for displaying all the actions you would like displayed. Rather than filling up the overflow menu with action items, you could choose to split the ActionBar so that it would appear at the bottom of the application for including the action items on the bottom bar. This same functionality can be achieved by including a Toolbar at the bottom of your application's layout.

Here, we see the Toolbar to be used as the bottom bar of the activity_styles_and_themes.xml file defined, which will appear at the bottom of the layout. Inside the Toolbar there is a LinearLayout with three ImageButton's with default Android icons applied as the android:src attribute. Here's the implementation for the Toolbar as the bottom bar:

```
<android.support.v7.widget.Toolbar

    android:id="@+id/bottom_bar"

    android:layout_width="match_parent"

    android:layout_height="wrap_content"

    android:layout_alignParentBottom="true"

    android:background="@color/default_toolbar"
```

```
        android:elevation="@dimen/midEle"
        android:minHeight="?attr/actionBarSize"
        android:theme="@style/Toolbar">

    <LinearLayout
        android:layout_width="match_parent"
        android:layout_height="match_parent"
        android:background="@color/transparent"
        android:orientation="horizontal">

        <ImageButton
            android:id="@+id/map_button"
            android:layout_width="wrap_content"
            android:layout_height="match_parent"
            android:contentDescription="@string/map"
            android:src="@android:drawable/ic_dialog_map" />

        <ImageButton
            android:id="@+id/email_button"
            android:layout_width="wrap_content"
            android:layout_height="match_parent"
            android:contentDescription="@string/email"
            android:src="@android:drawable/ic_dialog_email" />

        <ImageButton
            android:id="@+id/info_button"
            android:layout_width="wrap_content"
            android:layout_height="match_parent"
            android:contentDescription="@string/info"
            android:src="@android:drawable/ic_dialog_info" />
    </LinearLayout>
</android.support.v7.widget.Toolbar>
```

You will notice the ImageButton's laid out horizontally across the Toolbar in Figure 11.1.

Application Branding

To enhance your application's brand, you may want to consider styling a few attributes. Below is the application theme of `Brand.Green`. Notice the `android:windowBackground` attribute defined for controlling the color of the background area of the app; the `colorPrimaryDark` attribute for controlling the color of the status bar; the `colorPrimary` attribute for controlling the color of the `ActionBar/Toolbar`; the `colorAccent` attribute for coloring the control accents; the `colorControlHighlight` attribute for controlling the highlight color; the `android:textColor` attribute for controlling the color of text in the application; and the `android:textColorHint` color for controlling the color of the `TextInputLayout` label from the `hint` attribute of the `EditText`:

```
<style name="Brand.Green" parent="Brand">

    <!-- android:windowBackground colors the root background area of the app -->

    <item name="android:windowBackground">@color/theme_green_window_background</item>

    <!-- colorPrimaryDark colors the status bar -->

    <item name="colorPrimaryDark">@color/theme_green_primary_dark</item>

    <!-- colorPrimary colors the action bar and toolbar -->

    <item name="colorPrimary">@color/theme_green_primary</item>

    <!-- colorAccent colors the floating action button and accents of controls -->

    <item name="colorAccent">@color/theme_green_accent</item>

    <!-- colorControlHighlight controls the material ripple color -->

    <item name="colorControlHighlight">@color/theme_green_control_highlight</item>

    <!-- android:textColor controls the color of text in the app -->

    <item name="android:textColor">@color/theme_green_text_color</item>

    <!-- android:textColorHint controls the color of hint in the EditText -->

    <item name="android:textColorHint">@color/theme_green_primary_dark</item>

</style>
```

Here is the `Toolbar.Green` theme. Notice the `colorBackground` attribute is defined for controlling the overflow menu color. The `textColorPrimary` attribute controls the `Toolbar` title color, the `textColorSecondary` attribute controls the overflow icon color, and that `textColor` attribute controls the `Toolbar` text color—in this case—the color of the text in the overflow menu:

```
<style name="Toolbar.Green" parent="Toolbar">

    <!-- toolbar overflow background color controlled with colorBackground -->

    <item name="android:colorBackground">@color/theme_green_accent</item>

    <!-- toolbar title color controlled with textColorPrimary-->

    <item name="android:textColorPrimary">@color/theme_green_text_color</item>

    <!-- toolbar overflow icon color controlled with textColorSecondary -->
```

```
<item name="android:textColorSecondary">@color/theme_green_text_color</item>

<!-- toolbar overflow text color controlled with textColor -->

<item name="android:textColor">@color/theme_green_toolbar_overflow_text_
color</item>

</style>
```

To apply the `Brand.Green` theme, simply add it to the `android:theme` attribute of the `<application>` tag for global application styling, or the `<activity>` tag for a given `Activity` to style just that `Activity`. The code here shows applying the `Brand.Green` theme to the `GreenBrandActivity`:

```
<activity

    android:name="com.introtoandroid.stylesandthemes.GreenBrandActivity"

    android:label="@string/title_activity_green_brand"

    android:theme="@style/Brand.Green"/>
```

To apply the `Toolbar.Green` theme to a `Toolbar`, simply add it to the `android:theme` attribute of the `Toolbar`. The code here shows the application of the `Toolbar.Green` theme to the `Toolbar` widget of the `green_toolbar.xml` file:

```
android:background="@color/theme_green_primary "

android:theme="@style/Toolbar.Green"
```

Note that we have applied a `background` color to the `Toolbar` to help control the branding.

Dividers and Gaps

Another technique for creating visually appealing applications is to use dividers and gaps within your content layout. Dividers are small, 1-dp wide lines that appear to create visual divisions between content. Gaps are larger, sometimes 8dp, and make use of what's known as a white space for creating divisions in layouts. The `StylesAndThemes` application makes use of both dividers and gaps. Here is a divider:

```
<View

    android:background="@color/layout_divider_color"

    android:layout_width="match_parent"

    android:layout_height="1dp"

    android:alpha="0.1"/>
```

And here is a gap:

```
<View

    android:background="@android:color/transparent"

    android:layout_width="match_parent"

    android:layout_height="8dp"/>
```

The gap uses a background value of `transparent` so that the `android:windowBack ground` color shows through.

The `StylesAndThemes` application makes use of multiple dividers. Rather than applying these attributes directly to every single `View` that represents a divider, for example, a single divider style could be defined in the `styles.xml` file as shown here:

```xml
<style name="LayoutDivider">

    <item name="android:background">@color/layout_divider_color</item>

    <item name="android:layout_width">match_parent</item>

    <item name="android:layout_height">@dimen/divider</item>

    <item name="android:alpha">0.1</item>

</style>
```

Then, in your layout, you would only need to add a single line of code to achieve the same result. This is a great way to reuse code rather than repeating the same code everywhere. When you need to change how the style looks, you only have to make one change in the defined style, rather than having to update every single `View` in the layout. Here is the previously defined style applied to a `View` that acts as a divider:

```xml
<View style="@style/LayoutDivider" />
```

Menu

Another way to provide branding to your application is to style any menus that your application displays. Menus overlay other UI elements, so it is important that, in addition to complementary colors, any colors you apply to a menu have the proper contrast to your application's theme.

The Results Applied

Now that you've seen how to implement themes and styles for your application and its activities and views, it would be nice to see the result of those styles when applied. If you are not able to see this application in color, that's okay—effort has been made to make these themes and styles accessible with proper contrast when viewed in black and white. If you run the styles and themes application on your own device or emulator, you should be able to see the colors applied. If you're looking at the resulting image in this book in black and white, you'll see the difference in how the use of space has given this layout a much-needed facelift compared to that of the same layout seen in Figure 11.1. Figure 11.4 shows the results of those themes and styles applied to the `GreenBrandActivity`.

Typography

Another way to make your application stand out is to make use of different fonts. Fonts can provide attitude to your application. Some fonts may be more appropriate for serious applications such as business or finance, where other fonts may be more appropriate

Figure 11.4   The `GreenBrandActivity` layout
with themes and styles applied.

for more fun and easy-going themes such as a children's app or game. Here, we apply the
casual font to the `android:fontFamily` to various styles:

```
<style name="HeadingOrange">

    <item name="android:fontFamily">casual</item>

</style>


<style name="PrimaryTextViewOrange">

    <item name="android:fontFamily">casual</item>

</style>


<style name="SecondaryTextViewOrange">

    <item name="android:fontFamily">casual</item>

</style>


<style name="EditTextOrange">

    <item name="android:fontFamily">casual</item>

</style>
```

Figure 11.5   The casual font is applied to the
OrangeBrandActivity layout.

Figure 11.5 shows the casual font providing a more laid-back feel to the application.

Summary

In this chapter, you learned about the power of themes and styles, and how they can make even the most boring-looking application a visual stunner. You learned about applying themes and styles to your application's activities and views. You learned about style inheritance, merging and including layouts, and how to create application branding by using colors and applying those colors to particular attributes. You should now be capable of applying your own themes and styles to your applications.

Quiz Questions

1. True or false: Theme.Compat should be used for providing backward-compatible themes for your application.

2. What system attribute is colorPrimary used to color?

3. Which attributes are used for coloring the status bar?

4. True or false: The <insert> tag is used to include one layout inside another.

5. What View widget is useful for creating a bottom bar?

Exercises

1. In the Android API guide, "Styles and Themes," read the section "Style Properties" to learn more about styling properties for views here: *http://developer.android.com/guide/topics/ui/themes.html#Properties.*

2. Modify the StylesAndThemes application to include buttons; to style those buttons, follow the Android API guide "Styling Your Button" here: *http://d.android.com/guide/topics/ui/controls/button.html#Style.*

3. Modify the StylesAndThemes application to trigger a Dialog that displays when a TextView is clicked. Style the Dialog accordingly using the provided colors.

References and More Information

Android Training: "Maintaining Compatibility": "Define Alternative Styles":
http://d.android.com/training/material/compatibility.html#Theme
Android Training: "Styling the Action Bar":
http://developer.android.com/training/appbar/index.html
Android Training: Supporting Different Platform Versions: "Use Platform Styles and Themes":
http://d.android.com/training/basics/supporting-devices/platforms.html#style-themes
Android Training: "Using the Material Theme": "Customize the Color Palette":
http://d.android.com/training/material/theme.html#ColorPalette
Android Training: "Re-using Layouts with <include/>":
http://d.android.com/training/improving-layouts/reusing-layouts.html
Google Design Spec: "Style": "Color":
http://www.google.com/design/spec/style/color.html
Google Design Spec: "Style": "Imagery":
http://www.google.com/design/spec/style/imagery.html
Google Design Spec: "Style": "Typography":
http://www.google.com/design/spec/style/typography.html
Android API Guides: "Buttons": "Styling Your Button":
http://d.android.com/guide/topics/ui/controls/button.html#Style
Android API Guides: "Menus":
http://d.android.com/guide/topics/ui/menus.html
Android API Guides: "Styles and Themes":
http://d.android.com/guide/topics/ui/themes.html
Android API Guides: "Styles Resource":
http://d.android.com/guide/topics/resources/style-resource.html
Android SDK Reference regarding the application R.style class:
http://d.android.com/reference/android/R.style.html
Android SDK Reference regarding the application android.text.style package:
http://developer.android.com/reference/android/text/style/package-summary.html
Android SDK Reference regarding the application Resources.Theme class:
http://d.android.com/reference/android/content/res/Resources.Theme.html

12

Embracing Material Design

Android 5.0 API level 21 introduced the concept known as material design. Material design is an attempt by Google to create a standard for design and development of applications, and not just for Android. Material design is a specification—a set of rules that should remain standard across different platforms. Material design is branded as a visual language that is aimed at guiding designers and developers for using the best practices of visual, interaction, and motion design. Development using the material design concepts is platform specific, meaning the native Android material code you write for your Android application will not work for a Web application that is coded in HTML and JavaScript. In this chapter, we will introduce the Android development side of material design and how you can make your application use the material theme and APIs provided. By the end of the chapter, you should be comfortable implementing the most common material design tasks for Android application development.

Understanding Material

The material design standard is a specification that can be applied across platforms. Although it is a specification, that does not mean you must abide by all its rules—some of those rules may become outdated or replaced by better rules. It is meant to be a guideline and not a hard-and-fast means for dictating how you should design your application. With that said, the material specification provides many recommendations of best practices that Google has discovered. The development of material design is specific to the platform, and for Android there are specific APIs that help you add and implement material design in your application. In this chapter, you will be learning about the following material development concepts:

- Material Theme (`@android:style/Theme.Material` and `@style/Theme.AppCompat`)
- Lists and Cards (`RecyclerView` and `CardView`)
- View Shadows (`android:elevation`)
- Animations (circular reveal and `Activity` transitions)

> **Tip**
>
> The code example provided in this section is taken from the `SampleMaterial` application. The source code for this application is provided for download on the book's website (*http://introductiontoandroid.blogspot.com*).

The Default Material Theme

To get started working with material design in your Android application, you first need to make sure the Material theme is applied to your `styles.xml` file found in the `res/values/styles/` directory. We covered styles and themes in Chapter 11, "Appealing with Style." When targeting Android API Level 21 and higher, the default style applied to your Android application during project creation should be as follows:

```
<style name="AppTheme" parent="@android:style/Theme.Material"/>
```

The `SampleMaterial` Application

The `SampleMaterial` application demonstrates how to populate a list of names into the new `RecyclerView`. The `RecyclerView` is the recommended replacement for the `ListView` control. A `RecyclerView` allows you to add a very large number of items while still being able to scroll efficiently without slowing the user interface. This application also makes use of the new `CardView` that allows you to add rounded corners and shadows to the card, which may hold one or more views.

A `RecyclerView` is used for the list and a `CardView` is used for grouping `View` widgets together—each card represents a name, and names can be added, updated, and deleted from the list in their own card. When you scroll the list, each card will animate onto the screen using the new circular reveal animation. In addition, you are able to add a new card by clicking the `FloatingActionButton`, which makes use of the new material transition effects to transition the `FloatingActionButton` into the next Activity using a smooth animation. Figure 12.1 shows what the `SampleMaterial` application looks like after launching.

Implementing the `SampleMaterial` Application

This section will provide an in-depth explanation of how to implement various material concepts found in the `SampleMaterial` application. You will start by performing simple configurations, providing the required data, implementing the appropriate views, and coding the functionality. Let's get started!

Dependencies

For the `SampleMaterial` application, you will be using the material theme supplied with the support libraries. In addition, you will make use of various other support libraries that

Figure 12.1   The `SampleMaterial` application.

allow material components to work on versions of Android older than API Level 21. To add these dependencies, place the following lines in your `build.gradle` app module file in the dependencies section:

```
compile 'com.android.support:design:23.0.0'
compile 'com.android.support:appcompat-v7:23.0.0'
compile 'com.android.support:cardview-v7:23.0.0'
compile 'com.android.support:recyclerview-v7:23.0.0'
```

You are now set up to make use of material in your application. To learn more about Gradle and adding dependencies to your application, please see Appendix E, "Quick-Start: Gradle Build System."

Material Support Styles

The first thing you should do is make sure the Material theme support library is used for styling your application. In your `res/values/styles.xml`, replace the existing style with the following:

```
<style name="BaseTheme" parent="Theme.AppCompat.Light.DarkActionBar"/>
<style name="AppTheme" parent="BaseTheme"/>
```

In your `res/values-v21/styles.xml` file, replace the existing style with the following:

```
<style name="AppTheme" parent="BaseTheme"/>
```

Also, make sure that your `AndroidManifest.xml` file has this theme applied in the `<application>` tag as shown here:

```
android:theme="@style/AppTheme"
```

Showing the Dataset in the List

The first thing you want to do is show a list of names, initials, and colors associated with each `CardView` of the `RecyclerView`. To do so, you need to define those colors and names in your resource files.

Color Resources

In your `colors.xml` file, you want to define colors by their RGB values, provide a name for each color, and then create an `<integer-array>` with the name of `initial_colors` so that you can load the colors into your application code; you will learn how to do this in a later section of this chapter. Here is a sample of the `colors.xml` file:

```
<resources>

    <item name="blue" type="color">#2196f3</item>

    <item name="purple" type="color">#9c27b0</item>

    <item name="green" type="color">#1b5e20</item>

    <item name="orange" type="color">#ff5722</item>

    <item name="red" type="color">#f44336</item>

    <item name="indigo" type="color">#3f51b5</item>

    <item name="deep_purple" type="color">#673ab7</item>

    <item name="light_green" type="color">#689f38</item>

    <item name="teal" type="color">#009688</item>

    <item name="pink" type="color">#e91e63</item>


    <integer-array name="initial_colors">

        <item>@color/blue</item>

        <item>@color/purple</item>

        <item>@color/green</item>

        <item>@color/orange</item>

        <item>@color/red</item>

        <item>@color/indigo</item>
```

```xml
            <item>@color/deep_purple</item>

            <item>@color/light_green</item>

            <item>@color/teal</item>

            <item>@color/pink</item>

            <!-- more colors here -->

        </integer-array>

</resources>
```

String Resources

In your `strings.xml` file, you want to define a `<string-array>` with the name of `names_array` so that you can load the names into your application for each card. Here is a sample of the `strings.xml` file:

```xml
<resources>

    <string-array name="names_array">

        <item>Michael</item>

        <item>Jennifer</item>

        <item>Christopher</item>

        <item>Amy</item>

        <item>Jason</item>

        <item>Melissa</item>

        <item>David</item>

        <item>Michelle</item>

        <item>James</item>

        <item>Kimberly</item>

        <!-- more names here -->

    </string-array>

</resources>
```

Layout Resources

First, you need to create the main layout for the application. This layout will be a `RelativeLayout` and have two children views, a `RecyclerView` and a `FloatingActionButton`. Here are the contents of the `activity_sample_material.xml` layout file:

```xml
<RelativeLayout xmlns:android="http://schemas.android.com/apk/res/android"

    xmlns:tools="http://schemas.android.com/tools"

    android:layout_width="match_parent"

    android:layout_height="match_parent"
```

(Continues)

(Continued)

```
    android:paddingBottom="@dimen/activity_vertical_margin"
    android:paddingLeft="@dimen/activity_horizontal_margin"
    android:paddingRight="@dimen/activity_horizontal_margin"
    android:paddingTop="@dimen/activity_vertical_margin"
    tools:context=".SampleMaterialActivity">


    <android.support.v7.widget.RecyclerView
        android:id="@+id/recycler_view"
        android:layout_width="match_parent"
        android:layout_height="match_parent"
        android:scrollbars="vertical" />


    <android.support.design.widget.FloatingActionButton
        android:id="@+id/fab"
        android:layout_width="wrap_content"
        android:layout_height="wrap_content"
        android:layout_alignParentBottom="true"
        android:layout_alignParentEnd="true"
        android:layout_marginBottom="25dp"
        android:layout_marginEnd="25dp"
        android:clickable="true"
        android:contentDescription="@string/fab"
        android:elevation="6dp"
        android:src="@android:drawable/ic_input_add"
        android:transitionName="fab_transition"
        android:tint="@android:color/white" />


</RelativeLayout>
```

The RecyclerView defines the android:scrollbars attribute and sets the value to vertical, which allows the list to scroll vertically. The FloatingActionButton positions the button in the lower-right corner of the application, sets the android:elevation to 6dp so that the button appears to be floating above the layout, and provides the value of fab_transition for the android:transition name attribute that we will be using later for implementing the Activity transition.

Extending from `AppCompatActivity`

This application will also make use of the `AppCompatActivity` class for supporting material `Activity` APIs found in the `appcompat-v7` support library. Rather than your `SampleMaterialActivity` class extending the `Activity` class, have your application extend the `AppCompatActivity` class. The `onCreate()` method of this `Activity` starts as follows:

```
@Override
protected void onCreate(Bundle savedInstanceState) {
    super.onCreate(savedInstanceState);
    setContentView(R.layout.activity_sample_material);

    names = getResources().getStringArray(R.array.names_array);
    colors = getResources().getIntArray(R.array.initial_colors);

    initCards();

    if (adapter == null) {
        adapter = new SampleMaterialAdapter(this, cardsList);
    }
    recyclerView = (RecyclerView) findViewById(R.id.recycler_view);
    recyclerView.setAdapter(adapter);
    recyclerView.setLayoutManager(new LinearLayoutManager(this));

    // other functionality implemented here
}
```

The content view is set to the layout you defined previously, and that loads in the `names_array` and `initial_colors` array. The `initCards()` method then initializes the cards with the names and colors that you will see later in this chapter. An adapter is created and receives the list of cards, followed by setting the adapter to the `RecyclerView`.

Card Data Object

In order to make working with a card easy, you should create a `Card` data object for encapsulating the information of each `Card`. The `Card` data object is in the `card.java` file and is implemented like this:

```
public class Card {
    private long id;
    private String name;
```

(Continues)

(Continued)

```
    private int color_resource;

    public long getId() { return id; }

    public void setId(long id) { this.id = id; }

    public String getName() { return name; }

    public void setName(String name) { this.name = name; }

    public int getColorResource() { return color_resource;}

    public void setColorResource(int color_resource) {
        this.color_resource = color_resource;
    }
}
```

Each `Card` has three variables—an `id`, a `name`, and a `color_resource`—and getter and setter methods have also been included.

Initialize Cards

The `initCards()` method introduced earlier is implemented as follows:

```
private void initCards() {
    for (int i = 0; i < 50; i++) {
        Card card = new Card();
        card.setId((long) i);
        card.setName(names[i]);
        card.setColorResource(colors[i]);
        Log.d(DEBUG_TAG, "Card id " + card.getId() + ", name " +
                card.getName() + ", color " + card.getColorResource());
        cardsList.add(card);
    }
}
```

This method performs 50 iterations and makes 50 cards, each with an `id`, `name`, and `color_resource`, and adds each `Card` to the `cardsList` variable, which is defined as `ArrayList<Card>`.

Implementing the `RecyclerView` Adapter

Now that we have our data set, we need to bind this data to the `RecyclerView` so that the data can be made available to the layout. To do that, we use the `RecyclerView.Adapter` class that has been implemented in the `SampleMaterialAdapter.java` file as shown here:

```java
public class SampleMaterialAdapter extends
        RecyclerView.Adapter<SampleMaterialAdapter.ViewHolder> {
    private static final String DEBUG_TAG = "SampleMaterialAdapter";

    public Context context;
    public ArrayList<Card> cardsList;

    public SampleMaterialAdapter(Context context, ArrayList<Card> cardsList) {
        this.context = context;
        this.cardsList = cardsList;
    }

    @Override
    public int getItemCount() {
        if (cardsList.isEmpty()) {
            return 0;
        } else {
            return cardsList.size();
        }
    }

    @Override
    public long getItemId(int position) {
        return cardsList.get(position).getId();
    }

    @Override
    public ViewHolder onCreateViewHolder(ViewGroup viewGroup, int i) {
        LayoutInflater li = LayoutInflater.from(viewGroup.getContext());
        View v = li.inflate(R.layout.card_view_holder, viewGroup, false);
        return new ViewHolder(v);
    }
```

(Continues)

(Continued)

```
    @Override
    public void onBindViewHolder(ViewHolder viewHolder, int position) {
        String name = cardsList.get(position).getName();
        int color = cardsList.get(position).getColorResource();
        TextView initial = viewHolder.initial;
        TextView nameTextView = viewHolder.name;
        nameTextView.setText(name);
        initial.setBackgroundColor(color);
        initial.setText(Character.toString(name.charAt(0)));
    }


    // ViewHolder implemented here
}
```

The `SampleMaterialAdapter` class has an attribute for holding the list of cards in a `cardsList` variable. Notice a few method overrides in this class: the `getItemCount()` method returns the size of the `cardsList`, the `getItemId()` method returns the id of a particular `Card`, the `onCreateViewHolder()` method inflates the `card_view_holder` layout, and the `onBindViewHolder()` method binds the data set to the views found in the `card_view_holder` layout. This layout can be found in the `card_view_holder.xml` file and is defined here:

```
<?xml version="1.0" encoding="utf-8"?>
<android.support.v7.widget.CardView xmlns:android="http://schemas.android.com/
apk/res/android"
    xmlns:card_view="http://schemas.android.com/apk/res-auto"
    android:id="@+id/card_layout"
    android:layout_width="match_parent"
    android:layout_height="match_parent"
    android:layout_margin="3dp"
    android:clickable="true"
    android:foreground="?android:attr/selectableItemBackground"
    android:orientation="vertical"
    card_view:cardCornerRadius="10dp">

    <LinearLayout
        android:layout_width="match_parent"
        android:layout_height="match_parent"
```

```
    android:id="@+id/linear"
    android:background="@android:color/white"
    android:orientation="vertical"
    android:transitionName="layout_transition"
    android:padding="@dimen/padding">

    <TextView
        android:id="@+id/initial"
        android:layout_width="match_parent"
        android:layout_height="match_parent"
        android:gravity="center"
        android:transitionName="initial_transition"
        android:textColor="@android:color/white"
        android:textSize="@dimen/initial_size" />

    <LinearLayout
        android:layout_width="match_parent"
        android:layout_height="match_parent"
        android:background="@android:color/white"
        android:orientation="horizontal">

        <Button
            android:id="@+id/delete_button"
            android:layout_width="wrap_content"
            android:layout_height="match_parent"
            android:transitionName="delete_button_transition"
            android:text="@string/delete_button" />

        <TextView
            android:id="@+id/name"
            android:layout_width="match_parent"
            android:layout_height="wrap_content"
            android:transitionName="name_transition"
            android:textColor="@android:color/black"
            android:textSize="@dimen/text_size" />
    </LinearLayout>
```

(Continues)

(Continued)

```
    </LinearLayout>
</android.support.v7.widget.CardView>
```

The card_view_layout.xml file includes a CardView widget. The CardView includes a TextView for showing the initial of the name, a delete Button for deleting a Card, and a TextView for showing the name. The CardView also has two attributes defined; the first is android:clickable, which is set to true, and the second is android:foreground, which has the value of ?android:attr/selectableItemBackground. These attributes allow a CardView to listen for click events.

Implementing a `ViewHolder`

You need a way to encapsulate the information contained in each CardView of the RecyclerView, and the way to do that is by using the ViewHolder class of a RecyclerView. This class is defined inside the adapter shown earlier in this chapter. Here is the ViewHolder implementation that provides access to an itemView, and in this case, the itemView is equivalent to a CardView and its children:

```java
public class ViewHolder extends RecyclerView.ViewHolder {

    private TextView initial;

    private TextView name;

    private Button deleteButton;


    public ViewHolder(View v) {

        super(v);

        initial = (TextView) v.findViewById(R.id.initial);

        name = (TextView) v.findViewById(R.id.name);

        deleteButton = (Button) v.findViewById(R.id.delete_button);


        deleteButton.setOnClickListener(new View.OnClickListener() {

            // onClick implemented here

        });


        itemView.setOnClickListener(new View.OnClickListener() {

            // onClick implemented here

        });

    }

}
```

The `ViewHolder` defines a `TextView` for the `initial`, a `TextView` for the name, and a `Button` for the `deleteButton`.

Scrolling Animation with Circular Reveal

When each `Card` appears on the screen, the `Card` animates using the circular reveal animation that was added in API Level 21 in the `ViewAnimationUtils` class. Here is the `animateCircularReveal()` implementation using the animation that takes a `View` as input—in this case it will be a `CardView`:

```
public void animateCircularReveal(View view) {

    int centerX = 0;

    int centerY = 0;

    int startRadius = 0;

    int endRadius = Math.max(view.getWidth(), view.getHeight());

    Animator animation = ViewAnimationUtils.createCircularReveal(view,

            centerX, centerY, startRadius, endRadius);

    view.setVisibility(View.VISIBLE);

    animation.start();

}
```

The animation will begin in the upper-left corner of the `CardView` and will perform a circular reveal from that position, revealing the entire `Card` as the `RecyclerView` is scrolled. To make this work, you need to override the `onViewAttachedToWindow()` method to access the `ViewHolder` and pass the `itemView` of the `ViewHolder` to the `animateCircularReveal()` method as shown here:

```
@Override
public void onViewAttachedToWindow(ViewHolder viewHolder) {

    super.onViewAttachedToWindow(viewHolder);

    animateCircularReveal(viewHolder.itemView);

}
```

Figure 12.2 shows screenshots of the animation that reveals a particular card during scrolling. Because we can't show the animation here, we have included multiple screenshots.

Add Card Primary Action

Now that you know how to populate the list and animate during a scroll, you should learn how to add a new `Card` to the list. The `FloatingActionButton` must be configured to launch a new `Activity` for adding a new `Card`. Figure 12.3 shows the `FloatingActionButton`.

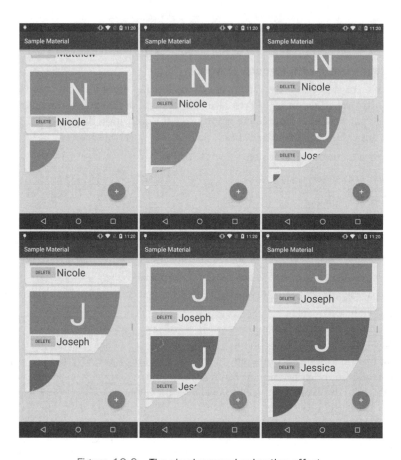

Figure 12.2   The circular reveal animation effect.

Figure 12.3   Primary action `FloatingActionButton` for
adding a new `Card`.

To configure the `FloatingActionButton`, simply add an `OnClickListener`
to the `FloatingActionButton` implemented in the `onCreate()` method of the
`SampleMaterialActivity` class as shown here:

```
FloatingActionButton fab = (FloatingActionButton) findViewById(R.id.fab);

fab.setOnClickListener(new View.OnClickListener() {

    @Override

    public void onClick(View v) {

        Pair<View, String> pair = Pair.create(v.findViewById(R.id.fab),

TRANSITION_FAB);


        ActivityOptionsCompat options;

        Activity act = SampleMaterialActivity.this;

        options = ActivityOptionsCompat.makeSceneTransitionAnimation(act, pair);


        Intent transitionIntent = new Intent(act, TransitionAddActivity.class);

        act.startActivityForResult(transitionIntent, adapter.getItemCount(),

options.toBundle());

    }

});
```

If you remember the `android:transitionName` attribute with a value of
`fab_transition` defined for the `FloatingActionButton`, the `OnClickListener` shown
above implements the transition animation. This is implemented with the
`ActivityOptionsCompat.makeSceneTransitionAnimation()` method. An `Intent` is
defined for launching the `TransitionAddActivity` class, which is launched with the
`startActivityForResult()` method passing in the size of the `adapter` with
`adapter.getItemCount()` so that a new `Card` can be added to the end of the list.

To complete the transition, a layout must be defined for the `TransitionAddActivity`
class. Here is the `activity_transition_add.xml` layout that receives the transition from
the `FloatingActionButton`:

```
<LinearLayout xmlns:android="http://schemas.android.com/apk/res/android"

    xmlns:tools="http://schemas.android.com/tools"

    android:id="@+id/linear"

    android:layout_width="match_parent"

    android:layout_height="match_parent"

    android:background="@android:color/white"

    android:orientation="vertical"

    android:padding="@dimen/padding"

    android:paddingBottom="@dimen/activity_vertical_margin"

    android:paddingLeft="@dimen/activity_horizontal_margin"
```

(Continues)

(*Continued*)

```
        android:paddingRight="@dimen/activity_horizontal_margin"
        android:paddingTop="@dimen/activity_vertical_margin"
        android:transitionName="fab_transition"
        tools:context="com.introtoandroid.samplematerial.TransitionAddActivity">

        <TextView
            android:id="@+id/initial"
            android:layout_width="match_parent"
            android:layout_height="0dp"
            android:layout_weight="1"
            android:gravity="center"
            android:textColor="@android:color/white"
            android:textSize="@dimen/initial_size" />

        <LinearLayout
            android:layout_width="match_parent"
            android:layout_height="0dp"
            android:layout_weight="1"
            android:background="@android:color/white"
            android:orientation="vertical">

            <EditText
                android:id="@+id/name"
                android:layout_width="match_parent"
                android:layout_height="wrap_content"
                android:inputType="textCapSentences"
                android:textColor="@android:color/black"
                android:textSize="@dimen/text_size" />

            <LinearLayout
                android:layout_width="match_parent"
                android:layout_height="wrap_content"
                android:background="@android:color/white"
                android:orientation="horizontal">
```

```
<Button

    android:id="@+id/add_button"

    android:layout_width="wrap_content"

    android:layout_height="wrap_content"

    android:text="@string/add_button" />

    </LinearLayout>

  </LinearLayout>

</LinearLayout>
```

The root `LinearLayout` shown above defines the `android:transitionName` attribute with a value of `fab_transition` to keep track of which views are animated during the transition. This animates the `FloatingActionButton` to transition into the `TransitionAddActivity`. Figure 12.4 shows multiple screenshots of the transition occurring over time. Notice the `FloatingActionButton` in the top-left screenshot, and in the top right, the `FloatingActionButton` appears to be transitioning. In the bottom-left screenshot, all the way to the bottom-right screenshot, you see the transition complete.

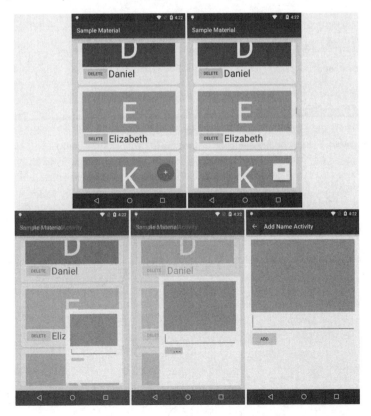

Figure 12.4   `FloatingActionButton` transition.

Inserting a New Card

Now the `TransitionAddActivity` class must be implemented. Here's the `onCreate()` method of the `Activity`:

```java
public class TransitionAddActivity extends AppCompatActivity {

    private EditText nameEditText;

    private TextView initialTextView;

    private int color;

    private Intent intent;

    private Random randomGenerator = new Random();

    @Override
    protected void onCreate(Bundle savedInstanceState) {
        super.onCreate(savedInstanceState);
        setContentView(R.layout.activity_transition_add);

        nameEditText = (EditText) findViewById(R.id.name);
        initialTextView = (TextView) findViewById(R.id.initial);
        Button add_button = (Button) findViewById(R.id.add_button);

        intent = getIntent();
        int[] colors = getResources().getIntArray(R.array.initial_colors);
        color = colors[randomGenerator.nextInt(50)];

        initialTextView.setText("");
        initialTextView.setBackgroundColor(color);

        nameEditText.addTextChangedListener(new TextWatcher() {
            @Override
            public void onTextChanged(CharSequence s, int start, int before, int
count) {
                if (count == 0) {
                    // add initialTextView
                    initialTextView.setText("");
                } else if (count == 1) {
                    // initialTextView set to first letter of nameEditText and
add name stringExtra
```

```java
                    initialTextView.setText(String.valueOf(s.charAt(0)));
                }
            }

            @Override
            public void beforeTextChanged(CharSequence s, int start, int count,
int after) {
            }

            @Override
            public void afterTextChanged(Editable s) {
            }
        });

        add_button.setOnClickListener(new View.OnClickListener() {
            @Override
            public void onClick(View v) {
                // must not be zero otherwise do not finish activity and report
Toast message
                String text = initialTextView.getText().toString().trim();
                if (TextUtils.isEmpty(text)) {
                    Toast.makeText(getApplicationContext(),
                            "Enter a valid name", Toast.LENGTH_SHORT).show();
                } else {
                    intent.putExtra(SampleMaterialActivity.EXTRA_NAME,
                            String.valueOf(nameEditText.getText()));
                    intent.putExtra(SampleMaterialActivity.EXTRA_INITIAL,
                            String.valueOf(nameEditText.getText().charAt(0)));
                    intent.putExtra(SampleMaterialActivity.EXTRA_COLOR, color);
                    setResult(RESULT_OK, intent);
                    supportFinishAfterTransition();
                }
            }
        });
    }
}
```

The method above loads the `activity_transition_add.xml` layout and configures an `OnClickListener` for the `add_button`, and it also implements a method for monitoring what `initial` to display when a user enters a name in the `EditText` field. When the `add_button` is clicked, there is a check to make sure the `EditText` field is not empty and, if there is a value for the `name`, the `initial`, and `color`, the new `Card` is passed back to the calling `Activity` with the `setResult()` method; the transition is then completed by calling the `supportFinishAfterTransition()` method. This method is required to perform the scene transition after finishing, and navigates the user back to the previous `Activity`. If you were to call the normal `finish()` method to complete the `Activity`, there would be no scene transition, so the `supportFinishAfterTransition()` method is required.

Completing the Transition and Reveal

The `SampleMaterialActivity` class must implement the `onActivityResult()` method to receive the resulting values of the `TransitionAddActivity`. Here is how the new Card is added to the list:

```
@Override
protected void onActivityResult(int requestCode, int resultCode, Intent data) {
    super.onActivityResult(requestCode, resultCode, data);

    Log.d(DEBUG_TAG, "requestCode is " + requestCode);
    // if adapter.getItemCount() is request code,
    // that means we are adding a new position
    // anything less than adapter.getItemCount()
    // means we are editing a particular position
    if (requestCode == adapter.getItemCount()) {
        if (resultCode == RESULT_OK) {
            // Make sure the Add request was successful
            // if add name, insert name in list
            String name = data.getStringExtra(EXTRA_NAME);
            int color = data.getIntExtra(EXTRA_COLOR, 0);
            adapter.addCard(name, color);
        }
    } else {
        // Anything other than adapter.getItemCount()
        // means editing a particular list item
        // the requestCode is the list item position
        if (resultCode == RESULT_OK) {
```

```
        // implement edit here

    }

  }

}
```

If the `requestCode` is the same value as the `adapter.getItemCount()` method, that means that the user is adding a new `Card`. This is where the new `Card` will be added and the name and `color` are passed to the `addCard()` method of the `adapter` to add the `Card`. Here is the `addCard()` method of the `SampleMaterialAdapter` class:

```
public void addCard(String name, int color) {

    Card card = new Card();

    card.setName(name);

    card.setColorResource(color);

    card.setId(getItemCount());

    cardsList.add(card);

    ((SampleMaterialActivity) context).doSmoothScroll(getItemCount());

    notifyItemInserted(cardsList.size());

}
```

This method simply creates a new `Card` data object, sets the `name`, the `color`, and the `id`, adds the `Card` to the `cardsList`, and then executes the `doSmoothScroll()` method of the calling `SampleMaterialActivity` context. This passes in the result of `getItemCount()` to determine where in the list to scroll to, and then calls the `notifyItemInserted()` method of the `RecyclerView.Adapter` class to update the `RecyclerView` and inform the `View` that a new item has been inserted. The `doSmoothScroll()` method then smoothly scrolls the `RecyclerView` list to the newly inserted item. Here is the `doSmoothScroll()` method implementation of the `SampleMaterialActivity` class:

```
public void doSmoothScroll(int position) {

    recyclerView.smoothScrollToPosition(position);

}
```

This code calls the `smoothScrollToPosition()` method of the `recyclerView` object, passing in the appropriate position to scroll to in the list.

To perform the circular reveal animation on the `View`, override the `onViewAttachedToWindow()` method of the `SampleMaterialAdapter` class, which provides access to the `ViewHolder` and then passes the `itemView` into the `animateCircularReveal()` method as shown here:

```
@Override

public void onViewAttachedToWindow(ViewHolder viewHolder) {
```

(Continues)

(Continued)

```
    super.onViewAttachedToWindow(viewHolder);

    animateCircularReveal(viewHolder.itemView);

}
```

Figure 12.5 shows a series of screenshots representing what the animation might look like as it executes.

Viewing/Editing a Card

Now that you can add a Card, you should also know how to view and edit a Card. To view a Card, you must set an OnClickListener on the itemView of the ViewHolder. Here is the OnClickListener of the itemView:

```
itemView.setOnClickListener(new View.OnClickListener() {

    @Override

    public void onClick(View v) {

        Pair<View, String> p1 = Pair.create((View) initial,
```

Figure 12.5   Adding and processing the result and inserting the new card.

```
                SampleMaterialActivity.TRANSITION_INITIAL);
        Pair<View, String> p2 = Pair.create((View) name,
                SampleMaterialActivity.TRANSITION_NAME);
        Pair<View, String> p3 = Pair.create((View) deleteButton,
                SampleMaterialActivity.TRANSITION_DELETE_BUTTON);


        ActivityOptionsCompat options;
        Activity act = (AppCompatActivity) context;
        options = ActivityOptionsCompat.makeSceneTransitionAnimation(act, p1, p2, p3);


        int requestCode = getAdapterPosition();
        String name = cardsList.get(requestCode).getName();
        int color = cardsList.get(requestCode).getColorResource();


        Log.d(DEBUG_TAG,
            "SampleMaterialAdapter itemView listener for Edit adapter position "
+
            requestCode);


        Intent transitionIntent = new Intent(context, TransitionEditActivity.class);
        transitionIntent.putExtra(SampleMaterialActivity.EXTRA_NAME, name);
        transitionIntent.putExtra(SampleMaterialActivity.EXTRA_INITIAL,
                Character.toString(name.charAt(0)));
        transitionIntent.putExtra(SampleMaterialActivity.EXTRA_COLOR, color);
        transitionIntent.putExtra(SampleMaterialActivity.EXTRA_UPDATE, false);
        transitionIntent.putExtra(SampleMaterialActivity.EXTRA_DELETE, false);
        ((AppCompatActivity) context).startActivityForResult(transitionIntent,
                requestCode, options.toBundle());
    }
});
```

This method creates another scene transition animation and this time animates the transition of three views. The `initial` of a particular `Card` in the list transitions into the `initial` of the `TransitionEditActivity`; the `name` of a particular `Card` in the list transitions into the `name` of the `TransitionEditActivity`; and the `deleteButton` of a particular `Card` in the list transitions into the `deleteButton` of the `TransitionEditActivity`. The startActivityForResult() method includes an Intent, which passes the name, initial, and color, and also passes the requestCode, which is the position of the Card in the list so that the onActivityResult() method is able to determine which Card to update.

The Edit Layout

To perform the transitions between the activities, the activity_transition_edit.xml layout defines the android:transitionName attributes for the views between which the transition occurs, as shown in the layout below:

```
<LinearLayout xmlns:android="http://schemas.android.com/apk/res/android"

    xmlns:tools="http://schemas.android.com/tools"

    android:id="@+id/linear"

    android:layout_width="match_parent"

    android:layout_height="match_parent"

    android:background="@android:color/white"

    android:orientation="vertical"

    android:padding="@dimen/padding"

    android:paddingBottom="@dimen/activity_vertical_margin"

    android:paddingLeft="@dimen/activity_horizontal_margin"

    android:paddingRight="@dimen/activity_horizontal_margin"

    android:paddingTop="@dimen/activity_vertical_margin"

    android:transitionName="layout_transition"

    tools:context="com.introtoandroid.samplematerial.TransitionEditActivity">


    <TextView

        android:id="@+id/initial"

        android:layout_width="match_parent"

        android:layout_height="0dp"

        android:layout_weight="1"

        android:gravity="center"

        android:textColor="@android:color/white"

        android:textSize="@dimen/initial_size"

        android:transitionName="initial_transition" />


    <LinearLayout

        android:layout_width="match_parent"

        android:layout_height="0dp"

        android:layout_weight="1"
```

```
    android:background="@android:color/white"
    android:orientation="vertical">

    <EditText
        android:id="@+id/name"
        android:layout_width="match_parent"
        android:layout_height="wrap_content"
        android:inputType="textCapSentences"
        android:textColor="@android:color/black"
        android:textSize="@dimen/text_size"
        android:transitionName="name_transition" />

    <LinearLayout
        android:layout_width="match_parent"
        android:layout_height="wrap_content"
        android:background="@android:color/white"
        android:orientation="horizontal"
        android:transitionName="delete_button_transition">

        <Button
            android:id="@+id/update_button"
            android:layout_width="wrap_content"
            android:layout_height="wrap_content"
            android:text="@string/update_button" />

        <Button
            android:id="@+id/delete_button"
            android:layout_width="wrap_content"
            android:layout_height="wrap_content"
            android:text="@string/delete_button" />
    </LinearLayout>
    </LinearLayout>
</LinearLayout>
```

Figure 12.6 shows a representation of what the transition looks like as it executes.

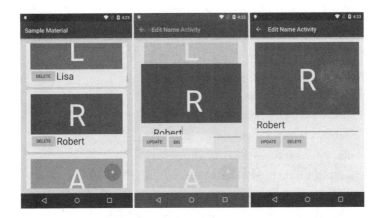

Figure 12.6   Viewing/editing card transition.

Edit Card Activity

Now let's take a look at the onCreate() method of the TransitionEditActivity class.
This class is very similar to the TransitionAddActivity class, but this class displays the
data of a particular Card and allows you to edit the name in the EditText field. This
Activity also allows you to update and delete the Card. Here is the
TransitionEditActivity class:

```
public class TransitionEditActivity extends AppCompatActivity {

    private EditText nameEditText;

    private TextView initialTextView;

    private Intent intent;


    @Override
    protected void onCreate(Bundle savedInstanceState) {

        super.onCreate(savedInstanceState);

        setContentView(R.layout.activity_transition_edit);


        nameEditText = (EditText) findViewById(R.id.name);

        initialTextView = (TextView) findViewById(R.id.initial);

        Button updateButton = (Button) findViewById(R.id.update_button);

        Button deleteButton = (Button) findViewById(R.id.delete_button);


        intent = getIntent();

        String nameExtra = intent.getStringExtra(SampleMaterialActivity.EXTRA_NAME);
```

```
String initialExtra =
        intent.getStringExtra(SampleMaterialActivity.EXTRA_INITIAL);
int colorExtra = intent.getIntExtra(SampleMaterialActivity.EXTRA_COLOR, 0);


nameEditText.setText(nameExtra);
nameEditText.setSelection(nameEditText.getText().length());
initialTextView.setText(initialExtra);
initialTextView.setBackgroundColor(colorExtra);


nameEditText.addTextChangedListener(new TextWatcher() {
    @Override
    public void onTextChanged(CharSequence s,
                int start, int before, int count) {
        if (s.length() == 0) {
            // update initialTextView
            initialTextView.setText("");
        } else if (s.length() >= 1) {
            // initialTextView set to first letter of
            // nameEditText and update name stringExtra
            initialTextView.setText(String.valueOf(s.charAt(0)));
            intent.putExtra(SampleMaterialActivity.EXTRA_UPDATE, true);
        }
    }


    @Override
    public void beforeTextChanged(CharSequence s,
            int start, int count, int after) {
    }


    @Override
    public void afterTextChanged(Editable s) {
    }
});
```

(Continues)

(Continued)

```
        updateButton.setOnClickListener(new View.OnClickListener() {
            @Override
            public void onClick(View v) {
                // must not be zero otherwise do not
                // finish activity and report Toast message
                String text = initialTextView.getText().toString().trim();
                if (TextUtils.isEmpty(text)) {
                    Toast.makeText(getApplicationContext(),
                            "Enter a valid name", Toast.LENGTH_SHORT).show();
                } else {
                    intent.putExtra(SampleMaterialActivity.EXTRA_UPDATE, true);
                    intent.putExtra(SampleMaterialActivity.EXTRA_NAME,
                            String.valueOf(nameEditText.getText()));
                    intent.putExtra(SampleMaterialActivity.EXTRA_INITIAL,
                            String.valueOf(nameEditText.getText().charAt(0)));
                    setResult(RESULT_OK, intent);
                    supportFinishAfterTransition();
                }
            }
        });


        // delete implemented here
    }
}
```

Pay particular attention to the `updateButton` with the `OnClickListener`. This method returns the results when the `updateButton` is clicked so that the `onActivityResult()` method of the `SampleMaterialActivity` is able to update the `Card` with the new data. Here is the `onActivityResult()` update implementation:

```
@Override
protected void onActivityResult(int requestCode, int resultCode, Intent data) {
    super.onActivityResult(requestCode, resultCode, data);

    if (requestCode == adapter.getItemCount()) {
        // add implemented here
    } else {
```

```
        if (resultCode == RESULT_OK) {
            // Make sure the request was successful
            RecyclerView.ViewHolder viewHolder =
                recyclerView.findViewHolderForAdapterPosition(requestCode);
            if (data.getExtras().getBoolean(EXTRA_DELETE, false)) {
                // delete implemented here
            } else if (data.getExtras().getBoolean(EXTRA_UPDATE)) {
                // if name changed, update user
                String name = data.getStringExtra(EXTRA_NAME);
                viewHolder.itemView.setVisibility(View.INVISIBLE);
                adapter.updateCard(name, requestCode);
            }
        }
    }
}
```

This method detects if an update has occurred, sets the visibility of the `CardView` to `View.INVISIBLE` so that the `View` animates when updated, and then calls the `updateCard()` method of the `adapter`, passing in the `name` and the `position` of the particular `Card` in the list. Here is the `updateCard()` method of the `SampleMaterialAdapter` class that sets the new `name` of the `Card` in the list and calls the `notifyItemChanged()` method of the adapter to update the item in the list:

```
public void updateCard(String name, int list_position) {
    cardsList.get(list_position).setName(name);
    Log.d(DEBUG_TAG, "list_position is " + list_position);
    notifyItemChanged(list_position);
}
```

Deleting a Card

Now that you know how to add and update a `Card`, the next step is to delete a `Card`. To delete a `Card`, you need to set an `OnClickListener` for the `deleteButton` of the `ViewHolder`. Here is the implementation:

```
deleteButton.setOnClickListener(new View.OnClickListener() {
    @Override
    public void onClick(View v) {
        animateCircularDelete(itemView, getAdapterPosition());
    }
});
```

When the button is clicked, the `animateCircularDelete()` method is called, passing in the `itemView`, which is a particular `CardView`, and also passing in the position of the `Card` in the list to be deleted. Here is the `animateCircularDelete()` method:

```java
public void animateCircularDelete(final View view, final int list_position) {

    int centerX = view.getWidth();

    int centerY = view.getHeight();

    int startRadius = view.getWidth();

    int endRadius = 0;

    Animator animation = ViewAnimationUtils.createCircularReveal(view,
            centerX, centerY, startRadius, endRadius);


    animation.addListener(new AnimatorListenerAdapter() {

        @Override

        public void onAnimationEnd(Animator animation) {

            super.onAnimationEnd(animation);


            Log.d(DEBUG_TAG,

                "SampleMaterialAdapter onAnimationEnd for Edit adapter position " +

                list_position);

            Log.d(DEBUG_TAG, "SampleMaterialAdapter onAnimationEnd for Edit
cardId " +

                    getItemId(list_position));


            view.setVisibility(View.INVISIBLE);

            cardsList.remove(list_ position);

            notifyItemRemoved(list_ position);

        }

    });

    animation.start();

}
```

This method animates the circular reveal from a different location of the `Card` so that the lower-right corner of the deleted `Card` is the last spot to disappear from the screen during the animation. At the end of the animation, the `Card` is removed from the `cardsList` and the `adapter` is notified that the item has been removed by calling the

`notifyItemRemoved()` method. You need to be sure to override the
`onViewDetachedFromWindow()` method and clear the animation with the `clearAnimation()`
method called on the `itemView` in the `SampleMaterialAdapter` class once the animation
completes. Here is the implementation:

```
@Override
public void onViewDetachedFromWindow(ViewHolder viewHolder) {
    super.onViewDetachedFromWindow(viewHolder);
    viewHolder.itemView.clearAnimation();
}
```

Figure 12.7 shows a representation of the delete animation occurring across multiple
screenshots until the `Card` is deleted and the list repositions the other cards accordingly.

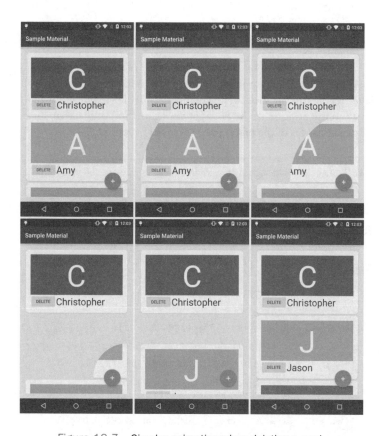

Figure 12.7   Circular animation when deleting a card.

You may also want to know how to delete a `Card` from the `TransitionEditActivity` class. Here is a `deleteButton` with an `OnClickListener()` for notifying the calling `Activity` that the `deleteButton` has been pressed:

```
@Override
protected void onCreate(Bundle savedInstanceState) {
    // other code implemented here


    deleteButton.setOnClickListener(new View.OnClickListener() {
        @Override
        public void onClick(View v) {
            intent.putExtra(SampleMaterialActivity.EXTRA_DELETE, true);
            setResult(RESULT_OK, intent);
            supportFinishAfterTransition();
        }
    });
}
```

The calling `Activity` is then notified of which `Card` to delete; it accesses the `Card` for deletion by retrieving the `ViewHolder` for that particular deleted position and then passes the `CardView` and the position to the `deleteCard()` method of the `adapter`. Here is the complete implementation of the `onActivityResult()` method:

```
@Override
protected void onActivityResult(int requestCode, int resultCode, Intent data) {
    super.onActivityResult(requestCode, resultCode, data);

    if (requestCode == adapter.getItemCount()) {
        // add implemented here
    } else {
        if (resultCode == RESULT_OK) {
            // Make sure the request was successful
            RecyclerView.ViewHolder viewHolder =
                    recyclerView.findViewHolderForAdapterPosition(requestCode);
            if (data.getExtras().getBoolean(EXTRA_DELETE, false)) {
                // The user is deleting a contact
                adapter.deleteCard(viewHolder.itemView, requestCode);
            } else if (data.getExtras().getBoolean(EXTRA_UPDATE)) {
                // updated implemented here
            }
        }
    }
}
```

```
        }
    }
}
```

And here is the `deleteCard()` method of the `SampleMaterialAdapter` class:

```
public void deleteCard(View view, int list_position) {

    animateCircularDelete(view, list_position);

}
```

Summary

This chapter introduced material design and showed you how to add the material theme and the material support libraries to your application. In addition, you also learned how to implement a circular reveal animation and scene transitions between activities. Further, you learned how to implement a `CardView`, a `RecyclerView`, `RecyclerView.Adapter`, and the `RecyclerView.ViewHolder`. You are now equipped for developing material Android applications.

Quiz Questions

1. How do you add the `CardView` support library to your application?

2. What attribute is used for defining a transition on a `View` within a layout?

3. What `Activity` class should you extend from when implementing material applications?

4. What method should you override for determining the size of a `RecyclerView.Adapter`?

5. True or false: you should override the `getId()` method of the `RecyclerView.Adapter` to determine the position of the item in the list.

6. How do you bind data to a `RecyclerView`?

Exercises

1. To learn more about what Google defines as material design, read through the material design specification found here:
   http://www.google.com/design/spec/material-design/introduction.html.

2. Read through the `RecyclerView` documentation found here to become familiar with all the classes available for use with the `RecyclerView`:
   http://d.android.com/reference/android/support/v7/widget/RecyclerView.html.

3. Modify the `SampleMaterial` application to support fragments, where adding and editing occurs within a `Fragment`.

References and More Information

Android Developers Blog: "AppCompat v21—Material Design for Pre-Lollipop Devices!":
http://android-developers.blogspot.com/2014/10/appcompat-v21-material-design-for-pre.html
Android Developers Blog: "Implementing Material Design in Your Android app":
http://android-developers.blogspot.com/2014/10/implementing-material-design-in-your.html
Android Design: "Material Design for Android":
http://d.android.com/design/material/index.html
Android Training: "Material Design for Developers":
http://d.android.com/training/material/index.html
Android Tools: "Support Library Features": "v7 appcompat library":
http://d.android.com/tools/support-library/features.html#v7-appcompat
Android Tools: "Support Library Features": "v7 recyclerview library":
http://d.android.com/tools/support-library/features.html#v7-recyclerview
Android Tools: "Support Library Features": "v7 cardview library":
http://d.android.com/tools/support-library/features.html#v7-cardview
Android SDK Reference regarding the application CardView class:
http://d.android.com/reference/android/support/v7/widget/CardView.html
Android SDK Reference regarding the application RecyclerView class:
http://d.android.com/reference/android/support/v7/widget/RecyclerView.html
Android SDK Reference regarding the application RecyclerView.Adapter class:
http://d.android.com/reference/android/support/v7/widget/RecyclerView.Adapter.html
Android SDK Reference regarding the application RecyclerView.ViewHolder class:
http://d.android.com/reference/android/support/v7/widget/RecyclerView.ViewHolder.html
Android Samples: "CardView":
http://d.android.com/samples/CardView/index.html
Android Samples: "RecyclerView":
http://d.android.com/samples/RecyclerView/index.html

13

Designing Compatible Applications

According to the *MOVR Mobile Overview Report, January–March 2015*, by ScientiaMobile, Inc., in the first quarter of 2015 there were over 5,600 different Android devices on the market worldwide—just from smartphones, tablets, and feature phones. In this chapter, you learn how to design and develop Android applications that are compatible with a variety of devices despite differences in screen size, hardware, or platform version. We offer numerous tips for designing and developing your application to be compatible with many different devices.

Maximizing Application Compatibility

With dozens of manufacturers developing Android devices, we've seen an explosion of different device models and form factors—each with its own market differentiators and unique characteristics. Users now have choices, but these choices come at a cost. This proliferation of devices has led to what some developers call *fragmentation* and others call *compatibility issues*. Terminology aside, it has become a challenging task to develop Android applications that support a broad range of devices, even when the devices are of the same form factor. Developers must contend with devices that support different platform versions (see Figure 13.1), hardware configurations (including optional hardware features) such as OpenGL versions (see Figure 13.2), and variations in screen sizes and densities (see Figure 13.3). The list of differentiators is lengthy and it grows with each new device.

Although fragmentation makes the Android app developer's life more complicated, it's still possible to develop for and support a variety of devices within a single application. When it comes to maximizing compatibility, you'll always want to use the following strategies:

- Whenever possible, choose the development option that is supported by the widest variety of devices. In many cases, you can detect device differences at runtime and provide different code paths to support different configurations. Just make sure you inform your quality assurance team of this sort of application logic so it can be understood and thoroughly tested.

- Whenever a development decision limits the compatibility of your application (for example, using an API that was introduced in a later API level or introducing a

Version	Codename	API	Distribution
2.2	Froyo	8	0.2%
2.3.3 - 2.3.7	Gingerbread	10	4.1%
4.0.3 - 4.0.4	Ice Cream Sandwich	15	3.7%
4.1.x	Jellybean	16	12.1%
4.2.x		17	15.2%
4.3		18	4.5%
4.4	KitKat	19	39.2%
5.0	Lollipop	21	15.9%
5.1		22	5.1%

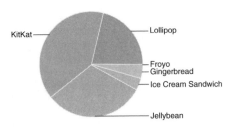

Data collected during a 7-day period ending on September 7, 2015.
Any versions with less than 0.1% distribution are not shown.

Figure 13.1   Android device statistics regarding platform version (source:
http://d.android.com/about/dashboards/index.html#Platform).

hardware requirement such as camera support), assess the risk and document this limitation. Determine whether you are going to provide an alternative solution for devices that do not support this requirement.

- Consider screen size and density differences when designing application user interfaces. It is often possible to design very flexible layouts that look reasonable on different screen resolutions and sizes, as well as in both portrait and landscape modes for mobile, and on round and rectangle Wear screens. However, if you don't consider these factors early on, you will likely have to make changes (sometimes painful ones) later to accommodate the differences.

- Test on a wide range of devices early in the development process to avoid unpleasant surprises late in the game. Make sure the devices have different hardware and

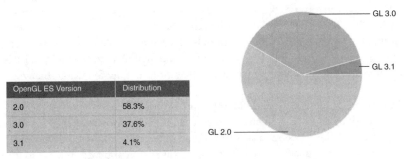

OpenGL ES Version	Distribution
2.0	58.3%
3.0	37.6%
3.1	4.1%

Data collected during a 7-day period ending on September 7, 2015.

Figure 13.2   Android device statistics regarding OpenGL versions (source:
http://d.android.com/about/dashboards/index.html#OpenGL).

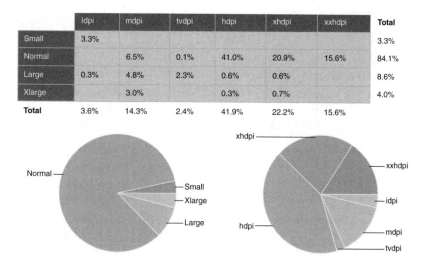

	ldpi	mdpi	tvdpi	hdpi	xhdpi	xxhdpi	Total
Small	3.3%						3.3%
Normal		6.5%	0.1%	41.0%	20.9%	15.6%	84.1%
Large	0.3%	4.8%	2.3%	0.6%	0.6%		8.6%
Xlarge		3.0%		0.3%	0.7%		4.0%
Total	3.6%	14.3%	2.4%	41.9%	22.2%	15.6%	

Data collected during a 7-day period ending on September 7, 2015.
Any screen configurations with less than 0.1% distribution are not shown.

Figure 13.3   Android device statistics regarding screen sizes and densities (source: *http://d.android.com/about/dashboards/index.html#Screens*).

software, including different versions of the Android platform, different screen sizes, and different hardware capabilities.

- Whenever necessary, provide alternative resources to help smooth over differences between device characteristics (we talk extensively about alternative resources later in this chapter).

- If you do introduce hardware and software requirements to your application, make sure you register this information in the Android manifest file using the appropriate tags. These tags, used by the Android platform as well as third parties such as Google Play, help ensure that your application is installed only on devices that are capable of meeting its requirements.

Now let's look at some of the strategies you can use to target different device configurations and languages.

Designing User Interfaces for Compatibility

Before we show you the many ways you can provide custom application resources and code to support specific device configurations, it's important to remember that you can often avoid their use in the first place. The trick is to design your initial default solution to be flexible enough to cover any variations. When it comes to user interfaces, keep them simple and don't overcrowd them. Also, take advantage of the many powerful tools at your disposal:

- As a rule of thumb, design for normal-size screens and medium resolution. Over time, devices trend toward larger screens with higher resolution.

- Use fragments to keep your screen designs independent from your application `Activity` classes and provide for flexible workflows.

- Leverage the various Android Support Library APIs to provide newer support libraries to older platform versions.

- For `View` and `Layout` control width and height attributes, use `match_parent` (also called the deprecated `fill_parent`) and `wrap_content` so that controls scale for different screen sizes and orientation changes, instead of using fixed pixel sizes.

- For dimensions, use the flexible units, such as `dp` and `sp`, as opposed to fixed-unit types, such as `pt`, `px`, `mm`, and `in`.

- Avoid using `AbsoluteLayout` and other pixel-perfect settings and attributes.

- Use flexible layout controls such as `RelativeLayout`, `LinearLayout`, `TableLayout`, `FrameLayout`, or a custom layout to design a screen that looks great in both portrait and landscape modes, as well as on a variety of different screen sizes and resolutions.

- Encapsulate screen content in scalable container controls such as `ViewPager`, `ScrollView`, `ListView`, and `RecyclerView`. Generally, you should scale and grow screens in only one direction (vertically or horizontally), not both.

- Don't provide exact position values for screen elements, sizes, and dimensions. Instead, use relative positions, weights, and gravity. Spending time up front to get this right saves time later.

- Provide application graphics of reasonable quality and always keep the original (larger) sizes around in case you need different versions for different resolutions at a later time. There is always a trade-off in terms of graphics quality versus file size. Find the sweet spot where the graphic scales reasonably well for changes in screen characteristics without bulking up your application or taking too long to display. Whenever possible, use stretchable graphics, such as Nine-Patch, which allow a graphic to change size based on the area in which it is displayed.

Tip

Looking for information about the device screen? Check out the `DisplayMetrics` utility class, which, when used in conjunction with the window manager, can determine all sorts of information about the display characteristics of the device at runtime, as shown here:

```
DisplayMetrics currentMetrics = new DisplayMetrics();

WindowManager wm = getWindowManager();

wm.getDefaultDisplay().getMetrics(currentMetrics);
```

You may also learn about a device configuration and user configurations, such as input modes, screen size and orientations, locales, and scaling at runtime, through the `Configuration` class as follows:

```
Configuration config = getResources().getConfiguration();
```

Working with Fragments

Fragments were discussed in detail in Chapter 9, "Partitioning with Fragments," but they deserve another mention here in relation to designing compatible applications. All applications can benefit from the screen workflow flexibility provided by Fragment-based designs. By decoupling screen functionality from specific Activity classes, you have the option of pairing up that functionality in different ways, depending on the screen size, orientation, and other hardware configuration options. As new types of Android devices hit the market, you'll be well placed for supporting them if you do this work up front—in short, future-proofing your user interfaces.

> **Tip**
>
> There's little excuse not to use fragments, even if you are supporting legacy Android versions as far back as Android 1.6 (nearly 100% of the market). Simply use the Android Support Library to include these features in your legacy code. With most non-Fragment-based APIs deprecated, it's clearly the path along which the platform designers are leading developers.

Leveraging the Various Android Support Library APIs

In addition to fragments, several other new features of the Android SDK are so important for future device compatibility that there are Android support libraries to bring these APIs to older device platform versions, some as far back as Android 1.6. In addition, there are certain modern features such as the RecyclerView that are only available through the support library, so even if you are not interested in targeting older devices, to implement newer features may require adding the appropriate support libraries. To use the Android Support Library APIs with your application, take the following steps:

1. Use the Android SDK Manager to download the Android Support Repository for Android Studio.
2. View your project in the Android view of Android Studio, and open the appropriate build.gradle module file.
3. Add the appropriate support libraries to the dependencies declaration with the version target to the build.gradle file.
4. Begin using the APIs available as part of the Android Support Library. For example, to create a class extending FragmentActivity, you need to import android.support.v4.app.FragmentActivity.

For a full list of the available APIs in the Android Support Library, see *http://d.android.com/ tools/support-library/features.html*.

Supporting Specific Screen Types

Although you generally want to try to develop your applications to be screen independent (supporting all types of screens, small and large, high density and low), when necessary you can explicitly specify the types of screens your application can support in the

Android manifest file. Here are some of the basics for supporting different screen types within your application:

- Explicitly state which screen sizes your application supports using the `<supports-screens>` Android manifest file tag. For more information on this Android manifest tag, see *http://d.android.com/guide/topics/manifest/supports-screens-element.html*.
- Design flexible layouts that work with different-size screens.
- Provide the most flexible default resources you can, and add appropriate alternative layout and drawable resources for different screen sizes, densities, aspect ratios, and orientations as needed.
- Test, test, test! Make sure you regularly review how your application behaves on devices with different screen sizes, densities, aspect ratios, and orientations as part of your quality-assurance testing cycle.

Tip

For a very detailed discussion of how to support different types of screens, from the smallest watches to the largest tablets and televisions, see the Android Developer website: *http://d.android.com/guide/practices/screens_support.html*.

It's also helpful to understand how legacy applications are automatically scaled for larger and newer devices using what is called *screen compatibility mode*. Depending on the version of the Android SDK that your application originally targeted, the behavior on newer platform versions may be subtly different. This mode is on by default but can be disabled by your application. Learn more about screen compatibility mode at the Android Developer website: *http://d.android.com/guide/practices/screen-compat-mode.html*.

Working with Nine-Patch Stretchable Graphics

Screens come in various dimensions. It can save you a lot of time if you use stretchable graphics to enable a single graphic to scale appropriately for different screen sizes and orientations, or different lengths of text. Android supports Nine-Patch Stretchable Graphics for this purpose. Nine-Patch Stretchable Graphics are simply PNG graphics that have patches, or areas of the image, defined to scale appropriately, instead of the entire image scaling as one unit. We discuss how to create stretchable graphics in Appendix D, "Mastery: Android SDK Tools."

Providing Alternative Application Resources

Few application user interfaces look perfect on every device. Most require some tweaking and some special-case handling. The Android platform allows you to organize your project resources so that you can tailor your applications to specific device criteria. It can be useful to think of the resources stored at the top of the resource hierarchy naming scheme as *default resources*, and the specialized versions of those resources as *alternative resources*.

Here are some reasons you might want to include alternative resources within your application:

- To support different user languages and locales
- To support different device screen sizes, densities, dimensions, orientations, and aspect ratios
- To support different device docking modes
- To support different device input methods
- To provide different resources depending on the device's Android platform version

Understanding How Resources Are Resolved

Here's how it works. Each time a resource is requested within an Android application, the Android operating system attempts to find the resource that is the best possible match for the job. In many cases, applications provide only one set of resources. Developers can include alternative versions of those same resources as part of their application packages. The Android operating system always attempts to load the most specific resources available—the developer does not have to worry about determining which resources to load because the operating system handles this task.

There are four important rules to remember when creating alternative resources:

1. The Android platform always loads the most specific, most appropriate resource available. If an alternative resource does not exist, the default resource is used. Therefore, it's important to know your target devices, to design for the defaults, and to add alternative resources judiciously in order to keep your projects manageable.

2. Alternative resources must always be named exactly the same as the default resources and must be stored in the appropriately named directory, as dictated by a special alternative resource qualifier. If a string is called `strHelpText` in the `res/values/strings.xml` file, it must be named the same in the `res/values-fr/strings.xml` (French) and `res/values-zh/strings.xml` (Chinese) string files. The same goes for all other types of resources, such as graphics or layout files.

3. Good application design dictates that alternative resources should almost always have a default counterpart so that regardless of the device configuration, some version of the resource will always load. The only time you can get away without a default resource is when you provide every kind of alternative resource. One of the first steps the system takes when finding a best matching resource is to eliminate resources that are contradictory to the current configuration. For example, in portrait mode, the system would not even attempt to use a landscape resource, even if that is the only resource available. Keep in mind that new alternative resource qualifiers are added over time, so although you might think your application provides complete coverage of all alternatives now, it might not do so in the future.

4. Don't go overboard creating alternative resources because they add to the size of your application package and can have performance implications. Instead, try to design your default resources to be flexible and scalable. For example, a good layout design can often support both landscape and portrait modes seamlessly—if you use appropriate layouts, user interface controls, and scalable graphics resources.

Organizing Alternative Resources with Qualifiers

Alternative resources can be created for many different criteria, including, but not limited to, screen characteristics, device input methods, and language or regional differences. These alternative resources are organized hierarchically within the res/ resource project directory. You use directory qualifiers (in the form of directory name suffixes) to specify a resource as an alternative resource to load in specific situations.

A simple example might help to drive this concept home. The most common example of when alternative resources are used has to do with the default application icon resources created as part of a new Android project in Android Studio. An application could simply provide a single application icon graphics resource, stored in the res/mipmap/ directory. However, different Android devices have different screen densities. Therefore, alternative resources are used instead: res/mipmap-hdpi/ic_launcher.png is an application icon suitable for high-density screens, res/mipmap-ldpi/ic_launcher.png is the application icon suitable for low-density screens, and so on. Note that in each case, the alternative resource is named the same. This is important. Alternative resources must use the same names as the default resources. This is how the Android system can match the appropriate resource to load—by its name.

Here are some additional important facts about alternative resources:

- Alternative resource directory qualifiers are always applied to the default resource directory name, for example, res/drawable-qualifier/, res/values-qualifier/, res/layout-qualifier/.

- Only one directory qualifier of a given type may be included in a resource directory name. Sometimes this has unfortunate consequences—you might be forced to include the same resource in multiple directories. For example, you cannot create an alternative resource directory called res/drawable-ldpi-mdpi/ to share the same icon graphic. Instead, you must create two directories: res/drawable-ldpi/ and res/drawable-mdpi/. Frankly, when you want different qualifiers to share resources instead of providing two copies of the same resource, you're often better off making the shared resources your default resources, and then providing alternative resources for those resources that do not match ldpi and mdpi—such as, hdpi. As we said, it's up to you how you go about organizing your resources; these are just our suggestions for keeping things under control.

- Alternative resource directory qualifiers (and resource filenames) must always be lowercase, with one exception: region qualifiers.

- Alternative resource directory qualifiers can be combined or chained, with each qualifier separated from the next by a dash. This enables developers to create very specific directory names and therefore very specialized alternative resources. These qualifiers must be applied in a specific order, and the Android operating system always attempts to load the most specific resource (that is, the resource with the longest matching path). For example, you can create an alternative resource directory for the French language (qualifier `fr`) in the Canadian region (qualifier `rCA`—CA is a region qualifier and is therefore capitalized) string resources (stored in the values directory) as follows: `res/values-fr-rCA/strings.xml`.

- You need to create alternative resources only for the specific resources you require—not for every resource in a given file. If you need to translate only half the strings in the default `strings.xml` file, provide alternative strings only for those specific string resources. In other words, the default `strings.xml` resource file might contain a superset of string resources and the alternative string resource files would contain a subset—only the strings requiring translation. Common examples of strings that do not get localized are company and brand names.

- No custom directory names or qualifiers are allowed. You may use only the qualifiers defined as part of the Android SDK. These qualifiers are listed in Table 13.1.

- Always try to include default resources—that is, those resources saved in directories without any qualifiers. These are the resources that the Android operating system will fall back on when no specific alternative resource matches the criteria. If you don't, the system falls back on the closest matching resource based upon the directory qualifiers, which could be one that might not make sense.

Now that you understand how alternative resources work, let's look at some of the directory qualifiers you can use to store alternative resources for different purposes. Qualifiers are tacked onto the existing resource directory name in a strict order, shown in descending order in Table 13.1.

Good examples of alternative resource directories with qualifiers are

- `res/values-en-rUS-port-finger/`
- `res/drawables-en-rUS-land-mdpi/`
- `res/values-en-qwerty/`

Bad examples of alternative resource directories with qualifiers are

- `res/values-en-rUS-rGB/`
- `res/values-en-rUS-port-FINGER-wheel/`
- `res/values-en-rUS-port-finger-custom/`
- `res/drawables-rUS-en/`

Table 13.1 **Important Alternative Resource Qualifiers**

Directory Qualifier	Example Values	Description
Mobile country code and mobile network code	mcc310 (United States) mcc310-mnc004 (United States, Verizon)	The mobile country code (MCC), optionally followed by a dash, and a mobile network code (MNC) from the SIM card in the device.
Language and region code	en (English) ja (Japanese) de (German) en-rUS (American English) en-rGB (British English)	The language code (ISO 639-1 two-letter language code), optionally followed by a dash, and the region code (a lowercase r followed by the region code as defined by ISO 3166-1-alpha-2).
Layout direction	ldltr ldrtl	The application's layout direction, either left to right or right to left. Resources such as layouts, values, or drawables can use this rule. Requires setting the application attribute supportsRtl as true in your manifest file. Added in API Level 17.
Screen pixel dimensions. Several qualifiers for specific screen dimensions, including smallest width, available width, and available height.	sw<N>dp (smallest width) w<N>dp (available width) h<N>dp (available height) Examples: sw320dp sw480dp sw600dp sw720dp h320dp h540dp h800dp w480dp w720dp w1080dp	DP-specific screen requirements. swXXXdp: Indicates the smallest width that this resource qualifier supports. wYYYdp: Indicates the minimum width. hZZZdp: Indicates the minimum height. The numeric value can be any width the developer desires, in dp units. Added in API Level 13.
Screen size	small normal large xlarge (added in API Level 9)	Generalized screen size. A small screen is generally a low-density QVGA or higher-density VGA screen. A normal screen is generally a medium-density HVGA screen or similar. A large screen has at least a medium-density VGA screen or other screen with more pixels than an HVGA display. An xlarge screen has at least a medium-density HVGA screen and is generally tablet size or larger. Added in API Level 4.

Table 13.1 **Continued**

Directory Qualifier	Example Values	Description
Screen aspect ratio	`long` `notlong`	Whether or not the device is a wide-screen device. WQVGA, WVGA, FWVGA screens are `long` screens. QVGA, HVGA, and VGA screens are `notlong` screens. Added in API Level 4.
Screen orientation	`port` `land`	When a device is in portrait mode, the `port` resources will be loaded. When the device is in landscape mode, the `land` resources will be loaded.

UI mode	`car`
	`desk`
	`appliance`
	`television`
	`watch` (added in API Level 20)
		Load specific resources when the device is in a `car` or `desk` dock.
		Load specific resources when the device is a `television` display.
		Load specific resources when the device is an `appliance` and has no display.
		Load specific resources when the device is a `watch` display.

Night mode	`night` `notnight`	Load specific resources when the device is in `night` mode or `notnight`. Added in API Level 8.

Screen pixel density	`ldpi`
	`mdpi`
	`hdpi`
	`xhdpi` (added in API Level 8)
	`xxhdpi` (added in API Level 16)
	`xxxhdpi` (added in API Level 18)
	`tvdpi` (added in API Level 13)
	`nodpi`
		Low-density screen resources (approx. 120dpi) should use the `ldpi` option.
		Medium-density screen resources (approx. 160dpi) should use the `mdpi` option.
		High-density screen resources (approx. 240dpi) should use the `hdpi` option.
		Extra-high-density screen resources (approx. 320dpi) should use the `xhdpi` option.
		Extra-extra-high-density screen resources (approx. 480dpi) should use the `xxhdpi` option.
		Extra-extra-extra-high-density screen resources (approx. 640dpi) should use the `xxxhdpi` option.
		Television screen resources (approx. 213dpi, between `mdpi` and `hdpi`) should use the `tvdpi` option.
		Use the `nodpi` option to specify resources that you do not want to be scaled to match the screen density of the device.
		Added in API Level 4.

(Continues)

Table 13.1 **Continued**

Directory Qualifier	Example Values	Description
Touchscreen type	notouch finger	Resources for devices without touchscreens should use the notouch option. Resources for devices with finger-style (capacitive) touchscreens should use the finger option.
Keyboard type and availability	keysexposed keyshidden keyssoft	Use the keysexposed option for resources when a keyboard is available (hardware or soft keyboard). Use the keyshidden option for resources when no hardware or software keyboard is available. Use the keyssoft option for resources when the soft keyboard is available.
Text input method	nokeys qwerty 12key	Use the nokeys option for resources when the device has no hardware keys for text input. Use the qwerty option for resources when the device has a QWERTY hardware keyboard for text input. Use the 12key option for resources when the device has a 12-key numeric keypad for text input.
Navigation key availability	navexposed navhidden	Use navexposed for resources when the navigational hardware buttons are available to the user. Use navhidden for resources when the navigational hardware buttons are not available to the user (such as when the phone case is slid shut).
Navigation method	nonav dpad trackball wheel	Use nonav if the device has no navigation buttons other than a touchscreen. Use dpad for resources where the primary navigation method is a directional pad. Use trackball for resources where the primary navigation method is a trackball. Use wheel for resources where the primary navigation method is a directional wheel.

Table 13.1 **Continued**

Directory Qualifier	Example Values	Description
Android platform	v3 (Android 1.5) v4 (Android 1.6) v7 (Android 2.1.X) v8 (Android 2.2.X) v9 (Android 2.3-2.3.2) v10 (Android 2.3.3–2.3.4) v12 (Android 3.1.X) v13 (Android 3.2.X) v14 (Android 4.0.X) v15 (Android 4.0.3) v16 (Android 4.1.2) v17 (Android 4.2.2) v18 (Android 4.3) v19 (Android 4.4) v20 (Android 4.4W.2) v21 (Android 5.0) v22 (Android 5.1) v22 (MNC preview) v23 (Android 6.0)	Load resources based on the Android platform version, as specified by the API level. This qualifier will load resources for the specified API level or higher. Note: There are some known issues with this qualifier. See the Android documentation for details.

The first bad example does not work because you can have only one qualifier of a given type, and this one violates that rule by including both rUS and rGB. The second bad example violates the rule that qualifiers (with the exception of the region) are always lowercase. The third bad example includes a custom attribute defined by the developer, but these are not currently supported. The last bad example violates the order in which the qualifiers must be placed: language first, then region, and so on.

Providing Resources for Different Orientations

Let's look at a very simple application that uses alternative resources to customize screen content for different orientations. The SimpleAltResources application (see the sample code for this chapter found on the book's website, *http://introductiontoandroid.blogspot.com*, for a complete implementation) has very little custom code to speak of (check the Activity class if you don't believe us); there were two lines of code written for adding the Android Design Support library ToolBar as the ActionBar, and rather than SimpleAltResourcesActivity extending Activity, we extend AppCompatActivity. Here are the two lines of code we added to the onCreate() method:

```
toolbar = (Toolbar) findViewById(R.id.toolbar);

setSupportActionBar(toolbar);
```

The interesting functionality depends on the resource folder qualifiers. These resources are as follows:

- The default resources for this application include the application icon in the `res/mipmap/` directory; a picture graphic stored in the `res/drawable/` directory; the layout file stored in the `res/layout/` directory; and the color, dimension, string, and style resources stored in the `res/values/` directory. These resources are loaded whenever a more specific resource is not available to load. They are the fallbacks.

- There is a portrait-mode alternative picture graphic stored in the `res/drawable-port/` directory. There are also portrait-mode-specific string and color resources stored in the `res/values-port/` directory. If the device is in portrait orientation, these resources—the portrait picture graphic, the strings, and the colors—are loaded and used by the default layout.

- There is a landscape-mode alternative picture graphic stored in the `res/drawable-land/` directory. There are landscape-mode-specific string and color (basically reversed background and foreground colors) resources stored in the `res/values-land/` directory as well. If the device is in landscape orientation, these resources—the landscape picture graphic, the strings, and the colors—are loaded and used by the default layout.

Figure 13.4 (left) shows the `Android` project view of Android Studio, with the `res/` directory fully expanded, revealing the different symbolic resource file names and subdirectories for different configurations. Note that these directories are only symbolic representations of their names, not their actual file system location. The `Android` project view shows how easy it is to determine what configuration a particular resource is for by displaying the appropriate resource qualifiers to the right of the filename in parentheses, even though these are only symbolic representations of the project hierarchy. For example, we see three `pic.jpg` files—the first has no qualifier, so that is the default `pic.jpg` resource, the second `pic.jpg` has the `(land)` qualifier to the right, and the third `pic.jpg` has the `(port)` qualifier to the right. Figure 13.4 (right) shows the traditional `Project` view of Android Studio, expanded to reveal the `res/` directory showing the actual file system names and locations of these directories. Rather than displaying a symbolic `(land)` file representation, the actual directory name contains the qualifier—for example, `values-land` and `values-port`—each of which contains a `colors.xml` file and `strings.xml` file (those files not shown for the traditional `Project` view).

Figure 13.5 illustrates how `SimpleAltResources` loads different resources based on the portrait orientation of the application at runtime. This figure shows the rendered resources, with a unique blue, white, and black color palette for the status bar, `TextView`, `ToolBar`, and navigation bar, and a unique image for the `ImageView`.

Figure 13.6 illustrates how `SimpleAltResources` loads different resources based on the landscape orientation of the application at runtime. This figure shows the rendered resources, with a unique red and black color palette for the status bar, `ToolBar`, `TextView`, and navigation bar, and a unique image for the `ImageView`.

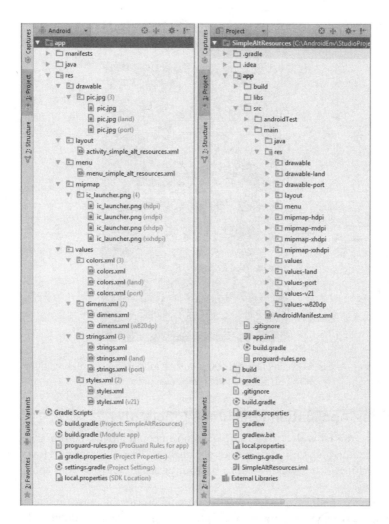

Figure 13.4   An expanded `Android` project view of Android Studio reveals the alternative resource files within the `res/` subdirectories by their symbolic name and project hierarchy location (left), and shows the traditional `Project` view that displays the `res/` subdirectories with their actual file system name and location (right).

Using Alternative Resources Programmatically

Currently, there is no easy way to request resources of a specific configuration programmatically. For example, the developer cannot programmatically request the French or English version of the string resource. Instead, the Android system determines the resource at runtime, and developers refer only to the general resource variable name.

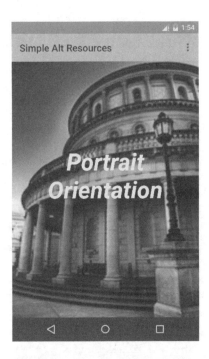

Figure 13.5   Using alternative resources for portrait orientation in the
SimpleAltResources application.

Organizing Application Resources Efficiently

It's easy to go too far with alternative resources. You could provide custom graphics for every different permutation of device screen, language, or input method. However, each time you include an application resource in your project, the size of your application package grows.

There are also performance issues with swapping out resources too frequently—usually when runtime configuration transitions occur. Each time a runtime event such as an orientation or keyboard state change occurs, the Android operating system restarts the underlying Activity and reloads the resources. If your application is loading a lot of resources and content, these changes come at a cost to application performance and responsiveness.

Choose your resource organization scheme carefully. Generally, you should make the most commonly used resources your defaults and then carefully overlay alternative resources only when necessary. For example, if you are writing an application that routinely shows videos or displays a game screen, you might want to make landscape-mode resources your defaults and provide alternative portrait-mode resources because they are not as likely to be used.

Figure 13.6   Using alternative resources for landscape orientation in the
SimpleAltResources application.

Retaining Data across Configuration Changes

An Activity can keep data around through these transitions by using the
onRetainNonConfigurationInstance() method to save data and the
getLastNonConfigurationInstance() method to restore this data after the transition.
This functionality can be especially helpful when your Activity has a lot of setup or
preloading to do. When using fragments, all you need to do is set use the
setRetainInstance() method to retain a Fragment instance across these changes.

Handling Configuration Changes

In cases where your Activity does not need to reload alternative resources on a specific
transition, you might want to consider having the Activity class handle the transition
to avoid having your Activity restart. A camera application could use this technique to
handle orientation changes without having to reinitialize the camera hardware internals,
redisplay the viewfinder window, or redisplay the camera controls (the Button controls
simply rotate in place to the new orientation—very slick).

For an Activity class to handle its own configuration changes, your application must

- Update the <activity> tag in the Android manifest file for that specific Activity
  class to include the android:configChanges attribute. This attribute must specify
  the types of changes the Activity class handles itself.
- Implement the onConfigurationChanged() method of the Activity class to handle the specific changes (by type).

Targeting Tablets and TVs

There has been tremendous growth in the types of devices supported by the Android platform. Whether we're talking tablets or TVs, there is something for everyone. These devices make for an exciting time for application developers. More devices mean more user groups and demographics are using the platform. These types of Android devices, however, pose some unique challenges for Android developers.

Targeting Tablet Devices

Tablets come in a variety of sizes and default orientations from many different manufacturers and carriers. Luckily, from a developer's perspective, tablets can be considered just another Android device, provided that you haven't made any unfortunate development assumptions.

Android tablets run the same platform versions that traditional smartphones do—there is nothing special that they require. These days, most tablets run Android Jelly Bean and higher. Here are some tips for designing, developing, and publishing Android applications for tablet devices:

- **Design flexible user interfaces:** Regardless of what devices your applications are targeting, use flexible layout designs. Use `RelativeLayout` to organize your user interfaces. Use relative dimension values such as `dp` instead of specific values such as `px`. Use stretchable graphics such as Nine-Patch.

- **Take advantage of fragments:** Fragments make for much more flexible user interface navigation by decoupling screen functionality from specific activities.

- **Leverage alternative resources:** Provide alternative resources for various device's screen sizes and densities.

- **Screen orientation:** Tablets often default to landscape mode, but this is not always the case. Some tablets, especially smaller ones, use portrait defaults.

- **Input mode differentiators:** Tablets often rely solely on touchscreen input. Some configurations also have a few other physical buttons, but this is unusual because typical hardware buttons have moved to the touchscreen.

- **UI navigational differences:** Users hold and tap on tablets in a different fashion from the way they do on smartphones. In portrait and landscape modes, tablet screens are substantially wider than their smartphone equivalents. Applications such as games that rely on the user cradling the device in his or her hands like a traditional game controller may struggle with all the extra room on a tablet. The user's thumbs might easily reach or access the two halves of a smartphone screen, but cannot do the same on a tablet.

- **Feature support:** Certain hardware and software features are not usually available on tablets. For example, telephony is not always available. This has implications for unique device identifiers; many developers used to rely on the telephony identifier that may not be present on tablets. The point is, hardware differences can also lead to other, less obvious impacts.

Targeting TV Devices

Android TV is another type of device that Android developers can target. Users can browse Google Play for compatible applications and download them much as they would to other Android devices.

In order to develop Android TV applications, developers use the Android SDK as well as the add-on for Android TV, which can be downloaded using the Android SDK Manager.

Android TV applications have a similar structure to smartphone and tablet applications, although there are some subtle differences between targeting Android TV devices and targeting smartphones and tablets. Let's look at some development tips for targeting Android TV devices:

- **Screen density and resolution:** Android TV applications should target resolutions of 1920 x 1080 pixels and allow the system to automatically resize the resources for you if your user should have a TV with a lower resolution.

- **Screen orientation:** Android TV devices need only landscape-oriented layouts.

- **Overscan margins:** Screen clipping can occur on Android TVs due to overscan. If you are using the v17 `Leanback` support classes, you have nothing to worry about; however, if you are not using those classes, be sure to define a 10% margin for your layouts so your screen elements are not affected by overscan clipping.

- **Not pixel perfect:** One caveat regarding Android TV development is not to rely on the exact number of pixels on the screen. Televisions don't always expose every single pixel. Therefore, your screen designs should be flexible enough to accommodate small adjustments when you've had a chance to test your applications on real Android TV devices.

- **Input mode limitations:** Unlike tablets or smartphones, Android TV devices are not within arm's reach and do not have touchscreens. This means no gestures, no multitouch, and so on. Android TV interface uses a directional pad remote (or D-pad)—that is, arrow keys for up, down, left, and right along with a `Select` button. Some configurations also have a game controller.

- **UI navigational differences:** The input type limitations with Android TV devices may mean you need to make some changes to your application's screen navigation. Users can't easily skip over focusable items on the screen. For instance, if your UI has a row of items, with the two most common on the far left and far right for convenient access with thumb clicks, these items may be inconveniently separated for the average Android TV user.

- **Android manifest file settings:** A number of Android manifest file settings should be configured appropriately for the Android TV. Review the Android TV training for details: *http://d.android.com/training/tv/start/start.html.*

- **Google Play filters:** Google Play uses Android manifest file settings to filter applications and provide them to the appropriate devices. Certain features, such as those defined using the `<uses-feature>` tag, may exclude your application from Android TV devices. If you have built a game, you should set the `android:isGame` attribute of the `<application>` tag in your manifest file so your app will be listed in the games section. One example of this is when applications require features such as touchscreen, camera, and telephony. For a complete list of features supported and unsupported by the Android TV, see "Handling TV Hardware": *http://d.android.com/training/tv/start/hardware.html*.

- **Feature support:** Certain hardware and software features (sensors, cameras, telephony, and so on) are not available on Android TV devices.

Tip

For more information on developing for Android TV devices, see the Android TV Android Developers Guide at *https://developers.google.com/tv/android/*.

Extending Your Application to Watches and Cars

With Android Wear and Android Auto being specialized versions of Android—Wear for running on watches, and Auto for running on dashboard console devices—there are many application compatibility differences when comparing a Wear or Auto application to one for smartphones, tablets, and TVs, or when comparing a Wear application to an Auto application.

Wear and Auto applications are designed to act as an extension to a handheld device—a smartphone or tablet. Integration with Wear may be performed with an application extension that gets installed on the Wear device. The extension is packaged with your handheld application and installed at the same time the handheld application installs. Integration also may not have an application extension to be installed on the Wear device; instead, the handheld device relays messages that are displayed on the screen of the Wear device in the form of a `Notification` using the `NotificationCompat` class.

There are minimal compatibility issues when your handheld application is only used to relay notifications for display on the Wear device; if those notifications contain icon images, resolution may need to be considered, but you must ensure the APIs used on the handheld remain compatible with the Android Wear API version paired with the handheld.

On the other hand, if the Wear integration requires a separate Wear application to be installed on the Wear device itself, you are now challenged with ensuring application compatibility across Wear devices, so things like layouts or device configurations are now more of an issue to contend with—in addition to compatibility issues you must maintain across handheld devices such as smartphones and tablets. The good news is that there are very few Android Wear devices on the market as of this writing, but this is surely going to change as more manufacturers move into the wearable device market.

For Android Auto, the dashboard console device acts as an extension to your handheld application and relays messages and audio, or allows for voice interaction or button presses on the console device, which means there is no application that needs to be installed on the console device. As of now, there are minimal compatibility issues to contend with, but make sure the APIs in your handheld application match up properly with the console device APIs.

Tip

To learn more about building applications for Android Wear, see *http://d.android.com/wear/index.html*. To learn more about building applications for Android Auto, see *http://d.android.com/auto/index.html*.

Ensuring Compatibility with `SafetyNet`

Even if you have implemented all of these compatibility design techniques, it does not mean your application is guaranteed to run as expected on the device on which it has been installed. How could this be, you may ask? Because Android is open source, anyone capable of building a hardware device could use Android as the operating system, without needing to pass any quality or compatibility requirements before going to market. In addition, you may come across a customer who replaced the stock Android of their device. This means you cannot guarantee that your application will perform as expected in this situation, even if you adhere to all of these compatibility recommendations.

With this in mind, Google Play has a service you can access called `SafetyNet` that will help you determine if a device is capable of running your application as intended. The AOSP does recommend to all hardware manufacturers that they build compatible devices, but that does not mean they will comply. In the hope that they do build compatible hardware devices, the AOSP has created the Compatibility Test Suite that allows manufacturers to check their device for compatibility against a series of manual or automatic tests. If a manufacturer passes these tests, Google records a profile for the device. That means the device is most likely configured to maintain compatibility for running your application as intended for the requirements you have specified in that application.

In order for you, the application developer, to use `SafetyNet`, you must agree to the Google API's Terms of Service. Once you have done so, you may make requests to the `SafetyNet` API to check if the device profile your application has been installed on matches the profile of a device that has passed the Compatibility Test Suite. If there is no match, you application may have problems running correctly—but maybe not; there really is no way to tell until the user reaches a part of your code that triggers an error. Unfortunately, there is nothing you can do in this situation until after the fact. On the other hand, if there is a profile match, your application may just run as expected, but really there are no guarantees other than that the device your application is running on is a match to a device profile that has passed the Compatibility Test Suite.

Tip

For more information on the `SafetyNet` API service, see *http://d.android.com/training/ safetynet/index.html*. For more information about Compatibility and the AOSP, see *https:// source.android.com/compatibility/index.html*.

Summary

Compatibility is a vast topic, and we've given you a lot to think about. During design and implementation, always consider if your choices are going to introduce roadblocks to device compatibility. Quality assurance personnel should always vary the devices used for testing as much as possible—certainly don't rely solely on emulator configurations for testing coverage. Use best practices that encourage compatibility, and do your best to keep compatibility-related resources and code streamlined and manageable.

If you take only two concepts away from this chapter, one should be that alternative resources and fragments can be used to great effect. They enable a flexibility that can go a long way toward achieving compatibility. The other is that certain Android manifest file tags can help ensure that your applications are installed only on devices that meet certain requirements. In addition, you learned about the compatibility similarities between smartphones, tablets, and TVs, and you should understand the differences in compatibility between handhelds and Wear, and handhelds and TV. Finally, to help you further determine if your application may work properly on the given device, you learned about a Google Play service that allows you to make API requests to determine if a device matches a compatibility profile that has passed the AOSP Compatibility Test Suite.

Quiz Questions

1. True or false: As a rule of thumb, to design user interfaces for compatibility, design for normal-size screens and medium resolution.

2. What percentage of Android devices currently on the market support the use of fragments?

3. What manifest file tag is used to explicitly state which screen sizes your application supports?

4. True or false: The directory `res/drawables-rGB-MDPI/` is a good example of an alternative resource directory with a qualifier.

5. What are the possible values for the layout direction's alternative resource directory qualifier?

6. True or false: You can request resources of a specific configuration programmatically.

7. What is the method call you should implement in your `Activity` class for handling configuration changes?

8. True or false: Your Android Auto applications are installed on a car's dashboard console device.

Exercises

1. Read through the "Best Practices" topic of the Android API Guides (*http://d.android.com/guide/practices/index.html*) to learn more about how to build apps that work for a wide range of devices.

2. Using the "Best Practices" Android API Guides, determine what the typical sizes in dp units are for small, normal, large, xlarge, xxlarge, and xxxlarge screens.

3. Using the "Best Practices" Android API Guides, determine what scaling ratio you should follow between the six screen densities of low, medium, high, extra-high, extra-extra-high, and extra-extra-extra-high.

4. Using the online documentation, determine the name of the SafetyNet attribute returned from the getJwsResult() method that tells you whether the device your application is being installed on matches a device profile that has passed the AOSP Compatibility Test Suite.

References and More Information

ScientiaMobile: Mobile Overview Report (MOVR) 2015 Q1:
  http://data.wurfl.io/MOVR/pdf/2015_q1/MOVR_2015_q1.pdf
Android SDK Reference regarding the application Dialog class:
  http://d.android.com/reference/android/app/Dialog.html
Android SDK Reference regarding the Android Support Library:
  http://d.android.com/tools/extras/support-library.html
Android API Guides: "Screen Compatibility Mode":
  http://d.android.com/guide/practices/screen-compat-mode.html
Android API Guides: "Providing Alternative Resources":
  http://d.android.com/guide/topics/resources/providing-resources.html#AlternativeResources
Android API Guides: "How Android Finds the Best-matching Resource":
  http://d.android.com/guide/topics/resources/providing-resources.html#BestMatch
Android API Guides: "Handling Runtime Changes":
  http://d.android.com/guide/topics/resources/runtime-changes.html
Android API Guides: "Device Compatibility":
  http://d.android.com/guide/practices/compatibility.html
Android API Guides: "Supporting Multiple Screens":
  http://d.android.com/guide/practices/screens_support.html
ISO 639-2 languages:
  http://www.loc.gov/standards/iso639-2/php/code_list.php
ISO 3166 country codes:
  http://www.iso.org/iso/home/standards/country_codes.htm

Android Training: "Building Apps for TV":
   http://d.android.com/training/tv/index.html
Android Training: "Building Apps for Wearables":
   http://d.android.com/training/building-wearables.html
Android Training: "Building Apps for Auto":
   http://d.android.com/training/auto/index.html

IV

Application
Development
Essentials

14
Using Android Preferences

Applications are about functionality and data. In this chapter, we explore the simplest way to store, manage, and share application data persistently within Android applications: by using shared preferences. The Android SDK includes a number of helpful APIs for storing and retrieving application preferences in different ways. Preferences are stored as groups of key/value pairs that can be used by the application. Shared preferences are most appropriate for storing simple kinds of data, such as application state and user settings, in a persistent fashion.

Working with Application Preferences

Many applications need a lightweight data storage mechanism called shared preferences for storing application state, simple user information, configuration options, and other such information. The Android SDK provides a simple preferences system for storing primitive application data at the `Activity` level as well as preferences shared across all of an application's activities.

> **Tip**
>
> Many of the code examples provided in this section are taken from the
> `SimplePreferences` application. The source code for the `SimplePreferences` application
> is provided for download on the book's website (*http://introductiontoandroid.blogspot.com*).

Determining When Preferences Are Appropriate

Application preferences are sets of data values that are stored *persistently*, meaning that the preference data persists across an application's lifecycle events. In other words, the application or device can be started and stopped—turned on and off—without losing the data.

Many simple data values can be stored as application preferences. For example, your application might want to store the username of the application's user. The application could use a single preference to store this information, as shown below:

- The data type of the preference is a `String`.
- The key for the stored value is a `String` called "UserName".
- The value for the data is the username "HarperLee1926".

Storing Different Types of Preference Values

Preferences are stored as groups of key/value pairs. The following data types are supported as preference-setting values:

- `Boolean` values
- `Float` values
- `Integer` values
- `Long` values
- `String` values
- A `Set` of multiple `String` values

Preference functionality can be found in the `SharedPreferences` interface of the `android.content` package. To add preferences support to your application, you must take the following steps:

1. Retrieve an instance of a `SharedPreferences` object.
2. Create a `SharedPreferences.Editor` to modify the preference content.
3. Make changes to the preferences using the `Editor`.
4. Commit your changes.

Creating Private Preferences for Use by a Single `Activity`

Individual activities can have their own private preferences, although they are still represented by the `SharedPreferences` class. These preferences are for the specific `Activity` only and are not shared with other activities within the application. The `Activity` gets only one group of private preferences, which are simply named after the `Activity` class. The following code retrieves an `Activity` class's private preferences, called from within the `Activity`:

```
import android.content.SharedPreferences;

...

SharedPreferences settingsActivity = getPreferences(MODE_PRIVATE);
```

You have now retrieved the private preferences for that specific `Activity` class. Because the underlying name is based on the `Activity` class, any change to the `Activity` class will change what preferences are read.

Creating Shared Preferences for Use by Multiple Activities

Creating shared preferences is similar. The only two differences are that we must name our preference set and use a different call to get the preference instance, as shown here:

```
import android.content.SharedPreferences;

...

SharedPreferences settings =

    getSharedPreferences("MyCustomSharedPreferences", MODE_PRIVATE);
```

You have now retrieved the shared preferences for the application. You can access these shared preferences by name from any `Activity` in the application. There is no limit to the number of different shared preferences you can create. For example, you could have some shared preferences called "UserNetworkPreferences" and others called "AppDisplayPreferences." How you organize shared preferences is up to you. However, you should declare the name of your preferences as a variable so that you can reuse the name across multiple activities consistently. Here is an example:

```
public static final String PREFERENCE_FILENAME = "AppPrefs";
```

Searching and Reading Preferences

Reading preferences is straightforward. Simply retrieve the `SharedPreferences` instance you want to read. You can check for a preference by name, retrieve strongly typed preferences, and register to listen for changes to the preferences. Table 14.1 describes some helpful methods in the `SharedPreferences` interface.

Table 14.1 Important **android.content.SharedPreferences** Methods

Method	Purpose
SharedPreferences.contains()	Sees whether a specific preference exists by name
SharedPreferences.edit()	Retrieves the Editor to change these preferences
SharedPreferences.getAll()	Retrieves a map of all preference key/value pairs
SharedPreferences.getBoolean()	Retrieves a specific Boolean-type preference by name
SharedPreferences.getFloat()	Retrieves a specific Float-type preference by name
SharedPreferences.getInt()	Retrieves a specific Integer-type preference by name
SharedPreferences.getLong()	Retrieves a specific Long-type preference by name
SharedPreferences.getString()	Retrieves a specific String-type preference by name
SharedPreferences.getStringSet()	Retrieves a specific Set of String preferences by name

Adding, Updating, and Deleting Preferences

To change preferences, you need to open the preference `Editor`, make your changes, and commit them. Table 14.2 describes some helpful methods in the `SharedPreferences.Editor` interface.

The following block of code retrieves an `Activity` class's private preferences, opens the preference `Editor`, adds a `Long`-type preference called `SomeLong`, and saves the change:

```
import android.content.SharedPreferences;

...

SharedPreferences settingsActivity = getPreferences(MODE_PRIVATE);

SharedPreferences.Editor prefEditor = settingsActivity.edit();

prefEditor.putLong("SomeLong", java.lang.Long.MIN_VALUE);

prefEditor.apply();
```

Table 14.2 Important **android.content.SharedPreferences.Editor** Methods

Method	Purpose
`SharedPreferences.Editor.clear()`	Removes all preferences. This operation happens before any put operation, regardless of when it is called within an editing session; then, all other changes are made and committed.
`SharedPreferences.Editor.remove()`	Removes a specific preference by name. This operation happens before any put operation, regardless of when it is called within an editing session; then, all other changes are made and committed.
`SharedPreferences.Editor.putBoolean()`	Sets a specific `Boolean`-type preference by name.
`SharedPreferences.Editor.putFloat()`	Sets a specific `Float`-type preference by name.
`SharedPreferences.Editor.putInt()`	Sets a specific `Integer`-type preference by name.
`SharedPreferences.Editor.putLong()`	Sets a specific `Long`-type preference by name.
`SharedPreferences.Editor.putString()`	Sets a specific `String`-type preference by name.
`SharedPreferences.Editor.putStringSet()`	Sets a specific `Set` of `String`-type preferences by name.
`SharedPreferences.Editor.commit()`	Commits all changes from this editing session.
`SharedPreferences.Editor.apply()`	Much like the `commit()` method, this method commits all preference changes from this editing session. However, this method commits the changes to in-memory `SharedPreferences` immediately, but commits the changes to disk asynchronously within the application lifecycle.

> **Tip**
>
> If you're targeting devices that run at least API Level 9 (Android 2.3 and higher), you would benefit from using the `apply()` method instead of the `commit()` method. However, if you need to support legacy versions of Android, you'll want to stick with the `commit()` method, or check at runtime before calling the most appropriate method. Even when you are writing as little as one preference, using `apply()` could smooth out the operation because any call to the file system may block for a noticeable (and therefore unacceptable) length of time.

Reacting to Preference Changes

Your application can listen for, and react to, changes to shared preferences by implementing a listener and registering it with the specific `SharedPreferences` object using the `registerOnSharedPreferenceChangeListener()` and `unregisterOnSharedPreferenceChangeListener()` methods. This interface class has just one callback, which passes to your code the shared preferences object that changed as well as which specific preference key name changed.

Finding Preferences Data on the File System

Internally, application preferences are stored as XML files. You can access the preferences file using the `File Explorer` via Android `Device Monitor`. You find these files on the Android file system in the following directory:

```
/data/data/<package name>/shared_prefs/<preferences filename>.xml
```

The preferences filename is the `Activity` class name for private preferences or the specific name you give for the shared preferences. Here is an example of the XML file contents of a preferences file with some simple values:

```
<?xml version="1.0" encoding="utf-8" standalone="yes" ?>

<map>

    <string name="String_Pref">Test String</string>

    <int name="Int_Pref" value="-2147483648" />

    <float name="Float_Pref" value="-Infinity" />

    <long name="Long_Pref" value="9223372036854775807" />

    <boolean name="Boolean_Pref" value="false" />

</map>
```

Understanding the application preferences file format can be helpful for testing purposes. You can use the Android `Device Monitor` to copy the preference files to and from the device. Since the shared preferences are just a file, regular file permissions apply. When creating the file, you specify the file's mode (permissions). This determines if the file is readable outside the existing package.

Note

For more information about using the Android `Device Monitor` and the `File Explorer`, please see Appendix C, "Quick-Start: Android `Device Monitor`."

Creating Manageable User Preferences

You now understand how to store and retrieve shared preferences programmatically. This works very well for keeping application state but what if you have a set of user settings and you want to create a simple, consistent, and platform-standard way in which the user can edit them? Good news! You can use the handy `PreferenceActivity` class (`android.preference.PreferenceActivity`) to easily achieve this goal.

Tip

Many of the code examples provided in this section are taken from the `SimpleUserPrefs` application. The source code for the `SimpleUserPrefs` application is provided for download on the book's website.

Implementing a `PreferenceActivity`-based solution requires the following steps:

1. Define the preference set in a preference resource file.
2. Implement a `PreferenceFragment` class and tie it to the preference resource file. Note that `PreferenceFragment` will work only on Android 3.0 and above. In the interest of backward compatibility, a `PreferenceActivity` without the `PreferenceFragment` can be used to support legacy platform versions as needed.
3. Implement a `PreferenceActivity` class and add the `PreferenceFragment` you just created.
4. Hook up the `Activity` within your application as you normally would. For example, register it in the manifest file, start the `Activity` as normal, and so on.

Now let's look at these steps in more detail.

Creating a Preference Resource File

First, you create an XML resource file to define the preferences your users are allowed to edit. A preference resource file contains a root-level `<PreferenceScreen>` tag, followed by various preference types. These preference types are based on the `Preference` class (`android.preference.Preference`) and its subclasses, such as `CheckBoxPreference`, `EditTextPreference`, `ListPreference`, `MultiSelectListPreference`, and more. Some preferences have been around since the Android SDK was first released, whereas others, such as the `MultiSelectListPreference` class, were introduced in Android API Level 11 and are not backward compatible with older devices.

Each preference should have some metadata, such as a title and some summary text that will be displayed to the user. You can also specify default values and, for those preferences that launch dialogs, the `Dialog` prompt. For the specific metadata associated with a given preference type, see its subclass attributes in the Android SDK documentation. Here are some common `Preference` attributes that most preferences should set:

- The `android:key` attribute is used to specify the key name for the shared preference.
- The `android:title` attribute is used to specify the friendly name of the preference, as shown on the editing screen.
- The `android:summary` attribute is used to give more details about the preference, as shown on the editing screen.
- The `android:defaultValue` attribute is used to specify a default value of the preference.

Like any resource files, preference resource files can use raw strings or reference string resources. The following example of a preference resource file does a bit of both (the string array resources are defined elsewhere in the `strings.xml` resource file):

```xml
<?xml version="1.0" encoding="utf-8"?>
<PreferenceScreen
    xmlns:android="http://schemas.android.com/apk/res/android">
    <EditTextPreference
        android:key="username"
        android:title="Username"
        android:summary="This is your ACME Service username"
        android:defaultValue=""
        android:dialogTitle="Enter your ACME Service username:" />
    <EditTextPreference
        android:key="email"
        android:title="Configure Email"
        android:summary="Enter your email address"
        android:defaultValue="your@email.com" />
    <PreferenceCategory
        android:title="Game Settings">
        <CheckBoxPreference
            android:key="bSoundOn"
            android:title="Enable Sound"
```

(Continues)

(Continued)

```
            android:summary="Turn sound on and off in the game"

            android:defaultValue="true" />

    <CheckBoxPreference

        android:key="bAllowCheats"

        android:title="Enable Cheating"

        android:summary="Turn the ability to cheat on and off in the game"

        android:defaultValue="false" />

</PreferenceCategory>

<PreferenceCategory

    android:title="Game Character Settings">

    <ListPreference

        android:key="gender"

        android:title="Game Character Gender"

        android:summary="This is the gender of your game character"

        android:entries="@array/char_gender_types"

        android:entryValues="@array/char_genders"

        android:dialogTitle="Choose a gender for your character:" />

    <ListPreference

        android:key="race"

        android:title="Game Character Race"

        android:summary="This is the race of your game character"

        android:entries="@array/char_race_types"

        android:entryValues="@array/char_races"

        android:dialogTitle="Choose a race for your character:" />

</PreferenceCategory>

</PreferenceScreen>
```

This XML preference file is organized into two categories and defines fields for collecting several pieces of information, including a username (String), sound setting (boolean),
cheat setting (boolean), character gender (fixed String), and character race (fixed String).

For instance, this example uses the CheckBoxPreference type to manage boolean
shared preference values, for example, game settings such as whether or not sound is enabled or whether cheating is allowed. Boolean values are checked on and off straight from
the screen. The example uses the EditTextPreference type to manage the username, and
it uses ListPreference types to allow the user to choose from a list of options. Finally,
the settings are organized into categories using <PreferenceCategory> tags.

Next, you need to wire up your PreferenceActivity class and tell it about your preference resource file.

Using the **PreferenceActivity** Class

The PreferenceActivity class (android.preference.PreferenceActivity) is a helper class that is capable of displaying a PreferenceFragment. This PreferenceFragment loads up your XML preference resource file and transforms it into a standard settings screen, much as you see in the Android device settings. Figure 14.1 shows what the screen for the preference resource file discussed in the previous section looks like when loaded into a PreferenceActivity class.

To wire up your new preference resource file, create a new class that extends the PreferenceActivity class within your application. Next, override the onCreate() method of your class. Retrieve the FragmentManager for the Activity, start a FragmentTransaction, insert your PreferenceFragment into the Activity, and then call commit(). Tie the preference resource file to the PreferenceFragment class using the addPreferencesFromResource() method. You will also want to retrieve an instance of the PreferenceManager (android.preference.PreferenceManager) and set the name of these preferences for use in the rest of your application at this time, if you're using a name other than the default. Here is the complete implementation of the SimpleUserPrefsActivity class, which encapsulates these steps:

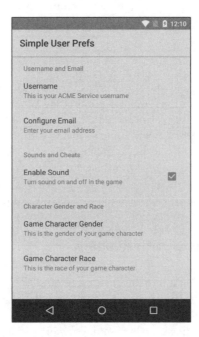

Figure 14.1   Game settings managed with PreferenceActivity.

```
public class SimpleUserPrefsActivity extends PreferenceActivity {

    @Override
    public void onCreate(Bundle savedInstanceState) {

        super.onCreate(savedInstanceState);

        FragmentManager manager = getFragmentManager();

        FragmentTransaction transaction = manager.beginTransaction();

        transaction.replace(android.R.id.content,
                new SimpleUserPrefsFragment());

        transaction.commit();

    }


    public static class SimpleUserPrefsFragment extends PreferenceFragment {

        @Override
        public void onCreate(Bundle savedInstanceState) {

            super.onCreate(savedInstanceState);

            PreferenceManager manager = getPreferenceManager();

            manager.setSharedPreferencesName("user_prefs");

            addPreferencesFromResource(R.xml.userprefs);

        }

    }

}
```

Now you can simply wire up the `Activity` as you normally would. Don't forget to register it within your application's Android manifest file. When you run the application and start the `UserPrefsActivity`, you should see a screen that looks like Figure 14.1. Trying to edit all other preferences will launch a dialog with the appropriate type of prompt (`EditText` or `Spinner` control), as shown in Figures 14.2 and 14.3.

Use the `EditTextPreference` type to manage `String` shared preference values, such as username, as shown in Figure 14.2.

Use the `ListPreference` type to force the user to choose from a list of options, as shown in Figure 14.3.

Organizing Preferences with Headers

The concept of `Preference` headers was added in Android 3.0 (API Level 11). The headers feature allows your application to present a list of options for navigating to setting subscreens. A very good example of a system application that uses the headers feature is the Android system Settings application. On large-screen devices, the left pane displays the setting list items and, depending on which setting item is selected, determines what setting options are displayed in the right pane. There are a few setup steps for making your application ready for incorporating the `Preference` headers feature:

1. Create individual `PreferenceFragment` classes for each setting collection.

Figure 14.2 Editing an `EditText` (`String`) preference.

2. Define the header list using the `<preference-headers>` tag in a new XML file.
3. Create a new `PreferenceActivity` class that calls the method `onBuildHeaders()` for loading the headers resource file.

Tip

Many of the code examples provided in this section are taken from the `UserPrefsHeaders` application. The source code for the `UserPrefsHeaders` application is provided for download on the book's website.

An example of a headers file follows, which groups settings into separate header entries:

```
<preference-headers xmlns:android="http://schemas.android.com/apk/res/android">
    <header
            android:fragment=
"com.introtoandroid.userprefs.UserPrefsHeadersActivity$UserNameFrag"
            android:title="Personal Settings"
            android:summary="Configure your personal settings" />
    <header
```

(Continues)

(Continued)

```
            android:fragment=
"com.introtoandroid.userprefs.UserPrefsHeadersActivity$GameSettingsFrag"
            android:title="Game Settings"
            android:summary="Configure your game settings" />
    <header
            android:fragment=
"com.introtoandroid.userprefs.UserPrefsHeadersActivity$CharSettingsFrag"
            android:title="Character Settings"
            android:summary="Configure your character settings" />
</preference-headers>
```

Here, we have defined some <header> entries within a <preference-headers> node. Each <header> defines just three attributes: android:fragment, android:title, and android:summary. Here is how our new UserPrefsHeadersActivity class should look:

```
public class UserPrefsHeadersActivity extends PreferenceActivity {
    /** Called when the activity is first created. */
    @Override
```

Figure 14.3 Editing a ListPreference (String array) preference.

```java
public void onCreate(Bundle savedInstanceState) {

    super.onCreate(savedInstanceState);

}


@Override
public void onBuildHeaders(List<Header> target) {

    loadHeadersFromResource(R.xml.preference_headers, target);

}


@Override
protected boolean isValidFragment(String fragmentName) {

    return UserNameFragment.class.getName().equals(fragmentName) ||

            GameSettingsFragment.class.getName().equals(fragmentName) ||

            CharacterSettingsFragment.class.getName().equals(fragmentName);

}


public static class UserNameFrag extends PreferenceFragment {

    @Override
    public void onCreate(Bundle savedInstanceState) {

        super.onCreate(savedInstanceState);

        PreferenceManager manager = getPreferenceManager();

        manager.setSharedPreferencesName("user_prefs");

        addPreferencesFromResource(R.xml.personal_settings);

    }

}


public static class GameSettingsFrag extends PreferenceFragment {

    @Override
    public void onCreate(Bundle savedInstanceState) {

        super.onCreate(savedInstanceState);

        PreferenceManager manager = getPreferenceManager();

        manager.setSharedPreferencesName("user_prefs");

        addPreferencesFromResource(R.xml.game_settings);

    }

}
```

(Continues)

(Continued)

```
    public static class CharSettingsFrag extends PreferenceFragment {
        @Override
        public void onCreate(Bundle savedInstanceState) {
            super.onCreate(savedInstanceState);
            PreferenceManager manager = getPreferenceManager();
            manager.setSharedPreferencesName("user_prefs");
            addPreferencesFromResource(R.xml.character_settings);
        }
    }
}
```

For the sake of clarity, we will show just one of the `<PreferenceScreen>` files:

```
<PreferenceScreen xmlns:android="http://schemas.android.com/apk/res/android">
    <PreferenceCategory
        android:title="Username and Email">

        <EditTextPreference
            android:key="username"
            android:title="Username"
            android:summary="This is your ACME Service username"
            android:defaultValue="username01"
            android:dialogTitle="Enter your ACME Service username:" />

        <EditTextPreference
            android:key="email"
            android:title="Configure Email"
            android:summary="Enter your email address"
            android:defaultValue="your@email.com" />
    </PreferenceCategory>
</PreferenceScreen>
```

Now that we have implemented our application, we are able to see the differences in how the settings are displayed on single-pane (see Figure 14.4) and two-pane screens (see Figure 14.5).

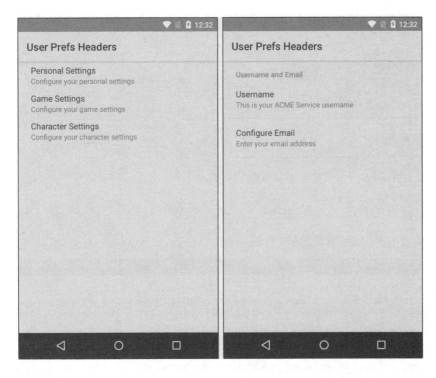

Figure 14.4   Preference headers appear on a small screen as a
single-pane layout, showing the headers layout (left) and the settings layout (right).

Tip

A headers list displayed on small-screen devices in single-pane mode can be cumbersome
to navigate. Instead, it is usually better for smaller-screen devices to present the settings
page directly, rather than showing the headers list that groups individual
PreferenceScreen items.

Auto Backup for Android Applications

Android Marshmallow introduced a new feature known as Auto Backup for Apps. You
can now easily implement a full data backup and restore for your applications that targets
Android Marshmallow. This new feature is useful for saving important information for
users in case they lose their device, upgrade it, or uninstall and reinstall your application,
preserving this important information with very little development effort on your part.

You should consider implementing backup and restore for application preferences. To
get your application to backup preference data, you simply add the android:allowBackup

Figure 14.5   `Preference` headers and settings appear on a large screen as a two-pane layout.

attribute set to the value of `true` and add the `android:fullBackupContent` attribute to the `<application>` tag in your Android manifest; then set that value to `true` or you may even define an XML resource file that specifies the data your application should include or exclude from backup and restore. Setting the `allowBackup` attribute to `false` prevents any of your application data from being automatically backed up.

To add the automatic backup functionality to our `SimplePreferences` application, the `<application>` tag would look like the following:

```
<application

    android:allowBackup="true"

    android:icon="@mipmap/ic_launcher"

    android:label="@string/app_name"

    android:theme="@style/AppTheme"

    android:fullBackupContent="true">
```

Now, when a user modifies his or her application preferences, your application is capable of backing up the data, which is encrypted and then uploaded to the user's Google Drive account. Your users may opt out of this feature if they so choose.

Application developers can save a reasonable amount of data (currently 25MB) for their users per Android app with Auto Backup. The data will be backed up every 24 hours, so if your users lose their device or uninstall your application, recovering the data for your users is really easy, as reinstalling will check the users' Google Drive to see if there is data for your application to restore.

To learn more about the Auto Backup service for configuring what data your application should or should not backup, and for the commands to test out this functionality with the `SimplePreferences` application, see *http://d.android.com/preview/backup/index.html.*

Summary

In this chapter, you learned about the variety of different ways to store and manage application data that is available on the Android platform. The method you use depends on what kind of data you need to store. With these skills, you are well on your way to leveraging one of the more powerful and unique features of Android. Use shared preferences to store simple application data, such as strings and numbers, in a persistent manner. You can also use the `PreferenceActivity` or `PreferenceFragment` class to simplify the creation of user preference screens within your application that use the standard look and feel of the platform on which your application is running. You learned how to use `Preference` headers for displaying your application preferences in either a single-pane or two-pane layout. In addition, you learned that you can perform a full data backup and restore for users when your application targets Android Marshmallow and newer.

Quiz Questions

1. What are the different data types supported as preference-setting values?
2. True or false: You use the `getPreferences()` method to retrieve the private preferences of a specific `Activity`.
3. What is the directory on the Android file system that stores application `Preference` XML files?
4. What are the common `Preference` attributes that most preferences should set?
5. What is the method call for accessing the `Preference` resource file from within a `PreferenceFragment`?
6. What is the `<application>` attribute for configuring Auto Backup for your applications that target Android Marshmallow and future versions?

Exercises

1. Using information gathered from the Android documentation, write a simple code snippet demonstrating how you would configure a preference item to launch an `Activity` instead of a setting screen.
2. Using the Android documentation, determine the `SharedPreferences` method call for listening for preference changes.
3. Using the `SimpleUserPrefs` and `UserPrefsHeaders` applications, modify the code to display only the `<preference-headers>` list on large screens in two-pane mode.

References and More Information

Android SDK Reference regarding the `SharedPreferences` interface:
  http://d.android.com/reference/android/content/SharedPreferences.html
Android SDK Reference regarding the `SharedPreferences.Editor` interface:
  http://d.android.com/reference/android/content/SharedPreferences.Editor.html
Android SDK Reference regarding the `PreferenceActivity` class:
  http://d.android.com/reference/android/preference/PreferenceActivity.html
Android SDK Reference regarding the `PreferenceScreen` class:
  http://d.android.com/reference/android/preference/PreferenceScreen.html
Android SDK Reference regarding the `PreferenceCategory` class:
  http://d.android.com/reference/android/preference/PreferenceCategory.html
Android SDK Reference regarding the `Preference` class:
  http://d.android.com/reference/android/preference/Preference.html
Android SDK Reference regarding the `CheckBoxPreference` class:
  http://d.android.com/reference/android/preference/CheckBoxPreference.html
Android SDK Reference regarding the `EditTextPreference` class:
  http://d.android.com/reference/android/preference/EditTextPreference.html
Android SDK Reference regarding the `ListPreference` class:
  http://d.android.com/reference/android/preference/ListPreference.html
Android Preview regarding Auto Backup for Apps:
  http://developer.android.com/preview/backup/index.html

15

Accessing Files and Directories

Android applications can store raw files on a device by using a variety of methods. The Android SDK includes a number of helpful APIs for working with private application and cache files, as well as for accessing external files on removable storage such as SD cards. Developers who need to store information safely and persistently will find the available file management APIs familiar and easy to use. In this chapter, we show you how to use the Android file system to read, write, and delete application data.

Working with Application Data on a Device

As discussed in Chapter 14, "Using Android Preferences," shared preferences provide a simple mechanism for storing simple application data persistently. However, many applications require a more robust solution that allows for any type of data to be stored and accessed in a persistent fashion. Some types of data that an application might want to store include the following:

- **Multimedia content such as images, sounds, video, and other complex information:** These types of data structures are not supported as shared preferences. You may, however, store a shared preference that includes the file path or URI to the multimedia and store the multimedia on the device's file system or download it only when needed.

- **Content downloaded from a network:** As mobile devices, Android devices are not guaranteed to have persistent network connections. Ideally, an application will download content from the network once and keep it as long as necessary. Sometimes data should be kept indefinitely, whereas other circumstances simply require data to be cached for a certain amount of time.

- **Complex content generated by the application:** Android devices function under stricter memory and storage constraints than desktop computers and servers do. Therefore, if your application has taken a long time to process data and come up with a result, that result should be stored for reuse, as opposed to re-creating it on demand.

Android applications can create and use directories and files to store their data in a variety of ways, some of which include the following:

- Storing private application data under the application directory
- Caching data under the application's cache directory
- Storing shared application data on external storage or on shared directory areas

Note

You can use the Android `Device Monitor` to copy files to and from a device. For more information about using Android `Device Monitor` and the `File Explorer`, please see Appendix C, "Quick-Start: Android `Device Monitor`."

Practicing Good File Management

You should follow a number of best practices when working with files on the Android file system. Here are a few of the most important ones:

- Anytime you read or write data to disk, you are performing intensive blocking operations and using valuable device resources. Therefore, in most cases, the file access functionality of your applications should not be performed on the main UI thread of the application. Instead, these operations should be handled asynchronously using threads, `AsyncTask` objects, or other asynchronous methods. Even working with small files can slow down the UI thread due to the nature of the underlying file system and hardware.

- Android devices have limited storage capacity. Therefore, to free up space on the device, store only what you need to store, and clean up old data when you no longer need it. Use external storage whenever it is appropriate to give the user more flexibility.

- Be a good citizen: be sure to check for availability of resources such as disk space and external storage opportunities prior to using them and causing errors or crashes. Also, don't forget to set appropriate file permissions for new files, and to release resources when you're not using them (in other words, if you open them, close them, and so on).

- Implement efficient file access algorithms for reading, writing, and parsing file contents. Use the many profiling tools available as part of the Android SDK to identify and improve the performance of your code. A good place to start is with the `StrictMode` API (`android.os.StrictMode`).

- If the data the application needs to store is well structured, you may want to consider using a SQLite database to store that application data.

- Test your application on real devices. Different devices have different processor speeds. Do not assume that because your application runs smoothly on the emulator it will run that way on real devices. If you're using external storage, test when external storage is not available.

Let's explore how file management is achieved on the Android platform.

Understanding Android File Permissions

Remember from Chapter 1, "Presenting Android," that each Android application is its own user on the underlying Linux operating system. It has its own application directory and files. Files created in the application's directory are private to that application by default.

Files can be created on the Android file system with different permissions. These permissions specify how a file is accessed. Permission modes are most commonly used when creating files. These permission modes are defined in the `Context` class (`android.content.Context`):

- `MODE_PRIVATE` (the default) is used to create a file that can be accessed only by the "owner" application itself. From a Linux perspective, this means the specific user identifier. The constant value of `MODE_PRIVATE` is `0`, so you may see this used in legacy code.

- `MODE_APPEND` is used to append data to the end of an existing file. The constant value of `MODE_APPEND` is `32768`.

Warning

Up until API Level 17, `MODE_WORLD_READABLE` and `MODE_WORLD_WRITEABLE` constants were viable options for exposing data to other applications, but they have now been deprecated. Using these constants in your applications may present security vulnerabilities when exposing data to other applications. Exposing your application's data using these two file permission settings is now discouraged. The new and recommended approach is to use API components specifically designed for exposing application data for reading and writing by others, which include using the `Service`, `ContentProvider`, and/or `BroadcastReceiver` APIs.

An application does not need any special Android manifest file permissions to access its own private file system area. With Android versions prior to 4.4, in order for your application to access external storage, it needed to register for the `READ_EXTERNAL_STORAGE` or `WRITE_EXTERNAL_STORAGE` permission. As of Android 4.4, you do not need to request those permissions to read or write private files to your application, only if your application needs access to the public external storage space.

Working with Files and Directories

Within the Android SDK, you can also find a variety of standard Java file utility classes (such as `java.io`) for handling different types of files, such as text files, binary files, and XML files. In Chapter 6, "Managing Application Resources," you learned that Android applications can also include raw and XML files as resources. Retrieving the file handle to a resource file is performed slightly differently from accessing files on the device file system, but once you have a file handle, either method allows you to perform read operations and other file operations in the same fashion. After all, a file is a file.

Clearly, Android application file resources are part of the application package and are therefore accessible only to the application itself. But what about file system files? Android application files are stored in a standard directory hierarchy on the Android file system.

Generally speaking, applications access the Android device file system using methods within the `Context` class (`android.content.Context`). The application, or any `Activity` class, can use the application `Context` to access its private application file directory or cache directory. From there, you can add, remove, and access files associated with your application. By default, these files are private to the application and cannot be accessed by other applications or by the user.

> **Tip**
>
> Many of the code examples provided in this section are taken from the `SimpleFiles` and `FileStreamOfConsciousness` applications. The `SimpleFiles` application demonstrates basic file and directory operations; it has no user interface (just `logcat` output). The `FileStreamOfConsciousness` application demonstrates how to log strings to a file as a chat stream; this application is multithreaded. The source code for these applications is provided for download on the book's website (*http://introductiontoandroid. blogspot.com*).

Exploring the Android Application Directories

Android application data is stored on the Android file system in the following top-level directory:

```
/data/data/<package name>/
```

Several default subdirectories are created for storing databases, preferences, and files as necessary. The actual location of these directories varies by device. You can also create other custom directories as needed. All file operations begin by interacting with the application `Context` object. Table 15.1 lists some important methods available for application file management. You can use all the standard `java.io` package utilities to work with `FileStream` objects.

Table 15.1 **Important `android.content.Context` File Management Methods**

Method	Purpose
`Context.deleteFile()`	Deletes a private application file by name. Note: You can also use the `File` class methods.
`Context.fileList()`	Gets a list of all files in the `files` subdirectory.
`Context.getCacheDir()`	Retrieves the application `cache` subdirectory.
`Context.getDir()`	Creates or retrieves an application subdirectory by name.
`Context.getExternalCacheDir()`	Retrieves the `cache` subdirectory on the external file system (API Level 8).
`Context.getExternalCacheDirs()`	Retrieves the `cache` subdirectories of the external file system from the emulated external partition of the internal storage device and from the external storage of the removable storage device (API Level 19).
`Context.getExternalFilesDir()`	Retrieves the `files` subdirectory on the external file system (API Level 8).
`Context.getExternalFilesDirs()`	Retrieves the `files` subdirectories of the external file system from the emulated external partition of the internal storage device and from the external storage of the removable storage device (API Level 19).
`Context.getFilesDir()`	Retrieves the application `files` subdirectory.
`Context.getFileStreamPath()`	Returns the absolute file path to the application `files` subdirectory.
`Context.getNoBackupFilesDir()`	Retrieves the application `files` subdirectory and files placed here will not be included for backup with Backup Manager (API 21).
`Context.openFileInput()`	Opens a private application file for reading.
`Context.openFileOutput()`	Opens a private application file for writing.

Creating and Writing to Files in the Default Application Directory

Android applications that require only the occasional file to be created should rely upon the helpful `Context` class method called `openFileOutput()`. Use this method to create files in the default location under the application data directory:

```
/data/data/<package name>/files/
```

For example, the following code snippet creates and opens a file called `Filename.txt`. We write a single line of text to the file and then close the file:

```
import java.io.FileOutputStream;

...

FileOutputStream fos;
```

(Continues)

(*Continued*)

```
String strFileContents = "Some text to write to the file.";
fos = openFileOutput("Filename.txt", MODE_PRIVATE);
fos.write(strFileContents.getBytes());
fos.close();
```

We can append data to the file by opening it with the mode set to MODE_APPEND:

```
import java.io.FileOutputStream;

...

FileOutputStream fos;
String strFileContents = "More text to write to the file.";
fos = openFileOutput("Filename.txt", MODE_APPEND);
fos.write(strFileContents.getBytes());
fos.close();
```

The file we created has the following path on the Android file system:

```
/data/data/<package name>/files/Filename.txt
```

Figure 15.1 shows a screen capture of an Activity that is configured to collect text input from a user, and then it writes the information to a text file when Send is clicked.

Figure 15.1   A screen capture of an Activity that is capable of writing to a text file.

Reading from Files in the Default Application Directory

Once again, we have a shortcut for reading files stored in the default `files` subdirectory. The following code snippet opens a file called `Filename.txt` for read operations:

```
import java.io.FileInputStream;

...

String strFileName = "Filename.txt";

FileInputStream fis = openFileInput(strFileName);
```

Figure 15.2 shows a screen capture of an `Activity` that is configured to read the information from a text file upon launching the `Activity`.

Reading Raw Files Byte by Byte

You handle file-reading and file-writing operations using standard Java methods. The `java.io.InputStreamReader` and `java.io.BufferedReader` are used for reading bytes

Figure 15.2   A screen capture of an `Activity` reading from a text file and displaying the contents.

and characters from different types of primitive file types. Here's a simple example of how to read a text file, line by line, and store it in a `StringBuffer`:

```
FileInputStream fis = openFileInput(filename);

StringBuffer sBuffer = new StringBuffer();

BufferedReader dataIO = new BufferedReader (new InputStreamReader(fis));

String strLine = null;


while ((strLine = dataIO.readLine()) != null) {

    sBuffer.append(strLine + "\n");

}


dataIO.close();

fis.close();
```

Reading XML Files

The Android SDK includes several utilities for working with XML files, including SAX, an XML Pull Parser, and limited DOM, Level 2 Core support. Table 15.2 lists the packages helpful for XML parsing on the Android platform.

Your XML parsing implementation will depend on which parser you choose to use. Back in Chapter 6, "Managing Application Resources," we discussed including raw XML resource files in your application package. Here is a simple example of how to load an XML resource file and parse it using an `XmlPullParser`.

The XML resource file contents, as defined in the res/xml/my_pets.xml file, are as follows:

```xml
<?xml version="1.0" encoding="UTF-8"?>

<!-- Our pet list -->

<pets>

    <pet type="Bunny" name="Bit"/>

    <pet type="Bunny" name="Nibble"/>

    <pet type="Bunny" name="Stack"/>

    <pet type="Bunny" name="Queue"/>

    <pet type="Bunny" name="Heap"/>

    <pet type="Bunny" name="Null"/>

    <pet type="Fish" name="Nigiri"/>

    <pet type="Fish" name="Sashimi II"/>

    <pet type="Lovebird" name="Kiwi"/>

</pets>
```

Table 15.2 **Important XML Utilities**

Package or Class	Purpose
android.sax.*	Framework to write standard SAX handlers
android.util.Xml	XML utilities, including the XMLPullParser creator
org.xml.sax.*	Core SAX functionality (project: *http://www.saxproject.org*)
javax.xml.*	SAX and limited DOM, Level 2 Core support
org.w3c.dom	Interfaces for DOM, Level 2 Core
org.xmlpull.*	XmlPullParser and XMLSerializer interfaces as well as a SAX2 Driver class (project: *http://xmlpull.org*)

The following code illustrates how to parse the preceding XML using a special pull parser designed for XML resource files:

```
XmlResourceParser myPets = getResources().getXml(R.xml.my_pets);
int eventType = -1;
while (eventType != XmlResourceParser.END_DOCUMENT) {
    if(eventType == XmlResourceParser.START_DOCUMENT) {
        Log.d(DEBUG_TAG, "Document Start");
    } else if(eventType == XmlResourceParser.START_TAG) {
        String strName = myPets.getName();
        if(strName.equals("pet")) {
            Log.d(DEBUG_TAG, "Found a PET");
            Log.d(DEBUG_TAG,
                "Name: "+myPets.getAttributeValue(null, "name"));
            Log.d(DEBUG_TAG,
                "Species: "+myPets.
                getAttributeValue(null, "type"));
        }
    }
    eventType = myPets.next();
}
Log.d(DEBUG_TAG, "Document End");
```

Tip

You can review the complete implementation of this parser in the ResourceRoundup project found in the Chapter 6 directory.

Supporting Adoptable Storage Devices

Android Marshmallow introduced a new feature for device users that allows them to adopt their external storage device—usually an SD card—by encrypting and formatting the SD card to function just like internal storage. This will allow users to transfer their applications and associated private files among the internal storage and the SD card, which functions just like internal storage. You need to make sure not to hard-code file path names with this new feature, since the file path names will dynamically change when users move your application and associated files from one storage device to the other. You should use the `Context` methods for determining path names—methods such as `getFilesDir()` and `getDir()`. To learn more about this new addition to Android Marshmallow and to see a list of the methods you should use for determining path names, see *http://d.android.com/preview/behavior-changes.html#behavior-adoptable-storage*.

Working with Other Directories and Files on the Android File System

Using `Context.openFileOutput()` and `Context.openFileInput()` method calls are great if you have a few files and you want them stored in the application's private `files` subdirectory, but if you have more sophisticated file management needs, you'll want to set up your own directory structure. To do this, you must interact with the Android file system using the standard `java.io.File` class methods.

The following code retrieves the `File` object for the `files` application subdirectory and retrieves a list of all filenames in that directory:

```
import java.io.File;

...

File pathForAppFiles = getFilesDir();
String[] fileList = pathForAppFiles.list();
```

Here is a more generic method to create a file on the file system. This method works anywhere on the Android file system you have permission to access, not just the `files` subdirectory:

```
import java.io.File;

import java.io.FileOutputStream;

...

File fileDir = getFilesDir();
String strNewFileName = "myFile.dat";
String strFileContents = "Some data for our file";


File newFile = new File(fileDir, strNewFileName);
newFile.createNewFile();
```

```
FileOutputStream fo =
    new FileOutputStream(newFile.getAbsolutePath());
fo.write(strFileContents.getBytes());
fo.close();
```

You can use `File` objects to manage files within a desired directory and create subdirectories. For example, you might want to store "track" files within "album" directories. Or perhaps you want to create a file in a directory other than the default. Let's say you want to cache some data to speed up your application's performance and how often it accesses the network. In this instance, you might want to create a cache file. There is also a special application directory for storing cache files. Cache files are stored in the following location on the Android file system, retrievable with a call to the `getCacheDir()` method:

```
/data/data/<package name>/cache/
```

The external cache directory, found via a call to the `getExternalCacheDir()` method, is not treated the same in that files are not automatically removed from it.

Warning

Applications are responsible for managing their own cache directory and keeping it to a reasonable size (1MB is commonly recommended). The system places no limit on the number of files in a cache directory. The Android file system deletes cache files from the internal cache directory (`getCacheDir()`) as needed when internal storage space is low, or when the user uninstalls the application.

The following code gets a `File` object for the `cache` application subdirectory, creates a new file in that specific directory, writes some data to the file, closes the file, and then deletes it:

```
File pathCacheDir = getCacheDir();
String strCacheFileName = "myCacheFile.cache";
String strFileContents = "Some data for our file";


File newCacheFile = new File(pathCacheDir, strCacheFileName);
newCacheFile.createNewFile();


FileOutputStream foCache =
    new FileOutputStream(newCacheFile.getAbsolutePath());
foCache.write(strFileContents.getBytes());
foCache.close();
newCacheFile.delete();
```

Creating and Writing Files to External Storage

Applications should store large amounts of data on external storage (using the SD card) rather than on limited internal storage. You can access external file storage, such as the SD card, from within your application as well. This is a little trickier than working within the confines of the application directory, as SD cards are removable, and so you need to check to see if the storage is mounted before use.

Tip

You can monitor file and directory activity on the Android file system using the `File Observer` class (`android.os.FileObserver`). You can monitor storage capacity using the `StatFs` class (`android.os.StatFs`).

You can access external storage on the device using the `Environment` class (`android.os.Environment`). Begin by using the `getExternalStorageState()` method to check the mount status of external storage. You can store private application files on external storage, or you can store public shared files such as media. If you want to store private application files, use the `getExternalFilesDir()` method of the `Context` class because these files will be cleaned up if the application is uninstalled later. The external cache is accessed using the similar `getExternalCacheDir()` method. However, if you want to store shared files such as pictures, movies, music, ringtones, or podcasts on external storage, you can use the `getExternalStoragePublicDirectory()` method of the `Environment` class to get the top-level directory used to store a specific file type.

Tip

Applications that use external storage are best tested on real hardware, as opposed to the emulator. You'll want to make sure you thoroughly test your application with various external storage states, including mounted, unmounted, and read-only modes. Each device may have different physical paths, so directory names should not be hard-coded.

Maintaining Backward Compatibility

Some Android devices format the internal storage device with two partitions—one to act as the internal storage, and another to emulate external storage. In addition, some of those devices include an SD card slot. This sounds like a useful feature, but with Android versions 4.3 and older, the `Context.getExternalFilesDir()` method would not allow access to the external SD card, as it would return path information for the emulated external storage. Android 4.4 added new methods that allow your application to access both the emulated external storage on the internal partition, and the SD card slot external storage with the method `Context.getExternalFilesDirs()`. This method returns an array including both external storage results. In addition, the Android Support v4 library includes a backward-compatible helper class to access this same method. Just include the

ContextCompat in place of Context, and call getExternalFilesDirs() to access both external storage areas on devices older than Android 4.4. We talk more about adding the Android Support library in Chapter 13, "Designing Compatible Applications."

Summary

There are a variety of ways to store and manage application data on the Android platform. The method you use depends on what kind of data you need to store. Applications have access to the underlying Android file system, where they can store their own private files, as well as limited access to the file system at large. It is important to follow best practices, such as performing disk operations asynchronously, when working on the Android file system, because mobile devices have limited storage and computing power. This chapter covered many different ways for working with files using both internal and external storage with many tips to help your development.

Quiz Questions

1. What are the constant values of the Android file permission modes of MODE_PRIVATE and MODE_APPEND?

2. True or false: Storing files using the MODE_WORLD_READABLE and MODE_WORLD_WRITEABLE permissions is the new recommended way for exposing your application's data to others.

3. What is the top-level directory for storing Android application data on the Android file system?

4. What is the name of the Context class method call for creating files under the application data directory?

5. What is the name of the Context class method call for retrieving the external cache directory?

6. True or false: The android.os.Environment.getExternalStorageMountStatus() method is used for determining the mount state of a device's external storage.

Exercises

1. Using the Android documentation, describe how to hide media files saved to a public external file directory to prevent Android's media scanner from including the media files in other applications.

2. Create an application that is able to display the result of whether the SD card is available or not prior to accessing the external storage system.

3. Create an application for storing image files to the Pictures directory of external storage.

References and More Information

Android SDK Reference regarding the `java.io` package:
  http://d.android.com/reference/java/io/package-summary.html
Android SDK Reference regarding the `Context` interface:
  http://d.android.com/reference/android/content/Context.html
Android SDK Reference regarding the `File` class:
  http://d.android.com/reference/java/io/File.html
Android SDK Reference regarding the `Environment` class:
  http://d.android.com/reference/android/os/Environment.html
Android Training: "Saving Files":
  http://d.android.com/training/basics/data-storage/files.html
Android API Guides: "Using the Internal Storage":
  http://d.android.com/guide/topics/data/data-storage.html#filesInternal
Android API Guides: "Using the External Storage":
  http://d.android.com/guide/topics/data/data-storage.html#filesExternal
Android API Guides: "App Install Location":
  http://d.android.com/guide/topics/data/install-location.html
Android API Guides: "<manifest>":
  http://d.android.com/guide/topics/manifest/manifest-element.html
Android SDK Reference regarding the `ContextCompat` class:
  http://d.android.com/reference/android/support/v4/content/ContextCompat.html

16

Saving with SQLite

There are many different ways for storing your Android applications' data. As you learned in Chapter 14, "Using Android Preferences," and in Chapter 15, "Accessing Files and Directories," there is definitely more than one way for accessing and storing your data. But what if you need to store structured data for your application, such as data more suited for storing in a database? That's where SQLite comes in. In this chapter, we are going to be modifying the SampleMaterial application found in Chapter 12, "Embracing Material Design," so that Card data is stored persistently in a SQLite database on the device and will survive various lifecycle events. By the end of this chapter, you will be confident in adding a SQLite database for your application.

SampleMaterial Upgraded with SQLite

The SampleMaterial application found in Chapter 12, "Embracing Material Design," shows you how to work with data in the application but fails when it comes to storing the data permanently so that it survives Android lifecycle events. When adding, updating, and deleting cards from the SampleMaterial application, and then clearing the SampleMaterial application from the Recent apps, the application is not able to remember what cards were added, updated, and deleted. So we updated the application to store the information in a SQLite database to keep track of the data permanently. Figure 16.1 shows the SampleSQLite application, which looks the same as the SampleMaterial application, but is backed by a SQLite database.

Working with Databases

The first thing that must be done is to define the database table that should be created for storing the cards in the database. Luckily, Android provides a helper class for defining a SQLite database table through Java code. That class is called SQLiteOpenHelper. You need to create a Java class that extends from the SQLiteOpenHelper, and this is where you can define a database name and version, and where you define the tables and columns. This is also where you create and upgrade your database. For the SampleSQLite application,

Figure 16.1   Showing the SampleSQLite application.

we created a CardsDBHelper class that extends from SQLiteOpenHelper, and here's the implementation that can be found in the CardsDBHelper.java file:

```java
public class CardsDBHelper extends SQLiteOpenHelper {
    private static final String DB_NAME = "cards.db";
    private static final int DB_VERSION = 1;

    public static final String TABLE_CARDS = "CARDS";
    public static final String COLUMN_ID = "_ID";
    public static final String COLUMN_NAME = "NAME";
    public static final String COLUMN_COLOR_RESOURCE = "COLOR_RESOURCE";

    private static final String TABLE_CREATE =
            "CREATE TABLE " + TABLE_CARDS + " (" +
```

```
                COLUMN_ID + " INTEGER PRIMARY KEY AUTOINCREMENT, " +

                COLUMN_NAME + " TEXT, " +

                COLUMN_COLOR_RESOURCE + " INTEGER" +

                ")";


    public CardsDBHelper(Context context) {

        super(context, DB_NAME, null, DB_VERSION);

    }


    @Override

    public void onCreate(SQLiteDatabase db) {

        db.execSQL(TABLE_CREATE);       }


    @Override

    public void onUpgrade(SQLiteDatabase db, int oldVersion, int newVersion) {

        db.execSQL("DROP TABLE IF EXISTS " + TABLE_CARDS);

        onCreate(db);

    }

}
```

This class starts off by defining a few `static final` variables for providing a name and version number, and an appropriate table name with table column names. Further, the `TABLE_CREATE` variable provides the SQL statement for creating the table in the database. The `CardsDBHelper` constructor accepts a `context` and this is where the database name and version are set. The `onCreate()` and `onUpgrade()` methods either create the new table or delete an existing table, and then create a new table.

You should also notice that the table provides one column for the `_ID` as an `INTEGER`, one column for the `NAME` as `TEXT`, and one column for the `COLOR_RESOURCE` as an `INTEGER`.

Note

The `SQLiteOpenHelper` class assumes version numbers will be increasing for an upgrade. That means if you are at version 1, and want to update your database, set the version number to 2 and increase the version number incrementally for additional versions.

Providing Data Access

Now that you are able to create a database, you need a way to access the database. To do so, you will create a class that provides access to the database from the `SQLiteDatabase`

class using the `SQLiteOpenHelper` class. This class is where we will be defining the
methods for adding, updating, deleting, and querying the database. The class for doing
this is provided in the `CardsData.java` file and a partial implementation can be
found here:

```java
public class CardsData {
    public static final String DEBUG_TAG = "CardsData";

    private SQLiteDatabase db;
    private SQLiteOpenHelper cardDbHelper;

    private static final String[] ALL_COLUMNS = {
            CardsDBHelper.COLUMN_ID,
            CardsDBHelper.COLUMN_NAME,
            CardsDBHelper.COLUMN_COLOR_RESOURCE
    };

    public CardsData(Context context) {
        this.cardDbHelper = new CardsDBHelper(context);
    }

    public void open() {
        db = cardDbHelper.getWritableDatabase();    }

    public void close() {
        if (cardDbHelper != null) {
            cardDbHelper.close();        }
    }
}
```

Notice the `CardsData()` constructor. This creates a new `CardsDBHelper()` object
that will allow us to access the database. The `open()` method is where the database is
created with the `getWritableDatabase()` method. The `close()` method is for closing
the database. It is important to close the database to release any resources obtained by
the object so that unexpected errors do not occur in your application during use. You
also want to open and close the database during your application's particular lifecycle
events so that you are only executing database operations at the times when you have the
appropriate access.

Updating the `SampleMaterialActivity` Class

The onCreate() method of the SampleMaterialActivity now creates a new data access object and opens the database. Here is the updated onCreate() method:

```java
public CardsData cardsData = new CardsData(this);


@Override
protected void onCreate(Bundle savedInstanceState) {
    super.onCreate(savedInstanceState);
    setContentView(R.layout.activity_sample_material);


    names = getResources().getStringArray(R.array.names_array);
    colors = getResources().getIntArray(R.array.initial_colors);


    recyclerView = (RecyclerView) findViewById(R.id.recycler_view);
    recyclerView.setLayoutManager(new LinearLayoutManager(this));


    new GetOrCreateCardsListTask().execute();


    FloatingActionButton fab = (FloatingActionButton) findViewById(R.id.fab);
    fab.setOnClickListener(new View.OnClickListener() {
        @Override
        public void onClick(View v) {
            Pair<View, String> pair = Pair.create(v.findViewById(R.id.fab),
                TRANSITION_FAB);


            ActivityOptionsCompat options;
            Activity act = SampleMaterialActivity.this;
options = ActivityOptionsCompat.makeSceneTransitionAnimation(act, pair);


Intent transitionIntent = new Intent(act, TransitionAddActivity.class);
            act.startActivityForResult(transitionIntent, adapter.getItemCount(),
options.toBundle());
        }
    });
}
```

Notice the new `GetOrCreateCardsListTask().execute()` method call. We cover this implementation later in this chapter. This method queries the database for all cards or fills the database with cards if it is empty.

Updating the `SampleMaterialAdapter` Constructor

An update in the `SampleMaterialAdapter` class is also needed, and the constructor is shown below:

```
public CardsData cardsData;

public SampleMaterialAdapter(Context context, ArrayList<Card> cardsList,
        CardsData cardsData) {

  this.context = context;

  this.cardsList = cardsList;

  this.cardsData = cardsData;

}
```

Notice a `CardsData` object is passed into the constructor to ensure the database is available to the `SampleMaterialAdapter` object once it is created.

Warning

Because database operations block the UI thread of your Android application, you should always run database operations in a background thread.

Database Operations Off the Main UI Thread

To make sure that the main UI thread of your Android application does not block during a potentially long-running database operation, you should run your database operations in a background thread. Here, we have implemented an `AsyncTask` for creating new cards in the database, and will subsequently update the UI only after the database operation is complete. Here is the `GetOrCreateCardsListTask` class that extends the `AsyncTask` class, which either retrieves all the cards from the database or creates them:

```
public class GetOrCreateCardsListTask extends AsyncTask<Void, Void,

ArrayList<Card>> {

  @Override
  protected ArrayList<Card> doInBackground(Void... params) {

    cardsData.open();

    cardsList = cardsData.getAll();

    if (cardsList.size() == 0) {

      for (int i = 0; i < 50; i++) {
```

```
            Card card = new Card();

            card.setName(names[i]);

            card.setColorResource(colors[i]);

            cardsList.add(card);

            cardsData.create(card);

            Log.d(DEBUG_TAG, "Card created with id " + card.getId() + ",
name " + card.getName() + ", color " + card.getColorResource());

        }

    }

    return cardsList;

}


    @Override
    protected void onPostExecute(ArrayList<Card> cards) {
        super.onPostExecute(cards);
        adapter = new SampleMaterialAdapter(SampleMaterialActivity.this,
                cardsList, cardsData);
        recyclerView.setAdapter(adapter);

    }

}
```

When this class is created and executed in the onCreate() method of the Activity, it overrides the doInBackground() method and creates a background task for retrieving all the cards from the database with the call to getAll(). If no items are returned, that means the database is empty and needs to be populated with entries. The for loop creates 50 Cards and each Card is added to the cardsList, and then created in the database with the call to create(). Once the background operation is complete, the onPostExecute() method, which was also overridden from the AsyncTask class, receives the cardsList result from the doInBackground() operation. It then uses the cardsList and cardsData to create a new SampleMaterialAdapter, and then adds that adapter to the recyclerView to update the UI once the entire background operation has completed.

Notice the AsyncTask class has three types defined; the first is of type Void, the second is also Void, and the third is ArrayList<Card>. These map to the Params, Progress, and Result generic types of an AsyncTask. The first Params is used as the parameter of the doInBackground() method, which are Void, and the third Result generic is used as the parameter of the onPostExecute() method. In this case, the second Void generic was not used, but would be used as the parameter for the onProgressUpdate() method of an AsyncTask.

> **Note**
>
> Note that you are not able to call UI operations on the `doInBackground()` method
> of an `AsyncTask`. Those operations need to be performed before or after the
> `doInBackground()` method, but if you need the UI to update only after the background
> operation has completed, you must perform those operations in the `onPostExecute()`
> method so the UI is updated appropriately.

Creating a Card in the Database

The magic happens in the call to `cardsData.create()`. This is where the `Card` is inserted
into the database. Here is the `create()` method definition found in the `CardsData` class:

```java
public Card create(Card card) {

    ContentValues values = new ContentValues();

    values.put(CardsDBHelper.COLUMN_NAME, card.getName());

    values.put(CardsDBHelper.COLUMN_COLOR_RESOURCE, card.getColorResource());

    long id = db.insert(CardsDBHelper.TABLE_CARDS, null, values);

    card.setId(id);

    Log.d(DEBUG_TAG, "Insert id is " + String.valueOf(card.getId()));

    return card;

}
```

The `create()` method accepts a `Card` data object. A `ContentValues` object is created
to temporarily store the data that will be inserted into the database in a structured format.
There are two `value.put()` calls that map the database column to a `Card` attribute. The
`insert()` method is then called on the cards table and the temporary values are passed in
for insertion. An `id` is returned from the call to `insert()` and that value is then set as the
id for the `Card`, and finally a `Card` object is returned. Figure 16.2 shows the `logcat` output of cards being inserted into the database.

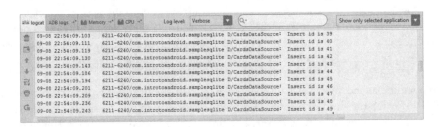

Figure 16.2 `logcat` output showing items inserted into the database.

Getting All Cards

Earlier, we mentioned the getAll() method that queries the database for all the cards in the cards table. Here is the implementation of the getAll() method:

```java
public ArrayList<Card> getAll() {

    ArrayList<Card> cards = new ArrayList<>();

    Cursor cursor = null;

    try {

        cursor = db.query(CardsDBHelper.TABLE_CARDS,

                COLUMNS, null, null, null, null, null);

        if (cursor.getCount() > 0) {

            while (cursor.moveToNext()) {

                Card card = new Card();

                card.setId(cursor.getLong(cursor

                        .getColumnIndex(CardsDBHelper.COLUMN_ID)));

                card.setName(cursor.getString(cursor

                        .getColumnIndex(CardsDBHelper.COLUMN_NAME)));

                card.setColorResource(cursor

                        .getInt(cursor.getColumnIndex(CardsDBHelper

                            .COLUMN_COLOR_RESOURCE)));

                    cards.add(card);

            }

        }

    } catch (Exception e){

        Log.d(DEBUG_TAG, "Exception raised with a value of " + e);

    } finally{

        if (cursor != null) {

            cursor.close();

        }

    }

    return cards;

}
```

A query is performed on the cards table inside a try statement with a call to query() that returns all columns for the query as a Cursor object. A Cursor allows you to access the results of the database query. First, we ensure that the Cursor count is greater than zero, otherwise no results will be returned from the query. Next, we iterate through all the cursor objects by calling the moveToNext() method on the cursor, and for each database item, we create a Card data object from the data in the Cursor and set the Cursor data to Card data. We also handle any exceptions that we may have encountered, and finally the Cursor object is closed and all cards are returned.

Adding a New Card

You already know how to insert cards into the database because we did that to initialize the database. So adding a new Card is very similar to how we initialized the database. The addCard() method of the SampleMaterialAdapter class needs a slight modification. This method executes AsyncTask to add a new card in the background. Here is the updated implementation of the addCard() method creating a CreateCardTask and executing the task:

```
public void addCard(String name, int color) {

    Card card = new Card();

    card.setName(name);

    card.setColorResource(color);

    new CreateCardTask().execute(card);

}


private class CreateCardTask extends AsyncTask<Card, Void, Card> {

    @Override

    protected Card doInBackground(Card... cards) {

        cardsData.create(cards[0]);

        cardsList.add(cards[0]);

        return cards[0];

    }


    @Override

    protected void onPostExecute(Card card) {

        super.onPostExecute(card);

        ((SampleMaterialActivity) context).doSmoothScroll(getItemCount() - 1);

        notifyItemInserted(getItemCount());

        Log.d(DEBUG_TAG, "Card created with id " + card.getId() + ", name " +

                card.getName() + ", color " + card.getColorResource());

    }

}
```

The doInBackground() method makes a call to the create() method of the cardsData object, and in the onPostExecute() method, a call to the doSmoothScroll() method of the calling Activity is made, then the adapter is notified that a new Card has been inserted.

Updating a Card

To update a Card, we first need a way to keep track of the position of a Card within the list. This is not the same as the database id because the id of the item in the database is not the same as the position of the item in the list. The database increments the id of a Card, so each new Card has an id one higher than the previous Card. The RecyclerView list, on the other hand, shifts positions as items are added and removed from the list.

First, let's update the Card data object found in the Card.java file and add a new listPosition attribute with the appropriate getter and setter methods as shown here:

```
private int listPosition = 0;


public int getListPosition() {

    return listPosition;

}


public void setListPosition(int listPosition) {

    this.listPosition = listPosition;

}
```

Next, update the updateCard() method of the SampleMaterialAdapter class and implement an UpdateCardTask class that extends AsyncTask as follows:

```
public void updateCard(String name, int list_position) {

    Card card = new Card();

    card.setName(name);

    card.setId(getItemId(list_position));

    card.setListPosition(list_position);

    new UpdateCardTask().execute(card);

}


private class UpdateCardTask extends AsyncTask<Card, Void, Card> {

    @Override

    protected Card doInBackground(Card... cards) {

        cardsData.update(cards[0].getId(), cards[0].getName());
```

(Continues)

(Continued)

```
        cardsList.get(cards[0].getListPosition()).setName(cards[0].getName());

        return cards[0];

    }


    @Override
    protected void onPostExecute(Card card) {
        super.onPostExecute(card);
        Log.d(DEBUG_TAG, "list_position is " + card.getListPosition());
        notifyItemChanged(card.getListPosition());

    }

}
```

The `UpdateCardTask` calls the `update()` method of the `cardsData` object in the `doInBackground()` method and then updates the `name` of the corresponding `Card` in the `cardsList` object and returns the `Card`. The `onPostExecute()` method then notifies the adapter that the item has changed with the `notifyItemChanged()` method call.

Finally, the `CardsData` class needs to implement the `update()` method to update the particular `Card` in the database. Here is the `update()` method:

```
public void update(long id, String name) {
    String whereClause = CardsDBHelper.COLUMN_ID + "=" + id;
    Log.d(DEBUG_TAG, "Update id is " + String.valueOf(id));
    ContentValues values = new ContentValues();
    values.put(CardsDBHelper.COLUMN_NAME, name);
    db.update(CardsDBHelper.TABLE_CARDS, values, whereClause, null);
}
```

The `update()` method accepts `id` and `name` parameters. A `whereClause` is then con-structed for matching the `id` of the `Card` with the appropriate `id` column in the database, and a new `ContentValues` object is created for adding the updated `name` for the particular `Card` to the appropriate `name` column. Finally, the `update()` method is executed on the database.

Deleting a Card

Now let's take a look at how to modify the deletion of cards. Remember the `animateCircularDelete()` method—this is where a `Card` was animated off the screen and deleted from the `cardsList` object. In the `onAnimationEnd()` method, construct a `Card` data object and pass that to the execute method of a `DeleteCardTask` object, which is an `AsyncTask`. Here are those implementations:

```
public void animateCircularDelete(final View view, final int list_position) {
    int centerX = view.getWidth();
```

```java
        int centerY = view.getHeight();
        int startRadius = view.getWidth();
        int endRadius = 0;
        Animator animation = ViewAnimationUtils.createCircularReveal(view,
                centerX, centerY, startRadius, endRadius);

        animation.addListener(new AnimatorListenerAdapter() {
            @Override
            public void onAnimationEnd(Animator animation) {
                super.onAnimationEnd(animation);
                view.setVisibility(View.INVISIBLE);
                Card card = new Card();
                card.setId(getItemId(list_position));
                card.setListPosition(list_position);
                new DeleteCardTask().execute(card);
            }
        });
        animation.start();
    }


    private class DeleteCardTask extends AsyncTask<Card, Void, Card> {
        @Override
        protected Card doInBackground(Card... cards) {
            cardsData.delete(cards[0].getId());
            cardsList.remove(cards[0].getListPosition());
            return cards[0];
        }


        @Override
        protected void onPostExecute(Card card) {
            super.onPostExecute(card);
            notifyItemRemoved(card.getListPosition());
        }
    }
}
```

The doInBackground() method of the DeleteCardTask calls the delete() method of the cardsData object and passes in the id of Card. Then the Card is removed from the cardsList object, and in the onPostExecute() method, the adapter is notified that an item has been removed by calling the notifyItemRemoved() method and passing in the list position of the Card that has been removed.

There is one last method to implement—the delete() method of the CardsData class. Here is that method:

```
public void delete(long cardId) {

    String whereClause = CardsDBHelper.COLUMN_ID + "=" + cardId;

    Log.d(DEBUG_TAG, "Delete position is " + String.valueOf(cardId));

    db.delete(CardsDBHelper.TABLE_CARDS, whereClause, null);

}
```

The delete() method of the CardsData class accepts an id of a Card, constructs a whereClause using that id, and then calls the delete() method on the cards table of the database, passing in the appropriate whereClause with the id of the Card to delete.

Summary

You now have a full implementation of a database that provides permanent storage for your application. In this chapter, you learned how to create a database. You also learned how to access the database for querying, inserting, updating, and deleting items from it. In addition, you also learned how to update the SampleMaterial application so that Card data is stored in a database. Finally, you learned how to perform your database operations off of the main UI thread by performing the operations in the background with an AsyncTask so as not to block the UI when running these blocking operations. You should now be ready to implement simple SQLite databases in your own applications.

Quiz Questions

1. What is the SQLiteDatabase method for creating a table?
2. What method provides access for reading and writing a database?
3. True or false: The async() method of an AsyncTask allows you to execute long-running operations off the main UI thread in the background.
4. True or false: The onAfterAsync() method of an AsyncTask allows you to execute UI methods after an AsyncTask completes.

Exercises

1. Read through the "Saving Data in SQL Databases" training in the Android documentation found here: *http://d.android.com/training/basics/data-storage/databases.html*.

2. Read through the "SQLiteDatabase" SDK reference to learn more about how to utilize a SQLite database here: *http://d.android.com/reference/android/database/sqlite/SQLiteDatabase.html*.

3. Modify the SampleSQLite application to support the deletion of all items from the database with a single database operation.

References and More Information

Android Tools: "sqlite3":
  http://d.android.com/tools/help/sqlite3.html
SQLite:
  http://www.sqlite.org/
Command Line Shell For SQLite:
  http://www.sqlite.org/cli.html
Android API Guides: "Content Providers":
  http://d.android.com/guide/topics/providers/content-providers.html
Android SDK Reference regarding the application android.database.sqlite package:
  http://d.android.com/reference/android/database/sqlite/package-summary.html
Android SDK Reference regarding the application AsyncTask class:
  http://d.android.com/reference/android/os/AsyncTask.html
Android SDK Reference regarding the application ContentValues class:
  http://d.android.com/reference/android/content/ContentValues.html
Android SDK Reference regarding the application SQLiteDatabase class:
  http://d.android.com/reference/android/database/sqlite/SQLiteDatabase.html
Android SDK Reference regarding the application SQLiteOpenHelper class:
  http://d.android.com/reference/android/database/sqlite/SQLiteOpenHelper.html
Android SDK Reference regarding the application Cursor class:
  http://d.android.com/reference/android/database/Cursor.html

17

Leveraging Content Providers

Applications can access data within other applications on the Android system through content provider interfaces and can expose internal application data to other applications by becoming a content provider. Content providers are the way applications can access user information, including contact data, images, audio and video on the device, and much more. In this chapter, we take a look at some of the content providers available on the Android platform and what you can do with them.

Warning

Always run content provider code on test devices, not on your personal devices. It is very easy to accidentally wipe out all of the Contacts database or other types of data on your devices. Consider this fair warning because we discuss operations such as how to query (generally safe) and modify (not so safe) various types of device data in this chapter.

Exploring Android's Content Providers

Android devices ship with a number of built-in applications, many of which expose their data as content providers. Your application can access content provider data from a variety of sources. You can find the content providers included with Android in the package `android.provider`. Table 17.1 lists some useful content providers in this package.

Now let's look at some of the most popular and official content providers in more detail.

Tip

The code examples provided in this chapter use the `CursorLoader` class for performing cursor queries on a background thread using the `loadInBackground()` method. This prevents your application from blocking on the UI thread when performing cursor queries. This approach has replaced the older `Activity` class method `managedQuery()` for performing cursor queries that block the UI thread and this method is officially deprecated. If you are targeting devices earlier than Honeycomb, you'll want to import the `CursorLoader` class from the Android Support Package using `android.support.v4.content.CursorLoader` rather than importing the class from `android.content.CursorLoader`.

Table 17.1 **Useful Built-in Content Providers**

Provider	Purpose
AlarmClock	Set alarms within the Alarm Clock application (API Level 9)
CalendarContract	Calendar and event information (API Level 14)
CallLog	Sent and received calls
ContactsContract	Phone contact database or phonebook (API Level 5)
DocumentsProvider	Read and write access for files on disk or in the cloud (API Level 19)
MediaStore	Audio/visual data on the phone and external storage
SearchRecentSuggestions	Search suggestions appropriate to the application
Settings	System-wide device settings and preferences
Telephony	SMS and MMS phone operation data (API Level 19)
UserDictionary	A dictionary of user-defined words for use with predictive text input (API Level 3)
VoicemailContract	A single unified place for the user to manage voicemail content from different sources (API Level 14)

Using the **MediaStore** Content Provider

You can use the MediaStore content provider to access media on the phone and on external storage devices. The primary types of media you can access are audio, images, and video. You can access these different types of media through their respective content provider classes under android.provider.MediaStore.

Most of the MediaStore classes allow full interaction with the data. You can retrieve, add, and delete media files from the device. There are also a handful of helper classes that define the most common data columns, data columns that can be requested.

Table 17.2 lists some commonly used classes you can find under android.provider.MediaStore.

Table 17.2 **Common MediaStore Classes**

Class	Purpose
Audio.Albums	Manages audio files organized by album
Audio.Artists	Manages audio files organized by artist
Audio.Genres	Manages audio files belonging to a particular genre
Audio.Media	Manages audio files on the device
Audio.Playlists	Manages audio files that are part of a particular playlist
Audio.Radio	Manages audio files related to radio (API Level 21)
Files	Lists all media files (API Level 11)
Images.Media	Manages image files on the device
Images.Thumbnails	Retrieves thumbnails for the image files
Video.Media	Manages video files on the device
Video.Thumbnails	Retrieves thumbnails for the video files (API Level 5)

Tip

Many of the code examples provided in this section are taken from the
`SimpleContentProvider` application. The source code for the
`SimpleContentProvider` application is provided for download on the book's website
(*http://introductiontoandroid.blogspot.com*).

The following code demonstrates how to request data from a content provider.
A query is made to the `MediaStore` to retrieve both the titles of all the audio files on the
SD card of the handset and their respective durations. This code requires that you load
some audio files onto the virtual SD card in the emulator.

```
String[] requestedColumns = {

    MediaStore.Audio.Media.TITLE,

    MediaStore.Audio.Media.DURATION

};


CursorLoader loader = new CursorLoader(this,

    MediaStore.Audio.Media.EXTERNAL_CONTENT_URI,

    requestedColumns, null, null, null);

Cursor cur = loader.loadInBackground();


Log.d(DEBUG_TAG, "Audio files: " + cur.getCount());

Log.d(DEBUG_TAG, "Columns: " + cur.getColumnCount());


int name = cur.getColumnIndex(MediaStore.Audio.Media.TITLE);

int length = cur.getColumnIndex(MediaStore.Audio.Media.DURATION);


cur.moveToFirst();

while (!cur.isAfterLast()) {

    Log.d(DEBUG_TAG, "Title" + cur.getString(name));

    Log.d(DEBUG_TAG, "Length: " +

        cur.getInt(length) / 1000 + " seconds");

    cur.moveToNext();

}
```

The `MediaStore.Audio.Media` class has predefined strings for every data field
(or column) exposed by the content provider. You can limit the audio file data fields
requested as part of the query by defining a `String` array with the column names
required. In this case, we limit the results to track only the title and the duration of each
audio file.

We then use a `CursorLoader` and access the cursor using a `loadInBackground()` method call. The first parameter of the `CursorLoader` is the application context. The second parameter is the predefined URI of the content provider you want to query. The third parameter is the list of columns to return (audio file titles and durations). The fourth and fifth parameters control any selection-filtering arguments, and the sixth parameter provides a sort method for the results. We leave the last three parameters `null` because we want all audio files at this location. By using the `loadInBackground()` method, we get a `Cursor` as a result. We then examine our `Cursor` for the results.

Accessing Content Providers That Require Permissions

Your application needs a special permission to access the information provided by the `MediaStore` content provider. You can declare the `<uses-permission>` tag by adding the following to your `AndroidManifest.xml` file:

```
<uses-permission

    android:name="android.permission.READ_EXTERNAL_STORAGE"/>
```

To further support the new app permissions model introduced in Android Marshmallow API Level 23 and newer, you can check if the permission has been accepted by the user of your application code, and if not, request the appropriate permission. Here is a simple implementation:

```
if (ActivityCompat.checkSelfPermission(this,

        Manifest.permission.READ_EXTERNAL_STORAGE)

        != PackageManager.PERMISSION_GRANTED) {

    ActivityCompat.requestPermissions(Activity.this,

        PERMISSIONS_EXTERNAL_STORAGE, REQUEST_EXTERNAL_STORAGE);

} else {

    // permission already accepted, continue as usual

}
```

The preceding code checks if the permission has been granted, and if not, requests the permission by displaying a request dialog asking for the user to accept the permission. You can learn more about permissions and the new permission model in Chapter 5, "Defining the Manifest," or you can see the full implementation in the `SimpleContentProvider` application that accompanies this chapter, found on the books website.

Although it's a tad confusing, there is no `MediaStore` provider permission. Instead, applications that access the `MediaStore` use the `READ_EXTERNAL_STORAGE` permission.

Tip

You can find all available permissions in the class `android.Manifest.permission`.

Using the `CallLog` Content Provider

Android has a content provider for accessing the call log on the handset via the class `android.provider.CallLog`. At first glance, the `CallLog` might not seem to be a useful provider for developers, but it has some nifty features. You can use the `CallLog` to filter recently dialed calls, received calls, and missed calls. The date and duration of each call are logged and tied back to the Contacts application for caller identification purposes.

The `CallLog` is a useful content provider for customer relationship management (CRM) applications. The user can also tag specific phone numbers with custom labels within the `Contacts` application.

To demonstrate how the `CallLog` content provider works, let's look at a hypothetical situation where we want to generate a report of all calls to a number with the custom label `HourlyClient123`. Android allows for custom labels on these numbers, which we leverage for this example:

```
String[] requestedColumns = {
    CallLog.Calls.CACHED_NUMBER_LABEL,
    CallLog.Calls.DURATION
};

CursorLoader loader = new CursorLoader(this,
    CallLog.Calls.CONTENT_URI,
    requestedColumns,
    CallLog.Calls.CACHED_NUMBER_LABEL + " = ?",
    new String[] { "HourlyClient123" },
    null);
Cursor calls = loader.loadInBackground();

Log.d(DEBUG_TAG, "Call count: " + calls.getCount());

int durIdx = calls.getColumnIndex(CallLog.Calls.DURATION);
int totalDuration = 0;

calls.moveToFirst();
while (!calls.isAfterLast()) {
    Log.d(DEBUG_TAG, "Duration: " + calls.getInt(durIdx));
    totalDuration += calls.getInt(durIdx);
    calls.moveToNext();
}

Log.d(DEBUG_TAG, "HourlyClient123 Total Call Duration: " + totalDuration);
```

This code is similar to the code shown for the MediaStore audio files. Again, we start with listing our requested columns: the call label and the duration of the call. This time, however, we don't want to get every call in the log, only those with a label of HourlyClient123. To filter the results of the query to this specific label, it is necessary to specify the fourth and fifth parameters of the CursorLoader. Together, these two parameters are equivalent to a database WHERE clause. The fourth parameter specifies the format of the WHERE clause with the column name by using selection parameters (shown as ?) for each selection argument value. The fifth parameter, the String array provides the values to substitute for each of the selection arguments (?), in order, as you would do for a simple SQLite database query.

We use the same method to iterate the records of the Cursor and add up all the call durations.

Adding Required Permissions for Accessing the CallLog Provider

Your application needs a special permission to access the information provided by the CallLog content provider. You can add the appropriate permissions by adding the following to your AndroidManifest.xml file:

```
<uses-permission

    android:name="android.permission.READ_CALL_LOG" />
```

To support the new apps permission model of Android Marshmallow 6.0 API Level 23 and newer, you need to ensure the READ_CALL_LOG permission has been accepted, or request it if the permission has not yet been accepted. Here is a code snippet showing how to perform the check:

```
if (ActivityCompat.checkSelfPermission(this, Manifest.permission.READ_CALL_LOG)

        != PackageManager.PERMISSION_GRANTED) {

    ActivityCompat.requestPermissions(MenuActivity.this,

        PERMISSIONS_CALL_LOG, REQUEST_CALL_LOG);

} else {

    // permission already accepted, continue as usual

}
```

Although the values are cached within the CallLog content provider, the data is similar to what you might find in the ContactsContract provider.

Using the CalendarContract Content Provider

Introduced officially in Android 4.0 (API Level 14), the CalendarContract content provider allows you to manage and interact with the user's calendar data on the device. You can use this content provider to create one-time and recurring events in a user's calendar, set reminders, and access and manipulate other calendar data, provided the device user has appropriately configured calendar accounts (for example, Microsoft Exchange). In addition to the fully featured content provider, you can also quickly trigger a new event to be added to the user's calendar using an `Intent`, as shown here:

```
Intent calIntent = new Intent(Intent.ACTION_INSERT);

calIntent.setData(CalendarContract.Events.CONTENT_URI);

calIntent.putExtra(CalendarContract.Events.TITLE,
    "My Winter Holiday Party");

calIntent.putExtra(CalendarContract.Events.EVENT_LOCATION,
    "My Ski Cabin at Tahoe");

calIntent.putExtra(CalendarContract.Events.DESCRIPTION,
    "Hot chocolate, eggnog and sledding.");

startActivity(calIntent);
```

Here, we seed the calendar event title, location, and description using the appropriate intent `Extras`. These fields will be set in a form that displays for the user, who will then need to confirm the event in the Calendar app. To learn more about the `CalendarContract` provider, see *http://d.android.com/guide/topics/providers/calendar-provider.html* and *http://d.android.com/reference/android/provider/CalendarContract.html*.

Using the `UserDictionary` Content Provider

Another useful content provider is the `UserDictionary` provider. You can use this content provider to predict a user's text input on text fields and other user input mechanisms. Individual words stored in the dictionary are weighted by frequency and organized by locale. You can use the `addWord()` method within the `UserDictionary.Words` class to add words to the custom user dictionary.

Using the `VoicemailContract` Content Provider

The `VoicemailContract` content provider was introduced in API Level 14. You can use this content provider to add new voicemail content to the shared provider so that all voicemail content is accessible in one place. Application permissions, such as the `ADD_VOICEMAIL` permission, are necessary for accessing this provider. For more information, see the Android SDK documentation for the `VoicemailContract` class at *http://d.android.com/reference/android/provider/VoicemailContract.html*.

Using the `Settings` Content Provider

Another useful content provider is the `Settings` provider. You can use this content provider to access the device settings and user preferences. Settings are organized much as they are in the Settings application—by category. You can find information about the `Settings` content provider in the `android.provider.Settings` class. If your application needs to modify system settings, you'll need to register the `WRITE_SETTINGS` or `WRITE_SECURE_SETTINGS` permissions in your application's Android manifest file.

Introducing the `ContactsContract` Content Providers

The Contacts database is one of the most commonly used applications on Android devices. People always want contact information handy for contacting friends, family, coworkers, and clients. Additionally, most devices show the identity of a contact based on the Contacts application, including nicknames, photos, or icons.

Android provides a built-in Contacts application, and the contact data is exposed to other Android applications using the content provider interface. As an application developer, this means you can leverage the user's contact data within your application for a more robust user experience.

The content provider for accessing user contacts was originally called `Contacts`. Android 2.0 (API Level 5) introduced an enhanced contacts-management content provider class to manage the data available from the user's contacts. This provider, called `ContactsContract`, includes a subclass called `ContactsContract.Contacts`. This is the preferred contacts content provider.

Your application needs special permission to access the private user information provided by the `ContactsContract` content provider. You must declare a `<uses-permission>` tag using the permission `READ_CONTACTS` to read this information. If your application modifies the Contacts database, you'll need the `WRITE_CONTACTS` permission as well.

Tip

Some of the code examples provided in this section are taken from the `SimpleContacts` application. The source code for the `SimpleContacts` application is provided for download on the book's website.

Working with the `ContactsContract` Content Provider

The more recent contacts content provider, `ContactsContract.Contacts`, introduced in API Level 5 (Android 2.0), provides a robust contact content provider that suits the more robust Contacts application that has evolved along with the Android platform.

Tip

The `ContactsContract` content provider was further enhanced in more recent versions of Android to incorporate substantive social networking features. Some of the new features include managing the device user's identity and favorite methods of communication with specific contacts, as well as an `INVITE_CONTACT` `Intent` type for applications used to make contact connections. The device user's personal profile is accessible through the `ContactsContract.Profile` class (which requires the `READ_PROFILE` application permission). The device user's preferred methods of communicating with specific contacts can be accessed through the new `ContactsContract.DataUsageFeedback` class. For more information, see the Android SDK documentation for the `android.provider.ContactsContract` class.

The following code utilizes the `ContactsContract` provider:

```
String[] requestedColumns = {

    ContactsContract.Contacts.DISPLAY_NAME,

    ContactsContract.CommonDataKinds.Phone.NUMBER,

};

CursorLoader loader = new CursorLoader(this,

    ContactsContract.Data.CONTENT_URI,

    requestedColumns, null, null, "display_name desc limit 1");

Cursor contacts = loader.loadInBackground();


int recordCount = contacts.getCount();

Log.d(DEBUG_TAG, "Contacts count: " + recordCount);


if (recordCount > 0) {

    int nameIdx = contacts

        .getColumnIndex(ContactsContract.Contacts.DISPLAY_NAME);

    int phoneIdx = contacts

        .getColumnIndex(ContactsContract.CommonDataKinds.Phone.NUMBER);


    contacts.moveToFirst();

    Log.d(DEBUG_TAG, "Name: " + contacts.getString(nameIdx));

    Log.d(DEBUG_TAG, "Phone: " + contacts.getString(phoneIdx));

}
```

First, we can see here that the code is using a query URI provided from the `ContactsContract` provider called `ContactsContract.Data.CONTENT_URI`. Second, you're requesting different column names. The column names of the `ContactsContract` provider are organized more thoroughly to allow for far more dynamic contact configurations. This can make your queries slightly more complex. Luckily, the `ContactsContract.CommonDataKinds` class has a number of frequently used columns defined together. Table 17.3 shows some of the commonly used classes that can help you work with the `ContactsContract` content provider.

Table 17.3 **Commonly Used `ContactsContract` Data Column Classes**

Class	Purpose
`ContactsContract.CommonDataKinds`	Defines a number of frequently used contact columns such as email, nickname, phone, and photo.
`ContactsContract.Contacts`	Defines the consolidated data associated with a contact. Some aggregation may be performed.
`ContactsContract.Data`	Defines the raw data associated with a single contact.
`ContactsContract.PhoneLookup`	Defines the phone columns and can be used to quickly look up a phone number for caller identification purposes.
`ContactsContract.StatusUpdates`	Defines the social networking columns and can be used to check the instant messaging status of a contact.
`ContactsContract.PinnedPositions`	Defines whether a contact has been pinned by the user so that applications may present the user an ordering of those pinned contacts. (API Level 21).

Tip

New additions have been made to the `ContactsContract` content provider in Android 5.0 (API Level 21), providing insight to contact snippets that match particular searches. You now have the ability to determine the search filters a contact has matched using `ContactsContract.SearchSnippets`. This is an extremely useful feature because, prior to this addition, there was no standard way for an application to determine which contacts had matched a particular search filter.

For more information on the `ContactsContract` provider, see the Android SDK documentation: *http://d.android.com/reference/android/provider/ContactsContract.html.*

Modifying Content Provider Data

Content providers are not only static sources of data. They can also be used to add, update, and delete data, if the content provider application has implemented this functionality. Your application must have the appropriate permissions (that is, `WRITE_CONTACTS` as opposed to `READ_CONTACTS`) to perform some of these actions. Let's use the `ContactsContract` content provider and give some examples of how to modify the Contacts database.

Adding Records

Using the `ContactsContract` content provider, we can, for example, add a new record to the Contacts database programmatically. The code that follows adds a new contact named `Ian Droid` with a phone number of `6505551212`, as shown here:

```
ArrayList<ContentProviderOperation> ops = new ArrayList

<ContentProviderOperation>();


int contactIdx = ops.size();
```

```
ContentProviderOperation.Builder op =
    ContentProviderOperation.newInsert(ContactsContract.RawContacts.CONTENT_URI);
op.withValue(ContactsContract.RawContacts.ACCOUNT_NAME, null);
op.withValue(ContactsContract.RawContacts.ACCOUNT_TYPE, null);
ops.add(op.build());


op = ContentProviderOperation.newInsert(ContactsContract.Data.CONTENT_URI);
op.withValue(ContactsContract.Data.MIMETYPE,
    ContactsContract.CommonDataKinds.StructuredName.CONTENT_ITEM_TYPE);
op.withValue(ContactsContract.CommonDataKinds.StructuredName.DISPLAY_NAME,
    "Ian Droid");
op.withValueBackReference(ContactsContract.Data.RAW_CONTACT_ID,
    contactIdx);
ops.add(op.build());


op = ContentProviderOperation.newInsert(ContactsContract.Data.CONTENT_URI);
op.withValue(ContactsContract.CommonDataKinds.Phone.NUMBER,
    "6505551212");
op.withValue(ContactsContract.CommonDataKinds.Phone.TYPE,
    ContactsContract.CommonDataKinds.Phone.TYPE_WORK);
op.withValue(ContactsContract.CommonDataKinds.Phone.MIMETYPE,
    ContactsContract.CommonDataKinds.Phone.CONTENT_ITEM_TYPE);
op.withValueBackReference(ContactsContract.Data.RAW_CONTACT_ID,
    contactIdx);
ops.add(op.build());


getContentResolver().applyBatch(ContactsContract.AUTHORITY, ops);
```

Here, we use the ContentProviderOperation class to create an ArrayList of operations to insert records into the Contacts database on the device. The first record we add with newInsert() is the ACCOUNT_NAME and ACCOUNT_TYPE of the contact. The second record we add with newInsert() is a name for the ContactsContract.CommonDataKinds.StructuredName.DISPLAY_NAME column. We need to create the contact with a name before we can assign information, such as phone numbers. Think of this as creating a row in a table that provides a one-to-many relationship to a phone number table. The third record we add with newInsert() is a phone number for the contact that we are adding to the Contacts database.

We insert the data in the database found at the `ContactsContract.Data.CONTENT_URI` path. We use a call to `getContentResolver().applyBatch()` to apply all three `ContentProvider` operations at once using the `ContentResolver` associated with our `Activity`.

> **Tip**
>
> At this point, you might be wondering how the structure of the data can be determined. The best way is to thoroughly examine the documentation for the specific content provider with which you want to integrate your application.

Updating Records

Inserting data isn't the only change you can make. You can update one or more rows as well. The following block of code shows how to update data within a content provider. In this case, we update a phone number field for a specific contact.

```
String selection = ContactsContract.Data.DISPLAY_NAME + " = ? AND " +
    ContactsContract.Data.MIMETYPE + " = ? AND " +
    ContactsContract.CommonDataKinds.Phone.TYPE + " = ? ";


String[] selectionArgs = new String[] {
    "Ian Droid",
    ContactsContract.CommonDataKinds.Phone.CONTENT_ITEM_TYPE,
    String.valueOf(ContactsContract.CommonDataKinds.Phone.TYPE_WORK)
};


ArrayList<ContentProviderOperation> ops =
    new ArrayList<ContentProviderOperation>();


ContentProviderOperation.Builder op =
    ContentProviderOperation.newUpdate(ContactsContract.Data.CONTENT_URI);
op.withSelection(selection, selectionArgs);
op.withValue(ContactsContract.CommonDataKinds.Phone.NUMBER, "6501234567");
ops.add(op.build());


getContentResolver().applyBatch(ContactsContract.AUTHORITY, ops);
```

Again, we use the `ContentProviderOperation` class to create an `ArrayList` of operations that update a record in the Contacts database on the device—in this case, the phone number field previously given a TYPE_WORK attribute. This replaces any current phone number stored in the NUMBER field with a TYPE_WORK attribute currently stored with the contact. We add the ContentProviderOperation with the newUpdate() method and, once again, use applyBatch() on the ContentResolver class to complete our change. We can then confirm that only one row was updated.

Deleting Records

Now that you have cluttered up your Contacts application with sample user data, you might want to delete some of it. Deleting data is fairly straightforward. Another reminder, however: you should use these examples only on a test device, so you don't accidentally delete all of your contact data from your device.

Deleting All Records

The following code deletes all rows at the given URI. Keep in mind that you should execute operations like this with extreme care.

```
ArrayList<ContentProviderOperation> ops =
    new ArrayList<ContentProviderOperation>();


ContentProviderOperation.Builder op =
    ContentProviderOperation.newDelete(ContactsContract.RawContacts.CONTENT_URI);
ops.add(op.build());


getContentResolver().applyBatch(ContactsContract.AUTHORITY, ops);
```

The newDelete() method deletes all rows at a given URI, which in this case includes all rows at the RawContacts.CONTENT_URI location (in other words, all contact entries).

Deleting Specific Records

Often, you want to select specific rows to delete by adding selection filters that will remove rows matching a particular pattern.

For example, the following newDelete() operation matches all contact records with the name Ian Droid, which we used when we created the contact previously in this chapter.

```
String selection = ContactsContract.Data.DISPLAY_NAME + " = ? ";
String[] selectionArgs = new String[] { "Ian Droid" };


ArrayList<ContentProviderOperation> ops =
    new ArrayList<ContentProviderOperation>();
```

(Continues)

(Continued)

```
ContentProviderOperation.Builder op =
    ContentProviderOperation.newDelete(ContactsContract.RawContacts.CONTENT_URI);
op.withSelection(selection, selectionArgs);
ops.add(op.build());


getContentResolver().applyBatch(ContactsContract.AUTHORITY, ops);
```

Using Third-Party Content Providers

Any application can implement a content provider to share its information safely and securely with other applications on a device. Some applications use content providers only to share information internally—within their own brand, for example. Others publish the specifications for their providers so that other applications can integrate with them.

If you poke around in the Android source code, or run across a content provider you want to use, consider this: a number of other content providers are available on the Android platform, especially those used by some of the typically installed Google applications (Calendar, Messaging, and so on). Be aware, though, that using undocumented content providers, simply because you happen to know how they work or have reverse-engineered them, is generally not a good idea. Use of undocumented and unofficial content providers can make your application unstable. This post on the Android Developers Blog makes a good case for why this sort of hacking should be discouraged in commercial applications: *http://android-developers.blogspot.com/2010/05/be-careful-with-content-providers.html*.

Summary

Your application can leverage the data available within other Android applications, if they expose that data as content providers. Content providers such as `MediaStore`, `CallLog`, and `ContactsContract` can be leveraged by other Android applications, resulting in a robust, immersive experience for users. Applications can also share data among themselves by becoming content providers. Becoming a content provider involves implementing a set of methods that manage how and what data you expose for use in other applications.

Quiz Questions

1. What is the name of the content provider for accessing media on the phone and on external storage devices?

2. True or false: The `MediaStore.Images.Thumbnails` class is for retrieving thumbnails for image files.

3. What permission is required for accessing information provided by the `CallLog` content provider?

4. What is the method call for adding words to the custom user dictionary of the UserDictionary provider?

5. True or false: The Contacts content provider was added in API Level 5.

Exercises

1. Using the Android documentation, determine all the tables associated with the ContactsContract content provider.

2. Create an application that is able to add words that a user enters into an EditText field to the UserDictionary content provider.

3. Create an application that is able to add an email address for a contact using the ContactsContract content provider. As we have said before, always run content provider code on test devices, not your personal devices.

References and More Information

Android API Guides: "Content Providers":
   http://d.android.com/guide/topics/providers/content-providers.html
Android API Guides: "Content Provider Testing":
   http://d.android.com/tools/testing/contentprovider_testing.html
Android SDK Reference regarding the android.provider package:
   http://d.android.com/reference/android/provider/package-summary.html
Android SDK Reference regarding the AlarmClock content provider:
   http://d.android.com/reference/android/provider/AlarmClock.html
Android SDK Reference regarding the CallLog content provider:
   http://d.android.com/reference/android/provider/CallLog.html
Android SDK Reference regarding the Contacts content provider:
   http://d.android.com/reference/android/provider/Contacts.html
Android SDK Reference regarding the ContactsContract content provider:
   http://d.android.com/reference/android/provider/ContactsContract.html
Android SDK Reference regarding the MediaStore content provider:
   http://d.android.com/reference/android/provider/MediaStore.html
Android SDK Reference regarding the Settings content provider:
   http://d.android.com/reference/android/provider/Settings.html
Android SDK Reference regarding the SearchRecentSuggestions content provider:
   http://d.android.com/reference/android/provider/SearchRecentSuggestions.html
Android SDK Reference regarding the UserDictionary content provider:
   http://d.android.com/reference/android/provider/UserDictionary.html

V

Application Delivery Essentials

18

Learning the Development Workflow

The Android development process is similar to the traditional desktop software process, with a couple of distinct differences. Understanding how these differences affect your Android development team is critical to running a successful project. This insight into the Android development process is invaluable to those new to Android development and to veteran developers alike, to those in management and planning, and to the developers and testers in the trenches. In this chapter, you learn about the peculiarities of Android development as they pertain to each stage of the software development process.

An Overview of the Android Development Process

Android development teams are often small in size and project schedules are short in length. The entire project lifecycle is often condensed, and whether you're a team of one or one hundred, understanding the Android development considerations for each part of the development process can save you a lot of wasted time and effort. Some hurdles an Android development team must overcome include:

- Choosing an appropriate software methodology
- Understanding how target devices dictate the functionality of your application
- Performing thorough, accurate, and ongoing feasibility analyses
- Mitigating the risks associated with preproduction devices
- Keeping track of device functionality through configuration management
- Designing a responsive, stable application on a memory-restrictive system
- Designing user interfaces for a variety of devices with different user experiences
- Testing the application thoroughly on the target devices
- Incorporating third-party requirements that affect where you can sell your application

- Deploying and maintaining an Android application
- Reviewing user feedback, crash reports, and ratings, as well as deploying timely application updates

Choosing a Software Methodology

Developers can easily adapt most modern software methodologies to Android development. Whether your team opts for traditional rapid application development (RAD) principles or more modern variants of agile software development, such as Scrum, Android applications have some unique requirements.

Understanding the Dangers of Waterfall Approaches

The short development cycle might tempt some to use a waterfall approach, but developers should beware of the inflexibility that comes with this choice. It is generally a bad idea to design and develop an entire Android application without taking into account the many changes that tend to occur during the development cycle (see Figure 18.1). Changes

Figure 18.1   The dangers of waterfall development (graphic courtesy of Amy Tam Badger).

to target devices (especially preproduction models, though sometimes shipping devices can have substantial software changes), ongoing feasibility, performance concerns, and the need for quality assurance (QA) to test early and often on the target devices themselves, (not just the emulator) make it difficult for strict waterfall approaches to succeed with Android projects.

Understanding the Value of Iteration

Because of the speed at which Android projects tend to progress, iterative methods have been the most successful strategies adapted to Android development. Rapid prototyping gives developers and QA personnel ample opportunity to evaluate the feasibility and performance of the Android application on the target devices and adapt as needed to the changes that inevitably occur over the course of the project.

Gathering Application Requirements

Despite the relative simplicity of an Android application's feature set compared to a traditional desktop application, requirements analyses for an Android application can be more complex. The Android user interface must be elegant and the application must be fault tolerant, not to mention responsive in a resource-constrained environment. You must often tailor requirements to work across a number of devices that might have vastly different user interfaces and input methods. Incorporating great variation in target platforms can make development assumptions tricky. It's not unlike the differences Web developers might need to accommodate when developing for different Web browsers (and versions of Web browsers).

Determining Project Requirements

When multiple devices are involved (which is almost always the case with Android), we have found several approaches to be helpful for determining project requirements. Each approach has its benefits and its drawbacks. These approaches are

- The lowest common denominator method
- The customization method

Using the Lowest Common Denominator Method

With the lowest common denominator method, you design the application to run *sufficiently* well across a number of devices. In this case, the primary target for which you develop is the device configuration with the fewest features—basically, the most inferior device. Only requirements that can be met by all devices are included in the specification in order to reach the broadest range of devices—requirements such as input methods, screen resolution, and the platform version. With this method, you'll often put a stake in the ground for a specific Android API level and then tailor your application further using Android manifest file settings and Google Play filters.

Note

The lowest common denominator method is roughly equivalent to developing a desktop application with these minimum system requirements—Windows XP and 512MB of RAM—on the assumption that the application will be forward compatible with the latest version of Windows (and every other version in between). It's not ideal, but in some cases the trade-offs are acceptable.

Some light customization, such as resources and the final compiled binary (and the version information), is usually feasible with the lowest common denominator method. The main benefit of this method is that there is only one major source code tree to work with; bugs are fixed in one place and the fixes apply for all devices. You can also easily add other devices without changing much code, provided they, too, meet the minimum hardware requirements. The drawbacks include the fact that the resulting generalized application does not maximize any device-specific features, nor can it take advantage of new platform features. Also, if a device-specific problem arises or you misjudge the lowest common denominator and later find that an individual device lacks the minimum requirements, the team might be forced to implement a workaround (hack) or branch the code at a later date, losing the early benefits of this method but keeping all the drawbacks.

Tip

The Android SDK makes it easy for developers to target multiple platform versions within a single application package. Developers should take care to identify target platforms early in the design phase. That said, over-the-air firmware updates to users do occur, so the platform version on a given device is likely to change over time. Always design your applications with forward compatibility in mind, and make contingency plans for distributing application upgrades to existing applications as necessary.

When using more modern SDK features, such as fragments or loaders, one of the easiest ways to get your application to support more devices is by using the Android Support Package and the support libraries. Using the support libraries will allow you to write your application following best practices such as supporting master-detail navigation flows, while allowing your application to also work on older devices that do not have built-in support for those modern SDK features. Increasing the market size for your application could be as simple as importing the support libraries to use in your application's code, rather than importing the standard SDK libraries.

Using the Customization Method

Google Play provides management capabilities to implement a customized application for particular devices by leveraging multiple APK support. Multiple APK support allows you to create multiple APKs of your application, each of which targets a specific set of device configurations or even a specific device. The different configurations that you are able to target are as follows:

- Different API levels
- Different GL textures
- Different screen sizes
- Different CPU architectures
- Any combination of different API levels, different GL textures, different screen sizes, and or different CPU architectures

This customization method gives you complete control over how your application functions on a specific set of target devices, or even one particular device, if you desire to have that level of fine-grained control over the capabilities your application provides. Google Play allows developers to tie multiple APK files together under a single product name. This allows developers to create optimal packages without including a lot of resources not needed by every device. For example, a "small-screen package" wouldn't need resources for tablets and televisions.

Tip

To learn more about how to implement and manage multiple APK support for your application, see the following URLs: *http://d.android.com/training/multiple-apks/index.html* and *http://d.android.com/google/play/publishing/multiple-apks.html*.

This method works well for specialized applications with a small number of target devices but does not scale easily from a build or product management perspective.

Generally, developers will come up with a core application framework (classes or packages) shared across all versions of the application. All versions of a client/server application would likely share the same server and interact with it in the same way, but the client implementation is tailored to take advantage of specific device features, when they are available. The primary benefit of this technique is that users receive an application that leverages all the features their device (or API level) has to offer. Some drawbacks include source code fragmentation (many branches of the same code), increased testing requirements, and the fact that it can be more difficult to add new devices in the future.

For customization, you should also think about which screen sizes you will support. You may have an application that should work only on small screens, such as smartphones, or you may want to support only tablets, Android TVs, Wear, or Auto. Regardless, you should provide screen-specific layouts, adding to your application manifest the types of screens your application supports for Google Play filtering, and packaging different drawable resource files.

Taking Advantage of the Best of Both Methods

In truth, Android development teams usually use a hybrid approach, incorporating some aspects from both methods. It's pretty common to see developers define classes of devices based on functionality. For example, a game application might group devices based on graphics performance, screen resolution, or input methods. A location-based service (LBS) application might group devices based on the available internal sensors. Other applications might develop one version for devices with built-in, front-facing cameras and one version for those without. These groupings are arbitrary and set by the developer to keep the code and testing manageable. They will, in large part, be driven by the details of a particular application and any support requirements. In many cases, these features can be detected at runtime as well, but add enough of them together and the code paths can become overly complex when having two or more applications would actually be easier.

Tip

A single, unified version of an application is usually cheaper to support than multiple versions. However, a game might sell better with custom versions that leverage the distinct advantages and features of a specific class of devices. A vertical business application would likely benefit more from a unified approach that works the same, is easier to train users across multiple devices, and would thus have lower support costs for the business.

Developing Use Cases for Android Applications

You should first write use cases in general terms for the application before adapting them to specific device classes, which impose their own limitations. For example, a high-level use case for an application might be "Enter Form Data," but the individual devices might use different input methods, such as hardware versus software keyboards, and so on. Following this approach allows you to chart application user flows independent of specific user interface components or user-experience best practices that are most appropriate for a given device, form factor, or even platform. Considering that the most successful mobile applications these days need to have both Android and iOS versions, starting your use case development independent from the platform can help keep your app's identity in parity, while still recognizing and embracing platform differences upon implementation.

Tip

Developing an application for multiple devices is much like developing an application for different operating systems and input devices (such as handling Mac keyboard shortcuts versus those on Windows)—you must account for both subtle and not-so-subtle differences. These differences might be obvious, such as not having a keyboard for input, or not so obvious, such as device-specific bugs or different conventions for soft keys. See Chapter 13, "Designing Compatible Applications," for a discussion of device compatibility.

Incorporating Third-Party Requirements and Recommendations

In addition to the requirements imposed by your internal requirements analyses, your team needs to incorporate any requirements imposed by others. Third-party requirements can come from any number of sources, including:

- Android SDK License Agreement requirements
- Google Play requirements (if applicable)
- Other Google license requirements (if applicable)
- Other third-party API requirements (if applicable)
- Other application store requirements (if applicable)
- Mobile carrier/operator requirements (if applicable)
- Application certification requirements (if applicable)
- Android design guidelines and recommendations (if applicable)
- Other third-party design guidelines and recommendations (if applicable)

Incorporating these requirements into your project plan early is essential not only for keeping your project on schedule, but also so that these requirements are built into the application from the ground up, as opposed to applied as an afterthought, which can be risky.

Managing a Device Database

As your Android development team builds applications for a growing number of devices, it becomes more and more important to keep track of your application's target devices and related information for revenue estimation and maintenance purposes. Creating a device database is a great way to keep track of both marketing and device specification details for target devices. When we say database, we mean anything from a Microsoft Excel spreadsheet to a SQL database. The point is that the information is shared across the team or company and kept up-to-date. It can also be helpful to break devices into classes, such as those that support OpenGL ES 3.0 or those without camera hardware.

Tip

Depending on the resources available to you, you may not be able to keep track of every single device you plan to target. In that case, you should, instead, keep track of the class of devices that you plan to target and gather and maintain statistics on common device characteristics rather than specific device characteristics.

The device database is best implemented early, when project requirements and target devices have just been determined. Figure 18.2 illustrates how you can track device information and how different members of the application development team can use it.

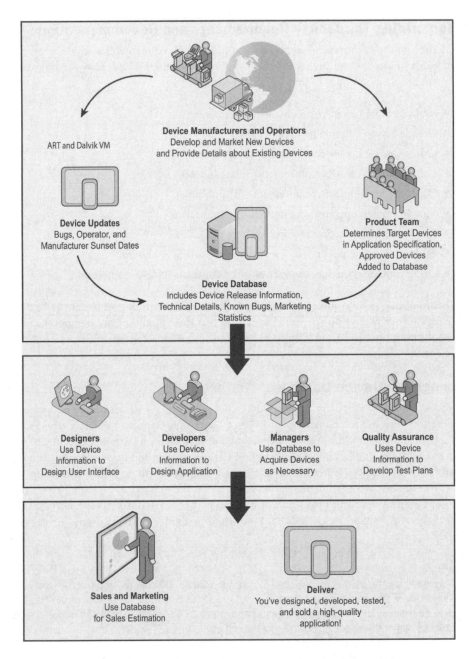

Figure 18.2   How a development team uses the device database.

Tip

Readers have asked us for our take on using personal devices for testing purposes. Is it safe? Is it smart? The short answer is that you can use your personal device for testing safely in most cases. It's highly unlikely that you will "break" or "brick" your device to the point where a factory reset won't fix it. However, protecting your data is another problem entirely. For example, if your application acts on the Contacts database, bugs or other coding mistakes may mess with your real contacts. Sometimes using personal devices is convenient, especially for small development teams without a big hardware budget. Make sure you understand the ramifications of doing so.

Determining Which Devices to Track

Some companies track only the devices they actively develop for, whereas others also track devices they might want to include in the future, or lower-priority devices. You can include devices in the database during the requirements phase of a project, as well as later if there are changes in a project's scope. You can also add devices as subsequent porting projects long after the initial application has been released.

Storing Device Data

You should design the device database to contain any information about a given device that would be helpful for developing and selling applications. This might require that someone be tasked with keeping track of a continual stream of information from carriers and manufacturers. Still, this information can be useful for all Android projects at a company. This data should include the following:

- Important device technical specification details (screen resolution, hardware details, supported media formats, input methods, and localization).

- Any known issues with devices (bugs and important limitations).

- Device manufacturer and carrier information (any firmware customizations, release and sunset dates, and expected user statistics, such as if a device is highly anticipated and expected to sell a lot, or is well received for vertical market applications, and so on).

- API-level data and firmware upgrade information. (As information becomes available, changes might have no impact on the application or warrant an entirely separate device entry; keep in mind that different manufacturers and carriers roll out upgrades on different schedules, so keeping track of this information at too fine-grained a level may not be feasible.)

- Actual testing of device information (which devices have been purchased or loaned through manufacturer or carrier loaner programs, how many are available, and so on).

You can also cross-reference the device manufacturer and carrier information with sales figures from the manufacturer, carrier, application stores, and internal metrics. Your application's ratings and reviews, as well as any crash reports by device, should also be documented.

The actual testing of device information is often best implemented as a library check-out system. Team members can reserve devices for testing and development purposes. When a loaner device needs to be returned to the manufacturer, it's easy to track. This also facilitates sharing devices across teams.

Using Device Data

Remember that the database can be used for multiple Android development projects. Device resources can be shared and sales statistics can be compared to see on which devices your applications perform best. Different team members (or roles) can use the device database in different ways:

- Product designers use the database to develop the most appropriate application user interface for the target devices.

- Media artists use the database to generate application assets such as graphics, videos, and audio in supported media file formats and resolutions appropriate for the target devices.

- Project managers use the database to determine the devices that must be acquired for development and testing purposes on the project and development priorities.

- Software developers use the database to design and develop applications compatible with target device specifications.

- QA personnel use the database to design and develop the target device specifications for test plans and to test the application thoroughly.

- Marketing and sales professionals use the database to estimate sales figures for released applications. For example, it is important to be aware that application sales will drop as device availability drops.

The information in the database can also help determine the most promising target devices for future development and porting. Android devices have built-in ways for users to report when their application crashes. When users report a crash, the information is sent to Google, and Google then presents it to you from within the Google Play Developer Console. Tracking this information will help you improve the quality of your applications over the long term.

Using Third-Party Device Databases

There are third-party databases for device information, including screen size, internal device details, and carrier support details, but subscribing to such information can be costly for a small company. Many Android developers instead choose to create a custom device database with only the devices they are interested in and the specific data they need for each device, which is often absent from open and free databases. WURFL (*http://wurfl.sourceforge.net*), for instance, is better for mobile Web development than for application development.

Assessing Project Risks

In addition to the normal risks any software project must identify, mobile projects need to be aware of the outside influences that can affect their project schedule and whether the project requirements can be met. Some of the risk factors include identifying and acquiring target devices and continually reassessing application feasibility.

Identifying Target Devices

Just as most sane software developers wouldn't write a desktop application without first deciding what operating systems (and their versions) the application will run on, Android developers must consider the target devices their application will run on. Each device has different capabilities, a different user interface, and unique limitations.

Target devices are generally determined in one of two ways:

- There's a popular "killer" device you want to develop for.
- You want to develop an application for maximum coverage.

In the first instance, you have your initial target device (or class of devices) figured out. In the second instance, you want to look at the available (and soon-to-be-available) devices on the market and adjust your application specifications to cover as many as is reasonably feasible.

Tip

On the Android platform, you normally do not target individual devices specifically; instead, you focus on device features or classes (for example, those running a specific platform version or having specific hardware configurations). You can limit the devices upon which your application will be installed using Android manifest tags, which act as market filters.

There may be instances when your application is targeting only a specific niche, such as Android TV or Android Wear. In this case, your application would probably not be useful for a smartphone or tablet; on the other hand, if your application is more general, such as a game, you should make every effort to determine the different targets and types of devices your application will work on, such as smartphones, phablets, tablets, and TVs.

Understanding How Manufacturers and Operators Fit In

It is also important to note that we've seen popular product lines, such as the Nexus, Galaxy, Moto, One, Desire, or Xperia line of Android devices, customized by a number of manufacturers. A carrier often ships its custom version of a device, including a different user experience or skin, as well as big bundles of custom applications (taking up a bunch of space on the device). The carrier might also disable specific device features, which could effectively make it impossible for your application to run. You must take all these factors into account when considering your application requirements and capabilities. Your application's running requirements must match the features shared across all target devices and, in all cases, appropriately handle optional feature use.

Understanding How Devices Come and Go over Time

New devices are developed all the time. Carriers and manufacturers retire (sunset) devices all the time. Different carriers might carry the same (or similar) device but might sunset (retire) the device at different times. A carrier may also release a particular device much sooner than other carriers, for various reasons.

Tip

Developers should set a policy, made clear to users, of how long an application will be supported after the carrier or manufacturer stops supporting a specific device. This policy might need to be different for various carriers because carriers impose their own support requirements.

Developers need to understand how different kinds of device models can move through the worldwide marketplace. Some devices are available (or become popular) only in certain geographic regions. Sometimes devices are released worldwide, but often they are only released regionally.

Historically, it has been common for a device (or new generation of devices) to become available initially in market-driving regions of eastern Asia, including South Korea and Japan, and then show up in Europe, North America, and Australia, where device users often upgrade every year or two and pay premium rates for applications. Finally, these same devices become available in Central and South America, China, and India, where subscribers often don't have landlines or the same levels of income. Regions such as China and India must often be treated as entirely separate mobile marketplaces—with more affordable devices requiring vastly different revenue models. Here, applications sell for less, but revenue is instead derived from the huge and growing subscriber base.

Acquiring Target Devices

The earlier you can get your hands on the target devices, the better off you are. Sometimes this is as easy as going to the store and buying a new device.

It is quite common for an application developer to target upcoming devices—those not yet shipped or available to consumers. There is a great competitive advantage to having your application ready to run the moment consumers have the device in their hands for the first time. For preproduction devices, you can join manufacturer and operator developer programs. These programs help you keep abreast of changes to the device lines (upcoming models, discontinued models). Many of these programs also include preproduction device loan programs, enabling developers to get their hands on the device before consumers do.

Tip

If you are just getting started acquiring Android devices, consider a Google Experience device, such as one of the Nexus handsets like the Nexus 4, 5, 6, 7, 9, or 10. See *http://www.google.com/nexus/* for more information and to see which Nexus devices are currently on the market, as some older devices like the 4, 7, and 10 may only be available through third parties.

There are risks for developers writing applications for specific preproduction devices because device shipment dates often slide and the platform might have unstable or bug-prone firmware. Devices can be delayed or canceled. Device features (especially new and interesting ones) are not set in stone until the device ships and the developer verifies that those features work as expected. Exciting new devices are announced all the time—devices you might want your application to support. Your project plan must be flexible enough to change and adapt with the market as necessary.

Tip

Sometimes you don't need to acquire specific devices to test with them. Various online services allow you to remotely install and test on real devices that are accessible and con-trollable through remote services. Most of these services have some sort of charge that must be weighed against the cost of actually owning the device outright.

Determining the Feasibility of Application Requirements

Android developers are at the mercy of the device limitations, which vary in terms of memory and processing power, screen type, and platform version. Mobile developers do not really have the luxury that traditional desktop application developers have of saying an application requires "more memory" or "more space." Device limitations are pretty much fixed, and if an Android application is to run, it runs within the device's limitations or not at all. Technically speaking, most Android devices have some hardware flexibility, such as the ability to use external storage devices such as SD cards, but we're still talking about limited resources.

You can do true feasibility assessment only on the physical device, not the software emulator. Your application might work beautifully in the emulator but falter on the actual device. Android developers must constantly revisit feasibility, application responsiveness, and performance throughout the development process.

Understanding Quality Assurance Risks

The QA team has its work cut out for it because the testing environment is generally less than ideal.

Testing Early, Testing Often

Get those target devices in hand as early as possible. For preproduction devices, it can take months to get the hardware from the manufacturer. Cooperating with carrier device loaner programs and buying devices from retail locations is frustrating but sometimes necessary. Don't wait until the last minute to gather the test hardware. We have seen many developers wonder why their applications run slowly on certain older devices only to realize that testing on a fast development computer or brand-new device with a dedicated network connection is not the same as testing on the actual device.

Testing on the Device

It cannot be said enough: `Testing on the emulator is helpful, but testing on the device is essential.` In reality, it doesn't matter if the application works on the emulator—no one uses an emulator in the real world.

Although you can perform factory resets on devices and wipe user data, there is often no easy way to completely "wipe" a device and return it to a clean starting state, so the QA team needs to determine and stick to a testing policy of what is considered a clean state on the device. Testers might need to learn to flash devices with different firmware versions and understand subtle differences between platform versions, as well as how underlying application data is stored on the device (for example, SQLite databases, private application files, and cache usage).

Mitigating the Risk of Limited Real-World Testing Opportunities

In some ways, every QA tester works within a controlled environment. This is doubly true for Android application testers. They often work with devices that are not on real networks and preproduction devices that might not match those in the field. In addition, because testing generally takes place in a lab, the location (including primary cell tower, satellite fixes and related device signal strength, availability of data services, LBS information, and locale information) is fixed. The QA team needs to get creative to mitigate the risks of testing too narrow a range of these factors. For example, it is essential to test all applications when the device has no signal (and in airplane mode and such) to make sure they don't crash and burn under such conditions that we all experience at some point. A variety of testing tools, some better suited to developers and white-box testers, are available to assist in application development. Some of the most suitable tools include UI/Application Exerciser Monkey, `monkeyrunner`, and `JUnit`.

Testing Client/Server and Cloud-Friendly Applications

Make sure the QA team understands its responsibilities. Android applications often have network components and server-side functionality. Make sure thorough server and service testing is part of the test plan—not just the client portion of the solution that is implemented on the device. This might require the development of desktop or Web applications to exercise network portions of the overall solution.

Writing Essential Project Documentation

You might think that with its shorter schedules, smaller teams, and simpler functionality, Android software project documentation would be less onerous. Unfortunately, this is not the case—quite the opposite. In addition to the traditional benefits good documentation provides any software project, it serves a variety of purposes in Android development. Consider documenting the following for your project:

- Requirements analysis and prioritization
- Risk assessment and management
- Application architecture and design
- Feasibility studies, including performance benchmarking
- Technical specifications (overall, server, device-specific client)
- Detailed user interface specifications (general, service specific)
- Test plans, test scripts, test cases (general, device specific)
- Scope change documentation

Much of this documentation is common in the average software development project. But perhaps your team finds that skimping on certain aspects of the documentation process has been doable in the past. Before you think of cutting corners in an Android development project, consider some of these documentation requirements for a successful project. Some project documentation might be simpler than that of larger-scale software projects, but other portions might need to be fleshed out in finer detail—especially user interface and feasibility studies.

Developing Test Plans for Quality Assurance Purposes

Quality assurance relies heavily on the functional specification documentation and the user interface documentation. Screen real estate is valuable on Android devices, and user experience is vital to the successful project. Test plans need to provide complete coverage of the application user interface, yet be flexible enough to address higher-level user experience issues that may meet the requirements of the test plan but just aren't positive experiences.

Understanding the Importance of User Interface Documentation

There's no such thing as a killer application with a poorly designed user interface. Thoughtful user interface design is one of the most important details to nail down during the design phase of any Android project. You must thoroughly document application workflow (application state) at the screen-by-screen level and can include detailed specifications for key usage patterns and how to fall back gracefully when certain keys or features are missing. You should clearly define usage cases in advance.

Leveraging Third-Party Testing Facilities

Some companies opt to have QA done off-site by a third party; most QA teams require detailed documentation, including use case workflow diagrams, to determine correct application behavior. If you do not provide adequate, detailed, and accurate documentation to the testing facility, you will not get deep, detailed, and accurate test results. By providing detailed documentation, you raise the bar from "it works" to "it works correctly." What might seem straightforward to some people might not be to others.

Providing Documentation Required by Third Parties

If you are required to submit your application for review to a software certification program, or in some cases to an Android application store, part of your submission is likely to be some documentation about your application. Some stores require, for example, that your application include a Help feature or technical support contact information. Certification programs might require you to provide detailed documentation on application functionality, user interface workflow, and application state diagrams.

Providing Documentation for Maintenance and Porting

Android applications are often ported to additional devices and other OS platforms. This porting work is frequently done by a third party, making the existence of thorough functional and technical specifications even more crucial.

Leveraging Configuration Management Systems

Many wonderful source control systems are out there for developers, and most that work well for traditional development work fine for a mobile project. Versioning your application, on the other hand, is not necessarily as straightforward as you might think.

Choosing a Source Control System

Android development considerations impose no surprise requirements for source control systems. Some considerations for developers evaluating how to handle configuration management for an Android project are

- Ability to keep track of source code (Java) and binaries (Android packages and so on)
- Ability to keep track of application resources by device configuration (graphics and so on)
- Integration with the developer's chosen development environment (Android Studio or Eclipse)

One point to consider is integration between the development environment (such as Android Studio) and your source control system. Common source control systems, such as Git, Subversion, CVS, and Mercurial, work well with Android Studio and Eclipse. Git source control is integrated with Android Studio. Check to see if your favorite source control system works with your chosen Android development environment.

Implementing an Application Version System That Works

Developers should also make an early decision on a versioning scheme that takes into account the device particulars and the software build. It is often not sufficient to version the software by build alone (that is, Version 1.0.1).

Android developers often combine the traditional versioning scheme with the target device configuration or device class supported (Version `API Level.Important Characteristic/ Device Class Name`.101). This helps QA, technical support personnel, and end users who might not know the model names or features of their devices or know them only by marketing names developers are often unaware of. For example, an application developed with camera support for API Level 11 might be versioned 11.15.101 (or 1115101), where 15 stands for "Camera Support," whereas the same application for a device without camera support might have a version such as 11.16.101 (or 1116101), where 16 stands for the "No Camera Support" source branch. If you had two different maintenance engineers supporting the different source code trees, you would know just by the version name to which version you should assign bug fixes. The numbers 15 and 16 do not officially map to the existence or nonexistence of a camera, but are used here as an example. You should come up with your own numbering system that maps to particular characteristics or device classes and makes sense to your Android development team.

Just to make things a tad more confusing, you need to plan your upgrade versions as well. If an upgrade spawns a rebuild of your application, you might want to version it appropriately: Version 11.15.101.Upg1, and so forth. Yes, this can get out of control, so don't go overboard, but if you design your versioning system intelligently up front, it can be useful later when you have different device builds floating around internally and with users. Finally, you also have to keep track of the `versionCode` attribute associated with your application.

Also, be aware of what distribution methods support multiple application packages or binaries as the same application and which require each binary to be managed independently. There are several good reasons not to have all of your code and resources in a single binary. Application package size, for example, can get large and unmanageable when the application attempts to support multiple device resolutions using alternative resources. There is a great write up on assigning codes to your different application versions here: *http://d.android.com/google/play/publishing/multiple-apks.html#CreatingApks*.

Designing Android Applications

When designing an application for Android, the developer must consider the constraints the device imposes and decide what type of application framework is best for a given project.

Understanding Android Device Limitations

Applications are expected to be fast, responsive, and stable, but developers must work with limited resources. You must keep in mind the memory and processing-power constraints of all target devices when designing and developing Android applications.

Exploring Common Android Application Architectures

Android applications have traditionally come in two basic models: stand-alone applications and network-driven applications.

Stand-alone applications are packaged with everything they require and rely on for the device to do all the heavy lifting. All processing is done locally, in memory, and is subject to the limitations of the device. Stand-alone applications might use network functions, but they do not rely on them for core application functionality. An example of a reasonable stand-alone application is a basic Solitaire game. A user can play the game when the device is in airplane mode without issue.

Network-driven applications provide a lightweight client on the device but rely on the network (or the cloud) to provide a good portion of their content and functionality. Network-driven applications are often used to offload intensive processing to a server. They also benefit from the ability to deliver additional content or functionality on the fly, long after the application has been installed. Developers also like network-driven applications because this architecture enables them to build one smart application server or cloud service with device clients for many different operating systems to support a larger audience of users. Good examples of network-driven applications include

- Applications that leverage cloud-based services, application servers, or Web services
- Customizable content such as social networking applications
- Applications with noncritical process- and memory-intensive operations that can be offloaded to a powerful server and the results delivered back to the client
- Any application that provides additional features at a later date without a full update to the binary

How much you rely on the network to assist in your application's functionality is up to you. You can use the network to provide only content updates (new messages from friends), or you can use it to dictate how your application looks and behaves (for instance, adding new menu options or features on the fly). If your application is truly network based, such as a Web app, and does not need access to any device-specific features, you may not even need to build a native application with an installable APK. In that case, you may prefer to have users access your application through a browser.

Designing for Extensibility and Maintenance

Applications can be written with a fixed user interface and a fixed feature set, but they don't have to be. Network-driven applications can be more complex to design but offer flexibility for the long term. Here's an example: Let's say you want to write a wallpaper application. Your application can be a stand-alone version, partially network driven, or completely network driven. Regardless, your application has two required functions:

- Display a set of images and allow the user to choose one.
- Take the chosen image and set it as the wallpaper on the device.

A super-simple stand-alone wallpaper application might come with a fixed set of wallpapers. If they're a generic size for all target devices, you might need to reformat them for the specific device. You could write this application, but it would waste space and processing. You can't update the wallpapers available, and it is generally just a bad design.

The partially network-driven wallpaper application might enable the user to browse a fixed menu of wallpaper categories that show images from a generic image server. The application downloads a specific graphic and then formats the image for the device. As the developer, you can add new wallpaper images to the server anytime, but you need to build a new application every time you want to add a new device configuration or screen size. If you want to change the menu to add live wallpapers at a later date, you need to write a new version of your application. This application design is feasible, but it isn't using its resources wisely and isn't particularly extensible. However, you could use the single application server and write applications for Android, iOS, Linux, and Windows clients, so you are still in a better position than you were with the stand-alone wallpaper application.

The fully network-driven version of the wallpaper application does the bare minimum on the device. The client enables the server to dictate what the client user interface looks like, what menus to display, and where to display them. The user browses the images from the application server just as he or she would with the partially network-driven version, but when the user chooses a wallpaper, the mobile application just sends a request to the server: "I want this wallpaper and I am this kind or type of device, with such-and-such screen resolution." The server formats and resizes the image (any process-intensive operations) and sends the perfectly tailored wallpaper down to the application, which the application then sets as the wallpaper. Adding support for more devices is straightforward: simply deploy the lightweight client with any necessary changes and add support for that device configuration to the server. Adding a new menu item is just a server change, resulting in all devices (or whichever devices the server dictates) getting that new category. You need to update the client only when a new function requires the client to change, such as to add support for live wallpapers. The response time of this application depends on network performance, but the application is the most extensible and dynamic. However, this application is basically useless when the device is in airplane mode.

Stand-alone applications are straightforward. This approach is great for one-shot applications and those that are meant to be network independent. Network-driven applications require a bit more forethought and are sometimes more complicated to develop, but might save a lot of time and provide users with fresh content and features for the long run.

Designing for Application Interoperability

Android application designers should consider how they will interface with other applications on the device, including other applications written by the same developer. Here are some issues to address:

- Will your application rely on other content providers?
- Are these content providers guaranteed to be installed on the device?
- Will your application act as a content provider? What data will it provide?
- Will your application have background features? Act as a service?
- Will your application rely on third-party services or optional components?
- Will your application use publicly documented Intent mechanisms to access third-party functionality? Will your application provide the same?
- How will your application's user experience suffer when optional components are not available?
- Will your application require substantial device resources such as battery life? Will it play nice?
- Will your application expose its functionality through a remote interface such as Android Interface Definition Language (AIDL)?

Developing Android Applications

Android application implementation follows the same principles as other platforms. The steps Android developers take during implementation are fairly straightforward:

- Write and compile the code.
- Run the application in the software emulator.
- Test and debug the application in the software emulator or test device.
- Package and deploy the application to the target devices.
- Test and debug the application on the target devices.
- Incorporate changes from the team and repeat until the application is complete.

Note

We talk more about development strategies for building solid Android applications in Chapter 20, "Delivering Quality Applications."

Testing Android Applications

Testers face many challenges, including device fragmentation (many devices, each with different features—some call this "compatibility"), defining device states (What is a clean state?), and handling real-world events (device calls, loss of coverage). Gathering the devices needed for testing can be costly and difficult.

The good news for Android QA teams is that the Android SDK includes a number of useful tools for testing applications on both the emulator and the device. There are many opportunities for leveraging white-box testing.

You must modify defect-tracking systems to handle testing across device configurations and carriers. For thorough testing, QA team members generally cannot be given the device and told to "try to break it." There are many shades of gray for testers between black-box and white-box testing. Testers should know their way around the Android emulator and the other utilities provided with the Android SDK. Android QA involves a lot of edge-case testing. Again, a preproduction model of a device might not be exactly the same as what eventually ships to consumers.

> **Note**
>
> We discuss testing Android applications in detail in Chapter 21, "Testing Your Applications."

Controlling the Test Release

In some situations, you may wish to take complete control of to whom your application will be released for testing. Rather than making your application available to the entire world all at once, releasing your application on a smaller scale may be the ideal test plan. Here are the common ways for controlling the test release of an application:

- **Private controlled testing:** In this situation, developers invite users to a controlled setting, such as an office. They observe users interacting with the application, and then make changes based on feedback from those test users. The developers then implement any updates, invite more testers to interact with the application, and so on, until the design receives positive feedback. Only then would they release the application to more users. Private testing usually involves not allowing the application to leave the facilities on a test user's device; sometimes you may even want to provide your own testing device to ensure that the application never leaves your facilities.

- **Private group testing:** In this situation, developers prove their APK file to a very small set of test users, and then collect feedback in a manner suitable for the situation. They then use the feedback to make the necessary changes, rerelease the APK to the same test users, or new test users, and continue receiving feedback and updating accordingly, until they begin receiving positive responses from users. The application is usually not on a strict lockdown policy, such as never leaving the building, but rather has a more limited but semi-open test distribution. One feature of Google Play that may help you facilitate this type of test release is a Private Channel Release. If you have a Google Apps domain, you can launch your application in a controlled and private way to users of your particular domain.

- **Google Play Staged Rollouts:** Google Play provides many new features for controlling to whom your application is released. Using these facilities may ease how you test your application with real users. Staged Rollouts is a feature of Google Play that allows you to offer your application to alpha and beta test groups for collecting early feedback, prior to releasing your application to all Google Play users.

Deploying Android Applications

Developers need to determine what methods they use to distribute applications. With Android, you have a number of options. You can market applications yourself and leverage marketplaces such as Google Play. Android marketplaces, such as Amazon Appstore for Android, also have Android distribution channels of which you can take advantage.

Note

We discuss publication of Android applications in detail in Chapter 22, "Distributing Your Applications."

Determining Target Markets

Developers must take into account any requirements imposed by third parties offering application distribution mechanisms. Specific distributors might impose rules for what types of applications they distribute on your behalf. They might impose quality requirements such as testing certifications (although none specific to Android applications existed at the time this book went to print) and accompanying technical support, documentation and adherence to common user interface workflow standards, and performance metrics for responsive applications. Distributors might also impose content restrictions such as barring objectionable content.

Tip

The most popular distribution channels for Android applications have been changing over time. Google Play remains the first stop in Android app publication, but both the Amazon Appstore and Facebook App Center have become effective hubs for Android app distribution. Other app stores are also available; some cater to special user groups and niche application genres, whereas others distribute for many different platforms.

Supporting and Maintaining Android Applications

Developers cannot just develop an application, publish it, and forget about it—even the simplest of applications likely requires some maintenance and the occasional upgrade. Generally speaking, Android application support requirements are minimal if you come from a traditional software background, but they do exist.

Carriers and operators generally serve as the front line of technical support to end users. As a developer, you aren't usually required to have 24/7 responsive technical support staff or toll-free device numbers and such. In fact, the bulk of application maintenance can fall on the server side and be limited to content maintenance—for example, posting new media such as audio, video, or other content. This may not seem obvious at first. After all, you've provided your email address and website when the user downloaded your application, right? Although that may be the case, your average user still calls the company on the bill first (in other words, the manufacturer or carrier) for support if the device is not functioning properly.

That said, the device firmware changes quickly, and Android development teams need to stay on top of the market. Here are some of the maintenance and support considerations unique to Android application development.

Track and Address Crashes Reported by Users

Google Play—the most popular way to distribute Android applications—has built-in features enabling users to submit crash and bug reports regarding an application. Monitor your developer account and address these issues in a timely fashion in order to maintain your credibility and keep your users happy.

Testing Firmware Upgrades

Android handsets receive frequent (some say *too* frequent) firmware upgrades. This means that the Android platform versions you initially tested and supported become obsolete and the handsets on which your application is installed can suddenly run new versions of the Android firmware. Although upgrades are supposed to be backward compatible, this hasn't always proven true. In fact, many developers have fallen victim to poor upgrade scenarios, in which their applications suddenly cease to function properly. Always retest your applications after a major or minor firmware upgrade occurs in the field.

Maintaining Adequate Application Documentation

Maintenance is often not performed by the same engineers who developed the application in the first place. Here, keeping adequate development and testing documentation, including specifications and test scripts, is even more vital.

Managing Live Server Changes

Always treat any live server and Web or cloud service with the care it deserves. This means you need to appropriately time your backups and upgrades. You need to safeguard data and maintain user privacy at all times. You should manage rollouts carefully because live Android application users might rely on the app's availability. Do not underestimate the server-side development or testing needs. Always test server rollouts and service upgrades in a safe testing environment before "going live."

Identifying Low-Risk Porting Opportunities

If you've implemented the device database we talked about previously in this chapter, now is the ideal time to analyze device similarities to identify easy porting projects. For example, you might discover that an application was originally developed for a specific class of device, but now several popular devices are on the market with similar specifications. Porting an existing application to these new devices is sometimes as straightforward as generating a new build (with appropriate versioning) and testing the application on the new devices. If you defined your device classes well, you might even get lucky and not have to make any changes at all when new devices come out.

Application Feature Selection

When determining what features your application will support, make sure to think about the costs versus the benefits of supporting a particular feature. Adding new features is always the easy part, but removing them from your application is not. Once users become accustomed to a feature, if that feature goes missing, your users may never use your application again. They may even go as far as writing a negative review and giving your app an extremely low rating. Always make sure that a particular feature is of use to the users of your application, rather than just cluttering a user interface with things for users to do, only to realize that you should not have added a given feature in the first place.

Summary

Android software development has evolved over time and differs in some important ways from traditional desktop software development. In this chapter, you gained some practical advice for adapting traditional software processes to Android—from identifying target devices to testing and deploying your application to the world. There's always room for improvement when it comes to software processes. Ideally, some of these insights can help you to avoid the pitfalls new Android app companies sometimes fall into or they can help to simply improve the processes of veteran teams.

Quiz Questions

1. True or false: The waterfall software methodology is preferable to the iteration and rapid prototyping approach for Android development.

2. What are the approaches the authors have found helpful for determining project requirements?

3. When is the best time to implement a device database?

4. True or false: Since the Android emulator has been made available, testing on real devices is not essential.

5. What are the steps Android developers take during implementation?

Exercises

1. Come up with an idea for an application, then determine and explain the best approach to take for discovering project requirements.

2. Create a list of requirements for the application idea you came up with in the previous exercise.

3. Identify the target devices for the application idea that you came up with in the first exercise, and create a simple device database outlining the important features that are relevant to your application idea.

References and More Information

Wikipedia on the software development process:
http://en.wikipedia.org/wiki/Software_development_process
Wikipedia on the Waterfall model:
http://en.wikipedia.org/wiki/Waterfall_model
Wikipedia on rapid application development (RAD):
http://en.wikipedia.org/wiki/Rapid_application_development
Wikipedia on iterative and incremental development:
http://en.wikipedia.org/wiki/Iterative_and_incremental_development
Wikipedia on Scrum (software development): *https://en.wikipedia.org/wiki/Scrum_(software_development)*
Extreme Programming:
http://www.extremeprogramming.org
Android Training: "Designing for Multiple Screens":
http://d.android.com/training/multiscreen/index.html
Android Training: "Creating Backward-Compatible UIs":
http://d.android.com/training/backward-compatible-ui/index.html

Android API Guides: "Supporting Multiple Screens":
http://d.android.com/guide/practices/screens_support.html
Android API Guides: "Supporting Tablets and Handsets":
http://d.android.com/guide/practices/tablets-and-handsets.html
Android Google Services: "Filters on Google Play":
http://d.android.com/google/play/filters.html

Planning the Experience

Knowing how to use the newest Android APIs is a great start, but there is more to building Android applications than just programming a bunch of code and adding more features to your application. Implementing a slick-looking user interface is also wonderful, but if your application is difficult to figure out how to use and it does not provide any real benefit to the user, it will most likely never become that "killer app." In order to truly set your application apart from the myriad of other applications available to users, you really must think differently about what user problem your application solves. Solving that problem in a graceful way—rather than developing an application that is just a collection of implemented Android features—is one of the best pieces of advice the authors have to share.

The purpose of this chapter is to present many different concepts and techniques that should enable you to make better decisions about how to design your application with your users in mind. The information presented in this chapter is not exhaustive, nor is it meant to be the default methodology that you have to use when planning your applications. Rather, the information should be adapted to fit your particular project. The authors have seen that the most successful projects are not always performed by developers who follow one particular rigorous development methodology that has been handed to them. Usually, the most successful projects are completed by developers who work together to create their own system and refine a methodology that works best for them, within their own resource constraints.

Thinking about Objectives

When starting a new Android development project, it is always a good idea to set some expectations early on, before writing code. The most helpful expectations to think about are in the form of objectives. Usually, there are at least two parties who have objectives in relation to a given Android development project, if not more. People who use your application obviously have reasons for doing so; therefore, they have objectives they are working to achieve with your application. On the other hand, you, the developer or team of developers, have reasons for building the application. In addition, besides users and team, there may be other stakeholders who have objectives in relation to your project.

User Objectives

Generally, users install an application because of a need they are trying to fulfill. User objectives may vary widely; for example, users who are forgetful may be looking for an application that can keep track of important information for them, such as a note-taking application or a calendar application. On the other hand, certain users may want to be entertained by a game, but have only short bursts of time they can devote to playing it.

Focusing your development efforts around a clear set of user objectives should help you determine who your target users will be. As an application developer, if you try to fulfill the objectives of too many different types of users, you may end up not pleasing any users at all. If you start development without determining who your target users are, you may end up building a note-taking game for a forgetful, busy user looking for an entertaining way to help them remember important information in short bursts.

Not only will knowing your users' objectives help you focus your development efforts on creating a superior experience for a particular type of user, but it will also help you discover if there are applications that may already be fulfilling the same or similar needs. Building an application that is just like other applications already available is not a good use of your efforts. But focusing in on the pain points that your target users have, and knowing what the current competition is, should help you make better decisions with your development efforts.

Take the time early on to think about what a realistic set of user objectives is for a particular need you want your application to fill, and think about how to differentiate yourself from the competition. Then design your application to fulfill those objectives. You may be pleasantly surprised when your users thank you for fulfilling their needs.

Team Objectives

Whether you are a team of one working alone in your bedroom, or one person on a team of many at a large corporation, you are probably building the application with specific objectives in mind. Those team objectives could be achieving 5,000 downloads in the first month or generating $50,000 in revenue in the first quarter. Other examples of team objectives could be releasing the first version of an application in one month, or something different altogether, such as generating a measurable quantity of brand recognition. The more measurable the objective, the better the decisions you make will be as your project progresses. Stay away from unmeasurable objectives, like "inspire people to write deep thoughts."

Whatever those team objectives are, it is a good idea to start thinking about them as early as possible. Fulfilling your users' objectives is only part of the equation. Failure to have a clear set of team objectives may result in developing software that is late or over budget, or it may even result in the project never being completed.

Objectives of Other Stakeholders

Not all Android application projects have other stakeholders involved, but some projects do. Other stakeholders could include advertisers that provide ads for placing within your application. Their objectives may be to maximize their revenues while maintaining their brand recognition without harming the users' experience of your application. Early in the planning process, think about other stakeholders in addition to your users and your team.

Not thinking up front about the needs of other stakeholders may result in harming any types of business partnerships that you may have developed with those stakeholders. Failure to consider their needs could damage your relationship.

Techniques for Focusing Your Product Efforts

Knowing that you should target your project efforts around a clear set of objectives is the first step. Now we will discuss practical techniques that you can begin using right now to help you think about what your users' objectives are and how you can fulfill them.

Personas

One way to keep your target users in mind during your Android project is to create a fictional persona. The purpose of using a persona during development is to think about your users' problems from their perspective. Defining a persona and the problems that persona has is just one way to fine-tune who your target users will be—and how to differentiate your product from the other available applications.

Personas are fairly easy to create. Some of the information that you should consider defining for your fictional personas includes

- Name
- Gender
- Age range
- Occupation
- Android sophistication level
- Favorite applications
- Most-used Android features
- Attitude toward or awareness of your application's objective
- Education
- Income
- Marital status
- Hobbies
- Problems for which the persona wants or needs a solution

This list is not comprehensive, but it is a good start to help you focus in on exactly who your target users are. You should create only one or two different personas. As we mentioned earlier in this chapter, if you try to please every single type of user, your application may never actually solve any particular need for any users at all.

You can create these personas on paper and keep them nearby and visible while you work. Sometimes it even helps to attach a picture of a person to this fictional character; that way, your character has a face to go with the name. Then, when you are making decisions for your Android application, you can refer to your target user's persona to see if you are fulfilling that user's needs.

User Story Mapping

User story mapping is one way to approach project planning and come to a shared understanding of what you are building by helping your team to discover who your actual target users are and what interactions they will be performing with your system. This is usually done by creating simple user stories that describe the most beneficial features of your application as functional details, collecting the minimal set of beneficial features—each in their simplest form—while still allowing users to complete the most important tasks they want and need to perform. Then you can order those stories in the flow required to complete a particular objective. Once the order of the minimum number of stories is determined to meet a particular objective, a product backlog can be arranged for each story in its simplest form. When iterating over time, more complexity may be added to the individual stories as the project evolves and user feedback is gathered, helping your team determine the best way to proceed with development.

The goals of user story mapping are to learn as quickly as possible what your users actually want—without just relying on assumptions—from user feedback; to drive features with benefits provided to users as the method for deciding what to build next; and, all the while, to arrive at a shared understanding with all project stakeholders. User story mapping is a fairly complex topic, and it is worth looking into for those who are interested in taking their project planning skills to another level. To learn more about user story mapping, see the following link: *http://www.agileproductdesign.com/blog/the_new_backlog.html*.

Entity Discovery and Organization

Early in your project's life, you should start thinking about the entities, classes, and objects that describe the information within your application. Drawing simple diagrams on paper can help you determine how to organize your code. Here are a few techniques that you can use:

- **Domain modeling:** A domain model provides names for all of the entities used within a project. The domain model usually evolves over the life of a project and includes the entity names, which should be nouns, and their relationships to other entities.

- **Class modeling:** A class model is very similar to a domain model, just more specific. A class model is usually derived from a domain model but includes much more detail—class names, attributes, operations, and relationships to other classes.

- **Entity relationship modeling:** An entity relationship model is used specifically for describing an application's data model. The data model describes the tables of a database. This diagram usually includes the entity names, their attributes, relationships to other entities, and cardinalities.

With the information you gather from these diagrams, combined with the Android classes that your project requires, it becomes increasingly important to think about where and how to implement classes in relation to one another as your project progresses. The larger your project gets without proper organization and planning, the more your code base resembles spaghetti code: that is, unstructured, tangled, overly complex, and very difficult to follow.

Planning User Interactions

Having an idea of the objectives a user seeks to accomplish in your application is a great foundation for moving your project forward. With this information in mind, you should take some time to plan how users will interact with your application and how they will proceed through the application to accomplish their desired tasks. You can begin planning user interactions by thinking about user flows and creating screen maps.

User Flows

A user flow is the path the user takes through an application to accomplish a particular goal. This goal may be closely related to one or more use stories, because a user must often take multiple actions in order to accomplish a particular goal. When designing user flows, remember to keep the steps to the minimum required in order to accomplish the goal while maintaining an optimal experience for the user. Too many steps may lead to unnecessary confusion or frustration.

You should also limit the number of user flows your application provides. As we mentioned earlier, you should not try to create a solution for every type of user. Instead, specialize by fulfilling a need that helps users make their lives easier. A few user flows per application are common, but you probably will design at least one or two key flows that a user performs frequently.

Screen Maps

One way to determine the user flows or key flows for your application is by designing a screen map, which is a way to visualize the relationships among the screens of your application. The organization of a screen map will vary from application to application. Some maps may involve just one or two screens, whereas others could have dozens.

You can assemble a screen map by first creating a list of all the screens that your application will need, and then connecting them to show their relationships.

Note

Not all user interactions may require you to build a screen within your application. For example, notifications for your application appear in the status bar, but you do not have to build the status bar. You just need to integrate with the Android APIs for displaying notifications to the user. Keep these things in mind when creating your user flows and screen maps.

When designing your screen maps, here are a few things you should be aware of:

- A screen does not necessarily mean you need an `Activity`. Instead, consider reusable fragments for displaying like content.

- Group content fragments together when in a multipane layout, but use them separately when in a single-pane layout.

- When possible, use one or more of the navigation design patterns that are commonly recommended for use in Android applications. We talk more about navigation techniques and design patterns in Chapter 10, "Architecting with Patterns."

Tip

To learn more about creating screen maps and planning your application's navigation, please read the Android documentation found here: *http://d.android.com/training/design-navigation/index.html*.

Communicating Your Application's Identity

To set your application apart from other applications, you should think about the identity that you would like users to associate with your product. Some of the most common ways to communicate identity are as follows:

- Develop consistent style guidelines and follow those guidelines throughout your application. To jump start this process, you should take a look at the material design specification here: *http://www.google.com/design/spec/material-design/introduction.html*.

- Choose a specific color palette and theme for your application. Use colors to establish uniformity or contrast among the different visual elements of your user interface. Style the various UI components such as the status bar, app bar, menus, action icons, views, layouts, and various other components to help make your application's brand stand out. The material design documentation provides an amazing visual color palette to simplify the process of choosing bold colors that work well in harmony with each other. You can find the color palette here: *http://www.google.com/design/spec/style/color.html#color-color-palette*.

- Create a unique application launcher icon that your users will remember. Try to associate the purpose of your application with the design of your icon. In addition, any other icons that you create should instantly communicate to users what the icon means.

- Use your application logo rather than your application icon when portraying your brand to users. Prior to API 21, it was recommended that you display the application icon and title on the app bar. As of API 21, using an icon and a title is discouraged, so you should consider using your brand's logo elsewhere in the application.

Many of the most successful application brands portray their brand logo on the launch screen of their launcher `Activity`, and keep it visible for a few seconds before transitioning to the actual application with which users interact. For inspiration on launch screens, see *http://www.google.com/design/spec/patterns/launch-screens.html*.

- Emphasize content with various font styles. Don't just stick to one font, style, color, size, or other attributes. To learn more about the material design typography recommendations, see *http://www.google.com/design/spec/style/typography.html*.

- Use white space or empty space effectively. To learn more about these material design layout recommendations, see *http://www.google.com/design/spec/layout/principles.html*.

- Do not cram user interface components together. Instead, use padding and margins to provide spacing between these components. To learn more about the material design metrics and spacing user interface components, see *http://www.google.com/design/spec/layout/metrics-keylines.html*.

- If you plan on having your application run on different-size displays, make sure it remains flexible with its layouts to accommodate differences across devices' displays.

Tip

For a comprehensive overview of style recommendations, see the Android documentation that can be found here: *http://d.android.com/design/style/index.html* and the material design specification here: *http://www.google.com/design/spec/material-design/introduction.html*.

Designing Screen Layouts

Before investing a great deal of time or money in developing your application, you should spend some time deciding how you would like your user interface layout to appear. There are a few different methods you can use for determining your screen layouts.

Sketches

You should start making decisions about your layouts very early on by quickly creating rough sketches, on paper or on a whiteboard, to determine how your screens and their visual components should be organized in their layouts. This is a very quick way to determine any screens that may be required and should help uncover any usability issues prior to investing a lot of time in writing code. Don't be concerned with accuracy or detail at this stage.

Wireframes

Wireframes are slightly more sophisticated and structured than sketches but serve a similar purpose. Once you determine that your sketches are appropriate, you can create a more structured wireframe to further solidify how the application layout should appear.

Wireframes typically do not involve details such as color, images, or typography. Like sketches, you can create wireframes on paper or on a whiteboard, with a little more attention to accuracy and detail. You may even want to consider using a software program for designing your wireframes.

Design Comps

A design comp is a high-fidelity mock-up of an application's layouts. Usually, it would be created in a graphic design program. In a design comp, your application's identity should be taken seriously, as this is usually the stage where major decisions on the branding of an application are made. You may even want more than one design comp created, to allow you to choose the one that best communicates your application's identity. A design comp is created prior to finalizing the design and identity, and prior to spending a great amount of time coding the design.

Tip

Google provides a great set of high-fidelity stencils, icons, colors, and fonts that can be used for making design comps. The stencils include realistic mock-ups of common Android user interface controls. When you are ready to create your design comps, you may opt to roll your own, although using these downloads will make your job a whole lot easier and save you a great amount of time. Many different formats are available for download, so you can choose your graphics editor of choice. You can download these files here: *http://d.android.com/design/downloads/index.html.*

Reacting Properly with Visual Feedback

Provide visual feedback that follows your style guidelines to let users know that something is about to happen or has already happened when they interact with the user interface, especially when the interaction involves initiating application operations or behaviors.

Some ways to provide visual feedback include

- Using color states, animations, and transitions.
- Displaying alert messages or dialogs to confirm or acknowledge before making a final decision. An alternative to confirming or acknowledging is the Undo pattern, similar to what is found in the Gmail application. When a user deletes an email, rather than asking for confirmation or acknowledgment, a Toast message with an Undo option is made available in case the message was unintentionally deleted.
- Using Toast messages to provide feedback that does not require important decisions to be confirmed or acknowledged.
- Using the Android Design Support library to maintain backward-compatible material designs for supporting Android devices, version 2.1 or newer. The following

blog post provides a great overview of this new addition to the Android SDK: *http://android-developers.blogspot.com/2015/05/android-design-support-library.html.*

- Displaying validation when users interact with forms or provide input, to let them know whether they have provided the correct information or format.

Tip

The material design specification provides a great resource for incorporating animation into your design to create responsive interaction. You can learn more about this feature here: *http://www.google.com/design/spec/animation/responsive-interaction.html.*

Observing Target Users for Usability

The quicker you present your design to actual target users, the quicker you will be able to discover any problems in your application's design. In addition, observing the users' interactions with your application and receiving their feedback could prove to be invaluable and help you get your design right.

You may want to start presenting your design to friends or family. This is definitely a cheap way to begin testing usability. The only problem is that your friends or family may not fit the profile of your target users. Therefore, you may need to use other means to find your target users. Once you have found them, have them test your design and see what you can learn from their interactions with it.

Mocking Up the Application

The fastest way to receive feedback on your design is to present your work to your target users even before you have written any code. You may be wondering how this is done, but the answer is simple. As we recommended earlier in this chapter, you may have already created rough sketches on paper. If so, presenting these mock-ups to users, without a real working application, is definitely the most cost-effective approach to testing your design up front, with very little effort.

UI Storyboards

A UI storyboard is usually a collection of screen mock-ups derived from designs. You may want to create a storyboard of all the screens required for your application, or you may decide that you just want to test the most important user flows. Usually, you would present the UI storyboard in paper format and ask a target user to begin using the storyboard as if it were an actual application.

There are drawbacks to presenting just a UI storyboard to a target user, especially because the design is not working on an actual device. But the immediate benefits that you receive may far outweigh the drawbacks. As we mentioned earlier, presenting a storyboard to a user, even if it is a series of paper mock-ups, may actually help you uncover major design issues early on.

Prototypes

You may consider building a prototype, which is similar to a UI storyboard, only more sophisticated in that the prototype actually works on a real device. Usually, the prototype's functionality is extremely limited and is definitely not meant to be a real application. Depending on the effort you want to invest, the prototype may be merely capable of navigating through your screens and can be used just to validate the user flows, or you may decide that you would like to spend more time providing it with some of the most important functions of your application.

A prototype usually does not have much styling, if any, but it should reflect how you presume the layout will actually appear. The main point of the prototype is not to impress users with the beauty of the application, but to help uncover any usability issues that may not be readily apparent. Presenting your target users a minimally functioning prototype is another great way to discover any usability issues early in the development process.

Testing the Release Build

To validate your design, you should present your release build to your target users prior to an official launch. Even if you have tested and verified your application's usability with UI storyboards or with a prototype, you still want to be sure that the real application does not have any major usability issues.

The release build is usually much more sophisticated than a prototype and more than likely has received styling and an application identity. Problems not apparent in the storyboard or prototype phases may be evident when your target users begin testing the release build. One reason for this could be due to any styling that may have been applied. Major styling decisions typically are not applied to storyboards or prototypes, so usability issues caused by styling will not be uncovered until real users test the release build.

Testing and validating your design prior to release is just as important and valuable to the overall success of your application as it is to the process early on in development.

Summary

In this chapter, you have learned many different methods for planning the Android application experience. You have learned how to think about your application from your users' perspective and have picked up valuable tips for how to structure your application. You have also learned that focusing on one or two key flows can help set your application apart from your competitors. You have also learned that getting your application in front of users as quickly as possible may be the best way to validate your design. Go forth with the knowledge learned in this chapter and begin creating incredible Android application experiences for your users!

Quiz Questions

1. What are the three types of objectives you should think about when planning your application?

2. What information should you consider defining for your personas?

3. What are the three techniques mentioned in this chapter for discovering and organizing information without your application's code?

4. What are two methods useful for planning user interactions with your application?

5. What are the various methods you can use for determining your screen layouts?

6. What are the two methods mentioned in this chapter for mocking up your application so that you can start receiving user feedback as early as possible?

Exercises

1. Come up with a simple application idea. Create your first persona, choose a problem he or she would like solved, and define a simple user story map for your idea that focuses on the primary benefits your solution provides rather than features.

2. Make a list of screens that will be required for implementing your idea, and then create a screen map.

3. Create a simple mock-up of your application on paper and ask someone to use the paper mock-up. Determine if there is anything wrong with your application or if there is anything you could do to improve the design after presenting it.

References and More Information

Wikipedia: persona (user experience):
   http://en.wikipedia.org/wiki/Persona_(user_experience)
Wikipedia: User story: *https://en.wikipedia.org/wiki/User_story*
Android Training: "Best Practices for User Experience & UI":
   http://d.android.com/training/best-ux.html
Android Design: "Patterns":
   http://d.android.com/design/patterns/index.html
Android API Guides: "Supporting Tablets and Handsets":
   http://d.android.com/guide/practices/tablets-and-handsets.html
Android Distribute: "App Quality":
   http://d.android.com/distribute/essentials/index.html
Android Distribute: "Build Better Apps: Know Your Flows":
   http://d.android.com/distribute/analyze/build-better-apps.html#flows
Android Design: "Downloads":
   http://d.android.com/design/downloads/index.html
YouTube: Android Developers Channel: "Android Design in Action":
   https://www.youtube.com/playlist?list=PLWz5rJ2EKKc8j2B95zGMb8muZvrIy-wcF

Delivering Quality Applications

In this chapter, we cover tips and techniques from our years in the trenches of mobile software design and development. We also warn you—the designers, developers, and managers of mobile applications—of the various and sundry pitfalls you should do your best to avoid. Reading this chapter all at one time when you're new to Android development might be a bit overwhelming. Instead, consider reading specific sections when planning the parts of the overall design process. Some of our advice might not be appropriate for your particular project, and processes can always be improved. Ideally, this information about how Android development projects succeed (or fail) will give you some insight into how you might improve the chances of success for your own projects.

Best Practices in Delivering Quality Applications

The "rules" of Android application design are straightforward and apply across all device platforms. These rules were crafted to remind us that our applications often play a secondary role on the device. Many Android devices are, at the end of the day, smartphones. These rules also make it clear that we do operate, to some extent, because of the infrastructure managed by the carriers and device manufacturers. These rules are echoed throughout the Android SDK License Agreement and third-party application marketplace terms and conditions.

The "rules" are as follows:

- Don't abuse the user's trust.
- Don't interfere with device telephony and messaging services (if applicable).
- Don't break or otherwise tamper with or exploit the device hardware, firmware, software, or OEM components.
- Don't abuse or cause problems on operator networks (if applicable).

Now, perhaps these rules sound like no-brainers, but even the most well-intentioned developers can accidentally break them if they aren't careful and don't test their applications thoroughly before distribution. This is especially true for applications that leverage networking support and low-level hardware APIs on the device, as well as for those that store private user data such as names, locations, and contact information.

Meeting Android Users' Demands

Android users also have their own set of demands for applications they install on their devices. Applications are expected to

- "Enchant me," "simplify my life," and "make me amazing" (from the Android design documentation found here: *http://d.android.com/design/get-started/creative-vision.html*)
- Have straightforward, intuitive user interfaces that are easy to get up and running
- Get the job done with minimal frustration to the user (provide visual feedback and follow common Android design patterns) and minimal impact on device performance (battery usage, network and data usage, and so on)
- Be available 24 hours a day, 7 days a week (remote servers or services that are always on, always available, and not running in someone's closet)
- Include a Help and/or About screen for feedback and support contact information
- Honor private user information and treat it with care

Designing User Interfaces for Android Devices

Designing effective user interfaces for Android devices, especially for applications that run on a number of different devices and form factors, is something of a black art. We've all seen bad Android application user interfaces. A frustrating user experience can turn a user off your brand while a good experience can win a user's loyalty. Great experiences give your application an edge over the competition, even if your functionality is similar. An elegant, well-designed user interface can win over users even when the application functionality is behind that of the competition. Said another way, doing something really well is more important than cramming too many features into an app and doing them badly.

Here are some tips for designing great Android user interfaces:

- Fill screens sparingly; too much information on one screen overwhelms the user.
- Be consistent with user interface workflows, menu types, and buttons. Also, consider making the user interface consistent with Android and Material Design patterns.
- Design your applications using fragments, even if you aren't targeting devices larger than a smartphone. (The Android Support Package makes this possible for nearly all target versions.)
- Make touch target sizes ("hit areas") large enough (48dp) and space them appropriately (8dp).
- Streamline common use cases with clear, consistent, and straightforward interfaces.
- Use big, readable fonts and large icons.
- Integrate tightly with other applications on the system using standardized controls, such as the `QuickContactBadge`, content providers, and search adapters.

- Keep localization in mind when designing text-heavy user interfaces. Some languages are lengthier than others.

- As much as possible, reduce the number of keys or clicks needed.

- Do not assume that specific input mechanisms (such as specific buttons or keys) are available on all devices.

- Try to design the default use case of each screen to require only the user's thumb or index finger. Special cases might require other buttons or input methods, but encourage "thumbing" by default.

- Size resources such as graphics appropriately for target devices. Do not include oversize resources and assets because they bulk up your application package, load more slowly, and are generally less efficient.

- In terms of "friendly" user interfaces, assume that users do not read the application permissions when they approve them to install your application. If your application does anything that could cause users to incur significant fees or it shares private information, consider informing users again (as appropriate) when your application performs such actions. Basically, take a "no surprises" approach, even if the permissions and your privacy policy also state the same thing.

Note

We discussed how to design Android applications that are compatible with a wide range of devices, including how to develop for different screen sizes and resolutions, in Chapter 13, "Designing Compatible Applications." We also discussed designing for the user experience in Chapter 19, "Planning the Experience."

Designing Stable and Responsive Android Applications

Android device hardware has come a long way in the past few years, but developers must still work with limited resources. Users do not usually have the luxury of upgrading the RAM and other hardware in Android devices. Android users may, however, take advantage of removable storage devices such as SD cards to provide some extra space for application and media storage, but some manufacturers use only built-in storage devices, preventing removable storage as an option. Spending some time up front to design a stable and responsive application is important for the success of the project. The following are some tips for designing robust and responsive Android applications:

- Don't perform resource-intensive or lengthy operations on the main UI thread. Always use asynchronous tasks, threads, or background services to offload blocking operations.

- Use efficient data structures and algorithms; these choices manifest themselves in app responsiveness and happy users.

- Use recursion with care; these functional areas should be code reviewed and performance tested.

- Keep application state at all times. The Android `Activity` back stack makes this work well, but you should take extra care to go above and beyond.

- Save your state using appropriate lifecycle callbacks, and assume that your application will be suspended or stopped at any moment. If your application is suspended or closed, you cannot expect a user to verify anything (click a button and so on). If your application resumes gracefully, your users will be grateful.

- Start up fast and resume fast. You cannot afford to have the user twiddling thumbs waiting for your application to start. Instead, you need to strike a delicate balance between preloading and on-demand data because your application might be suspended (or closed) with no notice.

- During long operations, keep users informed by using progress bars. Consider offloading heavy processing to a server instead of performing these operations on the device because they might drain battery life beyond the limits users are willing to accept.

- Ensure that long operations are likely to succeed before embarking on them. For example, if your application downloads large files, check for network connectivity, file size, and available space before attempting the download.

- Minimize the use of local storage because most devices have very limited amounts. Use external storage only when appropriate because some devices do not have external storage available. Be aware that SD cards (the most common external storage option) can be ejected and swapped; your application should handle this gracefully.

- Understand that data calls to content providers and across the AIDL barrier come at a cost to performance, so make these calls judiciously.

- Verify that your application resource consumption model matches your target audience. Gamers might anticipate shorter battery life on graphics-intensive games, but productivity or fitness applications should not drain the battery unnecessarily and should be lightweight for people "on the go" who do not always have their device charging.

Tip

Written by the Google Android team, the Android Developers Blog (*http://android-developers. blogspot.com*) is a fantastic resource. This blog provides detailed insight into the Android platform, often covering topics not discussed in the Android platform documentation. Here, you can find tips, tricks, best practices, and shortcuts on relevant Android development topics. Savvy Android developers visit this blog regularly and incorporate these practices and tips into their projects. Keep in mind that Google's Android Developer guys and gals are often focused on educating the rest of us about the latest API-level features; their techniques and advice may not always be suitable for implementation with older target platforms.

Designing Secure Android Applications

Many Android applications integrate with core applications such as the Phone, Camera, Location-Based Services, and Contacts. Make sure you take all the precautions necessary to secure and protect private user data such as names, locations, and contact information used by your application. This includes safeguarding personal user data on application servers and during network transmission.

> **Tip**
>
> If your application accesses, uses, or transmits private data, especially usernames, passwords, or contact information, it's a good idea to include an End User License Agreement (EULA) and a privacy policy with your application. Also keep in mind that privacy laws vary by country.

Handling Private Data

To begin with, limit the private or sensitive data your application stores as much as possible. Don't store this information in plain text, and don't transmit it over the network without safeguards. Do not try to work around any security mechanisms imposed by the Android framework. Store private user data in private application files, which are private to the application, and not in shared parts of the operating system. Do not expose application data in content providers without enforcing appropriate permissions on other applications. Use the encryption classes available in the Android framework when necessary. Consider using SQLCipher, an encrypted version of SQLite, where appropriate. SQLCipher is not built into Android, but you may download and configure this for inclusion in your application. To learn more about SQLCipher, see *https://guardianproject.info/code/sqlcipher*.

Transmitting Private Data

The same cautions about handling private data should apply to any remote network data storage (such as application servers or cloud storage) and network transmission. Make sure any servers or services that your application relies on are properly secured against identity or data theft and invasion of privacy. Treat any servers your application uses like any other part of the application: test these areas thoroughly. Any private data transmitted should be secured using typical security mechanisms such as SSL. The same rules apply when enabling your application for backups using services such as Android Backup Service or Auto Backup for Apps.

Designing Android Applications for Maximum Profit

For billing and revenue generation, Android applications generally fall into one or more of the following categories:

- Free applications (including those with advertising revenue)
- Single payment (pay once)

- In-app products (pay for specific content, such as a wallpapers, a Sword of Smiting, or a new level pack)
- Subscription billing (payments recurring on a schedule, often seen with productivity and service applications)
- Outside billing and membership supplementation (access to content such as premium TV for current paying subscribers)

Applications can use multiple types of billing, depending on which marketplaces and billing APIs they use. No specific billing APIs are built into the Android framework. With Android in general, third parties can provide billing methods or APIs, so technically the sky's the limit. There is an optional Google Play In-app Billing API add-on for use with Google Play (and only Google Play). Google Play provides support for accepting various payment methods for Google Play, including credit cards, PayPal, direct carrier billing, gift cards, and Google Play balance values.

When designing your Android applications, consider the functional areas where billing can come into play and factor this into your design. Consider the transactional integrity of specific workflow areas of the application for which the user can be charged. For example, if your application has the capability to deliver data to the device, make sure this process is transactional in nature so that if you decide to charge for this feature, you can drop in the billing code, and when the user pays, the delivery occurs or the entire transaction is rolled back.

Note

You will learn more about the different methods currently available to market your application in Chapter 22, "Distributing Your Applications."

Following the Android Application Quality Guidelines

Users' expectations of application quality rise with every new iteration of Android. Luckily, Google has invested a great deal of effort researching what a quality application is like, its employees have designed quite a few quality applications themselves, and the best part is that they have designed a set of standards that you can use to measure your application's quality.

There are six quality guidelines recommended in the Android documentation that you should seriously consider:

- **Core app quality:** Core app quality guidelines are the most basic standards that all of your applications should follow, and they should also be validated on each and every device that you plan on targeting. The core app quality guidelines include criteria for how to assess your application's visual design and user interaction, criteria for functional behavior, criteria for stability and performance criteria, and criteria for Google Play promotions. The guidelines also provide a sort of step-by-step procedural approach to testing your application to determine if it meets these recommended criteria. You can learn more about how to meet the core app quality guidelines here: *http://d.android.com/distribute/essentials/quality/core.html.*

- **Tablet app quality:** If you are building an application for tablets, you still need to make sure that you meet the core app quality criteria. In addition, Google provides an additional set of quality criteria for developers writing applications for tablets. You can learn more about the guidelines for tablet app quality here: *http://d.android. com/distribute/googleplay/quality/tablet.html.*

- **Wear app quality:** If you are building an application for Wear, there are different quality considerations you need to be aware of, but you should familiarize yourself with the core app quality criteria first. Wear apps have a minimum set of requirements to meet before they are made available in Google Play. You can learn more about how to meet the quality guidelines for Wear here: *http://d.android.com/ distribute/essentials/quality/wear.html.*

- **TV app quality:** If you are building an application for TV, in addition to following the core app quality guidelines, you also aim to meet all of the TV app quality criteria. TV apps have a minimum set of requirements to meet before they are made available in Google Play. You can learn more about the TV app quality guidelines here: *http://d.android.com/distribute/essentials/quality/tv.html.*

- **Auto app quality:** If you are building an application for Android Auto, you need to meet the core app quality criteria before moving onto meeting the Auto app quality guidelines. Auto apps have a minimum set of requirements to meet before they are made available in Google Play. You can learn more about the Auto app quality guidelines here: *http://d.android.com/distribute/essentials/quality/auto.html.*

- **Education guidelines:** If you are building an Educational app, you need to meet the core criteria and basic educational requirements. In addition to app quality and these basic requirements, you must also meet strict educational value parameters. Education apps have a minimum set of requirements to meet before they are made available in Google Play. You can learn more about the educational quality guidelines here: *https://developers.google.com/edu/guidelines.*

Even if your application meets the criteria and recommendations for creating a quality application, your efforts should not end there. User demand and application competition are setting the bar for quality higher and higher. To keep up with demand and to outshine your competition, the Android documentation provides a set of strategies that you can begin thinking about and implementing in your application quality analysis. To learn more about the strategies for continuously optimizing your application's quality, visit *http://developer.android.com/distribute/essentials/optimizing-your-app.html.*

Unless you are building a Wear, TV, Auto, or Education application, there are no requirements that your application actually adheres to these quality guidelines to be made available in Google Play, but if you would like your application to achieve success, these guidelines are where to begin focusing your efforts. For applications that require meeting a minimum set of standards, make sure you follow the suggested guidelines. In addition, Google provides many tools and resources useful for helping you meet these criteria in your application. You can learn more about those features here: *http://d.android.com/ distribute/essentials/index.html#tools.*

Leveraging Third-Party Quality Standards

Android marketplaces other than Google Play may implement and impose their own quality requirements, and certainly programs have been created with some recognized body's endorsement or stamp of approval. The Amazon Appstore for Android puts apps through some testing before they are made available for sale.

Warning

With Android, the market is expected to manage itself to a greater extent than in some other platform markets. Do not make the mistake of interpreting that as "no rules" when it really means "few rules imposed by the system." Strong licensing terms are in place to keep malware and other malicious code out of users' hands, and applications do indeed get removed for misbehavior, just as they do when they sneak through onto other platform markets.

Designing Android Applications for Ease of Maintenance and Upgrades

Generally speaking, it's best to make as few assumptions about the device configurations as possible when developing an Android application. You'll be rewarded later when you want to port your application or provide an easy upgrade. You should carefully consider what assumptions you make.

Leveraging Application Diagnostics

In addition to adequate documentation and easy-to-decipher code, you can leverage some tricks to help maintain and monitor Android applications in the field. Building lightweight auditing, logging, and reporting into your application can be highly useful for generating your own statistics and analytics. Relying on third-party information, such as that generated with market reports, could cause you to miss some key pieces of data that are useful to you. For example, you can easily keep track of

- How many users install the application
- How many users launch the application for the first time
- How many users regularly use the application

- What the most popular usage patterns and trends are
- What the least popular usage patterns and features are
- What devices (determined by application versioning or other relevant metrics) are the most popular

Often, you can translate these figures into rough estimates of expected sales, which you can later compare with actual sales figures from third-party marketplaces. You can streamline and, for example, make the most popular usage patterns the most visible and efficient in terms of user experience design. Sometimes you can even identify potential bugs, such as features that are not working at all, just by noting that a feature has never been used in the field. Finally, you can determine which device targets are most appropriate for your specific application and user base.

You can gather interesting information about your application from numerous sources, including the following:

- Google Play sales statistics, ratings, and bug/crash reports, as well as those available on other distribution channels.
- Application integration with statistics-gathering APIs such as Google Analytics or other third-party application monitoring services.
- For applications relying on network servers, quite a lot of information can be determined by looking at server-side statistics.
- Feedback sent directly to you, the developer, through email, user reviews, or other mechanisms made available to your users.

Tip

Never collect personal data without the user's knowledge and consent. Gathering anonymous diagnostics is fairly commonplace, but avoid keeping any data that can be considered private. Make sure your sample sizes are large enough to obfuscate any personal user details, and make sure to factor out any live QA testing data from your results (especially when considering sales figures).

Designing for Easy Updates and Upgrades

Android applications can easily be upgraded in the field. The application update and upgrade processes do pose some challenges to developers, though. When we say *updating*, we mean modifying the Android manifest version information and redeploying the updated application on users' devices. When we say *upgrading*, we mean creating an entirely new application package with new features and deploying it as a separate application that the user must choose to install and that does not replace the old application.

From an update perspective, you need to consider what conditions necessitate an update in the field. For example, do you draw the line at crashes or at feature requests? You also want to consider the frequency with which you deploy updates—you need to schedule updates so that they come up frequently enough to be truly useful, but not so often that users are constantly updating their application.

Tip

You should build application content updates into the application functionality as a feature (often network driven) as opposed to necessitating an over-the-air actual application update. By enabling your applications to retrieve fresh content on the fly, you keep your users happy longer and applications stay relevant.

When considering upgrades, decide the manner in which you will migrate users from one version of your application to the next. Will you leverage the Android Backup Service features so that your users can transition seamlessly from one device to the next, or will you provide your own backup solution? Consider how you will inform users of existing applications that a major new version is available.

Tip

Google provides a service known as the Android Backup Service that allows developers to make user application data persistent in the cloud for easy restoration. This service is used for storing application data and settings and is not meant to be a database back end for your application. To learn more about the Android Backup Service, see *http://d.android.com/google/backup/index.html*.

Leveraging Android Tools for Application Design

The Android SDK and developer community provide a number of useful tools and resources for application design. You might want to leverage the following tools during this phase of your development project:

- The Android Studio Layout Editor is a good place to start for rapid proof of concept. You can find more about the Layout Editor here: *http://d.android.com/sdk/installing/studio-layout.html*.
- Use the Android emulator before you have specific devices. You can use different AVD configurations to simulate different device configurations and platform versions.
- The Android `Device Monitor` tool is very useful for memory profiling.
- The Hierarchy Viewer in Pixel Perfect mode enables accurate user interface design. Along with `lint`, it can also be used to optimize your layout designs.

- The Draw Nine-Patch tool can create stretchable graphics for mobile use.
- The `uiautomatorviewer` tool can help you determine how your user interface is actually structured.
- Real devices are your most important tool. Use real devices for feasibility research and application proof-of-concept work whenever possible. Do not design solely using the emulator. The Developer Options within the Settings application are useful tools for developing and debugging on actual hardware.
- The technical specifications for specific devices, often available from manufacturers and carriers, can be invaluable for determining the configuration details of target devices.

Avoiding Silly Mistakes in Android Application Design

Last but not least, here is a list of some of the silly mistakes Android designers should do their best to avoid:

- Designing or developing for months without performing feasibility testing on the device (basically "waterfall testing")
- Designing for a single device, platform, language, or hardware configuration
- Designing as if your device has a large amount of storage and processing power and is always plugged into a power source
- Developing for the wrong version of the Android SDK (verify the device SDK version)
- Trying to adapt applications to smaller screens after the fact by having the device "scale"
- Deploying oversize graphics and media assets with an application instead of sizing them appropriately

Best Practices in Delivering Quality Android Applications

Developing applications for Android is not that different from traditional desktop development. However, developers might find developing Android applications more restrictive and, especially, resource constrained because mobile devices are not yet as powerful as desktop machines. Again, let's start with these best practices or "rules" for Android application development:

- Test assumptions regarding feasibility early and often on the target devices.
- Keep application size as small and efficient as possible.

- Choose efficient data structures and algorithms appropriate to Android devices with constrained resources.
- Exercise prudent memory management.
- Assume that devices are running primarily on battery power.

Designing a Development Process That Works for Android Development

A successful project's backbone is a good software process. It ensures standards and good communication, and it reduces risks. We talked about the overall Android development process in Chapter 18, "Learning the Development Workflow." Again, here are a few general tips for successful Android development processes:

- Use an iterative development process.
- Use a regular, reproducible build process with adequate versioning.
- Communicate scope changes to all parties—changes often affect testing most of all.

Testing the Feasibility of Your Application Early and Often

It cannot be said enough: you must test developer assumptions on real devices. There is nothing worse than designing and developing an application for a few months only to find that it needs serious redesign to work on an actual device. Just because your application works on the emulator does not, *in any way*, guarantee that it will run properly on the device. Some functional areas to examine carefully for feasibility include

- Functionality that interacts with peripherals and device hardware
- Network speed and latency
- Memory footprint and usage
- Algorithm efficiency
- User interface suitability for different screen sizes, resolutions, and form factors
- Device input method assumptions
- File size and storage usage

We know, we sound like a broken record—but, truly, we've seen this mistake of inadequate feasibility testing made over and over again. Projects are especially vulnerable to this when target devices aren't yet available. What happens is that engineers are forced closer to the waterfall method of software development with a big, bad surprise that comes after weeks or months of development on some vanilla-style emulator.

We don't need to explain again why waterfall approaches are dangerous, do we? You can never be too cautious about this stuff. Think of this as the preflight safety speech of Android software development.

Using Coding Standards, Reviews, and Unit Tests to Improve Code Quality

Developers who spend the time and effort necessary to develop efficient Android applications are rewarded by their users. The following list is representative of some of the efforts you can make:

- Centralizing core features in shared Java packages. (If you have shared C or C++ libraries, consider using the Android NDK.)
- Developing for compatible versions of the Android SDK (know your target devices).
- Using the right level of optimization, including coding with RenderScript or using the NDK, where appropriate.
- Using built-in controls and widgets appropriate to the application, customizing only where needed.

You can use system services to determine important device characteristics (screen type, language, date, time, input methods, available hardware, and so on). If you make any changes to system settings from within your application, be sure to change the settings back when your application exits or pauses, if appropriate.

Defining Coding Standards

Developing a set of well-communicated coding standards for the development team can help drive home some of the important requirements of Android applications. Some standards might include

- Implementing robust error handling as well as handling exceptions gracefully.
- Moving lengthy, process-intensive, or blocking operations off the main UI thread.
- Avoiding creating unnecessary objects while running critical sections of code.
- Releasing objects and resources you aren't actively using.
- Practicing prudent memory management. Memory leaks can render your application useless.
- Using resources appropriately for future localization. Don't hard-code strings and other assets in code or layout files.
- Avoiding obfuscation in the code itself unless you're doing so for a specific reason (such as using the Google Play Licensing service). Comments are worthwhile. However, you should consider obfuscation later in the development process to protect against software piracy using built-in ProGuard support.
- Considering the use of standard document generation tools such as `javadoc`.
- Instituting and enforcing naming conventions—in code and in database schema design.

Performing Code Reviews

Performing code inspections can improve the quality of project code, help enforce coding standards, and identify problems before QA gets its hands on a build and spends time and resources testing it.

It can also be helpful to pair developers with the QA personnel who test the developers' specific functional areas in order to build a closer relationship between the teams. If testers understand how the application and Android operating system function, they can test the application more thoroughly and successfully. This might or might not be done as part of a formal code review process. For example, a tester can identify defects related to type safety just by noting the type of input expected (but not validated) on a layout's form field or by reviewing the Submit or Save button-handling functions with the developer. This would help circumvent the time spent to file, review, fix, and retest validation defects. Reviewing the code in advance doesn't reduce the testing burden but rather helps reduce the number of easily caught defects.

Developing Code Diagnostics

The Android SDK provides a number of packages related to code diagnostics. Building a framework for logging, unit testing, and exercising your application to gather important diagnostic information, such as the frequency of method calls and performance of algorithms, can help you develop a solid, efficient, and effective mobile application. It should be noted that diagnostic hooks are almost always removed prior to application publication because they impose significant performance reductions and greatly reduce responsiveness.

Using Application Logging

In Chapter 3, "Creating Your First Application," we discussed how to leverage the built-in logging class android.util.Log to implement diagnostic logging, which can be monitored via a number of Android tools, such as the logcat utility (available within Android Studio and the Android Device Monitor).

Developing Unit Tests

Unit testing can help developers move one step closer to the elusive 100% of code coverage testing. The Android SDK includes extensions to the JUnit framework for testing Android applications. Automated testing is accomplished by creating test cases, in Java code, that verify the application works the way you designed it. You can do this automated testing for both unit testing and functional testing, including user interface testing.

Basic JUnit support is provided through the junit.framework and junit.runner packages. Here, you find the familiar framework for running basic unit tests with helper classes for individual test cases. You can combine these test cases into test suites. There are utility classes for your standard assertions and test result logic.

The Android-specific unit-testing classes are part of the android.test package, which includes an extensive array of testing tools designed specifically for Android applications.

This package builds upon the `JUnit` framework and adds many interesting features, such as the following:

- Simplified hooking of test instrumentation (`android.app.Instrumentation`) with `android.test.InstrumentationTestRunner`, which you can run via `adb` shell commands
- Performance testing (`android.test.PerformanceTestCase`)
- Single `Activity` (or `Context`) testing (`android.test.ActivityUnitTestCase`)
- Full application testing (`android.test.ApplicationTestCase`)
- Services testing (`android.test.ServiceTestCase`)
- Utilities for generating events such as touch events (`android.test.TouchUtils`)
- Many more specialized assertions (`android.test.MoreAsserts`)
- The Android Testing Support Library with `AndroidJUnitRunner` (`android.support.test.runner.AndroidJUnitRunner`), UI testing with `Espresso` (`android.support.test.espresso`), and UI Automator (`android.support.test.uiautomator`)
- Mock and stub utility classes (`android.test.mock`)
- `View` validation (`android.test.ViewAsserts`)

Handling Defects Occurring on a Single Device

Occasionally, you have a situation in which you need to provide code for a specific device. Google and the Android team tell you that when this happens, it's a bug, so you should tell them about it. By all means, do so. However, this won't help you in the short term, nor will it help you if they fix it in a subsequent revision of the platform but carriers don't roll out the update and fix for months, if ever, to specific devices.

Handling bugs that occur only on a single device can be tricky. You don't want to branch code unnecessarily, so here are some of your choices:

- If possible, keep the client generic and use the server to serve up device-specific items.
- If the conditions can be determined programmatically on the client, try to craft a generic solution that enables developers to continue to develop under one source code tree, without branching.
- If the device is not a high-priority target, consider dropping it from your requirements if the cost-benefit ratio suggests that a workaround is not cost-effective. Not all markets support excluding individual devices, but Google Play does.
- If required, branch the code to implement the fix. Make sure to set your Android manifest file settings such that the branched application version is installed only on the appropriate devices.
- If all else fails, document the problem only and wait for the underlying "bug" to be addressed. Keep your users in the loop.

Leveraging Android Tools for Development

The Android SDK comes with a number of useful tools and resources for application development. The development community adds even more useful utilities to the mix. You might want to leverage the following tools during this phase of your development project:

- Android Studio
- The Android emulator and physical devices for testing
- The Android `Device Monitor` tool for debugging and interaction with the emulator or device
- The ADB tool for logging, debugging, and shell access tools
- The `sqlite3` command-line tool for application database access (available via the `adb` shell)
- Android Support Packages for including the support libraries to avoid writing custom case code
- The `uiautomatorviewer` tool for helping you test and optimize your user interfaces.
- The Hierarchy Viewer for user interface debugging of views

Numerous other tools also are available as part of the Android SDK. See the Android documentation for more details.

Avoiding Silly Mistakes in Android Application Development

Here are some of the frustrating and silly mistakes Android developers should try to avoid:

- Forgetting to register new activities, services, and necessary permissions to the `AndroidManifest.xml` file
- Forgetting to display `Toast` messages using the `show()` method
- Hard-coding information such as network information, test user information, and other data into the application
- Forgetting to disable diagnostic logging before release
- Forgetting to remove test-configured email addresses or websites in code before release
- Distributing live applications with debug mode enabled

Summary

Be responsive, stable, and secure—these are the tenets of Android development. In this chapter, we armed you—the software designers, developers, and project managers—with tips, tricks, and best practices for Android application design and development based on real-world knowledge and experience from veteran Android developers. Feel free to pick and choose which information works well for your specific project, and keep in mind that the software process, especially the mobile software process, is always open to improvement.

Quiz Questions

1. What are some application diagnostics that you should consider keeping track of?
2. What is the difference between designing for updates and designing for upgrades?
3. What are some of the Android tools recommended to leverage during application design?
4. True or false: One best practice is to assume that devices are primarily running while plugged in.
5. What are some of the Android tools recommended to leverage during development?
6. True or false: It is a good practice to enable diagnostic logging before release.
7. True or false: Always distribute your live applications with debug mode enabled.

Exercises

1. Read the Android documentation training titled "Best Practices for Security & Privacy": (*http://d.android.com/training/best-security.html*).
2. Read the Android documentation training titled "Best Practices for Interaction and Engagement": (*http://d.android.com/training/best-ux.html*).
3. Read the Android documentation training titled "Best Practices for Background Jobs": (*http://d.android.com/training/best-background.html*)

References and More Information

Android Training: "Performance Tips":
  http://d.android.com/training/articles/perf-tips.html
Android Training: "Keeping Your App Responsive":
  http://d.android.com/training/articles/perf-anr.html
Android Training: "Designing for Seamlessness":
  http://d.android.com/guide/practices/seamlessness.html
Android API Guides: "User Interface":
  http://d.android.com/guide/topics/ui/index.html
Android Design: "Android Design Principles":
  http://d.android.com/design/get-started/principles.html
Android Distribute: Essentials: "Essentials for a Successful App":
  http://d.android.com/distribute/essentials/index.html
Analytics SDK for Android: "Add Analytics to Your Android App":
  https://developers.google.com/analytics/devguides/collection/android/v4/

21

Testing Your Applications

Test early, test often, test on the device. That is the quality assurance mantra we consider most important when it comes to testing Android applications. Testing your applications need not be an onerous process. Instead, you can adapt traditional QA techniques, such as automation and unit testing, to the Android platform with relative ease. In this chapter, we discuss our tips and tricks for testing Android applications. We also warn you—the project managers, software developers, and testers of mobile applications—of the various and sundry pitfalls you should do your best to avoid. We also provide a practical example, in addition to introducing many tools available for automating Android application testing.

Best Practices in Testing Mobile Applications

Like all software projects, mobile development projects benefit from a well-designed defect-tracking system, regularly scheduled builds, and planned, systematic testing. There are also plentiful opportunities for white-box and black-box testing, as well as opportunities for automation.

Designing a Mobile Application Defect-Tracking System

You can customize most defect-tracking systems to work for the testing of mobile applications. The defect-tracking system must encompass the tracking of issues for specific device defects and problems related to any centralized application servers (if applicable).

Logging Important Defect Information

A good mobile defect-tracking system includes the following information about a typical device defect:

- Application build version information, language, and so on
- Device configuration and state information, including device type, Android platform version, and important specs
- Screen orientation, network state, sensor information
- Steps to reproduce the problem using specific details about exactly which input methods were used (touch versus click)

■ Device screenshots that can be taken using Android `Device Monitor` or the Hierarchy Viewer tool provided with the Android SDK, or by using the screen shot shortcut key command provided by your device manufacturer. See your device owner's manual to learn the key shortcut command for your particular device, as the command may vary by device.

Tip

It can be helpful to develop a simple glossary of standardized terms for certain actions on the devices, such as touch-mode gestures, click versus tap, long click versus press and hold, clear versus back, and so on. This helps make the steps to reproduce a defect more precise for all parties involved.

Redefining the Term Defect for Mobile Applications

It's also important to consider the larger definition of the term defect. Defects might occur on all devices or on only some devices. Defects might also occur in other parts of the application environment, such as on a remote application server. Some types of defects typical of mobile applications include the following:

■ Crashing, unexpected terminations, forced closures, app not responding (ANR) events, and various other terms used for unexpected behavior that result in the application no longer running or responding

■ Features not functioning correctly (improper implementation)

■ Using too much disk space on the device

■ Inadequate input validation (typically, "button mashing")

■ State management problems (startup, shutdown, suspend, resume, power off)

■ Responsiveness problems (slow startup, shutdown, suspend, resume)

■ Inadequate state change testing (failures during interstate changes, such as an unexpected interruption during resume)

■ Usability issues related to input methods, font sizes, and cluttered screen real estate; cosmetic problems that cause the screen to display incorrectly

■ Pausing or "freezing" on the main UI thread (failure to implement asynchronous tasks, threading)

■ Feedback indicators missing (failure to indicate progress)

■ Integration with other applications on the device causing problems

■ Application "not playing nicely" on the device (draining battery, disabling power-saving mode, overusing network resources, incurring extensive user charges, obnoxious notifications)

■ Using too much memory, not freeing memory or releasing resources appropriately, and not stopping worker threads when tasks are finished

■ Not conforming to third-party agreements, such as the Android SDK License Agreement, Google Maps API terms, app store terms, or any other terms that apply to the application

- Application client or server not handling protected/private data securely, including ensuring that remote servers or services have adequate uptime and security measures taken

Managing the Testing Environment

Testing mobile applications poses a unique challenge to the QA team, especially in terms of configuration management. The difficulty of such testing is often underestimated. Don't make the mistake of thinking that mobile applications are easier to test because they have fewer features than desktop applications and are, therefore, simpler to validate. The vast variety of Android devices available on the market today makes testing different installation environments tricky.

Warning

Ensure that all changes in project scope are reviewed by the QA team. Adding new devices sometimes has little impact on the development schedule but can have significant consequences in terms of testing schedules.

Managing Device Configurations

Device fragmentation is one of the biggest challenges the mobile tester faces. Android devices come in various form factors with different screens, platform versions, and underlying hardware. They come with a variety of input methods such as hardware buttons, keyboards, and touchscreens. They come with optional features, such as cameras, enhanced graphics support, fingerprint readers, and even 3D displays. Many Android devices are smartphones, but non-phone devices such as tablets, TVs, wearables, and other devices are becoming more and more popular with each Android SDK release. Keeping track of all the devices, their abilities, and so on is a big job, and much of the work falls on the testing team.

QA personnel must have a detailed understanding of the functionality of each target device, including familiarity with what features are available and any device-specific idiosyncrasies that exist. Whenever possible, testers should test each device as it is used in the field, which might not be the device's default configuration or language. This means changing input modes, screen orientations, and locale settings. It also means testing with battery power, not just plugging the device into a power source while sitting at a desk.

Tip

Be aware that third-party firmware modifications can affect how your application works on the device. For example, let's assume you've gotten your hands on an unbranded version of a target device and testing has gone well. However, if certain carriers take that same device but remove some default applications and load it up with others, this is valuable information to the tester. Many devices ditch the stock Android user experience for more custom user interfaces, like HTC's Sense and Samsung's TouchWiz user interfaces. Just because your application runs flawlessly on the "vanilla" device doesn't mean that this is how most users' devices are configured by default. Do your best to get test devices that closely resemble the devices users will have in the field. The various default styles may not display as you expect with your user interface.

One hundred percent testing coverage is impossible, so QA must develop priorities thoughtfully. As we discussed in Chapter 18, "Learning the Development Workflow," developing a device database can greatly reduce the confusion of mobile configuration management, help determine testing priorities, and keep track of physical hardware available for testing. Using AVD configurations, the emulator is also an effective tool for extending coverage to simulate devices and situations that would not be covered otherwise.

Tip

If you have trouble configuring devices for real-life situations, you might want to look into the device "labs" available through some carriers. Instead of participating in loaner programs, developers visit the carrier's on-site lab where they can rent time on specific devices. Here, a developer can install an application and test it—not ideal for recurring testing but much better than no testing—and some labs are staffed with experts to help out with device-specific issues. In addition, there are various cloud-based device testing services you may utilize that allow you to deploy your application on hundreds of devices at once while performing automated testing. These cloud services have a cost associated with their use and could become very expensive very quickly.

Determining Clean Starting State on a Device

There is currently no good way to "image" a device so that you can return to the same starting state again and again. The QA testing team needs to define what a "clean" device is for the purposes of test cases. This can involve a specific uninstall process, some manual cleanup, or sometimes a factory reset.

Tip

Using the Android SDK tools, such as Android `Device Monitor` and ADB, developers and testers can have access to the Android file system, including application SQLite databases. These tools can be used to monitor and manipulate data on the emulator. For example, testers might use the `sqlite3` command-line interface to "wipe" an application database or fill it with test data for specific test scenarios. For use on devices, you may need to "root" the devices first. Rooting a device is beyond the scope of this book, and we do not recommend doing so on test devices.

While we're on the topic of "clean" states, here is another issue to consider: You may have heard that you can "root" most Android devices, allowing access to underlying device features not openly accessible through the public Android SDK. Certainly there are apps (and developers writing apps) that require this kind of access (some are even published on Google Play). Generally speaking, though, we feel that rooted devices do not make good testing and development devices for most teams. You want to develop and test on devices that resemble those in the hands of users; most users do not root their devices.

Mimicking Real-World Activities

It is nearly impossible (and certainly not cost-effective for most companies) to set up a complete isolated environment for mobile application testing. It's fairly common for networked applications to be tested against test (mock) application servers and then go "live" on production servers with similar configurations. However, in terms of device configuration, mobile software testers must use real devices with real service to test mobile applications properly. If the device is a phone, it needs to be able to make and receive phone calls, send and receive text messages, determine location using LBS services, and basically do anything a phone would normally do.

Testing a mobile application involves more than just making sure the application works properly. In the real world, your application does not exist in a vacuum but is one of many installed on the device. Testing a mobile application involves ensuring that the software integrates well with other device functions and applications. For example, let's say you were developing a game. Testers must verify that calls received while the game is being played cause the game to pause automatically (keep state) and that calls can be answered or ignored without issue.

This also means testers must install other applications on the device. A good place to start is with the most popular applications for the device. Testing your application with these other applications installed, combined with real use, can reveal integration issues or usage patterns that don't mesh well with the rest of the device.

Sometimes testers need to be creative when it comes to reproducing certain types of events. For example, testers must ensure that an application behaves appropriately when mobile handsets lose network connectivity or coverage.

Tip

Unlike with some other mobile platforms, testers actually have to take special steps to make most Android devices lose coverage above and beyond holding them wrong. To test loss of signal, you could go out and test your application in a highway tunnel or elevator, or you could just place the device in the refrigerator. Don't leave it in the cold too long, though, because this will drain the battery. Tin cans work great, too, especially those that have cookies in them. First, eat the cookies; then place the device in the can to seal off the signal. This advice also holds true for testing applications that leverage location-based services.

Maximizing Testing Coverage

All test teams strive for 100% testing coverage, but most also realize such a goal is not reasonable or cost-effective (especially with dozens of Android devices available around the world). Testers must do their best to cover a wide range of scenarios, the depth and breadth of which can be daunting—especially for those new to mobile. Let's look at several specific types of testing and how QA teams have found ways—some tried-and-true and others innovative—to maximize coverage.

Validating Builds and Designing Smoke Tests

In addition to a regular build process, it can be helpful to institute a build acceptance test policy (also sometimes called build validation, smoke testing, or sanity testing). Build acceptance tests are short and targeted at key functionality to determine whether the build is good enough for more thorough testing to be completed. This is also an opportunity to quickly verify bug fixes expected to be in the build before a complete retesting cycle occurs. Consider developing build acceptance tests for multiple Android platform versions to run simultaneously.

Automating Testing

Mobile build acceptance testing is frequently done manually on the highest-priority target device; however, this is also an ideal situation for an automated "sanity" test. By creating an automated test script that runs using the Android SDK's test tool, called `monkeyrunner`, the team can increase its level of confidence that a build is worth further testing, and the number of bad builds delivered to QA can be minimized. Based on a set of Python APIs, you can write scripts that install and run applications on emulators and devices, send specific keystrokes, and take screenshots. When combined with the `JUnit` unit-testing framework, you can develop powerful automated test suites.

Testing on the Emulator versus the Device

When you can get your hands on the actual device your users have, focus your testing there. However, devices and the service contracts that generally come with them can be expensive. Your test team cannot be expected to set up test environments on every carrier or in every country where your application is used. There are times when the Android emulator can reduce costs and improve testing coverage. Some of the benefits of using the emulator include

- The ability to simulate devices when they are not available or in short supply
- The ability to test difficult test scenarios not feasible on live devices
- The ability to be automated like any other desktop software

Testing Before Devices Are Available Using the Emulator

Developers frequently target up-and-coming devices or platform versions not yet available to the general public. These devices are often highly anticipated, and developers who are ready with applications for these devices on Day 1 of release often experience a sales bump because fewer applications are available to their users—less competition, more sales.

The latest version of the Android SDK is usually released to developers several months prior to when the general public receives over-the-air updates. Also, developers can sometimes gain access to preproduction devices through carrier and manufacturer developer programs. However, developers and testers should be aware of the dangers of testing on preproduction devices. The hardware is generally beta quality. The final technical specifications and firmware can change without notice. Release dates can slip, and the device might never reach production.

When preproduction devices cannot be acquired, testers can do some functional testing using emulator AVD configurations that attempt to closely match the target platform, thus lessening the risks for a compact testing cycle when these devices go live and allowing developers to release applications faster.

Understanding the Dangers of Relying on the Emulator

Unfortunately, the emulator is more of a generic Android device that only simulates many of the device internals—despite all the options available within the AVD configuration.

Tip

As part of the test plan, consider developing a document that describes the specific AVD configurations used for testing different device configurations.

The emulator does not represent the specific implementation of the Android platform that is unique to a given device. It does not use the same hardware to determine signal, networking, or location information. The emulator can "pretend" to make and receive calls and messages, or take pictures or video. At the end of the day, however, it doesn't matter if the application works on the emulator if it doesn't work on the actual device.

Testing Strategies: Black- and White-Box Testing

The Android tools provide ample resources for black-box and white-box testing:

- Black-box testers might require only testing devices and test documentation. For black-box testing, it is even more important that testers have a working knowledge of the specific devices, so providing device manuals and technical specifications also helps with more thorough testing. In addition to such details, knowing device nuances as well as device standards can greatly help with usability testing. For example, if a dock is available for the device, knowing that it's either landscape or portrait mode is useful.

White-box testing has never been easier on mobile. White-box testers can leverage the many affordable tools, including Android Studio (which is available for free) and the many debugging tools available as part of the Android SDK. White-box testers especially use the Android emulator, `Device Monitor`, and ADB. They can also take advantage of the powerful testing APIs such as `AndroidJUnitRunner`, `Espresso`, `uiautomator`, and the Hierarchy Viewer for user interface debugging. For these tasks, the tester requires a computer with a development environment similar to the developer's as well as knowledge of Java, Python, and the various typical tools available for developers.

Testing Mobile Application Servers and Services

Testers often focus on the client portion of the application and sometimes neglect to thoroughly test the server portion. Many mobile applications rely on networking or the cloud. If your application depends on a server or remote service to operate, testing the server side of your application is vital. Even if the service is not your own, you need to test thoroughly against it so you know it behaves as the application expects it to behave.

Warning

Users expect applications to be available anytime, day or night, 24/7. Minimize server or service downtimes and make sure the application notifies users appropriately (and doesn't crash and burn) if a service is unavailable. If the service is outside your control, it might be worthwhile to look at what service-level agreements are offered.

Here are some guidelines for testing remote servers or services:

- Version your server builds. You should manage server rollouts like any other part of the build process. The server should be versioned and rolled out in a reproducible way.

- Use test servers. Often, QA tests against a mock server in a controlled environment. This is especially true if the live server is already operational with real users.

- Verify scalability. Test the server or service under load, including stress testing (many users, simulated clients).

- Test the server security (hacking, SQL injection, and such).

- Ensure data transmissions to and from the server are secure and not easily sniffed (SSL, HTTPS, and valid certificates).

- Ensure that your application handles remote server maintenance or service interruptions gracefully—scheduled or otherwise.

- Test your old clients against new servers to ensure expected, graceful application behavior. Consider versioning your server communications and protocols in addition to your client builds.

- Test server upgrades and rollbacks, and develop a plan for how you are going to inform users if and when services are down.

These types of testing offer yet more opportunities for automated testing to be employed.

Testing an Application's Visual Appeal and Usability

Testing a mobile application is not only about finding dysfunctional features, but also about evaluating the usability of the application. Report areas of the application that lack visual appeal or are difficult to navigate or use. We like to use the walking-and-chewing-gum analogy when it comes to mobile user interfaces. Mobile users frequently do not give the application their full attention. Instead, they walk or do something else while they use it. Applications should be as easy for the user as chewing gum.

Tip

Consider conducting usability studies to collect feedback from people who are not familiar with the application. Relying solely on the product team members, who see the application regularly, can blind the team to application flaws.

Handling Specialized Test Scenarios

In addition to functional testing, there are a few other specialized testing scenarios that any QA team should consider.

Testing Application Integration Points

It's necessary to test how the application behaves with other parts of the Android operating system. For example:

- Ensuring that interruptions from the operating system are handled properly (incoming messages, calls, and powering off)

- Validating content provider data exposed by your application, including such uses as through a Live Folder
- Validating functionality triggered in other applications via an `Intent`
- Validating any known functionality triggered in your application via an `Intent`
- Validating any secondary entry points to your application as defined in `AndroidManifest.xml`, such as application shortcuts
- Validating alternative forms of your application, such as App Widgets
- Validating service-related features, if applicable

Testing Application Upgrades

When possible, perform upgrade tests of both the client and the server or service side of things. If upgrade support is planned, have development create a mock upgraded Android application so QA can validate that data migration occurs properly, even if the upgraded application does nothing with the data.

Tip

Users receive Android platform updates over the air on a regular basis. The platform version on which your application is installed might change over time. Some developers have found that firmware upgrades have broken their applications, necessitating upgrades. Always retest your applications when a new version of the SDK is released, so that you can upgrade users before your applications have a chance to break in the field.

If your application is backed by an underlying database, you'll want to test versioning your database. Does a database upgrade migrate existing data or delete it? Does the migration work from all versions of the application to the current version, or just the last version?

You should also apply these same testing and versioning principles to APIs of networked applications. If your application makes use of a REST API, having proper versioning of the REST API ensures that your networking code works as expected.

Testing Device Upgrades

Applications are increasingly using the cloud and backup services available on the Android platform. This means that users who upgrade their devices can seamlessly move their data from one device to another. So if they drop their smartphone in a hot tub or crack their tablet screen, their application data can often be salvaged. If your application leverages these services, make sure you test whether these transitions work.

Testing Product Internationalization

It's a good idea to test internationalization support early in the development process—on both the client and the server or services. You're likely to run into some problems in this area related to screen real estate and issues with strings, dates, times, and formatting.

Tip

If your application will be localized for multiple languages, test in a foreign language—especially a verbose one. The application might look flawless in English but be unusable in German, where words are generally longer.

Testing for Conformance

Make sure to review any policies, agreements, and terms to which your application must conform and make sure your application complies. For example, Android applications by default must conform to the Google Play Developer Distribution Agreement and, when applicable, other Google Play services terms of service. Other distribution means and add-on packages may add further terms that your application must abide by.

Installation Testing

Generally speaking, installation of Android applications is straightforward; however, you need to test installations on devices with low resources and low memory as well as test installation from the specific marketplaces when your application "goes live." If the manifest install location allows external media, be sure to test various low or missing resource scenarios.

Backup Testing

Don't forget to test features that are not readily apparent to the user, such as the backup and restore services and the sync features.

Performance Testing

Application performance matters in the mobile world. The Android SDK has support for calculating performance benchmarks within an application and monitoring memory and resource usage. Testers should familiarize themselves with these utilities and use them often to help identify performance bottlenecks, dangerous memory leaks, and misused resources.

One common performance issue we see frequently with new Android developers is that they try to do everything on the main UI thread. Time- and resource-intensive work, such as network downloads, XML parsing, graphics rendering, and other such tasks should be moved off the main UI thread so that the user interface remains responsive. This helps avoid so-called force close (or FC) issues and negative reviews that say as much.

The Debug class (`android.os.Debug`) has been around since Android was first released. This class provides a number of methods for generating trace logs that can then be analyzed using the `traceview` test tool. Android includes a class called `StrictMode` (`android.os.StrictMode`) that can be used to monitor applications, track down latency issues, and banish ANRs. There's also a great write-up about `StrictMode` on the Android Developers Blog, available at *http://android-developers.blogspot.com/2010/12/new-gingerbread-api-strictmode.html*.

Here's another good example of a common performance issue we see from new Android application developers: Many do not realize that, by default, Android screens (backed by activities) are restarted every time the screen orientation changes. Unless the developer takes the appropriate actions, nothing is cached by default. Even basic applications really need to take care of how their lifecycle management works. Tools are available to do this efficiently, yet we frequently run into very inefficient ways of doing this—usually due to not handling lifecycle events at all.

Testing In-App Billing

Billing is too important to leave to guesswork. Test it. The Google Play Developer Console allows developers to test application billing. Testing in-app billing requires an actual device with the most recent version of Google Play installed. Making sure billing works correctly could help prevent loss of revenue.

Testing for the Unexpected

Regardless of the workflow you design, understand that users do random, unexpected things—on purpose and by accident. Some users are "button mashers," whereas others forget to set the keypad lock before putting the device in their pocket, resulting in a weird set of key presses. Rotating the screen frequently, sliding a physical keyboard in and out, or fiddling with other settings often triggers unexpected configuration changes. A phone call or text message inevitably comes in during the most remote edge cases. Your application must be robust enough to handle this. The Exerciser Monkey command-line tool can help you test for this type of event.

Testing to Increase Your Chances of Creating a "Killer App"

Every mobile developer wants to create a "killer app"—those applications that go viral, rocket to the top of the charts, and make millions a month. Most people think that if they just find the right idea, they'll have a killer app on their hands. Developers are always scouring the top-ten lists and Google Play's Editors' Choice category, trying to figure out how to develop the next great app. But let us tell you a little secret: if there's one thing that all "killer apps" share, it's a higher-than-average quality standard. No clunky, slow, obnoxious, or difficult-to-use application ever makes it to the big leagues. Testing and enforcing quality standards can mean the difference between a mediocre application and a killer app.

If you spend any time examining the mobile marketplace, you'll notice that a number of larger mobile development companies publish a variety of high-quality applications with a shared look and feel. These companies leverage user interface consistency, as well as shared and above-average quality standards to build brand loyalty and increase market share, while hedging their bets that perhaps just one of their many applications will have that magical combination of a great idea and quality design. Other, smaller companies often have the great ideas but struggle with the quality aspects of mobile software development. The inevitable result is that the mobile marketplace is full of fantastic application ideas badly executed with poor user interfaces and crippling defects.

Leveraging Android SDK Tools for Android Application Testing

The Android SDK and developer community provide a number of useful tools and resources for application testing and quality assurance. You might want to leverage the following tools during this phase of your development project:

- The physical devices for testing and bug reproduction
- The Android emulator for automated testing and testing of builds when devices are not available

- The Android `Device Monitor` tool for debugging and interaction with the emulator or device, as well as for taking screenshots
- The ADB tool for logging, debugging, and shell access tools
- The Exerciser Monkey command-line tool for stress testing of input (available via the `adb` shell command)
- The `monkeyrunner` API for automating running unit test suites and for writing functional and framework unit tests
- The `AndroidJUnitRunner` API for running Junit3 and Junit4 `Instrumentation` tests
- The `Espresso` functional UI testing framework
- The `uiautomator` testing framework, a command-line tool and a set of APIs for automating user interface tests to run on one or more devices by writing UI functional test cases
- The `UiAutomation` class used for automating and simulating user interactions that span multiple applications, allowing you to inspect the user interface to determine if your tests have passed or failed
- The `uiautomatorviewer` tool, which helps you understand the `View` hierarchy of your layout by scanning the views displayed on the screen of an actual Android device for creating very detailed tests
- The `logcat` command-line tool, which can be used to view log data generated by the application (best used with debug versions of your application)
- The `traceview` application, which can be used to view and interpret the tracing log files you can generate from your app
- The `sqlite3` command-line tool for application database access (available via the `adb` shell command)
- The Hierarchy Viewer for user interface debugging, performance tweaking, and pixel-perfect screenshots of the device
- The `lint` tool, which can be used to optimize the layout resources of an application
- The `systrace` tool for analyzing the display and performance execution times of your application's processes
- The `bmgr` command-line tool, which can help test the backup management features of your application, if applicable

It should be noted that although we have used the Android tools, such as the Android emulator and `Device Monitor` debugging tools, with Android Studio, these are stand-alone tools that can be used by QA personnel without the need for source code or a development environment.

Tip

The tools discussed in Appendix D, "Mastery: Android SDK Tools," and throughout this book are valuable not just to developers; these tools provide testers with much more control over device configuration.

Avoiding Silly Mistakes in Android Application Testing

Here are some of the frustrating and silly mistakes and pitfalls that Android testers should try to avoid:

- Not testing the server or service components used by an application as thoroughly as the client side.
- Not testing with the appropriate version of the Android SDK (device versus development build versions).
- Not testing on the device and assuming the emulator is enough.
- Not testing the live application using the same system that users have (billing, installation, and such). Buy your own app.
- Neglecting to test your application on enough representative device configurations.
- Neglecting to test all entry points to the application.
- Neglecting to test in different coverage areas and network speeds.
- Neglecting to test using battery power. Don't always have the device plugged in.

Android Application Testing Essentials

The Android SDK offers many different methods for testing your application. Some test methods available must be run exclusively from within Android Studio, others exclusively from the command-line, but you are able to run some of them using either Android Studio or the command-line. Many of these test methods require writing a test program to run against your application.

Writing a test program to run against your application may sound intimidating at first. After all, you are writing a lot of code already just to build an application. If you are new to the concept of writing test code, you may be wondering why you should spend the time learning how to write more code to test your application.

The answer is simple. Writing tests helps automate a great amount of the testing process, rather than having to manually verify that your code is working correctly. An example should help. Let's say you build an application that allows users to create, read, update, and delete data. Many times these actions are performed on a data model. Writing tests against the data model allows you to verify that the data model's code is functioning as it should, providing the correct results when queried, storing the correct results when saved, and deleting the correct information when deleted.

On the other hand, when a user takes an action within your application, you usually would like to provide some sort of visual feedback. Writing tests against your views allows you to verify that when a user does take a particular action, the views are displaying the correct information every step of the way.

Tip

Tests should be designed to determine what the results of your application code should be. As long as your application's requirements remain the same, your tests should always expect the same results, even if you change your application's underlying code. In the case that one of your tests fails, as long as the expectation is the same and you have written your tests correctly, you probably have made a mistake somewhere in your application's logic.

You may be thinking that your app is too simple for testing or that there is no way that an error could possibly be in your code because you are sure that you have covered every possible scenario. If you believe this to be true, and even though you programmed the application to do only what the app is supposed to do, just remember that your users are not programmers, nor do they limit their expectations to what you believe your application provides. Your users may think your application provides a scenario that you have not actually created for them, and when they try to use this imagined scenario, your application will more than likely explode in their hands. That is when the negative reviews start rolling in. Even if the feature never existed in the first place, your users most likely don't care and will blame the problem on you even if it wasn't your fault they tried to do something they weren't supposed to.

Since you are the application programmer, you are bound to come across one or two errors while coding. As your application grows, and you release new features, how do you know for sure that the results you expected last week are still the same as the results your application is providing this week?

Unit Testing with JUnit

One way to ensure that your application is working properly, and continues to work properly over long periods of time, is to write unit tests. A unit test is designed to test small units of your application's logic. For example, you may always expect a particular value to be created when a user does something. A unit test ensures that every time your code changes, the actual result of that unit of code is as expected. The alternative way to test whether your application is creating that particular value properly would be to install your application and try out each and every feature in every possible order while taking into account every possible scenario to see if the result is as expected every time you update your code. This method quickly becomes cumbersome and time-consuming as your application grows and becomes very difficult to track.

Android provides unit testing based on the JUnit testing framework. Many of Android's testing classes directly inherit their functionality from JUnit. This means that you can write unit tests to test Java code, or you can write more Android-specific tests. Both JUnit and the Android SDK tools testing classes are available from within Android Studio. Unit testing is a very big topic. The content in this section is not meant to be comprehensive, but rather to serve as an introduction to how you can start unit testing your Android applications to create software that is less error prone.

There are two approaches to writing unit tests. One approach is to write the application first and then write the tests last. The other approach is to write the tests first and then write the application code last. We will be working with an application that has already been written to ease ourselves into understanding unit tests. There are many reasons you would want to write your tests before your application logic; this approach is known as Test-Driven Development (TDD).

We will not cover TDD in this book, but once you have a feel for how we create our first working test project, you should be more comfortable moving on to the test-first approach. We will point out that using TDD helps with deciding up front what your application results should be, and therefore you can write your unit tests with those results in mind. Knowing what the expected results should be without having written the application logic means that your tests will fail. Once you have written your tests and they fail, you then move on to writing your application, knowing what results to produce, until all your tests pass.

Just to clarify, this does not mean that you write every single one of your tests up front before writing any code. Instead, you write a single unit test and then move on to writing the application code to make that individual unit test pass. Once we are through, you should be able to see how TDD could have been applied to the following example. TDD is a vast topic, and there are many great resources out there for learning it.

Introducing the `PasswordMatcher` Application

In order to learn how to perform unit testing, we first need an application that we can unit test. We have provided a simple application that shows two `EditText` fields with an `inputType` of `textPassword`. This means that any text typed into the fields will be anonymous. We also have a `Button` with an `onClick` listener that determines if the two passwords entered into each of the `EditText` boxes are equal. Figure 21.1 shows what the user interface for the application looks like.

| Tip
Many of the code samples provided in this chapter are taken from the `PasswordMatcher` application. The source code for this application is provided for download on the book's website (*http://introductiontoandroid.blogspot.com*).

Figure 21.1   The PasswordMatcher application showing two EditText
boxes and a Button.

Let's take a look at the contents of the layout file for the PasswordMatcher
application. The name of the file is activity_password_matcher.xml.

```
<LinearLayout xmlns:android="http://schemas.android.com/apk/res/android"
    xmlns:tools="http://schemas.android.com/tools"
    android:layout_width="match_parent"
    android:layout_height="match_parent"
    android:orientation="vertical"
    android:paddingBottom="@dimen/activity_vertical_margin"
    android:paddingLeft="@dimen/activity_horizontal_margin"
    android:paddingRight="@dimen/activity_horizontal_margin"
    android:paddingTop="@dimen/activity_vertical_margin"
    tools:context=".PasswordMatcherActivity" >
    <TextView
        android:id="@+id/title"
        android:layout_width="match_parent"
```

```
        android:layout_height="wrap_content"
        android:contentDescription="@string/display_title"
        android:text="@string/match_passwords_title" />
    <EditText
        android:id="@+id/password"
        android:layout_width="match_parent"
        android:layout_height="wrap_content"
        android:hint="@string/password"
        android:inputType="textPassword"
        android:text="" />
    <EditText
        android:id="@+id/matchingPassword"
        android:layout_width="match_parent"
        android:layout_height="wrap_content"
        android:hint="@string/matching_password"
        android:inputType="textPassword"
        android:text="" />
    <Button
        android:id="@+id/matchButton"
        android:layout_width="wrap_content"
        android:layout_height="wrap_content"
        android:contentDescription="@string/submit_match_password_button"
        android:text="@string/match_password_button" />
    <TextView
        android:id="@+id/passwordResult"
        android:layout_width="match_parent"
        android:layout_height="wrap_content"
        android:contentDescription="@string/match_password_notice"
        android:visibility="gone" />
</LinearLayout>
```

The layout is a LinearLayout that contains a TextView for displaying our application title, two EditText views with the text initially set to be an empty string, a Button, and a final TextView for displaying the results of our Button onClick response that has a visibility of GONE. This visibility setting means that the TextView will not appear when the application is first launched, nor will it take up any visual space.

The code for our `PasswordMatcherActivity` is as follows:

```java
public class PasswordMatcherActivity extends Activity {
    EditText password;
    EditText matchingPassword;
    TextView passwordResult;

    @Override
    protected void onCreate(Bundle savedInstanceState) {
        super.onCreate(savedInstanceState);
        setContentView(R.layout.activity_password_matcher);

        password = (EditText) findViewById(R.id.password);
        matchingPassword = (EditText) findViewById(R.id.matchingPassword);
        passwordResult = (TextView) findViewById(R.id.passwordResult);

        Button button = (Button) findViewById(R.id.matchButton);
        button.setOnClickListener(new View.OnClickListener() {
            @Override
            public void onClick(View v) {
                String p = password.getText().toString();
                String mp = matchingPassword.getText().toString();

                if (p.equals(mp) && !p.isEmpty() && !mp.isEmpty()) {
                    passwordResult.setVisibility(View.VISIBLE);
                    passwordResult.setText(R.string.passwords_match_notice);
                    passwordResult.setTextColor(getResources().getColor(
                            R.color.green));
                } else {
                    passwordResult.setVisibility(View.VISIBLE);
                    passwordResult.setText(R.string.passwords_do_not_match_
                            notice);
                    passwordResult.setTextColor(getResources().getColor(
                            R.color.red));
                }
            }
```

```
        });
    }
}
```

   As you can see, the `onClick` method checks to see that our two passwords are equal and that they are not empty. If either of the passwords is empty or they are not equal, we change the visibility setting of the `TextView` to `View.VISIBLE`, set the text to display an error message, and set the text color to red. If the passwords are equal and not empty, we change the visibility setting of the `TextView` to `View.VISIBLE`, set the text to display a success message, and set the text color to green.

Determining What Our Tests Should Prove

Let's think about what results our application should produce. Our application requests the user to input data into two text fields, and then responds with a result when the user clicks the button. Here are the results that we would like our tests to make sure our application produces:

- When a user leaves either one or both of the password fields empty, assert that our application has displayed a red error message.
- When a user enters two passwords that do not match, assert that our application has displayed a red error message.
- When a user enters two matching passwords, assert that our application has displayed a green success message.

   Now that we know what results our application should produce, we are set up pretty well for knowing how to write our tests. In order to make sure our application produces those results, we will write tests that assert these assumptions, and that the actual results are as expected.

Creating a Run Configuration for Test Code

In order to write our tests, we must first create a new test class named `PasswordMatcherTest` in our `app/src/androidTest/java/com.introtoandroid.passwordmatcher` directory. Luckily for us, this directory was created for us automatically when we created our application. Our test class will go here.

   You will notice a class file named `ApplicationTest` already located in that directory. The `ApplicationTest` class is where you are able to write tests against your application classes. We will not be working with application test cases in this example, as we are only concerned with writing `Activity` test cases using the `ActivityInstrumentationTestCase2` for testing the `PasswordMatcherActivity` class.

The steps for creating the `PasswordMatcherTest` java class are as follows:

1. In Android Studio, select the `Edit Configurations...` option from the `Run/Debug Configurations` drop-down (see Figure 21.2).

2. On the `Run/Debug Configurations` window, click the `Add New Configuration` icon ( ) and choose `Android Tests` (see Figure 21.3).

3. A new `Android Tests` configuration will appear for editing. Provide a `Name` such as `app tests`, select the `Module` of app from the drop-down, and select the `Show chooser dialog` option of the `Target Device` setting (see Figure 21.4).

4. Click the `OK` button and you should now see the `app tests` configuration selected as the `Run/Debug Configuration` (see Figure 21.5).

5. Now we need to create the `PasswordMatcherTest` class. If you are working in the symbolic `Android` view of Android Studio, which is the default project view, right-click the app/java/com.introtoandroid.passwordmatcher (androidTest) directory, and select `New, Java Class`. If you are working in the traditional `Project` view of Android Studio, right-click the app/src/androidTest/java/com.introtoandroid.passwordmatcher directory and select `New, Java Class`. The `Create New Class` dialog will appear; then enter the `Name` of `PasswordMatcherTest` (Figure 21.6). Click `OK` to create the `PasswordMatcherTest` class.

Now that our test class has been created, in Figure 21.7 we can see the folder structure showing the `PasswordMatcherTest` class, visible from the symbolic `Android` view (left) and from the traditional `Project` view (right).

Let's go ahead and prepare the class for writing our test code by following these steps:

1. In the `PasswordMatcherTest` file, import the `ActivityInstrumentationTestCase2` class. This class allows us to write functional tests for the `PasswordMatcherActivity` class. The import should look as follows:

   ```
   import android.test.ActivityInstrumentationTestCase2;
   ```

2. We must also extend the `PasswordMatcherTest` class with the `ActivityInstrumentationTestCase2` and provide the `PasswordMatcherActivity`

Figure 21.2   Selecting the `Edit Configurations`... option of Android Studio for creating a test configuration.

Figure 21.3   Adding a new `Android Tests` configuration.

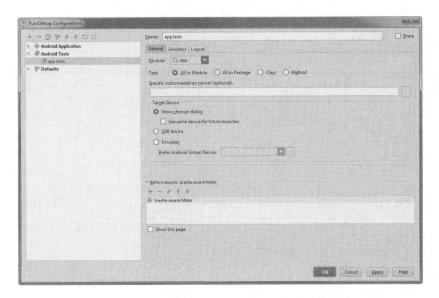

Figure 21.4   Configuring the `app tests` configuration.

Figure 21.5   The app tests configuration selected.

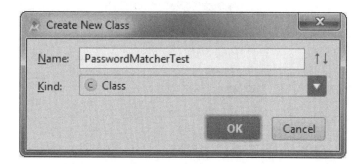

Figure 21.6   Creating the PasswordMatcherTest class.

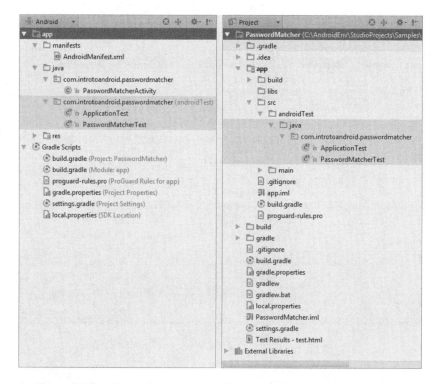

Figure 21.7   Viewing the test project directory structure from the symbolic
Android view (left) and from the traditional Project view (right).

as the type for the `ActivityInstrumentationTestCase2` class. The class should be extended as follows:

```
public class PasswordMatcherTest extends
    ActivityInstrumentationTestCase2<PasswordMatcherActivity> { … }
```

3. We have one more addition that must be made before we can write any test code, and that is to add a class constructor. Go ahead and add the following code to your class:

```
public PasswordMatcherTest() {
    super(PasswordMatcherActivity.class);
}
```

We are now ready to begin writing our tests for this project.

Writing the Tests

There are a few standard steps to take when writing tests. First, we need to create a setup method that will provide our test class with any information that we will need to access from within the tests. This is the place where we want to access our `PasswordMatcherActivity`, which will allow us to gain access to any of the views that we may need throughout the tests. We must create a few variables for accessing our views in addition to importing any classes that may be required. Here are the import statements:

```
import android.widget.Button;

import android.widget.EditText;

import android.widget.TextView;
```

Here are the variables we need to access in our test project:

```
TextView title;

EditText password;

EditText matchingPassword;

Button button;

TextView passwordResult;

PasswordMatcherActivity passwordMatcherActivity;
```

And here is our `setUp()` method:

```
protected void setUp() throws Exception {
    super.setUp();
    passwordMatcherActivity = getActivity();
    title = (TextView) passwordMatcherActivity.findViewById(R.id.title);
    password = (EditText) passwordMatcherActivity.findViewById(R.id.password);
```

(Continues)

(Continued)

```
    matchingPassword = (EditText)

            passwordMatcherActivity.findViewById(R.id.matchingPassword);

    button = (Button) passwordMatcherActivity.findViewById(R.id.matchButton);

    passwordResult = (TextView)

    passwordMatcherActivity.findViewById(R.id.passwordResult);

}
```

The `setup()` method gets the `PasswordMatcherActivity` using the `getActivity()` method, so that we can start accessing our views using the `findViewById` method.

Now we can begin writing test cases to ensure that our application is behaving correctly. We should start by testing the initial state of the application to make sure the starting state is correct. Even though the initial state will always be the same, it is a good idea to know that the application starts as expected, because if something is not working correctly when our application begins changing state, we have already verified that our starting state is as expected, and that rules out the starting state from being the culprit.

Tip

When using `JUnit 3` for Android testing, all test case methods must begin with the word `test`, such as `testPreConditions()` or `testMatchingPasswords()`. Prepending the word `test` to method names lets `JUnit 3` know that the method is in fact a test method and not just a standard method. Only the methods that start with the word `test` will be run as test cases.

The elements of our application that change their state during execution are the two `EditText` elements and the `TextView` result notice. Ensuring that our test starts with the correct inputs gives us confidence that our actual test methods will start with the correct values. Let's begin by writing our very first test case for making sure the starting state of our application is as expected.

```
public void testPreConditions() {

    String t = title.getText().toString();

    assertEquals(passwordMatcherActivity.getResources()

            .getString(R.string.match_passwords_title), t);

    String p = password.getText().toString();

    String pHint = password.getHint().toString();

    int pInput = password.getInputType();

    assertEquals(EMPTY_STRING, p);

    assertEquals(passwordMatcherActivity.getResources()

            .getString(R.string.password), pHint);
```

```
    assertEquals(129, pInput);

    String mp = matchingPassword.getText().toString();

    String mpHint = matchingPassword.getHint().toString();

    int mpInput = matchingPassword.getInputType();

    assertEquals(EMPTY_STRING, mp);

    assertEquals(passwordMatcherActivity.getResources()
            .getString(R.string.matching_password), mpHint);

    assertEquals(129, mpInput);

    String b = button.getText().toString();

    assertEquals(passwordMatcherActivity.getResources()
            .getString(R.string.match_password_button), b);

    int visibility = passwordResult.getVisibility();

    assertEquals(View.GONE, visibility);

}
```

Android Unit-Testing APIs and Assertions

Before we run our first test, let's take a moment to introduce assertions. If you are new to unit testing, you probably have not yet been exposed to the assert methods. An assertion compares the expected value the application should be creating (the expected value provided by you) with the actual value that the test receives upon running the application.

There are many standard JUnit assertion methods that you have at your disposal, but there are also many Android-specific assertion methods.

The testPreConditions() method begins by getting the text value of the TextView with the id of title. We then use the assertEquals() method and pass in the value that our test expects the text attribute to be, with the value that the getText() method actually provides. When you run the test, if the values are equal, this means that one particular assertion of the test passes. We continue getting the text value, hint value, and inputType of both EditText fields, and use the assertEquals() method to make sure the expected value matches the actual value. We also get the text value of the Button and check to see if it matches the expected value. We finish the method by making sure that the visibility of the passwordResult notice is not showing and is equal to the View.GONE value.

If all of the assertions pass, this means that the entire test should pass and that the starting values of our application are the values they are supposed to be.

Running Your First Test Using Android Studio

To run your first test using Android Studio, select your app tests configuration (see Figure 21.5) in Android Studio, and then click the Run ▶ icon.

Note

Make sure that you have an emulator running on your computer, or that you have a real device connected to your computer on which your tests will run. If you have more than one device or emulator attached to your computer, you may be presented with a selection UI to choose a device on which to run the test.

Your test should begin running, and you must wait until the test completes to determine if it passes or fails.

Analyzing the Test Results

Once the test completes, you should see the Run tab open within Android Studio. If your test has been written correctly, you should see the results, shown in Figure 21.8, that indicate the test has passed.

Notice that the testPreConditions() method was run in Figure 21.8. An icon 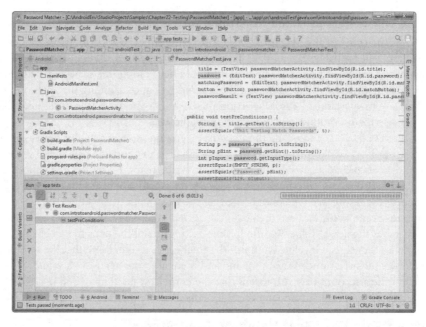 provides a visual indication that the test run completed successfully. Also note the time it took to complete the testPreConditions() method.

Figure 21.8   Android Studio showing that the testPreConditions() method has passed.

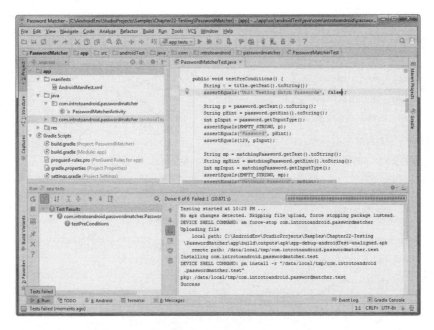

Figure 21.9   Android Studio showing that the `testPreConditions()` method has failed the test.

A failed test means that the expected results do not match the actual results. The ⬤ icon lets you know that a test has failed. In the case that the test failed, you would see a window like the one depicted in Figure 21.9.

Adding Additional Tests

The test project includes a few additional tests, but we will cover only one of those tests here, as they are very similar. Please see the `PasswordMatcherTest` class for the full code listing that provides all the test methods. The test that we will discuss is the `testMatchingPasswords()` method. As the name of the method suggests, this test will determine if the passwords we provide the application match and, if so, will let us know if the expected visual outcome of the test matches what the application actually outputs when provided with the matching password inputs.

Here is our `testMatchingPasswords()` method:

```
public void testMatchingPasswords() {

    TouchUtils.clickView(this, password);
```

(Continues)

(*Continued*)

```
    sendKeys(GOOD_PASSWORD);

    TouchUtils.clickView(this, matchingPassword);

    sendKeys(GOOD_PASSWORD);

    TouchUtils.clickView(this, button);

    String p = password.getText().toString();

    assertEquals("abc123", p);

    String mp = matchingPassword.getText().toString();

    assertEquals("abc123", mp);

    assertEquals(p, mp);

    int visibility = passwordResult.getVisibility();

    assertEquals(View.VISIBLE, visibility);

    String notice = passwordResult.getText().toString();

    assertEquals(passwordMatcherActivity.getResources()

            .getString(R.string.passwords_match_notice), notice);

    int noticeColor = passwordResult.getCurrentTextColor();

    assertEquals(passwordMatcherActivity.getResources()

            .getColor(R.color.green), noticeColor);

}
```

This test does a few things. Since we have initialized our views in the setUp() method, we can begin testing our application. We start the method by calling the TouchUtils.clickView() method. The TouchUtils class provides methods for simulating touch events within our application. Calling the clickView() method on the password EditText field grabs the focus of the field and allows the test to use the sendKeys() method to enter a GOOD_PASSWORD value into the EditText field. We continue the test by grabbing the focus of the matchingPassword EditText field and use the sendKeys() method for the test to enter the same GOOD_PASSWORD value into the second EditText field. We then use the getText() method to get the text value of each of the EditText values to ensure that the values are equal to the GOOD_PASSWORD value the test entered, and then check to make sure that both EditText values are equal to each other. The test then checks the passwordResult TextView to see if the visibility has been set to View.VISIBLE and further checks to see if the value of the text is actually what we expect the value to be. Finally, we get the text color value of the passwordResult TextView and check to make sure that the value is equal to green.

When you run the test, you should see the PasswordMatcher application start up, and you should also notice that both EditText values automatically begin receiving password input into their respective fields, followed by the Button named Match Passwords receiving a click. After the `Button` receives the click from the test, you should finally see the `TextView` display as visible, and the `PasswordMatcherActivity` should now display a green success notice that reads `Passwords match!` (see Figure 21.10).

After we run our test, we should see that the test passes, and this means that the application responded as expected (see Figure 21.11).

Here are just a few classes, located in the `android.test` package that you may want to be aware of. For a full listing with descriptions, see the Android documentation here: *http://d.android.com/reference/android/test/package-summary.html*.

- **`ActivityInstrumentationTestCase2<?>:`** used for functional testing of a single `Activity`
- **`MoreAsserts:`** used to provide additional assertion methods specific to Android
- **`TouchUtils:`** used to perform touch events
- **`ViewAsserts:`** used to provide assertion methods for making assertions about views

Figure 21.10   The `PasswordMatcher` application displays a `TextView` with a green color indicating that the passwords entered match.

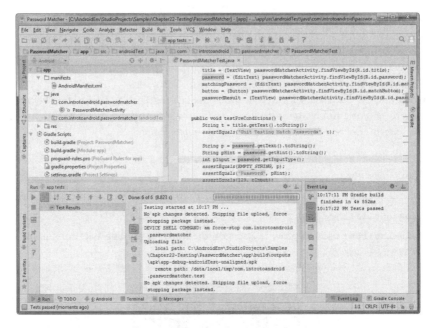

Figure 21.11   Android Studio displaying a successful test run.

More Android Automated Testing Programs and APIs

Automated testing is a very powerful tool that you should use when developing your Android applications. JUnit for Android is just one of the automated testing tools that the Android SDK provides. The Android SDK provides other tools for testing applications and it provides a Testing Support Library. Here are some of the tools available for testing your applications:

- **UI/Application Exerciser Monkey:** This program, named monkey, can be run from the command-line using an adb shell command. Use this tool for stress testing your application, which generates and sends your test device random events while your application is running. This is useful for uncovering bugs that may be present when random events are thrown at your application.

- **monkeyrunner:** This is a testing API for writing Python programs that take control of the automated testing process. A monkeyrunner program runs outside the Android emulator or device and can be used for running unit tests, installing and uninstalling your .apk file, testing across multiple devices, taking screenshots of your application during a running test cycle, and providing many more useful features.

- **AndroidJUnitRunner:** This is a test runner that is compatible with JUnit 3 or JUnit 4 and serves as a replacement for the InstrumentationTestRunner class, which is only compatible with JUnit 3 and is included in the Testing Support Library.

- **Espresso:** This is a UI testing framework useful for testing application user flows within a single application and works with AndroidJUnitRunner; it is also included in the Testing Support Library.

- **uiautomator:** This is a testing framework and command-line tool that was added in API Level 16. The uiautomator tool is used for running tests from the command-line using an adb shell command. You can use this tool for automating user interface tests across one or more devices and for automating the functional testing of your user interface.

- **UiAutomation:** This is a testing class for simulating user events and for leveraging the AccessibilityService APIs for inspecting user interfaces during automated tests. You can use this class for simulating user events that span multiple applications and it is included in the Testing Support Library.

Summary

In this chapter, we armed you—the keepers of application quality—with real-world knowledge for testing Android applications, in addition to introducing a real example of how to test your Android applications with unit tests.

Whether you're a team of one or one hundred, testing your applications is critical for project success. Luckily, the Android SDK provides a number of tools for testing applications, as well as a powerful unit-testing framework and other sophisticated testing APIs. By following standard QA techniques and leveraging these tools, you can ensure that the application you deliver to your users is the best it can be.

Quiz Questions

1. True or false: One typical defect common to mobile applications is an application using too much disk space on the device.

2. Name three specialized test scenarios that any QA team should consider.

3. What is the name of the unit-testing library available for testing Android applications?

4. When using JUnit 3 for testing Android applications, with what prefix must your test methods begin?

5. True or false: Testing the default starting values of your application is overkill.

6. What Android test class is used for performing touch events from within unit tests?

Exercises

1. Read through the Testing section within the Tools documentation, at the following URL: *http://d.android.com/tools/testing/index.html*.

2. Using the `PasswordMatcher` project, determine how to run the tests from the command-line and provide the command for doing so.

3. Add an additional test method to the `PasswordMatcherTest` class that uses a method from the `ViewAsserts` class to determine if each of the views of the `PasswordMatcherActivity` is on the screen. Write the method and make sure the test passes.

References and More Information

Android Tools: "Testing":
   http://d.android.com/tools/testing/index.html
Android Tools: "Android Testing Tools":
   http://d.android.com/tools/testing/testing-tools.html
Android Tools: "`monkeyrunner`":
   http://d.android.com/tools/help/monkeyrunner_concepts.html
Android Tools: "UI/Application Exerciser Monkey":
   http://d.android.com/tools/help/monkey.html
Android Training: "Automating User Interface Tests":
   http://d.android.com/training/testing/ui-testing/index.html
Android Reference: "`AndroidJUnitRunner`":
   http://d.android.com/reference/android/support/test/runner/AndroidJUnitRunner.html
Android Reference: "`android.support.test.espresso`":
   http://d.android.com/reference/android/support/test/espresso/package-summary.html
Android Reference: "`UiAutomation`":
   http://d.android.com/reference/android/app/UiAutomation.html
Wikipedia on software testing:
   http://en.wikipedia.org/wiki/Software_testing

22

Distributing Your Applications

After you've developed and tested your application, the next logical step is to publish it so that other people can enjoy it. You might even want to make some money. A variety of distribution opportunities are available to Android application developers. Many developers choose to sell their applications through mobile marketplaces such as Google Play. Others develop their own distribution mechanisms; for example, they might sell their applications from a website. You may even want to have fine-grained control over who can install your application using features found within the Google Play Developer Console. Regardless, developers should consider which distribution options they plan to use during the application design and development process because some distribution choices might require code changes or impose restrictions on content.

Choosing the Right Distribution Model

The application distribution methods you choose to employ depend on your goals and target users. Here are some questions you should ask yourself:

- Is your application ready for prime time, or are you considering a beta period to iron out the kinks?
- Are you trying to reach the broadest audience, or have you developed a vertical market application? Determine who your users are, which devices they are using, and their preferred methods for seeking out and downloading applications.
- How will you price your application? Is it freeware or shareware? Are the payment models (single payment versus subscription model versus ad-driven revenue) you require available on the distribution mechanisms you want to leverage?
- Where do you plan to distribute? Verify that any application markets you plan to use are capable of distributing within given countries or regions.
- Are you willing to share a portion of your profits? Distribution mechanisms such as Google Play take a percentage of each sale in exchange for hosting your application and distributing and collecting application revenue on your behalf.

- Do you require complete control over the distribution process, or are you willing to work within the boundaries and requirements imposed by third-party marketplaces? This might require compliance with further license agreements and terms.

- If you plan to distribute yourself, how will you do so? You might need to develop more services to manage users, deploy applications, and collect payments. If so, how will you protect user data? With what trade laws must you comply?

- Have you considered creating a free trial version of your application? If the distribution system under consideration has a return policy, consider the ramifications. You need to ensure that your application has safeguards to minimize the number of users who buy your app, use it, and return it for a full refund. For example, a game might include safeguards such as a free trial version and a full-scale version with more game levels than could possibly be completed within the refundable time period.

Protecting Your Intellectual Property

You've spent time, money, and effort to build a valuable Android application. Now you want to distribute it, but perhaps you are concerned about reverse engineering of trade secrets and software piracy. As technology rapidly advances, it's impossible to perfectly protect against either.

If you're accustomed to developing Java applications, you might be familiar with code obfuscation tools. These are designed to strip easy-to-read information from compiled Java byte codes, making the decompiled application more difficult to understand and reverse engineer. Some tools, such as ProGuard (*http://proguard.sourceforge.net*), support Android applications because they can run after the `.jar` file is created and before it's converted to the final package file used with Android. ProGuard support is built into Android projects created with Android Studio.

Google Play also supports a licensing service called Google Play Licensing. The License Verification Library (LVL), for use within your application, performs the license verification between your app and the licensing service. This is available as an SDK developer tool but works on Android API Level 3 and higher. It applies to any application distributed through Google Play, both free and purchased. It requires application support—code additions—to be fully utilized, and you should seriously consider obfuscating your code if you use it. The service's primary purpose is to verify that a paid application installed on a device was properly purchased by the user, and in the case of a free application, it is used to request the expansion files associated with your free application. You can find out more about app licensing at the Android Developer website, *http://d.android.com/google/play/licensing/index.html*.

You may also be concerned about rogue applications impersonating your brand or committing trademark and/or copyright infringement. Google has many mechanisms set up for reporting infringements, so if this does occur, you should report those infringements to protect your brand. In addition to using the mechanisms Google provides for reporting infringements, you may also need to consult with legal counsel.

Following the Policies of Google Play

When you publish your application to Google Play, you must agree to certain policies that Google enforces. One of those policies is the Developer Distribution Agreement, which can be found here: *http://play.google.com/about/developer-distribution-agreement.html*. By accepting the agreement, you are agreeing not to perform certain prohibited actions that are outlined within the agreement.

Another term of service that you agree to is the Developer Program Policies as defined here: *http://play.google.com/about/developer-content-policy.html*. This includes rules that prohibit spam, restrict content, and govern ad implementations, and it even outlines subscription and cancellation policies. Staying up-to-date on the current policies of Google Play is very important to avoid any negative repercussions for failure to comply with them.

Billing the User

Unlike some other mobile platforms you might have used, the Android SDK does not currently provide built-in billing APIs that work directly from within applications. Instead, billing APIs are normally add-on APIs that are provided by the distribution channels.

For selling your applications on Google Play, you must register for a Google payments merchant account. Once registered with the Google Play Developer Console, you need to set up a merchant account.

Google Play allows you to sell your application in more than 130 different countries, enabling you to accept the currencies that your users are used to spending. Users will be able to make purchases from their Android devices or from the Web, and Google Play provides an easy way to track and manage the entire process. Google Play accepts many different forms of payment, including direct carrier billing, credit card, gift card, or a stored Google Play balance. Any revenue that you generate is paid out to you in monthly installments to your Google Wallet Merchant account.

If an application needs to charge ad hoc fees for goods sold within the application (that is, subscriptions or in-app products), the application developer must implement an in-app billing mechanism. Google Play provides an In-app Billing API for billing support within any application published to Google Play (*http://d.android.com/google/play/billing/index.html*). Android Pay is another method that allows you to sell physical goods and services within your application.

Building your own in-app billing system? Most Android devices can leverage the Internet, so using online billing services and APIs—PayPal, Amazon, or others, for example—is a common choice. Check with your preferred billing service to make sure it specifically allows mobile use and that the billing methods your application requires are available, feasible, and legal for your target users. Similarly, make sure any distribution channels you plan to use allow these billing mechanisms (as opposed to their own).

Leveraging Ad Revenue

Another method to make money from users is to have an ad-supported mobile business model. Android itself has no specific rules against using advertisements within applications. However, different markets may impose their own rules for what's allowed. For instance, Google's AdMob Ads service allows developers to place ads within their applications. (Read more at *https://developers.google.com/admob/android/start*.) Several other companies provide similar services.

Collecting Statistics Regarding Your Application

Before you publish, you may want to consider adding some statistics collection to your application to determine how your users use it. You can write your own statistics-collection mechanisms, or you can use third-party add-ons such as the Google Analytics SDK v4 for Android (*https://developers.google.com/analytics/devguides/collection/android/v4/*). Ensure that you always inform your users if you are collecting information about them, and incorporate your plans into your clearly defined EULA and privacy policy. Statistics can help you see not just how many people are using your application, but also how they are actually using it.

Now let's look at the steps you need to take to package and publish your application.

Packaging Your Application for Publication

Developers must take several steps when preparing an Android application for publication and distribution. Your application must also meet several important requirements imposed by the marketplaces. The following steps are required for publishing an application:

1. Prepare and perform a release candidate build of the application. You can do this by configuring the Gradle build system, which allows you to build different variants of your application, such as free or paid, or debug or release. We introduce how to leverage the Gradle build system for this purpose in Appendix E, "Quick-Start: Gradle Build System."

2. Verify that all requirements for the marketplace are met, such as configuring the `build.gradle` file and the Android manifest file properly. For example, make sure the application name and version information are correct, and the `debuggable` attribute is set to `false`.

3. Package and digitally sign the application.

4. Test the packaged application release thoroughly.

5. Update and include all the required resources for the release.

6. Make sure that your servers or the services used by your application are stable and production ready.

7. Publish the application.

The preceding steps are required but not sufficient to guarantee a successful deployment. Developers should also take these steps:

1. Thoroughly test the application on all target handsets.
2. Turn off debugging, including Log statements and any other logging.
3. Verify permissions, making sure to add those for services used and to remove any that aren't used, regardless of whether they are enforced by the handsets.
4. Test the final, signed version with all debugging and logging turned off.

Now, let's explore each of these steps in more detail, in the order they might be performed.

Preparing Your Code for Packaging

An application that has undergone a thorough testing cycle might need changes made to it before it is ready for a production release. These changes convert it from a debuggable, preproduction application into a release-ready application.

Setting the Application Name and Icon

An Android application has default settings for the icon and label. The icon appears in the application launcher and can appear in various other locations, including marketplaces. As such, an application is required to have an icon. You should supply alternative icon drawable resources for various screen resolutions. The label, or application name, is also displayed in similar locations and defaults to the package name. You should choose a short, user-friendly name that displays under the application icon in launcher screens.

Versioning the Application

Next, proper versioning is required, especially if updates could occur in the future. The version name is up to the developer. The version code, though, is used internally by the Android system to determine if an application is an update. You should increment the version code for each new update of an application. The exact value doesn't matter, but it must be greater than the previous version code. Versioning is discussed in Appendix E, "Quick-Start: Gradle Build System."

Verifying the Target Platforms

Make sure your application sets the defaultConfig element in the build.gradle file correctly. This is used to specify the minimum and target SDK versions that the application can run on. This is perhaps the most important setting after the application name and version information.

Configuring the Android Manifest for Filtering

If you plan to publish through Google Play, you should read up on how this distribution system uses certain tags within the Android manifest file to filter applications available to users. Many of these tags, such as `<supports-screens>`, `<uses-configuration>`, `<uses-feature>`, and `<uses-permission>` were discussed in Chapter 5, "Defining the Manifest." Set each of these items carefully, because you don't want to accidentally put too many restrictions on your application. Make sure you test your application thoroughly after configuring these Android manifest file settings. For more information on how Google Play filters work, see *http://d.android.com/google/play/filters.html*.

Preparing Your Application Package for Google Play

Google Play has strict requirements for application packages. When you upload your application to the Android Developer Console, the package is verified and any problems are communicated to you. Most often, problems occur when you have not properly configured your `build.gradle` file or the Android manifest file.

Google Play uses the `versionName` element of the `defaultConfig` tag within the `build.gradle` file to display version information to users. It also uses the `versionCode` element internally to handle application upgrades. The `android:icon` and `android:label` attributes of the `<application>` tag within the Android manifest file must also be present because both are used by Google Play to display the application name to the user with a visual icon.

Disabling Debugging and Logging

Next, you should turn off debugging and logging. Disabling debugging involves removing the `android:debuggable` attribute from the `<application>` tag of the `AndroidManifest.xml` file or setting it to `false`. You can turn off the logging code within Java in a variety of different ways, from just commenting it out to using the Gradle build system for handling this. We talk more about the Gradle build system in Appendix E, "Quick-Start: Gradle Build System."

> **Tip**
>
> A common method for conditionally compiling debug code is to use a class interface with a single, `public static final boolean` that's set to `true` or `false`. When this is used with an `if` statement and set to `false`, because it's immutable the compiler should not include the unreachable code, and it certainly won't be executed. We recommend using some method other than just commenting out the `Log` lines and other debug code.

Verifying Application Permissions

Finally, the permissions used by the application should be reviewed. Include all permissions that the application requires, and remove any that are not used. Users appreciate this.

Packing and Signing Your Application

Now that the application is ready for publication, the file package—the `.apk` file—needs to be prepared for release. The package manager of an Android device will not install a package that has not been digitally signed. Throughout the development process, the

Android tools have accomplished this through signing with a debug key. The debug key cannot be used for publishing an application to the wider world. Instead, you need to use a true key to digitally sign the application. You can use the private key to digitally sign the release package files of your Android application, as well as any upgrades. This ensures that the application (as a complete entity) is coming from you, the developer, and not some other source (imposters!).

> **Warning**
>
> A private key identifies the developer and is critical to building trust relationships between developers and users. It is very important to secure private key information.

Google Play requires that your application's digital signature validity period end after October 22, 2033. This date might seem like a long way off and, for mobile, it certainly is. However, because an application must use the same key for upgrading and because applications that are designed to work closely together with special privileges and trust relationships must also be signed with the same key, the key could be chained forward through many applications. Thus, Google is mandating that the key be valid for the foreseeable future so application updates and upgrades are performed smoothly for users.

> **Note**
>
> Finding a third-party certificate authority that will issue a key is optional, but self-signing is the most straightforward solution. Within Google Play, there is no benefit to using a third-party certificate authority.

Although self-signing is typical of Android applications, and a certificate authority is not required, creating a suitable key and securing it properly are critical. The digital signature for Android applications can impact certain functionality. The expiry of the signature is verified at installation time, but after it's installed, an application continues to function even if the signature has expired.

You can export and sign your Android package file from within Android Studio as follows (or you can use the command-line tools):

1. In Android Studio, select `Build` from the menu and choose `Generate Signed APK`. You will be presented with a `Generate Signed APK` dialog as seen in Figure 22.1.

2. On the `Key store path` entry, click the `Create new…` option and the `New Key Store` dialog will be displayed as seen in Figure 22.2. (If you already have a key store, rather than clicking `Create new…` on the `Generate Signed APK` dialog, click `Choose existing…` to select your key store file from your file system, enter the correct `Key store password`, choose the appropriate `Key alias`, then enter the `Key password`, and skip to step 5 below).

3. On the `New Key Store` dialog, enter the details of the key as shown in Figure 22.2.

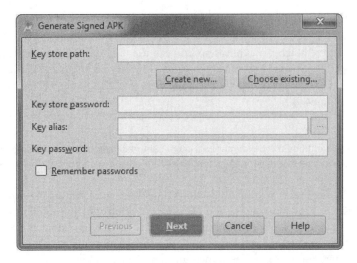

Figure 22.1   Generate Signed APK dialog of Android Studio.

Figure 22.2   New Key Store dialog of Android Studio.

Warning

Make sure you choose a strong password for the key store. Remember where the key store is located, too. The same key is required to publish an upgrade to your application. If the key is checked into a revision-control system, the password helps protect it. However, you should consider adding an extra layer of privilege required to get to the key.

4. Click the OK button. The Generate Signed APK dialog should now look similar to Figure 22.3.

5. Click the Next button.

6. Select an appropriate APK Destination Folder for your application and click Finish (see Figure 22.4).

You have now created a fully signed and certified application package file. The application package is ready for publication. For more information about signing, and to learn how to automatically sign your application during the Android Studio build process, see the Android Developer website: *http://d.android.com/tools/publishing/app-signing.html*.

Note

If you are not using Android Studio, you can use the keytool and jarsigner command-line tools available within the JDK, in addition to the zipalign utility provided with the Android SDK, to create a suitable key and sign an application package file (.apk). Although zipalign is not directly related to signing, it optimizes the application package for more efficient use on Android.

Figure 22.3   Generate Signed APK information completely filled out.

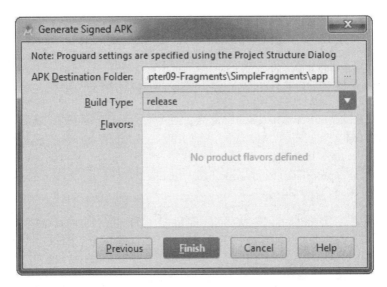

Figure 22.4   Generate Signed APK with an
APK Destination Folder selected.

Testing the Release Version of Your Application Package

Now that you have configured your application for production, you should perform a final full testing cycle, paying special attention to subtle changes to the installation process. An important part of this process is to verify that you have disabled all debugging features so that logging has no negative impact on the functionality and performance of the application.

Including All Required Resources

Before releasing your application, you need to make sure that all the required resources are available for access from your application. Testing that these resources are working properly and are accessible is extremely important. Also, be sure that the most recent versions of these resources are included.

Readying Your Servers or Services

Make sure that your servers or any third-party services that your application accesses are stable and work well in a production setting. The last thing you want is to have a strong application with a weak back end. If your application is accessible via the Web, and not just a stand-alone application, ensuring proper and stable access to your servers and services should be a priority.

Distributing Your Application

Now that you've prepared your application for publication, it's time to get it out to users—for fun and profit. Before you publish, you may want to consider setting up an application website, tech support email address, help and feedback forum, Twitter/ Facebook/Google+/social network du jour account, and any other infrastructure you may want or need to support your published application.

Publishing to Google Play

Google Play is the most popular mechanism for distributing Android applications at the time of this writing. This is where a typical user purchases and downloads applications. As of this writing, it's available to most, but not all, Android devices. As such, we show you how to check your package for preparedness, sign up for a Google Play Developer Console account, and submit your application for download to Google Play.

Note

Google Play is updated frequently. We have made every attempt to provide the latest steps for uploading and managing applications. However, these steps and the user interfaces described in this section may change at any time. Please login to and review the Google Play Developer Console website (*https://play.google.com/apps/publish*) for the latest information.

Signing Up for Publishing to Google Play

To publish applications through Google Play, you must register for a publisher account and set up a Google Payments merchant account.

Note

As of this writing, only developers ("merchants") residing in certain approved countries may sell priced applications on Google Play due to international laws. Developers from many other countries can register for publisher accounts, but they may publish only free applications at this time. For a complete list of supported publisher countries, see *https://support.google.com/googleplay/android-developer/table/3539140*.

To sign up for a Google Play publisher account, you need to follow these steps:

1. Go to the Google Play Developer Console website at *https://play.google.com/apps/ publish*.

2. Sign in with the Google account you want to use. If you do not yet have a Google account, click the Create account link and create one first.

3. You must first agree to the Google Play Developer distribution agreement by ticking the check box, as shown in Figure 22.5, and then pressing Continue to payment. As of this writing, a $25 (USD) one-time registration fee is required to publish applications.

4. Note that Google Wallet is used for registration payment processing, so you must also set up a Google Wallet account if you don't already have one, as shown in Figure 22.6.

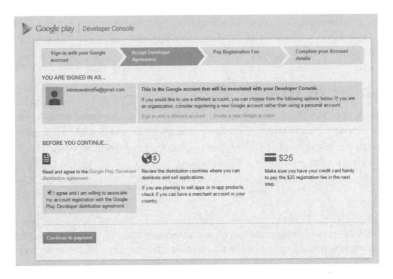

Figure 22.5   Accepting the Google Play Developer Distribution Agreement.

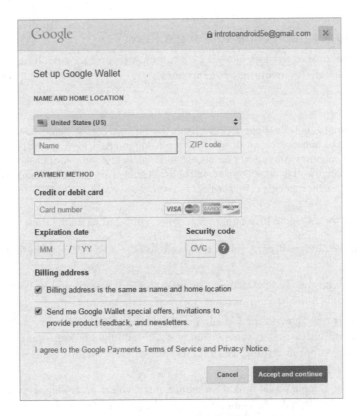

Figure 22.6   Setting up a Google Wallet account.

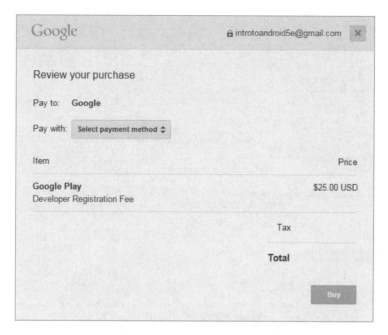

Figure 22.7   Accepting the $25 registration fee.

5. Once you have set up the Google Wallet account, you must then accept the $25 registration fee (shown in Figure 22.7).

6. You then proceed to Complete your Account details (see Figure 22.8). Enter the required information and click Complete registration.

Tip

Always print out the actual agreement you sign as part of the registration process, in case it changes in the future.

When you successfully complete these steps, you are presented with the home screen of the Google Play Developer Console, as seen in Figure 22.9. Signing up and paying to be an Android Developer does not create a Google Wallet Merchant account. A merchant account is used for payment processing purposes. From the Developer Console, you should be able to set up a merchant account by following the link in the lower-right section of the screen. If you are creating a paid app, feel free to set this up at any time.

Uploading Your Application to Google Play

Now that you have an account registered for publishing applications to Google Play and have a signed application package, you are ready to upload it for publication.

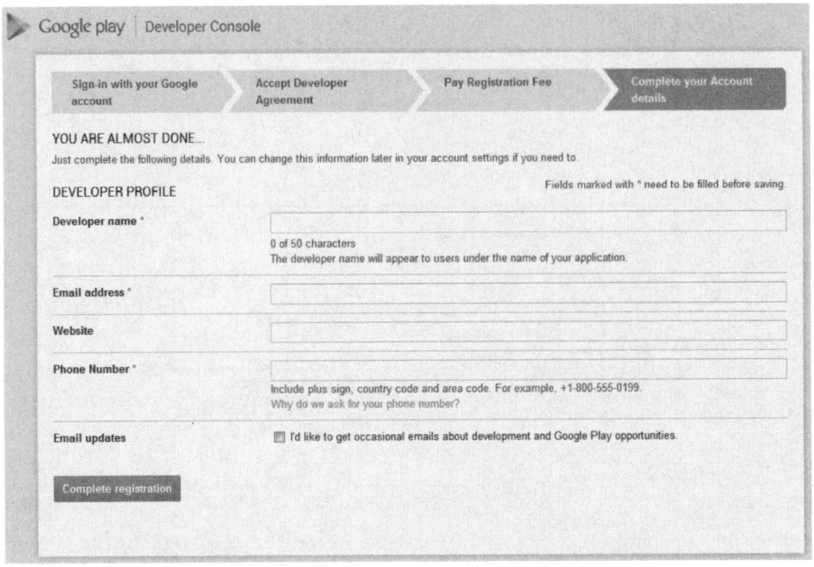

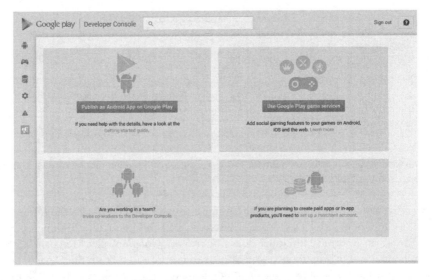

Figure 22.8   Complete your Account details page.

Figure 22.9   The Developer Console start page.

From the main page of the Google Play Developer Console website, sign in and click the Publish an Android App on Google Play button. You should now see an Add New Application dialog, as seen in Figure 22.10.

From this page, you can create a new listing in the Developer Console for your application. In order to publish a new application, enter a Title and click the Upload APK button on this dialog. You will now see a new application listing requesting that you `Upload your first APK to Production` (see Figure 22.11). There are three options for uploading presented: Production, Beta Testing, and Alpha Testing. The Beta and Alpha Testing options are for performing a Staged Rollout, which will be discussed later in this chapter.

When you click the `Upload your first APK to Production` button, you are presented with a dialog that allows you to upload an `.apk` file from your file system by dragging and dropping the file onto the upload space or by browsing and selecting the file.

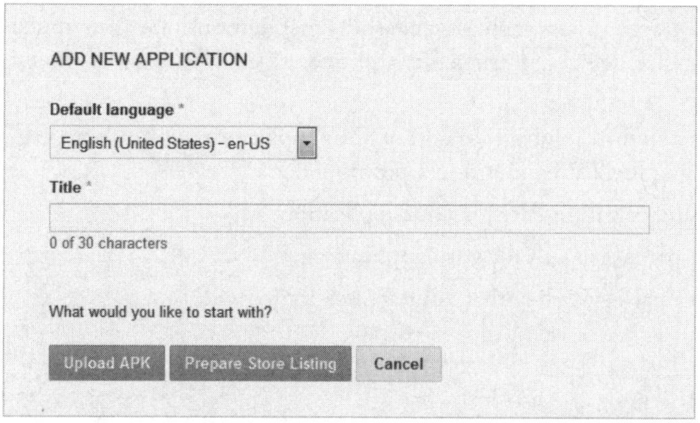

ADD NEW APPLICATION

Default language *

English (United States) - en-US

Title *

0 of 30 characters

What would you like to start with?

Upload APK   Prepare Store Listing   Cancel

Figure 22.10   The `Add New Application` dialog.

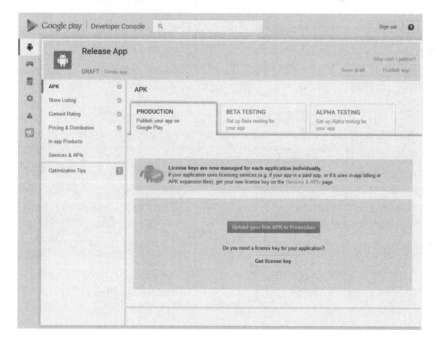

Figure 22.11   Google Play application upload form.

Uploading Application Marketing Assets

The Store Listing tab associated with your application begins with the Product Details section (see Figure 22.12). Here, you can perform the following tasks:

- Manage translations by purchasing translations or providing your own application translations

- Enter an application title, short description, and full description

- Upload graphic assets such as screenshots that demonstrate your application on different-size devices, in particular a phone, a 7-inch tablet, a 10-inch tablet, and a TV

- Provide a high-resolution version of your application icon, a feature graphic, a promo graphic, TV banner, and a promo video

- Enter categorization data for your application

- Provide contact details for your application

- Link to a privacy policy that your application provides

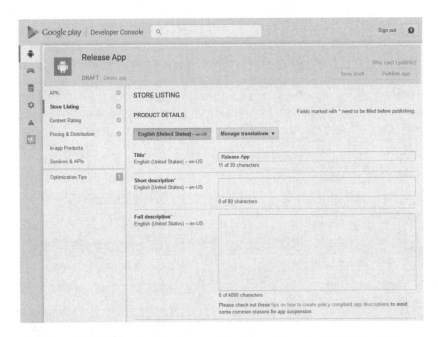

Figure 22.12   Google Play Store Listing and Product Details form.

Configuring Pricing and Distribution Details

The `Pricing & Distribution` tab associated with your application allows you to enter pricing information for your application (see Figure 22.13). Here, you can do the following:

- Specify whether the application is free or paid
- Specify the countries where you would like to distribute your application
- Opt-in to Android Wear, Designed for Families, and Google Play for Education distribution
- Provide consent for acknowledging marketing opt-out, and that your application abides by the Android Content Guidelines and export laws of your country

Note

Currently, a 30% transaction fee is imposed for hosting applications within Google Play. Prices can range from $0.99 to $200 (USD), and similar ranges are available in other supported currencies. For more details, see *https://support.google.com/googleplay/ android-developer/answer/112622* and *https://support.google.com/googleplay/ android-developer/table/3541286*.

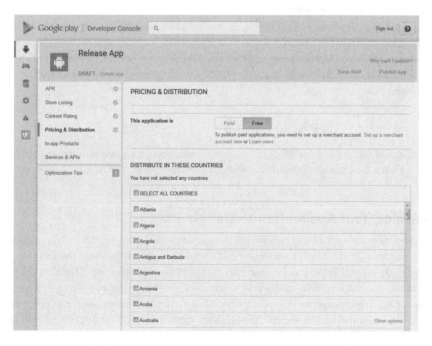

Figure 22.13   Developer Console `Pricing & Distribution` tab.

Configuring Additional Application Options

There are a few other tabs associated with your application that allow you to configure additional setup tasks:

- Supply an International Age Rating Coalition (IARC) content rating to your application.
- Specify in-app products for your application. This requires adding the BILLING permission to your APK and setting up a merchant account.
- Manage services and APIs such as Google Cloud Messaging (GCM), Licensing & In-app Billing, Google Play Game Services, and App Indexing from Google Search.
- Implement additional optimization tips for improving your app listing on Google Play.

Managing Other Developer Console Options

In addition to managing your applications, you can also set up Google Play Game Services and review detailed financial reports for your paid applications. To review financial reports, you must have a merchant account set up to enable paid apps. Financial information is downloadable in CSV format.

Google Play Game Services

The Google Play game services APIs allow you to add leaderboards, achievements, real-time and multiplayer features, and events and quests services, and to save game data by enabling the Saved Games service. From the Developer Console, you must accept the Google APIs terms of service before you can begin integrating Game Services into your application.

Note

Google Play Game Services APIs provide many useful tools for game developers, but there are no rules prohibiting non-game applications from using these APIs.

Publishing Your Application to Google Play

Once you have entered all the required information, you should be ready to transition your application from a draft to publishing it on Google Play. Once you publish, your application will appear in Google Play. Some publishers have reported that their applications are not available until a few hours after publishing, so you may need to wait before seeing the application in Google Play. After publication, you can see average ratings, installs, and crash statistics in the All Applications section of the Developer Console (see Figure 22.14).

Figure 22.14   Viewing application statistics within the Google Play
Developer Console.

Tip

Receiving crash reports from a specific device? Check your application's market filters in
the Android manifest file. Are you including and excluding the appropriate devices? You can
also exclude specific devices by adjusting the Supported Devices settings of the application
listing.

Managing Your Application on Google Play

Once you've published your application to Google Play, you will need to manage it. Some
considerations include understanding how the Google Play return policy works, managing
application upgrades, and, if necessary, removing your application from publication.

Understanding the Google Play Application Return Policy

Google Play currently has a 2-hour refund policy on applications. That is to say, a user can
try out an application for 2 hours and then return it for a full refund. However, this applies
only to the first download and first return. If a particular user has already returned your
application and wants to "try it again," he or she must make a final purchase—and can't
return it a second time. Although this limits abuse, you should still be aware that if your
application has limited reuse appeal, you might find that you have a return rate that's too
high and you will need to pursue other methods of monetization.

Upgrading Your Application on Google Play

You can upgrade existing applications from the Google Play Developer Console. Simply upload a new version of the same application after incrementing the version of your application in the build.gradle app module file, using the versionCode and versionName elements. When you publish it, users receive an Update Available notification, prompting them to download the upgrade. You can learn more about the build.gradle file and the versionCode and versionName elements in Appendix E, "Quick-Start: Gradle Build System."

> **Warning**
>
> Application updates must be signed with the same private key as the original application. For security reasons, the Android package manager does not install the update over the existing application if the key is different. This means you need to keep the key corresponding with the application in a secure, easy-to-find location for future use.

Removing Your Application from Google Play

You can also use the Unpublish action in the Google Play Developer Console to remove the application from Google Play. The Unpublish action is immediate, but your application entry in the Google Play store application might be cached on handsets that have viewed or downloaded your application. Keep in mind that unpublishing the application makes it unavailable to new users but does not remove it from existing users' devices.

Google Play Staged Rollouts

In case you are not yet ready to offer your application for download to the entire world, you are able to distribute it as a prerelease version using Staged Rollouts. This allows you to define alpha and beta test groups, so you are able to generate feedback prior to offering your application to all of Google Play. Any reviews provided will not be visible in the Google Play store, which provides you an opportunity to fix any defects that may generate negative reviews before they affect the perception of your application.

Just know that when you add users to a particular test group, and you upgrade your application from a previous test group, those users will not see the updates unless they are in both test groups. For example, users in the alpha test group will not see the beta updates unless they are also in the beta test group.

Publishing to the Google Play Private Channel

If you have a Google Apps domain, Google allows you to launch and distribute your application in a private way to the users of your Google Apps domain. The distribution occurs through the Google Play store and can be useful if your application should be restricted to only those within your organization. Rather than having to set up your own distribution mechanisms for internal distribution, you are able to leverage all of the powerful features that Google Play provides, without needing to make your application available to users other than the group that should have access. To learn more about using a Private Channel, see *https://support.google.com/googleplay/android-developer/answer/2623322*.

Translating Your Application

Since Google Play is available to users in more than 130 different countries, and growing, you should think about translating your application into different languages early in the development process. There are simple measures that you can take to prepare your application for localization, including the following:

- Design your application with localization in mind from Day 1.
- Know which languages you may want to target first.
- Do not hard-code strings into your application. Instead, use string resources for any text, so when the time comes, all you need to do is have the string resources translated.
- Opt for professional translations by native speakers rather than using free services like Google Translate if you are able to afford it. Google Translate is not a professional translation service so the translations may be incorrect.
- The Google Play Developer Console offers professional translations through Google Play. You are able to hire professional translators to translate the string resources you provide. This helps to streamline the translation process and provides a simple way to find translators. Any translations that you purchase are a direct business relationship between you and the company providing the services, and not between you and Google.
- Make sure once your application has been translated that you also test the application in each language. Some translations may require more textual content or right-to-left language support, thereby pushing your user interface out of whack. Testing for this scenario is important because users won't want to use an application that does not display properly.

Tip

For tips on how to prepare your application for localization, you should read the "Localization Checklist" article here: *http://d.android.com/distribute/tools/localization-checklist.html*.

Publishing Using Other Alternatives

Google Play is not the only place available to distribute your Android applications. Many alternative distribution mechanisms are available to developers. Application requirements, royalty rates, and licensing agreements vary by store. Third-party application stores are free to enforce whatever rules they want on the applications they accept, so read the fine print carefully. They might enforce content guidelines, require additional technical support, and enforce digital signing requirements. Only you and your team can determine which are suitable for your specific needs.

Tip

Android is an open platform, which means there is nothing to prevent a handset manufacturer or an operator (or even you) from developing an Android application store.

Here are a few alternative marketplaces where you might consider distributing your Android applications:

- **Amazon Appstore** is an example of an Android-specific distribution website for free and paid applications (*https://developer.amazon.com/appsandservices*).
- **Samsung Galaxy Apps** is an app store managed by one of the most successful Android device manufacturers on the market (*http://seller.samsungapps.com*).
- **GetJar** boasts about having over 200 million users, so this is definitely an Android market to consider adding your application to (*http://developer.getjar.mobi/*).
- **Soc.io Mall** (formerly AndAppStore) is an Android-specific distribution site for free applications, e-books, and music using an on-device store (*http://soc.io/Home*).
- **SlideME** distributes mobile applications across a wide range of devices and is headquartered in Seattle, Washington (*http://slideme.org/developers*).
- **Anzhi** is an app store in China with 25 million active users, and sometimes can be found pre-installed on devices, so be prepared with a translation of your app in Chinese (*http://dev.anzhi.com/*).
- **Opera Mobile Store** claims to have 105 million visitors per month and over 2 million apps downloaded every day from over 230 countries (*https://publishers.apps.opera.com/*).

Self-Publishing Your Application

You can distribute Android applications directly from a website, server, or email. The self-publishing method is most appropriate for vertical market applications, content companies developing mobile marketplaces, and big-brand websites wanting to drive users to their branded Android applications. It can also be a good way to get beta feedback from end users.

Although self-distribution is perhaps the easiest method of application distribution, it might also be the hardest in which to market, protect, and make money. The only requirement for self-distribution is to have a place to host the application package file.

There are downsides to self-distribution: Google Play services will not be available. The Google Play licensing service will not be available to help you protect your application from piracy. In addition, Google Play's In-app Billing service is not available to apps outside Google Play; therefore, you will have to manage the billing aspects yourself. Furthermore, end users must configure their devices to allow packages from unknown sources. This setting is found under the Security section of the device's Settings application, as shown in Figure 22.15. This option is not available on all consumer devices in the market.

After that, the final step the user must take is to enter the URL of the application package into the Web browser on the handset and download the file (or click a link to it). When the file is downloaded, the standard Android install process occurs, asking the user to confirm the permissions and, optionally, to confirm an update or replacement of an existing application if a version is already installed. You also need to implement your own way to notify the user when the application has been updated.

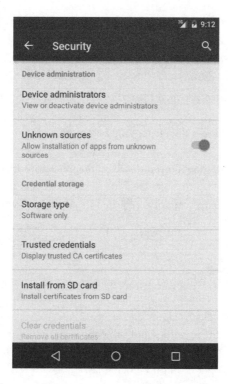

Figure 22.15   Settings application showing the Unknown sources setting turned on for installing from sources other than Google Play.

Summary

You've now learned how to design, develop, test, and deploy professional-grade Android applications. In this final chapter, you learned how to prepare your application package for publication using a variety of revenue models. You also learned about different distribution strategies. Whether you publish through Google Play, alternative markets, your own website, email, or some combination of these options, you can now build a robust application from the ground up and distribute it for profit (or fame!).

So, now it's time to go out there, fire up your favorite IDE, and build some amazing applications. We want to encourage you to think outside the box. The Android platform leaves the developer with a lot more freedom and flexibility than most other mobile platforms. Take advantage of this. Use what works and reinvent what doesn't. You might find yourself with a killer app.

Finally, if you're so inclined, we'd love to know about all the exciting applications you're building. You'll find our contact information in the Introduction to this book. Best of luck!

Quiz Questions

1. What is the name of the obfuscation tool provided with the Android SDK?
2. True or false: The In-app Billing APIs have been added to the Android SDK.
3. What is the name of the Google third-party add-on for collecting statistics regarding your application?
4. What is the difference between the `build.gradle` elements `versionName` and `versionCode`?
5. True or false: You should disable logging before uploading your application to Google Play.
6. True or false: You are not allowed to self-sign applications that you want to upload to Google Play.
7. What type of merchant account is required for Google Play in order to create paid applications?

Exercises

1. Read through the "Publishing Overview" section and accompanying subsections from the Android documentation found here: *http://d.android.com/tools/publishing/publishing_overview.html*.
2. Read through all of the sections and subsections in the Distribute tab on the Android Developers website found here: *http://d.android.com/distribute/index.html*.
3. Publish your first application on Google Play.

References and More Information

The Google Play website:
https://play.google.com/store
Android Tools: "Publishing Overview":
http://d.android.com/tools/publishing/publishing_overview.html
Android Developers Distribute: Google Play: "Developer Console":
http://d.android.com/distribute/googleplay/developer-console.html
Android Tools: "ProGuard":
http://d.android.com/tools/help/proguard.html
Android Google Services: "Filters on Google Play":
http://d.android.com/google/play/filters.html
Android Google Services: Google Play Distribution: "App Licensing":
http://d.android.com/google/play/licensing/index.html
Google Developers: "Play Games Services for Android":
https://developers.google.com/games/services/android/quickstart
Android Developers Blog: "Native RTL support in Android 4.2":
http://android-developers.blogspot.com/2013/03/native-rtl-support-in-android-42.html
Google Play Developer Console Help: "Google Play Apps Policy Center":
https://support.google.com/googleplay/android-developer/answer/4430948

VI

Appendixes

Tips and Tricks: Android Studio

Android Studio—a special version of the JetBrains IntelliJ IDEA Community Edition IDE—includes everything you need to get started developing professional Android applications. Android Studio is the official IDE for Android application development and is recommended. In addition, you may choose to use IntelliJ IDEA Community or Ultimate Editions for developing your Android applications—the same capabilities of Android Studio are available for these editions. Eclipse with the ADT plugin used to be a viable Android development environment before IntelliJ-based IDEs, but this approach is not recommended and support for Eclipse will no longer be available.

In this appendix, we provide a number of helpful tips and tricks for using Android Studio to develop Android applications quickly and effectively. Even though you may choose to use IntelliJ IDEA instead of Android Studio, the instructions provided within this appendix apply to using either Android Studio or IntelliJ IDEA. Since Android Studio and IntelliJ IDEA provide equivalent IDE and Android development capabilities, from here on, we will refer only to Android Studio.

Organizing Your Android Studio Workspace

In this section, we provide a number of tips and tricks to help you organize your Android Studio workspace for optimum Android development.

Integrating with Source Control Services

Android Studio integrates with many source control technologies. This allows Android Studio to manage checking out projects and files from local and remote version control, checking in a project or file to local or remote version control, updating a project or file, and showing a file's status, as well as a number of other tasks, depending on the support of the integration.

Tip

Source control integrations are available for GitHub, CVS, Git, Subversion, Mercurial, and Google Cloud.

Generally speaking, not all files are suitable for source control. For Android projects, any file within the `bin/`, `gen/`, `build/`, `.idea/`, and `.gradle/` directories shouldn't be in source control. You can add file suffixes such as `*.apk`, `*.ap_`, `*.class`, `*.dex`, `local.properties`, `*.iml`, and `*.log`. Conveniently, this applies to all integrated source control systems.

Repositioning Windows within Android Studio

Android Studio provides some pretty decent layouts by default. However, not everyone works the same way. We feel that some may like to tailor the layouts to suit their Android development workflow.

> **Tip**
>
> Experiment with organizing your layout to find one that suits your workflow. Each window has its own layout, too.

For instance, the `TODO` window is usually found on the bottom of Android Studio. This works fine because this tab is only a few lines high. But if your project has a long list of `TODO` items and you are not able to view the entire list with only a few lines visible, you may want to reposition the `TODO` window to the right or left of Android Studio, so that your `TODO` list displays more of the `TODO` items when you view this window. Luckily, moving a window in Android Studio is easy: simply drag the window tab to the left, right, top, or bottom, and move it to a new location on the IDE, such as the right side of Android Studio where the other window tabs are displayed. This provides the much-needed vertical space to see the dozens of `TODO` items your project may have. You may also right-click a window tab, choose `Move to`, and then choose from the available options, which will be `Right`, `Left`, `Top`, or `Bottom`, depending on where the window tab is currently located.

> **Tip**
>
> If you mess up a layout or just want to start fresh, you can reset it by choosing `Window, Restore Default Layout`.

Resizing the Editor Window

Sometimes you might find that the editor window of an open file is just too small, especially with all the extra tool windows and tabs surrounding it. Try this: double-click the tab of the source file that you want to edit. Boom! It's now nearly the full Android Studio window size! Double-click to return the editor window to normal. (`Ctrl+Shift+F12` works on Windows, `Command+Shift+F12` on the Mac.)

Resizing Tool Windows

You can resize entire tool windows, too. For instance, if you need more screen space to review the logcat output, found within the tool windows section at the bottom labeled `Android`, you can double-click the top bar of the `Android` tool window to expand the window to the full Android Studio windows size. Or, with the `Android` tool window in focus, you can use `Ctrl+Shift+Up` on Windows or `Command+Shift+Up` on the Mac to gradually increase the window size, or `Ctrl+Shift+Down` on Windows or `Command+Shift+Down` on the Mac to gradually decrease the window size.

Viewing Editor Windows Side by Side

Ever wish you could see two source files at once? Well, you can! Simply right-click a source file tab and choose `Move right` or `Move down`. You will then see each source file docked either side by side with another file (shown in Figure A.1) or below another file (shown in Figure A.2). This creates a parallel editor area where you can drag and rearrange other file tabs as well.

Viewing Two Sections of the Same File

Ever wish you could see two places at once in the same source file? You can! Make sure the file is open and focused, right-click the source file tab, and then choose `Split Vertically` or `Split Horizontally`. A second editor tab for the same file comes up either to the side or below. With the previous tip, you can now have two different views of the same file side by side (see Figure A.3) or (see Figure A.4).

If you have split your source file views and would like to return to a non-split view, simply right-click the source file tab and select `Unsplit` .

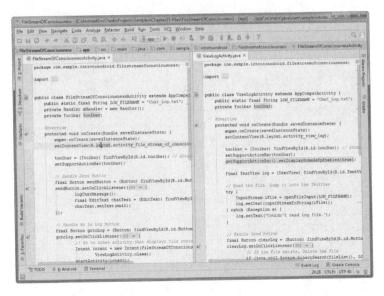

Figure A.1   Two windows showing different files docked side by side.

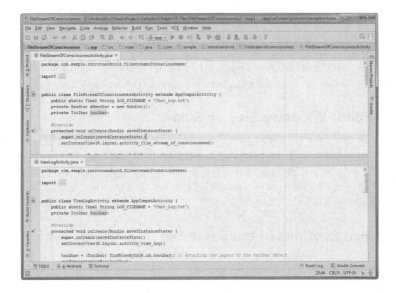

Figure A.2 Two windows showing different files docked one above the other.

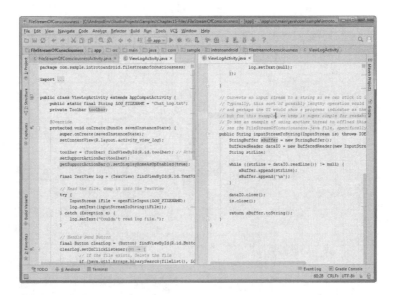

Figure A.3 Viewing different sections of the same file in two different windows side by side.

Figure A.4   Viewing different sections of the same file in two different windows, one above the other.

Closing Unwanted Tabs

Ever feel like you have far too many tabs open for files you're no longer editing? We do! There are a number of solutions to this problem. First, you can right-click a file tab and choose `Close Others` to close all other open files. You can quickly close specific tabs by middle-clicking each tab. (This even works on a Mac with a mouse that can middle-click, such as one with a scroll wheel.) You can even limit closing tabs to a particular vertical or horizontal split by right-clicking a source file tab and choosing `Close All in Group`.

Keeping Editor Windows under Control

Finally, you can use the Android Studio setting that limits the number of open file editors:

1. Open the Android Studio's `Settings` dialog found under the `File` menu option.
2. Expand `Editor`, choose `General`, and then choose `Editor Tabs`.
3. Edit the value in `Tab limit` found under the `Tab Closing Policy`.

This will cause old editor windows to close infrequently used files when new ones are opened. The default value is set to 10, which seems to be a good number to use for the `Tab limit` option to keep the clutter down but to have enough editors open to still get work done and have reference code open.

Creating Custom Log Filters

Every Android log statement includes a tag. You can use these tags with filters defined in `logcat`. To add a new filter, you must change the logcat filtering drop-down option found on the logcat menu bar, to the `Edit Filter Configuration` option, rather than the default option of `Show only selected application`. The `Create New Logcat Filter` dialog will appear, and you can modify the current filter or you can click the green plus sign button to add a new filter. Name the filter—perhaps using the tag name—and define any filtering parameters you would like to use, such as the `Log_Tag` or `Package Name`. Now `logcat` will only show messages that contain this tag. In addition, you can create filters that display items by severity level.

Android convention has largely settled on creating tags based on the name of the class. You see this frequently in the code provided with this book. Note that we create a constant in each class with the same variable name to simplify each logging call. Here's an example:

```
public static final String DEBUG_TAG = "MyClassName";
```

This convention isn't a requirement, though. You could organize tags around specific tasks that span many activities, or you could use any other logical organization that works for your needs. Another, simpler way to do this is as follows:

```
private final String DEBUG_TAG = getClass().getSimpleName();
```

Although not as efficient at runtime, this code can help you avoid copy-and-paste errors. If you've ever been looking over a log file and had a misnamed debug tag string mislead you, this trick may be useful to you.

Searching Your Project

You have several ways to easily search your project files from within Android Studio. The IDE search options—found under the search icon displayed to the far right of the Android Studio toolbar—allow you to search everywhere—including non-project files if so desired. Most frequently, we use the `Find` search option found on the toolbar—you can also activate the `Find` command by pressing `Ctrl+F` on Windows or `Command+F` on the Mac— which allows you to search for text within the files.

Organizing Android Studio Tasks

By default, any comment that starts with `// TODO` will show up on the `TODO` tab window of Android Studio. This can be helpful for tagging code areas that require further implementation. You can click a specific `TODO` item and it will take you straight to the comment in the file so you can implement the item at a later time.

You can also create custom comment filters above and beyond `TODO` items. We often leave comments with people's initials to make it easy for them to find specific functional areas of the application for code review. Here's an example:

```
// LED: Does this look right to you?
```

```
// JAJ: Related to Bug 1234. Can you fix this?
```

```
// SAC: This will have to be incremented for the next build
```

When you have to implement something that is less than ideal, you might also use a special comment such as // HACK to flag that code as subject to further review. To add custom filters to your TODO list, edit your Android Studio Settings (available at File, Settings on Windows and at Android Studio, Preferences on the Mac) and navigate to Editor, TODO. Add a new pattern by clicking the green plus symbol found in the Patterns section, typing HACK as the value for Patterns, and then clicking OK. Add any patterns you want to flag. So, for instance, something with your initials might be high priority that you'll look at right away, but a HACK flag may be a low priority because, presumably, it works but maybe not in the best way possible.

Writing Code in Java

In this section, we provide a number of tips and tricks to help you implement the code for your Android applications.

Using Autocomplete

Autocomplete is a great feature that speeds up code entry. If this feature hasn't appeared for you yet or has gone away, you can bring it up by pressing Ctrl+Space. Autocomplete not only saves time in typing but also can be used to jog your memory about methods—or to help you find a new method. You can scroll through all the methods of a class and even see the Javadoc's associated with them. You can easily find static methods by using the class name or the instance variable name. You follow the class or variable name with a dot (and maybe Ctrl+Space) and then scroll through all the names. Then you can start typing the first part of a name to filter the results.

Creating New Classes and Methods

You can quickly create a new Java class and corresponding source file by right-clicking the package to create it in, then choosing New, and then choosing one of the many different types of classes you can create. You then follow a wizard for defining the class to your requirements.

Along the same lines as creating new classes, you can quickly create method stubs within a class in the editor by choosing Code, and then choosing Override Methods, Implement Methods, Delegate Methods, or Generate. Then you follow the associated wizard to choose the methods for which you're creating stubs.

Organizing Imports

When referencing a class in your code for the first time, you can hover over the newly used class name, press Alt+Enter, and then choose Import class to have Android Studio quickly add the proper import statement.

In addition, the `Optimize Imports` command (`Ctrl+Alt+O`) causes Android Studio to automatically optimize your imports by removing any unused imports.

If there is any ambiguity in the name of a class during automatic import, the Android Studio prompts you for the package to import.

Finally, you can configure Android Studio to automatically import on the fly. You may also create an exclude from imports list by package or class name to exclude those from the auto import feature.

To configure automatic imports, perform the following steps:

1. Choose `File`, then `Settings` on Windows, or `Android Studio`, then `Preferences` on the Mac.

2. Expand `Editor`, then `General`, and choose `Auto Import`.

3. Check `Optimize imports on the fly`, and/or `Add unambiguous imports on the fly`, and then click `OK`.

Reformatting Code

Android Studio has a built-in mechanism for reformatting Java code. Reformatting code with a tool is useful for keeping the style consistent, applying a new style to old code, or matching styles with a different client or target (such as a book or an article).

To quickly reformat a small block of code, select the code and press `Ctrl+Alt+L` on Windows (or `Command+Alt+L` on the Mac). The code is reformatted to the current settings. If no code is selected, the entire file is formatted. Occasionally, you need to select more code—such as an entire method—to get the indentation levels and brace matching correct.

Android Studio reformatting settings are found in the `Settings` under `Editor`, `Code Style`, and you can further narrow reformatting options by selecting `Java` or `XML`. You can configure these settings on a per-project basis, and you can apply and modify dozens of rules to suit your own style.

Renaming Almost Anything

Android Studio's `Rename` tool is quite powerful. You can use it to rename variables, methods, class names, package names, project names, and more. Most often, you can simply right-click the item you want to rename and then choose `Refactor`, `Rename`. If you are renaming a top-level class in a file, the filename has to be changed as well. Android Studio usually handles the source control changes required to do this if the file is being tracked by source control. If Android Studio can determine that the item is in reference to the identically named item being renamed, all instances of the name are renamed as well. If renaming options are selected, this means even comments, strings, variables, tests, text, and inheritors are updated with the new name. Quite handy!

Refactoring Code

Do you find yourself writing a whole bunch of repeating sections of code that look, for instance, like the following?

```
TextView nameCol = new TextView(this);

nameCol.setTextColor(getResources().getColor(R.color.title_color));

nameCol.setTextSize(getResources().

getDimension(R.dimen.help_text_size));

nameCol.setText(scoreUserName);

table.addView(nameCol);
```

This code sets text color, text size, and text value. If you've written two or more blocks that look like this, your code could benefit from refactoring. Android Studio provides useful refactoring tools, two in particular for extracting code by Variable and Method, to speed up this task and make it almost trivial.

Extracting Variables

Follow these steps to extract a Variable:

1. Select the expression getResources().getColor(R.color.title_color).

2. Right-click and choose Refactor, Extract, Variable (or press Ctrl+Alt+V on Windows and Command+Alt+V on the Mac).

3. In the editing box that appears, enter the name for the variable. If a Multiple occurrences found message appears, choose either Replace this occurrence only, or Replace all X occurrences, then enter the name for the variable. Then watch the magic happen.

4. Repeat steps 1–3 for the text size.

The result should now look like this:

```
int textColor = getResources().getColor(R.color.title_color);

float textSize = getResources().getDimension(R.dimen.help_text_size);

TextView nameCol = new TextView(this);

nameCol.setTextColor(textColor);

nameCol.setTextSize(textSize);

nameCol.setText(scoreUserName);

table.addView(nameCol);
```

All repeated sections of the last five lines also have this change made. How convenient is that?

Extracting Methods

Now you're ready for the second tool. Follow these steps to extract a `Method`:

1. Select all five lines of the first block of code.
2. Right-click and choose `Refactor, Extract, Method` (or press `Ctrl+Alt+M` on Windows or `Command+Alt+M` on the Mac).
3. Name the method, select a `Visibility` level, select the `Parameters` to include, choose the parameters `Type`, then enter a `Name` for the parameter variables, and finally click `OK` and watch the magic happen.

By default, the new method is below your current one. If the other blocks of code are actually identical (meaning the statements of the other blocks are in the exact same order), the types are all the same, and so on, they will also be replaced with calls to this new method. You can see this in the count of additional occurrences shown in the `Extract Method` dialog. If that count doesn't match what you expect, check that the code follows exactly the same pattern. Now you should have code that looks similar to the following:

```
addTextToRowWithValues(newRow, scoreUserName, textColor, textSize);
```

It is easier to work with this code than with the original code, and it was created with almost no typing! If you had ten instances before refactoring, you've saved a lot of time by using a useful Android Studio feature.

Reorganizing Code

Sometimes, reformatting code isn't enough to make it clean and readable. Over the course of developing a complex `Activity`, you might end up with a number of embedded classes and methods strewn about the file. A quick Android Studio trick comes to the rescue. With the file in question open in the editor, highlight the code you would like to move.

Simply click and drag the code that you highlighted and place the code where you would like it to appear directly in the editor. Do you have a method that is called only from a certain class but is available to all? Just drag it into that class. You can even drag highlighted code across files in the editor by selecting, dragging, and then dropping. In addition, you can also copy code by holding down the `Ctrl` key while dragging your selection to the desired location.

Using Intention Actions

The `Intention Actions` feature—accessible by hovering the mouse over possible problematic code while clicking `Alt+Enter` or by clicking the lightbulb icon to the left of the line of code in question—isn't just for fixing possible issues. It brings up a menu of various tasks that can be performed on the highlighted code, and it shows what changes may take effect. One useful `Intention Action`—`Extract string resource`—is a type of `Intention Action` that allows you to extract a string resource from a string literal in your code and quickly move it into an Android string resource file, where the code is automatically updated to use the string resource. Consider how Extract String resource would work on the following two lines:

```
Log.v(DEBUG_TAG, "Something happened");

String otherString = "This is a string literal.";
```

The updated Java code is shown here:

```
Log.v(DEBUG_TAG, getString(R.string.something_happened));

String otherString = getString(R.string.string_literal);
```

And these entries have been added to the string resource file:

```
<string name="something_happened">Something happened</string>

<string name="string_literal">This is a string literal.</string>
```

The process also brings up a dialog for customizing the string name and indicating which alternative resource file it should appear in, if any.

The Intention Actions feature can be used in layout files with many Android-specific options for performing tasks such as extracting dimensions and strings.

Providing Javadoc-Style Documentation

Regular code comments are useful (when done right). Comments in Javadoc style appear in code completion dialogs and other places, thus making them even more useful. To quickly add Javadoc style comments to a method or class, simply type /**, then press the Enter or Return key, and a Javadoc-style comment block will appear with associated parameter and return attributes already listed.

Resolving Mysterious Build Errors

Occasionally, you might find that Android Studio finds build errors where there were none just moments before. In such a situation, you can try a couple of quick Android Studio tricks.

A first method is to try synchronizing the project to refresh dependencies if there were any changes made to your Gradle script. Simply right-click the project and choose Synchronize "MyApp" or press Ctrl+Alt+Y. This may just work or it may display error messages that help you debug what is wrong when building your project.

Another method you can try is to run the Clean project command. Android Studio runs the make command on the project, and then rebuilds the project.

Summary

In this appendix, you have learned useful tips and techniques for leveraging many powerful features provided with Android Studio. You have learned quite a few tips for organizing your Android Studio IDE. You have also learned useful tricks for writing code for your applications in Java. The many features of Android Studio make developing Android applications a pleasant experience.

Quiz Questions

1. True or false: It is possible to use source control from within the Android Studio.
2. What is the keyboard shortcut for maximizing the editor window within Android Studio?
3. Describe how to view two source-file windows at once.
4. True or false: It is not possible to view two different sections of the same file in two different windows within Android Studio.
5. What is the keyboard shortcut for reformatting Java code?
6. What is the keyboard shortcut for extracting a variable?
7. What is the keyboard shortcut for using `Intention Actions`?

Exercises

1. Practice using the various keyboard shortcuts mentioned throughout this appendix.
2. Use the Android Studio or IntelliJ IDEA documentation or the Internet to discover at least one other useful keyboard shortcut for Android development that was not mentioned in this appendix.
3. Practice rearranging the various UI elements within Android Studio until you are comfortable with your arrangement.

References and More Information

Android Tools: "Android Studio Overview":
   http://d.android.com/tools/studio/index.html
Android Tools: "Android Studio Tips and Tricks":
   http://d.android.com/sdk/installing/studio-tips.html
IntelliJ IDEA Help: "Quick Start":
   https://www.jetbrains.com/idea/help/intellij-idea-quick-start-guide.html
IntelliJ IDEA Help: "Keyboard Shortcuts You Cannot Miss":
   https://www.jetbrains.com/idea/help/keyboard-shortcuts-you-cannot-miss.html
Oracle Java SE Documentation: "How to Write Doc Comments for the Javadoc Tool":
   http://www.oracle.com/technetwork/java/javase/documentation/index-137868.html

B

Quick–Start: Android Emulator

The most useful tool provided with the Android SDK is the emulator. Developers use the emulator to quickly develop Android applications for a variety of hardware. This Quick-Start is not a complete documentation of the emulator commands, but is instead designed to get you up and running with common tasks. Please see the emulator documentation provided with the Android SDK for a complete list of features and commands.

The Android emulator is integrated with Android Studio, or accessible with command-line instructions. The emulator is also available within the `tools/` subdirectory of the Android SDK and you can launch it as a separate process. The best way to launch the emulator is by using the Android Virtual Device Manager. We focus this appendix on using the emulator and Android Virtual Device Manager packaged with Android Studio.

Simulating Reality: The Emulator's Purpose

The Android emulator (see Figure B.1) simulates a real device environment where your applications run. As a developer, you can configure the emulator to closely resemble the devices on which you plan to deploy your applications.

Here are some tips for using the emulator effectively:

- You can use keyboard commands to easily interact with the emulator.
- Mouse clicking within the emulator window works, as do scrolling and dragging. The keyboard arrow buttons also work. Don't forget the side buttons, such as the volume control—these work, too.
- If your computer has an Internet connection, so does your emulator. The browser works. You can toggle networking using the F8 key.
- Different Android platform versions show slightly different underlying user experiences (the basics of the Android operating system) on the emulator. For example, older platform targets have a basic Home screen and use an application drawer to store installed applications, whereas the newer platform versions such as Android Marshmallow and newer use sleeker controls. The emulator uses the basic user interface, which is frequently overridden, or skinned, by manufacturers and carriers.

Figure B.1   An Android emulator showing physical keys without
the system navigation bar.

In other words, the operating system features of the emulator might not match what real users see.

- The Settings application can be useful for managing system settings. You can use the Settings application to configure the user settings available within the emulator, including networking, screen options, and locale options.

- The Dev Tools application can be useful for setting development options. These include many useful tools, from a terminal emulator to a list of installed packages. Additionally, tools for accounts and sync testing are available. JUnit tests can be launched directly from here.

- To switch between portrait and landscape modes of the emulator, use the 7 and 9 keys on the numeric keypad (or the Ctrl+F11 and Ctrl+F12 keys).

- You can use the F6 key to emulate a trackball with your trackball-equipped mouse. This takes over exclusive control of your mouse, so you must use F6 to get control back again.

- For an emulator with physical keys, the Menu button is a context menu for the given screen. Keep in mind that newer devices do not always have the physical keys such as Home, Menu, Back, and Search. Emulator configurations without physical keys will usually display the system navigation bar, which includes navigation controls for Home, Back, and Recents, and pressing and holding the Home control will bring up a Search control.

- Invoke the application lifecycle: To easily stop an application, just press Home (on the emulator) and you'll get onPause() and onStop() Activity lifecycle events. To resume, launch the application again. To pause the application, press the Power button (on the emulator). Only the onPause() method will be called. You'll need to press the Power button a second time to activate the display to be able to unlock the emulator to see the onResume() method call.

- Notifications such as incoming SMS messages appear in the status bar, along with indicators for simulated battery life, signal strength and speed, and so on.

Warning

One of the most important things to remember when working with the emulator is that it is a powerful tool, but it is no substitute for testing on the true target device. The emulator often provides a much more consistent user experience than a physical device, which moves around in the physical world, through tunnels and cell signal dead zones, with many other applications running and sucking down battery and resources. Always budget time and resources to thoroughly exercise your applications on target physical devices and in common situations as part of your testing process.

Working with Android Virtual Devices

The Android emulator is a not a real device, but a generic Android system simulator for testing purposes. Developers can simulate different types of Android devices by creating AVD configurations.

Tip

It can be helpful to think of an AVD as providing the emulator's personality. Without an AVD, an emulator is an empty shell, not unlike a CPU with no attached peripherals.

Using AVD configurations, Android emulators can simulate

- Different device types such as phone, tablet, Android Wear, or Android TV
- Different target platform versions

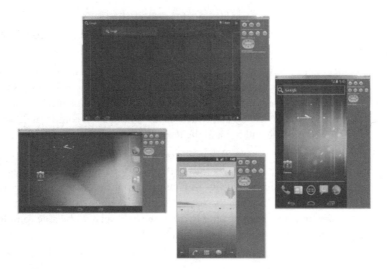

Figure B.2   AVD configurations described in different emulator settings.

- Different input methods
- Different orientations such as portrait, landscape, or both
- Different network types, speeds, and strengths
- Different device skins
- Different emulated performance options
- Different underlying hardware configurations
- Different RAM, VM heap, and internal storage configurations
- Different external storage configurations

Each emulator configuration is unique, as described within its AVD profile, and stores its data persistently, including installed applications, modified settings, and the contents of its emulated SD card. A number of emulator instances with different AVD configurations are shown in Figure B.2.

Using the Android Virtual Device Manager

To run an application in the Android emulator, you must configure an Android Virtual Device (AVD). To create and manage AVDs, you can use the Android Virtual Device Manager from within Android Studio, or use the `android` command-line tool provided with the Android SDK in the `tools/` subdirectory. Each AVD configuration contains important information describing a specific type of Android device, including the following:

- The friendly, descriptive name for the configuration
- The target Android platform version

- The screen size, density, and resolution
- Hardware configuration details and features, including how much RAM is available, which input methods exist, and optional hardware details such as camera support
- Simulated external storage (virtual SD cards)

Creating an AVD

Follow these steps to create an AVD configuration within Android Studio:

1. Launch the Android Virtual Device Manager from within Android Studio by clicking the little green Android device icon ( ) on the toolbar. You can also launch it by selecting `Tools`, `Android`, and then `AVD Manager` from the Android Studio menu.

2. If there are no configured AVDs on your system, you will be presented with a screen to create virtual devices (see Figure B.3). If there are already configured AVDs on your system, they are displayed as a list inside the Android Virtual Device Manager (see Figure B.4).

3. Click the `Create a virtual device` button (see Figure B.3) or the `Create Virtual Device` button (see Figure B.4) to create a new AVD.

4. Choose a Device definition for the AVD (see Figure B.5). In this case, we can choose the `Nexus 5, 4.95", 1080 × 1920, xxhdpi` device from the device options of the `Phone` category and then click `Next`.

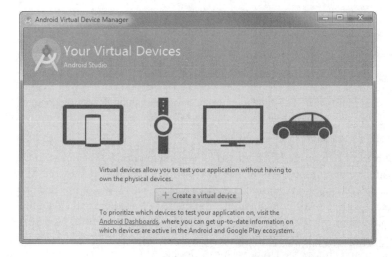

Figure B.3   No configured AVD's on the system.

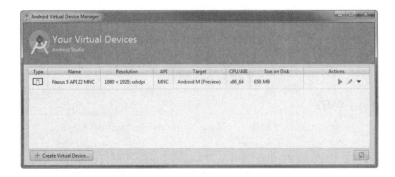

Figure B.4   An already configured AVD on the system.

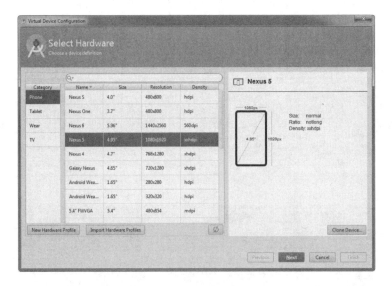

Figure B.5   Selecting a hardware device definition, Nexus 5 phone,
for the AVD.

5. Select a system image (see Figure B.6). This represents the version of the Android
   platform running on the emulator. The platform is represented by the API level. For
   example, to support Android 5.1.1 API Level 22, select one of the Lollipop release
   names with the ABI you would like to target, such as x86 or x86_64. However, this
   is also where you decide whether or not to include the optional Google APIs. If
   your application relies on the Maps application and other Google Android services,
   you should choose the target with the Google APIs. For a complete list of API levels
   and which Android platforms they represent, see *http://d.android.com/guide/topics/*

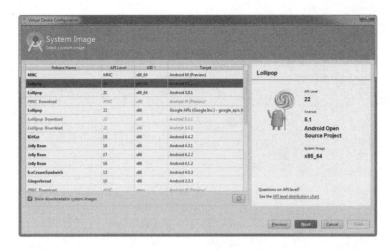

Figure B.6   Selecting a system image for the AVD, showing both
downloaded and available for download system images.

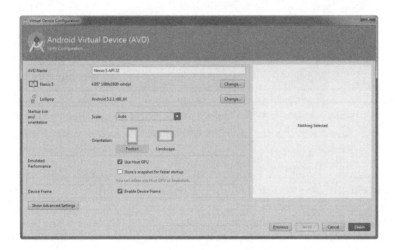

Figure B.7   A sample AVD configuration with basic settings configured
before creation.

manifest/uses-sdk-element.html#ApiLevels. Once you have selected your system image, click `Next`.

6. Choose a name for the AVD (see Figure B.7). If you are trying to simulate a specific device, you might want to name it as such. For example, a name such as `Nexus 5 API 22` might refer to an AVD that simulates the Nexus 5 running the Android 5.1.1 platform. Click the `Show Advanced Settings` button.

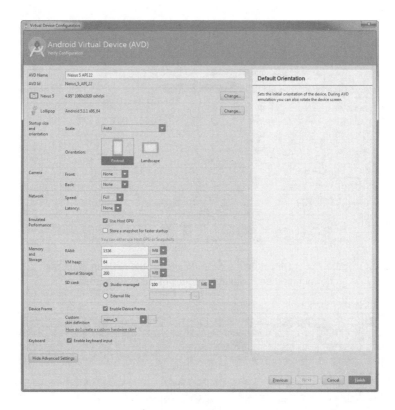

Figure B.8   A sample AVD configuration with advanced settings configured
before creation.

7. The advanced settings (see Figure B.8) are where you can configure or modify other
hardware characteristics that you would like enabled or disabled. If your application
will be using a front and/or back camera, you may choose to emulate these cameras
or, provided your host computer has camera hardware, you may attach them to your
AVD. You may also configure network settings and latency to simulate the speed of
the devices' network transfer rate. You may also configure memory and storage options, such as RAM, VM heap, internal storage space, and SD card capacity. Each SD
card image takes up space on your hard drive and takes a long time to generate; don't
make your card capacities too large, or they will hog your hard drive space. The minimum is 10MB. Choose a reasonable size, such as 1024MB or less. Just make sure you
have adequate disk space on your development computer and choose an appropriate
size for your testing needs. If you're dealing with large files within your application,
you may need to allocate much more capacity than the default. If you want to disal-
low using your host computer's hardware keyboard, or remove the skin and hardware
controls when running the emulator, you may deselect the default options.

8. Continue to configure or modify any other hardware characteristics that you would like enabled or disabled. We have found it easier to keep these options enabled. There are also Emulated Performance options you should consider enabling: `Store a snapshot for faster startup` or `Use Host GPU`. The snapshot setting eliminates the wait time for launching an AVD by persisting the AVD's state between executions, and the GPU setting leverages the host's graphics processor for rendering OpenGL ES within the AVD. Note that you are only able to choose one or the other, not both at the same time. `Use Host GPU` is the default option selected.

9. Once you have configured your AVD, click the `Finish` button and wait for the operation to complete. Because the Android Virtual Device Manager formats the memory allocated for SD card images, creating an AVD configuration sometimes takes a few moments.

Creating AVDs with Custom Hardware Settings

As mentioned earlier, you can choose specific hardware configuration settings within your AVD configurations. You need to know what the default settings are to determine whether you need to override them. Some of the hardware options available are shown in Table B.1.

Tip

You can save time, money, and a lot of grief by spending a bit of time up front configuring AVDs that closely match the hardware on which your application will run. Share the specific settings with your fellow developers and testers. We often create device-specific AVDs and name them after the device.

Table B.1 **Important Hardware Profile Options**

Hardware Property Option	Description	Default Value
Device RAM size `hw.ramSize`	Physical RAM on the device, in megabytes	96
Touchscreen support `hw.touchScreen`	Touchscreen exists on the device	Yes
Trackball support `hw.trackBall`	Trackball exists on the device	Yes
Keyboard support `hw.keyboard`	QWERTY keyboard exists on the device	Yes
GPU emulation `hw.gpu.enabled`	Emulate OpenGL ES GPU	Yes

(Continues)

Table B.1 **Continued**

Hardware Property Option	Description	Default Value
D-pad support `hw.dPad`	Directional pad exists on the device	Yes
GSM modem support `hw.gsmModem`	GSM modem exists on the device	Yes
Camera support `hw.camera`	Camera exists on the device	No

Camera pixels (horizontal)
`hw.camera.`
`maxHorizontalPixels`
	Maximum horizontal camera pixels	640

Camera pixels (vertical)
`hw.camera.`
`maxVerticalPixels`
	Maximum vertical camera pixels	480

GPS support `hw.gps`	GPS exists on the device	Yes
Battery support `hw.battery`	Device can run on a battery	Yes
Accelerometer support `hw.accelerometer`	Accelerometer exists on the device	Yes
Audio recording support `hw.audioInput`	Device can record audio	Yes
Audio playback support `hw.audioOutput`	Device can play audio	Yes
SD card support `hw.sdCard`	Device supports removable SD card	Yes
Cache partition support `disk.cachePartition`	Device supports cache partition	Yes
Cache partition size `disk.cachePartition.size`	Device cache partition size in megabytes	66MB
Abstracted LCD density `hw.lcd.density`	Generalized screen density	160

Launching the Emulator with a Specific AVD

After you have configured the AVD you want to use, you are ready to launch the emulator. Although there are a number of ways to do this, here are four methods you will likely use on a regular basis:

- From within Android Studio, you can configure the application's `Run/Debug` configurations to use a specific AVD.
- From within Android Studio, you can configure the application's `Run/Debug` configurations to enable the developer to choose an AVD manually upon launch from a chooser dialog.

- From within Android Studio, you can launch an emulator directly from within the Android Virtual Device Manager.
- The emulator is available within the `tools/` directory of the Android SDK and can be launched as a separate process from the command-line (generally necessary only if you are not using Android Studio).

Maintaining Emulator Performance

The Android emulator is slow if you do not choose any special configuration options when setting up your virtual devices or if you do not follow well-known tricks. That said, here are a few tips that will help ensure the best and speediest emulator experience possible:

- Enable the `Store a snapshot for faster startup` feature in your AVD. Then, before you start using your AVD, launch it once, let it boot up, and shut it down to set a baseline snapshot. This is especially important with the newest platform versions such as Jelly Bean. Subsequent launches will be faster and more stable. You can even turn off saving a new snapshot to speed up exiting and turn on `Use Host GPU`, and it will continue to use the old snapshot while the responsiveness of the emulator instance will be faster because the GPU is now helping to improve the performance of the emulator instance.
- Launch your emulator instances before you need them, such as when you first launch Android Studio, so that when you're ready to debug, they're already running.
- Keep the emulator running in the background between debugging sessions in order to quickly install, reinstall, and debug your applications. This saves valuable minutes of waiting for the emulator to boot up. Instead, simply launch the `Debug` configuration from Android Studio and the debugger reattaches.
- Keep in mind that application performance is much slower when the debugger is attached. This applies to both running in the emulator and on a device.
- If you've been using an emulator for testing many apps, or just need a very clean environment, consider re-creating the AVD from scratch. This will give you a new environment clean of any past changes or modifications. This can help speed up the emulator, too, if you have lots of apps installed.

Tip

If your development machine has an Intel processor that supports hardware Virtualization Technology (VT), you can take advantage of a special Android emulator system image that Intel provides to further speed up your development environment. When installing Android Studio, make sure to install the Intel Hardware Accelerated Execution Manager (Intel HAXM) and then download any Intel x86 or x86_64 Atom system images you might need using the Android SDK Manager. The emulator will be accelerated using your development machine's CPU hardware. To learn more about configuring virtual machine acceleration, see the following URL: *http://d.android.com/tools/devices/emulator.html#acceleration*.

Launching an Emulator to Run an Application

The most common way to launch the emulator involves launching a specific emulator instance with a specific AVD configuration, either through the Android Virtual Device Manager or by choosing a specific emulator in the Run/Debug Configurations options for your project in Android Studio and installing or reinstalling the latest incarnation of your application.

The default Run/Debug Configurations available when you first created your application might look something like Figure B.9, which includes a single module named app.

Tip

Remember that you can create multiple Run/Debug Configurations for different application modules, each with different options, using different startup options and even different AVDs.

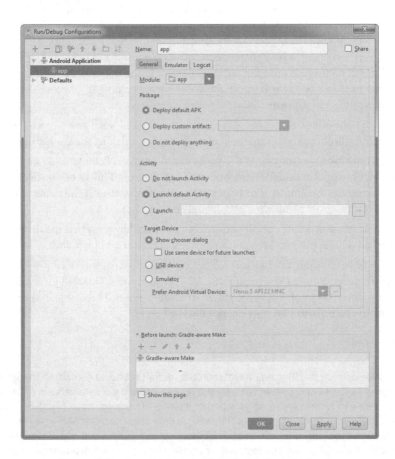

Figure B.9   A run/debug configuration in Android Studio.

To edit an existing run/debug configuration, or to create a new run/debug configuration for a specific project within Android Studio, take the following steps:

1. Choose `Run, Edit Configurations` or click the default project configuration, usually named `app` unless you provided a different name at project creation, and choose `Edit Configurations` (see Figure B.10).

2. On the `Run/Debug Configurations` dialog, select the configuration you would like to edit (see Figure B.11, left), or to create a new configuration, click the `Add New Configuration` symbol (⊞) or press `Alt+Insert` and select `Android Application` (see Figure B.11, right).

Figure B.10   Accessing the run/debug configuration settings from the `Edit Configurations` drop-down of the default `app` module in Android Studio.

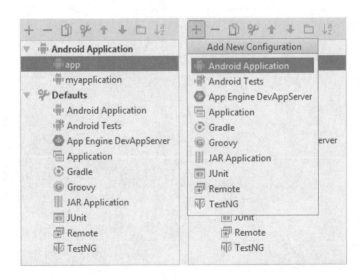

Figure B.11   Listing the existing run/debug configurations (left) and adding a new `Android Application` run/debug configuration (right).

3. Name your run/debug configuration.

4. Select the appropriate `Module` if your project has more than one.

5. In the `Target Device` settings, choose an appropriate option. Either select the `Show chooser dialog` option, which will allow you to choose from a list of running devices, hardware or Emulator, or allow you to launch an emulator; or select the `USB device` option, which will launch your application on connected USB devices; or select the `Emulator` option and then choose a specific AVD by selecting one from the `Prefer Android Virtual Device` drop-down to use with the emulator (only those matching your application's target SDK are available from the drop-down).

6. Configure any emulator startup options on the `Emulator` tab (Figure B.12). You can enter any options not specifically configured for the emulator on the tab as normal command-line options in the `Additional command line options` field. The Android

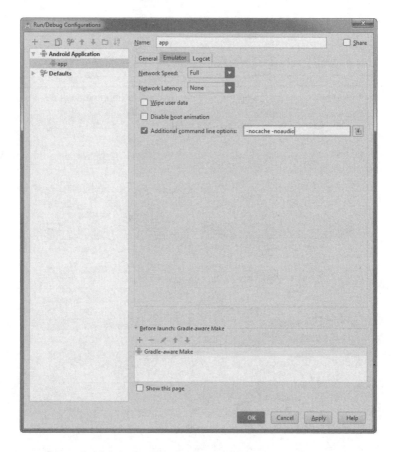

Figure B.12   Configuring emulator command-line options from
the `Emulator` tab of the `Run/Debug Configurations` settings of
Android Studio.

emulator has a number of configuration options above and beyond those set in the AVD profile. Make sure the box for `Additional command line options` is checked and enter the options you need in the text box to the right. You may also set these options when the emulator is launched from the command-line. Some emulator startup settings include numerous disk image, debug, media, network, system, UI, and help settings. For a complete list of emulator startup options, consult the Android emulator documentation: *http://d.android.com/tools/help/emulator.html#startup-options*.

7. The `Logcat` tab (see Figure B.13) of the `Run/Debug Configurations` settings allows you to select or deselect particular options for controlling the behavior of Logcat while you run/debug your application. At the time of this writing, there are only three options available for selecting, as seen in Figure B.13. As you become more comfortable with these default settings, feel free to experiment with their different options to see what works best for you.

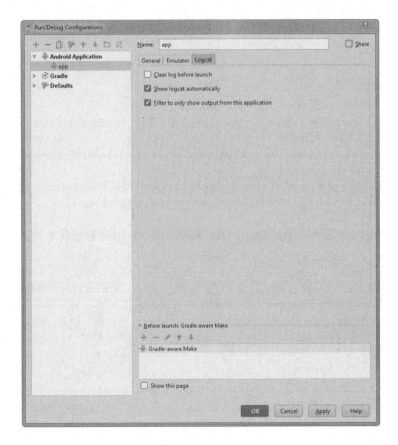

Figure B.13   Configuring options on the `Logcat` tab of the `Run/Debug Configurations` settings of Android Studio.

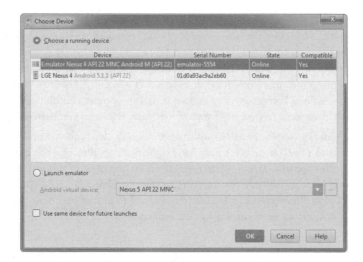

Figure B.14   The device chooser with an emulator and a USB device
running.

You can create multiple run/debug configurations as outlined above. If you set a specific AVD for use in the `Target Device` settings, that AVD is used with the emulator
whenever you debug your application in Android Studio. However, if you select the `Show
chooser dialog` option, you are prompted to select from a list of USB devices or running
emulators in the device chooser when you first try to debug the application, as shown in
Figure B.14. After you have launched the application for installation, Android Studio pairs
the device with your project for the duration of your debugging session.

Launching an Emulator from the Android Virtual Device Manager

Sometimes you just want to launch an emulator on the fly—for example, to have a second
emulator running to interact with your first emulator to simulate calls, text messages, and
such. In this case, you can simply launch it from the Android Virtual Device Manager. To
do this, take the following steps:

1. Launch the Android Virtual Device Manager from within Android Studio (🖳) on
   the toolbar. You can also launch it by selecting `Tools`, `AVD Manager` from the Android Studio menu.

2. Select an existing AVD configuration from the list or create a new AVD that
   matches your requirements.

3. Hit the `Launch` button (▶). The emulator now launches with the AVD you
   requested.

Warning

You cannot run multiple instances of the same AVD configuration simultaneously. If you think about it, this makes sense because the AVD configuration keeps the state and persistent data. If you need more than one of the same configurations running simultaneously, create different AVDs with the same configuration.

Configuring the GPS Location of the Emulator

To develop and test applications that use Google Maps support with location-based services, you need to create an AVD with a target that includes the Google APIs. After you have created the appropriate AVD and launched the emulator, you need to configure its location. The emulator does not have location sensors, so the first thing you need to do is seed your emulator with GPS coordinates.

To configure your emulator with pretend coordinates, launch your emulator (if it is not already running) with an AVD supporting the Google APIs and follow the steps described below.

In the emulator:

1. Press the Home button to return to the Home screen if you are not already there.
2. Find and launch the Maps application.
3. If this is the first time you've launched the Maps application, click through the various startup dialogs.
4. Choose the My Location floating action button (see Figure B.15) and enable location on the device if it is not already enabled.

In Android Studio:

1. Click the Android Device Monitor icon on the toolbar of Android Studio and wait for Device Monitor to launch.

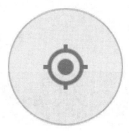

Figure B.15   The Maps application's My Location floating action button.

2. In Device Monitor, make sure your device is selected in the Devices pane.

3. You should see an Emulator Control pane on the upper-right side, so make this the active pane. Scroll down to the Location Controls.

4. Manually enter the longitude and latitude of your location. Note that they are in reverse order. For example, Yosemite National Park has the coordinates Longitude: –119.532836 and Latitude: 37.992920.

5. Click Send.

Back in the emulator, notice that the map now shows the location you seeded. Your screen should display your location as Yosemite National Park, as shown in Figure B.16. This location persists across emulator launches.

You can also use GPX 1.1 coordinate files to send a series of GPS locations through Device Monitor to the emulator, if you prefer. GPX 1.0 files are not supported by Device Monitor.

Tip

Wondering where we got the coordinates for Yosemite? To find a specific set of coordinates for use, you can go to *http://maps.google.com*. Navigate to the location for which you want the coordinates. Next, right-click the location and choose "What's here?" The latitude and longitude will be placed near the search field.

Figure B.16   Setting the location of the emulator to Yosemite National Park.

Calling between Two Emulator Instances

You can have two emulator instances call each other using the `Dialer` application provided on the emulator. The emulator's "phone number" is its port number, which can be found in the title bar of the emulator window. To simulate a phone call between two emulators, you must perform the following steps:

1. Launch two different AVDs so two emulators are running simultaneously. (Using the Android AVD and SDK Manager is easiest.)
2. Note the port number of the emulator you want to receive the call.
3. In the emulator that makes the call, launch the `Dialer` application.
4. Type the port number you noted as the number to call. Press Enter (or Send).
5. You see (and hear) an incoming call on the receiving emulator instance. Figure B.17 shows an emulator with port 5554 (left) using the `Dialer` application to call the emulator on port 5556 (right).
6. Answer the incoming call by pressing Answer.
7. Pretend to chat for a bit. Figure B.18 shows a call in progress.
8. You can end either emulator call at any time by pressing the End key.

Figure B.17 Simulating a phone call between two emulators.

Figure B.18   Two emulators with a phone call in progress.

Messaging between Two Emulator Instances

You can send SMS messages between two emulators, exactly as previously described for simulating calls, by using the emulator port numbers as SMS addresses. To simulate a text message between two emulators, you must perform the following steps:

1. Launch two instances of the emulator.

2. Note the port number of the emulator you want to receive the text message.

3. In the emulator that sends the text, launch the `Messaging` application.

4. Type the port number you noted as the "To" field for the text message. Enter a text message, as shown in Figure B.19 (left). Press the `Send` button.

5. You see (and hear) an incoming text message on the receiving emulator instance. Figure B.19 (center) shows an emulator with port 5556 receiving a text message from the emulator on port 5554 (left).

6. View the text message by pulling down the `status bar` or launching the `Messaging` app.

7. Pretend to chat for a bit. Figure B.19 (right) shows a text message conversation in progress.

Figure B.19   Emulator at port 5554 (left) crafting a text message to send to another emulator at port 5556 (center and right).

Interacting with the Emulator through the Console

In addition to using Device Monitor to interact with the emulator, you can also connect directly to the Emulator console using a Telnet connection and then issuing commands. For example, to connect to the Emulator console of the emulator using port 5554, you would do the following:

```
telnet localhost 5554
```

You can use the Emulator console to issue commands to the emulator. To end the session, just type quit or exit. You can shut down this instance of the emulator using the kill command.

Warning

You may need to enable Telnet on your system in order to proceed through the following sections if this has not already been done.

Using the Console to Simulate Incoming Calls

You can simulate incoming calls to the emulator from specified numbers. The console command for issuing an incoming call is shown here:

```
gsm call <number>
```

Figure B.20   Incoming call from 521-5556 (configured as a contact named
Anne Droid), prompted via the Emulator console.

For example, to simulate an incoming call from the number 521-5556, you would issue
the following console command:

```
gsm call 5215556
```

The result of this command in the emulator is shown in Figure B.20. The name "Anne
Droid" shows up because we have an entry in the Contacts database that ties the phone
number 521-5556 to a contact named Anne Droid.

Using the Console to Simulate SMS Messages

You can simulate SMS messages to the emulator from specified numbers as well, just as
you can from Device Monitor. The command for issuing an incoming SMS is shown
here:

```
sms send <number> <message>
```

For example, to simulate an incoming SMS from the number 521-5556, you would
issue the following command:

```
sms send 5215556 What's up!
```

Figure B.21   An incoming SMS in the status bar from 521-5556 (configured as a contact named Anne Droid) is prompted via the Emulator console. The left image shows the SMS arrival with the SMS icon smiley face in the status bar, and the right image shows the incoming message as a notification.

In the emulator, you get a notification on the far left of the `status bar` informing you of a new SMS message. You can pull down the `status bar` to see the new message or launch the `Messaging` application. The result of the preceding command in the emulator is shown in Figure B.21.

Using the Console to Send GPS Coordinates

You can use the Emulator console to issue GPS commands to the emulator. The command for a simple GPS fix is shown here:

```
geo fix <longitude> <latitude> [<altitude>]
```

For instance, to set the fix for the emulator to the top of Mount Everest, launch the `Maps` application in the emulator by selecting `All Apps`, `Maps`, `My Location`. Then, within the Emulator console, issue the following command to set the device's coordinates appropriately:

```
geo fix 86.929837 27.99003 8850
```

Using the Console to Monitor Network Status

You can monitor the network status of the emulator and change the network speed and latency on the fly. The command for displaying network status is shown here:

```
network status
```

Typical results from this request look something like this:

```
Current network status:
  download speed:        0 bits/s (0.0 KB/s)
  upload speed:          0 bits/s (0.0 KB/s)
  minimum latency: 0 ms
  maximum latency: 0 ms
OK
```

Using the Console to Manipulate Power Settings

You can manage "fake" power settings on the emulator using the power commands. You can turn the battery capacity to 99% charged as follows:

```
power capacity 99
```

You can turn the AC charging state to off (or on) as follows:

```
power ac off
```

You can turn the battery status to the options unknown, charging, discharging, not-charging, or full as follows:

```
power status full
```

You can turn the battery present state to true (or false) as follows:

```
power present true
```

You can turn the battery health state to the options unknown, good, overheat, dead, overvoltage, or failure as follows:

```
power health good
```

You can show the current power settings by issuing the following command:

```
power display
```

Typical results from this request look something like this:

```
AC: offline
status: Full
```

```
health: Good
present: true
capacity: 99
OK
```

Using Other Console Commands

There are also commands for simulating hardware events, port redirection, and checking, starting, and stopping the virtual machine. For example, quality assurance personnel will want to check out the event subcommands, which can be used to simulate key events for automation purposes. It's likely this is the same interface used by the UI/Application Exerciser Monkey, which presses random keys and tries to crash your application.

Personalizing the Emulator

Here are a few more tips for using the emulator, just for fun:

- On the Home screen, press and hold the screen to change the wallpaper.
- If you press and hold an icon (usually an application icon) from within the All Apps launcher, you can place a shortcut to it on your Home screen for easy access. Newer platform versions also enable other options, such as uninstalling the application or getting more information, which is very handy.
- If you press and hold an icon on your Home screen, you can move it around or dump it into the trash to get it off the screen.
- Press and fling the device's Home screen to the left and right for more space. Depending on which version of Android you're running, you find a number of other pages, with App Widgets such as Google Search and lots of empty space where you can place other Home screen items.
- A way to add widgets to your Home screen is to launch the All Apps screen, then navigate to Widgets. There are many different widgets available, and selecting one is how you can add those widgets to your Home screen, as shown in Figure B.22.

In other words, the emulator can be personalized in many of the same ways as a regular device. Making these types of changes can be useful for comprehensive application testing.

Understanding Emulator Limitations

The emulator is powerful, but it has several important limitations:

- It is not a device, so it does not reflect actual behavior, only simulated behavior. Simulated behavior is generally more consistent (less random) than what users experience in real life on real devices.

Figure B.22   Customizing the emulator Home screen by adding the Home
screen tips App Widget.

- It simulates phone calls and messaging, but you cannot place or receive true calls or SMS messages. There is no support for MMS.
- It has a limited ability to determine device state (network state, battery charge).
- It has a limited ability to simulate peripherals (headphones, sensor data).
- There is limited API support (for example, no SIP or third-party hardware API support). When developing certain categories of applications, such as augmented reality applications, 3D games, and applications that rely on sensor data, you're better off using the real hardware.
- Performance is limited (modern devices often perform much better than the emulator at many tasks, such as video and animation).
- There is limited support for manufacturer- or operator-specific device characteristics, themes, or user experiences. Some manufacturers have provided emulator add-ons to more closely mimic the behavior of specific devices.
- On Android 4.0 and later, the emulator can use attached Web cameras to emulate device hardware cameras. On previous versions of the tools, the camera would respond but took fake pictures.
- There is no USB, Bluetooth, or NFC support.

Summary

In this appendix, you learned about one of the most useful tools incorporated with the Android SDK, the Android emulator. The Android emulator is available as part of Android Studio and is also available from the command-line. The emulator is an effective development tool for simulating real devices. When your application requires testing on many different device configurations, rather than purchasing every device you would like to support, the Android Virtual Device Manager allows for varying emulator configurations, making testing cost-effective. Even though the emulator has limitations and is not meant to be a replacement for testing on real hardware, you have learned much of what the emulator has to offer and have discovered firsthand just how close to reality the emulator performs.

Quiz Questions

1. What is the keyboard shortcut to toggle networking of an emulator?
2. What is the keyboard shortcut for toggling between portrait and landscape modes?
3. What is the keyboard shortcut for emulating a trackball with your mouse?
4. Which `Activity` lifecycle events does pressing the `Home` key invoke?
5. What is the hardware configuration property for supporting GPU emulation within your AVD configurations?
6. What is the command for connecting to an emulator from the console?
7. What is the command for a simple GPS fix?

Exercises

1. Using the Android documentation, devise a list of the Android emulator category command-line parameters.
2. Using the Android documentation, name the command-line option for enabling GPU emulation.
3. Using the Android documentation, design a command for creating an AVD from the command-line.

References and More Information

Android Tools: "Managing Virtual Devices":
   http://d.android.com/tools/devices/index.html
Android Tools: "Managing AVDs with AVD Manager":
   http://d.android.com/tools/devices/managing-avds.html
Android Tools: "Managing AVDs from the Command Line":
   http://d.android.com/tools/devices/managing-avds-cmdline.html

Android Tools: "Android Emulator":
  http://d.android.com/tools/help/emulator.html
Android Tools: "Using the Emulator":
  http://d.android.com/tools/devices/emulator.html
Android Tools: "android":
  http://d.android.com/tools/help/android.html

C

Quick-Start:
Android **Device Monitor**

The Android `Device Monitor` is a debugging tool provided with the Android SDK. Developers use `Device Monitor` to provide a window into the emulator or the actual device for debugging purposes as well as for file and process management. It's a blend of several tools: a task manager, a profiler, a file explorer, an emulator console, and a logging console. This Quick-Start is not a complete documentation of `Device Monitor` functionality. Instead, it is designed to get you up and running with common tasks. See the `Device Monitor` documentation provided with the Android SDK for a complete list of features.

Using `Device Monitor` with Android Studio and as a Stand-Alone Application

If you use Android Studio, the `Device Monitor` tool is integrated with your development environment. You are able to launch `Device Monitor` by clicking the Android icon ( ) found on the toolbar. By using `Device Monitor` integrated with Android Studio (shown in Figure C.1, using the `File Explorer` to browse files on the emulator instance), you can explore any emulator instances running on the development machine and any Android devices connected via USB.

If you're not using Android Studio, the `Device Monitor` tool is also available within the `tools/` directory of the Android SDK, and you can launch it as a separate application by running the `monitor` command, in which case it runs in its own process.

> **Tip**
>
> There should be only one instance of `Device Monitor` running at a given time. Other `Device Monitor` launches are ignored; if you have `Device Monitor` running from Android Studio and try to launch `Device Monitor` from the command-line, you might see question marks instead of process names, and you will see debug output stating that the instance of `Device Monitor` is being ignored.

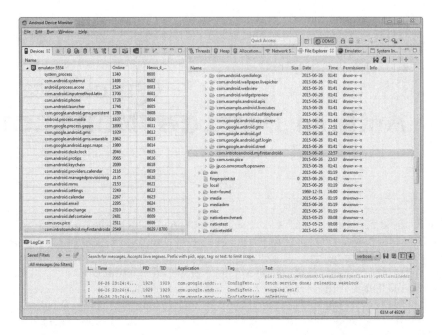

Figure C.1   After launching `Device Monitor` from Android Studio, with one emulator connected.

Warning

Not all `Device Monitor` features are available for both emulators and devices. Certain features, such as the `Emulator Control` features, are available only for emulators. Most devices are more secure than the emulator. Thus, the `File Explorer` may be limited to just public areas of the device, unlike on the emulator.

Getting Up to Speed Using Key Features of `Device Monitor`

Whether you use `Device Monitor` from Android Studio or as a stand-alone tool, be aware of a few key features:

- The `Devices` pane displays running emulators and connected devices in the top-left corner.
- The set of `Threads`, `Heap`, `Allocation Tracker`, `Network Statistics`, `File Explorer`, and `System Information` tabs on the right side are populated with data when a specific process on an emulator or device is highlighted in the `Devices` pane.

- The `Emulator Control` pane provides features such as the ability to send GPS information and to simulate incoming calls and SMS messages to emulators.

- The `LogCat` window enables you to monitor the output of the Android logging console for a given device or emulator. This is where calls to `Log.i()`, `Log.e()`, and other log messages display.

Now let's look at how to use each of these `Device Monitor` features in more detail.

Tip

`Device Monitor` has another viewing perspective that provides direct access to the Hierarchy Viewer tool, which can be used for debugging and performance-tuning your application's user interface. You can open this perspective by choosing `Window, Open Perspective...`. See Appendix D, "Mastery: Android SDK Tools," for more details about this tool.

Working with Processes, Threads, and the Heap

One of the most useful features of `Device Monitor` is the ability to interact with processes. Each Android application runs in its own VM with its own user ID on the operating system. Using the `Devices` pane of `Device Monitor`, you can browse all instances of the VM running on a device, each identified by its package name. For example, you can perform the following tasks:

- Attach and debug applications
- Monitor threads
- Monitor the heap
- Stop processes
- Force garbage collection (GC)

Attaching a Debugger to an Android Application

Although you'll use Android Studio debug configurations to launch and debug your applications most of the time, you can also use `Device Monitor` to choose which application to debug and attach directly. To attach a debugger to a process, you need to have the package source code open in your Android Studio workspace. Now perform the following steps to debug:

1. On the emulator or device, verify that the application you want to debug is running.

2. In `Device Monitor`, find that application's package name in the `Devices` pane and highlight it.

3. Click the little green bug button (![bug]) to debug that application.

4. Switch to the `Debug` perspective of the Android Studio as necessary; debug as you would normally.

Stopping a Process

You can use `Device Monitor` to kill an Android application by following these steps:

1. On the emulator or device, verify that the application you want to stop is running.
2. In `Device Monitor`, find that application's package name in the `Devices` pane and highlight it.
3. Click the red stop sign button (▣) to stop that process.

Monitoring Thread Activity of an Android Application

You can use `Device Monitor` to monitor thread activity of an individual Android application by following these steps:

1. On the emulator or device, verify that the application you want to monitor is running.
2. In `Device Monitor`, find that application's package name in the `Devices` pane and highlight it.
3. Click the button with three black arrows (▦) to display the threads of that application. They appear in the right portion of the `Threads` pane.
4. On the `Threads` pane, you can choose a specific thread and click the `Refresh` button to drill down within that thread. The resulting classes in use display below.

Note
You can also start thread profiling using the button with three black arrows and a red dot (▦).

For example, in Figure C.2, we see the `Threads` pane contents for the package named `com.introtoandroid.myfirstandroidapp` running on the emulator.

Monitoring Heap Activity

You can use `Device Monitor` to monitor the heap statistics of an individual Android application. The heap statistics are updated after every garbage collection (GC) via these steps:

1. On the emulator or device, verify that the application you want to monitor is running.
2. In `Device Monitor`, find that application's package name in the `Devices` pane and highlight it.

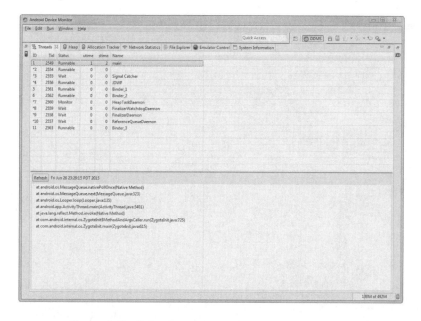

Figure C.2   Using the Device Monitor Threads pane.

3. Click the green cylinder button ( ) to display the heap information for that application. The statistics appear in the Heap pane. This data updates after every GC. You can also cause GC operations from the Heap pane using the button Cause GC.

4. On the Heap pane, you can choose a specific type of object. The resulting graph in use displays at the bottom of the Heap pane, as shown in Figure C.3.

Tip

When using the Allocation Tracker and Heap monitor, keep in mind that not all the memory your app uses will be accounted for in this view. This tool shows the allocations within the Dalvik VM. Some calls allocate memory on the native heap. For example, many image manipulation calls in the SDK will result in memory allocated natively and will not show up in this view.

Prompting Garbage Collection

You can use Device Monitor to force GC to run by following these steps:

1. On the emulator or device, verify that the application you want to run GC for is running.

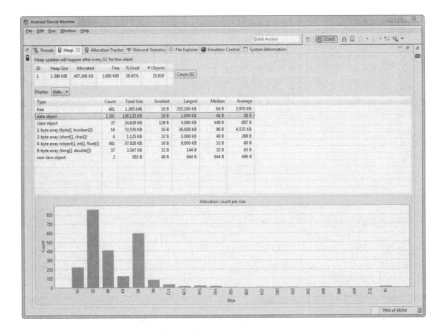

Figure C.3   Using the `Device Monitor Heap` pane.

2. In `Device Monitor`, find that application's package name in the `Devices` pane and highlight it.

3. Click the garbage can button (🗑) to cause GC to run for the application. The results can be viewed in the `Heap` pane.

Creating and Using an HPROF File

`HPROF` files can be used to inspect the heap and for profiling and performance purposes. You can use `Device Monitor` to create an `HPROF` file for your application by following these steps:

1. On the emulator or device, verify that the application you want the `HPROF` data for is running.

2. In `Device Monitor`, find that application's package name in the `Devices` pane and highlight it.

3. Click the `HPROF` button (📲) to create an `HPROF` dump to be generated for the application. The files will be generated in the `captures/` directory, which is located inside the root directory of your application.

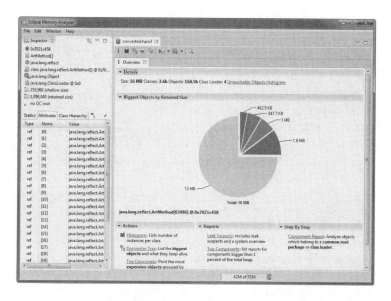

Figure C.4   Using the Memory Analyzer stand-alone tool
to inspect converted `HPROF` profiling information.

Once you have Android-generated `HPROF` data, you can convert it to a standard `HPROF` file format using the Android SDK tool called `hprof-conv`. You can use whichever profiling tool you prefer to examine the information.

For example, in Figure C.4, you can see the converted `HPROF` dump response in the stand-alone tool called Memory Analyzer (mat).

> **Note**
>
> You can generate `HPROF` files in Android using several other methods. For example, you can do it programmatically using the `Debug` class. The `monkey` tool also has options for generating `HPROF` files as it runs. You can also generate `HPROF` files using Android Studio.

Using the `Allocation Tracker`

You can use `Device Monitor` to monitor memory allocated by a specific Android application. The memory allocation statistics are updated on demand by the developer. Follow these steps to track memory allocations:

1. On the emulator or device, verify that the application you want to monitor is running.

2. In `Device Monitor`, find that application's package name in the `Devices` pane and highlight it.

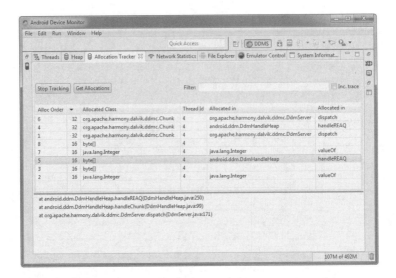

Figure C.5   Using the Device Monitor Allocation Tracker pane.

3. Switch to the Allocation Tracker pane on the right pane.

4. Click the Start Tracking button to start tracking memory allocations and the Get Allocations button to get the allocations at a given time.

5. To stop tracking allocations, click the Stop Tracking button.

For example, in Figure C.5, we see the Allocation Tracker pane contents for an application running on the emulator.

The Android documentation has a brief tutorial on how to capture a heap dump with Device Monitor, including instructions on how to view the heap dump using the Memory Analyzer tool here: *http://d.android.com/tools/debugging/debugging-memory.html#HeapDump*. In addition, the Android developer website has a write-up on memory analysis at *http://android-developers.blogspot.com/2011/03/memory-analysis-for-android.html*.

Viewing Network Statistics

You can use Device Monitor to analyze the network usage of your applications. This tool is useful for providing information about when your application performs network data transfers. The Android class TrafficStats is used to add network statistics analysis code to your application. To distinguish among different types of data transfers in your application, you simply apply a TrafficStats tag in your code before executing the transfer. Knowing network statistics should help you make better decisions about how to optimize your network data transfer code. In Figure C.6, we see the Network Statistics pane contents for a hardware device.

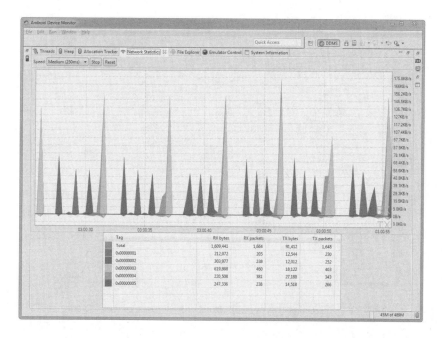

Figure C.6   Using the `Device Monitor Network Statistics` pane.

Working with the `File Explorer`

You can use `Device Monitor` to browse and interact with the Android file system on an emulator or device (although it's somewhat limited on devices without root access). You can access application files, directories, and databases, as well as pull and push files to the Android system, provided you have the appropriate permissions.

For example, in Figure C.7, we see the `File Explorer` pane contents for the emulator.

Browsing the File System of an Emulator or Device

To browse the Android file system, follow these steps:

1. In `Device Monitor`, choose the emulator or device you want to browse in the `Devices` pane.

2. Switch to the `File Explorer` pane. You see a directory hierarchy.

3. Browse to a directory or file location.

Table C.1 shows some important areas of the Android file system. Although the exact directories may vary from device to device, the directories listed are the most common.

Keep in mind that directory listings in the `File Explorer` might take a moment to update when contents change.

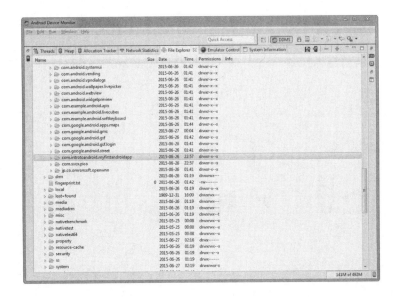

Figure C.7   Using the `Device Monitor File Explorer` pane.

Table C.1 **Important Directories in the Android File System**

Directory	Purpose
`/data/app/`	Where Android APK files are stored.
`/data/data/<packagename>/`	Application top-level directory; for example: `/data/data/com.introtoandroid.myfirstandroidapp/`.
`/data/data/<packagename>/shared_prefs/`	Application shared preferences directory. Named preferences are stored as XML files.
`/data/data/<packagename>/files/`	Application file directory.
`/data/data/<packagename>/cache/`	Application cache directory.
`/data/data/<packagename>/databases/`	Application database directory; for example: `/data/data/com.introtoandroid.pettracker/databases/test.db`.
`/mnt/sdcard/`	External storage (SD card).
`/mnt/sdcard/download/`	Where browser images are saved.

Note

Some device directories, such as the `/data` directory, might not be accessible from the `Device Monitor File Explorer`.

Copying Files from the Emulator or Device

You can use the `File Explorer` to copy files or directories from an emulator or a device file system to your computer by following these steps:

1. Using the `File Explorer`, browse to the file or directory to copy and highlight it.
2. From the top-right corner of the `File Explorer`, click the disk button with the arrow ( ) to pull the file from the device. Alternatively, you can pull down the drop-down menu next to the buttons and choose `Pull File`.
3. Type in the path where you want to save the file or directory on your computer and click `Save`.

Copying Files to the Emulator or Device

You can use the `File Explorer` to copy files to an emulator or a device file system from your computer by following these steps:

1. Using the `File Explorer`, browse to the file or directory to copy and highlight it.
2. From the top-right corner of the `File Explorer`, click the phone button with the arrow ( ) to push a file to the device. Alternatively, you can pull down the drop-down menu next to the buttons and choose `Push File`.
3. Select the file or directory on your computer and click `Open`.

> **Tip**
>
> The `File Explorer` also supports some drag-and-drop operations. This is the only way to push directories to the Android file system; however, copying directories to the Android file system is not recommended because there's no delete option for them. You need to delete directories programmatically if you have the permissions to do so. Alternatively, the `adb` shell can be used with `rmdir`, but you still need permissions. That said, you can drag a file or directory from your computer to the `File Explorer` and drop it in the location you want.

Deleting Files on the Emulator or Device

You can use the `File Explorer` to delete files (one at a time, and not directories) on the emulator or device file system. Follow these steps:

1. Using the `File Explorer`, browse to the file you want to delete and highlight it.
2. In the top-right corner of the `File Explorer`, click the red minus button ( ) to delete the file.

Warning
Be careful. There is no confirmation. The file is deleted immediately and is not recoverable.

Working with the `Emulator Control`

You can use `Device Monitor` to interact with instances of the emulator using the `Emulator Control` pane. You must select the emulator you want to interact with for the `Emulator Control` pane to work. You can use the `Emulator Control` pane to do the following:

- Change telephony status
- Simulate incoming voice calls
- Simulate incoming SMS messages
- Send a location fix (GPS coordinates)

Changing Telephony Status

To simulate changing the telephony status using the `Emulator Control` pane (shown in Figure C.8), use the following steps:

1. In `Device Monitor`, choose the emulator whose telephony status you want to change.

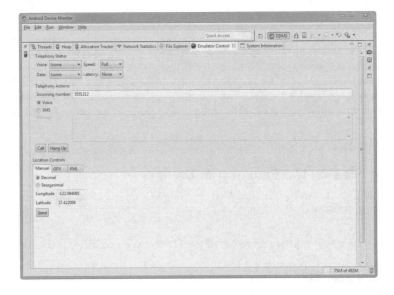

Figure C.8   Using the `Device Monitor Emulator Control` pane.

2. Switch to the `Emulator Control` pane. You work with the `Telephony Status`.

3. Select the desired options from `Voice`, `Speed`, `Data`, and `Latency`.

4. For example, when changing the `Data` option from `Home` to `Roaming`, you should see a notification in the `status bar` that the device is now in roaming mode.

Simulating Incoming Voice Calls

To simulate an incoming voice call using the `Emulator Control` pane (shown in Figure C.8), use the following steps:

1. In `Device Monitor`, choose the emulator you want to call in the `Devices` pane.

2. Switch to the `Emulator Control` pane. You work with the `Telephony Actions`.

3. Input the incoming phone number. This can include only numbers, +, and #.

4. Select the `Voice` radio button.

5. Click the `Send` button.

6. In the emulator, your phone is ringing. Answer the call.

7. The emulator can end the call as normal, or you can end the call in `Device Monitor` using the `Hang Up` button.

Simulating Incoming SMS Messages

`Device Monitor` provides the most stable method for sending incoming SMS messages to the emulator. You send an SMS much as you initiated the voice call. To simulate an incoming SMS message using the `Emulator Control` pane (shown in Figure C.8, top), use the following steps:

1. In `Device Monitor`, choose the emulator you want to send a message to in the `Devices` pane.

2. Switch to the `Emulator Control` pane. You work with the `Telephony Actions`.

3. Input the incoming phone number. This may include only numbers, +, and #.

4. Select the `SMS` radio button.

5. Type in your SMS message.

6. Click the `Send` button.

7. Over in the emulator, you receive an SMS notification.

Sending a Location Fix

The steps for sending GPS coordinates to the emulator are covered in Appendix B, "Quick-Start: Android Emulator." Simply input the GPS information into the `Emulator Control` pane (shown in Figure C.8, bottom), click `Send`, and use the `Maps` application on the emulator to get the current position.

Working with the `System Information` Pane

You can use `Device Monitor` to analyze the system information of instances of the emulator using the `System Information` pane. You must select the emulator you want to analyze for the `System Information` pane to work. You can use the `System Information` pane as shown here:

1. In `Device Monitor`, choose the emulator or device you want to analyze.

2. Switch to the `System Information` pane.

3. Select from the drop-down the type of `System Information` you are interested in analyzing.

4. If the screen is blank, you may need to click the `Update from Device` button.

5. You should now see a chart displaying the `System Information`, as shown in Figure C.9.

Taking Screen Captures of the Emulator and Device Screens

You can take screen captures of the emulator and the device from `Device Monitor`. The device captures are most useful for debugging, and this makes the `Device Monitor` tool

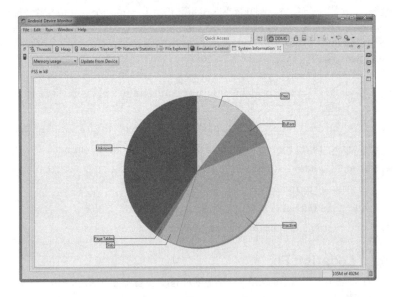

Figure C.9 Using the `Device Monitor` `System Information` pane.

appropriate for quality assurance personnel and developers. To capture a screenshot, take the following steps:

1. In `Device Monitor`, choose the emulator or device you want to capture in the `Devices` pane.

2. On the device or emulator, make sure you have the screen you want to capture.

3. Click the multicolored square picture button (🖼) to take a screen capture. A capture window launches, as shown in Figure C.10.

4. Within the capture window, click the `Save` button to save the screen capture. Similarly, the `Copy` button stores the screenshot in your clipboard, the `Refresh` button updates the screenshot if the underlying device or emulator screen has changed since you launched the capture window, and the `Rotate` button rotates the screenshot 90 degrees.

Working with Application Logging

The `LogCat` tool is integrated into `Device Monitor`. It is provided as a pane along the bottom of the `Device Monitor` user interface. You can control how much information displays by choosing an option from the log type filter drop-down. The default option is verbose (show everything). The other options correspond to `debug`, `info`, `warn`, `error`,

Figure C.10   Using `Device Monitor` to take a screenshot.

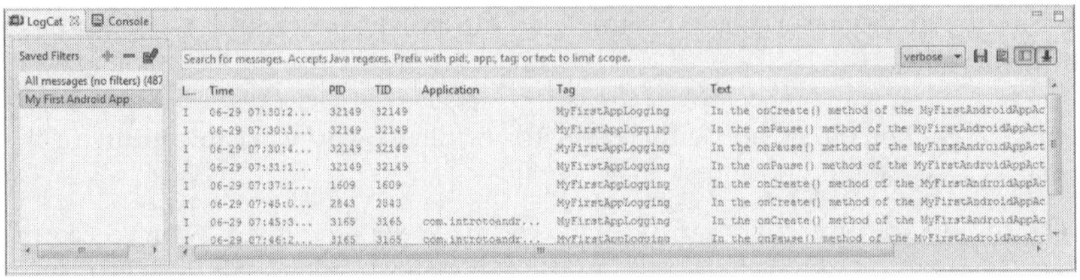

Figure C.11   Using the `Device Monitor LogCat` logging pane
with a custom filter.

and `assert`. When selected, only log entries for that level of severity and worse will display. You can filter the `LogCat` results to show just search results by using the search entry field, which fully supports regular expressions. Search terms can be limited in scope with prefixes, such as `text:`, to limit the following term to just the log message text.

You can also create saved filters to display only the `LogCat` information associated with particular attributes. You can use the plus (+) button to add a saved filter and show only log entries matching a tag, message, process ID, name, or log level. The strings for each attribute filter can also be Java-style regular expressions.

For example, suppose your application does this:

```
public static final String DEBUG_TAG = "MyFirstAppLogging";

Log.i(DEBUG_TAG,

    "In the onCreate() method of the MyFirstAndroidAppActivity Class.");
```

You can create a `LogCat` filter using the plus button ([+]). Name the filter and set the log tag to the string matching your debug tag:

```
MyFirstAppLogging
```

The `LogCat` pane with the resulting filters is shown in Figure C.11.

Summary

In this appendix, you have learned many valuable features that `Device Monitor` provides. `Device Monitor` can be launched from within Android Studio or from the command-line. You learned that `Device Monitor` provides tools for monitoring your application's performance while running on an emulator or a device. You also learned that `Device Monitor` allows you to interact directly with the file system of an emulator or a device. You should also feel comfortable interacting with an emulator or device, performing actions such as phone calls, SMS, taking screenshots, or even logging application data.

Quiz Questions

1. What is the name of the Android SDK directory where the command-line `monitor` application resides?

2. True or false: The `Device Monitor` tab for sending GPS coordinates to a device or emulator is called the `Emulator Control` tab.

3. Name some of the tasks that you can perform with the `Threads` and `Heap` tabs.

4. What is the name of the class used for adding network statistics analysis code to your application?

5. True or false: The `LogCat` tool is not part of `Device Monitor`.

Exercises

1. Launch a sample application, on either an emulator or a device, and practice analyzing the application using the various `Device Monitor` tabs.

2. Practice interacting with an emulator or device by sending calls, SMS messages, and GPS coordinates, and then take screen captures of each interaction using `Device Monitor`.

3. Practice adding log statements to a sample application, and then use `LogCat` to view the logging information.

References and More Information

Android Tools: "Device Monitor":
   http://d.android.com/tools/help/monitor.html
Android Tools: "HPROF Converter":
   http://d.android.com/tools/help/hprof-conv.html
Android Reference: "TrafficStats":
   http://d.android.com/reference/android/net/TrafficStats.html
Android Tools: "Reading and Writing Logs":
   http://d.android.com/tools/debugging/debugging-log.html
Android Reference: "Log":
   http://d.android.com/reference/android/util/Log.html

D

Mastery:
Android SDK Tools

Android developers are fortunate to have many tools at their disposal to help facilitate the design and development of quality applications. Some of the Android SDK tools are integrated by default into Android Studio, or integrated with Eclipse after installing the ADT plugin, whereas other Android SDK tools must be used from the command-line. In this appendix, we walk through a number of the most important tools available for use with Android. Knowledge of SDK tools will help you develop Android applications faster and with fewer roadblocks.

Note

This appendix covers the existing tools available at the time of this writing. To see exactly which tools were used during the writing of this book, check out the book's Introduction and read the section "Development Environments Used in This Book."

The Android SDK tools are updated frequently. We have made every attempt to provide the latest steps for the latest tools. However, these steps and the user interfaces described in this appendix may change at any time. Please review the Android Development website (*http://d.android.com/tools/help/index.html*) and our book's website (*http://introductiontoandroid.blogspot.com*) for the latest information.

Using the Android Documentation

Although it is not a tool per se, the Android documentation is a key resource for Android developers. An HTML version of the Android documentation is provided in the docs/ subfolder of the Android SDK, and the documentation should always be your first stop when you encounter a problem. You can also access the latest help documentation online at the Android Developer website, *http://developer.android.com/index.html* (or *http://d.android.com* for short). The Android documentation is organized and searchable, and is divided into three main categories with several sections per category, as shown in Figure D.1:

- **Design:** This tab provides information about designing Android applications.
  - **Up and running with material design:** This section provides an introduction to material design, with download links for designers and articles written by Google about material design.
  - **Pure Android:** This section includes Android design best practices and training for helping you develop applications that deliver a high-quality user experience.
  - **Resources:** This section includes links to material design resources such as layout templates, sticker sheets, icons, fonts, color palettes, and more.
- **Develop:** This tab provides information for developing Android applications.
  - **Training:** The training section includes tutorials for using specific classes and provides code samples that you are free to use within your applications. The tutorials are listed in order of how one should proceed through the Android development learning process, and many important topics are discussed in depth. These trainings are an invaluable resource to Android developers.
  - **API Guides:** This tab provides in-depth explanations of many Android topics, classes, or packages. Although related to the Training section, the API Guides provide a much deeper explanation of particular features of the Android API.
  - **Reference:** This tab includes a searchable package and class index of all Android APIs provided as part of the Android SDK in a Javadoc-style format. You will spend most of your time on this tab, looking up Java class documentation, checking method parameters, and performing other similar tasks.
  - **Tools:** The Tools tab is the definitive resource for learning about Android Studio and the SDK tools. Many of these tools are covered throughout this book and are usable from either your IDE or the command-line. One particular section of the Tools tab, the Tools Help section, is particularly useful for learning how to use both the SDK Tools and the Platform Tools. This is also where you download Android Studio and the SDK tools, available for Windows, Mac, and Linux.
  - **Google Services:** This tab provides tutorials, code samples, and API guides for integrating Google services into your Android application, and will help you learn what you need to know about Google Play developer tools.
  - **Samples:** This tab provides many sample applications categorized by topic, to help you learn exactly how to use particular APIs. You can browse the various sample projects, or you can download them to your system so that you can import into your IDE and run them on your devices and emulators to see how important features have been implemented.
  - **Preview:** This tab provides information about the current preview release of Android. Here, you will learn about features that are coming to the next version of Android, and how to get started with developing for these new APIs.

- **Distribute:** This tab provides information about distributing Android applications.

  - **Google Play:** This tab provides an introduction to Google Play. Having a good understanding of Google Play is important before launching your application. This section provides an overview of Google Play and introduces the various opportunities and programs Google Play provides developers.

  - **Essentials:** This tab provides in-depth explanations of the different quality guidelines developers should follow when building their applications. There is also a section dedicated to tools and resources—checklists, guidelines, generators, and more—that will help you make better applications.

  - **Get Users:** The Get Users section teaches you what you need to know about user acquisition. Topics covered include creating a quality Play store listing, using ads, search, internationalization, and invites to grow, along with other content worth looking into for growing your user base.

  - **Engage & Retain:** This tab covers techniques that go beyond getting users. Here, you will learn about techniques you can implement for keeping your users active with your application.

  - **Earn:** This section covers the many different ways you can monetize your application. Monetization topics covered include discussions about freemium, premium, subscription, ad revenue, e-commerce, and other business models for generating income from your users.

  - **Analyze:** The Analyze tab discusses topics to educate you on tracking and analytics. You will learn how proper tracking can be incorporated into your application, and you will also learn about how to use the data gathered for improving your applications.

  - **Stories:** This section highlights some applications that have been successfully distributed within Google Play. Learning how others have achieved success is always helpful for understanding how those principles may be applied to your application.

Figure D.1 shows a screenshot of the Android SDK Reference tab of the website.

Now is a good time to learn your way around the Android SDK documentation. First, check out the online documentation, and then try the local documentation.

Tip

Different features of the Android SDK are applicable to different versions of the platform. New APIs, classes, interfaces, and methods have been introduced over time. Therefore, each item in the documentation was tagged with the API level when it was first introduced. To see whether an item is available in a specific platform version, check its API level, usually listed along the right side of the documentation. You can also filter the documentation to a specific API level, so that it displays only the SDK features available for that platform version (see Figure D.1, left center).

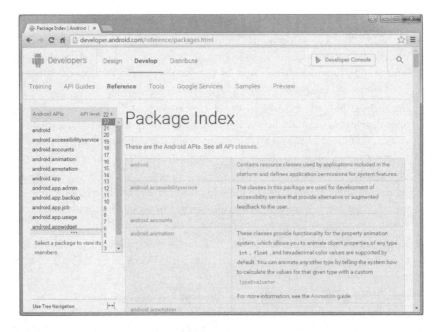

Figure D.1   The Android Developer website.

Keep in mind that this book is designed to be a companion guide in your journey to mastering Android development. It covers Android fundamentals and tries to distill a lot of information into an easily digestible format to get you up and running quickly. It then provides you with a thorough understanding of what is available and feasible on the Android platform. It is not an exhaustive SDK reference, but rather a guide to best practices. You'll need to become intimately familiar with the Android SDK Java class documentation in order to be successful at designing and developing Android applications in the long run.

Leveraging the Android Emulator

Although we introduced the Android emulator as a core tool in Chapter 2, "Setting Up for Development," it's worth mentioning again. The Android emulator is probably the most powerful tool at a developer's disposal, along with the Android SDK and Android Virtual Device Managers (which we also talked about fairly extensively in other chapters of this book). It is important for developers to learn to use the emulator and understand its limitations. The Android emulator is integrated with Android Studio. For more information about the emulator, please check out Appendix B, "Quick-Start: Android Emulator." We suggest that you review that detailed appendix after you have looked over the other materials covered in this appendix.

Figure D.2   The Android emulator in action running the `Support App Navigation` sample application.

Figure D.2 shows a sample application included with the Android SDK called `Support App Navigation` and what it looks like when running in the Android emulator.

You can also find exhaustive information about the emulator on the Android Developer website: *http://d.android.com/tools/help/emulator.html.*

Viewing Application Log Data with `logcat`

You learned how to log application information in Chapter 3, "Creating Your First Application," using the `android.util.Log` class. The log output appears in the `logcat` tool window of Android Studio. You can also interact with `logcat` directly.

Even when you have a great debugger, incorporating logging support into your applications is very useful. You can then monitor your application's log output, generated on either the emulator or an attached device. Log information can be invaluable for tracking down difficult bugs and reporting application state during the development phase of a project.

Log data is categorized by severity. When you create a new class in your project, we recommend defining a unique debug tag string for that class so that you can easily track down where a log message originated. You can use this tag to filter the logging data and find only the messages you are interested in. You can use the `logcat` utility from within Android Studio to filter your log messages to the debug tag string you supplied for your application. To learn how to do this, check out the "Creating Custom Log Filters" section in Appendix A, "Tips and Tricks: Android Studio."

Finally, there are some performance trade-offs to consider when it comes to logging. Excessive logging impacts device and application performance. At a minimum, debug and verbose logging should be used only for development purposes and should be removed prior to application publication.

Debugging Applications with `Device Monitor`

When it comes to debugging on the emulator or device, you need to turn your attention to the Android `Device Monitor` tool. `Device Monitor` is a debugging utility that is integrated into Android Studio. It is also available as a stand-alone executable in the `tools/` subdirectory of the Android SDK installation.

The `Device Monitor` available from Android Studio (see Figure D.3) provides a number of useful features for interacting with emulators and handsets, and debugging applications. You use `Device Monitor` to view and manage processes and threads running on the device, view heap data, and attach to processes to debug, as well as a variety of other tasks.

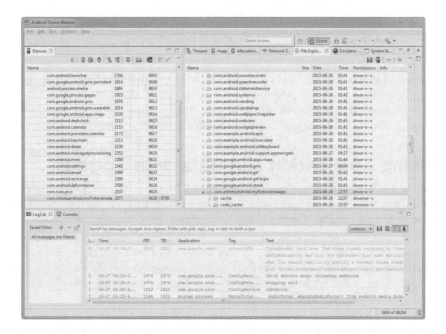

Figure D.3   `Device Monitor` launched from Android Studio.

You can find out all about the Android `Device Monitor` and how to use its features in Appendix C, "Quick-Start: Android `Device Monitor`." We suggest that you review that detailed appendix after you have looked over the other material covered in this appendix.

Using Android Debug Bridge (ADB)

The Android Debug Bridge (ADB) is a client/server command-line tool that enables developers to debug Android code on the emulator and the device using Android Studio. Both the `Device Monitor` and the Android SDK tools use ADB to facilitate interaction between the development environment and the device (or emulator). You can find the `adb` command-line tool in the `platform-tools/` directory of the Android SDK.

Developers can also use ADB to interact with the device file system, install and uninstall Android applications manually, and issue shell commands. For example, the `logcat` and `sqlite3` shell commands enable you to access logging data and application databases.

For an exhaustive ADB reference, see the Android SDK documentation at *http://d.android.com/tools/help/adb.html*.

Using the Layout Editor

Android Studio is a solid, well-designed development environment for Java applications. When using Android Studio, you have access to a bunch of simple Android-specific tools to help you design, develop, debug, and publish applications. Like all applications, Android apps are made up of functionality (Java code) and data (resources such as strings and graphics). The functionality is handled with the Android Studio Java editor, compiler, and the Gradle build system. The Android SDK tools integrated into Android Studio add numerous special editors for creating Android-specific resource files to encapsulate application data such as strings and user interface resource templates called layouts.

Android layout (user interface templates) resources are technically XML files. However, some people prefer to be able to drag and drop controls, move them around, and preview what the user interface will look like to an actual user. Android Studio has amazing support for designing your layouts visually with the layout editor.

The layout editor loads whenever you open an XML file within the `res/layout/` project directory hierarchy. You can use the layout editor in `Design` view, which allows you to drag and drop controls and see what your application will look like with a variety of AVD-style configuration options (Android API level, screen resolution, orientation, theme, and more), as shown in Figure D.4. You can also switch to `Text` view to edit controls directly or set specific properties.

We discussed the details of designing and developing user interfaces, as well as working with layouts and user interface controls, in Chapter 7, "Exploring Building Blocks," and Chapter 8, "Positioning with Layouts." For now, we just want you to be aware that your application's user interface components are generally stored as resources, and that the Android SDK provides some helpful tools for designing and managing these resources.

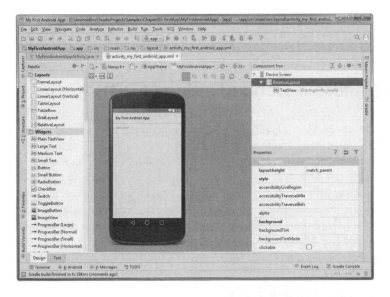

Figure D.4   Using the layout editor in Android Studio in `Design` view.

Using the Android Hierarchy Viewer

The Android Hierarchy Viewer is a tool that identifies layout component relationships (the hierarchy) and helps developers design, debug, and profile their user interfaces. Developers can use this tool to inspect the user interface control properties and develop pixel-perfect layouts. The Hierarchy Viewer is available as a perspective in the Android `Device Monitor`, and also as a stand-alone executable in the `tools/` subdirectory of your Android SDK installation, which has been deprecated.

The Hierarchy Viewer is a visual tool that can be used to inspect your application user interfaces in ways that allow you to identify and improve your layout designs. You can drill down on specific user interface controls and inspect their properties at runtime. You can save screenshots of the current application state on the emulator or the device.

The Hierarchy Viewer application is divided into two main modes:

- **Layout View mode:** This mode shows the hierarchy of user interface controls loaded by your application in tree form. You can zoom in and select specific controls to find out lots of information about their current state; there is also profiling information to help you optimize your controls.

- **Pixel Perfect mode:** This mode shows the user interface pixels in a zoomed-in grid fashion. This is useful for designers who need to look at very specific layout arrangements or line up views on top of images.

You can switch between the modes by moving between the `Hierarchy View` and `Pixel Perfect` perspectives of `Device Monitor`.

Launching the Hierarchy Viewer

To launch the Hierarchy Viewer with your application in the emulator, perform the following steps:

1. Launch your Android application in the emulator.
2. Launch `Device Monitor` and make sure the application process is selected in the `Devices` view.
3. Switch to the `Hierarchy View` perspective in `Device Monitor`. As an alternative to `Device Monitor`, navigate to the Android SDK `tools/` subdirectory and launch the Hierarchy Viewer application (`hierarchyviewer`), but note the stand-alone version has been deprecated in favor of the `Device Monitor` integration.
4. Choose your emulator instance from the `Device` listing.
5. Select the application you want to view from the options available. The application must be running on that emulator to show up on the list.

Working in Layout View Mode

The Layout View mode is displayed within the `Hierarchy View` perspective of `Device Monitor` and is invaluable for debugging drawing issues related to your application's user interface controls. If you wonder why something isn't drawing correctly, try launching the `Hierarchy View` perspective and checking the properties for that control at runtime.

Note

When you load an application in the Hierarchy Viewer, you will want to be aware of the fact that your application user interface does not begin at the root of the hierarchy in the tree view. In fact, there are several layers of layout controls above your application content that will appear as parent controls of your content. For example, the system `status bar` is a higher-level control. Your application contents are actually child controls within a `FrameLayout` control called `@id/content`. When you load layout contents using the `setContentView()` method within your `Activity` class, you are specifying what to load within this high-level `FrameLayout`.

Figure D.5 shows the `Device Monitor` in the `Hierarchy View` perspective showing the tree view and loaded in Layout View mode.

When you first load your application in Layout View mode, you will see several panes of information. The main pane shows the parent/child control relationships as a tree view. Each tree node represents a user interface control on the screen and shows the control's unique identifier, type, and profiling information for optimization purposes (more on this in a moment). There are also a number of smaller panes on the right side of the screen. The loupe/zoom pane allows you to quickly navigate a large tree view. The property pane shows the various properties for each tree node, when highlighted. The wireframe model

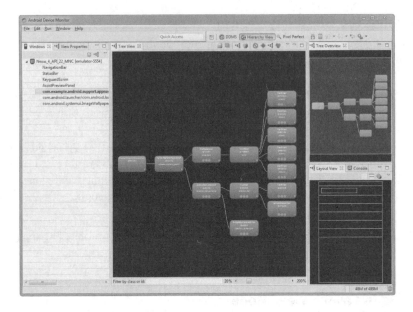

Figure D.5   The Hierarchy View perspective (Layout View mode).

of the currently loaded user interface is displayed, with a red box highlighting the currently selected control. To the far left, there is the Windows pane, which lists the currently running devices and their running applications.

> **Tip**
>
> You'll have better luck navigating your application View objects with the Hierarchy View perspective if you set your View object ID properties to friendly names you can remember instead of the autogenerated sequential ID tags provided by default. For example, a Button control called SubmitButton is more descriptive than Button01.

You can use the Hierarchy View perspective to interact and debug your application user interface.

Optimizing Your User Interface

You can also use the Hierarchy Viewer to optimize your user interface contents. If you have used this tool before, you may have noticed little red, yellow, or green dots in the tree view. These are performance indicators for each specific control:

- The left dot represents how long the measuring operation for this view takes.
- The middle dot represents how long the layout-rendering operation for this view takes.
- The right dot represents how long the drawing operation for this view takes.

Indicators represent how each control renders in relation to other controls in the tree. They are not a strict representation of a bad or good control, per se. A red dot means that this view renders the slowest, compared to all views in the hierarchy. A yellow dot means that this view renders in the bottom 50% of all views in the hierarchy. A green dot means that this view renders in the top 50% of all views in the hierarchy. When you click a specific view within the tree, you will also see the actual performance times on which these indicators are based.

> **Tip**
>
> The Hierarchy Viewer provides control-level precision profiling. However, it won't tell you if your user interface layouts are organized in the most efficient way. For that, you'll want to check out the `lint` command-line tool available in the `tools/` subdirectory of the Android SDK installation. This tool is also integrated into Android Studio and runs automatically when you compile your application. This tool will help you identify unnecessary layout controls in your user interface, among other inefficiencies. Find out more at the Android Developer website: *http://d.android.com/tools/debugging/debugging-ui.html#lint*.

Working in Pixel Perfect Mode

You can use the `Pixel Perfect` mode to closely inspect your application user interface. You can also load PNG mock-up files to overlay your user interface and adjust your application's look. You can access the `Pixel Perfect` mode by selecting the perspective of the same name in `Device Monitor`.

Figure D.6 illustrates how you can inspect the currently running application screen at the pixel level by using the loupe feature of this mode.

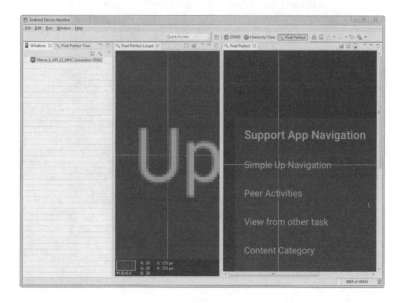

Figure D.6   The Hierarchy Viewer tool (`Pixel Perfect` mode).

Working with Nine-Patch Stretchable Graphics

Android supports Nine-Patch Stretchable Graphics, which provide flexibility for supporting different user interface characteristics, orientations, and device screens. Nine-Patch Stretchable Graphics can be created from PNG files using the draw9patch tool included with the tools/ subdirectory of the Android SDK.

Nine-Patch Stretchable Graphics are simply PNG graphics that have patches, or areas of the image, defined to scale appropriately, instead of the entire image being scaled as one unit. Figure D.7 illustrates how the image (shown as the square) is divided into nine patches. Often, the center segment is transparent.

The interface for the draw9patch tool is straightforward. In the left pane, you can define the guides to your graphic to specify how it scales when stretched. In the right pane, you can preview how your graphic behaves when scaled with the patches you defined. Figure D.8 shows a simple PNG file loaded in the tool, prior to its guides being set.

To create a Nine-Patch Stretchable Graphic file from a PNG file using the draw9patch tool, perform the following steps:

1. Launch draw9patch in your Android SDK tools subdirectory.
2. Drag a PNG file onto the pane (or use File, Open Nine-Patch).
3. Click the Show patches check box at the bottom of the left pane.

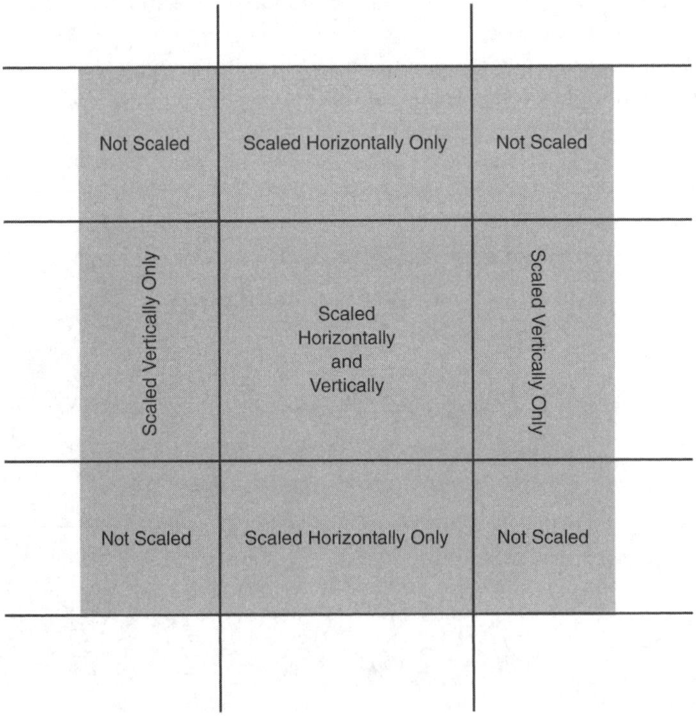

Figure D.7   How a Nine-Patch graphic of a square is scaled.

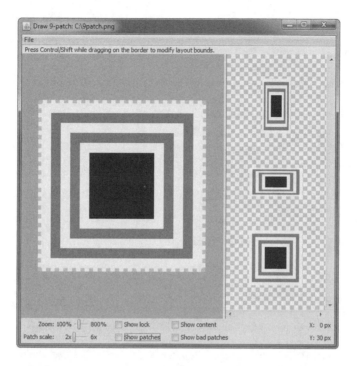

Figure D.8   A simple PNG file before Nine-Patch processing.

4. Set your `Patch scale` appropriately (set it higher to see more marked results).

5. Click along the left edge of your graphic to set a horizontal patch guide.

6. Click along the top edge of your graphic to set a vertical patch guide.

7. View the results in the right pane; move the patch guides until the graphic stretches as desired. Figures D.9 and D.10 illustrate two possible guide configurations.

8. To delete a patch guide, press `Shift` and click the guide pixel (black) or left-click the guide pixel.

9. Save your graphics file. Nine-Patch graphics should end with the extension `.9.png` (for example, `little_black_box.9.png`).

10. Include your graphics file as a resource in your Android project and use it just as you would a normal PNG file.

Working with Other Android Tools

Although we've already covered the most important tools, a number of other special-purpose utilities are included with the Android SDK. Many of these tools provide the underlying functionality that has been integrated into Android Studio. However, if you are not using Android Studio, these tools may be used on the command-line.

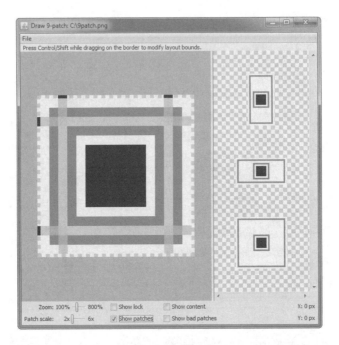

Figure D.9   A Nine-Patch PNG file after Nine-Patch processing with some patch guides defined.

A complete list of the development tools that come as part of the Android SDK is available on the Android Developer website at *http://d.android.com/tools/help/index.html*. There, you'll find a description of each tool as well as a link to its official documentation. Here is a list of some useful tools we haven't yet discussed:

- **android:** This command-line tool provides much the same functionality as the Android SDK and Android Virtual Device Managers; it also helps you create and manage projects if you are not using Android Studio.
- **bmgr:** This shell tool is accessed through the adb command-line to interact with the Backup Manager.
- **dmtracedump, hprof-conv, traceview:** These tools are used for diagnostics, debug logging, and profiling of applications.
- **jobb:** This tool is for encrypting and decrypting your expansion APK files to and from the Opaque Binary Blob (OBB) format.
- **lint:** This tool is integrated into Android Studio and runs automatically upon compilation of your application. In addition, it can be run as a command-line tool for inspecting your code for potential bugs and it provides improvement suggestions when found.

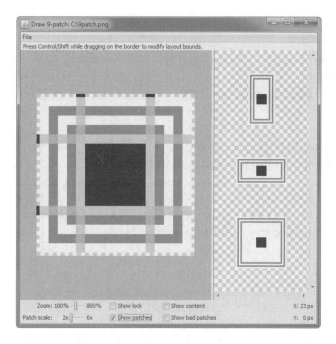

Figure D.10   A Nine-Patch PNG file after Nine-Patch processing with some different patch guides defined.

- **etc1tool:** This command-line tool lets you convert between PNG files and compressed Ericsson Texture Compression (ETC1) files. The specification for ETC1 is available at *http://www.khronos.org/registry/gles/extensions/OES/OES_compressed_ETC1_RGB8_texture.txt*.

- **logcat:** This shell tool is accessed through the adb command-line to interact with the platform logging tool. Although you'll normally access log output through Android Studio, you can also use this shell tool to capture, clear, and redirect log output (a useful feature if you're doing any automation, or not using Android Studio). Although the command-line logcat tool is used to provide better filters, the Android Studio logcat tool window has brought this filtering power to the graphical version.

- **mksdcard:** This command-line tool lets you create SD card disk images independent of a specific AVD.

- **monkey, monkeyrunner:** These are tools you can use to test your application and implement automated testing suites. We discussed unit testing and test opportunities for applications in Chapter 21, "Testing Your Applications."

- **ProGuard:** This is a tool for obfuscating and optimizing application code. We talked more about ProGuard, and specifically how to protect the intellectual property of an application, in Chapter 22, "Distributing Your Applications."

- **sqlite3:** This shell tool is accessed through the `adb` command-line to interact with SQLite databases.

- **systrace:** This is a performance-analysis tool for learning about the execution of applications.

- **Tracer for OpenGL ES:** This tool allows you to analyze the execution of OpenGL ES code to understand how an application is processing and executing graphics.

- **uiautomator:** This is an automated functional UI testing framework for creating and running user interface tests for an application.

- **zipalign:** This command-line tool is used to align an APK file after it has been signed for publication. This tool is necessary only if you do not use Android Studio Export Wizard to compile, package, sign, and align your application. We discussed these steps in Chapter 22, "Distributing Your Applications."

Summary

The Android SDK ships with a number of powerful tools to help with common Android development tasks. The Android documentation is an essential reference for developers. The Android emulator can be used for running and debugging Android applications virtually, without the need for an actual device. The `Device Monitor` debugging tool, which is accessible from within Android Studio, is useful for monitoring emulators and devices. ADB is the powerful command-line tool behind many of the features of `Device Monitor`. The Hierarchy Viewer and `lint` tools can be used to design and optimize your user interface controls, and the Nine-Patch tool allows you to create stretchable graphics for use within your apps. There are also a number of other useful tools to help developers with different development tasks, from design to development, testing, and publication.

Quiz Questions

1. True or false: `Device Monitor` is available as a stand-alone executable.
2. Which SDK subdirectory folder holds the `adb` command-line tool?
3. What are the two views for working with Android layout files using the Android Studio?
4. Which tool is used for inspecting and optimizing the user interface?

Exercises

1. Using the Android documentation as a reference, create a list of the `logcat` command-line options.
2. Using the Android documentation as a reference, determine which `adb` command is used for printing a list of all attached emulator instances.

3. Using the Android documentation as a reference, describe how to use `Device Monitor` for tracking the memory allocation of objects.

References and More Information

Android Developers "Package Index" reference:
http://d.android.com/reference/packages.html
Android Tools: "Android Emulator":
http://d.android.com/tools/help/emulator.html
Android Tools: "`Device Monitor`":
http://d.android.com/tools/help/monitor.html
Android Tools: "`android`":
http://d.android.com/tools/help/android.html
Android Tools: "Android Debug Bridge":
http://d.android.com/tools/help/adb.html
Android Tools: "`logcat`":
http://d.android.com/tools/help/logcat.html
Android Tools: "Draw 9-Patch":
http://d.android.com/tools/help/draw9patch.html
Android Tools: "Optimizing Your UI":
http://d.android.com/tools/debugging/debugging-ui.html
Android Tools: "Profiling with Hierarchy Viewer":
http://d.android.com/tools/performance/hierarchy-viewer/profiling.html
Android Tools: "Using the Layout Editor":
http://d.android.com/sdk/installing/studio-layout.html

E

Quick-Start: Gradle Build System

When programming Android applications, you're most likely to create many files that include numerous lines of source code. The question remains—how does all that source code you just wrote actually become an Android application? The answer—the Gradle build system. Gradle is an open-source tool used to automate the building, running, testing, and packaging of your Android application. Gradle is built directly into Android Studio and you're also able to run Gradle from the command-line.

Gradle, by itself, is an extremely powerful tool, but when it is combined with Android Studio, you are able to manage complex Android application builds. Gradle is important to learn because when you want to create different builds of the same application—for example, a free version and a paid version—rather than creating two separate Android Studio projects, you can create and manage the building of both applications from within one Android Studio project. In this appendix, you are going to learn about Gradle, the different builds files included with your application, the syntax for scripting your build files, and you will learn more about the options available for including in your build files. By the end of this appendix, you should be comfortable managing a more complex Android application build using Android Studio and Gradle.

Tip

Many of the code examples provided in this appendix are taken from the `SimpleGradleBuild` application. The source code for this application is provided for download on the book's website (*http://introductiontoandroid.blogspot.com*).

Gradle Build Files

Your Gradle build files are the files named `build.gradle`. Depending on how you've set up your project, you will have two or more `build.gradle` files. One `build.gradle` file is for global project build configuration settings and resides in your project root directory. The other `build.gradle` file(s) will be found in your application module(s), one per module.

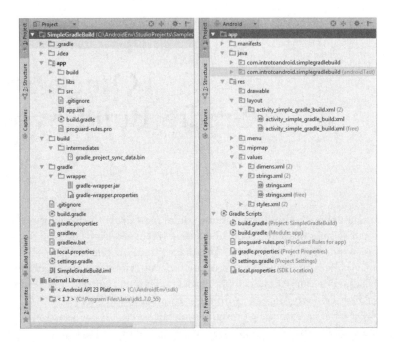

Figure E.1 In the `Project` view on the left, notice various Gradle files scattered throughout the directory structure of your application; in the `Android` view on the right, notice the section named `Gradle Scripts` that groups the important Gradle files for your application project.

The `build.gradle` files are plain text files that rely on Groovy syntax, which is a powerful domain-specific language (DSL) that can be used for creating readable build and automation scripts. You use the Groovy syntax to define how you would like your project built by declaring reserved elements and providing attributes and values. The elements you declare, and the attributes and values you give them, determine how your project and application modules will be built. To learn more about Groovy, see the groovy language website at *http://www.groovy-lang.org*.

Figure E.1 shows the various ways to access the Gradle build files. On the left, you will notice the `Project` view displaying the file system hierarchy of the `SimpleGradleBuild` project, and you should notice that the Gradle files are scattered throughout the project directories. On the right, you will notice the `Android` symbolic view showing a `Gradle Scripts` section that groups all the Gradle files together.

Project Settings

The `build.gradle` project file is for defining global build settings that are common to all application modules and subprojects. The file starts with the build script declaration, which defines the repository to use. The repositories available to choose from are J Center, Maven Central, and Ivy.

Note

You define the path to the Android SDK using the `ANDROID_HOME` environment variable on your system or by setting the `sdk.dir` in the `local.properties` file. For example, to set the location of the SDK on Windows using the `sdk.dir` setting, simply write this code:

```
sdk.dir=C\:\\path\\to\\sdk
```

To set the location on Mac OS X, write this code:

```
sdk.dir=/Applications/Android Studio.app/sdk
```

Below, you'll see the top-level project configuration settings of the `build.gradle` file of the `SimpleGradleBuild` project.

```
buildscript {

    repositories {

        jcenter()

    }

    dependencies {

        classpath 'com.android.tools.build:gradle:1.3.0'


        // NOTE: Do not place your application dependencies here; they belong
        // in the individual module build.gradle files

    }

}


allprojects {

    repositories {

        jcenter()

    }

}
```

Note

The location for including application modules in Android Studio projects is defined in the `settings.gradle` file. To include a module, simply include the named module. For example, to include a module named `app`, simply type:

```
include ':app'
```

Module Settings

You will spend most of your time marking up the `build.gradle` file of your application modules. The module settings are where you configure particular Android SDK settings such as the `compileSdkVersion` and `buildToolsVersion`. These settings are placed inside the `android` element. You also include `defaultConfig` settings and `buildTypes`. Here is a breakdown of some elements for a module build file:

- **Applying the Android Gradle Plugin:** The first line of your `build.gradle` file is used for including the `android` plug-in. You do so by including the following line:
  `apply plugin: 'com.android.application'`
- **Android Settings:** The `compileSdkVersion` and `buildToolsVersion` are used for declaring the appropriate version numbers for your requirements.
  - **Default Configurations:** The `defaultConfig` element is used for providing an `applicationId`, `minSdkVersion`, `targetSdkVersion`, `versionCode`, and `versionName`
  - **Product Flavors:** The `productFlavors` element is where you define different versions of your application.
  - **Build Types:** The `buildTypes` element is where you configure `ProGuard` settings, application signing, version suffixes, and various other build properties.
  - **Dependencies:** The `dependencies` element is where you configure local, remote, and module dependencies.

Support Library Dependencies

One type of dependency you will most likely use frequently will be the support libraries. The dependencies element is where you would include a particular support library. Later in this appendix, we show you how to include support library dependencies in your project, but first let's take a look at some important Android support libraries (see Table E.1) that you should be aware of.

Understanding the Gradle Wrapper

The Gradle wrapper can be found in the `gradle/wrapper/` directory relative to your project root and includes the `gradle-wrapper.jar` file and the `gradle-wrapper.properties` file. There is also the `gradlew` shell script for Windows, Mac, and Linux, which can be found in your project root. Rather than installing Gradle on your system, you should use the Gradle wrapper included in your project. If you try to build your application using different Gradle wrapper files or a locally installed version of Gradle, your application may not build correctly.

> **Warning**
>
> Never use Gradle wrapper files or Java `.jar` files from sources that you do not trust as they could be intended to harm your computer.

Table E.1 **Important Android Support Libraries**

Version	Identifier	Description
v4 Support Library	`com.android.support:` `support-v4:23.0.0`	Includes backward-compatible support for Android versions API level 4 and newer for using `Fragment`, `NotificationCompat`, `LocalBroadcastManager`, `ViewPager`, `PagerTitleStrip`, `PagerTabStrip`, `DrawerLayout`, `SlidingPaneLayout`, `Loader`, `FileProvider`, and more.
Multidex Support Library	`com.android.support:` `multidex:1.0.0`	This library is required if your application has more than 65,536 methods.
v7 appcompat library	`com.android.support:` `appcompat-v7:21.0.0`	Includes backward-compatible support for Android versions API level 7 and newer for using `ActionBar`, `AppCompatActivity`, `AppCompatDialog`, and `ShareActionProvider`.
v7 cardview library	`com.android.support:` `cardview-v7:21.0.0`	Includes backward-compatible support for Android versions API level 7 and newer for using the `CardView` widget.
v7 gridlayout library	`com.android.support:` `gridlayout-v7:21.0.0`	Includes backward-compatible support for Android versions API level 7 and newer for using the `GridLayout` class.
v7 mediarouter library	`com.android.support:` `mediarouter-v7:21.0.0`	Includes backward-compatible support for Android versions API level 7 and newer for using the `MediaRouter`, `MediaRouteProvider`, and other related classes.
v7 palette library	`com.android.support:` `palette-v7:21.0.0`	Includes backward-compatible support for Android versions API level 7 and newer for using the `Palette` class, useful for color extraction from images.
v7 recyclerview library	`com.android.support:` `recyclerview-v7:21.0.0`	Includes backward-compatible support for Android versions API level 7 and newer for using the `RecyclerView` class and widget.

(Continues)

Table E.1 **Continued**

Version	Identifier	Description
v7 Preference Support Library	`com.android.support:` `preference-v7:23.0.0`	Includes backward-compatible support for Android versions API level 7 and newer for using the `CheckBoxPreference` and `ListPreference` classes and other interfaces.

v8 renderscript library	`defaultConfig {`
	`    renderscriptTargetApi`
	`18`
	`    renderscriptSupport`
	`ModeEnabled true`
	`}`
		Includes backward-compatible support for Android versions API level 8 and newer for using the `Renderscript` framework.

v13 Support Library	`com.android.support:` `support-v13:18.0.0`	Includes backward-compatible support for Android versions API level 13 and newer for using fragments with `FragmentsCompat`.
v14 Preference Support Library	`com.android.support:` `preference-v14:23.0.0`	Includes backward-compatible support for Android versions API level 14 and newer.
v17 Preference Support Library for TV	`com.android.support:` `preference-v17:23.0.0`	Includes backward-compatible support for Android versions API level 17 and newer for using `BaseLeanbackPreferenceFragment` and `LeanbackPreferenceFragment`, and other classes.
v17 Leanback Library	`com.android.support:` `leanback-v17:21.0.0`	Includes backward-compatible support for Android versions API level 17 and newer for using `BrowserFragment`, `DetailsFragment`, `PlaybackOverlayFragment`, and `SearchFragment`.

Annotations Support Library	`com.android.support:`
	`support-annotations:`
	`22.0.0`
		This library is used for adding annotation metadata support.

Design Support Library	`com.android.support:` `design:22.2.1`	This library is used for adding material design support to your application.
Custom Tabs Support Library	`com.android.support:` `customtabs:23.0.0`	This library is used for adding custom tabs support to your application.
Percent Support Library	`com.android.support:` `percent:23.0.0`	This library is used for adding percent dimension support to your application.

Table E.1 **Continued**

Version	Identifier	Description
App Recommendation Support Library for TV	`com.android.support:` `app.recommendation-` `app:23.0.0`	Library is used for adding app recommendation support to your TV application.
Data Binding Library	Release candidate 1 beta version: `com.android.databinding:` `dataBinder:1.0-rc1` Currently requires declaring: `com.android.tools.` `build:gradle:1.3.0-beta4` Apply the plugin in each module: `apply plugin:` `'com.android.application'` `apply plugin:` `'com.android.databinding'`	This library is used for adding data binding support to your application and is currently in beta release.

You may be wondering if you should include the Gradle wrapper in your source control repository such as GitHub. You should always include Gradle wrapper files to ensure that your application will build properly.

Using Android Studio to Configure Your Builds

You can edit your build configuration files directly by editing the text or you can use the built-in module setting dialog for configuring your build.gradle file through user interface controls and form fields. This section covers using Android Studio and the project's module settings for configuring your build.gradle file.

Syncing Your Project

Every time you update your Gradle files, Android Studio prompts you to perform a Sync Now operation to update the configuration changes you've made. To avoid hunting down nonexistent bugs in your code, always make sure your files are in sync, otherwise your project may display errors if your build configuration is out of sync. Figure E.2 shows the app module build.gradle file requiring project sync and it displays the link for the Sync Now task.

Configuring the Android Properties

In order to configure the Android properties of the build.gradle file using a graphical user interface, you first need to open the Project Structure dialog. To open the

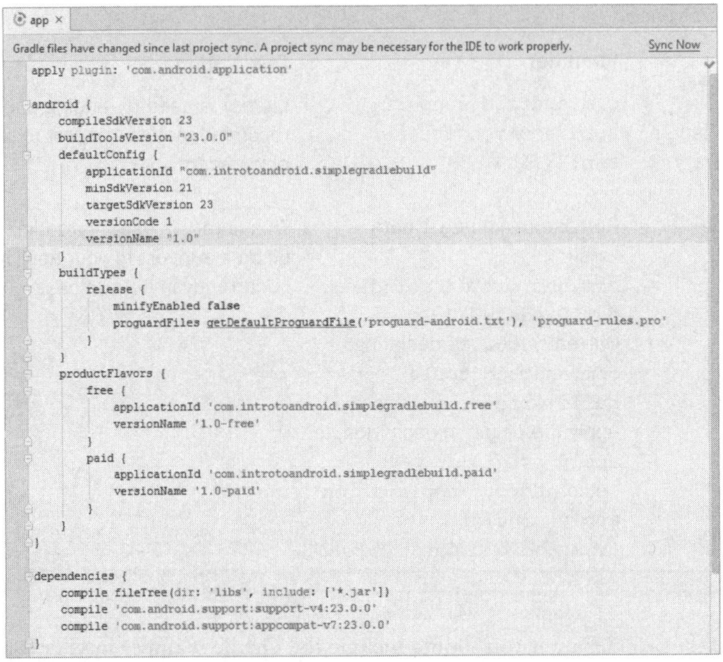

Figure E.2   The Android Studio prompt for the `Sync Now` task (top right).

`Project Structure` dialog, right-click the project root directory and a menu appears. You will see an `Open Module Settings` selection at the bottom of the menu. Click the `Open Module Settings`. Figure E.3 shows the menu presented upon right-clicking with the `Open Module Settings` option highlighted.

Once the `Project Structure` dialog has been opened, you should see the `Project Structure` dialog like that shown in Figure E.4. This dialog provides an overview of your `Project Structure` and displays, at the far left, any application modules your project has listed under the `Modules` section. Make sure a module is selected to edit the `build.gradle` file here. The `Properties` tab allows you to configure the `android` properties of the `build.gradle` file.

The code below shows the same options specified as those configured on the `Properties` tab of the `Project Structure` dialog (Figure E.4):

```
android {

    compileSdkVersion 23

    buildToolsVersion "23.0.0"

    ...

}
```

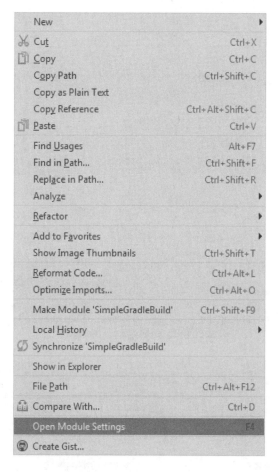

Figure E.3   Opening the `Project Structure` dialog via the `Open Module Settings` option.

Working with Signing Options

When working with the debug version of your application, you are not required to provide a secure certificate for signing your application. If you're working with the release version of your application, you will need to provide a release key for signing your application. Figure E.5 shows the `Signing` tab of the `Project Structure` dialog. You can add signing settings on this tab.

Configuring Different Build Flavors

The `Flavors` tab of the module settings allows you to add, remove, and configure different `productFlavors` for creating different versions of your app—for example, both a

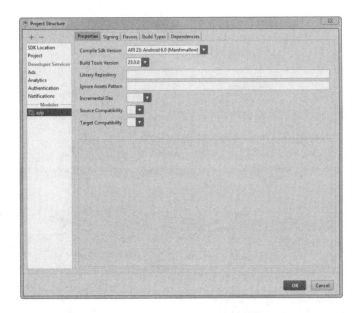

Figure E.4   Editing the `Properties` of the `build.gradle` file from the `Project Structure` dialog.

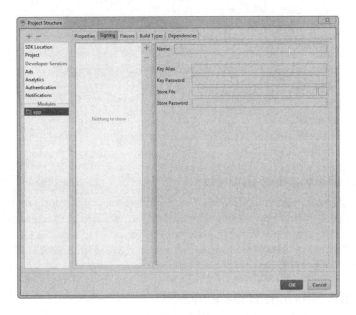

Figure E.5   The `Signing` settings of the `build.gradle` file in the `Project Structure` dialog.

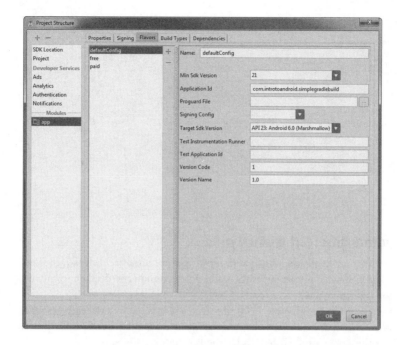

Figure E.6   Editing the `productFlavors` of the `build.gradle` file from the `Project Structure` dialog.

free and a paid version. You are also able to configure the `defaultConfig` options on the `Flavors` tab. Figure E.6 shows the `Flavors` tab with the `defaultConfig` option showing, along with a `free` and `paid` flavor option.

The code below shows the `defaultConfig`, `free`, and `paid` elements specified as those configured on the `Flavors` tab of the `Project Structure` dialog:

```
...

defaultConfig {

    applicationId "com.introtoandroid.simplegradlebuild"

    minSdkVersion 21

    targetSdkVersion 23

    versionCode 1

    versionName "1.0"

}

...

productFlavors {

    free {
```

(Continues)

```
(Continued)
        applicationId 'com.introtoandroid.simplegradlebuild.free'

        versionName '1.0-free'

    }

    paid {

        applicationId 'com.introtoandroid.simplegradlebuild.paid'

        versionName '1.0-paid'

    }

}
...
```

Configuring Different Build Types

The Build Types tab allows you to add, remove, and configure different build types such as debug and release. Figure E.7 shows the debug build type displaying the available options for configuration.

When editing the Build Types from the Project Structure dialog, you will notice both a debug and release entry, but when editing the build.gradle file directly, you will not see the debug entry listed under the buildTypes section.

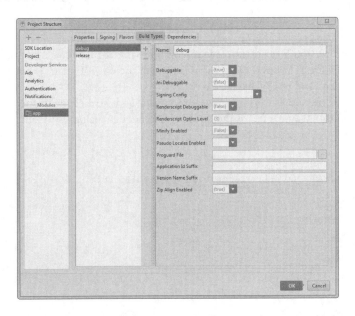

Figure E.7   Editing the Build Types of the build.gradle file from the
Project Structure dialog.

```
buildTypes {

    release {

        minifyEnabled false

        proguardFiles getDefaultProguardFile('proguard-android.txt'),

                'proguard-rules.pro'

    }

}
```

If you would like to see the debug entry listed in the buildTypes section, you need to enter it manually. The following code shows a debug entry:

```
buildTypes {

    release {

        minifyEnabled false

        proguardFiles getDefaultProguardFile('proguard-android.txt'),

                'proguard-rules.pro'

    }

    debug {

        debuggable true

    }

}
```

Configuring Application Dependencies

The Dependencies tab allows you to add, remove, reorder, and change the scope of your module dependencies. Figure E.8 shows the Dependencies tab with a local dependency defined and two module dependencies for including the support-v4 library and the appcompat-v7 library, each with the scope of compile.

Adding Library Dependencies

If you wanted to add a module library dependency, a dialog appears after clicking the add icon and presents a list of the available module libraries. Figure E.9 shows the Choose Library Dependency dialog.

Here, you will notice the dependencies listed in the app module build.gradle file. These are the same as those from the Dependencies tab of the Project Structure dialog:

```
dependencies {

    compile fileTree(dir: 'libs', include: ['*.jar'])

    compile 'com.android.support:support-v4:23.0.0'

    compile 'com.android.support:appcompat-v7:23.0.0'

}
```

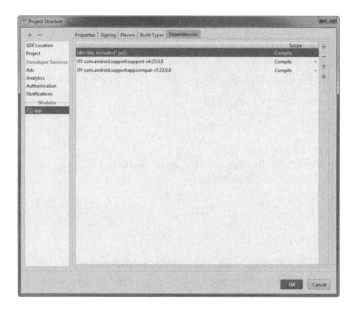

Figure E.8   The Dependencies of the build.gradle file from the
Project Structure dialog.

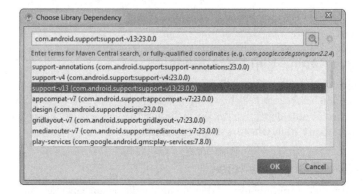

Figure E.9   Adding a new library dependency from the Dependencies tab
of the Project Structure dialog.

Building Different APK Variants

In order to be able to build different APK variants, you need to create the appropriate
build variant directories and files. Now that you have configured the productFlavors of
free and paid, the following steps will allow you to build these variants:

1. Create a `free/` and `paid/` directory on your `app/src/` path.

2. Create a `res/` resource directory with a `layout/` and `values/` subdirectory in both the `free/` and `paid/` directories you just created.

3. In the `layout/` directory of the `free` flavor, create an XML file that has the same name of the XML file in your `app/src/main/res/layout` directory. In our case, the file is named `activity_simple_gradle_build.xml`. For the layout of the `free` flavor, create a relative layout with the child `TextView` and set the `text` attribute to `@string/hello_free_world`. Here is the `TextView`:

```
<TextView
    android:layout_width="wrap_content"
    android:layout_height="wrap_content"
    android:text="@string/hello_free_world" />
```

Do the same for the `paid` flavor, but set the text attribute of the `TextView` to `@string/hello_paid_world`. Here is the `TextView`:

```
<TextView
    android:layout_width="wrap_content"
    android:layout_height="wrap_content"
    android:text="@string/hello_paid_world" />
```

4. In the `values/` directory of the `free` flavor, create an XML file that has the same name of the XML file in your `app/src/main/res/values` directory. Name the file `strings.xml` and, for the `free` flavor, put the following in the file:

```
<resources>
    <string name="hello_free_world">Hello free world!</string>
</resources>
```

For the `paid` flavor, put the following in the `strings.xml` file:

```
<resources>
    <string name="hello_paid_world">Hello paid world!</string>
</resources>
```

5. Now you're ready to build the variants. From Android Studio, you are able to open the `Build Variants` tab found on the far left toward the bottom of the IDE (see Figure E.10, right). With the `Build Variants` tab open you can choose which `Build Variant` you would like to build. Select either the `freeDebug` or `paidDebug` and then build or run your project. After you have built both variants, you will now have an `outputs/` folder where the `free` and `paid` APK variants have been created (see Figure E.10, right-center).

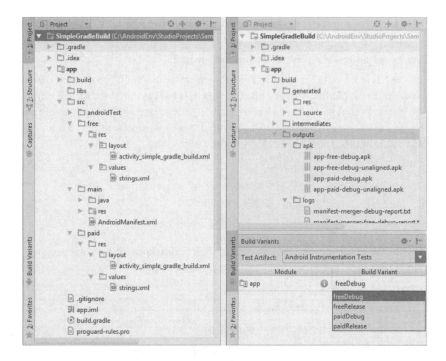

Figure E.10   Here is the `SimpleGradleBuild` project hierarchy with
`free/` and `paid/` directories in the `app/src/` folder for managing different
`productFlavors` (left), and the `app/build/outputs/apk/` folder that
shows the created APK files after building the project and how to switch
between `Build Variants` (right).

The result of building different APK variants is shown in Figure E.11. The `freeDebug` build variant is running on the left on an emulator, and the build process determined the appropriate layout and string file for displaying the text "Hello free world!" The `paidDebug` build variant is running on the right on an emulator, and the build process determined the appropriate layout and string file for displaying the text "Hello paid world!"

Running Different Gradle Build Tasks

Android Studio provides a number of different Gradle build tasks that you can execute on your project to verify if the project, its modules, and its source files have been configured properly. Figure E.12 shows the `install` tasks that you have available for the `app` module. These tasks are specific to the configuration of your project.

You can run these Gradle build tasks by double-clicking a task. You will then see Android Studio executing the task and the results will be displayed similar to what is seen in Figure E.13, where the results of executing the `androidDependencies` task are listed in the `android` folder of the `SimpleGradleBuild`.

Figure E.11   Two different product flavors of the `SimpleGradleBuild`
application, the `free` version (left) and the `paid` version (right).

Figure E.12 The Gradle projects tab of the SimpleGradleBuild
application with various Gradle tasks available.

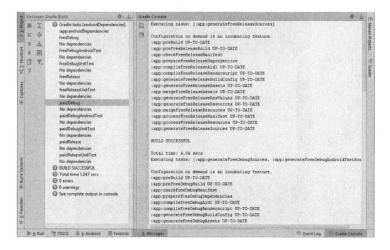

Figure E.13   The results of running the `androidDependencies` task.

Summary

This appendix described the Gradle build system and how it is integrated with Android Studio. You learned the basics of Gradle and how to configure different application build types and product flavors. You also learned how to edit the `build.gradle` files by using the Groovy syntax with plain text or by using a graphical user interface. You also learned about the various support libraries you can use for module dependencies in your application. You should now be comfortable using Gradle and configuring your project for creating different product flavors and build variants.

Quiz Questions

1. True or false: The `gradlew` and `gradlew.bat` files are used for configuring your Gradle settings using plain text.

2. True or false: Gnarly is the name of the domain-specific language used for scripting your Gradle build files.

3. What is the `settings.gradle` file used for?

4. Why is it preferable to use the Gradle wrapper rather than using your own installation of Gradle on your system?

5. What element is used for defining the `compileSdkVersion` and `buildToolsVersion`?

Exercises

1. Familiarize yourself with the "Gradle Build Language Reference" found here: *https://docs.gradle.org/current/dsl*.

2. Read the "Signing Your Applications" article found with the online documentation here: *http://d.android.com/tools/publishing/app-signing.html*.

3. Expand on the `SimpleGradleBuild` application to include the `signingConfigs` element for both the `free` and `paid` version `release` build.

References and More Information

Android Tools: "Build System Overview":
   http://d.android.com/sdk/installing/studio-build.html
Android Tools: "Configuring Gradle Builds":
   http://d.android.com/tools/building/configuring-gradle.html
Android Tools: "Android Plugin for Gradle":
   http://d.android.com/tools/building/plugin-for-gradle.html
Android Tools: "Manifest Merging":
   http://d.android.com/tools/building/manifest-merge.html
Android Tools: "Building Apps with Over 65K Methods":
   http://d.android.com/tools/building/multidex.html
Android Tools: "Support Library":
   http://d.android.com/tools/support-library/index.html
Android Tools: "Data Binding Guide":
   http://d.android.com/tools/data-binding/guide.html
Android Tools Project Site: "Gradle Plugin User Guide":
   http://tools.android.com/tech-docs/new-build-system/user-guide
"Gradle Build Language Reference":
   https://docs.gradle.org/current/dsl/
"Gradle: The New Android Build System":
   https://gradle.org/the-new-gradle-android-build-system/

Answers to Quiz Questions

Chapter 1: Presenting Android

1. Android Open Source Project
2. True
3. Android, Inc.
4. G1 was the name. HTC was the manufacturer. T-Mobile was the carrier.
5. Fire OS

Chapter 2: Setting Up for Development

1. Version 7
2. Unknown sources
3. USB debugging
4. android.jar
5. junit.*
6. Google Mobile Ads SDK

Chapter 3: Creating Your First Application

1. The e means ERROR, w means WARN, i means INFO, v means VERBOSE, and d means DEBUG.
2. Step into is F7. Step over is F8. Step out is Shift+F8.
3. Ctrl+Alt+O on Windows and ^+Option+O on a Mac.
4. Clicking on the far-left column of the intended line of code or pressing Ctrl+F8 on Windows and Command+F8 on a Mac.
5. Go to Settings, Developer Options, and under Debugging, turn on USB debugging.

Chapter 4: Understanding Application Components

1. `Context`
2. `getApplicationContext()`
3. `getResources()`
4. `getSharedPreferences()`
5. `getAssets()`
6. The "back stack"
7. `onSaveInstanceState()`
8. `sendBroadcast()`

Chapter 5: Defining the Manifest

1. `<uses-configuration>`
2. `<uses-feature>`
3. `<supports-screens>`
4. `<permission>`
5. `android.permission.USE_FINGERPRINT`

Chapter 6: Managing Application Resources

1. False
2. Property animations, tweened animations, color state lists, drawables, mipmaps, layouts, menus, arbitrary raw files, simple values, arbitrary XML
3. `getString()`
4. `getStringArray()`
5. PNG, Nine-Patch Stretchable Images, JPEG, GIF, WEBP
6. `@resource_type/variable_name`

Chapter 7: Exploring Building Blocks

1. `findViewById()`
2. `getText()`
3. `EditText`
4. `AutoCompleteTextView, MultiAutoCompleteTextView`
5. False
6. False

Chapter 8: Positioning with Layouts

1. False
2. True
3. `setContentView()`
4. False
5. `android:layout_attribute_name="value"`
6. False
7. `ScrollView`
8. `Toolbar`, `SwipeRefreshLayout`, `RecyclerView`, `CardView`, `ViewPager`, `DrawerLayout`

Chapter 9: Partitioning with Fragments

1. `FragmentManager`
2. `getFragmentManager()` or `getSupportFragmentManager()`
3. The fully qualified `Fragment` class name
4. False
5. `DialogFragment`, `ListFragment`, `PreferenceFragment`, `WebViewFragment`, `BrowserFragment`, `DetailsFragment`, `VerticalGridFragment`, `SeachFragment`, `RowsFragment`, `HeadersFragment`, `GuidedStepFragment`, `ErrorFragment`, and `PlaybackOverlayFragment`
6. `ListView`
7. Using the Android Support Library package

Chapter 10: Architecting with Patterns

1. The activities must reside on the same hierarchy level within the application, and a simple call to `startActivity()` is all that is required.
2. Define the `parentActivityName` and use the correct `Activity`.
3. `onBackPressed()`
4. `setDisplayHomeAsUpEnabled(true);`
5. `getActionBar().hide();`
6. False
7. `dismiss()`
8. `AlertDialog`

Chapter 11: Appealing with Style

1. False
2. `ActionBar`
3. `statusBarColor`
4. False
5. `Toolbar`

Chapter 12: Embracing Material Design

1. You add the `compile 'com.android.support:cardview-v7:23.0.0'` line to the dependencies of the `build.gradle` file of your app module.
2. `android:transitionName="transition"`
3. `AppCompatActivity`
4. `getItemCount()`
5. False; `getItemId()` is the method to override.
6. Implement a `RecyclerView.Adapter` and a `RecyclerView.ViewHolder`, and override the appropriate `RecyclerView.Adapter` methods for binding data to the view.

Chapter 13: Designing Compatible Applications

1. True
2. 99%
3. `<supports-screens>`
4. False
5. `ldltr, ldrtl`
6. False
7. `onConfigurationChanged()`
8. False

Chapter 14: Using Android Preferences

1. `Boolean, Float, Integer, Long, String, String Set`
2. True
3. `/data/data/<package name>/shared_prefs/<preferences filename>.xml`
4. `android:key, android:title, android:summary, android:defaultValue`
5. `addPreferencesFromResource()`
6. `android:fullBackupContent`

Chapter 15: Accessing Files and Directories

1. `0,32768`
2. False
3. `/data/data/<package name>/`
4. `openFileOutput()`
5. `getExternalCacheDir()`
6. False

Chapter 16: Saving with SQLite

1. `execSQL()`
2. `getWritableDatabase()`
3. False
4. False

Chapter 17: Leveraging Content Providers

1. `MediaStore`
2. True
3. `READ_CONTACTS`
4. `addWord()`
5. False

Chapter 18: Learning the Development Workflow

1. False
2. The lowest common denominator method and the customization method
3. Early, when project requirements are just determined and target devices are determined
4. False
5. Write and compile the code, run the application in the software emulator, test and debug the application in the software emulator or test device, package and deploy the application to the target devices, test and debug the application on the target devices, and incorporate changes from the team and repeat until the application is complete.

Chapter 19: Planning the Experience

1. User, team, and other stakeholder objectives
2. Name, gender, age range, occupation, Android sophistication level, favorite applications, most-used Android features, attitude toward or awareness of your application's objectives, education, income, marital status, hobbies, and problems the persona wants or needs a solution to
3. Domain modeling, class modeling, and entity relationship modeling
4. User flows and screen maps
5. Sketches, wireframes, and design comps
6. UI storyboarding and prototyping

Chapter 20: Delivering Quality Applications

1. How many users install the application, how many users launch the application for the first time, how many users regularly use the application, what the most popular usage patterns and trends are, what the least popular usage patterns and features are, what devices are the most popular
2. Updating means modifying the Android manifest version information and redeploying the updated application on users' devices. Upgrading means creating an entirely new application package with new features and deploying it as a separate application that the user needs to choose to install and that does not replace the old application.
3. The Android emulator using different AVDs, Android Device Monitor, Hierarchy Viewer in Pixel Perfect View, Draw Nine-Patch tool, real devices, technical specifications for specific devices
4. False
5. Android Studio, the Android emulator, physical devices, Android Device Monitor, adb, sqlite3, the Hierarchy Viewer
6. False
7. False

Chapter 21: Testing Your Applications

1. True
2. Test application integration points, test application upgrades, test device upgrades, test product internationalization, test for conformance, installation testing, backup testing, performance testing, test in-app billing, test for the unexpected, and test to increase your chances of creating a "killer app"

3. JUnit

4. test

5. False

6. TouchUtils

Chapter 22: Distributing Your Applications

1. ProGuard

2. False

3. Google Analytics SDK v4 for Android

4. versionName is used to display application version information to users, and versionCode is an integer that Google Play uses internally to handle application upgrades.

5. True

6. False

7. A Google Payments merchant account

Appendix A: Tips and Tricks: Android Studio

1. True

2. Ctrl+Shift+F12 on Windows, Command+Shift+F12 on the Mac

3. With two source file windows open, right-click the tab for a source file and select Move Right or Move Down.

4. False

5. Ctrl+Alt+L on Windows, Command+Alt+L on the Mac

6. Ctrl+Alt+V on Windows, Command+Alt+V on the Mac

7. Alt+Enter

Appendix B: Quick-Start: Android Emulator

1. F8

2. Ctrl+F11/Ctrl+F12

3. F6

4. onPause() and onStop()

5. hw.gpu.enabled

6. telnet localhost <port>

7. geo fix <longitude> <latitude> [<altitude>]

Appendix C: Quick-Start: Android Device Monitor

1. `tools/`
2. True
3. Attach and debug applications, monitor threads, monitor the heap, stop processes, force garbage collection
4. `TrafficStats`
5. False

Appendix D: Mastery: Android SDK Tools

1. True
2. `platform-tools/`
3. Design view, Text view
4. Hierarchy Viewer

Appendix E: Quick-Start: Gradle Build System

1. False
2. False
3. The `settings.gradle` file is used for defining the inclusion of application modules.
4. Gradle wrapper ensures you will always be able to build your application.
5. The `android` element of your application module `build.gradle` file

Index

A

B

F

N

O

REGISTER YOUR PRODUCT at informit.com/register

Access Additional Benefits and SAVE 35% on Your Next Purchase

- Download available product updates.

- Access bonus material when applicable.

- Receive exclusive offers on new editions and related products.
  (Just check the box to hear from us when setting up your account.)

- Get a coupon for 35% for your next purchase, valid for 30 days. Your code will
  be available in your InformIT cart. (You will also find it in the Manage Codes
  section of your account page.)

Registration benefits vary by product. Benefits will be listed on your account page
under Registered Products.

InformIT.com–The Trusted Technology Learning Source

InformIT is the online home of information technology brands at Pearson, the world's foremost
education company. At InformIT.com you can

- Shop our books, eBooks, software, and video training.
- Take advantage of our special offers and promotions (informit.com/promotions).
- Sign up for special offers and content newsletters (informit.com/newsletters).
- Read free articles and blogs by information technology experts.
- Access thousands of free chapters and video lessons.

Connect with InformIT–Visit informit.com/community

Learn about InformIT community events and programs.

informIT.com
the trusted technology learning source

Addison-Wesley • Cisco Press • IBM Press • Microsoft Press • Pearson IT Certification • Prentice Hall • Que • Sams • VMware Press

ALWAYS LEARNING   PEARSON